A HISTORY OF YORKSHIRE:
'COUNTY OF THE BROAD ACRES'

'County of the Broad Acres' was a description of Yorkshire first used
in late Victorian times. The earliest reference was, appropriately, in
the context of cricket matches.

For Emma and Jonathan

A History of Yorkshire:
'County of the Broad Acres'

David Hey

Carnegie Publishing

Also published by Carnegie:
Prof. David Hey, *A History of Sheffield*
Malcolm Neesam, *Harrogate Great Chronicle, 1332–1841* (2005)

Town and city histories available from Carnegie:
Prof. John K. Walton, *Blackpool*
Dr Graham Davis and Penny Bonsall, *Bath*
Peter Aughton, *Bristol: A People's History*
Dr John A. Hargreaves, *Halifax*
Dr Andrew White (ed.), *A History of Lancaster*
Peter Aughton, *Liverpool: A People's History*
Prof. Alan Kidd, *Manchester*
Dr Jeffrey Hill, *Nelson*

Forthcoming town and city histories:
Prof. Carl Chinn, *Birmingham*
Dr Derek Beattie, *Blackburn*
Dr John Doran, *Chester*
Dr John A. Hargreaves, *Huddersfield*
Dr Andrew White, *Kendal*
Prof. Trevor Rowley, *A History of Oxford*
Dr Mark Freeman, *A History of St Albans*
Prof. Bill Sheils, *A History of York*

Full details on www.carnegiepublishing.com

A History of Yorkshire: 'County of the Broad Acres'

Copyright © David Hey, 2005

First published in 2005 by
Carnegie Publishing Ltd
Chatsworth Road,
Lancaster LA1 4SL
www.carnegiepublishing.com

British Library Cataloguing-in-Publication data
A catalogue record for this book is available from the British Library

ISBN 10: 1-85936-122-6
ISBN 13: 978-1-85936-122-1

Designed, typeset and originated by Carnegie Publishing
Printed and bound by CPI, Bath Press

half title page A club cricket match at Almondbury, Huddersfield.
PHOTOGRAPH: CARNEGIE, 2004

frontispiece
Castle Hill, Almondbury. Queen Victoria's Tower tops this striking landmark to the south of Huddersfield. The hilltop was occupied by Stone Age people and in the mid-first millennium BC it was fortified by a great ditch and rampart. These defences were reused and greatly enlarged by the Norman lords of the Honour of Pontefract when they converted it into a motte-and-bailey castle. The earthwork gave the nearby settlement of Almondbury its name.
PHOTOGRAPH: CARNEGIE 2004

Contents

Execution day, York, 1820. Thomas Rowlandson's depiction of a crowd which had assembled to see a public hanging. York was an assize city and convicted criminals were executed in front of the law courts and prison in what had once been the bailey of York Castle.
YORK MUSEUMS TRUST (YORK ART GALLERY)

Preface

W RITING a history of Yorkshire from prehistoric times to the present day is either a brave or a foolhardy venture. Clearly, no one person can be an expert in every period over such a wide range of time. Nor can any one author have read every publication in the vast literature that is available. To a large extent, such a history is written from a personal point of view. This has its advantages as well as disadvantages, for it reflects the author's enthusiasms and particular expertise.

This view of the county's history is different from many others in coming from south-west Yorkshire, in particular from the parish of Penistone. South Yorkshire is perhaps the least fashionable part of the county, but its varied landscapes and range of evidence about the past offer a good base from which to start. I have ancestors from all three ridings, and know every part of Yorkshire 'on the ground', sometimes as a mere tourist, but usually as a determined investigator of the county's history. My early interests were in the early modern period and the origins of the Industrial Revolution, so it was relatively easy to move both forwards into the modern age and backwards into the Middle Ages. I can claim no expertise in prehistory, but in my retirement, reading about prehistory and visiting major sites from Orkney to Brittany and from the Boyne Valley to Flag Fen has become a great interest.

Twenty years ago Longman published my *Yorkshire from AD 1000*. The later chapters of the present book use much of this material and may be considered an extended and up-to-date version of this earlier work. There is, however, a great deal that is new. In particular, the book is richly illustrated and the captions are designed to add considerably to the text and to reinforce the emphasis on the wealth of visual evidence for the history of the county.

I am very grateful to all at Carnegie Publishing who have been so active in producing this book. Claire Walker has been busy behind the scenes, but my principal debt is to Alistair Hodge, whose enthusiasm for combining social and economic history with landscape history matches mine and who has toured many parts of Yorkshire to take photographs. The Bibliography is an acknowledgement of how much this general survey of Yorkshire's history is dependent on the publications of numerous scholars, many of whom are personal friends. The book is also a tribute to an era that is sadly almost past, when tutors in University extra-mural departments were able to teach whatever interested them and to inspire others to pursue their own research.

David Hey

Introduction

THE HISTORIC COUNTY of Yorkshire lasted for about a thousand years and was by far the largest in England. Even though it was dismantled into five parts in 1974, its distinctive identity is still recognised by its own people and by outsiders. It covered more than 3¾ million acres and accounted for about an eighth of the whole of the country. The West Riding itself was bigger than any other English county except Lincolnshire and the North Riding was the fourth in size. Yorkshire stretched from the river Tees in the north to the Humber in the south and from the North Sea to the highest points of the Pennines, reaching in one place to within 10 miles of the Irish Sea. The date that it became a county cannot be fixed precisely, but it appears to have been created during the late tenth or the early eleventh century, about the same time as the other Danelaw counties of Derbyshire, Leicestershire, Lincolnshire and Nottinghamshire. The earliest surviving reference to Yorkshire is from the *Anglo-Saxon Chronicle* in 1065. When Domesday Book was compiled in 1086, the counties of Lancashire, Westmorland, Cumberland, Durham and Northumberland had not been created. Yorkshire was close to the northern frontier of William the Conqueror's England.

The territory that became Yorkshire in the late Anglo-Scandinavian period had an identity in much earlier times. It seems to have been the district which was settled by the Danish army that captured York in 876 and it was perhaps the territory of the Anglian kingdom of Deira at its greatest extent before it was united with Bernicia to form the kingdom of Northumbria. Certainly, Yorkshire's southern boundary followed that of Northumbria in the ninth and tenth centuries, though it was adjusted where it met Nottinghamshire in the Norman period. Some readjustment of the north-western border may also have been necessary at the same time. Earlier still, the Romans had taken a crucial first step towards creating an identity for the future county when they built a major fort and civilian settlement at York in the late first century, but in pre-historic times people had different loyalties and attachments.

The history of Yorkshire has been deeply influenced by the great variety of soils and geological formations that are found within the county. Life on the Pennines or the North York Moors has always been a very different experience from life in low-lying agricultural districts such as Holderness and the Humberhead Levels. In many ways, the farmers of the Vale of York have had more in common with those of the Midland Plain than with the miners, steel workers and textile workers of their own county. As in other parts of England, people felt that they belonged to their parish and to a wider neighbourhood that was bounded by the nearest market towns and which they called their 'country', a term that survived well into the twentieth century. Relatively few people travelled to other parts of Yorkshire or had any contact with the 'strangers' who lived beyond the district with which they were familiar. Although the Elizabethan and Stuart gentry were conscious of belonging to Yorkshire and contemporary outsiders made comments (usually adverse) on Yorkshiremen as a breed set apart from the rest, ordinary folk did not have this sense of belonging to the county until relatively late in its history. A few literary references can be found in the late eighteenth century and the Romanticism that led Scotsmen to wearing kilts in newly devised 'clan tartans' in the early nineteenth century had some effect in Yorkshire, when the white rose of the medieval house of York was adopted as the county badge, but it was not until the great industrial changes of the Victorian era that the sentiment took hold. The success of the Yorkshire County Cricket Club from the 1890s onwards seems to have been the great stimulus that united Yorkshire people and gave them a sense of their superiority.

Yorkshire's western boundary runs along the Pennines, whose peaks rise to

View towards York Minster from Clifford's Tower. The slender tower and spire of St Mary's, Castlegate, is in the Perpendicular Gothic style of the late Middle Ages. A church has occupied this site since before the Norman Conquest. Fairfax House in the foreground is one of the best of several brick town houses which were occupied by Yorkshire gentry families. Designed by John Carr, York's famous architect, and completed by 1755, it was bought by Charles Gregory, ninth Viscount Fairfax, who completely remodelled the interior. It has been restored and opened to the public as one of the finest Georgian town houses in the country.

PHOTOGRAPH: CARNEGIE, 2005

2,415 feet at Whernside and where the rainfall is over 70 inches per annum. Early writers, starting with William Camden and Roger Dodsworth, often compared this range of hills with the Italian Apennines, or in Daniel Defoe's case with the Andes. Then in the mid eighteenth century Charles Bertram (1723–65) cleverly forged a medieval chronicle with Roman-sounding names, including *Alpes Penini*, and 'the Pennines', or 'the Pennine chain' became accepted as an authentic ancient name. It continued in use even after the forgery was exposed, though the people who lived on these hills long used various local names instead. The Yorkshire Pennines are divided into two geological series. The northerly parts, from the Stainmore Pass in Teesdale as far south as Craven are mainly composed of carboniferous limestone, which produces spectacular natural scenery, rich lead veins, upland heaths and rough hill pastures. South of Skipton the limestone gives way to the sandstones and shales of the millstone grit measures, with rocky escarpments, extensive peat bogs with cotton grass and soft rushes, and drier parts supporting bilberries and heather, various species of grass, and an increasing amount of bracken. The Pennine foothills were amongst the last parts of England to be settled, and although some hamlets were founded before the Norman Conquest, many more started as medieval clearances. Except in the lower parts of the more fertile dales, farmers concentrated upon livestock and many were dependent upon mining or a craft for a sufficient livelihood. Some districts prospered through having this dual economy and upper Calderdale became one of the wonders of the Tudor age when contemporaries were astonished that so much wealth could be generated in such bleak countryside. During the Industrial Revolution the valley bottoms in West Yorkshire were transformed into mill towns and in Hallamshire the metalworkers used the rivers to power their forges and grinding wheels, while the hills above were enclosed with stone walls to extend the limits of cultivation or to preserve enormous stretches or moorland for grouse shooting.

Further east, the gentler slopes of the coal-measure sandstones supported medieval market towns, villages, hamlets and scattered farmsteads in a pleasant, wooded countryside before they too were altered almost beyond recognition by industrialisation. The coal and iron seams had long been exploited in a modest way, but the landscape had not been seriously disfigured by these activities before the second half of the eighteenth century. In 1769 Arthur Young wrote, 'The country between Sheffield and Barnsley is fine, it abounds with the beauties of landscape', but when William Cobbett made the reverse journey two generations later he remarked, 'All the way along from Leeds to Sheffield it is coal and iron and iron and coal'. The West Riding had lagged behind the two other ridings in the Middle Ages, but during the sixteenth and seventeenth centuries its industrial success attracted much comment and by the Victorian era its population had far outstripped the rest. By then it had become one of the most advanced industrial economies in the world.

In Queen Anne's reign the North York Moors (whose old name was Blackamore) were described as 'very barren grownde and covered with ling

'The country between Sheffield and Barnsley is fine, it abounds with the beauties of landscape.'

ARTHUR YOUNG, 1769

and bent throughout'. This bleak plateau, much of it over 1,000 feet, is now highly valued scenery in summer time, but it provided only the roughest grazing and even its dales have never afforded an easy living. The farmers had limited opportunities to combine husbandry with a craft and were always amongst the poorest and most backward in the country. Canon J. C. Atkinson's memories of *Forty Years in a Moorland Parish*, published in 1891, tell of an insular world that still relied on magic and superstition. Nor did Camden think much of Yorkshire's other hilly district, the Wolds. He wrote, 'The middle is nothing but a heap of mountains, called Yorkeswold'. The verdict was too harsh, for though the High Wolds were given over to sheep-runs and rabbit warrens, the lower slopes supported small market towns and villages with large, arable fields. This crescent-shaped range of chalk hills, stretching from the Humber to Flamborough Head and rarely rising above 800 feet, has long been a sheep-and-corn district with a character of its own. The numerous prehistoric features in the landscape attest to its popularity with settlers over the centuries. But settlements have come and gone and the Wolds are also the setting for Wharram Percy, Britain's most famous deserted medieval village.

These hills frame the horizons of the vast Vale of York and the smaller vales of Pickering, Mowbray and Cleveland, extensive acres of flat farming land that receive only 24 inches of rain per annum. Upon entering Yorkshire, Henry VIII was taken from Doncaster to Scawsby Lees to see 'one of the greatest and richest valleys' that Bishop Tunstall had discovered 'in all his travels thro' Europe'. Later that century, Camden found that these lowland districts were 'pretty fruitful'. Farming systems varied according to the quality of the soils, which ranged from the fruitful earths covering the magnesian limestone belt to the ill-drained carrs of the Humberhead Levels and parts of the Vale of Pickering. All the Pennine rivers, except the Tees, find their way into the Ouse and Humber, which was a great benefit in terms of inland transport but an occasional serious problem because of flooding. Light, well-drained soils produced good crops, but elsewhere in the vales it made more sense for farmers to concentrate on livestock. Wherever possible, each community tried to balance its resources; thus the townships and parishes of the Vale of Pickering extended in long, narrow strips on to the North York Moors and in the south of the county several townships had detached pastures in Hatfield Chase and other low-lying areas.

To the east of the Wolds lies another rich agricultural district that was formerly troubled by drainage problems. Slow-moving streams and hundreds of meres once produced a watery surface, but now only Hornsea Mere is left. In the Middle Ages the special character of Holderness was emphasised by the fact that it was almost an island, remote from the rest of England except by sea, cut off by the extensive carrs of the Hull valley in the west and the Earl's Dyke to the north, and constantly eroded along its North Sea and Humber shores. Every slight rise supports a straggling village that has been rebuilt in brick during the eighteenth and nineteenth centuries. Daniel Defoe could not

'We have been looked upon as rude and barbarous people ...'

John Cary's Map of Yorkshire, 1787, shows the old boundaries of the county and its ridings, together with towns, great houses, roads, rivers and canals. The map was part of a small-scale atlas of Britain which had run to no fewer than 43 editions by 1835.

find anything remarkable near the coast – 'not a port, not a gentleman's seat, not a town of note' – but along the banks of the Humber splendid churches reflect the medieval wealth of the ports and market towns. In the Middle Ages this was one of the more prosperous parts of England.

The history of Yorkshire is therefore not a unified story. The contrasting and changing fortunes of these natural sub-regions within the county will be a major theme in the chapters that follow. Even within these districts, the way that one community developed was often markedly different from the experience of its neighbours. In South Yorkshire the village of Frickley has almost disappeared off the map, but a mile to both the north and to the south the pit villages of South Kirkby and Thurnscoe sprawl across the countryside. Adwick-le-Street is a populous parish, but just across the A1 motorway the tiny estate village at Brodsworth is hidden in the dry valley below a mid nineteenth-century hall and a medieval church. The West Riding has some of the largest industrial conurbations in the country, but in the two other ridings old market towns flourish and village life has been little affected by industry. Outsiders may recognise a Yorkshire accent, but local people can place a speaker much more precisely in a particular 'country'. It is this diversity of experience within the historic county of Yorkshire that we must try to capture.

'A Yorkshireman born and bred, I care not who knows it; I hope true Yorkshire never denies his county.'

1650

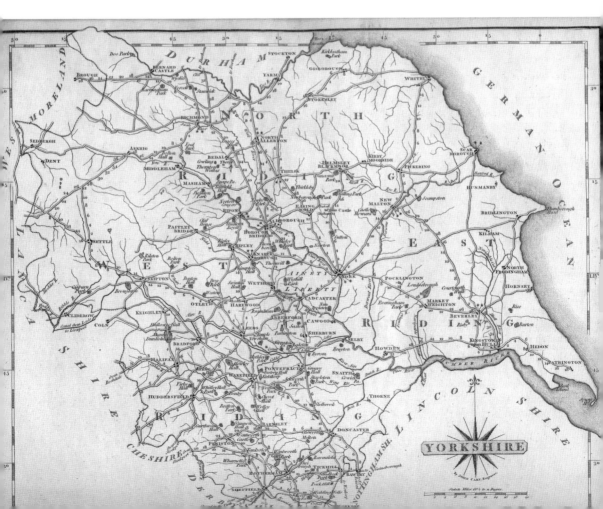

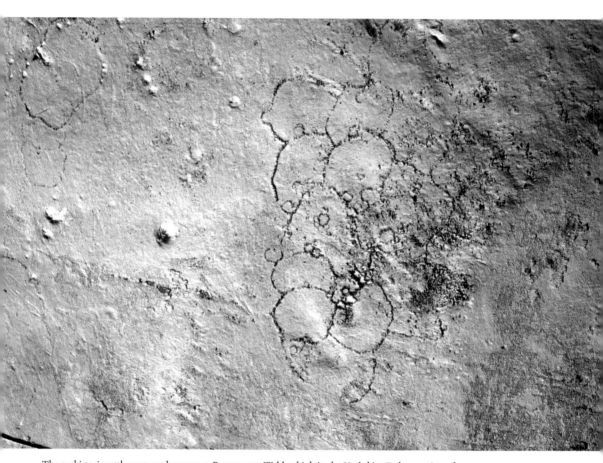

The prehistoric settlement on the moor at Burton cum Walden high in the Yorkshire Dales consists of a group of at least 14 hut circles surrounded by irregular enclosures. The huts vary in size from 4 to 10 metres in diameter and are mostly incorporated into the enclosure walls. The average sized enclosure was about 50 by 40 metres. About 250 metres away is a contemporary field system, well defined by boulder walling. Aerial photography and field surveys have brought many such sites to light in recent decades.

R. WHITE, YORKSHIRE DALES NATIONAL PARK AUTHORITY

CHAPTER I | *Prehistory and the Roman Empire*

The Stone Age

By about 10,000 BC the ice that had covered much of northern Britain had retreated and much of the open tundra land had been replaced by a wooded landscape of birch, hazel and pine trees. Around 5,900 BC rising sea levels cut Britain off from the continent of Europe and summer temperatures rose to

2–3°C higher than they are today. The winters became milder; oak, ash, elm and lime began to spread on deep, rich soils, and alder and willow started to grow in the wetlands. The reindeer and bison that had flourished in colder conditions became extinct and in their place came red and roe deer, elk, wild cattle, horses and pigs and a great variety of small mammals. Armed with new tools and weapons made from flint, Stone Age people followed these animals over extensive hunting grounds in regular seasonal patterns.

The enormously long period of prehistory is traditionally divided into a three-age system based on the tools that were used for hunting, butchering meat, felling trees, building houses, cutting out clothes and numerous other everyday tasks. The Stone, Bronze and Iron Ages were not distinct eras but gradually merged into each other and retained many old characteristics. Flint and other stone tools were used for half a million years until about 500 BC, well into the Iron Age, and the transition from bronze to iron tools took several centuries to complete. The divisions are useful aids to our understanding as

below A barbed harpoon point, made from deer antler, found during the nineteenth-century excavations of Victoria Cave, near Settle (*right*), and dated to about 11,000 years ago. The tip is broken. As it may have been embedded in a scavenging or dying animal, it does not provide evidence that humans definitely occupied the cave.
YDNPA HISTORIC ENVIRONMENT RECORD

0   50   100
mm

7

long as we think more in terms of continuity than of change. Old ideas about new technologies being brought into Britain by successive waves of invaders have been discarded in favour of an approach that emphasises continuity from the 'hunter-gatherers' who first settled here when the climate began to change dramatically.

The earliest evidence of human activity in what is now Yorkshire comes from limestone caves or rock shelters. Two miles north of Settle, a steep climb by lane and footpath takes us out of Langcliffe to Victoria Cave, high above the Ribble valley. Here has been found an antler point that had been used as a weapon or harpoon by hunters during the Upper Paleolithic or Old Stone Age, which ended about 8,000 BC. Animal bones from much earlier times that were found within this shallow shelter have been identified as those of mammoth, rhinoceros and hippopotamus. Other slight evidence of human occupation has been found in Attermire Cave nearby, at Calf Hole Cave near Grassington, at Dowkerbottom Cave in Wharfedale and at Deadman's Cave, Anston, in South Yorkshire, but little or no evidence of Old Stone Age groups has been found elsewhere in Yorkshire. Few people had ventured this far north.

The Mesolithic era or Middle Stone Age, which lasted from around 8,000 BC to about 4,500 BC, is distinguished by the flint tools and flakes that have been found where hunters settled for the summer season. Mesolithic people were far more numerous than their predecessors. They lived in all types of countryside, from the tops of the moors to the lowest river valleys, though they have left no marks on the landscape. Scatters of flints have been found below exposed peat deposits on the Pennine moors – near Broomhead, Deepcar, Dunford, Marsden, Meltham and Saddleworth in the south-west, on Baildon Moor, above the Wharfe valley and around Grassington, Kettlewell and Kilnsey. The sheltered sides of valleys and fertile lowlands no doubt provided more congenial homes. Flint implements have been discovered on and around the Wolds, where small areas of chalk downland were cleared, and in the Vale of York, while bone points and harpoon heads have been picked up at several places in Holderness near Hornsea. Over 780 worked, Mesolithic flint tools have been found at Stone Carr, on a sand and gravel island in the lower Hull valley. Mesolithic people perhaps moved from one recognised site to another in a regular annual progression following the herds, for they were largely reliant on hunting. Whether they had domesticated cattle, sheep and pigs and whether they grew cereals is a matter for lively debate amongst prehistorians. The distinction between herding prey and farming livestock is not a sharp one.

Adam Sedgwick (1785–1873), a native of Dent, was one of the leading figures in the new science of geology. He became Woodwardian Professor of Geology at Cambridge, President of the Geological Society, President of the British Association, Fellow of the Royal Society, and recipient of the prestigious Copley and Wollaston medals. His memorial is a huge slab of granite and public water supply in the street approaching the church. The photograph was taken in 1882.

The discovery of fresh evidence and the development of new archaeological techniques stimulate interpretations that are very different from those that were fashionable only a generation ago. The most famous Mesolithic site in Britain is that at Star Carr, a couple of miles south of Seamer in the Vale of Pickering, although there is nothing to see now above ground. It is difficult to imagine that this district was once a large, shallow lake surrounded by fairly well-wooded countryside. Excavations undertaken between 1949 and 1951 on the fenland fringes by an outflow channel of the lake unearthed a small settlement which was interpreted as a winter/spring base camp. No dwellings were found but, judging by the numerous wood and bone objects which were preserved by water-logging, it was thought that a family group of about twenty-four members lived there. A brushwood platform was interpreted as a landing place and the discovery of a wooden paddle suggested that boats or canoes had been used, perhaps for fishing or for hunting wildfowl and beavers. Antlers of red and roe deer had been fashioned into a variety of barbed spearheads, and discarded bones proved that the diet included wild beef, venison, pork, hares and hedgehogs; and that pine martens, foxes and beavers were hunted for their pelts. The bones of a domesticated dog which were found are the earliest yet known in Britain. Hollowed-out stag 'frontlets', consisting of part of the skull and the stumps of the antlers, were interpreted as ceremonial costume worn by priests or dancers in magic rituals, although other prehistorians argued they were used as disguises for stalking deer. Since 1976 a great deal more research has been carried out on both the finds and the environment and improved techniques have led to new interpretations. Radiocarbon dating suggests that the site was occupied around the mid-eighth millennium BC. The vegetation was burned deliberately and regularly and the large quantities of wood that were preserved in the waterlogged conditions have provided the earliest evidence for worked timber anywhere in the world. The Vale of Pickering Research Project has now identified a number of similar sites in the vicinity. The many thousands of fashioned flints which have been found not far away at Seamer Carr support the idea that Star Carr was not simply a seasonal base-camp, for prey was available for hunting all year round. Some prehistorians now think that the timber platform may have been not a landing place but a religious site which crossed the boundary between land and water.

Polished stone axe heads on display at the Dales Countryside Museum. They were probably made on the slopes of Pike o' Stickle, Great Langdale, in the Lake District, the source of many of the most prestigious axes of the Neolithic period.

The population of Britain in the Mesolithic era is thought to have been only a few thousands, but DNA tests suggest that they, rather than new settlers from the continent of Europe, were the ancestors of the much more numerous families of the Neolithic period (the New Stone Age), which lasted from around 4,500 to about 2,200 BC. Neolithic people were

The Rudston Monolith. Remarkably, this huge, roughly cut block of Jurassic gritstone was dragged here from a quarry 28 miles to the north to stand in a major Neolithic ceremonial area. This has been a sacred site for thousands of years, one that the early Christians sought to adapt to their own purposes. The monolith now stands in the churchyard, a few feet away from All Saints church. It was probably topped with a cross in the early Christian era, for the village name is derived from Old English words meaning rood (i.e. cross) stone. The top of the stone was covered with lead in 1773 to protect it from the weather, but this was removed later.

PHOTOGRAPH: CARNEGIE, 2005

definitely farmers rather than hunters. They tilled the land, kept domesticated animals, and made distinctive 'grooved ware' pottery of a coarse fabric which they decorated with repeated patterns made by a piece of cord or bone. Their flint and stone axes have been found in large numbers, particularly on the Wolds, whose light soils were easily cleared of open woodland and scrub to form grazing grounds. Many small pits containing pottery and high-quality flint implements have been discovered on the lower Wold slopes at Carnaby, for example. The countryside as we know it was first fashioned at this time, but we have very little evidence of actual settlement sites. Instead, we know the Neolithic people as the builders of our first great monuments – the henges, stone circles, barrows and hilltop enclosures surrounded by banks and wooden palisades – that still adorn the landscape. The Wolds provide particularly rich evidence of the elaborate social and burial rituals that were associated with barrows or 'howes', the *tumuli* of Ordnance Survey maps.

Two of the three surviving 'Devil's Arrows'. One is surrounded by trees and the other two are in the middle of a field near the A1, so it is difficult now to appreciate the context in which these stones were originally placed.

PHOTOGRAPHS: CARNEGIE, 2005

About a dozen Neolithic long barrows have been identified on the Wolds, though none is now clearly recognisable. A typical example that has been excavated is that at Willerby Wold, Staxton, six miles south of Scarborough. Burial rituals took place at the concave forecourt at the eastern end of the barrow, then after six bodies or more were laid to rest in a timber chamber the whole structure was set on fire and abandoned. Much more evident in the landscape are the later round barrows. Crop marks seen from the air show that round barrows were distributed widely across the Wolds. The largest one, known as Willy Howe, stands in what prehistorians describe as 'the Rudston/Burton Fleming ceremonial landscape'.

Another outstanding example is the huge mound of Duggleby Howe, which can be seen from a road near Duggleby village on the northern flanks of the Wolds. The excavation by J. R. Mortimer in 1890 demonstrated that a man had been buried in a shaft that had been dug into the chalk. The body was accompanied into the after-life by six flint arrowheads, a bone pin, two beaver teeth and twelve boar tusks, personal belongings which were perhaps meant to symbolise feasting and prowess at hunting. The shaft was then filled with the remains of two other people and a separate skull. Further burials were made at the top of the shaft and another person was interred in a second, shallower shaft alongside the first. The mound that was piled above the shafts contained a further eight burials, then at a later stage 53 cremations were inserted into the

crest of the mound as it continued to grow in size. The cremated bodies were accompanied by curved bone pins, polished-edged flint knives, and other characteristic late Neolithic equipment. Aerial photography has since revealed that Duggleby Howe was sited at the exact centre of a circular, ditched earthwork that is as large as the celebrated henges of Wessex.

The Wolds also possesses the largest standing stone from prehistoric Britain. The Rudston Monolith is an enormous Jurassic gritstone block, 6 feet wide and rising 25½ feet out of the ground. Geologists tell us that the stone must have been moved from an outcrop at Grosmont 28 miles away on the North York Moors. It cannot be dated accurately, but aerial photography has revealed a unique arrangement of four later Neolithic avenues (cursuses) converging on the hillock on which the stone stands above the Gypsey Race. Here was a complex of monuments comparable to the ceremonial focus at Duggleby. A similar line of three erect stones, now marked by grooves through natural erosion and known as the Devil's Arrows, stand half-a-mile or so west of Boroughbridge. They were hewn out of millstone grit and transported from at least 10 miles away. The line once numbered four, or perhaps five, giant stones.

Circular, sacred spaces defined by a ditch and an outer bank and known to us as henges were constructed throughout the later Neolithic period and the early Bronze Age. They vary greatly in size and frequently have standing stones within or around them and one or more entrances. They were the cathedrals of their day, spiritual and social centres which attracted pilgrims from miles around. Hundreds survive in Britain, but few have been found elsewhere in Europe. At Thornborough, near Ripon on the north side of the river Ure, a remarkable group of three henges were arranged at roughly equal intervals in a line with a slight kink, along a previous cursus that stretched for over a mile. Each of the henges measured 240 feet in diameter and was defined by a bank 5 feet high, a deep internal ditch and opposing pairs of entrances. The banks are best preserved within the northern henge, which is covered with trees. Nothing has been found inside the henges, for sacred places would have been kept clean, but small pieces of worked flints from the surrounding fields have been dated to around 3,500 BC. Two remarkable discoveries have been made. First, excavations have shown that enormous quantities of white gypsum crystals had been dug from pits and brought a few miles downstream in a massive communal effort to give the banks a glistening, white appearance comparable to that of the great henges on the chalk downs of Wessex. Secondly, computer analysis has revealed that the alignment of the henges is an exact

The huge, round mound, known as Duggleby Howe and dated to the late Neolithic Age, is set in the middle of an earlier, circular earthwork, which has been interpreted as a causewayed camp. The mound is much larger than the typical round barrows of the Early Bronze Age and the whole complex is comparable in size with the great henge monuments of Wessex.

Limited excavation has shown that the mound was used for burials at different phases. Some skeletons were placed in crouched positions, while other bodies were cremated. One adult was accompanied by six arrowheads, a bone pin, two beaver incisors and twelve boar tusks, personal belongings that were perhaps symbols of feasting and of hunting prowess. The chalk mound which covered the burials was sealed beneath a layer of clay.

NATIONAL MONUMENT RECORD

match with that of the three central stars of the belt of Orion, which appears framed in the night sky from August. Other, simple henges have been identified nearby. The Thornborough district was clearly an area of great spiritual significance to Neolithic people and perhaps to their descendants in the early Bronze Age.

Henges were also constructed on the Pennines, notably at Castle Dykes near Aysgarth in Wensleydale. Neolithic and Bronze Age sites have been located in mid-Wharfedale, along the watersheds and slopes of the Aire to the south and the Washburn to the north. Families no doubt chose to settle in the better farming areas on the lower ground, but the evidence has been destroyed by the activities of their successors. A dozen or so Neolithic or early Bronze Age long barrows survive in prominent positions high on the North York Moors, for

Rock art, Addingham High Moor. The moors around Ilkley contain some of the best examples of rock surfaces with prehistoric cup-and-ring markings and other designs. Their exact date and purpose remain contentious. The more complex designs, such as that of the so-called 'swastika stone' shown here, tend to be in areas with large numbers of rock art. This stone is located in a commanding position overlooking the upper reaches of Wharfedale.

PHOTOGRAPH: CARNEGIE, 2005

left This remarkable series of three late Neolithic henges at Thornborough is unparalleled in Britain. The slight kink in the line joining the henges has been shown to be an exact match with that of the central stars of Orion's belt. Each henge is defined by a bank and deep, internal ditch. On the ground, the central henge is the easiest to view, from the lane which cuts across the middle of the photograph. Plans to quarry even nearer to the site are being actively contested.

NATIONAL MONUMENT RECORD

example at Scamridge, Kepwick and Great Ayton Moor. They seem not only to have commemorated the remains of the dead but to have marked the territories of various groups of people. A definite pattern cannot be discovered, however, for so many have disappeared over time. The practice of barrow building continued late into the Bronze Age.

Other evidence for prehistoric activity is not immediately obvious. In the last 25 years or so prehistorians have come to realise just how widespread are the symbols and images which were cut into rock surfaces by Neolithic and Bronze Age people. The best collection of rock art is on Rombalds Moor, Ilkley, which has Neolithic stone circles, numerous cairns, and a remarkable number of carvings on the rocks around the edge of the moor. Their precise meaning is not

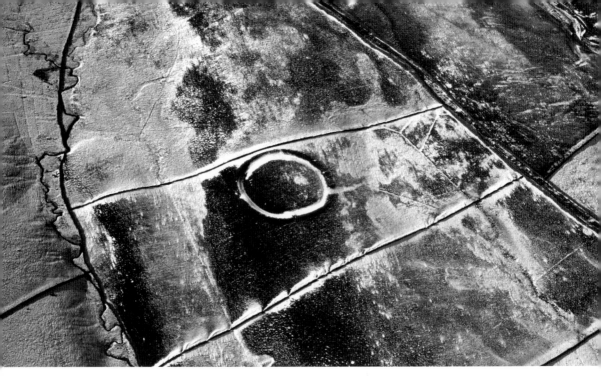

The Neolithic henge at Castle Dykes, Aysgarth. Situated high on the southern flank of Wensleydale, this roughly circular enclosure commands extensive views to the north, west and east. A little over 75 metres across, it has a single entrance on the eastern side and is defined by a bank and an internal ditch, about 2 metres deep. A number of short stones are thought to have once formed a circle around the inner slope of the bank. Henges were probably used as ritual centres to mark the passing seasons and for social gatherings and trade.

known but it is clear they were positioned at points which people driving livestock had to pass on their way to the upland grazing grounds in the spring. Some of these places offer extensive views of the lower levels. Further south on the Pennines, most of the evidence of Neolithic occupation comes from isolated surface finds of flint tools imported from the Wolds. Flamborough Head is known to have been one of the few sources of good quality work-able flint in northern England. In the waterlogged lowland districts a variety of woodwork has been excavated. Neolithic people had already discovered what Oliver Rackham has described as 'the key to woodland manage-ment: that the regrowth shoots from a stump are more useful than the original tree'. Coppice-woods, which were cut on various rotations, must already have been a con-spicuous part of the landscape. We divide the long period of prehistory, for our convenience and understanding, into the ages from which stone, bronze and iron tools sur-vive, but of course most prehistoric artefacts were wooden and if more survived we would think instead in terms of inventions and fashions in woodworking.

The Bronze Age

The Stone Age merged into the Bronze Age of around 2,200–700 BC by a gradual process of change. Stone and flint implements remained in use, but axes and other tools of bronze became increasingly common for hunting, clearing and cultivating, and for prestigious gifts and offerings at religious sites. Evidence of everyday life remains difficult to find, but tombs and ceremonial centres have left an exceptionally rich record up to about 1,400 BC. The most familiar survival is the round barrow, the form of burial mound which first appeared in the Neolithic period and which became the dominant type in the first half of the second millennium BC. The most prominent barrows were the tombs of important individuals who were accompanied into the after-life by significant objects, known to archaeologists as grave goods, but others were family cemeteries that were used over the generations. The contents of these barrows suggest that the social divisions within local Bronze Age societies were much more sharply defined than in the Neolithic period. However, round barrows were just one of several methods of burial. Some people were interred in a stone cist, often with a food vessel placed beside them, and from the middle of the second millennium BC the favoured method was cremation, with the ashes placed in a cinerary urn in an unmarked cemetery.

About 600 food vessels and cremation urns have been found in barrows on the Wolds. Most of the smaller barrows have been ploughed out in recent times, but some are still prominent, grass-covered mounds and many more are visible at certain times of the year as slight humps in the cultivated fields. Scattered tools and weapons have been found, especially on the light soils, and although settlement sites have rarely been identified enough evidence survives to show that by the later Bronze Age farmers were separating their arable lands from their livestock pastures with banks and ditches or by a line of pits. An open, cleared landscape in the Driffield area was divided into compact units by linear earthworks and to the west, for about six miles, a ceremonial area included more than 40 round barrows strung out along the floor of the broad valley. The Wolds and the Hambleton and Tabular Hills were becoming managed landscapes.

One of the most important sites to have been excavated on the Wolds is that at Thwing, where a circular outer ditch formed a formidable defensive barrier with vertical sides to a depth of more than 10 feet. Just inside the ditch, a rampart of chalk rubble had been built around a reinforcing box framework of timber posts. About 50 feet inside the rampart bank, an older, circular ditch about 6½ feet deep protected an inner area 165 feet in diameter, at the centre of which stood an unusually large, round timber building. Here the excavators found bones of cattle, sheep, pigs, horses and deer, various small bronze items, evidence of weaving, and a quern that had been used for grinding grain. These domestic relics suggest that the central structure was a dwelling, but its great diameter of about 92 feet and the henge-like nature of the encircling

Castle Dykes.
PHOTOGRAPH: CARNEGIE, 2005

earthworks, with opposing entrances, invite comparison with ancient Neolithic ritual centres. Thwing was not only a ring fort, but like the naturally defensive site of Castle Hill, Scarborough, it was a centre for bronze-making and other crafts that used materials from distant sources.

Holderness has few spectacular earthworks from the Bronze Age, but the range of axes, tools and prestige weapons such as rapiers and swords that have been found there is greater than in any other part of Yorkshire. The high-quality artefacts that have been recovered in drainage operations seem to have been deliberately placed in water as votive offerings. In 1998 a small and badly damaged late Neolithic or early Bronze Age henge was discovered there when the North Sea washed away parts of the beach. About a third of the henge had been destroyed, but enough remained to indicate an outer circular ditch and bank over 30 yards in diameter and a second inner ditch and bank. A nearby Bronze Age barrow was erected over a Neolithic house and various pits and hearths. A second barrow, exposed by the North Sea, 50 yards to the south, had been built over a hearth. Monuments were built on Easington Beach over a long period of some 1,500 years. The most spectacular Bronze Age discoveries in the low-lying lands around the Humber have been the log-boats. Since 1937 the remains of four boats, made of carefully jointed planks sewn together with yew withies, have been found on the Humber foreshore at North Ferriby, a site which has been described as 'the world's oldest boatyard', and the remains of other boats have been discovered at Kilnsea near Spurn Head and well up the River Don at Templeborough. Recent experiments with a reconstruction of the first North Ferriby boat have proved that Bronze

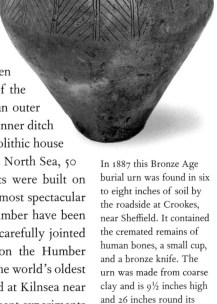

In 1887 this Bronze Age burial urn was found in six to eight inches of soil by the roadside at Crookes, near Sheffield. It contained the cremated remains of human bones, a small cup, and a bronze knife. The urn was made from coarse clay and is 9½ inches high and 26 inches round its largest circumference.
SHEFFIELD GALLERIES & MUSEUMS TRUST

One of the Bronze Age trackways on the Humber foreshore at Melton during excavation in 1998 as part of the Humber Wetlands project. The tracks were constructed of hurdles, using coppiced hazel and some alder, willow and poplar, and fixed in place by vertical stakes. The trackways were aligned parallel to the river.
BY COURTESY OF THE HUMBER WETLANDS PROJECT

Age people would have had no difficulty in sailing down the Humber and crossing the North Sea. Trackways and a fish-trap are among many discoveries from this period. Two trackways were constructed from hurdle panels of woven hazel rods, which were secured in position by posts driven into the saltmarsh creeks, probably to allow access to fertile saltmarsh pasture. The rods and posts suggest that the local woods were carefully managed under a coppice system.

The better-drained soils of the central lowlands have long been intensively farmed and most of the prehistoric monuments have been levelled, but crop marks revealed by aerial photography and finds of axes, spearheads and rapiers suggest plenty of human activity during the Bronze Age in the Vale of Pickering and on both sides of the Vale of York, extending into the Vale of Mowbray and the lowland parts of Craven. As the climate deteriorated in the late second millennium BC the Humber wetlands spread into the southern Vale of York. Peat had begun to form on Thorne and Hatfield Moors in the Neolithic period, but it became much more widespread during the Bronze Age. Further west, the dry, fertile lands of the magnesian limestone outcrop were attractive to settlers, but the evidence on the coal-measure sandstones has been largely destroyed by later activities. The Humber Wetlands Project has shown how old ideas about the prehistoric period can be overturned by intensive surveys and excavations. Our knowledge of the Bronze Age in some parts of Yorkshire remains fragmentary.

The North York Moors have preserved some of the best landscape evidence from the Bronze Age. Burial mounds with evocative names like Shunner Howe, Lilla Howe and Swarth Howe, derived from Old Norse *haugr*, stand out on the skyline. Along Three Howes Rigg, a mile north of Castleton, a line of large barrows commands a panoramic view of the Esk valley. Many of the round barrows have traditional names, like Robin Hood's Butts, Obstruch Rook and Hob-on-the-Hill. Until well into the nineteenth century countryfolk believed

Late Bronze Age spearhead on display in the Dales Countryside Museum. This well-preserved example was probably not a hunting or fighting weapon but a prestigious item for parades and displays. It may have been deposited in a lake as a votive offering.
OUT OF OBLIVION, YORKSHIRE DALES NATIONAL PARK AUTHORITY

in hobgoblins who were supposed to live in the barrows, emerging at night to plague or help the farmers as the mood took them. In his *Forty Years in a Moorland Parish* (1891), Canon J. C. Atkinson recounted many such tales told by his elderly Danby parishioners.

The silhouettes of two barrows high on the North York Moors.

About 200 barrows on the North York Moors have been excavated and recorded, mostly by the unsophisticated methods of nineteenth-century antiquarians such as Atkinson or John Walker Ord, whose *History of Cleveland* (1846) described a typical expedition on which he helped to dig two barrows in a day. Eighty per cent of the excavated barrows contained Bronze Age pottery and 60 per cent had cremated human bones, but very little else was found. Sometimes the barrows contained later cremations in addition to the early ones in the middle of the mound. The barrows which were placed at panoramic viewpoints – such as Swarth Howe, high on the Whitby–Guisborough road looking down to the coast – contain more elaborate articles, some of them cast in bronze. Loose Howe, on the watershed above Rosedale, contained two bronze daggers, a stone ceremonial axe, an oak coffin with a lid and an oak boat or canoe. These finds reinforce the idea that society was becoming more hierarchical. The prominent positions of many round barrows on the watersheds – often in long lines spaced out on the ridges – suggests that they may have acted also as boundary markers, defining the ancestral lands of local groups. But other round barrows, such as those in the cemetery on the Eston Hills, were erected in large groups and some were built on or close to early dwelling sites.

Field walls were built from around 1500 BC onwards to enclose small parcels of cleared land on the North York Moors. These enclosures look as if they were irregular-shaped garden plots which were cultivated by people who were mainly concerned with livestock. The remains of 70 or so prehistoric farms on the North York Moors are most conspicuous in Upper Ryedale and Eskdale or at Thompson's Rigg near Blakey Topping and Harland Moor north of Gillamoor. Most farms were small but some were several acres in size, with extensive grazing grounds stretching over the moors beyond a ditch and a bank. The moors now seem an unlikely environment for growing crops, but conditions there have degenerated since the early Bronze Age, at which time the climate was warmer, woods were abundant, and the pastures were more nourishing and less peaty than they are now. As the trees were felled and the rainfall became heavier, the over-exploited soils became thinner and less fertile. Stones had to be cleared from the fields and piled into cairns, often against large earthfast boulders. We see these fields as they were when they were abandoned, followed by the spread of peat bogs and two or three thousand years of erosion. When the remains of stone walls that wind among the scattered cairns are mapped they can be recognised as ancient field boundaries. Occasionally a carved stone, a stone cist or early Bronze Age pottery has been found amongst the cairns, but excavation has rarely yielded anything other than a few pieces of charcoal. It appears that most cairns were the result of field clearance. As no Bronze Age houses have been discovered alongside the cairns, the settlements were probably sited in the valleys by the arable land and meadows. Prehistoric farmers had similar requirements to their medieval descendants and it is likely that present-day township boundaries which stretch from the valleys on to the moors have their roots in the Bronze Age.

Scamridge Dykes. This spectacular complex of prehistoric dykes, curving six abreast in a huge arc across the North York Moors, are interpreted as boundary earthworks where no natural markers suffice. Their impressive size and replication suggest that they marked a major tribal boundary.

Ingleborough from the
south, now one of the
challenges on the 'Three
Peaks Walk' (with
Whernside and Pen-y-
Ghent). The Iron Age
hillfort occupies a large
proportion of the summit
seen here.

PHOTOGRAPH: CARNEGIE, 2005

The dykes (long ditches and banks) which sometimes run for miles across the countryside marked boundaries which are often still in use, especially on the limestone hills just off the moors. They have been dated from about 1000 BC onwards, much later than the round barrows and the first fields, and they are thought to have been a response to the inevitable disputes over resources when the population began to grow. Much of the Cleave Dyke on the western scarp of the Hambleton Hills has been ploughed out, but the Steeple Cross, Hesketh and Casten Dykes which run off it are major earthworks which mark territorial boundaries similar to those made by the lines of Bronze Age barrows on the Snilesworth area to the north. The dykes and the river valleys enclose territories that include grazing on the moors, arable land on the lower hills, meadows in the dales and access to river water. East of Newton Dale, major prehistoric dykes form boundaries across the Tabular Hills. These impressive multiple dykes are much larger than Cleave Dyke and seem to have marked the territories of powerful groups of people. Scamridge Dykes, which sweep six abreast in a huge arc from the scarp near Cockmoor to the head of Kirkdale, Ebberston, and the great Double Dykes on Sproxton Moor are thought to have been major tribal boundaries.

Although Bronze Age activity on the Pennines is far less evident than on the North York Moors, it survives in greater variety than for any other period of prehistory. Barrows, cairns, stone circles and field walls can be seen in the right conditions – when the sun is low or the snow is melting, when the trees have lost their leaves and the bracken has withered – scattered along the outcrops of millstone grit and the dale sides in the northern parts and to a limited extent in the southwest. Small, unspectacular stone circles were not difficult to build. It seems that each family group had one for its own ceremonies and rituals. Families lived nearby in small, circular houses which were built with a timber frame and roofed with thatch.

The Iron Age

Prehistorians define the era from about 700 BC to the Roman occupation as the Iron Age, for this was a time of a serious clearing of the woods using iron axes and iron ploughshares. Continuity with the Bronze Age is nevertheless far more evident than change. Most families still lived in thatched round houses, though new styles became apparent which continued into the Romano-British period, and the great majority earned their living through farming. For the first time, we can put a name to the people who lived between the Humber and what became lowland Scotland. Between the first century AD and the Roman invasion they were known as the Brigantes, a name whose literal meaning was the 'high ones', though whether this had the sense of 'warlords' or 'upland dwellers' is uncertain. The Roman geographer Ptolemy wrote that their territory stretched from sea to sea. If so, they must have included a group known as the Parisi who controlled what later became the East Riding of Yorkshire.

Ingleborough: one of
Yorkshire's most dramatic
Iron Age hill forts, whose
earthworks surrounding
the summit of the hill are
well preserved. The
rampart was constructed
with dry stone walling,
consisting of rubble placed
between flat, upright
stones. The stone
foundations of at least 20
hut circles have been
identified within the 15-
acre enclosure, mostly in
the more sheltered eastern
side. As there is no
permanent water supply, it
is likely that the dwellings
were occupied only in the
summer months, when
livestock was grazed on
the higher pastures.
Ingleborough may also
have been a tribal centre
used for ritual purposes
and as an expression of
royal authority.

R. WHITE, YORKSHIRE DALES NATIONAL
PARK AUTHORITY

The Brigantes formed the largest group of people in Iron Age Britain, but they were far from being the richest or the most advanced, preferring to live in farmsteads and hamlets rather than towns. Pollen analysis, radio-carbon dates and the discovery of rotary 'beehive' querns point to a major extension of farming from the middle Iron Age onwards. The lowland countryside became quite thickly populated, but the surviving visual evidence of farming activity comes mostly from the uplands, where there has been less disturbance in later times. Some of the best-preserved field patterns from Iron Age Britain run along the dalesides, notably at Grassington in Upper Wharfedale. They are mostly rectangular or square-shaped, but small paddocks or yards and groups of 'house-platforms' and larger 'settlement-platforms', approached by hollo-ways, are cut into the hillsides. Aerial photographs have revealed how the land in central Swaledale was divided into large estates, but on the ground these divisions appear only as low, ruined walls. On Marrick Moor, Harkerside and Calverside, near Reeth, estates were defined by a long 'top wall' and by water-courses. These 'co-axial' land division systems (as they are known to prehistorians) are also evident in Wensleydale and in Upper Wharfedale, near Conistone. Likewise, on the North York Moors 'cross-ridge dykes', which run across the necks of spurs between the valleys, subdivide the countryside into separate estates. Those at Levisham and Horness Ridge date from the late Iron Age or Roman periods, but others, for example the Double Dykes on Danby Rigg, are from the Dark Ages following the collapse of the Roman Empire. On the Wolds, much of the once-extensive network of dykes was obliterated by ploughing during the twentieth century, but the many short stretches that survive include good examples near Huggate and Millington, along with the remnants of a triple dyke near Langton.

Farming on the light soils of the Wolds became more intense and the growing population spread along the valleys and into those parts of the Wolds that had been previously considered marginal. Excavations in the 1950s showed that a site in a commanding position at Staple Howe, Knapton, seven miles east of Malton, was first settled by a farming family around 500 BC. An oval-shaped house with a gabled roof rising from walls made of stone and rammed chalk was surrounded by farmyards and defended by a wooden palisade around the edge of the natural chalk hillock. About 100 years later, this house was replaced by a pair of round houses with wooden walls and conical roofs supported by central posts. Both houses had hearths and ovens and entrances that faced south east to catch the light and to avoid the worst weather. A loom was found in one house and a granary was located close by. On the Wolds, circular houses were often occupied continuously over a long period of time. Small, short-horned cattle, Soay- or Shetland-type sheep, and goats, pigs and horses were reared while barley, emmer wheat and spelt wheat were grown in fields that were less than half-an-acre in size. The evidence of large-scale and sudden clearance of the woods towards the end of the Iron Age suggests that the landscape was by then fully occupied by farming families.

The Wolds also provide the best evidence of Iron Age burial customs. Elsewhere, the lack of graves leads us to suppose that bodies were cast into lakes, rivers or swamps. Large cemeteries of scores or even hundreds of small, square-ditched barrows dating from the fourth to the first century BC have been found on the lower slopes of the Wolds, notably at Arras, Driffield, Eastburn, Garton and Rudston. Over 100 of the 500 or so mounds at Dane's Graves, Driffield, have been excavated at various times, mainly by the late nineteenth-century antiquarian, J. R. Mortimer. The interred bodies that lay in crouched positions in pits at the centre of the mounds were accompanied by grave goods such as jewellery and food offerings in a pot. The varied quantity of grave goods suggests a society differentiated by rank and status. The finds are displayed in the Yorkshire Museum and the British Museum.

The cemetery at Arras, near Market Weighton, has given its name to the distinctive cultural tradition of the people on the Wolds which began in the late fifth or early fourth century BC. It was once thought that this culture was imported by an immigrant tribe, known from Roman literary sources as the Parisi, who possibly originated from the Marne region of northern France, but current thinking is that it was developed by native people who had contacts across the sea. The crouched burials and the grave goods are peculiarly British in style and, while other features were influenced by Continental practices, they need not be explained by invasion. The twenty most spectacular graves among the thousands which have been examined are those where the corpse of an important person was buried beneath a dismantled two-wheeled vehicle (which was originally referred to as a chariot but is now thought of as a carriage or the equivalent of the Victorian trap). In a barrow at Garton Slack the body was placed instead on top of the wheels of the dismantled vehicle, together with a whip and harness fittings. Food for the after-life was provided in the form of a pig's head, which was split in two. The vehicle had twelve-spoke wheels with a diameter of 2 feet 9½ inches, rimmed with iron tyres. Such vehicles were prestigious but were not used in battle, other than perhaps to convey warriors to the battlefield. The grave was covered by a square, earthen barrow surrounded by a ditch. The traces of a round building found close by were interpreted as a mortuary house, where funeral rituals might have been performed before the burial.

In 2001 a similar burial was excavated on the prominent hill above Wetwang Slack, close to where three previous 'carriage' burials had been found. It has been dated provisionally to the fourth or third century BC. The body was identified as that of a mature woman who was laid in a small hollow in the southern end of the grave, probably on a mat, hide or sheet. Joints of pork and several split pig skulls were placed over the upper part of her body and an iron mirror rested on her legs. The dismantled two-wheeled vehicle was then placed in her grave. A reconstruction of the vehicle used in BBC TV's *Meet the Ancestors* is now on display in the British Museum. Most 'chariot' burials are from the Wolds, though one was found recently at Newbridge, near

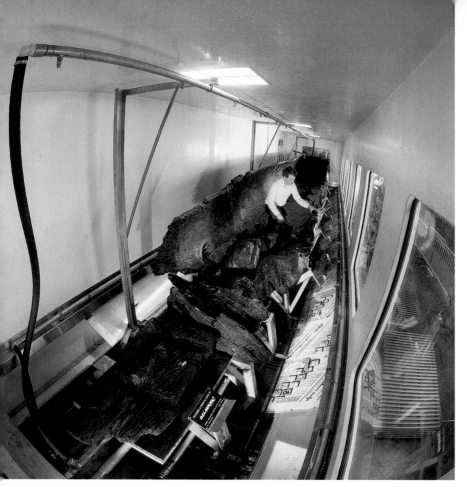

The Hasholme Boat. Now preserved in Hull Museum, this remarkable Iron Age boat was discovered during land drainage works in 1984 deep below marshy carr lands next to the River Foulness at Hasholme Hall. At that time, the wetlands of the Humber Estuary were more extensive than at present. The boat was over 41 feet long and 5 feet wide and weighed about 6 tonnes. It was made from a single, hollowed-out oak tree that was felled between 322 and 277 BC, and could seat a crew of up to 20. As it was decorated, it presumably had some status, but on its final journey over 2,000 years ago, it was carrying a cargo which included sides of beef and timber. It is thought to have capsized after an accident.

HULL AND EAST RIDING MUSEUM

below Now on display in the Hull and East Riding Museum, this reconstruction of an Iron Age 'chariot' or cart was made for the BBC TV *Meet the Ancestors* programme. It was based on the excavated finds in a woman's grave on the east side of Wetwang village, on a prominent hill above Wetwang Slack, in 2001. The burial has been dated to the fourth or third century BC. Although the long axle had long since rotted away, the shape of the voids allowed this reconstruction, which is considerably different from earlier interpretations. The burial was found unexpectedly during the excavation of a medieval manorial complex before the building of a new housing estate. Over the upper part of the woman's body were placed joints of pig, an iron mirror and other metal objects, including horse bits.

HULL AND EAST RIDING MUSEUM

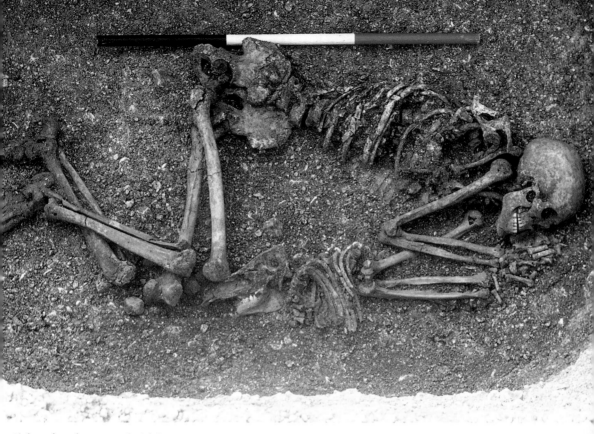

Skeleton from the Iron Age burial site at Wetwang.
HULL AND EAST RIDING MUSEUM

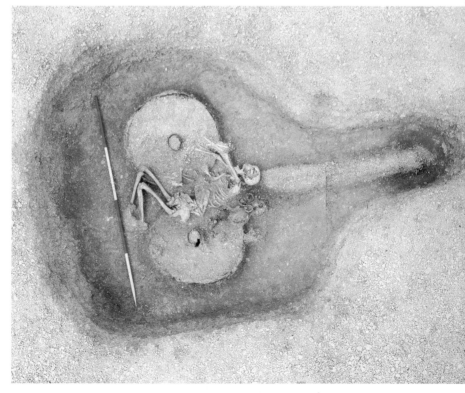

A view from above of the second of three 'chariot' burials at the large Iron Age cemetery at Wetwang Slack, excavated by John Dent in 1984. The outline of the vehicle that accompanied the body can be seen as two wheels and a long axle. Such vehicles were once thought to be military chariots, and the name has stuck, but they were more likely to have been carts or carriages for everyday use. The vehicle was dismantled before being placed in the grave. Although similar graves have been found elsewhere, they are particularly associated with the Wolds escarpment.
HULL AND EAST RIDING MUSEUM

Edinburgh, and in 2004 a fine example was unearthed at Ferrybridge, well to the west of the Ouse. Here the 'chariot' had been placed intact in an upright position behind the body of a man who had died in his thirties. He was accompanied by some joints of pork but no weapons. The iron tyres and various fittings were well preserved and the spokes of the wooden wheels were outlined by stains in the earth. The ditch surrounding the grave contained bones from at least 250 two-to-three year old cattle and from other livestock, suggesting that the funeral was celebrated with a large feast.

Our richest evidence for the Iron Age comes from burials. A previous excavation at Wetwang Slack had revealed a large cemetery near an open settlement of round houses. Although the original barrow mounds had disappeared under the plough, their positions were still marked by their surrounding rectangular ditches in a clear linear arrangement. The barrows varied considerably in size, the largest measuring 29 feet by 26 feet. Only the graves of adults were found within them, for children were buried close by in flat graves or in existing barrow mounds. Most of the corpses had been placed in plank coffins, usually on their left side in a crouched position with the head to the north. They were accompanied by pork or other food offerings and by personal belongings. Women wore bronze and iron bracelets, necklaces and pendants made of blue glass beads, or of jet, amber, bronze and stone, and iron pins and brooches were used as dress fittings. The men were buried with their iron swords and iron-bound wooden shields. The cemetery was dated to the second and first centuries BC; after the Roman conquest a native farm was built over it. There is now little to see on the ground, but the best finds from excavations on the Wolds are on display in Hull Museum.

We now know that large numbers of people also settled in lowland districts during the Iron Age. In 1984 the Humberside Wetlands Project found a massive Iron Age log-boat that was preserved at Hasholme in the shallow Foulness Valley in what was once part of a tidal area that extended from the Humber as far north as Market Weighton. The boat, which was dated to the third century BC and is now on display in Hull Museums, had sunk with a cargo of beef. It demonstrates that the design of carpenters' joints was as masterly then as it is now. Prehistoric woodworkers had grasped that timber-framed buildings could be made from small trees and that managed coppices, cut to a rotation system, would yield a regular supply of underwood for poles, fencing, the laying of tracks, fuel and many other purposes. Dozens of iron smelting sites, including one of the biggest and oldest slag heaps yet found in Iron Age Britain, have been discovered in the Humberside wetlands in recent years. Local bog ore deposits were used and the waterways provided the communications. Several Iron Age settlements have also been identified further east in Holderness, including the so-called 'lake villages' at Barmston and Ulrome, south of Bridlington.

In other parts of Yorkshire the most obvious Iron Age features in the landscape are the hillforts and other defended sites, some of which started off as simpler Bronze Age earthworks. Although they are not as common or as

dramatic as those in the south of England or the Scottish borders, these hill forts are widespread. Their construction indicates population growth and a pressure on available resources that forced the inhabitants to defend their territories. On the crest of Eston Nab an impressive D-shaped rampart rises above the Tees. On the south-west edge of the Hambleton Hills the earthworks around Roulston Scar were identified by an English Heritage survey in 2001 as those of a promontory fort, roughly triangular in shape, with an almost complete circuit of 1.3 miles and an internal area of 60½ acres. But most earthworks were much smaller than this and those which surrounded a single farmstead may have had status rather than defence in mind, rather like the moated houses of medieval times. It has been suggested that during the Iron Age every well-defined knoll in Swaledale was 'fortified' or at any rate occupied by a high-status residence. Even the Wolds and the Tabular Hills have some examples.

On the edges of the Pennines, the origins of Castle Hill, Almondbury, whose timber-laced and vitrified ramparts enclose one of the two most dramatic hill forts in Yorkshire, are uncertain, for no absolute dating evidence for the initial construction of the fort has been found, but a late Bronze Age date is thought likely. The ramparts of the second stage date from the seventh century BC or even earlier, but the stone-revetted rampart with a timber-lace core of the third phase is likely to be sixth century BC, well into the Iron Age. The fort was

The Iron Age earthworks at Stanwick, thought to mark the site of the Brigantian capital, are difficult to visualise at ground level. These grass-covered ramparts in the Tofts, near the medieval parish church, are the easiest to spot.

abandoned in the fourth century BC and not used again until a large Norman castle was erected on the same site, re-using the old defences. The same thing happened at Barwick-in-Elmet.

The other dramatic defences are those of the thick gritstone wall that encircles the top of Ingleborough, the loftiest hill fort in Britain. Unlikely as it now seems, about 20 circular stone buildings provided shelter within the fort. They must surely have been occupied only in summer. The well-preserved hill fort at Wincobank, overlooking the river Don, has been radio-carbon dated to around 500 BC. Other Iron Age forts have been identified at Brierley Common, Sutton Common and Castle Hill, Wentbridge, and smaller, rectangular earthworks survive in the south-west Pennines at Meg Dyke (Barkisland), Oldfield Hill (Meltham) and Royd Edge (Meltham). Large labour forces were needed to build the hill forts and the surrounding farms must have been able to provide considerable amounts of food.

The substantial, sprawling set of earthworks that cover about 750 acres at Stanwick, north of Richmond, probably enclosed the tribal capital of the Brigantes in the last century BC and up to and after the Roman Conquest. Stanwick has by far the most extensive Iron Age ramparts in Britain, but it occupies a lowland site and is now covered by fields and lanes and therefore lacks grandeur. The visitor sees great banks and ditches, including an excavated and exposed section of rampart, but at ground level it is impossible to sense

One of the most dramatic sections of rampart at Stanwick is completely tree-covered. The renowned archaeologist Sir Mortimer Wheeler excavated and reconstructed one section in the 1930s.

The bailey, Castle Hill, Almondbury. The De Lacis, Norman lords of the newly created Honour of Pontefract, chose this prehistoric site as the centre of the western parts of their huge lordship. The inner rampart of the ancient hill fort was strengthened as the outer defence and a deep ditch (seen here) was dug to separate the new motte from the bailey. An estate map drawn by William Senior in 1634 has the words 'The scite of the towne' written across the bailey and in 1584 two men held 'one burgage upon the top of the Castle Hill'. The attempt to found a borough here seems to have been abandoned by the late thirteenth century. In 1294 Henry de Laci obtained a grant of a weekly market and three-day fair at Almondbury and the market town developed around the parish church.

PHOTOGRAPH: CARNEGIE, 2004

any pattern. The best view is from the raised, circular churchyard of the medieval church of St John, a surprisingly large building for a parish that now has few inhabitants. To the west of the churchyard at the heart of the fort is an oval enclosure known as the Tofts, a strongpoint whose ramparts rise some 24 feet above the surrounding ditch. From the Tofts, it is possible to see much of the outer circuit of ramparts, now grass-covered but once faced in drystone walling, that rise from wide and deep ditches. The main north-west entrance to the huge complex was both massive and elaborate. Excavations and surveys have revealed a long and complicated history that began as a series of unenclosed settlements surrounded by fields and paddocks. The purpose of the enormous ramparts was not defence but an impressive political statement of the power and authority of the Brigantian leaders. Excavations in the 1980s unearthed sophisticated imports from Italy, including rare forms of Samian pottery, amphorae and volcanic glass. Unique in northern Britain in its vast scale, Stanwick resembles the great tribal centres of the south. Impossible to defend, it was more a town than a fort and the Tofts was probably the usual residence of Queen Cartimandua, the last ruler of the Brigantes.

In recent decades aerial photography has revealed the crop marks of large numbers of Iron Age farmsteads, particularly on the fertile soils that overlie the narrow belt of magnesian limestone that runs through central Yorkshire as far north as Tadcaster. In the later Iron Age the number of these roundhouses, surrounded by a ditch, increased so much that it was common to align them in 'ladder settlements', linked by a droveway. The density of Iron Age settlement was unsuspected before it was revealed from the air and from field surveys such as those that have been undertaken between the Aire and the Wharfe, where the remains of field walls, banks and enclosures have been detected. During the long centuries of prehistory the landscape had evolved gradually and without any major disruption. The Iron Age population of Britain probably reached over 1 million and it is clear that a great deal of land was being tilled or used for grazing long before the Roman invasion.

Romans and Britons

The Roman army that landed in Britain in AD 43 reached the East Midlands within a couple of years, but the initial advance came to a stop at the River Don, which must have been the southern boundary of the Brigantes. Queen Cartimandua accepted the role of client-ruler of the North and used Roman support to maintain her position against the forces of her estranged husband Venutius. Her dependency was demonstrated in AD 51 when she rewarded the Romans by handing over Caractacus, a British leader who had sought asylum in her territory. During the reign of Nero (54–68) the Romans built a fort at Templeborough on the southern banks of the Don, opposite the Iron Age hill fort at Wincobank. Whether or not Wincobank had been re-fortified at this time is not known, but

Roman bath house, Templeborough under excavation. The Roman fort at Templeborough, west of Rotherham, was the site of one of Britain's first 'rescue' excavations, when a munitions factory owned by Steel, Peech & Tozer was built over the ruins during the First World War. Two hundred years earlier, Daniel Defoe had written that the foundations of the fort were 'very plain to be seen, and, I suppose, may remain so to the end of time'. The Roman name of the fort is not known and 'Templeborough' seems to have been an antiquarian fancy which was not recorded before 1559. On Jeffreys' map of Yorkshire (1771) the site was named Brough Hill.

the positioning of the Roman fort was surely symbolic. The foundations at Templeborough were plain to see until 1916, when they were obliterated by a steel works. Before the site was destroyed excavators identified three phases of building. The first fort housed 800 men, including 240 cavalry; a new fort in the second century accommodated 500 soldiers; the third phase was dated to the late third or early fourth century. Finds from the site are on display in the Clifton Park Museum, Rotherham. So far, this is the only Roman fort in south Yorkshire that has been dated securely to the time when Nero was emperor.

Brigantia retained its semi-independence until AD 69 when Cartimandua divorced Venutius and co-habited with his armour-bearer. Venutius immediately launched a major revolt against the queen and her Roman supporters. In response, the Ninth Legion of the Roman Army, under the command of Quintus Petillius Cerialis, moved from Lincoln, where it had been stationed about 25 years. It has long been thought that the army marched along a military road known as Ermine Street to the prehistoric ferrying point across the Humber and then along the western edge of the Wolds, but the absence of forts suggests that this route was created in more settled times. The Romans subsequently defended the river crossing by building a fort at Brough-on-Humber. Little is now visible of the fort, which fell out of use in the second century, nor of the later town, which may have been *Petuaria*, the name recorded by Ptolemy as the tribal capital of the Parisi; an inscription bearing this name was found when the amphitheatre was excavated. A civilian settlement, or *vicus*, grew up north west of the fort. From Brough the road headed along the Wolds escarpment before branching off to York or continuing north to a fort that was built at an important crossing of the River Derwent at Old Malton. This was probably bigger than the slightly later one whose ramparts are still visible as grassy slopes. Whether it was known as *Derventio* or *Delgovica* is now disputed, for a site at Stamford Bridge has claims to have been *Derventio*. The original fort was abandoned by the close of the first century, but a new garrison was established at Malton about 160 as a convenient posting for a unit that was no longer needed further north. Malton was an important route centre and in the late second and third centuries a small town was established on the other side of the Derwent at Norton.

The original Roman road from Lincoln was probably that which headed for the Vale of York across the River Don. We do not have any precise information that allows us to date this road, nor the erection of timber forts along it. The general assumption is that these forts date from AD 69 to 71, but those to the south of the Don may have been earlier foundations, for like Templeborough they lay outside Brigantia. Aerial photographs have identified a first-century fort, which was enlarged in the fourth century, near the inland port of Bawtry, whence Derbyshire lead was exported, and a much larger fort, which was capable of housing 3,000 men, by the River Torne at Rossington Bridge, close to a major industrial site where pottery was made and iron was smelted. The fort at *Danum*, where the road crossed the Don at the highest point of

below Aerial view of Castleford. The view looking south of where the Roman road from Tadcaster to Doncaster crossed the confluence of the rivers Aire and Calder. The Roman fort of *Lagentium*, which was capable of housing 500 soldiers, was established at this strategic site in the late first century AD and the accompanying civilian settlement (*vicus*) developed into a thriving town. There is little from the Roman period to see above ground but recent excavations have unearthed significant finds which had been preserved by the waterlogged conditions. Castleford – which was recorded as *aet Ceaster forda* in 948 – takes its name from 'the ford by the fortification'.

WWW.WEBBAVIATION.CO.UK

navigation for vessels coming up the river from the Humber, stood on the south bank of the river, as did Templeborough. It was rebuilt and enlarged twice during the second century. The shape of its earthworks determined the medieval town plan of Doncaster, but the associated civilian settlement, which was enclosed by deep ditches, is known only from small-scale excavation.

Within the territory of the Brigantes, north of the Don, a section of the raised 'Roman Ridge' road can still be followed between the Sun Inn and the Red House, where it still acts as a parish boundary as it heads towards another fort that has been revealed by aerial photography at Robin Hood's Well. Further north, the Roman road crossed the river Aire by its confluence with the Calder. On the south bank of the river the present town of Castleford overlies a timber fort that was known to the Romans as *Lagentium*. Defended by a ditch and a massive bank, it was capable of housing 500 soldiers until its closure about the year 100. Recent excavations have proved the existence of an adjacent civilian settlement dating from the time of the initial Roman advance. The waterlogged terrain has preserved numerous finds, including the seeds of imported figs, grapes and walnuts and large numbers of sheep and other animal bones, which show that Castleford was not just a garrison but a thriving town in the late first century. The *vicus* apparently failed to survive beyond the end of the second century, but evidence for some sort of occupation has been found for the late Roman period.

The Roman road then followed the crest of the magnesian limestone before

Mastiles Lane marching camp. This large Roman camp, covering about 20 acres, lies on a plateau high in upper Wharfedale. It is thought to date from the second half of the first century AD, when the Brigantes rebelled against the Roman governor of Britain, Petillius Cerialis. The enclosing ditch and bank are well preserved. The camp is surrounded by a flat open area suitable for gathering and training a large force of soldiers.

R. WHITE, YORKSHIRE DALES NATIONAL PARK AUTHORITY

turning north-east to Tadcaster (*Calcaria*), where one branch continued to York and the other headed north as Dere Street through the Roman forts at Newton Kyme, Roecliffe, Aldborough, Healam Bridge, and Catterick, and so on to Piercebridge and Corbridge near Hadrian's Wall. The Romans also used the major north–south prehistoric road that ran along the crest of the magnesian limestone and named it Ricknield Street. It entered Yorkshire at Ricknield-thorpe and crossed the Don at Strafford Sands (the later meeting-place of the wapentake of Strafforth). In the Middle Ages this road acted as the boundary of several parishes up to its junction with the road from Doncaster near Thorpe Audlin. After the construction of Hadrian's Wall, most if not all the forts other than that at York were abandoned, but some were re-occupied about 161–163, when the Roman army left Scotland upon the death of Antoninus Pius.

The final choice of base for the Ninth Legion was a new site where the Foss flows into the Ouse at *Eboracum*, modern York. The name seems to have referred to a yew grove. The Ninth Legion stayed there until about 120, when they were replaced by the Sixth Legion. Their 65-acre fort was built to the usual playing-card shaped design and was defended by a ditch, rampart, timber gates and towers. It quickly became the military capital of northern Britain. The civilian settlement on the south-western bank of the Ouse began to flourish in the mid to late second century, so that by the time of the Emperor Septimus Severus, who died in York in 211, *Eboracum* was the largest town in the North. Soon afterwards, it was promoted to the rare status of *colonia*. In time, the pronunciation of *Eboracum* changed, so that it was known as *Evorog* to the British and became *Eoforwic* under the Angles, *Jorvik* under the Vikings, and eventually York. In choosing the site of *Eboracum*, the Romans made a decision which was to have had profound consequences for the later history of Yorkshire.

York had a pivotal position in the Roman road system. It was linked to Dere Street and so to Aldborough (*Isurium Brigantium*), which became the second most important Roman town in the Vale of York. Aldborough began to grow in the more peaceful time of the 120s around the fort that the Ninth Legion had built to the south of the River Ure. Its Roman name was probably derived from the river and its second element suggests that here was the capital of the Brigantes once they came under direct Roman rule and Stanwick had been abandoned. Part of the second-century town wall and north gate, with its defensive towers, can be seen in the grounds of the museum, which are entered almost secretly from the narrow road that passes through the present village of Aldborough, 'the old fort'. Two mosaic pavements from wealthy town houses are exposed *in situ*, but the famous one depicting the legend of Romulus and Remus has been removed to Leeds City Museum. The medieval church of St Andrew stands at the centre of the Roman settlement, but little of the site has been excavated. In 2001 aerial photographs of crop marks revealed much of the Roman street grid, but we get little sense of the hustle and bustle of the Roman town from the peaceful nature of present-day Aldborough. Another fort and its *vicus* on Dere Street have recently been discovered nearby at Roecliffe. They date from the time of the Roman advance *c.* 71 but they were abandoned during the following decade, perhaps in favour of Aldborough. Dere Street was a major military road with numerous forts, many of which did not last long.

There is even less to see at Catterick (*Cataractonium*), the next fort and town to the north along Dere Street. Here the native British may have met Italians, Greeks and North Africans, for the late second-century fort was probably home

Map of Roman York. The fortress known as *Eboracum* was constructed at the confluence of the Foss and the Ouse on a site that had apparently not been settled before. A civilian settlement, that eventually acquired the status of colonia, was enclosed within walls on the south bank of the Ouse. These two components of Roman York have had a lasting effect on the city's topography.

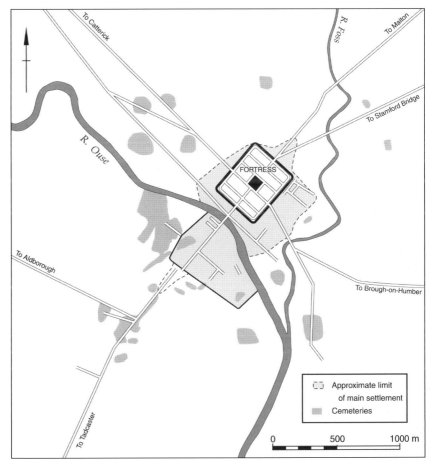

YORK ARCHAEOLOGICAL TRUST

The largest visible section of the Roman town wall at Aldborough, with part of a contemporary interval tower. Both were once 12 feet high. The bank to the left is all that remains of the original rampart.
PHOTOGRAPH: CARNEGIE, 2005

to cavalry from the Balkans. A continuing programme of excavations since 1981 has established a complex sequence, beginning with a fort that was built on the south side of the River Swale during the time that Agricola was governor of Britain (77–83). This fort had walls and a grid of streets covering 25 acres, but it was abandoned about 120. A *vicus* that had grown to the north of the fort survived and about 160 a second fort was built. A riverside settlement then developed well over a mile to the south, with leather working its speciality; hides processed there were exported across northern Britain. In the early fourth century a wall was erected around the small town, which was occupied until the end of the Roman Empire and possibly beyond.

Roman mosaic, Aldborough. Only a small part of the Roman town of *Isurium Brigantium* has been excavated. This star or flower mosaic is still *in situ* under a protective shelter in a part of the Roman settlement that is now under grass. It is one of fourteen mosaics that have been discovered at Aldborough.
PHOTOGRAPH: CARNEGIE, 2005

Once they controlled the Vale of York, the Ninth Legion pushed on into the Pennines, where they established a series of forts and marching camps each capable of accommodating 500 or 1,000 soldiers, notably at Bainbridge, Elslack, Ilkley, and at Slack, high above the Calder valley. The earthworks of the fort at Bainbridge (*Virosidum*) and its

Aerial view of the earthworks of the Roman fort of *Virosidum* at Brough by Bainbridge, founded c.AD 90–105 above the River Bain, a tributary of the Ure, and rebuilt in stone in the middle of the second century.
R. WHITE, YORKSHIRE DALES NATIONAL PARK AUTHORITY

above The Roman fort at Ilkley is still marked by a very distinct earthen mound and on its west side a section of wall has been exposed. The parish church is built on part of the site, which originally covered over 2 acres. Excavations in 1919–21 revealed that the timber fort which was founded about AD 79 was replaced by a stone fort in the second century and abandoned late in the third. It is now thought that this is not the fort that was known as *Olicana*.

PHOTOGRAPH: CARNEGIE, 2005

Wade's Causeway is the name given to the Roman military road across Wheeldale Moor. What we see now are the foundations of the road, rather than its finished surface. Wade was a post-Roman saga hero.

PHOTOGRAPH: CARNEGIE, 2005

vicus occupy a knoll above the medieval village. At Ilkley the layout of the Roman camp is still preserved in the townscape and the parish church, which stands within the fort, re-used much of the Roman stone. A stretch of the fort wall can be seen behind the museum. The fort had to be rebuilt in the early third century, after its destruction by Scots who had taken advantage of the withdrawal of Roman troops, and a civilian settlement grew up alongside it. It has long been assumed that this was Ptolemy's *Olicana*, but it seems more likely that this name was given to the fort at Elslack. The Romans were obliged to maintain these upland forts and to build link roads to protect their lead mines and their lines of communication across the Pennines. A well-preserved marching camp is clearly visible as low earthworks on either side of Mastiles Lane. During the second half of the third century regular threats came from Scotland and from Anglo-Saxon sea-pirates, so many of the northern forts underwent extensive reconstruction.

The Romans also built a road across the North York Moors. A dramatic length of Wade's Causeway, named after the legendary giant Wade, survives

on Wheeldale Moor, where it is one of the very few Roman roads in the country where the rough stone slabs of the foundations of the road are exposed to view. Its date is uncertain, but it seems to link the Roman fort at Lease Rigg with the military camps at Cawthorn, perhaps as a through route from the coast all the way to Malton. But some archaeologists argue that it was built in the late fourth century when new coastal stations were erected to defend the district from raiders.

The earthworks at Cawthorn, which date from around 100, are among the best-preserved examples of Roman military construction south of Hadrian's Wall, but their exact purpose is problematical for they form a unique group in a good strategic position on the northern scarp edge of the Tabular Hills. Recent survey work has concluded that they consist of a marching camp, two forts and an annexe. The two forts lie to the east and west of the camp and their defences are much more pronounced. Neither Cawthorn nor Lease Rigg has produced finds that are later than the early second century and it is almost certain that the troops were removed when Hadrian built his frontier wall in the 120s. Garrisons over much of eastern Brigantia were removed at that time and many soldiers were transferred from the Pennine forts too. The Romans have left few other obvious traces in the landscape of the North York Moors.

About the time that Constantine was acclaimed Emperor at York in 306 the fortress walls were extensively rebuilt, and in particular the great river front was restored with a series of towers that made it one of the grandest examples of the military architecture of the age. Some of the buildings within the fort were faced with imported marble. York was now one of the great military centres of the Roman Empire. The magnificent sight of *Eboracum*, directly overlooking the civil city across the river, demonstrated the power of the Roman army. The fort has had a lasting influence of the layout of the present city and many original features remain to be seen. The lines of two of the main streets through the fort are followed by the present Stonegate and Petergate, which leads to the site of the Roman gateway at Bootham Bar. Surviving sections of the Roman fortress wall underlie the medieval city wall. Near Monk Bar part of an interval tower and the rounded remains of the east corner tower ('the Aldwark Tower') are visible. In the Museum Gardens the lower section of the Multangular Tower formed the south-west corner of the early fourth-century fortress. Behind it a stretch of the fortress wall has been exposed below the

This modern statue of Constantine outside York Minster commemorates the man who was proclaimed Roman Emperor at York in AD 306 and who made Christianity the official religion of the Empire.

PHOTOGRAPH: CARNEGIE, 2005

This re-erected column near York Minster gives some idea of the former size of the fortress buildings of *Eboracum*.

Viking, Norman and medieval successors. The so-called 'Anglian Tower' which was inserted into it may well be late Roman in date. Part of the *principia* can be seen in the Undercroft Museum in York Minster and a tall column has been re-erected to the south of the Minster. A section of a fourth-century bath house can be viewed in the cellars of the Roman Bath Inn in St Sampson's Square and a vaulted sewer has been discovered at the corner of Swinegate and Church Street.

The large Roman civilian town that grew rapidly during the late second and early third centuries across the Ouse in the Micklegate/Bishophill area has less to show within its walls, but an imperial palace was built here and it is likely that the original church of the reign of Emperor Constantine was erected alongside it. The bishop of York is known to have attended the Council of Arles (Provence) in 314. Many of York's medieval churches incorporate re-used Roman masonry and part of a Roman tomb relief is preserved in St Martin-cum-Gregory, Micklegate. In the early fourth century York was a flourishing commercial and manufacturing centre and the most important port in the North. It was, however, the only large Roman town north of the Humber. Aldborough, Brough, Castleford, Catterick, Doncaster and Malton were of no great significance and they all seem to have declined long before the withdrawal of the Roman army.

Throughout the period of Roman occupation, the cosmopolitan ranks of the Roman forces formed only a tiny proportion of the population of the northern half of Britain. Life in much of the countryside continued as before, little touched by Roman influence. The Romans did not replace one culture by another in this peripheral part of their vast empire. Few Roman artefacts have been recovered from some of the excavated rural sites and though the main routes were well-engineered roads for the army the native population used the lanes and tracks that were familiar to their ancestors and which are mostly still in use today. The Romans had only a modest effect on the rural economy of much of northern Britain. The few villas which have been located in lowland areas near York, Malton and Brough date mostly from the late third or early fourth century and are small in size. They were built on the sites of Iron Age farmsteads and they did not specialise in the growing of cereals like the grand villas of southern Britain. The general state of the present landscape had been formed already by prehistoric farmers whose descendants continued to use traditional methods during the Roman occupation.

Nevertheless, the Roman conquest undoubtedly had an impact on the rural economy of some parts of the North. The demand from York for food and goods must have had a considerable effect on the surrounding countryside. The long period of relative peace and prosperity encouraged population growth and more intensive land use and settlement. A great deal of waste-land was brought under cultivation. The Humber Wetlands Project has discovered a range of Roman settlements, the largest at Trent Falls, where the rivers Ouse, Don and Trent combine to form the Humber. The best example of Roman-period

Cawthorn Camps. This series of four Roman camps has long puzzled archaeologists. The general opinion is that they were army practice camps, but that the one seen on the bottom left was a more permanent fort which stood in a convenient position between the forts at Malton and Lease Rigg. The camps have not been thoroughly excavated, but the finds suggest that they were abandoned upon the building of Hadrian's Wall in the AD 120s.

NATIONAL MONUMENT RECORD

ingenuity in the wetlands comes from the roads that were built, notably a 'turf-and-timber' road near the Roman fort at Bawtry, which had been constructed as a raft that floated on the waterlogged peat. The structure of the long bridge that carried the road over the river Idle consisted of parallel rows of three oak posts, which had been driven into the clay beneath the water and peat. The quality of the carpentry was outstanding.

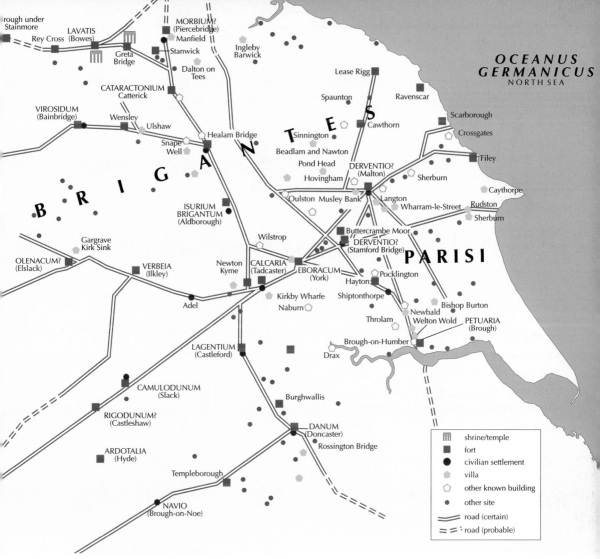

Map labels (north to south, west to east):

OCEANUS GERMANICUS
NORTH SEA

rough under Stainmore
Rey Cross
LAVATIS (Bowes)
MORBIUM? (Piercebridge)
Manfield
Stanwick
Ingleby Barwick
Greta Bridge
Dalton on Tees
Lease Rigg
CATARACTONIUM Catterick
Spaunton
Ravenscar
Scarborough
VIROSIDUM (Bainbridge)
Wensley
Ulshaw
Healam Bridge
Cawthorn
Crossgates
Snape Well
Sinnington
Beadlam and Nawton
Pond Head
DERVENTIO? (Malton)
Filey
Hovingham
Sherburn
Caythorpe
ISURIUM BRIGANTUM (Aldborough)
Oulston Musley Bank
Langton
Wharram-le-Street
Rudston
Sherburn
Gargrave Kirk Sink
Wilstrop
Buttercrambe Moor
DERVENTIO? (Stamford Bridge)
PARISI
OLENACUM? (Elslack)
VERBEIA (Ilkley)
Newton Kyme
CALCARIA (Tadcaster)
EBORACUM (York)
Pocklington
Hayton
Adel
Kirkby Wharfe
Naburn
Shiptonthorpe
Bishop Burton
Newbald
Throlam
Welton Wold
PETUARIA (Brough)
LAGENTIUM (Castleford)
Brough-on-Humber
Drax
CAMULODUNUM (Slack)
Burghwallis
RIGODUNUM? (Castleshaw)
DANUM (Doncaster)
Rossington Bridge
ARDOTALIA (Hyde)
Templeborough
NAVIO (Brough-on-Noe)

B R I G A N T E S

Legend:
- shrine/temple
- fort
- civilian settlement
- villa
- other known building
- other site
- road (certain)
- road (probable)

above Roman Yorkshire.
DRAWN BY I. FRONTANI

left The Multangular Tower, York. Seen from the Museum Gardens, the lower part of this ten-sided structure is the exterior of the west angle tower of the Roman legionary fortress. It dates from the fourth century AD, perhaps from the time of Constantinus I, and survives up to 17 feet high. The larger stones of the top 11 feet date from the thirteenth century.

PHOTOGRAPH: CARNEGIE, 2005

Aerial photographs taken by Derrick Riley during the 1970s and 1980s revealed an astonishing number of small farms and field systems dating from the late Iron Age and Roman periods on the magnesian limestone belt and the adjacent bunter sandstones of south Yorkshire and north Nottinghamshire. The field systems were on a very large scale and were not previously suspected. They formed a planned system of land use, covering large tracts of the countryside in 'brickwork patterns'. They were created earlier than the Roman road from Lincoln to Doncaster but continued in use in the latter part of the Roman period and were abandoned after the withdrawal of the Romans when rising sea levels flooded the whole area. Did the Romans drain Hatfield Chase by dykes, including the construction of the north arm of the river Don? Thorne and Hatfield peat moors and the marshy 'carrs' of alder and willow remained the haunts of brown bear, boar, beaver, wolf and the red and roe deer which were hunted by the inhabitants of Roman Doncaster, but most of the meat that was consumed there came from domesticated animals that were reared on the mixed-farming lands of the magnesian limestone and bunter sandstones. The plant remains from excavated sites at *Danum* included wheat and barley and large quantities of apple pips.

Pollen analysis has shown that the landscape of much of the wetlands had been cleared of trees before the arrival of the Romans. Even the large 'bog oaks' that have been ploughed up on the Hatfield Levels or found below the peat on Thorne Moors were sometimes felled by the axe or by burning. The clearance of woods peaked during the Roman occupation until large tracts of the countryside had little more woodland than they have today. The remaining woods were carefully managed to provide fuel and building materials. Those in the eastern half of south Yorkshire were dominated by lime trees, rather than by the oaks which were dominant on the heavier claylands of the west and on glacial deposits, while birch and pine grew on the poorer, sandy soils. The clay soils in the western half of south Yorkshire do not produce the crop marks that reveal the extent and nature of farming in the Roman period. This was a wood-pasture district that was very different in character from the magnesian limestone belt and the wetlands further east.

In the Burton Fleming–Rudston–Kilham area of the Wolds, an almost complete Romano-British landscape with fields, trackways and native farms has been reconstructed by the use of aerial photographs. Other evidence of widespread native Romano-British settlement has come from excavations near Holme-upon-Spalding Moor, a low-lying area dominated by coppiced woodland that fuelled local pottery kilns and an iron furnace. Yet the people who lived and worked in this district possessed very few artefacts and their buildings and farm enclosures showed almost no signs of outside influence during the Roman period. By contrast, excavations at Hayton and Shiptonthorpe, near Pocklington, have revealed new, second-century settlements that had no direct military connections but which sprawled along either side of the road from Brough to York and which proved to be rich in the full range of Roman artefacts.

Further north, the Romans found prosperous farms and settlements scattered across the Tabular Hills, where the fertility of good farm land could be maintained indefinitely by the manure of farm animals in fallow periods. Iron Age people had settled also on those parts of the boulder clays of Cleveland and the Vales of Mowbray and York which had adequate natural drainage. Some farmers had even moved into areas that were less well drained, for aerial photographs have revealed field systems in the flat carrs of the Vale of Pickering. By the time that the Romans arrived, the native people in the dales leading on to the North York Moors had acquired a pattern of fields that resembles those of the present day. Their mixed farming economy and sophisticated skills in wood and metal working formed a lifestyle which continued well into the nineteenth century. In each of these districts life in the countryside was little different under the Romans. The over-grazing of the uplands by herds of cattle, however, meant that many young trees failed to survive and the moors degenerated to their present peaty condition.

Throughout the Highland Zone of Britain Roman influence was diluted. No towns or villas were erected on the hills or the fringes of the moors. Yet the discovery at Stannington of a bronze sheet diploma shows that a soldier in the Roman army retired to farm there, near the limits of cultivation which were not reached until parliamentary enclosure of the moors in the late eighteenth century. The native people farmed landscapes that were essentially similar to those of today. In the Pennine dales the characteristic field systems were small in scale and defined by low walls, perhaps topped by hedges. The best-known field systems from the Roman period are those near Grassington, which are arranged on a co-axial pattern, but similar landscapes appear throughout Wharfedale and others are known in Wensleydale, Littondale and Ribblesdale. It has been argued that as later farmers generally avoided unnecessary work by fitting their fields into those already in existence, it is likely that some of the medieval strip-fields in Swaledale that run up and down slope between Reeth and Healaugh, and below Harkerside, are based on field systems which were in use in Roman times.

Some rural districts were changed by the rural industries that the Romans developed to support their army or to send finished products to other parts of their empire. At least 76 pottery kilns have been located in a large industrial complex at Rossington Bridge and Cantley, where coarse grey drinking vessels, bowls, jars and dishes were made for sale as far north as the Antonine Wall in lowland Scotland, over a long period of time from the second to the fourth century. Other potteries have been excavated at Crambeck, Knapton and Norton, close to the forts at Malton and York, and at Tholam near Brough-on-Humber. An iron furnace has also been discovered at Cantley and many more must have served the demands of the

Cantley was a major centre of Roman pottery manufacture from the second half of the second century to the mid fourth century. Excavations have revealed no fewer than 41 kilns, which specialised in the production of coarse grey table and kitchen ware, including bowls, vases, storage jars and cullinders for the Roman army.

army and the native population. The physical evidence for Roman coal, ironstone and lead mining has vanished under later activities, but two pigs of lead cast in AD 81, bearing an imperial inscription on one side and the abbreviation 'Brig' for Brigantia on the other, were discovered on Heyshaw Moor in 1731; other pigs that have been found date to the reigns of Trajan (98–117) and Hadrian (117–38). Jet was obtained from the coastal cliffs around Whitby and a considerable number of beehive querns were shaped in quarries on the North York Moors or on the Pennine escarpments, especially in the Baildon area of the Aire valley, to the west of Shipley, and at Wharncliffe, whose name is derived from 'quern-cliff'.

Few forts survive as prominent monuments today, though evidence suggests

that about 40 were constructed within Yorkshire during the long period of Roman occupation. Some known Roman names have not been identified with certainty, nor is the exact nature of Roman sites at Adel, Wetherby and Cleckheaton properly understood. Occasional raids on the coasts of Britain in the late second and third centuries developed into a large-scale attack in 367, after which the Roman army erected signal towers in strongly defended fortlets. The foundations of the one on the headland occupied by Scarborough Castle have been exposed. Others were built on Carr Naze, Filey, a site that is now partly destroyed by cliff erosion, on Beacon Hill at Flamborough, at Goldsborough, Huntcliff and Ravenscar, and perhaps at unknown sites, now washed away by the sea, further south in Holderness. We know little about the last decades of the Roman Empire. Many forts were abandoned long before the final withdrawal of the Romans in the early fifth century. The end came in 410 when the cities of Britain who appealed to their emperor for assistance were told to fend for themselves.

Aerial view of Scarborough with the foundations of the Roman signal tower clearly visible, partly eroded at the edge of the cliff.

CHAPTER 2 | *Britons, Angles and Vikings*

D URING THE THREE OR FOUR CENTURIES of Roman occupation the native people of Britain continued to farm their land in much the same way as did their distant ancestors. It seems likely that most of us are descended from the prehistoric people of these islands, but as they were illiterate the only written records that we have are those of their conquerors. Once the Romans had departed, we have even less contemporary evidence on what was going on. This once led historians to the view that the Roman withdrawal was a catastrophe and that the weak and divided native British were driven out of the country that became England by successive waves of invading Anglo-Saxons. There seemed much to commend this viewpoint, for the Roman towns had collapsed and surviving British place-names were scarce on the ground, while Bede's great *Ecclesiastical History of the English People*, written in 731, offered an unrivalled account of the English triumph over a backward, uncivilised people.

Nowadays, we are far less sure that this is an adequate report of what happened. The archaeological record has failed to find evidence of mass invasions from across the North Sea. Life in the countryside seems to have continued much as before. Perhaps the ubiquitous English place-names merely represent the replacement of one ruling class by another and the gradual adoption of the new language? Is there a later parallel with South America, where Spanish and Portuguese are now spoken, even though the conquering force was small and migration from Europe was limited? Was Bede's hostile account of the British merely the biased view of the triumphant English? The documentary and archaeological evidence for this period is thin, so different cases can be argued. It is generally agreed, however, that the withdrawal of Roman troops left Britain with no effective national government and that native warriors re-emerged as tribal leaders.

The abandonment of the Roman forts and the collapse of towns and markets must have had adverse economic consequences. Archaeologists have found that several feet of silt overlie the Roman remains in York and by the fifth century, and probably long before, the Roman settlements at Aldborough, Brough,

Catterick, Doncaster and Malton no longer supported urban activities. Life in the North was entirely rural and even in the countryside numerous sites which had been occupied during the Roman period were abandoned. Some cultivated land reverted to wood, heath or fen and as sea levels rose the Humberhead Levels and much of the southern Vale of York and the Vale of Pickering were flooded. The 'brickwork' patterns of fields in the lowlands south east of Doncaster disappeared until they were recovered by aerial photography over 1,500 years later. It has been argued that the native population shrank, perhaps because of an outbreak of plague, that settlement retreated in a comparable manner to the decay that followed the Black Death in the Middle Ages, and that the economy did not recover to the level that had been achieved under the Roman Empire until the late Anglo-Scandinavian period. Nevertheless, it is clear that in some parts of the countryside the pattern of land use that had been established under the Romans survived for centuries with little change. On the Wolds at Elmswell and around Wharram Percy, for example, there are few signs of a break in occupation. Anglian pottery has been found by many of the farmsteads and hamlets which were there in late Roman times.

The arrival of the Angles

The traditional story is that Anglo-Saxon mercenaries served in the Roman army from the late fourth century onwards to help defend the empire against the northern tribes, and that after the Roman withdrawal, a British tribal leader called Vortigern invited other mercenaries, who subsequently rebelled and seized control of East Anglia. In the mid fifth century, over a generation after the collapse of Roman government, Angles from the Schleswig-Holstein peninsula sailed up the Humber and the Derwent and established the kingdom of Deira, a name whose meaning is unknown, but which at first perhaps covered the territory which had been controlled during the Iron Age by the Parisi. Defined by the North Sea to the east and the Humber to the south, the kingdom of Deira stretched to the Tees in the north and to the flooded landscape of the Vale of York in the west. By the early seventh century it had expanded westwards over the whole of the territory that was to become Yorkshire and York had become its capital. The Angles gave their name to the country that was eventually called England.

The warriors of Deira were similar in character to the tribal leaders of the British kingdoms, though their skeletons show that they were taller and more muscular. The struggle for supremacy between the fifth and seventh centuries was waged between small bands of fighters, for most of the native population were not involved in warfare. The ultimate victory of the English warriors meant that the British aristocracy were replaced and that an unknown number of new settlers arrived as farmers, but most native families continued their lives undisturbed. It made no sense for the conquering armies to kill or drive away the families who worked the land, produced the food and paid the taxes.

The general consensus in recent years has been that the early Anglo-Saxons lived in scattered settlements and that villages were not created until the eighth or ninth centuries or later. The intensive excavations at Wharram Percy were influential in promoting this view and there can be little doubt that in many, perhaps most, cases this model is correct. However, the ongoing excavations at West Heslerton, where the Wolds descend northwards into the Vale of Pickering, have produced convincing evidence of a large village that was continually occupied from about 380, that is towards the end of the Roman occupation, to about 850, when the site was abandoned. The post holes of over 150 timber-framed buildings, with a consistent, rectangular ground plan that was very different from that of the native round houses, together with numerous smaller, sunken structures that served as granaries and outbuildings have been discovered in the most extensively excavated site of early Anglo-Saxon settlement in England. The houses were up to 30 feet long by 15 feet broad and the construction methods appear to have been sophisticated. The whole site was in use for most of its life and was organised into zones with different functions. No grand buildings were found, so perhaps this was a village of ordinary farmers with roughly equal status. A similar settlement has recently been located 1½ miles away, so it may turn out that such villages typified the pattern of early settlement around the Vale of Pickering.

Just beyond the settlement at West Heslerton lay a large, contemporary cemetery, which has been totally excavated. Here, and at many other early Anglian burial grounds, the skeletons show no evidence of violent death in warfare. The population appear to have been generally healthy, though the average lifespan was not much more than 40. Accepted opinions have had to be revised now that DNA analysis has revealed that some of the bodies that were accompanied with swords were female and that those skeletons that were adorned with beads and brooches were sometimes male. The evidence from the graves, including that of the new technique known as stable isotope analysis, which determines where people came from by an examination of their teeth enamel, does not support the idea that the early Anglian settlements were dominated by marauding warriors from across the sea. The local community at West Heslerton seems to have been essentially egalitarian.

The Angles found a foothold on the fertile soils of the lower Wolds, particularly on the western margins. The archaeological evidence comes largely from pagan cemeteries which have been found by the Humber and near the old Roman roads from Brough to Malton and York. At Sancton, on the edge of the Wolds near where these Roman roads divide, a large cemetery was in use from the first half of the fifth to the seventh century. The remains of 454 people have been identified in cremation urns, though the site probably contained many more. Contemporary cremation cemeteries have also been discovered at the Mount and Heworth to the south and east of York. Evidence from burial practices has shown that by the later fifth century Anglian material culture, including styles of dress and ornamentation, had spread from the Wolds into

Holderness and the Vales of Pickering, Mowbray and Cleveland. But archaeologists are no longer convinced that burial customs and dress fashions identify all these people as Angles. Could it be that over time the native British accepted these new ways? So far, DNA studies have not resolved the problem.

Abundant archaeological evidence from the sixth century onwards has been found in cemeteries in the Driffield district, including those at Cottam, Eastburn, Garton-on-the-Wolds, Kelleythorpe, Kilham and Nafferton. The fact that some of the graves around Driffield were placed in symbolic relationship with prehistoric burial sites and that 125 graves were dug near a Bronze Age barrow at West Heslerton suggests that these were the final resting places of native people, who wished to be buried near their ancestors. The range of burial practices (which mostly involved inhumation rather than cremation) and the variety of dress fasteners, brooches, weapons and other grave goods that have been found suggest that the background of the Angles was more complex than Bede imagined and that native Britons also contributed to the development of the new culture. When Christianity was gradually adopted in Deira during the seventh and eighth centuries the pagan cemeteries were replaced by new ones in churchyards which are mostly still in use and which have therefore not been excavated to reveal their secrets.

By the early seventh century the principal pagan shrine of the kingdom of Deira was at Goodmanham, not far from Sancton and the junction of the

Tor Dyke is a 2 kilometre long earthwork which stretches across the head of a valley between Upper Wharfedale and Coverdale. It has been cut into the limestone scar, then at the end of the scar the line was continued by a substantial artificial rampart. The dyke is thought to have been the north-eastern boundary of the British kingdom of Craven before it fell to Anglian invaders.
R. WHITE, YORKSHIRE DALES NATIONAL PARK AUTHORITY

Roman roads that headed north from the former fort at Brough. In 625 King Edwin was celebrating the pagan festival of Easter at his nearby, but as yet unidentified, royal palace when he survived an assassination attempt. It was probably here that Edwin held the conference which agreed to convert to Christianity, when one of his warriors famously compared life with the flight of a sparrow through a well-lit hall before returning to the outer darkness. At the end of the conference, the priest Coifi rode to Goodmanham to lead the destruction of the pagan temple.

The archaeological evidence for this period is so dependent on burials and cremations that it is difficult to obtain a balanced view of society as a whole. From their base on the Wolds the Anglian warriors gradually imposed their authority on the countryside between the Vale of York and the North Sea. Like their British opponents, they fought for honour and glory, for the spoils of war and for the regular payments and dues that they could impose on the lower ranks of society. Their material culture and language was not shared by the majority of the population. Even in Deira the natives probably still thought of themselves as Britons. By the end of the sixth century, however, the Angles of Deira were strong enough to conquer the British forces to the north and west of their kingdom. About the year 600 they were victorious at the battle of Catterick, where several British warriors were killed. Their leader, Aethelfrith, was soon able to unite Deira with Bernicia, the territory that lay north of the Tees, to form the new kingdom of Northumbria. Before his death in battle on his southern border near the river Idle in 616 he had become the most powerful king in Britain. By 627 both Catterick and York were prominent places within the Deiran part of Northumbria.

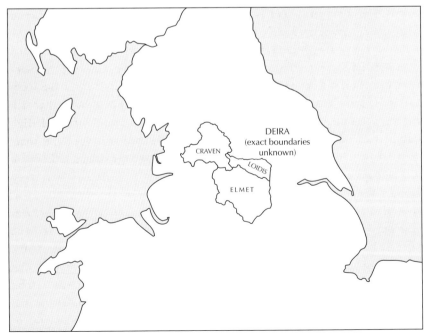

Map showing the approximate boundaries of the British kingdoms of Craven and Elmet, with its sub-division, or *regio*, of *Loidis*, before they fell to the Anglian kingdom of Deira in the early seventh century. How far northwards Deira had expanded from its original base in what later became the East Riding is uncertain. It was soon to be united with Bernicia to form the kingdom of Northumbria. Re-drawn after P. N. Wood, 'The Little British Kingdom of Craven', *Northern History*, XXXII (1996), pp. 1–20.

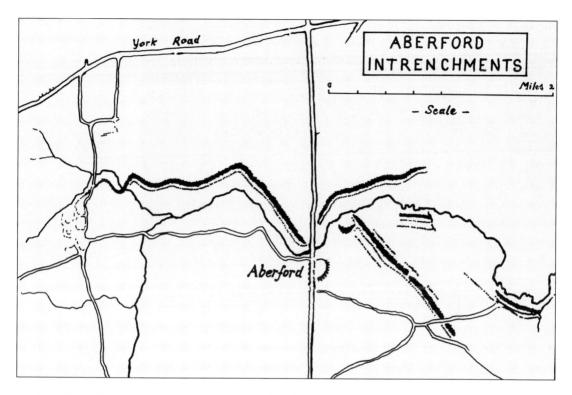

York Road

ABERFORD INTRENCHMENTS

Miles 2

– Scale –

Aberford

To the west of Deira lay the British kingdoms of Craven and Elmet. Craven stretched across the upper dales of the Wharfe and the Aire to Dentdale and the Ribble valley. The name was recorded as Cravescire in Domesday Book, and after the Norman conquest it became a rural deanery and the wapentake of Staincliffe. It seems to have fallen to the Northumbrians in the early seventh century, about the same time as Elmet, the much more populous and powerful kingdom that lay immediately to the south. Elmet stretched from the Wharfe to the Don, whose tributaries the Sheaf and Meersbrook both have names that were derived from words meaning a boundary. To the west the Pennines formed a natural frontier; to the east the limit of the kingdom in the early seventh century was the narrow belt of magnesian limestone, where Barwick and Sherburn retain their '-in-Elmet' names. South Kirkby, Sutton and High Melton were also named in this way during the Middle Ages. The small kingdom of Loidis, whose name is preserved in Leeds, Ledsham and Ledston, was perhaps a sub-division of Elmet and Hallamshire may well have been another. We do not have the evidence to decide whether the complex series of dykes that were dug near the borders of Elmet were constructed to defend that kingdom or whether they date from the later time of conflict between Northumbria and Mercia, but they are impressive in their size and complexity. The largest surviving dykes are those found near Aberford, especially that known as Becca Banks, while in the south the so-called Roman Rig runs parallel to the Don for about ten miles in two branches from Sheffield to Kilnhurst and Swinton. Similar dykes, placed 500 yards apart at Grinton and Fremington in

St Oswald's Church, Oswaldkirk. Sited where the Hambleton Hills descend to the Vale of Pickering, this typical medieval church is distinguished by its dedication and the place-name. Oswald was the early Christian king of Northumbria who invited Aidan to found a monastery at Lindisfarne. He was killed in battle in 642 by the pagan king Penda of Mercia and his body mutilated. Seventy English churches were dedicated to St Oswald, king and martyr.

PHOTOGRAPH: CARNEGIE, 2005

upper Swaledale, seem to have been constructed by the British to try to stop the Anglian advance.

In 617 Edwin, the next great ruler of Northumbria, conquered Elmet and expelled its king, Ceretic. For a time it was not apparent that this victory would be permanent, but the British never recovered, even after Edwin was killed by the combined forces of Cadwallon of Gwynedd and Penda of Mercia at the battle of Hatfield (north Nottinghamshire) in 633 and buried nearby at Edwinstowe. The following year Oswald, son of Aethelfrith, managed to reassert Northumbrian independence, but in 641 Penda was again victorious and the Mercians penetrated deep into Elmet until his death in 655 at a battle

St Oswald's Church, Castle Bolton. Oswald dedications continued to be made late in the Middle Ages. This small church alongside Sir Richard Scrope's castle dates from the end of the fourteenth century.

PHOTOGRAPH: CARNEGIE, 2005

The tower of St Mary Bishophill Junior, York. The tower was built in three phases before the Norman Conquest. Re-used Roman material forms the base, herringbone patterns characterise the middle, and the twin belfry openings in the top stage are in the late northern style. The church stands in the southern part of the city, off Micklegate.

PHOTOGRAPH: CARNEGIE, 2005

near where the Roman road from Doncaster to Tadcaster crossed the river Went. The kingdom of Northumbria survived further attacks until the Vikings arrived in 867, though their kings were regularly killed in battle, assassinated in power struggles, or sent into exile. Meanwhile, life went on much as before for most of their subjects.

The victorious Deirans moved from their original base on the Wolds to establish their new capital of Northumbria at York, or *Eoforwic* as it was then called. King Edwin was baptised there in 627, in a little wooden church that was soon replaced by a stone building dedicated to St Peter. The site has not been discovered, though it is likely to have stood near the present minster. The old Roman defences were strengthened and surviving Roman buildings perhaps gave the place the feel of an ancient capital, but new buildings that can be dated from the seventh to the ninth centuries have been found only in Fishergate, just beyond the confluence of the Ouse and the Foss. Even there, the buildings were not packed together. The building of new churches, notably St Mary Bishophill Junior and the unidentified church of Holy Wisdom, implies a growing population, but *Eoforwic* seems to have remained a small place until it was captured by the Vikings.

We do not know when the native population of the kingdom of Northumbria started to speak Old English, but no doubt it was a very long drawn-out process. Most Yorkshire place-names were not recorded before Domesday Book was compiled in 1086 and even the earliest surviving documents are from

All Saints Church, Sherburn-in-Elmet. The village name preserves the memory of the British kingdom of Elmet, which survived until the early seventh century. The church stands in a prominent position, away from the later village centre, and served a large parish. It is likely that it was an early Christian centre. It became a seat of the Archbishop of York, which helps to explain why the church was already a large, aisled building by the twelfth century. Much of the late Norman church survives, hidden from view by the later exterior. The chancel was rebuilt in Early English Gothic in the thirteenth century; the rest is in the Perpendicular style of the late Middle Ages.

PHOTOGRAPH: AUTHOR

the late seventh century, long after the Angles arrived, so we have no way of knowing how many British names survive in part in an altered form or were translated into Old English. The gradual transformation of *Eboracum* via *Eoforwic* and *Jorvik* into York demonstrates the possibilities. Most of our rivers still have their British or even earlier names and some prominent topographical features retain British name elements. For example, Chevet, Crigglestone, Pen-y-Ghent and Penistone are among the names that refer to ridges or hills. The long survival of some distinctive British communities into the Anglo-Scandinavian period is evident from place-names that incorporate the English term *walh*, which was used pejoratively, or the Viking word *brettas*. These have given us place-names such as Wales and Walton and the various Brettons, while Cumberworth is derived from the folk-name *cymri*, but such names form only a small minority of those recorded in Domesday Book. By then, the essentially English character of the place-names of Craven and Elmet was as obvious as it was in the eastern half of Yorkshire, where the Anglians first gained a foothold.

The place-name element *eccles*, which refers to a church served by a group of priests, has a shared origin with the Welsh *eglwys* and is regarded as firm evidence of the survival of Christianity from the time of the Roman Empire. No *eccles* names have been recorded in the original kingdom of Deira, where the Angles were pagans until the conversion of King Edwin, but nine are known in the former kingdom of Elmet. The outstanding example is Ecclesfield, whose medieval parish covered the whole of the 71,526 acres of Hallamshire. It seems that at least some British religious and secular units continued uninterrupted when Elmet fell, though *The Life of St Wilfrid*, written about 715, says that British clergy fled from their churches when the Angles invaded the northwest. Few people in the countryside in the western half of Yorkshire would have lived far from a church in the sixth and seventh centuries.

When Augustine arrived at Canterbury in 597 to convert the pagan English, the Celtic church had long been active in the North from the community that Columba had founded on the island of Iona. The conversion of the Angles of Northumbria began when King Edwin's marriage alliance with the royal family of Kent led to his baptism at York on Easter day 627 by Paulinus of Canterbury. The mass baptisms that followed included a great event in the river Swale at Catterick, but Paulinus was forced to flee six years later when Edwin was killed in battle. Edwin's successor, Oswald, was

The crypt of Ripon Minster was built by St Wilfrid in the 670s on the model of holy places in Rome. It is similar to that at Hexham, also founded by Wilfrid, a cosmopolitan figure who was the leading advocate of the Roman form of Christianity in the North of England. The rest of his abbey were destroyed in 950. The crypt became a famous place of pilgrimage.
BY KIND PERMISSION OF THE CHAPTER OF RIPON CATHEDRAL

sympathetic to the Celtic church and about 634 he invited Aidan and other monks from Iona to found a monastery at Lindisfarne as a base for converting Northumbria. Soon afterwards, Aidan established a monastery high on the cliffs above Whitby with the royal-born Hilda as abbess. The remains of a large number of wattle and daub houses on stone footings, all enclosed within a ditch, have been recovered by excavation close to the later medieval abbey. From Whitby, a cell was established at Hackness on a remote site in Forge Valley and in 659 Cedd built a monastery at Lastingham, which Bede described as being 'amid some steep and remote hills which seemed better fitted for the haunts of robbers and the dens of wild beasts than for human habitation'. For a generation or so the austere, monastic, Celtic form of Christianity was more influential in Northumbria than the episcopal system that was centred on Rome. The issue was resolved in 663 when King Oswy convened a synod at Whitby, where the Roman case advocated by Wilfrid, Abbot of Ripon, won the day against the arguments of Colman, Bishop of Lindisfarne. The synod was a turning point in the history of the English church.

New stone churches, built in the Roman style, were erected by Wilfrid at Ripon and Hexham and by Benedict Biscop at Jarrow and Monkwearmouth. The crypt beneath Ripon cathedral, where Wilfrid is buried, is the only surviving part of his church. He was appointed bishop of York in 669 and his successors were archbishops from 735. By then, the triumph of the Roman form of Christianity was complete and Bede was writing contemptuously of the

The nave of St Peter's Church, Conisbrough. The proportions of the nave and its great quoin stones, arranged in a side-alternate manner, as at Ledsham, suggest an eighth-century date for this minster church, whose territory stretched from the River Don to Yorkshire's southern boundary. The Normans knocked arches through the nave walls to create aisles.

Celtic tradition. During the eighth century York Minster and the chief Northumbrian monasteries were the recognised intellectual leaders of Christianity both in England and abroad and Alcuin of York was invited by Emperor Charlemagne to head the school at his royal palace in Aachen.

Christianity was imposed on the population from above. The major monasteries were royal foundations and little is known about organised religion beyond their walls. Even as late as the early eleventh century Archbishop Wulfstan II was constantly preaching against the dangers of pagan practices. These rituals were not displaced but were gradually absorbed into the Christian religion. The prehistoric monolith at Rudston seems to have been surmounted by a cross, hence the place-name meaning 'rood stone', and a church was built alongside it. Holy wells that had been used from time immemorial were now

left All Saints Church, Ledsham. Ledsham, Ledston and Leeds formed part of the early Anglian territory of 'Loidis'. That part of All S that is built of brown sandstone forms one of Yorkshire's outstanding early churches. The tall, box-shaped nave survives almost intact a the lower part of the tower originally formed a two-storeyed, western porch. In their monumental study, *Anglo-Saxon Architecture*, H. M. Joan Taylor argued that the dimensions of the nave, the use of large quoins, arranged in a side-alternate manner, and other evidence sug a similar date to the eighth-century Northumbrian churches at Escomb and Jarrow in County Durham.
PHOTOGRAPH: CARNEGIE, 2005

right Ecclesfield church. In the early seventeenth century, the Yorkshire antiquary, Roger Dodsworth, noted that local people called the church 'The Minster of the Moors'. St Mary's once served the whole of Hallamshire and Ecclesfield's Celtic place-name implies that a Christian community had been established here before the arrival of the pagan Anglo-Saxons. The church was rebuilt in the Perpendicul Gothic style between 1480 and 1520, but internal evidence shows that it replaced a substantial aisled building which had been completed about 1200. A crude Anglo-Saxon cross shaft was dug up outside the west door in 1893. Dodsworth went on to describe the building as ' fairest church for stone, wood, glase, and neat keeping, that ever I came in of contry church'.
PHOTOGRAPH: CARNEGIE 2004

left Anglo-Saxon Cross, Masham. The surviving lower part of a weather-beaten, round-shafted cross stands near the south door of St Mary's Church. The rich carvings suggest that Masham was an important monastic site in the Anglian period. Fragments of a pre-Conquest cross head and a rectangular-shafted cross are preserved within the church.
PHOTOGRAPH: AUTHOR

right Anglian crosses, All Saints' Church, Ilkley. Once standing in the churchyard, these crosses form a remarkable collection of ninth-century sculpture. The tallest cross shows the figure of Christ and various beasts; the sides are decorated with vine scrolls and the rear with the symbols of the four evangelists; the head was added a thousand years later. The other two crosses are also carved with beasts and vine scrolls in panels.
PHOTOGRAPH: CARNEGIE, 2005

dedicated to St Mary or to St Helen, the mother of Emperor Constantine, who may have replaced the Celtic deity Elen in popular imagination. St Helen wells are particular numerous in Yorkshire, Lancashire and Lincolnshire and that at Thorp Arch was venerated until modern times.

The evidence for the spread of Christianity comes mostly from the writings of Bede, the authors of numerous lives of saints, and the compilers of *The Anglo-Saxon Chronicle*, all of whom saw history through English eyes. We have to look at more tenuous evidence to learn something of the continued British influence that came from the various *eccles* and of the Christian centres that lay beyond the famous Northumbrian monasteries, especially in the districts where the population was thin on the ground. Some of these early centres can be identified by surviving architectural features or stone crosses, others by their later role as mother churches with huge parishes. It is clear that the religious communities that were mentioned in the literature of the eighth century were not the only ones that were around.

The important early church of All Saints at Ledsham served the old district of *Loidis* in the same way that Ecclesfield was the ecclesiastical centre of Hallamshire. Remarkably, much of the nave and the lower part of the tower, including the doorway into the south porch, survives intact from the eighth century. The small, blocked-in windows high in the nave wall, the chancel arch and the massive, side-alternate quoins define a narrow, box-like nave similar to that of the contemporary Northumbrian church at Escomb, County Durham. The nave of St Peter's, Conisbrough has a similar design and may be as early. During the twelfth century the Normans remodelled this church, but blocked-in windows and an entrance to a former porticus, or side-chapel, can be seen high above the new arches. Conisbrough's name means the 'king's fort' at the centre of a huge lordship. The church continued to serve a large parish with many detached portions until well into the Middle Ages.

Minster churches such as these were typically royal foundations for religious communities in the seventh or eighth centuries. King Edwin's estate at *Campodonum* in 'the forest of Elmet' had a church by 632, but its former whereabouts remains a matter of scholarly dispute. King Oswy (642–70) founded a monastery at West Gilling in repentance for a murder and a house of Benedictine monks was established at Ripon to replace the earlier community 'who followed Irish ways'. A group of canons were still there in the eleventh century, when the medieval liberty of Ripon stretched far over the surrounding countryside and included several sub-manors and outlying townships. The large estate centred on Otley, which was granted to Wilfrid, had a monastery by the eighth century. The two outstanding crosses there seem to have been commissioned by one of Wilfrid's successors as archbishop, yet Otley was not mentioned in surviving documents before the tenth century. One of the crosses bears the images of the four evangelists. Yorkshire has an important group of elaborately carved crosses from the pre-Viking era. Three at Ilkley date from 800–850 and a badly eroded cross from the same period stands in the churchyard at Masham. The large number of early crosses that were found at Dewsbury suggest that here was the minster centre for the huge manor of Wakefield. The remarkable frieze at All Saints, Hovingham, is thought to have been the side of a shrine, but the identity of the saint who was venerated there is unknown. The quality of the sculpture and the theological scholarship that

Anglian frieze, All Saints Church, Hovingham, showing scenes from the Annunciation. It dates from *c*.800 and may have been the side of a reliquary shrine to a local saint. The church also has a west tower in the Northumbrian style, with part of a ninth-century cross incorporated in its upper stage. Yet we have no documentary evidence for a church before the Norman Conquest.

inspired it show that Hovingham must have been an important religious centre that would otherwise have been unknown to us.

A letter from Pope Paul I to the king of Northumbria in 757–58 mentions a monastery at Coxwold, another not far away at Stonegrave, and a third at *Donaemuthe*, near Adlingfleet where the Don flows into the Trent. Elsewhere in Yorkshire, the evidence for early minster churches is more elusive, for the original buildings have been replaced in later styles. At Sherburn-in-Elmet the church of All Saints was rebuilt by the Normans but it stands within a prominent earthwork that hints at the early importance of the site and it served a large medieval parish. Other important minster churches at the centres of royal estates included those at Beverley, Bridlington, Catterick and Northallerton. The sites of many other small monastic houses remain unknown for they never recovered from the devastation of the Viking attacks in the ninth century. Bede feared that the transfer of estates to monasteries had become so common in his time that the kingdom would be weakened militarily.

The early Anglian settlements seem to have been founded within a framework of large estates or 'folk territories', some of which were already ancient. Balne, Hatfield and Lindrick are amongst the districts whose special character was already recognised. The names of particular settlements were rarely documented before the eighth century, by which time some were being abandoned in favour of new locations nearby. Place-names ending in -*ham*, such as Bramham, Ledsham or Rotherham, are thought to be amongst the earliest for they are found close to Roman roads or settlements. Some of the tribal leaders who led the way into new territory are commemorated in -*inga* or -*ingham* names, such as Addingham, Everingham, Headingley, Knottingley or Pickering. Goodmanham was known to Bede as *Godmundingaham*. But throughout England the largest group of place-names that were recorded by 731, when Bede wrote his great history, refer to features of the landscape. The lack of records before Domesday Book for the great majority of Yorkshire names means that we cannot place them in a firm historical context, nor can we be certain of their original forms. If Brinsford could change to Brinsworth, Greasbrook to Greasbrough, and Brekesherth to Brightside in the later Middle Ages, we must accept that others had probably changed during the long centuries of the Angles and the Vikings before they were written down for the first time in 1086. The significance of place-names to an understanding of settlement history remains a matter of much debate, though it is now generally recognised that the dominance of Anglian names, even in Craven and Elmet, does not mean that the native people were driven out or killed.

The large number of Anglian place-names that end in -ton or -ley are thought to date from after 750, with some minor names ending in -ley not appearing until after the Norman Conquest. These groups of place-names are the easiest to interpret, for -*tun* meant a settlement or small estate in countryside that had been cleared for arable farming and -*leah* referred to a clearing in a wood or a wood pasture. The first element of such names was often the personal name of the man who had the same status as a later lord of the manor. Some of the -*leahs* had probably been cleared well before the Angles arrived. They were found amongst managed woods where the farmers had a more pastoral economy than those who lived and worked in districts such as the narrow band of magnesian limestone whose fertile soils had long been used for growing cereals. Both types of names were relatively late formations within an older framework of large estates.

Several places with names ending in -*feld*, which referred to extensive pastures in a woodland landscape, were the centres of large estates. Driffield, Huddersfield and Wakefield are important examples and the three divisions of Hallamshire were Bradfield, Ecclesfield and Sheffield. Some places with -*wic* names, notably Stanwick, were early trading centres, yet others, such as Adwick-upon-Dearne seem to have been mere dairy farms. The -*burh* names have a wide range of reference to defensive structures. Almondbury and Ingleborough were Iron Age forts, Aldborough and Brough-on-Humber were Roman sites, but those along the Don at Barnburgh, Conisbrough, Mexborough and Sprotborough or along the Dearne at Kexbrough, Measbrough, Stainborough and Worsbrough point to Anglian defences erected during the conflicts between Northumbria and Mercia.

The English place-names within the old territory of Elmet contain many Mercian elements. This must mean that the Angles of Northumbria lost control of this district for long periods of time, during which new settlers arrived from the Midlands. For example, the Mercian place-name ending -*worth*, meaning an enclosure, is common to the south of the river Wharfe but rare in the North and East Ridings and specialist words like *iecels*, 'land added to an estate', as in Ickles near Rotherham, are found only to the west of the Great North Road in the southern part of the county. Numerous minor place-names that were formed after the Norman Conquest, such as *rod*, 'clearing' (which developed into the many -*royd* names of West Yorkshire), *pightel*, 'enclosure', *wang*, 'meadow' and dialect pronunciations such as *owler* for alder, are Mercian dialect forms that passed into northern speech. Mercian infiltration into Northumbria is also suggested by the positioning of Doncaster, Conisbrough, Rotherham and Sheffield on the south bank of the Don, which had long served as a frontier.

The Vikings

The Viking era in Northumbria opened in 793 with a traumatic attack on the monastery at Lindisfarne. The pagan warriors who sailed across the North Sea in their distinctive long ships were young aristocrats with poor prospects in their native countries where land was becoming scarce. Norwegians raided Orkney, the Western Isles and Ireland and Danes crossed the sea to plunder Northumbria's long and vulnerable coastline. In 866 a 'great army' of Danes sailed from the Low Countries to East Anglia. Their precise numbers are not known, but they stretched to thousands of soldiers who formed the largest force

to land in England before the Norman Conquest. They made rapid progress after their first winter, when they learned that Northumbria was in the throes of civil war between two rival claimants to the throne. In the summer of 867 they sailed up the Humber and took York with little resistance. At first, they were content with a client ruler and the taxes they imposed, but in 869 they returned for a whole year. In 870 they conquered the kingdom of East Anglia and four years later they defeated the Mercians. The account of their triumph which was written in the *Anglo-Saxon Chronicle* says that in 875 the great Danish army split into two and Halfdan led his troops to Tynemouth and then to York. The chronicler went on to report that in 876 Halfdan 'shared out the land of the Northumbrians, and they proceeded to plough and support themselves'. Northumbria was divided between the old Bernician territory to the north of the Tees, which remained under Anglian rulers in the late-ninth and early-tenth centuries, and a new Danish kingdom of York, which was allied to the Danish lordships in eastern Mercia and East Anglia. This kingdom seems to have covered the same territory that the Deirans had occupied at the height of their power. In time, it became the county of Yorkshire.

We know almost as little of the details of the Danish conquest and the tenth-century infiltration of groups of Norwegian Vikings from Ireland, western Scotland and Wales as we do of the earlier success of the Angles. The documentary and archaeological record is meagre before the spectacular discoveries from tenth-century *Jorvik*. Our only guides are the numerous Viking place-names and the survival of administrative units that ranged from ridings and wapentakes to things and bierlows.

Large numbers of Yorkshire settlements have Viking names that end in -by, -thorpe and -thwaite. In the North Riding 223 out of the 649 names that were recorded in Domesday Book are of Scandinavian origin and a further 66 are hybrids or English names that were influenced by Scandinavian speech. The East Riding has a similar proportion, but the Viking presence was less pronounced further inland in the West Riding, except in the countryside around York and Doncaster. The significance of all these names is a matter of scholarly debate, for it is agreed that the soldiers of Halfdan's army could not have filled all the settlements that have Danish names. Do the place-names simply demonstrate that a Viking elite took over the old estates and created smaller units that became the later manors and should we see the retired soldiers as

Viking sculpture, All Saints Church, Harewood. This fragment of a cross shaft was discovered in 1981 behind the Ryther monument. It seems to depict a boar hunt and has interlace decoration at the back and sides. It is thus similar in style to tenth- and eleventh-century sculptures that have been found elsewhere in Yorkshire.

PHOTOGRAPH: CARNEGIE, 2005

the ancestors of later thegns and minor lords? Or did large numbers of immigrant farmers sail across the North Sea once the conquest was complete, and is this why so many field names and other minor names have a Scandinavian origin and why Danish and Old Norse speech has had such a lasting influence on our language? Seventy per cent of the recorded personal names in the Yorkshire folios of Domesday Book were Scandinavian. So far DNA studies have failed to settle the matter.

Sometimes the Vikings replaced the Anglian name of a settlement with a new one in their own tongue, but it seems that total renaming was unusual. More commonly, as at Barnburgh, Mexborough and Thurlstone, existing settlements kept their Anglian place-name endings but took the name of their new lord as their first element. As Viking personal names were very different from the Anglian ones, we can distinguish them readily. More subtle changes occurred where Scandinavian words and forms replaced their English equivalents, so that Middleton might become Melton and Stainton could be pronounced Stanton. The numerous villages with Kirk, Kirby or Kirkby names are often sited on fertile lands, so perhaps they refer to existing churches that served Anglian settlements rather than to new church buildings once the Vikings became Christian? We can rarely be confident that a Viking place-name indicates a new settlement, though on the whole those places that have Danish names are scattered around earlier English ones on less desirable land. The various Denbys and Denabys distinguished groups of Danes who lived in neighbourhoods that were farmed mainly by the descendants of Britons and Angles.

In the first half of the tenth century groups of Norwegian Vikings from Ireland, Wales and western Scotland crossed the Pennines to settle on the marginal land that was still unoccupied. Names such as Crosland, Fixby, Golcar and elements in Greetland and Rastrick seem to have a Norwegian origin. Even so, less than a quarter of the West Riding's place-names are of Scandinavian origin, although another 10 per cent have been influenced by the Old Norse language in one way or another. It is not easy to separate minor place-names of Danish and Norwegian origin, though *torp* (thorpe) and *both* (booth) are Danish and *gil* (gill), *skali* (scholes), *brekka* (breck) and *slakki* (slack) are Norwegian. One of the lords of Ecclesfield in 1066 was called Norman, a 'north man' from Norway.

The numerous minor place-names that have a Scandinavian origin seem to imply a considerable expansion of secondary settlement during the Viking era and beyond. Thwaites were clearings, meadows or paddocks, thorpes were secondary settlements, and booths were cattle-rearing farms. The name Scholes or Scales often indicated a herdsman's hut or shieling on a summer pasture, but later on it simply denoted a labourer's cottage or a place where cows were milked on the edges of the commons. Carr names such as Deepcar and Potteric Carr were given to low-lying marshy areas overgrown with brushwood, such as alder or willow, and islands of dry land in the marshes were identified by the Old Norse word *holmr*, which has produced names such as Almholme, Lindholme and Shaftholme. Kirk Bramwith and South Bramwith are named from a wood overgrown with broom and minor names such as Loundside, The Lund and Lundwood come from an Old Norse word for a wood, perhaps in the sense of sacred grove.

Yorkshire's three ridings take their names from the Old Danish word *thrithing*, meaning a third part. Lindsey (the northern part of Lincolnshire) is the only other district to have ridings. The Yorkshire ridings were subdivided into wapentakes, a word that was derived from the symbolic flourishing of weapons at assemblies to signal agreement on matters of law and order. The Viking wapentakes seem to have been created gradually through the amalgamation of smaller units known as hundreds. By the time of Domesday Book the change to wapentakes was complete in the North and West Ridings but the conversion of the 18 hundreds of the East Riding into six wapentakes was not finished until the middle of the twelfth century. The new wapentake of Dickering, for example, covered roughly the same area as the three Domesday Book hundreds of Burton, Hunthou and Turbar. The meetings of wapentake assemblies were originally held in the open air at prominent and convenient sites, such as the crossing of the River Don at Strafford Sands or by tall crosses such as Ewcross, Staincross or Osgoldcross. Wapentakes lost their judicial functions in the later Middle Ages but they were still used for collecting taxes and raising the militia in the nineteenth century. They and the ridings were abolished in 1974. Other ancient units, which probably disappeared when the wapentakes were formed, took their names from the Old Danish word for an assembly. One met at Tingley, 'the mound where the thing or council met', and

Micklegate Bar, York. Micklegate was the 'great street' of *Jorvik*, Viking York, the principal highway into the city from the south and west. Micklegate Bar was one of the four entrances through the city walls. Its arch is Norman, but the super-structure was redesigned in the fourteenth century when the present city walls were built. Until the 1820s the Norman arch was approached through a barbican. Here, distinguished visitors were received by the mayor and corporation and escorted into the city. Here, too, were displayed the heads of executed traitors.

another at Morthen, 'the moorland assembly' near the village of Morthen; the old district name survives in Brampton-en-le-Morthen and Laughton-en-le-Morthen and was once applied to nearby Aston and Dinnington. The smallest administrative district of all was that of the township or vill, which the Vikings called a *byjar-log*, 'the law of the village'. The name long survived in South Yorkshire as Brightside Bierlow and Ecclesall Bierlow, two of the townships of Sheffield parish, as Greasbrough Bierlow in the parish of Rotherham, and a little further north as Brampton Bierlow, a suffix that distinguished the settlement from Brampton-en-le-Morthen a few miles away.

The Vikings destroyed all the early monasteries in the North and grabbed the estates for themselves. After their depredations, the nearest monastery to York was at Peterborough over 100 miles away. But some of the minster churches escaped the plundering and the relative lack of pagan grave goods and the discovery of Viking weapons in churchyards suggest that the invaders soon accepted native religious customs. In time, their leaders were converted to Christianity and their lifestyles were little different from those of the English kings to the south of Watling Street, which had become the agreed boundary of the Danelaw. From *c.* 882 to 895 *Jorvik* was ruled by a Christian king, Guthfrith, a Viking who was buried in York Minster.

A remarkable amount of Viking-age sculpture with a mixture of pagan and Christian elements survives in the old kingdom of York and its dependent territories in southern and central Cumbria. A cross at St Andrew's church, Middleton, depicts a warrior with a sword, shield, axe and spear. The River Tees appears to have been a major cultural barrier, for both the place-names and the distribution of surviving stone crosses and hogback tombstones show

Viking York. These tenth-century timber walls, discovered during the Coppergate excavations in the late 1970s, stand about a metre high. Solid oak planks were laid horizontally on thick beams that formed the foundations and upright posts reached up to roofs made of wooden shingles. These houses-cum-workshops of the coopers or woodworkers of Coppergate were set end-on to the street front. Many of York's central streets have names that end in the Old Norse *gata*, meaning 'street'. Coppergate formed part of the commercial heart of the Vikings' major city. Part of it has been reconstructed in the Jorvik Museum.

YORK ARCHAEOLOGICAL TRUST

Amber beads. The Coppergate excavations changed the popular image of the Vikings as brutal marauders. They were now seen as craftsmen and artists. In Coppergate a back room had been used as a workshop where jewellery was made, including these amber beads. The raw material was probably imported from the Baltic.

that the Vikings did not penetrate far into the Anglian kingdom of Northumberland, which was centred on Bamburgh. Anglian sculpture had been produced in monasteries, but the sculpture of the Viking era was a lay art, employing knotwork as the dominant motif and various shapes and designs that were peculiar to particular districts. Pagan stories of Wayland the Smith, Sigurd the Volsung (especially dragon-killing and heart-roasting) and Thor's fishing expedition were prominent parts of the Scandinavian mythology that was depicted on the sculptured stones. At Leeds a cross shaft combines Christian and pagan features by showing Wayland escaping with his wings and tools, accompanied by evangelists and ecclesiastics. Hogback tombstones, three-dimensional monuments that are often over four feet long, are distributed widely over the northern parts of Yorkshire. During the restoration of Brompton church, near Northallerton, in 1867 no fewer than eleven hogback tombstones were discovered. They are shaped like a building with walls and a roof and at each end beasts cling on to the gables and bite into the ridge. Other hogbacks with end-beats are found in neighbouring parishes between Brompton and the Tees. They were the distinctive art of Norwegian and Irish-Norse settlers from about 920 until the Norman Conquest.

Our sketchy appreciation of the Viking presence in the countryside of the kingdom of York is in marked contrast to the detailed knowledge that has been acquired from excavations at *Jorvik*, where a protective, oxygen-free environment of centuries of rubbish has preserved a huge range of objects made from organic materials such as leather, cloth and wood and simple domestic goods such as cooking pots and wooden cups, together with mass-produced silver brooches. *Jorvik* has become one of the most important archaeological sites in Britain. York's present street pattern was created in the tenth century with names such as Stonegate and Petergate which contain the Scandinavian element *gata*. From the south the curving line of Micklegate, the 'great street', passed through the former Roman colonia down to a new bridge over the Ouse. The excavations in Coppergate showed that the boundaries of the properties that stretched back from the new streets changed little over the next thousand years. The walls of the three adjacent timber buildings that were recovered – the best that have ever been found from this era – were made of several courses of horizontal plank cladding, supported on the inside by squared uprights. These were the houses and workshops of woodworkers and other craftsmen, including coiners or die-cutters. Finds from the excavations included jewellery made of amber and glass, combs made from antlers, various objects carved from bone, brooches and dress pins, fragments of clothing and hundreds of pairs of leather shoes. The excavations doubled the number of Viking artefacts that had been previously found in Britain and led to a reappraisal of the Vikings that emphasised the creative abilities of the citizens. Tenth-century *Jorvik* was a boom town with densely packed streets full of traders and craftsmen. By 1066 it was the second largest city in England with a lay-out that is still recognisable today.

The rulers of the Viking kingdom of York spent most of their time at their capital city for, unlike the earlier kings of Northumbria, they had no concerns north of the river Tees. The royal palace may be identified with *Conungsgurtha* ('King's Court') and the residence of the earls with *Earlsburgh*, the site now occupied by the ruins of St Mary's abbey. The walls of the old Roman fort were re-fortified with clay banks and *Jorvik* became a great capital and trading centre, which imported high-quality goods from Norway and the Baltic Sea. Animal hides, oils and fats came from the Arctic, pottery, ivory and silks from the Mediterranean, and jewellery, pottery and quern-stones from down the Rhine. *Jorvik*'s rural hinterland provided the beef and dairy produce that formed a major part of the diet of the townsmen and the everyday pottery was made locally. In more distant parts of the kingdom of York, however, the Viking contribution to the economy was modest.

By the tenth century the people of Yorkshire had mixed cultural origins and they were markedly less 'English' than those who lived further south. Their leaders did not take part in what has been seen as a struggle for English independence led by the kings of Wessex. When Athelstan became the ruler of Northumbria in 927, he was resented as an outsider. He was succeeded by the Norwegian warrior, Olaf, and later by another Norwegian, Eric Bloodaxe, but from 954 Northumbria was again ruled by Saxon kings whose policy was to appoint local earls but to encourage southern thegns to infiltrate the Viking kingdom. Yorkshire was first recorded as a name of a county in 1065, by which time the kingdom of York had been absorbed into the English kingdom for a century. Nevertheless, the Viking presence remained stronger here than anywhere else in the country.

Before the Norman Conquest

From the tenth century onwards, some of the large 'folk territories' or 'multiple estates' began to be broken into smaller manors with resident lords. Meanwhile, fresh grants by English kings, such as those by Athelstan to the minsters at York and Beverley, did little to restore the estates that the Vikings had confiscated from the monasteries and which they had divided into numerous small manors that were named after their new owners. The extensive estates or 'shires' that the kings and great lords of Northumbria had owned before the Viking invasion, such as Allertonshire, Burghshire, Coxwoldshire, Hallamshire, Howdenshire, Mashamshire, Riponshire and Sowerbyshire, began to fragment. as grants of small manors were made to younger children or to favoured followers. Domesday Book reveals that this process was well underway on some estates before the Norman Conquest, but others, such as Hallamshire, remained largely intact until their Norman lords created sub-manors and made generous donations to religious bodies.

The 'shires' contained every type of land, ranging from rough moorland and woodland pasture to good-quality arable and meadow. The lords farmed little land of their own and depended on the rents and dues of their tenants. An outstanding example is Burghshire, which stretched from the Pennine moors down to the lower valleys of the Ure, Nidd and Wharfe and which was named after its administrative centre at Aldborough, the successor to the old Roman town. Sixty of the 135 vills that were recorded within this shire in Domesday Book were wholly or partly royal possessions. By that time, the estate had two centres, at Aldborough and Knaresborough (which subsequently became the headquarters of a royal hunting forest), but the mixture of dependent properties known as berewicks and sokelands suggests that originally all had formed part of a single shire.

A complex pattern of landownership is evident from the Yorkshire folios of Domesday Book; nevertheless 40 per cent of the entries were concerned with berewicks and sokelands within the old shires and other large estates. The privileged tenants known as sokemen accounted for less than nine per cent of the recorded population of Yorkshire. Their largest numbers were in the multiple estates centred on Conisbrough, Northallerton, Wakefield and West Gilling. Over three-quarters of the West Riding's sokemen were found in the south-east, 120 of them in 24 places within the extensive lordship of Conisbrough, which stretched from the Don to the southern border of the county and eastwards into the lowlands of Hatfield, Thorne and Fishlake, though none was recorded in the central township. Another 40 belonged to the soke of Doncaster and a further 21 were listed in the outlying parts of the soke of Laughton-en-le-Morthen. Although sokemen were largely confined to the Danelaw, their privileges went back to Anglian times.

The creation of numerous small, independent manors had profound consequences. The new lords of the manor gave their names to the settlements that they dominated from their manor houses and regarded their estates as family properties which they passed on to their descendants. They were normally resident on their manors and they made sure that their peasants paid full dues and worked the prescribed number of days ploughing, sowing, weeding and harvesting the demesne lands. Many of the new manors were situated at the edges of the old multiple estates, but some were formed from scattered strips within the open fields and meadows and from associated pastures and commons. The divisions between the intermingled properties of different manors sometimes persisted until Victorian times and were recorded on the first editions of six-inch Ordnance Survey maps, but they did not affect the practical, communal farming arrangements of the villagers.

By the tenth and eleventh centuries much of the land in Yorkshire had been farmed for hundreds if not thousands of years and many of the estate and field boundaries were ancient. As the population grew, some of the pastures that had once been grazed on the edges of the woods, moors and fens and then abandoned after the departure of the Romans were cleared again, but the most striking changes in the landscape came on the corn-growing lands, when many

Holy Trinity church, Little Ouseburn. Even small medieval churches have contrasting architectural styles. Here the tower has Perpendicular Gothic battlements and pinnacles but is mostly early Norman, unbuttressed and with twin belfry-openings on each side. The chancel has Early English lancet windows, while the nave and aisle are Perpendicular in style. The isolated position of the church suggests that the settlement has moved since Norman times.
PHOTOGRAPH: CARNEGIE, 2005

of our villages assumed their present shapes and farmers began to practise common-field agriculture. Although excavations at West Heslerton have shown that post-Roman houses around the Vale of Pickering were clustered together, in most parts of England before the tenth century the typical settlement pattern was one of scattered farmsteads and small groups of houses whose occupiers farmed their land in individual plots. Excavations at Wharram Percy, on the Wolds, first cast doubts on the old notion that the original Anglo-Saxon settlers had introduced nucleated villages surrounded by open fields. The consensus of opinion now is that the change came much later and was not completed until well after the Norman Conquest. Although the new villages often kept the same names as the previous, dispersed communities, they were laid out in a radically different form.

These changes cannot be dated precisely, for we have no documentary evidence of the process. The regularity of some village plans along a road or around a green is striking even today and in many other cases nineteenth-century tithe award maps or the first edition of the six-inch Ordnance Survey maps enable historical geographers to measure the tofts and crofts and house plots and to prove a symmetrical arrangement. We cannot tell whether the new system was imposed from above or whether the local villagers planned the changes themselves after the harvest had been gathered, but it is noticeable that in the Vale of Pickering, where some classic examples of planned settlements are found, villages that had just one manorial lord were the most likely to be re-planned. Sometimes, the process might have been a gradual one and many other villages started as two or three groups of properties that were eventually joined together by new houses and cottages in the gaps. It seems likely that the open-field system was introduced at the same time as the village was planned, but we cannot be certain of this and we know that it often took a long time before a three-field system was fully developed. Originally, it seems, each farmer had a share of the good and the bad land in scattered strips within two or three open fields, with a share in the meadows and common rights on the pastures and wastes.

By the time of the Norman Conquest the present pattern of villages in Holderness was well established. This district had become one of the most densely populated parts of England, where peasant farmers cultivated their village cornfields right up to their parish boundaries. The acreage that was under the plough in the Domesday Book entry for Kilham in 1086 was exactly the same as that recorded in a survey in 1729. The only parishes in this district that still had any woods were those on the eastern slopes of the Wolds between Cave, Cottingham and Beverley. Domesday Book notes the names of 45 pre-Conquest freeholders who held land in Holderness, sometimes jointly and often in small parcels, but the name suggests that the district was once a single unit, for a 'hold' was a Danish nobleman. Perhaps that was when the distinctive field systems of Holderness came into being? Throughout the district, the cornfields of each village were laid out in long, parallel strips or 'lands'. These were often over 1,000 yards long and in some townships they stretched for over a mile. Even so, the arable was usually divided into just two communal fields which were rarely sub-divided into furlongs. The fields of each township had the same number of lands and each had the same proportion of broad and narrow lands lying in the same relative position to each other. The system of ownership was by 'sun-division', whereby each farmer had regularly placed strips in the fields that faced towards and away from the sun. The regularity of this pattern throughout Holderness suggests that it was imposed from above.

But Holderness villages do not have the regular plans of their fields. Many are strung out for over a mile and their structures seem to confirm the Domesday Book entries which reveal that before the Norman Conquest most villages were divided between two or more manorial lords. The villages on the Wolds are also irregular in shape, but here too the cornfields were usually laid out in two large fields divided into long lands. The light woods that had given the district its name had gone long before 1066 and the arable was tilled every-where except on the poorer soils of the High Wolds. One of the few charters to survive from before the Norman Conquest – a grant of an estate at Newbald on the western edge of the Wolds in 963 – shows that the boundary ran through dry valleys and along a prehistoric dyke towards Bronze Age burial mounds, but off the hills it followed watercourses and the edges of the cornfields. Its line can be identified as that of the medieval parish boundary. Another early charter from Holderness – a grant from King Cnut to the Archbishop of York of an estate at Pocklington in 1033 – also records boundary points that can be identified with those of the medieval parish. In waterlogged areas in the Hull valley, however, such as the marshy district between Wawne, Sutton, Rise and Routh, the township and parish boundaries were not agreed until the thirteenth century.

Planned villages arranged around a street or a green can be found also in the Vale of York. Their origins cannot be fixed firmly in time and many may date from after the Norman Conquest rather than from the Anglo-Scandinavian period. The corn-growing fields in the Vale of York were less extensive than those further east, but they appear to have been planned and were sometimes arranged by the 'sun-division' method. By 1140 at the latest, 16 original house plots were arranged in a regular pattern around the village street at Wheldrake and about 350 acres of surrounding arable land had been enclosed by a turf dyke. Elsewhere in these central parts of the county, much of the landscape was wooded and the watterlogged carrs near the Ouse and the Humber were sparsely settled, despite some early attempts at draining and diking.

The villages and hamlets on the coal-measure sandstones further west were also surrounded by open fields that were divided into strips for the communal growing of cereals, but most of the land in this district was farmed as wood pasture with extensive commons. The place-names need to be interpreted within the framework of the old estates. In the medieval parish of Royston, for instance, Carlton was where the churls or free peasants lived, Notton was where castrated rams were fattened, and Woolley was a wood pasture where wolves were still a hazard to the flocks of sheep.

The farmers in the hamlets that nestled high on the Pennines grew oats and rye in the strips of their small 'townfields' and hay in their hill meadows, while grazing their livestock on the commons and in pastures that had been cleared from the edges of the woods and moors in a piecemeal fashion. Place-names such as Onesacre, Thurgoland and Hunshelf, that were recorded in Domesday Book, refer to late settlements on relatively unproductive land. Some enclosures on the moorland edges were set aside as specialist cattle-rearing farms, known as booths or tunstalls. Other Old English and Scandinavian words were used for particular features in the landscape – for example a greave was a coppice wood, and a hirst was a wood on a hill – but the scarcity of documentary records for most localities before the late twelfth century means that we cannot usually put a firm date on them.

Although only 18 Yorkshire charters and wills date from before the Norman Conquest, they provide enough evidence to suggest that most medieval township boundaries were already established by the mid tenth century. A charter of 959 for the old 'multiple estate' of Howden mentions eight dependent settlements, all of which were described in Domesday Book as berewicks: Barn Hill, Belby, Caville, Eastrington, Hive, Kelpin, Knedlington and Thorpe. Six of the eight had Anglian names and the whole territory was bounded by the Ouse, Derwent, Aire and Foulness. Some of the places that were mentioned in other charters were not recorded in Domesday Book, which was concerned with estates rather than settlements. Large manors in the upland districts probably had many unrecorded small settlements. The brief entries in the Yorkshire folios of Domesday Book should be read warily, for they omit much essential information. They do not mention pastures, which must have covered far greater acreages than cereals, only two moors are named, and the total absence of recorded woodland in some districts is suspect. Woods were usually recorded as woodland pasture, where pigs grazed, but some were referred to as coppices, the carefully managed underwoods that were felled on rotation. The place-names Pilley and Shafton were derived from coppice woods where poles and shafts were made. Wood-pastures were a distinctive feature of the manors on the coal-measure sandstones, but the adjacent manors on the belt of magnesian limestone had been largely cleared of trees long before the Norman Conquest.

Over 1,800 Yorkshire place-names were recorded in Domesday Book. Five out of every six of the hamlets and villages that were settled before the end of the Middle Ages were in existence by 1066. Many of these settlements were already ancient by that time, though few have left earlier records. Most of their names have Old English, Old Danish or Old Norse elements and in many cases a mixture of two of these. The Viking presence is obvious in about 37 per cent of the Yorkshire place-names that were formed before the Norman Conquest. The great majority of Yorkshire people lived in the countryside, but Domesday Book shows that York was already a bustling place, second only to London in

left Ripon Minster. The church of St Peter and St Wilfrid is built above the crypt of the church that Wilfrid erected about 670. Nothing of the original church or monastery survives above ground level, for it was destroyed in 950. It then became a collegiate church for Ripon's large parish and was elevated to cathedral status in 1836. The present building is a mixture of styles, starting with a total reconstruction in the late thirteenth and early fourteenth centuries under the direction of Roger de Pont L'Évêque, Archbishop of York. The transepts and much of the choir are from this period, but the east end had to be rebuilt after it collapsed in 1288 and the crossing tower was reconstructed after a destructive thunderstorm in 1458 caused a great deal of damage. The nave is Perpendicular Gothic of the early sixteenth century. The three towers were topped with wooden spires until the seventeenth century. The church, by then a cathedral, was thoroughly restored in Victorian times under Sir George Gilbert Scott.

above When the village church of St John the Baptist at Kirk Hammerton, nine miles west of York, was greatly extended in 1891, the previous, late Anglo-Saxon church was preserved intact on the southern side of the new building. It stands on a knoll or mound and is one of the most complete survivals from about the time of the Norman Conquest. It has been argued that it may be as late as c.1100, though built in the old style that was familiar to the local masons. It can be categorised as 'Saxo-Norman overlap'. Even although it was erected many centuries after the fall of the Roman Empire, the builders seem to have re-used enormous stones from a nearby Roman fort or other structure. Roughly squared, greyish-brown stones were laid in irregular courses and even larger stones were selected for the quoins at the corners of the nave and chancel. The simple tower was added soon afterwards; the windows were inserted much later.

Tucked away in the valley named after it, about 4 miles east of Helmsley, St Gregory's Church, Kirkdale, was rebuilt not long before the Conquest. The tall, narrow nave is from that time, incorporating carved stones from the earlier church and perhaps the large quoins at its south-west corner. In the later Middle Ages windows were inserted and a porch added. The tower and chancel are nineteenth-century.

This Anglo-Scandinavian cross-shaft is one of many stones from the earlier church and churchyard that were re-used as humble building materials when the church was rebuilt in the eleventh century. It was placed in the nave wall and would originally have been plastered over.

This Anglo-Saxon inscription alongside the sundial above the south door of St Gregory's church tells how Orm, the son of Gamel, had bought the church when it was broken and fallen and had made it anew from the ground in honour of Christ and St Gregory, in the days of Edward the king and Tosti the earl. It dates from between 1055 and 1065.

PHOTOGRAPHS: CARNEGIE, 2005

size and importance. York was one of the greatest centres of North Sea trade and, with Chester, one of the only two towns north of the Trent where coins were minted The anonymous *Life of St Oswald* describes York about 980 as a densely populated city with rich Scandinavian merchants, but also with many poor buildings. Domesday Book informs us that by the reign of Edward the

Confessor York had between 1,600 and 1,800 houses and at least 14 churches, of which the tower of St Mary Bishophill Junior is the outstanding survivor.

The change from large estates to numerous small manors prompted the building of parish churches and the fragmenting of the old minster territories. The new lords of the manor, including those of Viking descent who had converted to Christianity, built their own places of worship close to their manor houses and appointed rectors to serve the parishes or chapelries which often followed the same boundaries as the manors. The survival of various payments to 'mother churches' in the later Middle Ages and sometimes well beyond helps us to reconstruct the districts that were served by some of the minster churches, such as Dewsbury, Otley and West Gilling, before they were subdivided into parishes. We are reliant on these clues, for we have very little other evidence. By the time of the Norman Conquest, the parochial system that survived into Victorian times was well established, though some churches long remained chapels-of-ease.

The medieval diocese of York stretched beyond the boundaries of the old Danish kingdom to include Nottinghamshire, which formed one of the five archdeaconries. This arrangement dates from mid tenth-century grants which compensated the Archbishop for his losses during the Viking invasion. Then, in 956 Archbishop Osketel acquired a large estate centred upon Southwell and two years later he received the equally generous gift of Scrooby and Sutton, just south of the Yorkshire border. The old minsters at Beverley, Ripon and Southwell became great collegiate churches that were in practice sub-cathedrals for the huge diocese of York.

The recovery and then rapid expansion of organised Christianity throughout Yorkshire is evident from the large quantity of church architecture and sculpture that survives from the period 950–1100. But of the 200 or so churches that date at least in part from before the end of the twelfth century few seem to be much earlier than 1050. One of the most complete examples at Kirk Hammerton is thought by some to have been built as late as the last quarter of the eleventh century or even the first years of the twelfth. Several churches that have been excavated in recent years were rebuilt in stone during this period after an earlier phase in wood. The place-names Felkirk and Woodkirk denote timber-framed churches and the Domesday Book entry for Old Byland refers to a wooden church, so perhaps it was common for the new parishes to be served by a wooden building until the final years of the Anglo-Scandinavian era.

At St Bartholomew's church at Aldbrough, in Holderness, a sundial that is built into the nave wall is inscribed 'Ulf had this church built for himself and for Gunwara's soul'. The contemporary church of St Mary, Castlegate, York, was built by Grim and Aese. Even before the Norman Conquest, many Yorkshire churches had been rebuilt, repaired and improved. The most famous example is the secluded church of St Gregory, Kirkdale, near Kirkbymoorside, where a sundial is inscribed 'Orm, son of Gamal, acquired the church of St Gregory when it was tumbled and ruined, and had it rebuilt from the ground

Anglian cross, St James's Church, Nunburnholme. Dating from about the year 1000, this is the finest cross in the East Riding. The figures below the arches on each side have not been identified, but a seated Virgin and Child in profile is recognisable. Small monsters, including a centaur, are also depicted.

PHOTOGRAPH: CARNEGIE, 2005

in honour of Christ and St Gregory, in the days of Edward the King and Tosti the Earl', i.e. between 1055 and 1065. Several neighbouring parishes along the northern edge of the Vale of Pickering, including those at Appleton-le-Street, Hovingham, Kirkby-moorside, Middleton and the royal minster at Pickering, have churches or stone crosses that date in part from the same era. Other Yorkshire churches with eleventh-century towers include those at Little Ouseburn, Skipwith and Wharram-le-Street, while All Saints, Kirkby Hill, two miles to the north of Aldborough, incorporates Roman masonry and has a nave whose corner stones are arranged in the typical side-alternate style of the period. In the border zone of South Yorkshire a mixture of styles is evident, with 'Mercian-type' long-and-short quoins at Laughton-en-le-Morthen and Bolton-upon-Dearne, a tower constructed with different techniques at Brodsworth, and stones arranged in herringbone patterns in the tower at Maltby. Three of these churches are on the magnesian limestone, the most densely settled part of medieval South Yorkshire, where the parishes were small and the churches numerous. The excavation of St Wilfrid's, Hickleton, showed that the first building on the site was a single-cell church, which had begun as a chapel-of-ease in the parish of Barnburgh; a silver penny minted at York in 905 was found at the lowest level of construction.

The large numbers of stone crosses that survive from the Anglo-Scandinavian era add further proof that Christianity was by then triumphant in Yorkshire. About one-quarter of the medieval parish churches in the Yorkshire countryside have pre-Conquest carved stones standing erect, embedded in the fabric, or reassembled after discovery. A fine mid eleventh-century cross stands over 11 feet tall in St Peter's church, Leeds. The best cross in the East Riding, at Nunburnholme, dates from the mid tenth century. Many others are only of poor quality and often owe their survival to their re-use as common building stone by Norman masons, but as they are often placed in unexceptional village churches they are collectively important in showing how widespread was the provision of places of worship before the Norman Conquest. Domesday Book seriously under-records this provision, for only 45 of the 140 Yorkshire churches that have crosses were mentioned there. Neither Aldbrough nor Wharram-le-Street are among the 167 churches that appear in the Yorkshire

section of Domesday Book, despite the clear architectural evidence that they date from before 1066.

Of the six northern counties, only Yorkshire was created before the Norman Conquest. The Domesday Book entries for Yorkshire were arranged under York and the three ridings, except that Craven was not yet incorporated within the West Riding. Beyond the county's north-western border, Amounderness, Cartmel, Furness, Kentdale and parts of Copeland and Lonsdale were attached to Yorkshire for administrative convenience. Each of these districts remained within the diocese of York and the archdeaconry of Richmond long after the creation of Lancashire, Westmorland and Cumberland in the twelfth century. Yorkshire's southern boundary with Nottinghamshire was not finalised until the Norman period and though the sea formed an obvious boundary to the east, the coastline has changed considerably. The Holderness coast has been severely eroded since at least the thirteenth century and a strip of land, perhaps a mile wide and containing 16 townships that were recorded in Domesday Book, has been lost.

When Eric Bloodaxe was killed at the battle of Stainmore in 954 and the kingdom of York was annexed to Wessex, a local earl was, prudently, left in charge. The place-names of north-west Yorkshire suggest that the leading local inhabitants there were a mixture of Norwegians, Irish-Norse and Strathclyde Britons, as in Cumbria. The Yorkshire nobility had developed a strong tradition of separatism and of empathy with the warriors of Scandinavia. The Danish kings who ruled England between 1016 and 1042 also preferred to appoint Scandinavians as earls of York. In 1055 Edward the Confessor appointed Tostig, Harold's brother, as earl, but ten years later he was expelled by the northern nobles, who invited Morcar, the younger brother of Edwin, Earl of Mercia, to take his place. When Tostig and Harold Hardrada of Norway invaded Yorkshire in 1066 Edwin and Morcar insisted that King Harold marry their sister as the price of their support. The invaders were defeated at Stamford Bridge, but Harold had little time to celebrate, for news soon arrived of a new invasion on the south coast of England. The Norman victory at Hastings on 14 October 1066 was one of the most decisive turning points in English history. All parts of the land were soon to feel its impact.

| *The Normans*

T HE STRONGEST RESISTANCE to William the Conqueror came from
the north of England. In the spring of 1068 Earls Edwin and Morcar led
a revolt against the taxes that he had levied and for a time it seemed possible
that the old kingdom of York might be revived with the help of the Danes or
the Scots. William's triumph was by no means a foregone conclusion as his
army marched north, but the rebels failed to gain support and were forced to
flee from York. The Conqueror ordered the construction of a motte-and-bailey
castle and left William Malet in charge of a garrison of 500 men, but another
rebellion broke out in the following year and the Norman army at Durham was
massacred. William returned to York, erected a second castle and placed

William fitz Osbern in command. Which of the two surviving castle earthworks came first is not known. The motte-and-bailey that was erected where the Foss flowed into the Ouse was strengthened in the thirteenth century by Clifford's Tower and became known as York Castle; the other one can be identified with the mound known as Baile Hill or Old Baile, which rises just inside the city walls on the opposite bank of the Ouse.

In September 1069 the rebels again came down from the hills to attack Fitz Osbern's troops, but their Danish allies, who had sailed up the Humber, eventually made peace with William and departed. Although it was not obvious at the time, the great era of the Vikings was over. William's army spent Christmas in York, but the threat of renewed guerilla activity if they left remained real. The exasperated William decided that the rebels had to be exterminated by a ruthless campaign, so horrific even by the violent standards of the age that it became known as the infamous 'harrying of the North'. His army marched into the countryside around York and Durham, killed everyone they could find, and burned down villages and hamlets, so that the guerillas had no food or other means of support. The *Anglo-Saxon Chronicle* says that William 'laid waste all the shire' and Ordericus Vitalis, writing from Normandy about 1125, claimed that

'*Castles he caused to be made, and poor men to be greatly oppressed.*'

ANGLO-SAXON CHRONICLE

> Nowhere else had William shown so much cruelty. Shamefully he succumbed to this vice, for he made no effort to restrain his fury and punished the innocent with the guilty. In his anger he commanded that all crops and herds, chattels and food of every kind should be brought together and burned to ashes with consuming fire, so that the whole region north of the Humber might be stripped of all means of sustenance. In consequence so serious a scarcity was felt in England, and so terrible a famine fell upon the humble and defenceless populace, that more than 100,000 Christian folks of both sexes, young and old alike, perished of hunger.

A later writer, Symeon of Durham, believed that 'Between York and Durham no village was inhabited'. He had heard that the countryside lay desolate for nine years, deserted except by bandits and wild animals.

There can be little doubt about the brutality of the campaign, even if we regard Orderic's figure of 100,000 deaths as the wild guess of someone who was born after the event, but it is difficult to judge the geographical extent of the devastation and the long-term effects of this barbarity. Earlier historians assumed that the numerous entries in Domesday Book that ended 'now it is waste' provided clear evidence of the destruction of settlements 17 years before the survey. No fewer than 480 Yorkshire vills (or townships) were returned as wholly waste, and another 314 as partly so: 367 in the North Riding, 267 in the West Riding and 160 in the East Riding. Waste vills were recorded in most English counties, but not on the large scale of Yorkshire. Later historians have shown, however, that 'waste' was often used as an administrative term for estates that no longer existed or had been amalgamated and in cases of doubtful ownership. Some vills that were described as waste were nevertheless given a value. The interpretation of Domesday Book is a highly technical matter, but the present consensus is that the entries for Yorkshire and Cheshire do not provide convincing evidence of the lasting effects of the harrying.

In 1086 the Pickering estate had a much lower value than it had 20 years earlier, but the nearby Coxwold estate had doubled in value and had more than twice the number of plough-teams. Little or no waste was recorded in the vills that were sited along major invasion routes, such as the lower reaches of the Ouse and the approach to Stamford Bridge from Bridlington, whereas plenty of waste vills were noted in areas that lay well away from York, such as Holderness or parts of South Yorkshire. In the northwest of the county, the wapentakes of Ewcross and Staincliffe provided many examples of waste vills, but immediately beyond their boundaries the neighbouring vills were apparently thriving. Domesday Book does not seem to be a reliable guide to the extent and ferocity of the harrying. Can we believe that the comparatively small army that the Normans had in the north could have wreaked so much damage that huge tracts of land still lay devastated 17 years later? It is difficult to accept that as many as 480 settlements, that is over a quarter of those recorded in the Yorkshire folios of Domesday Book, had no inhabitants in 1086, yet nearly all of them were subsequently resettled with their former place-names and boundaries intact.

Lordships and castles

Throughout England, the Normans consolidated their victory by forcing the natives to construct earthen castles, the likes of which had never been seen before. The *Anglo-Saxon Chronicle* observed of William: 'Castles he caused to be made, and poor men to be greatly oppressed'. The earliest type is thought to have been the ringwork, a circular enclosure formed by a bank and ditch. A good example is to be seen at Kippax, alongside the early Norman church. Another stands above the river Esk at Castleton, high on the North York Moors. This type of structure was soon abandoned in favour of the more complex motte-and-bailey castle. Mottes were great conical mounds with flat tops that

The motte-and-bailey castle at Mexborough, on the northern bank of the River Don opposite Conisbrough Castle, defended the important crossing at Strafford Sands, the meeting place of the wapentake. It may have replaced the earlier fort that gave Mexborough its name. Like so many of the Norman military earthworks, it was never developed into a stone castle.

PHOTOGRAPH: AUTHOR

In 1066 Kippax was the head of a large estate belonging to Edwin, Earl of Mercia. After the Norman Conquest it became the administrative centre of the northern part of Ilbert de Laci's huge honour of Pontefract. The bank of the early Norman ringwork is well preserved, immediately north-west of St Mary's church. The church was built soon after the Conquest, presumably by local masons who had long been familiar with the herringbone technique that allowed the use of poor-quality masonry. Both ringwork and church date from the time when the Normans were establishing control of Yorkshire.

PHOTOGRAPH: CARNEGIE 2005

Herringbone stonework on the tower of Kippax church.

PHOTOGRAPH: CARNEGIE 2005

supported wooden towers surrounded by a palisade of stakes; they acted as last refuges against attacks. Baileys were large enclosures which were defended by high banks and deep ditches; they contained domestic and service buildings, such as stables and barns. Good examples survive in South Yorkshire at Bradfield, Laughton-en-le-Morthen, Mexborough and Thorne. Some were erected during the long civil war of the reign of King Stephen (1135–54), when a hostile account in the *Anglo-Saxon Chronicle* noted that the barons 'filled the whole land with these castles. They sorely burdened the unhappy people of the country with forced labour on the castles. And when the castles were made they filled them with devils and wicked men'. In this poorly recorded period it remains impossible to date the construction of motte-and-bailey earthworks precisely and to say how long they continued in use. Pottery that was found

The Norman fortification of Burton-in-Lonsdale began with a simple ringwork, consisting of a mound surrounded by a ditch. This was probably erected in William the Conqueror's reign by the new lord, Ivo Taillebois, the king's steward, who was also granted Kendal. The ringwork was later enlarged into a motte-and-bailey castle, either under Ivo's successor, Robert de Stuteville, who was a major landowner in Yorkshire during William Rufus's reign, or by William of Lancaster, who was lord during the civil war of the reign of King Stephen. The Anglo-Saxon place-name suggests that there was an earlier fort on or near this site. All Saints Church, in the background, was completely rebuilt in 1868–76.

PHOTOGRAPH: CARNEGIE, 2005

during excavations at Castle Hill, Bardsey, dates from the twelfth and thirteenth centuries. Former ringworks appear to have been converted into motte-and-bailey castles at Burton-in-Lonsdale and Castle Hill, Mirfield, where the bailey now encloses the cemetery of the parish church. Some sites are difficult to interpret because the character of the local topography has changed considerably

Set high in Wensleydale, the Norman castle at Middleham replaced an earlier motte-and-bailey nearby. It was built in the late twelfth century for Robert de Fitz-Ranulf on a site that was not the best as far as defence was concerned. The keep was much more spacious than was usual and the windows and other architectural features relate to domestic arrangements rather than military considerations. Late in the thirteenth century, a massive curtain wall, 4 feet 6 inches thick, enclosed the keep. The whole structure seems to have been designed to impress rather than intimidate.

PHOTOGRAPH: CARNEGIE, 2005

since the Norman period. At Skipsea the motte is linked to the bailey by a cause-way which once spanned the tidal mere that separated them, and at Langthwaite, two miles north of Doncaster, a low-lying motte-and-bailey which now looks difficult to defend was originally surrounded by marshes.

In more settled times, many of these earthworks became obsolete, though a few remained outlying administrative centres of the great Norman lordships. Kimberworth, Laughton and Mexborough served in this capacity for the honour of Tickhill, and Almondbury, Kippax and Mirfield acted as similar centres for the honour of Pontefract. During the twelfth century, only the major sites were converted into castles with stone keeps, gatehouses and curtain walls whose towers soared at intervals above deep defensive ditches. The earliest keeps were rectangular in plan, following the sturdy examples of the Tower of London and Colchester Castle. Those at Richmond and Middleham are particularly fine examples of splendid residences rather than military strongholds.

In the late-eleventh and early-twelfth centuries the Norman kings treated Yorkshire as a border zone that had to be governed by some of their most trusted companions. The fear of new revolts and of Scottish or perhaps Viking attacks prompted William I and his sons to create huge lordships, known as castellanies or honours, around the major castles that defended the Vale of York and blocked the routes that came down from the Pennines. Domesday Book reveals that Yorkshire was controlled by only 28 tenants-in-chief and king's thegns compared to the 69 who shared responsibility for the smaller, neighbouring county of Lincolnshire. The same policy of appointing ruthless

The barons 'filled the whole land with these castles. They sorely burdened the unhappy people of the country with forced labour on the castles. And when the castles were made they filled them with devils and wicked men.'

ANGLO-SAXON CHRONICLE

SOUTH VIEW OF CONISBOROUGH CASTLE.

The romantic ruins of Conisbrough Castle, drawn in 1785. Hameline Plantagenet's cylindrical tower, built in the 1170s, still stands almost to its full height, for it was not fortified by Royalist troops during the Civil War of the 1640s and therefore not ordered to be demolished by the victorious parliamentarians afterwards. It had reached this ruined state through lack of care and the plundering of stone for buildings.
BY COURTESY OF THE YORKSHIRE ARCHAEOLOGICAL SOCIETY

barons who were determined to hang on to their spoils of the conquest was applied to the Welsh borders. Medieval castles are now a proud part of our heritage, but they were once the overbearing symbols of a brutal army of occupation.

One of the Conqueror's most trusted advisors was William de Warenne, the younger son of a powerful family that had taken their name from Varenne, near Dieppe. A commander at the battle of Hastings, he was soon rewarded with extensive estates, including the great lordship of Conisbrough, which had belonged to King Harold. He also built castles and priories at Lewes (Sussex) and Castle Acre (Norfolk). By the time of Domesday Book, Conisbrough was the most advanced Norman lordship in Yorkshire, a great, complex manor that had risen in value since the conquest. Warenne's stronghold was replaced by the present castle in the 1170s by Hameline Plantagenet, who had married the heiress of the family. The 90-feet high keep occupies a commanding position above an ancient crossing of the river Don. Built of local magnesian limestone, it was a larger version of the castle on the Warenne's Normandy estate at Mortemer and had the new cylindrical plan that had first been used at Orford (Suffolk). The main entrance is 20 feet above the spreading plinth and the six buttresses that support the 25-feet thick walls of the unlit basement, and the main living room on the first floor and the solar above are approached by an internal staircase. The designs of the joints of their great fireplaces appear to have been introduced into this country by men who had fought in the crusades. On the top floor were a small guard room, two cisterns, an oven and a dovecote,

Castle Hill, Sandal. About 1107 William de Warenne II, one of the mightiest of the Norman barons, was granted the huge manor of Wakefield by King Henry I. His castle was erected to the south of Wakefield at Sandal. The reclining figures on the bank side of the enormous motte give some idea of the vast scale of the castle. Only a few fragments of the walls survive, but the outline of this giant earthwork is still plain to see. Wakefield was a royal manor at the time of the Civil War and so the castle was demolished by order of Parliament in the late 1640s.

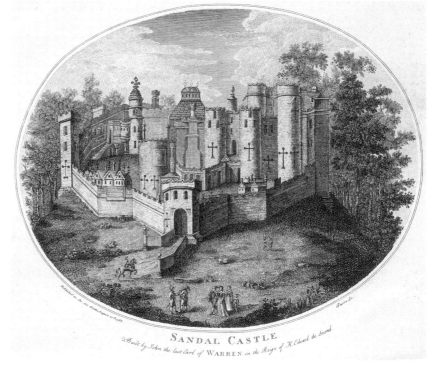

SANDAL CASTLE
Built by John the last Earl of WARREN in the Reign of K. Edward the Second.

Conisbrough's name means 'the king's stronghold', for this had been a seat of the kings of Northumbria. After the Norman Conquest this lordship was given to one of the Conqueror's mightiest barons, William de Warenne, who also had great estates in other parts of the country. The late twelfth-century keep, now cleaned and restored, rises behind the curtain wall, towers and barbican.
AUTHOR COLLECTION

which were sheltered by a conical roof. The curtain wall of the inner bailey, which enclosed several buildings whose foundations have been exposed by excavation, appears to be contemporary with the keep, though its towers were added about 20 years later. Conisbrough Castle remains the mightiest medieval military monument in South Yorkshire.

There is even less still standing at the Warennes' other Yorkshire castle, at Sandal within the manor of Wakefield, though the earthworks are impressive. In 1107 Henry I gave this huge manor, which stretched over the Pennines to the county's western boundary, to William de Warenne II. William's motte-and-bailey castle was replaced in the thirteenth century by a stone structure with a circular keep and four smaller towers crowning the motte; these were defended by a barbican and connected to the bailey by two drawbridges. The buildings within the curving line of the bailey included a great hall and kitchens. Excavations have revealed the entire ground plan of the castle in what is now a public park.

The defences of the Vale of York were strengthened by adding two new honours to these ancient royal lordships. The honour of Pontefract stretched across to the Pennines alongside the manor of Wakefield, while the honour of Tickhill was a southern neighbour of the lordship of Conisbrough. Pontefract Castle guarded the route over the moors through the Aire Gap and was built on the old Roman road from Doncaster to Catterick, while the eastern boundary of the honour followed the alternative route north from Doncaster to York. The king granted this new lordship to Ilbert de Laci, a powerful baron from Lassy, south of Bayeux, whose brother had a similar estate on the border with Wales. Pontefract takes its name from the old French words *pont freit* for broken bridge (hence the pronunciation Pomfret), because the castle and the town that grew alongside it were sited away from the previous manorial centre at Tanshelf. The keep, curtain wall and towers of the castle were destroyed after the parliamentarian victory in the Civil War in the 1640s, but an idea of their former size can be obtained from the sad ruins. The keep had been the most spectacular in Yorkshire.

The keep at Tickhill suffered the same fate. Little is known about the first Norman lord of the honour of Tickhill, Roger de Busli, who came from Bully-le-Vicompte, near Neufchâtel-en-Brai in Normandy. His motte-and-bailey castle was erected at the edge of the great swamp that divided Yorkshire from Nottinghamshire. At the other side of the swamp, Blyth acted as a second centre of the honour and was chosen as the site of the Benedictine priory that Roger founded. The new honour was made up of numerous manors in Nottinghamshire, Derbyshire and South Yorkshire, including Earl Edwin's estate at Laughton-en-le-Morthen. Roger's successor, Robert de Belleme, lost all by resisting the succession of Henry I and in 1102 the honour passed to the Crown. In 1129–30 King Henry built a shell keep, a curtain wall and a gatehouse at Tickhill and between 1178 and 1182 Henry II built a new, eleven-sided keep, a stone bridge and a higher curtain wall with four towers. Meanwhile, a successful new borough had been laid out near the castle, as at Pontefract.

'Roger, the man of Roger de Busli', one of the principal tenants of the honour of Tickhill at the time of the Domesday survey, can be identified with Roger de Louvetot, who came from a village that lay to the north of the river Seine in Normandy. His successor, William de Louvetot, became lord of both Hallamshire and Worksop and the tenant of the Pagnells' lands in South Yorkshire. In the early twelfth century William built substantial motte-and-bailey castles at Sheffield and Worksop and probably that at Bailey Hill, Bradfield. Sheffield Castle was destroyed in the Barons' War of 1266, but four years later Thomas de Furnival began work on an enormous stone castle, which dominated the town until it was dismantled in the late 1640s, after being fortified by the royalists in the Civil War.

The same pattern of development is evident in the rest of Yorkshire. After the suppression of the northern revolt the former estates of Earls Edwin and

Richmond Castle. Work began on the castle in 1071, when the Honour of Richmond was created to quell opposition to the Norman Conquest. The herringbone masonry, seen here in part of the curtain wall, supports this early date. The tower keep was built over the gatehouse about a century later. It is over 100 feet high and is one of the best-preserved keeps in the country.

Morcar were confiscated and turned into Norman castellanies, with many extra manors. By 1088 Yorkshire was the only county north of the Humber and Mersey that was fully under Norman control, with an archbishop, a sheriff, a mint, and two castles at York. The tenants-in-chief who were recorded in Domesday Book included William de Percy (from Percy-en-Auge, Eure) and Osbern de Archis (from Arques-la-Bataille, near Dieppe), whose families are commemorated in the place-names Bolton Percy and Thorp Arch. In many other parts of Yorkshire the ruins of formidable medieval castles still impress us with a sense of Norman might.

In the north of the county, the honour of Richmond was one of the three largest lordships that were created by William the Conqueror. He placed it in the safe hands of his cousin, Alan the Red, brother of the Duke of Brittany. The Bretons had played a key role at the battle of Hastings. Alan also held estates in eastern England and by the time of Domesday Book he was one of the richest and most powerful of the Norman barons. Two of his brothers succeeded him in turn after his death in 1093, and the family held on to the Richmond estate until 1399. Alan began work on his castle in 1071, once the northern rebellion had been put down. The cliff-top site high above the river Swale was given the appropriate Norman French name of Richmond, the 'strong hill'. From the beginning, stone curtain walls defended the other two sides of the triangular bailey. The use of herringbone masonry suggests that these walls, together with the original gatehouse and Scolland's Hall, were finished by the end of the twelfth century. The principal rooms in this two-storeyed hall, which were reached by an outside staircase, are of great architectural interest in providing the earliest example of this type of domestic accommodation in the whole of Europe. The remarkably well-preserved keep

Richmond Castle.
J. M. W. Turner's dramatic view of Richmond Castle on the cliff top above the River Swale. The original castle was built by Alan Rufus, lord of the enormous new Honour of Richmond that William the Conqueror had given him to subdue the North. Much of the curtain wall is Alan's work. The massive keep was erected over the gatehouse a hundred years later. Richmond was a Norman French name, meaning 'strong hill', an obvious attribution from this viewpoint.

BY COURTESY OF GROVE RARE BOOKS, BOLTON ABBEY

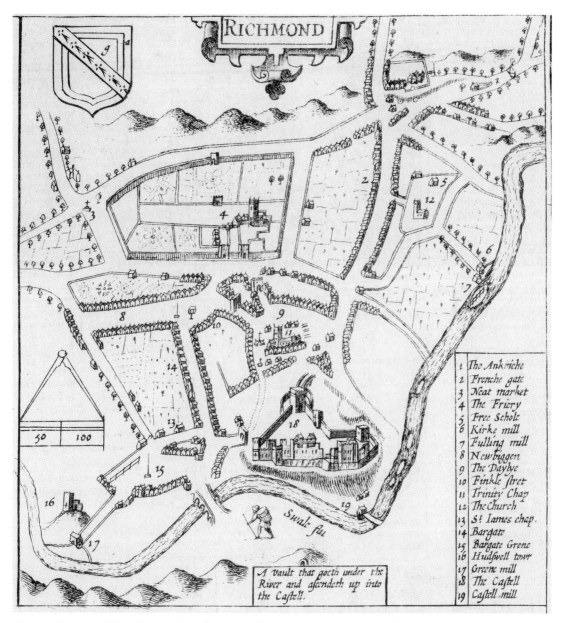

RICHMOND

1	The Ankriche
2	Frenche gate
3	Neat market
4	The Friery
5	Free Schole
6	Kirke mill
7	Fulling mill
8	Newbiggen
9	The Daybe
10	Finkle stret
11	Trinity Chap
12	The Church
13	St Iames chap.
14	Bargate
15	Bargate Grene
16	Hudswell towr
17	Greene mill
18	The Castell
19	Castell mill

A Vault that goeth under the River and ascendeth up into the Castell.

Swale flu

John Speed's map of Richmond, 1610. The medieval plan of the town that the Normans built by Alan Rufus' castle at Richmond was well preserved in the seventeenth century. Much of it is still obvious on the ground today. This was border territory and William the Conqueror provided Alan with an enormous lordship or honour, one of the largest in the kingdom.

that was raised over 100 feet high above the gatehouse during the third quarter of the twelfth century was used purely for military purposes. Its positioning at the entrance to the castle is unique. Richmond was also the first English castle to have three towers projecting from its curtain wall; one of the two surviving towers contains the tiny castle chapel. The outer bailey, which enclosed a large open space beyond the entrance to the castle, was later converted into a market

place and in the fourteenth century town walls were built on top of the curving line of the defences. Shop frontages preserve the line, but only two sections of walling and the remains of two of the four bars survive and much of the original space has been encroached upon by Holy Trinity church and other buildings. The honour of Richmond comprised 440 dependent manors, scattered through many parts of England, but in Yorkshire this new lordship formed an unusually large and compact unit of 199 manors and 43 outlying properties near the junction of the main roads from Scotland through the Vale of York.

Alan the Red also built a motte-and-bailey castle at Middleham to guard Coverdale and the road from Richmond to Skipton. The massive stone keep that was begun in the 1170s on a nearby site was different from that at Richmond in sacrificing some military austerity to improve the comfort of its chambers. One of the largest keeps in England, it stood on a 40-feet high mound and was surrounded by a formidable ditch. In the thirteenth and fourteenth centuries other buildings were constructed up to the curtain wall, which was heightened and provided with a gatehouse and corner towers. This was a lesson that the English had learned during the crusades. At Bowes, however, a smaller hall keep that was built in the 1170s and 1180s by Richard the engineer for Henry II, was never extended with other buildings or a curtain wall. At Knaresborough the royal castle occupies a high, rocky site above the river Nidd, similar to that at Richmond. Much of the curtain wall and its towers survive around the two baileys, but the keep was rebuilt for Edward II early in the fourteenth century. Skipton Castle was another Norman stronghold that was rebuilt at that time. The original motte-and-bailey had been constructed by Robert de Rumily, who had been granted the new honour by William II. The formidable defences are particularly impressive at the rear.

In the eastern part of the county the threat of renewed Viking invasions was met by incorporating all the pre-Conquest estates (except those that belonged

Knaresborough Castle. The ruins of the keep of the medieval royal castle are now contained within a public garden high above the River Nidd. The castle is first recorded in 1129–30, but the surviving structures date mostly from the first half of the fourteenth century. About 1540 John Leland wrote, 'The castel stondith magnificently and strongly on a rok, and hath a very depe diche, hewing out of the rok, wher it is not defendid with the ryver of Nidde … I numberid 11 or 12 towres.' In a survey of 1538 the keep was described as 'a marvelous hows of strenth, the walles thereof iiij [4] yards thik and more, and is of fyne hewin stone, clene pullished within and without, and strongly fortified with worke and man's ingyne to abide all assaults'. The curtain wall was 40 feet high where it joined the keep. The castle was sleighted by order of Parliament at the end of the Civil War.

PHOTOGRAPH: AUTHOR

Skipsea Castle and church. It is hard to realise from this peaceful rural scene that here was a major Norman castle and a short-lived borough. The motte of Drogo (or Drew) de Bevrere's castle that appears on the horizon to the right was once surrounded by the waters of a Holderness mere. A causey linked the motte to a bailey on higher ground. The foundations of the gatehouse leading into the bailey are seen in the foreground. Henry III ordered the destruction of the castle after a rebellion in 1221. Skipsea church was built at the same time as the castle and enlarged in the late Middle Ages.

PHOTOGRAPHS: CARNEGIE, 2005

to the Church) into the lordship of Holderness, governed from Skipsea Castle. The first lord was Drogo or Drew de la Beuvriere, a Fleming who had fought at Hastings and who also held extensive properties in Lincolnshire. He returned to the continent, perhaps in disgrace, in 1086–87 and Holderness was regranted to Odo or Eudo of Champagne and his wife, Adelaide of Aumale, the king's sister. The massive motte that rises nearly 50 feet above the former glacial mere at Skipsea was linked by a causeway to an 8-acre bailey. Its present desolate condition dates from its destruction by Henry III after he had put down a rebellion in 1221. The knights who supported the lords of Holderness had unusually large, though scattered, estates in this fertile part of the land. The Conqueror clearly felt that he had to reward men upon whom he could rely to rule this border zone with a firm hand.

William le Gros, Count of Aumale, chose the dramatic headland that projects between the two bays at Scarborough to build a castle after he had been created Earl of Yorkshire for his role in the 1138 Battle of the Standard near Northallerton, which had stopped a Scottish invasion. King Henry II turned Scarborough into a royal castle and between 1158 and 1169 he built the keep and curtain wall. His son, King John, spent the large sum of £2,000 on improving the castle with sturdier walls and semicircular towers until it was one of the strongest in England. A great hall occupied the first floor of the mighty keep, whose ruined appearance dates from its partial demolition in the late 1640s after the Civil War. It rises majestically above the medieval borough and harbour and the later spa town and resort.

Pickering Castle also has extensive remains. As part of his attempt to subdue the North, William I erected a motte-and-bailey castle here to control the royal honour that stretched from the Vale of Pickering up on to the North York Moors. A hundred years later, the inner bailey was given stone walls and then a shell keep was erected on top of the enormous motte and a curtain wall with interval towers was added to protect the domestic and administrative buildings. At Helmsley, the earliest masonry of another castle on the southern edge of the moors dates from around 1200 when Robert de Roos was lord. The ruined keep is a striking landmark but the defences relied more on the curtain wall and its towers and the deep ditches that were cut through the rock. In the mid thirteenth century the two gatehouses were strengthened with barbicans.

The properties of some of the new lordships were intermingled with other estates. The 215 manors held by Robert, Count of Mortain, half-brother of the Conqueror, were scattered across Yorkshire and he had no castle in the county.

The ruined shell keep and curtain walls at Pickering Castle date from the late twelfth century, but we can still get a strong sense of the earlier Norman motte-and-bailey castle, partly preserved by earthworks.

Robert took his title from Mortagne, in La Manche, and he was the largest landowner after the king until he was banished after an unsuccessful rebellion in 1088. His Yorkshire estates were divided between his two principal tenants, Nigel Fossard and Richard de Sourdeval, who came from a small place near Montagne. Richard's daughter was the second wife of Ralph Pagnell, who hailed from Calvados and whose first wife had been a sister or daughter of Ilbert de Laci of Pontefract Castle. His Yorkshire estates were centred on Hooton Pagnell, which had belonged to Earl Edwin of Mercia before the Conquest, but he built no castle there. Domesday Book records Nigel Fossard as tenant-in-chief of the barony of Mulgrave, where the remains of the castle date from the thirteenth century and later. Nigel's motte-and-bailey castles at Doncaster and Langthwaite were never rebuilt in stone. His estates eventually passed to eight successive generations of Peter de Mauleys.

Some of the Norman lordships that were named in Domesday Book had not then achieved their final forms. By the end of the eleventh century Norman control of the North was insecure and few Yorkshire castles had been built of stone. William II and Henry I made extensive changes after the rebellions that broke out upon their successions in 1088 and 1100. The barons who had fought on the losing sides lost everything. Soon, the Norman landholding class in northern England were mostly Henry's new men. Robert de Brus, from Brix, La Manche, was given a large estate in Yorkshire by the king in 1106 and the Mowbray fee was put together in Yorkshire, Lincolnshire and the Midlands for Nigel D'Aubigny before about 1114. It consisted at first of 60 knights' fees, but reached 100 under Nigel's son, Roger de Mowbray. The manors of Burton-in-Lonsdale and Kirkby Malzeard were incorporated within it in the mid twelfth century. Courts were held at Masham and Kirkby Malzeard and at Crowle in Lincolnshire.

Henry I's reign was followed by two decades of civil war in which the barons were divided between supporters of the rival claims to the throne of Stephen and Matilda. Many lesser lords took advantage of the troubles to build their own castles. By the second half of the twelfth century some Yorkshire estates were nominally held by an overlord who never visited the place. Real power lay with the resident sub-tenants, the favoured retainers from the ranks of the knights.

Knights were not recorded by name in the Yorkshire section of Domesday Book and they rarely appeared in other records until well into the twelfth or thirteenth centuries. In these early years their surnames were not fixed and

Aerial view of Pickering. In the Middle Ages the mighty Norman castle at the northern edge of the town served the huge Honour of Pickering, which stretched from the Vale of Pickering on to the North York Moors. The barbican to the south was eventually incorporated within the town and converted into burgage plots for the leading inhabitants. The main street, known as Castlegate and Burgate, links the castle with the parish church, which was probably the focal point of the settlement before the Norman Conquest. The market place is aligned at right angles at the end of this street, leading from the church along the ancient route from west to east. A charter for a Monday market was obtained in 1201, but markets and fairs were probably held here in much earlier times.

hereditary so their family trees are difficult to trace. The origins of some knights can be recognised from the Norman place-names that they chose for their surnames – Bosville, Mounteney, Reineville, Savile and so on – but other minor lords who may have been Normans took their surnames from their English manors. Few knights claimed descent from Anglo-Scandinavian ancestors, though the Fitzwilliams were an outstanding exception. Many of these knightly families remained leading landowners in Yorkshire for centuries,

An outbuilding to the west of the great Elizabethan house at Burton Agnes retains the name of Old Hall. Its brick exterior masks the fact that here are the substantial remains of a late Norman hall, built by Roger de Stuteville about 1170–75. The undercroft has a rib-vaulted roof supported by short, thick piers. A spiral staircase in the corner leads to the spacious principal floor above, where a fifteenth-century roof and a blocked-in traceried window can be seen.

PHOTOGRAPHS: CARNEGIE, 2005

above The exterior of the Old Hall was remodelled to match the later, Elizabethan Hall.

right The living quarters were on the first floor, which was reached from the undercroft via a spiral staircase. The bricked-in doorway to the left is Norman, but the roof is fifteenth century.

PHOTOGRAPHS: CARNEGIE, 2005

but several others eventually failed in the male line. The Newmarch family, who came from Neufmarché, not far from Roger de Busli's stronghold in Normandy, had one of the most important tenancies in the honour of Tickhill, with four knights' fees based at Bentley. The De Reinevilles, who derived their surname from a hamlet near Lassy, the Norman home of the De Lacis, were principal tenants of the honour of Pontefract, with four knights' fees based at Campsall. The Mounteneys moved from Montigny, near Louvetot, to the Hallamshire sub-manors of Shirecliffe and Cowley. The Bosvilles came from Beuzeville-la-Giffarde, a hamlet not far from Varenne, the home of their patrons; in the mid twelfth century Elias de Bosville granted Harthill church on the southern boundary of Yorkshire to the Cluniac priory that William de Warenne had founded at Lewes. The Vavasours, who took their name from a Norman French word for a vassal-in-chief or a feudal tenant below the rank of baron, began with Malger, one of the Domesday Book tenants of William de Perci. Malger was a Norman personal name which was used by later generations of the family, notably Sir Mauger Vavasour, the builder of the Elizabethan Weston Hall in lower Wharfedale.

These minor lords spent most of their time on their own estates, except when they were summoned to a baronial castle or called away on military service. Later on, they lived in moated manor houses, but in the twelfth century their favoured type of residence was the first-floor hall. The finest surviving example in Yorkshire stands beside the Elizabethan hall at Burton Agnes, though its exterior is masked by later brick walls and sash windows. Erected by Roger de Stuteville in the early 1170s, it is entered through a vaulted undercroft whose thick round piers are decorated with water-leaf capitals. A spiral stair in the north-west corner leads up to the former hall, which was re-roofed in the fifteenth century. Parts of contemporary halls in South Yorkshire survive, though much disguised, at Hatfield Old Manor House and Hooton Levitt.

Monasteries

The formidable castles that were erected by the Norman barons were matched by the splendid abbeys and priories that were reared in the two centuries following the Conquest. The old Anglian monasteries had been plundered and

Kirkstall Abbey, by Thomas Taylor, from *Loidis and Elmete*, by T.D.Whitaker (1816). Thomas Taylor's drawing of the abbey ruins seen across the cloisters shows how Kirkstall was built during the second half of the twelfth century and hardly altered before its dissolution. It is the country's most complete Norman Cistercian abbey, for unlike Fountains and Rievaulx it was never rebuilt in Early English Gothic. The doorways, windows and buttresses are uniform in style. The crossing tower of the church, which was heightened in the early sixteenth century, is the only addition in this view. The abbey accommodated up to 36 monks and many more lay brothers. At its dissolution in 1540 it still had 31 monks.

The crypt, St Mary's Church, Lastingham. In his *History of the English Church and People*, completed in AD 731, the Venerable Bede provides an account of the foundation of a monastery at Lastingham by St Cedd. To fulfil a prophecy of Isaiah, Cedd chose a site among some high, remote hills that were more suitable for the dens of robbers and the haunts of wild beasts than for human habitation. Cedd later became Bishop of Lichfield and his brother Chad became Abbot of Lastingham.

In 1078 Stephen, the abbot of Whitby, and some of his monks restored the monastery at Lastingham as a small Benedictine house. The crypt, seen here, is their work, but the new church above was not complete when the monks moved to St Mary's Abbey, York ten years later. Pilgrims entered the crypt to pray at the shrine of St Cedd. The vault is supported by four columns and the crypt extends into an apse (rounded end). Some carved stones from the crypt date from the eighth to the tenth century.
AUTHOR COLLECTION

destroyed so savagely by the early Vikings that none survived north of the River Trent. The re-establishment of old foundations and the creation of new monasteries was a deliberate policy to strengthen the Norman hold on England. In Yorkshire the achievement was such that within a hundred years of the 'harrying of the North' the county's monasteries were among the most successful in the land. They soon became as famous in their own time as their substantial ruins are today.

At first the Benedictine order was favoured. The Conqueror himself led the way in 1069 with the foundation of Selby Abbey, which soon became one of the richest monasteries in the North. The present church – the finest surviving Norman ecclesiastical building in Yorkshire – dates from about 1100, when Hugh de Laci was abbot. He seems to have employed the master mason who had supervised the construction of Durham Cathedral, for the same patterns are incised on the enormous piers in the nave. In the late 1070s Reinfrid, one of the Conqueror's knights who had viewed with sadness the ruined monasteries at Jarrow, Monkwearmouth, Whitby and York, took monastic vows and, together with Aldwin, the future prior of Durham, determined to restore them. In 1078 Stephen, the first abbot of Whitby, moved across the moors to the site of the ruined monastery of Lastingham to build a crypt that still acts as a shrine to the original founder, St Cedd. He also began a new abbey church above the crypt, but in 1088 he and his monks departed for York, where William II founded St Mary's Abbey on or close to what appears to have been the site of the former monastery of Galmanho. The foundations of the Norman church of the abbey are marked in the ground alongside the beautiful limestone walls that were erected in the late thirteenth century. Across the Ouse, the Benedictine priory that Ralph Pagnell founded in 1089 as a cell of the monastery of Marmoutier (Normandy) survives in part as the parish church of Holy Trinity, Micklegate.

Selby Abbey. The west front of the Benedictine abbey church is illuminated by the setting sun. This was the laymen's entrance; the monks were seated at the east end. The architectural history of this front extends over 700 years. The lower parts, including the doorway, the rounded windows, and the flat buttresses are late Norman work. Above are Early English windows and blank lancets, and a large window which was inserted much later in Perpendicular style. The central gable was added in 1873; the two towers were added in the early twentieth century; and the pinnacles were replaced with higher ones as late as 1935.

PHOTOGRAPH: CARNEGIE, 2005

Pagnell was typical of the first two generations of Normans who granted part of their English estates to monasteries in their native land. Marmoutier had other cells at Allerton Mauleverer and Headley, Aumale had a cell at Burstall, and St Wandrille's abbey built a small priory at Ecclesfield. The Yorkshire Benedictine abbeys also founded cells on their distant properties. Whitby had them at Goathland, Hackness, Middlesbrough and York; Selby had one at Snaith; and the ruins of St Martin's Priory that had been founded from St Mary's Abbey, York, in 1137 are visible in a public garden at Richmond.

The reformed Benedictine order which had been founded at Cluny (Burgundy) in 910 also attracted royal and baronial support. The Cluniacs emphasised liturgy and architectural splendour. Their first, and richest, house in England was the priory which William de Warenne and his wife founded at

Bridlington Priory. On display in the north aisle of the nave are re-erected parts of the twelfth-century cloister, with twin colonettes, zigzag decoration and finely carved capitals. Most of the Augustinian priory buildings were demolished late in the reign of Henry VIII.
PHOTOGRAPH: CARNEGIE, 2005

Guisborough Priory. The ruined wall at the east end rises to a surprising height, given that the rest of this Augustinian priory is marked only by its foundations. The priory was rebuilt in the Geometric Decorated style after a disastrous fire in 1289. The great east window was one of the largest in Yorkshire at that time. The church was 352 feet long and had twin towers at the western end.
PHOTOGRAPH: CARNEGIE, 2005

Lewes (Sussex) after a visit to Cluny. The tithes and other dues from the Warennes' Yorkshire estates formed a major part of the endowment. About 1090 Robert de Laci founded a Cluniac priory at Pontefract, near his castle, but nothing now survives above ground level. Monk Bretton Priory was founded from Pontefract about 1154, when Adam fitz Swein, the grandson of an Englishman who had retained his estates after the Norman Conquest, donated seven acres of land, but in 1281, after much quarrelling, the monks of Monk Bretton broke their links with Pontefract and became Benedictines. Arthington Nunnery was the only other Cluniac house in Yorkshire; none was founded in either the East or the North Ridings.

Fresh enthusiasm came in the early years of the twelfth century from the Augustinians, or the Austin canons as they were usually known. Starting in Italy and France and arriving in Colchester in 1103, they were not a strict monastic order, but rather groups of priests who shared a common life and served their local communities. Archbishop Thurstan was an enthusiastic supporter and by 1140 seven priories had been established in Yorkshire. The archbishop founded Nostell Priory in 1114–19 and attracted a royal endowment. It soon became an important house, but the only standing remains are of two late-medieval ranges of outbuildings in the grounds of the eighteenth-century house. About the same time,

Walter de Gant endowed another important Austin priory at Bridlington. Nothing survives of the original foundation, but the western part of the enormously long church that was erected in the thirteenth century and later remains in use. A third Austin priory at Guisborough had also been started before 1120 with a generous endowment from Robert de Brus, who appointed his brother as the first prior. Shortly afterwards, William Meschin and his wife, Cecilia, founded a priory at Embsay, but the land was infertile and so, in 1154–55, the canons moved four miles to Bolton, where their buildings now form a celebrated, picturesque ruin on the banks of the Wharfe. Kirkham Priory was established by Walter L'Espec about 1122 and not long afterwards other Austin houses were founded at Drax, Healaugh, Marton, Newburgh, North Ferriby and Warter.

Yorkshire has the greatest collection of monasteries in the country, headed by a magnificent series of Cistercian abbeys. This order of white monks was founded at Cîteaux (Burgundy) in 1098 in a desire to return to the simplicity and austerity of the early Benedictines. The monks renounced wealth and luxury and refused gifts of prosperous estates, seeking instead a frugal life of devotion and meditation on the edge of moors, marshes or woods. By the end of the twelfth century over 100 Cistercian houses had been founded in England and Wales. Each was laid out to a standard plan, whereby the monks were separated from the much larger numbers of lay brothers who did the manual work and who worshipped in the western part of the church only at the beginning and end of each day. Before the catastrophe of the Black Death, lay brothers were essential to the running of the monastic economy and that of the outlying granges.

The first Cistercian house was founded in 1128 at Waverley (Surrey). Four

The Romantic artists of the late eighteenth and early nineteenth centuries delighted in portraying ruined abbeys, where vegetation sprouted from the crumbling masonry. This drawing of the interior of Fountains Abbey, published by R. Metcalfe of Ripon, looks down the thirteenth-century choir, where the Cistercian monks chanted and prayed, into the Norman nave where the lay brothers worshipped. Abbot Marmaduke Huby's tower rises above the ruins on the north side of the church. From T. Sopwith's *Eight Views of Fountains Abbey*.
BY COURTESY OF GROVE RARE BOOKS, BOLTON ABBEY

Rievaulx Abbey from the south-east one early summer's morning. The idyllic rural setting enhances the romantic appeal of the abbey ruins. Rievaulx is as famous now as it was in its hey-day. In the Middle Ages this valley was much busier and noisier, for the abbey community was large and its industrial concerns included tanning and the forging of iron.
PHOTOGRAPH: CARNEGIE, 2005

years later, Walter L'Espec, lord of Helmsley and founder of Kirkham Priory, offered a wild site in the Rye Valley, on the edge of the North York Moors, to 13 monks from Clairvaux and soon Rievaulx became the most famous Cistercian abbey in twelfth-century England. Within two or three decades it had 140 monks and more than 500 lay brothers, led by St Ailrid, the greatest abbot of his age, teacher, author, administrator and confidant of kings and barons. Rievaulx's high reputation was matched by its glorious architecture. Building stones from Penny Piece quarry were brought on rafts down the old course of the Rye before the monks diverted the river and their magnificent church was erected on a north–south axis to fit it into the restricted position that was available below the steep slope of the valley side. The lay brothers' part of the church retains enough Norman work, especially in the bare walls of the transepts, to suggest its original austere appearance, but the monks' choir was rebuilt in the lighter, soaring Gothic style of the thirteenth century.

The determination of the early Cistercians to eschew all decoration is still plain to see at Kirkstall Abbey, which was established on the banks of the Aire in 1152 after an aborted start at Barnoldswick. Many of the buildings that were erected in the second half of the twelfth century survive up to the level of the

The nave of the abbey church, Rievaulx, was built for the 500–600 lay-brothers. The lower parts of the walls and the square bases of the aisle piers are all that remains of the building that was erected between 1135 and 1140 in plain, Romanesque style. The stones are of a redder colour than those that were used to raise the monks' part of the church at the eastern end in Early English Gothic style during the thirteenth century.

PHOTOGRAPH: CARNEGIE, 2005

eaves. They were paid for out of the profits of the wool trade and little was changed or added in the later Middle Ages. Kirkstall was not plundered at the Dissolution and remains the outstanding example of Cistercian architecture from the Norman period.

The successful establishment of Rievaulx Abbey inspired 13 Benedictine monks to leave St Mary's Abbey, York, for a desolate site in Skeldale, where Archbishop Thurstan had donated an uncultivated tract of land, watered by pure springs or fountains, for the foundation of another Cistercian abbey. Its success hung in the balance until 1135, when Hugh, the former Dean of York, arrived with money and a library. Fountains Abbey quickly grew into the richest and one of the most celebrated Cistercian monasteries in England. By the end of the twelfth century it had over 50 monks and more than 200 lay brothers. The nave of the abbey church and the long, vaulted cellarium are justly famous pieces of Norman architecture. Fountains, too, escaped the worst pillaging at the Dissolution and remains the most complete Cistercian abbey, as famous now as it was in the Middle Ages.

The monks of Byland Abbey came together as a Cistercian community in 1134 at Calder (Cumberland), but after four years they were forced to flee from Scottish raiders to Hood, near Thirsk. Their new site proved too small, so in 1143 they moved to Old Byland and removed the village to a new site so that they could worship undisturbed. Their desire for solitude was thwarted by the

Medieval floor tiles, Rievaulx Abbey. These decorative tiles are still *in situ* in the nave (the lay brothers' part) of the abbey church. Most of the abbey's buildings were floored with similar tiles that were laid from the thirteenth to the fifteenth centuries. They are among the best preserved in the country.

PHOTOGRAPH: CARNEGIE, 2005

The Undercroft, West Range, Fountains Abbey. The undercroft below the sleeping quarters of the lay brothers stretches from the nave of the church to the River Skell. It dates from the late twelfth century and was used as a great cellar at the northern end and as the lay brothers' refectory to the south. The monks would not have known this uninterrupted view, for the spaces were partitioned.

PHOTOGRAPH: CARNEGIE, 2005

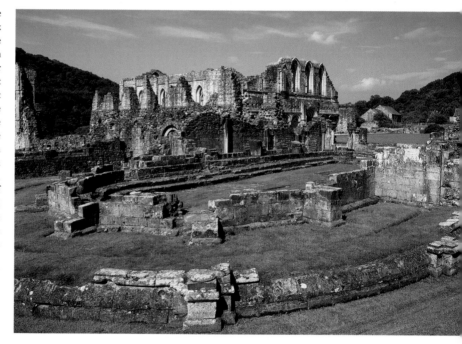

The foundations of the Chapter House, Rievaulx Abbey. Built in the middle years of the twelfth century as the business or management centre, it retains its rounded apse at the eastern end. In the foreground are the foundations of the surrounding arcade, a unique feature in a Cistercian house. A chapter of the rule of St Benedict was read before each meeting to the monks sitting on stone benches. The first abbots were buried here.

PHOTOGRAPH: CARNEGIE, 2005

distant sound of the bells of Rievaulx Abbey, so in 1147 they moved a little further to their present site, which had to be cleared of trees and drained by huge ditches. Three decades later, Byland Abbey had 36 monks, 100 lay brothers and a wide reputation for its spirituality. The spectacular rose window at the west end of their church was finished by 1225 and the monastery was laid out as a perfect model of Cistercian planning.

Yorkshire had three more Cistercian monasteries. The abbey that was resited at Jervaulx in 1156 has extensive remains, dating from the thirteenth century. Meaux Abbey in Holderness was founded from Fountains in 1150. A hundred years later it housed 60 monks and 90 lay brothers, so it was clearly an important establishment, but the destruction at the Dissolution was so comprehensive that nothing now remains above ground level. The final one occupies a lonely site at Roche on the boundary of the parishes of Laughton and Maltby that was landscaped by 'Capability' Brown in the eighteenth century. Founded in 1138 by two local lords, Roche Abbey soon flourished and by the 1170s the monks had started an ambitious rebuilding programme. The transepts and choir rank with Canterbury and Wells Cathedrals as the earliest English examples that survive of Gothic architecture. The magnesian limestone walls of the rib-vaulted transepts stand three storeys high, but their thickness and the blind recesses of the triforium hark back to the Romanesque style and so do not quite achieve the lightness of touch of the fully fledged Early English Gothic. Roche was badly affected by the Dissolution but the standard Cistercian plan is evident from the foundations.

Another order of canons, the Premonstratensians, began in 1120 at Prémontré in northern France. The canons combined preaching at parish churches with manual labour, devotion and scholarship, whilst following the communal life on the Cistercian model. They had only three abbeys in Yorkshire, though another at Beauchief (Derbyshire) had endowments of land in and around Hallamshire. In 1151 Roald, constable of Richmond, founded Easby Abbey, whose ruins now adorn the banks of the Swale. A second abbey was started at Swainby about 1187 but was soon transferred to Coverham, and in 1198 Egglestone Abbey was founded from Easby. Meanwhile, the Gilbertines, the only order of canons to originate in England, had spread from their base

Drawn by the young J. M. W. Turner as a romantic ruin on the banks of the Tees, the Premonstratensian Egglestone Abbey was founded in the 1190s, a mile or so south of Barnard Castle. It was always a small institution and never had more than 15 canons. The shell of the church dates from the second half of thirteenth century, but the east range of the monastic quarters were converted into a house by Robert Strelly, who was granted the property in 1548. The ground plan of the entire abbey remains clear from the surviving foundations. This engraving was reproduced as plate 16 in *A History of Richmondshire*, by T. D. Whitaker in 1823.

in Lincolnshire, where Gilbert, the parish priest of Sempringham, had built a small convent. The four Yorkshire houses consisted of Ellerton and St Andrew's, York, both of which have vanished, and two more substantial sites at Old Malton and at Watton in the East Riding. Watton Priory was founded as a double house for canons and nuns by Eustace Fitzjohn in the middle years of the twelfth century. The entire ground plan has been revealed by excavation and the prior's fifteenth-century brick house survives intact with its angle turrets reaching towards the sky and its famous oriel window casting light into the interior.

By the middle of the twelfth century Yorkshire had many small and poorly endowed nunneries, mostly Benedictine or Cistercian foundations, which are commemorated in two instances by the place-names Nun Appleton and Nun Monkton. Early examples from the 1130s include St Clement's, York, Handall near Whitby, and Kirklees. The remains of Yorkshire nunneries are generally unimpressive, though at Arthington the Cluniac nunnery was rebuilt after the

St Leonard's Hospital, York. At the entrance to the Museum Gardens this gaunt shell is all that remains of Yorkshire's largest medieval hospital. Founded in the twelfth century, it was restored by John Romanus, the treasurer of York Minster, in the second quarter of the thirteenth century in Early English Gothic style. In 1280 it accommodated 229 sick people as well as the staff. The undercroft housed the infirmary and the gabled first floor contained the chapel. The hospital grounds once extended as far as the present theatre and the Multangular Tower.

PHOTOGRAPH: CARNEGIE, 2005

Dissolution as a three-storeyed Elizabethan house. The Cistercian nunnery at Hampole achieved a wider fame because of its association with Richard Rolle, the hermit and prolific author of popular religious works, who died there in 1349.

The 90 or so hospitals founded as charitable institutions in Yorkshire during the Middle Ages were supervised by clergymen and nuns. The chapel was always a focal point within the complex of buildings. The largest hospital in Yorkshire was St Leonard's, York, a twelfth-century institution alongside St Mary's Abbey that accommodated 229 sick people when a count was made in 1280. The ruins of the vaulted undercroft of the infirmary hall and the chapel above make a striking spectacle at the entrance to the Museum Gardens; the hospital grounds once extended as far as the present civic theatre. York had 19 hospitals at different times in the Middle Ages and Beverley had ten; in all, 72 of Yorkshire's towns had 72 medieval hospitals. Many are commemorated merely by a foundation charter and perhaps the place-name Spital Hill.

The military orders that were created to protect pilgrims and guard holy places after Jerusalem had fallen to the crusaders in 1099 attracted numerous small donations of land from ordinary farming families. The Yorkshire

right Representation of Hell, York Minster. This fantastic stone carving from the Norman period, now on display in the undercroft museum, shows the damned in a cauldron, brought to the boil by devils stoking the fire. It is not known where this terrifying sculpture was displayed, but it was perhaps part of an external frieze.

BY COURTESY OF THE DEAN AND CHAPTER, YORK MINSTER

The Hospitium, St Mary's Abbey, York, was the guest house. Set low in the abbey grounds by the banks of the River Ouse, it has been largely rebuilt, but preserves the idea of a stone ground floor and a timber-framed upper floor.

PHOTOGRAPH: CARNEGIE, 2005

headquarters of the Knights of the Hospital of St John of Jerusalem were at Beverley, Mount St John, and Newland near Drax, those of the Knights Templar were at Temple Newsam, Templehirst and eight other small places, but hardly any physical remains survive. The policy of both the Hospitallers and the Templars was to let their scattered lands to peasant farmers. Every parish had men of religion amongst its landlords.

The Norman enthusiasm for founding abbeys and priories petered out by about 1220. During the twelfth and thirteenth centuries monas-

teries had built up their estates as the faithful continued to grant them land to clear from the wastes. For example, in the late twelfth century the Cistercians of Kirkstall Abbey were granted property in Seacroft, where they were allowed to 'make their hedges and to build folds and sheep houses' and in the early thirteenth century the monks of Byland Abbey were granted pasture for 360 sheep in Upper Whitley with 'all necessaries from the wood for making their sheep-cote in Kotrode, and for making a hedge and enclosure round the sheep-cote'. The Cistercians were particularly active in creating a system of granges, whereby lay brothers and hired labourers farmed their outlying properties. The grange buildings differed from those of ordinary farms only in having a chapel in their midst. Excavated sites, such as Cayton, Kildwick, Morker and Sutton, have revealed the foundations of labourers' cottages. As grants were usually of waste land on the margins of cultivation, granges were often isolated from village communities. For instance, in the 1160s Meaux Abbey was granted land and pasture for 300 sheep 'outside the ditches of the town' of Dunnington on the low-lying moor towards Beeford. By draining and reclaiming land, the monks eventually built up a farm of 408 acres around their moated site of Moor Grange.

In Yorkshire, the Cistercians were the most celebrated of the monastic sheep farmers. In their hey-day the shepherds of Fountains Abbey kept up to 18,000 sheep on Malham Moor and thousands more in other parts of the Dales. The abbey owned over 90 square miles of pastures in Wharfedale, all enclosed within a continuous boundary wall and clearly separated from the sheep pastures of other monasteries. The Pennine sheep-runs were internationally famous, for most of the wool was sold to Italian merchants, but other parts of Yorkshire were also grazed by monastic flocks, notably the High Wolds and the marshes of Holderness. By the 1270s Meaux Abbey had more than 11,000 sheep and over 1,000 beasts in Holderness. Meanwhile, Kirkstall Abbey held most of the land in Bessacarr, south-east of Doncaster, where they grazed their sheep, horses and cows. Several monasteries exploited the peat deposits of Inclesmoor, a few miles away. Cistercian monks were also active in mining and smelting the minerals on their estates, particularly iron ore. For example, in the 1150s Rievaulx Abbey obtained a grant of 'all the iron mines and minerals of Stainborough with wood necessary to make charcoal', and in 1161 Kirkstead Abbey (Lincolnshire) gained rights to mine and forge iron on the boundary of Ecclesfield and Kimberworth. Further north, by the 1190s the monks of Byland Abbey were forging iron at their granges at Bentley and Denby within the townships of Emley and Upper Whitley. Many of the Cinder Hills place-names on the Tankersley seam of ironstone (which stretched southwards from near the River Wharfe to Staveley in Derbyshire) commemorate monastic iron works. The contribution of the monasteries to the development of the medieval economy was a considerable one.

Towns

Secular lords were just as keen to increase their revenues. One way to do this was to establish a borough alongside their castle, or at a new site by a road junction or a navigable river, and to design a rectangular or triangular area for a weekly market and an annual fair. Many of Yorkshire's old market towns and present-day cities were created in the eleventh and twelfth centuries. Decisions made by Norman lords have had lasting effects on their topography, especially where the streets were laid out in a grid pattern around the market place. Some of the attempts to create boroughs were doomed to failure, but by the thirteenth century Yorkshire had well over 40 successful towns – many more than it had at the time of the Norman Conquest.

Three of the earliest and most successful of the new boroughs were created at the centres of the new honours of Richmond, Pontefract and Tickhill. At Richmond, the regular properties of the leading townsmen – known to historians as burgage plots – stretched back from the market place and, beyond the town walls, along Bargate and Frenchgate. The parish church of St Mary occupied an inconvenient position near Frenchgate, well away from the castle, while in the market place Holy Trinity had no churchyard and the status merely of a chapel. Both churches contain Norman work, but perhaps St Mary's was built on the site of an earlier church before the new town was laid out in the shadow of the castle? The Norman town plan is well preserved and Frenchgate is surely a significant name, both here and at Doncaster.

The Norman town of Pontefract replaced the previous estate centre at Tanshelf, though All Saints remained the parish church. The curving lines of Back Northgate and Walkergate defined the town's limits inside the ditch of the outer bailey of the castle. The parallel streets of Northgate and Southgate zig-zagged into Baxtergate and Finkle Street (a common name in the North for a dog-legged lane) and at the centre Micklegate served as a market place. In the middle of the thirteenth century a second borough, known as West Cheap, was planned around the church of St Giles. Its market place is now much encroached upon, but the street names – Market Place, Wool Market, Shoe Market Street, Corn Market, Beast Fair, Horse Fair, Roper Gate, Salter Row and Middle Row – speak of the old trading activities. Pontefract was one of the most successful of the new towns of the Norman period.

Pontefract and Tickhill were the only towns in the West Riding which had burgesses recorded in Domesday Book. At that time, the estate at Tickhill was still known by its old name of Dadsley. The abandoned site of All Hallows church and the positions of Dadsley Well Farm and Dadsley Lane suggest that the pre-Conquest centre was north of the new town that was designed alongside the bailey of Roger de Busli's castle. The market place was sited beyond the castle ditch in Sunderland and burgage plots stretched back from the main streets. When St Mary's replaced All Hallows as the parish church in the late twelfth century, it had to be placed in an obscure position beyond Castle Green and the back lane of the town. Tickhill flourished under the Normans but declined in the later Middle Ages, leaving the town plan well preserved.

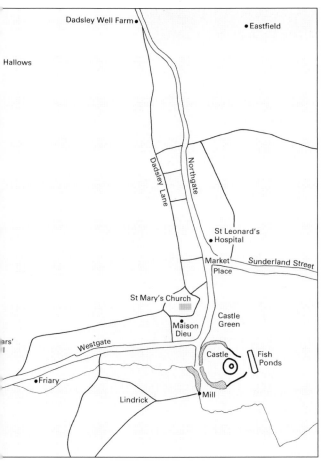

Plan of medieval Tickhill, showing places mentioned in the text.

In South Yorkshire Tickhill was at first more successful than any town except Doncaster, where the Fossards erected a castle on the site of a Roman fort and Anglo-Scandinavian burh at a strategic crossing of the Don. Medieval burgage plots have been identified at the heart of the town in French Gate, High Street,

Aerial view of Tickhill from the south-east. Although modern housing has spread across the fields, the medieval plan of the settlement is well preserved and the former dominance of the castle is evident.

St Sepulchre Gate, Baxter Gate and Scot Lane. Richard I's borough charter of 1194 confirmed what were already the ancient privileges of the burgesses. The present street pattern in the centre of Doncaster has been shaped by the town ditch, which had been dug out by 1215 and which was not infilled until 1734. During the Middle Ages the water from the Cheswold, the original course of the river Don, flowed along it, forming an effective barrier. The earthen bank which rose from the ditch never had walls, but four substantial stone gates or bars at St Mary's bridge, St Sepulchre Gate, Hall Gate and Sun Bar marked the entrances to the town. The Great North Road passed through it and an enormous market place was laid out near the wharf, which for nine months of the year could be reached by light craft that came up the Don. Like many other early market places, it formed an extension of the churchyard. The Norman church of St Mary Magdalene, which occupied the site of the Victorian Corn Exchange, became a chapel when St George's church was built upon the ruins of the motte-and-bailey castle, but 'the Maudlens' long remained a distinctive part of the market place. Doncaster has lost its medieval buildings but its Norman town plan can still be traced on the ground.

Plan of medieval Doncaster, showing places mentioned in the text.

Map labels:

River Don

Town Mills

Great North Road

River Don

The Marsh

River Don

River

Cheswold

Frenchgate

St George's

To Sheffield

St Sepulchre Gate

High Street

Hall Gate

Market Place

Horse Fair

Key

1. Hall Cross
2. Pinfold
3. Butchers' Cross
.... Medieval town ditch

Great North Road   Town Field

At Sheffield William de Louvetot was active in promoting the town that was centred on the market place that stretched up the hill from his castle. He built the town mill, a bridge across the river Don, the hospital of St Leonard and a church that soon became independent of the ancient minster at Ecclesfield. Burgesses lived and traded in the best positions by the market place and the High Street long before their status was formally recognised in 1297, but they remained dependent on the barons whose castle and huge deer park dominated the town until the middle years of the seventeenth century.

In the North Riding several boroughs began to flourish under the protection of a castle. At Scarborough the town that grew around St Mary's church and the harbour below the castle achieved borough status in the middle of the twelfth century; it became known as the Old Town when Newborough was added to the south. At Helmsley, where an earlier settlement was perhaps clustered around the church, a large market place (now much encroached upon) was laid out to the east of the castle, with the properties of the burgesses stretching away on either side; the borough charter can be dated to between 1186 and 1210. At Pickering the borough was in existence long before the charter of 1201; the market place extends from the churchyard on an old east–west route, well south of the castle. At Kirkbymoorside too the market developed alongside the church, with the small Stuteville and Neville castles

St Mary's Church, Scarborough. Just below the castle, but high above Oldborough and the harbour, St Mary's was founded as the parish church by Count William of Aumale in the reign of King Stephen (1135–54). In 1189 the tithes of the parish were granted to the abbey of Cîteaux in Burgundy, the mother house of the Cistercian order.

Before its partial destruction in the Civil War, St Mary's was one of the finest parish churches in Yorkshire. The chancel had aisles on both sides; the central tower had transepts; the nave had towers at the western ends of its immediate aisles; to the north stood an extra aisle dedicated to St Nicholas; and to the south the aisle extended into four chapels. The chancel was destroyed during the seige of Scarborough castle in 1645 and the crossing tower collapsed fourteen years later.

This view of the west front shows the bases of the original Norman towers. The gable between them and the outer wall of St Nicholas' aisle were reconstructed in the nineteenth century.

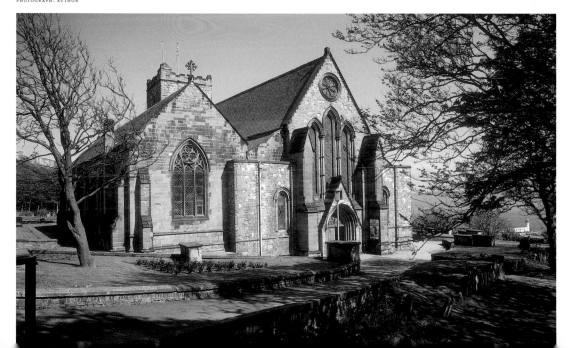

The large market place at Helmsley, sited alongside the churchyard and close to the castle, was once even bigger, but the distant shops in this view are the successors of the medieval stalls and butchers' shops which gradually filled much of the space to the south. A charter was granted in 1191 for a Saturday market and three one-day fairs and the leading townsmen occupied burgage plots on the west and east sides of the market place.

PHOTOGRAPH: CARNEGIE, 2005

well beyond; the borough was first recorded between 1154 and 1179. At Stokesley the large area that was devoted to markets and fairs is immediately obvious, though the castle and the burgesses have long since disappeared. At Skipton the broad High Street that descends from the castle and Holy Trinity church hosted the markets and fairs and fronted the burgage plots; borough status was confirmed in 1266. And at Knaresborough a Wednesday market was held in the space to the north of the castle and burgage plots stretched back from High Street, Finkle Street, Gracious Street and Briggate.

One of the most successful medieval boroughs in the north of the county was that at Thirsk, where remarkable evidence of the development of the town plan can be observed on the ground. The castle that was built about 1130 by

Thirsk Market Place. The enormous, rectangular market place was laid out by the middle of the twelfth century. It replaced the former market place on the other side of the Cod Beck, which stood near Robert de Mowbray's castle and the parish church of St Mary's. Thirsk flourished as a borough and market town serving the Vale of Mowbray and neighbouring parts of the North York Moors. In Victorian times the market place was remarkably free of traffic on the days when a market was not held.
BY COURTESY OF THE YORKSHIRE ARCHAEOLOGICAL SOCIETY

Roger de Mowbray was dismantled in 1176, but the manor house that succeeded it remained intact until it was destroyed by the Scots in 1326. A 400-acre park and extensive woods stretched beyond. By 1145 Roger de Mowbray had founded a borough, with 52 burgage plots arranged on the east side of the Cod Beck, around St James' Green and along Micklegate (Long Street) and Ingramgate in what is now a quiet part of the town. A weekly market was held on Mondays and annual fairs were arranged at the feasts of St James and St Luke. By the late fourteenth century, however, this site was abandoned in favour of the present Market Place, which was laid out as a huge rectangle on the opposite bank of the stream.

These towns depended for their success on the continued importance of the castles which they served. The deserted site of the borough of Skipsea by the ruined castle that was once the military and administrative centre of the new honour of Holderness forms a poignant contrast. Almondbury, Harewood and Skelton are three other places where castles failed to nourish successful boroughs. A seventeenth-century map marks the abandoned burgage plots within the outer bailey of Almondbury castle, high on the bleak hill that had been occupied first as a prehistoric fort.

The Archbishop of York was a patron of boroughs on some of his extensive estates. At Ripon the original settlement spread around St Wilfrid's, which had become a great collegiate church, but in the twelfth-century a huge, rectangular market place surrounded by burgage plots was staked out further west. It retains its shape and the original pattern of streets leading into it is largely unchanged. The weekly corn market and regular sheep and cattle fairs soon made Ripon a prosperous town. At Beverley, too, the ancient church had been rebuilt as a college of secular canons. By the reign of Henry I, and probably long before, a large triangular market place tapered from the minster towards the area that is still known as the Wednesday Market. Encroachments disguise its original size, for it extended to Highgate and Eastgate. As at Pontefract, the commercial

A detail of the town map of Ripon from Jeffreys' map of Yorkshire, 1771. The town was still contained within its medieval limits and had plenty of spaces for gardens and orchards. The Minster stood apart from the commercial heart of the town, where the huge Market Place had been partly encroached upon by buildings in its northern part. All the streets were known as 'gates', from the old Viking word that had passed into northern speech. Their winding courses reflect their unplanned development.

success of the town led to the creation of an extra market square – the Saturday Market – and the chapel-of-ease of St Mary. Another chapel, dedicated to St Nicholas, the patron saint of seafarers, stood near the navigable river Hull, the main artery for the export of Beverley cloths. Like Doncaster, Beverley was enclosed by a ditch and an earthen bank with bars at the principal entrances. On the western side of the town the road known as The Leases still follows the line of this ditch. Beyond lay the open fields, the extensive common pastures, and the archbishop's park. Burgesses were also encouraged to settle at another of the archbishop's market towns, at Otley, which prospered in a modest way, but a similar scheme at Brough-on-Humber failed in face of competition from Kingston-upon-Hull, one of Yorkshire's most successful medieval new towns. Further down the river, the archbishop's market town and inland port at Patrington survived longer until it too succumbed to the dominance of Hull.

The Bishop of Durham sponsored a small borough by his manor house and the collegiate church at Howden, which retains its character as a small market town. His scheme at Northallerton was more successful in the long run. The town was laid out to the east of his palace as the focal point of the Liberty of Allertonshire, an old Northumbrian shire that extended up to the Tees and controlled the route out of Scotland through the Vale of Mowbray. The pattern of burgage plots leading off the long, tapering High Street has survived, though the palace is but a ruined earthwork.

Abbeys and priories also took the initiative in founding new towns at their gates. When the Benedictine abbey was built at Selby, the existing settlement was altered out of recognition. A broad market place was laid out to the west of the abbey church and access to the staithes on a sharp bend of the Ouse was provided along Finkle Street and the broad Micklegate. Selby soon flourished both as an inland port and a market centre. At Whitby the Benedictines established a borough down below their abbey on both sides of the river Esk, which provided the safest natural harbour between the Tees and the Humber. Long flights of steps lead up the steep hillsides from the harbour. The moorland hinterland offered little opportunities for trade, so the burgesses were dependent on sea traffic and fishing. The Old Town at Bridlington was a mile inland from the small settlement that was clustered around the harbour. It already had burgesses at the time of Domesday Book, pre-dating the Augustinian priory. Burgage plots extended back from the wide High Street to the two back lanes. In 1200 the Augustinians obtained a charter to confirm the market and fair. The Augustinian order was also responsible for the market by their priory at Guisborough.

By no means all the Norman new towns were founded near castles or religious houses. Some were ancient centres of large estates, others were speculative ventures by lords of the manor. Pocklington, the only other East Riding town to have burgesses recorded in Domesday Book, was the centre of a large parish of 26,360 acres which included nine other settlements, each with a subordinate chapel. In the thirteenth century a new market place was designed for the ancient fairs and markets. Another old estate got a new commercial centre in the third quarter of the twelfth century when burgesses were attracted to a market place that was laid out at a crossroads well away from the settlement around the church at Old Malton. At Driffield, Sherburn-in-Elmet and Masham, comparable centres of ancient estates, the markets and fairs were not recorded until the thirteenth century and burgesses were not invited to settle, but in the West Riding a new town within an old estate was founded in 1207 by Maurice de Gant, lord of the manor of Leeds. The Anglo-

Scandinavian village was focused on Kirkgate by St Peter's church, but Gant planned his town further west, by the crossing of the river Aire, where the broad market street of Briggate led up to Headrow. The pattern of the 60 medieval burgage plots is partly intact, serving in Victorian times as long, narrow inn yards and shopping arcades.

Other Victorian towns that started off as small, medieval boroughs include Bingley, Bradford, Halifax and Rotherham, though the evidence comes from after the Norman period. Barnsley was a Norman new town, without burgesses, that was laid out on a new site, half-a-mile away from Old Barnsley, by the Cluniacs of Pontefract Priory, who had become lords of the manor. The markets and fairs were at first accommodated on Market Hill, then from 1249 on May Day Green, at the junction of important thorough-fares. Market Weighton's market charter dates from 1252, but as it lay at the junction of two early routes from the Wolds and the Vale of York it may have been an older trading centre. The triangular market space has been encroached upon, but long, curving properties, especially on the south side, are reminiscent of burgage plots. Of course, even the successful towns were very small by later standards, and in the Middle

Old Town, Whitby. The original settlement at Whitby stood on the east side of the harbour, below the abbey and the parish church on the cliff top, and close to the Market Place. These (demolished) cottages stretched up Boulby Bank from Church Street (or Kirkgate as it was known in 1318). They were built of brick and roofed with pantiles and were approached by verandahs on two or three levels.

Ages they rarely contained more than 1–2,000 people. The surrounding countryside could be seen from the market place.

Many of the successful new towns – and some of the failures – were sited alongside navigable rivers or on the coast. One that triumphed was Yarm, whose name was derived from a dam for catching fish that had been constructed within a loop of the river Tees 18 miles from the estuary. The recording of Yarm in Domesday Book and the position of the Norman church of St Mary Magdalene on the river bank away from the grid pattern of the planned town suggest that a small port was functioning here before Robert de Brus designed a borough with a regular pattern of narrow streets or wynds leading off a broad, curving High Street which accommodated the Thursday markets and annual fairs. The Tees was tidal up to four miles beyond Yarm, which acted as the nearest river port for the lead smelters of the Yorkshire Dales and the bridging point for traffic heading north from York and Thirsk. Despite its success – in 1295 it returned a member to Parliament – Yarm remained a chapelry of Kirk Levington until the nineteenth century, just as Barnsley stayed within the parish of Silkstone.

Bawtry's development was very similar to that of Yarm. Here, too, a small river port exported Derbyshire lead and other heavy goods from a wharf by St Nicholas' church, long before a new town was planned on a grid system around a large, rectangular market place. The borough was founded about 1200 between the river Idle and the Roman road, both of which served as the county boundary. Bawtry stuck out like the proverbial sore thumb into Nottingham-shire and long remained part of the Nottinghamshire parish of Blyth and the deanery of Retford. The Great North Road was diverted into the market place and Bawtry thrived both as a river port and as a thoroughfare town. Although nearly all its medieval buildings have gone, Bawtry's medieval topography is remarkably well preserved.

Upstream from the Humber, the Ouse was by far the busiest river for

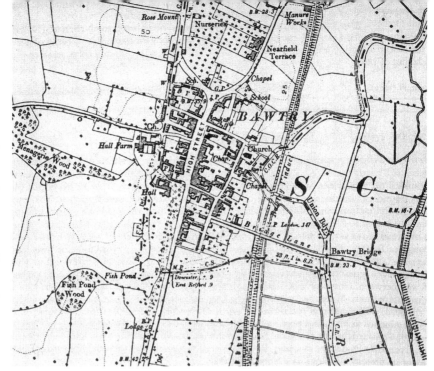

Bawtry. This first edition of the six-inch Ordnance Survey map reveals the regular plan of the medieval town, with the High Street serving as an enormous, rectangular market place and fair ground. The Yorkshire county boundary – marked by dots and dashes – encloses the town on three sides. The town was laid out on a grid plan between the winding course of the River Idle in the east and the Roman road heading for Doncaster in the west. The Great North Road was diverted through the centre of the town before rejoining its old line. A small river port at the highest point of navigation on the Idle existed before the market town was created c.1200.

The church of St Nicholas, patron saint of seafarers, stood on the banks of the river, just outside the grid pattern of the new town. Both the lord of the manor and the burgesses had staithes at Bawtry Wharf. Bawtry was the port for South Yorkshire metalware and Derbyshire lead and millstones until the Don Navigation and the Chesterfield Canal by-passed the town in the eighteenth century.

commercial traffic. Its importance to York was clear to the compilers of Domesday Book. It was tidal for most of its course and light boats were able to penetrate its tributaries as far inland as Doncaster on the Don, Knottingley on the Aire, Stamford Bridge on the Derwent, Tadcaster on the Wharfe and Boroughbridge on the Ure. Boroughbridge was a new town to the south of the bridge that was built over the Ure about 1145, at the edge of the manor and parish of Aldborough, and by 1165 it had achieved the status of a borough. The medieval street plan is preserved in Micklegate, Fishergate, Horsefair and St James' Square. Boroughbridge flourished as a river port where the Great North Road was joined by the road from York.

Another borough-port was laid out in a grid pattern by the Count of Aumale during the first half of the twelfth century at Hedon, 'the heather-covered hill' at the southern end of the parish of Preston. The town grew to three times its present size and supported three churches, including the splendid St Augustine's, the only one still standing and a monument to the wealth generated by trade in wool and hides in the later Middle Ages. In time, however, the narrow creek leading from the town to the Humber proved to be inadequate in face of competition from a rival port that had been established during the third quarter of the twelfth century by the Cistercian monks of Meaux. The monks knew this port as Wyke, meaning a creek, for it did not acquire the name of Kingston-upon-Hull (or Hull as it has always been known for short) until 1293, when Edward I bought the manor. They diverted the last few hundred yards of the old course of the river Hull into a straight channel and marked out a new town on a grid pattern. Goods from Holderness and the Wolds were brought down this channel and facilities were provided for the traffic that had sailed down the Ouse to reload. In 1193, for example, wool contributed by

Micklegate Bar. This upper part to the entrance to the city from the south was reared above the Norman arch in the fourteenth century, when the present walls were rebuilt. It was meant to be an imposing gateway where important people could be welcomed with ceremony, as much as a forbidding barrier.

PHOTOGRAPH: CARNEGIE, 2005

below Walmgate Bar, York. This bar guarding the eastern entrance to the medieval city of York contains Norman work but is essentially fourteenth-century in date. It is the only one of York's four bars to keep its barbican, a long extension designed to channel visitors under a portcullis and through wooden doors.

PHOTOGRAPH: CARNEGIE, 2005

The walls of York. The walls that encircle the medieval city are built on banks above much earlier foundations. Excavations in the Museum Gardens, south of Bootham Bar, have revealed a succession of defences, starting at the lowest level with the Roman wall to the Multangular Tower. The base of the small tower seen in the centre of the picture fills a breach in the Roman wall and so at first was thought to be Anglian. Most archaeologists now think that it is late Roman. To the right of the tower, and partly in the shadow, the different levels of the Viking, Norman and medieval banks are marked with green grass. The different layers of masonry are evident on the left side of the photograph. At the extreme right is the medieval boundary wall of St Leonard's hospital.

PHOTOGRAPH: AUTHOR

Bases of Norman piers, York Minster. The Norman cathedral which was demolished to make way for the present Gothic structure must have been a magnificent sight. The bases of the arches of the crypt that was erected for Archbishop Roger of Pont l'Évêque's church in the 1160s remain *in situ* and are reminiscent of the piers in the naves of Durham Cathedral and Selby Abbey.

BY COURTESY OF THE DEAN AND CHAPTER, YORK MINSTER

Yorkshire monasteries towards Richard I's ransom was sent from Wyke. By the close of the thirteenth century London and Boston were the only ports that had more trade.

During the Norman period York was by far the largest town in the county and the only one that was walled. The bars at Bootham, Micklegate and Walmgate are still entered under their Norman archways. York had suffered terribly from the Conqueror's harrying, but it soon recovered its position as the leading city in the North. The new minster church started by Thomas, the treasurer of Bayeux, who became Archbishop of York in 1070, was probably completed before his death in 1100. The 7 feet-thick walls incorporated much Roman masonry that had been plastered and painted with red lines to simulate new ashlar blocks and the church was set out at 45 degrees across the old Roman fortress to achieve the correct liturgical alignment. The 362 feet-long building comprised an aisleless nave, a crossing and transepts, and a choir with three apses at its eastern end. After it had been seriously damaged by fire in 1137, Archbishop Roger of Pont L'Évêque supervised the construction of a new choir and eight-bay crypt and the addition of two western towers. The crypt survives, but nearly all the Norman church above ground level was replaced later in the Middle Ages, starting with the transepts, which date from the time of Archbishop Walter de Grey (1216–55). The famous Five Sisters window in the north transept contains tall lancets filled with austere grisaille glass and supported by Purbeck marble shafts.

Thomas of Bayeux was generous in restoring old estates and granting new properties to the canons who served the minster. The arrangement whereby York and eight other English medieval cathedrals were run by secular canons rather than by monks began about 1090. The dean, precentor, chancellor and treasurer had their own houses near the archbishop's palace behind the minster, while the other members of the chapter were funded by the separate endowments of 36 prebends. The wealth generated by these endowments ranged widely, but those of the York treasureship and of Masham (which had been founded in the late twelfth century by Roger de Mowbray for a kinsman) were thought to be two of the richest plums in Christendom. Henry I made the substantial donations of the prebends of Driffield and Laughton-en-le-Morthen, for he regarded the minster as an important centre of loyalty to the throne. The Norman kings rarely ventured into the northern parts of their kingdom and so were depended upon the steadfastness of the Archbishop of York and the Bishop of Durham, together with the chapters of their cathedrals. This dependency led Henry to accept the Pope's decision to restore the independency of the see of York that had been had lost at the time of the Norman Conquest.

The excavation of St Helen's churchyard, by the north wall of York, has shown that skulls of the Norman period were of a markedly different type than earlier ones, thus suggesting immigration into the devastated city, perhaps from the Yorkshire countryside. The mosaic of winding streets bequeathed by the

St Mary's Church, Masham. The peculiar jurisdiction of Masham was once described as 'the richest plum in Christendom'. Its name has been preserved by the local brewery's Old Peculier beer. St Mary's Church served a large parish and so is a suitably large building, heightened in the later Middle Ages. The town is arranged around an enormous market place, with ample room for its sheep fairs. The lower part of the tower is Norman. It was built against the west wall of an earlier church, whose large, side-alternate quoins suggest a date from the time of the Kingdom of Northumbria. The original external face of the north wall has a square-sectioned string-course which dates it to the same period. The interior view looks down the nave into the chancel.

PHOTOGRAPH: AUTHOR
PHOTOGRAPH: CARNEGIE, 2005

Vikings was preserved intact when new houses were erected, except in the area that had been razed before the construction of York Castle. Nearly all the houses were timber-framed, in sharp contrast to the castle and numerous religious buildings, but a Norman stone building is incorporated in Gray's Court and at the end of a passage leading off Stonegate an upstairs window and the faint outline of a first-floor hall and undercroft survive from a twelfth-century house that may have resembled those that still stand on Steep Hill, Lincoln.

Very little is known about the daily lives of the citizens of York during the twelfth and thirteenth centuries, but hostility to one distinctive group in the reign of Richard I is well recorded. The Jewish community in York consisted of about 40 households in Coney Street, the largest gathering of Jews outside London, and their burial ground lay beyond the northern city wall at Jewbury. The anti-semitism that was whipped to fever pitch by the propaganda of the crusades broke out in rioting and plundering that forced the Jews to seek safety within York Castle on the night of 16 March 1190. The castle was set on fire by a mob determined on murder, so when all was lost, Jewish fathers cut the throats of their wives and children and then in turn submitted to the knife of their rabbi. At dawn the few remaining Jews walked out of the burnt-out castle and appealed for mercy in return for Christian baptism, but although they had been given a promise of safety all were killed. The mob were encouraged in their brutality by neighbouring landowners who owed huge debts to the Jewish money-lenders – Richard Malbisse of Acaster Malbis and Copmanthorpe,

left The interior of Clifford's Tower was gutted by fire after a gunpowder explosion in 1648, so the tower survives only as an empty shell.

PHOTOGRAPH: CARNEGIE, 2005

right Bainbridge. It was claimed in 1227 that Bainbridge had been founded by the lords of Middleham to provide each of twelve foresters with a house and nine acres of land. The fact that the village is arranged around an unusually large green suggests an element of planning. On a glacial mound overlooking the village stands the Roman fort of *Virosidum* (see the aerial photograph on page 38).

PHOTOGRAPH: CARNEGIE, 2005

William Percy of Bolton Percy, Alan Malekale, Marmaduke Darell and Philip de Fauconberg — middle-ranking barons who were connected by blood and ties of friendship. Despite their high rank, they did not escape justice and were forced to pay their debts. Within a few years other Jews had settled in York and by 1218 they formed one of England's ten specially protected urban communities. They soon prospered and in 1255 paid more tax than the Jews of any other provincial city, but under Edward I they faced further hostility and in 1290 the King expelled them all from England.

The countryside

The Norman kings turned huge stretches of the countryside into royal forests that were subject to distinctive laws. The term 'forest' was used in a legal rather than a descriptive sense, for the forests were wooded only in parts and contained land that was farmed by peasants. Within the forest boundaries, however, forest laws prevented the clearing of new land for farming, forbade the peasants from fencing their crops to keep out the game, imposed harsh penalties on poachers, and demanded that peasant dogs should be maimed so that they could not chase the deer and wild boar.

The Forest of Pickering was one of the largest, extending on to the North York Moors until it was 16 miles long and four miles wide and including more dense woodland than any other Yorkshire forest. Other parts of the North York Moors were included within the neighbouring Forest of Spaunton and large tracts of the Pennine moors around the upper reaches of the rivers were incorporated into similar private jurisdictions. The Forest of Wensleydale was 18 miles long and six miles wide, the Forest of Barden was granted to Robert de

Rumily by William I, and the lords of Richmond hunted in the New Forest in Swaledale and their chase in Arkengarthdale. Together with the Lancashire Forests of Bowland and Rossendale, which stretched over the moors to the Yorkshire boundary, and the neighbouring moorland estates of the Cistercian abbeys, they reserved enormous stretches of the countryside to great landlords, with lasting consequences for the rest of society right up to the recent legislation on 'the right to roam'. The Forest of Knaresborough was the largest of all the Yorkshire forests, being 20 miles long and eight miles broad and covering most of lower Nidderdale. Together with the area known as the Liberty on the other side of the River Nidd, it formed the honour of Knaresborough and was probably already old when it was first recorded in 1167. Further south, the Warennes hunted in the Forest of Sowerbyshire and in the upper reaches of the river Holme within their huge manor of Wakefield, while the Louvetots of Hallamshire set aside a large park near Sheffield Castle and extensive chases in the moorland valleys of the Rivelin and the Loxley. Chases were the baronial equivalent of the royal forests, though in practice forest was a term that was used rather loosely. In lowland Yorkshire, too, huge areas were brought under forest law. The Forest of Galtres extended 20 miles north-west of York as far as Aldborough and 15 miles north to Crayke Hill. A perambulation of 1316 shows that it covered 100,000 acres and included 60 townships. South of York, all the land between the Ouse and the Derwent formed another royal forest.

The forests grew to their largest extent under Henry II (1154–89), but during the following century some were 'disafforested' and by the fifteenth century most had fallen out of use. In their heyday they were administered by a host of officials, the chief of whom were of gentry rank with offices that sometimes became hereditary. The warden of a forest, together with his foresters and woodwards, applied forest laws through local courts and organised peasant agriculture in much the same way as any lord of the manor. Tenant farmers had common rights within the forest, as in other manors. In the Forest of Galtres, for example, the inhabitants of Easingwold and Huby had common grazing pastures for their oxen, cows, horses, and swine, but sheep and goats were prohibited. Each township had its special responsibilities, such as looking after the hounds or the construction and maintenance of the ditches, banks and pales around the woods. The clearing of new land was allowed under the control of forest officials but unlicensed clearances were not tolerated. One striking piece of evidence of authorised expansion comes from 1227, when Ranulph, son of Robert, claimed that his ancestors had created the village of Bainbridge in the Forest of Wensleydale in order to accommodate 12 foresters, each with a house and nine acres of land.

The private deer parks of the barons were enclosed well away from the royal forests. The earliest were associated with great castles and they sometimes remain distinctive landscapes. Conisbrough Parks is still the name of the countryside to the south of the castle and Pontefract Park is now used for horse racing and a golf course. The exceptionally large Haverah Park,

Knaresborough, was created about 1173 when William de Stuteville overrode the rights of his tenants by enclosing 2,250 acres of common pasture. In time, deer parks became a widespread feature of the rural landscape, with 73 known examples in the West Riding, 67 in the North Riding, and nearly 50 in the East Riding, with indications of many more, but they date mostly from the thirteenth and fourteenth centuries.

Many Yorkshire villages, especially those in the Vales of York, Mowbray and Pickering, still have a regular appearance that betray their planned origins. This regularity is even clearer on old maps, which show that the tofts around each house were exactly the same size. As we have seen, this process probably began in the ninth century and continued till the fourteenth. We lack documentary evidence to date them precisely, but it is possible that many were created in their present form during the late eleventh and twelfth centuries, after the harrying of the North. These planned villages are characteristic of townships which belonged to one or other of the Domesday Book tenants-in-chief but which had no land that the tenants worked directly for the lord. Sometimes, as at Huby, two rows face each other across the road or green, but more often, as at Gate Helmsley, just one row was laid out, and on other sites such as Attercliffe or Nun Monkton, three rows of houses were arranged around a triangular green. Occasionally, the curious positions of a parish church within or outside the regular plan of the village suggests that the core of an earlier settlement lay around it.

Fieldwork and the study of old maps has shown that planned forms were normal in the Vale of Pickering, more so than in any other part of Yorkshire. Appleton-le-Moors, four miles north-west of Pickering, is one of the most striking examples of a village where the houses face each other across a street that has only narrow grass verges and no lanes leading off it. The strict regularity of the plan is observed also in the crofts that extend to the two back-lanes, which run parallel to the main street and form a boundary between the village and its fields. Some of the crofts have merged into larger units over the centuries, but the original pattern can be discerned readily. The Abbot of St Mary's, York, was lord of the manor and it may have been during the time of Abbot Savary (1147–61), whose relations lived in Appleton, that the village was replanned and a neighbouring settlement (recorded as Baschebi in Domesday Book) was incorporated within it.

Medieval planning is also evident in the lay-out of the corn-growing fields. The two or three large open fields that were characteristic of most villages and the one or two 'townfields' of the hamlets were divided into furlongs for cropping purposes, with the individual strips of each farmer scattered within them. Sometimes the arable land was divided in the strict manner known as 'sun-division', so that each peasant got a fair share of good and poor soils. At Middleton, near Pickering, the shapes of former blocks of strips into which the open fields were divided are preserved by later hedges. Elsewhere, they are outlined by the old ploughing patterns of ridge-and-furrow that have survived in fields that have long ago been put down to grass. The strips have the shape of an inverted S that allowed the ox-plough teams to turn when they reached the headland. The evidence for open-field agriculture is much fuller in the later Middle Ages, but it is clear that in the Norman period field systems were still developing.

The corn mills that were recorded in considerable numbers in the Yorkshire folios of Domesday Book were water-powered and often on sites that remained in use well into the twentieth century. The first reference to a windmill in England is from 1185, when a post mill was recorded at Weedley, near South Cave, on the edge of the Wolds. The first English reference to a fulling mill comes from the same year, in a survey of the Knights Templar lands at Temple Newsam. The earlier practice had been to scour, thicken and felt cloth by 'walking', that is trampling by foot, and so for a long time afterwards fulling mills were known as walk mills. We have little information about the mining of coal or lead in the Norman period, but have some early evidence for the mining and forging of iron. The ore was mined in shallow bell-pits, washed and crushed, then smelted into wrought iron by the bloomery process, which used charcoal as fuel to achieve temperatures of 1,100–1,300°C. Impurities in the iron were then removed by repeated hammering. Two Yorkshire settlements that took their names from these activities were recorded in Domesday Book: Kirk Smeaton was the 'farmstead of the smiths' and Orgreave, 'a pit from which ore was dug'; the same survey also recorded six smiths at Hessle, near Hemsworth. Later in the Middle Ages substantial advances in iron making were achieved by the Cistercians.

Parish churches

The parish church was often the only stone building in a medieval village. Even most manor houses were timber framed. Once their victory was secure and the national population began to grow, Norman lords built new churches and chapels-of-ease and re-designed many of the existing ones. By 1200 the medieval parish system was more-or-less the same as it was 600 years later. Yorkshire has over 500 medieval parish churches, half of which retain some Norman work, mostly as nave arcades, chancel arches and splayed windows. Other, demolished buildings can be recognised as Norman from old illustrations or written descriptions before their replacement in Victorian times. Norman features survive particularly in small parishes where the population did not grow in the later Middle Ages, parishes whose fertile soils had attracted early settlers, so that villages were only a mile or two apart. In towns and villages that continued to expand, churches were enlarged and rebuilt, so now little survives from the twelfth century or, as at Rotherham, the size of the previous Norman church can be judged only from exposed foundations.

The earliest Norman churches had thick walls, filled with rubble and cemented by poor-quality mortar, and naves supported by low, rounded arches

St Nicholas' Church, Askham Bryan. This fine example of a small Norman village church in the Vale of York was built of magnesian limestone, presumably brought from Tadcaster, a few miles to the south-west. The nave and chancel were built as one unit and the church never acquired the dignity of a tower. The Norman-style bellcote was added in the nineteenth century, perhaps replacing an original one. The only piece of display is the south porch, which is entered through a Norman arch, supported by columns and adorned with zig-zag decoration. The windows preserve Norman forms but have been restored and 'improved'. The population of the village remained small so the church never needed to be extended.

PHOTOGRAPH: AUTHOR

Norman doorway, St John the Baptist's Church, Adel. This simple building consists only of nave and chancel, dating from the mid twelfth century, but it is made memorable by the ornamentation of the south doorway, which is projected almost like a porch. In the gable are representations of the Lamb of God, Christ in Majesty, and the symbols of the four evangelists. The four orders which frame the door have zigzag and animal decorations and the capitals of the columns have intertwined bands and leaves. Above the gable can be seen some of the carved heads of the corbel table that runs round the church. Inside, the chancel arch is also sumptuously decorated in the Norman style.

PHOTOGRAPH: CARNEGIE, 2005

and sturdy piers. They were built by native craftsmen who used the same styles of their Anglo-Scandinavian predecessors. At Kippax the tower, nave and chancel of the church that stands by the early Norman ringwork have the tall, narrow proportions and herringbone walling that were favoured before the Conquest. Further south at Burghwallis, the display of herringbone patterns is dazzling on a sunny day. At Bulmer, the former head of a deanery and wapentake, but now a Castle Howard estate village, the side-walls of the nave of the parish church and the lower part of the north chancel wall, are of the 'overlap' period around the Conquest and the head of an Anglian wheel cross suggests an even longer history, appropriate to a church dedicated to St Martin. On the Wolds at Weaverthorpe, old traditions were still being pursued in the early twelfth century when a tall, slim tower, nave and chancel were erected; a sundial that is set in the tympanum over the south door informs us that the church was built by Herbert the Chamberlain of Winchester.

By the middle years of the twelfth century the Normans were building churches in a more confident and decorative style. Yorkshire has some outstanding rural churches from these decades, especially in the central Vale of York. The small church of St John the Baptist, Adel, consists only of a nave and chancel, with a bellcote that was 'renewed' in 1839. The corbel table under the eaves is carved with fanciful heads and above the decorative string course rise small slit windows, deeply splayed on the inside. But the feature that captures immediate attention is the main doorway, which is carved with intertwined bands and leaves, animals, zigzag and beakhead decoration; in the gable the figure of Christ is surrounded by the symbols of the evangelists. St Mary's, Birkin, is built on a larger scale than Adel. The unbuttressed west tower and the eastern apse, supported by shallow pilaster-buttresses, are typically Norman, though the south aisle was added in the fourteenth century. The shafted windows above the string course are larger than those at Adel, but other features, such as the corbel table and the south doorway, which is adorned with medallions and zigzag and beakhead decoration, are comparable. Yorkshire has more beakhead decoration than any other county.

Most of the smaller churches and chapels-of-ease that are recognisable as Norman date from the 1140s and 1150s. They range from the chapel-of-ease that Otto de Tilli built at Thorpe-in-Balne in the parish of Barnby

Norman font, Thorpe Salvin The church of St Peter's contains the finest Romanesque font in Yorkshire. Dating from the second half of the twelfth century, the carvings represent a baptismal scene and the four seasons against a frame of Norman arches under a band of leaves. Here we see a harvesting scene to represent summer and a hunting expedition for autumn. Spring is depicted by sowing and winter by a man warming his legs before a fire. The baptism scene involves a priest holding a child by a font, with his parents and godparents in attendance.
AUTHOR COLLECTION

Dun, whose ruined nave is now used as a barn, to the heavily restored and enlarged St Mary's, Armthorpe, which started as a chapel-of-ease within Kirk Sandall parish. Some of the small churches have interesting pieces of sculpture, such as the crudely carved dragon with a tail shaped like an arrow in the tympanum of St Helen's, Austerfield, and the remarkable font at Thorpe Salvin, a masterpiece of Norman carving depicting a baptism scene and the four seasons. The most complete Norman church in the East Riding is St Nicholas, Newbald, a cruciform and aisleless structure with four doorways and the usual corbel table, round-arched windows and plaster buttresses. Begun about 1140, it was completed when the crossing tower was finished shortly after 1200. St Mary, Kirkburn, is a contemporary building, though the chancel was rebuilt in Victorian times. None of the many churches in the North Riding which retain some Norman features is truly outstanding.

The humble, little church at Adwick-upon-Dearne has never been enlarged or restored, for the population of this small parish remained modest and in Victorian times the manor had an absentee landlord. Consequently, the church still has its original Norman bellcote, a very rare survival. Even the towers that the Normans built on to their larger churches have usually been heightened or replaced, though a beautiful example survives at St Mary Magdalene, Campsall, once an important centre within the honour of Pontefract. Attractive combinations of Norman and late-medieval architecture can be seen a few miles away

Norman door, Stillingfleet church. All the major styles of English medieval architecture can be found at St Helen's church, but it is the south door which is justly famous. By the middle decades of the twelfth century the Normans were building and decorating even their small rural churches with more confidence. The door at Stillingfleet is thought to date from the 1160s. Dragons, fabulous beasts biting a roll-moulding, human heads, zigzag and other designs provide a display to strike a parishioner with awe as he or she entered the church. The ironwork on the wooden door may be contemporary with the masonry, but it may well be even earlier. It appears to depict a ship of the Viking era.

at the large, cruciform church of All Saints, Arksey, and at St Wilfrid, Brayton, which has a tall, unbuttressed Norman tower with twin bell-openings, a corbel table and a fine south doorway.

Yorkshire has a rich collection of 30 Norman doorways with decorative carvings. An outstanding example at Stillingfleet is thought to date from the 1160s, though the ironwork on the wooden door may well be earlier, for it has been forged into the shape of a Viking ship. The stone carvings of the surrounds include amongst their designs fabulous beasts biting a roll-moulding, human heads and zigzag. The other memorable doorway is the only Norman feature to survive in the fine late-medieval church of St Cuthbert, Fishlake. The four orders of the doorway are carved with medallions that contain pairs of seated and standing figures, animals, leaves and human heads. The sculptor is thought to have been a master craftsman who had worked at the Cluniac priory at Pontefract and whose other commissions included work at St Peter's, Conisbrough, where a tomb chest commemorating the third William de Warenne is carved in a chaotic group of scenes that include a standing bishop, a man fighting a dragon with another man lying below, two knights fighting on horseback, animals in medallions, signs of the Zodiac and Adam and Eve with the serpent in a tree. In their churches, as well as their monasteries and castles, the Normans have left a rich legacy in Yorkshire.

St Nicholas's Church, Newbald. The East Riding's best Norman parish church, St Nicholas's has a central tower but no aisles. The round-arched windows, the zigzag, scallop capitals and other decoration around the doorways, the carved heads of the corbel table under the roofline, and the flat buttresses place it in the middle years of the twelfth century, though the crossing tower was not completed until the early years of the following century.
PHOTOGRAPH: CARNEGIE, 2005

CHAPTER 4

Growth and Disaster,
1200–1400

Lynchets on the southern slopes below Elbolton and Kail Hill, near Thorpe and Burnsall. On hillsides in upland limestone country such as this, cultivation terraces were created by piling the stones that had been cleared so as to create flat land that was easier to plough, as well as to increase the depth of soil. They seem to have been created in the thirteenth and early fourteenth centuries when population pressure forced communities to find fresh plough land, but after the Black Death had reduced the population considerably the terraces once more became pastures and meadows. The lynchets have remained a striking feature of the upper Wharfedale landscape.

YDNPA, HISTORIC ENVIRONMENT RECORD

B ETWEEN THE NORMAN CONQUEST and the early years of the fourteenth century the population of England more than doubled and may have trebled. The available sources do not provide firm figures, but estimates based on Domesday Book suggest that in 1086 the national population was between 1.5 million and 2.25 million. Some historians think that by 1300 this number had risen to as much as 5 or 6 million. This growth came to a sudden end in the second decade of the fourteenth century, when pestilence and harvest failure caused a decline of at least 15 per cent. Then in 1348–50 the Black Death killed at least a third, perhaps half the people of England, and further outbreaks of plague, especially in 1360–62 and 1369, reduced the national population to between 2.2 and 3 million. Levels continued to fall during the next hundred years, so that by the third quarter of the fifteenth century the English population may have gone down to barely 2 million. This demographic background is crucial to an understanding of the later Middle Ages.

Castles and manor houses

The feudal barons remained as mighty as their Norman predecessors. The castles that had been erected in the twelfth century were usually strong enough to need little further embellishment, except to make the domestic accommodation more comfortable, though after its destruction in the Barons' War of 1266 Sheffield Castle had to be built anew. Starting in 1270, Thomas de Furnival planned a castle that was as grand as those that Edward I was to build later in the century in north Wales. It dominated the town of Sheffield for nearly four centuries at the confluence of the Sheaf and the Don, with a huge deer park extending across 2,461 acres from the eastern edge of the town over that part of the present city that is still known as Park Hill and The Manor. De Furnival needed a royal licence to 'crenellate', or fortify, his building. During the thirteenth and fourteenth centuries 51 of these licences were granted for properties in Yorkshire, ranging from the Archbishop of York's manor house at Cawood in 1272 and William le Vavasour's castle at Hazlewood in 1290 to the walls of the town of Hull in 1321 and 1327.

By the thirteenth century the crown's authority in Yorkshire was secure enough for some of its estates to be granted to favourites and junior members of the royal family. Knaresborough was given away in 1229, Richmond about 1240, and Pickering in 1267. Edward III granted most of the crown property in Yorkshire to his sons, John of Gaunt, Duke of Lancaster, and Edmund Langley, Duke of York. When John de Warenne, eighth Earl of Surrey, died without heirs in 1347, all his estates north of the Trent, including the Yorkshire lordships of Conisbrough and Wakefield, were forfeited to the crown and given to the Duke of York. Then, in 1372 the estates that had passed to the crown after the execution of Thomas, Earl of Lancaster, 50 years earlier, were given to the Duke of Lancaster. They included the great honours of Pontefract, Tickhill, Pickering and Knaresborough, the lordships of Bradford and Snaith, and parts of Yorkshire that lay adjacent to the honour of Clitheroe. Together, they made the Duchy of Lancaster the largest landowner in Yorkshire.

Outbreaks of civil war and the threat of invasion from north of the border meant that castles still needed stout defences, but by the early fourteenth century the old reliance on a keep had been abandoned. At Skipton Robert Clifford designed a new castle with a forbidding gatehouse and six massive round towers grouped together. In the later fourteenth and fifteenth centuries some of the smaller castles that were erected within Norman motte-and-baileys, such as those at Crayke, Harewood and Whorlton, were little more than large tower houses. Another favoured design was to arrange buildings around a courtyard with massive towers in the corners. The Latimers' castle at Danby led the way in Yorkshire, but the finest examples from the fourteenth century are at Bolton in Wensleydale and Sheriff Hutton on the edge of the Forest of Galtres.

In the early fourteenth century Sir Henry Scrope, Chief Justice and Chief

A View of Bolton Castle. 1787

Baron of the Exchequer, had established an estate in Wensleydale, centred on Bolton, but it was Sir Richard, the first Lord Scrope, who erected the castle, enclosed a park, built a church, and perhaps laid out the village on a regular plan of two rows on either side of a green. Work on the castle began in 1378 and took 18 years to complete; the timbers had to be brought by oxen all the way from the Cumberland Forest of Ingleby. Three of the four powerful corner towers survive almost to their original height, but despite their grim appearance, when Sir Edward Knollys came on a visit in 1568 he described the building not as a castle but as 'the highest walled house that I have seen'. The three-storeyed buildings that rise around a rectangular courtyard within the walls are also partly preserved.

Sheriff Hutton took its name from Bertram of Bulmer, Sheriff of York, who had erected a motte-and-bailey castle and a church there about 1140. The manor eventually passed to the Nevilles of Raby Castle (county Durham), who enclosed a park and established a weekly market in the village. In 1382 John Neville was granted a licence to crenellate which allowed him to choose a different site for a huge new castle, similar in design to that at Bolton, with tall corner towers four or five storeys high and almost equally tall domestic buildings arranged around a courtyard. His son, Ralph, was ennobled as Earl of Westmorland by Richard II and his numerous children married into most of the leading families in the land. With the addition of Middleham Castle and large estates in Cumberland, the Nevilles rivalled the Percies as the leading family in northern England until all their property was forfeited to the crown in 1471 and shared between Edward IV's two brothers. Richard, Duke of Gloucester – the future Richard III – was given Sheriff Hutton and Middleham, together with part of the Cumberland estates. In the 1540s John Leland thought that Sheriff Hutton was the best princely lodging in the North, but by the

Castle Bolton from the south-west. Yorkshire's finest surviving example of a late-medieval castle, where the domestic accommodation was arranged around a courtyard between sturdy corner towers.

PHOTOGRAPH: CARNEGIE, 2005

The ruins of Sheriff Hutton Castle. This former stronghold of the Neville family on the edge of the Forest of Galtres was built from 1382 by John de Neville, one of the leading noblemen in the North. The four angle towers and part of the gatehouse preserve the outline of this quadrangular, brick palace, which was already ruinous by the early seventeenth century.

PHOTOGRAPH: CARNEGIE, 2005

Aerial view of Pontefract Castle. This once mighty castle has been reduced to pitiful ruins in a public garden, but the lower part of the keep still stands on solid rock and parts of the curtain wall enclose the former inner bailey. Founded by Ilbert de Laci on a new site away from the old settlement at Tanshelf, it served an enormous Norman honour which stretched across the centre of the West Riding. A new borough was founded to the west of the castle. In the early fourteenth century Pontefract Castle was the chief residence of Thomas, Earl of Lancaster. After his execution in 1322, it passed to the Duchy of Lancaster and eventually to the Crown. Richard II was imprisoned and probably murdered here. The castle was dismantled in 1649 after it had been fortified by royalists during the Civil War.

following century it had fallen into ruin. Nowadays, the shattered towers and gatehouse pierce the skyline arrestingly, but little else remains.

About the same time as the Scropes were at work on Bolton Castle and the Nevilles were busy at Sheriff Hutton, Sir Thomas Percy began to erect a similar building at his family's main Yorkshire seat at Wressle, seven miles east of Selby. Leland thought that it was one of the best houses in the North, constructed 'of very fair and great squaird stone', but now only the substantial shell of the hall range, set between two towers, is standing. The fortunes of the Percies had risen in the early fourteenth century when Henry Percy had bought the Northumberland estates of Alnwick and Warkworth and had been rewarded for his vigorous leadership in the wars against Scotland by large grants of confiscated estates in the borders. In 1308 he had obtained licences to crenellate his Yorkshire manor houses at Spofforth and Leconfield. In the West Riding the Percies held the manors of Healaugh, Leathley, Linton, Spofforth and Tadcaster, as well as lands in Craven, Ribblesdale and Langstrothdale. In the North Riding they held Asenby, Gristhwaite, Kirk Leavington, Seamer, Throxenby and Topcliffe and in the East Riding they were lords of Arras, Catton, Gembling, Leconfield, Nafferton, Pocklington, Scorborough, Wansford, Wasplington and Wressle. Henry Percy's grandson and namesake became the first Earl of Northumberland, Earl Marshal of England, and warden of the northern marches, and was connected by kinship with nearly all the leading families in the land. Only the Duchy of Lancaster held more land in the North. The family's position began to crumble in 1399, when Henry IV, the son of John of Gaunt, Duke of Lancaster, ousted his cousin, Richard II, and then had him murdered at Pontefract castle. The Percies wavered in their loyalty, but then rebelled. In 1403 Henry Hotspur, the son of the Earl of Northumberland, was killed at the battle of Shrewsbury and in 1408 Earl Henry was killed at the battle of Bramham Moor. Earl Henry's head was stuck on a tower in the middle of London bridge and the rest of his body was quartered, pickled in spices, and taken on tour to be exhibited in Lincoln, York, Newcastle and Berwick.

Lesser lords also kept security in mind when they built their manor houses. The outstanding survivor is Markenfield Hall, three miles south of Ripon, which dates from 1310, when John de Markenfield obtained a licence to crenellate a building faced with dressed stone and set within a complicated system of moats. The ground floor was occupied by a large kitchen and servants' quarters. The first floor, which was reached by an external staircase and porch and lit by large windows in a contemporary Geometric design, contained the hall, solar and chapel, and the chambers on the upper floor were used as bedrooms. Another sturdy manor house at Rothwell (now demolished) was described in 1341 as containing a 'hall, chapel, chambers, kitchen, bakehouse, brewery, barn, oxstalls, stables, and other houses necessary for the residence of the lord, built and enclosed within stone walls'.

Moated manor houses sometimes succeeded Norman motte-and-bailey castles as the residence of the lord. The Fossards' castle at Langthwaite, to the north of Doncaster, was replaced by the Ratcliffe moat on the opposite bank of the stream and at Topcliffe the Percies' moat is close to the older earthworks. Most Yorkshire moats date from the thirteenth and fourteenth centuries, especially from 1250 to 1325; Baynard Castle at Cottingham, for example, was said to be 'well constructed with a double ditch enclosed by a wall' by 1282. No doubt lords had defence partly in mind when they constructed a moat, but precautions were often minimal and prestige seems to have been at least as important as security. Monasteries, minor lords and even freeholders followed the fashion. An extensive moat system at Thorpe-in-Balne enclosed not only the manor house and its outbuildings but also the fishponds and a Norman chapel-of-ease.

Rothwell contained a '... hall, chapel, chambers, kitchen, bakehouse, brewery, barn, oxstalls, stables, and other houses necessary for the residence of the lord, built and enclosed within stone walls.'

[1341]

The Long Barn, Whiston, near Rotherham, was erected as an estate barn for the Furnivals, lords of Hallamshire. Recent dendrochronology tests have proved that the original five bays, seen here before the barn's conversion into a village hall, date from 1223–52, making this Yorkshire's earliest surviving timber-framed building. The other bays date from the seventeenth century, when the barn was extended.

The wealthiest medieval lords built their castles and manor houses in stone, but everyone else used oak or, if timber was not available, humble materials such as cobbles or mud. The earliest surviving timber-framed building in Yorkshire is probably the long barn that the Furnivals, lords of Hallamshire, built at Whiston. The posts, arcade plates and connecting braces of the original five bays display carpentry techniques that are not found elsewhere in the county and which are paralleled in Essex barns of the early thirteenth century. They have been dated by dendrochronology to 1233–52. In midland and southern England some surviving cruck frames date from the thirteenth century, but northern examples are later. The only examples in Yorkshire of the more sophisticated base-cruck buildings with crown-post roofs are Baxby

The outbuildings of the farmstead within the moats at Thorpe-in-Balne include a dilapidated barn that was once a Norman chapel-of-ease within the parish of Barnby Dun. It was erected by Otto de Tilli, seneschal of the lordship of Conisbrough, in the mid-twelfth century. The nave was still standing in the 1820s, but now only the former chancel survives.

below Lady Row, Goodramgate, York. In October 1315 the Archbishop of York granted permission to the vicar of Holy Trinity church to erect a row of buildings on the edge of the churchyard. The rents were used to endow a chantry in the church. The plot measured 18 feet in width and 128 feet in length and was divided originally between ten buildings with a single room on each of two floors. The row of tenements or cottages was roofed in a continuous frame, with the upper storey jettied over the lower one. This modest accommodation for poor craftsmen or journeymen provided a ground-floor living room and workplace and an upper chamber and store. These cottages were unheated, so its occupants would have had to use the common bakehouse for cooking. This is the oldest surviving row of houses in England with a secure date.

PHOTOGRAPH: CARNEGIE, 2005

manor house in the parish of Husthwaite and the heavily restored Canons' Garth at Helmsley, both of which date from about 1300.

The earliest timber-framed buildings that survive in York are a group of small cottages built with overhanging chambers in Goodramgate about 1320. In the countryside cottages from this period are known only from foundations exposed during the excavation of deserted villages. They normally had just one room that was open to the roof and was heated by a central hearth; air and light came through narrow, unglazed windows. A cottage that was excavated at Wharram Percy measured only 20 feet by 10 feet. Such dwellings were supported by crude cruck frames rising from rubble foundations and infilled with whatever could be obtained locally. Documentary evidence points to the use of crucks even in the East Riding, where few timber-framed houses survive. In 1599, for example, a survey of Settrington noted that all the houses and cottages were reared on crucks. In the North Riding, the manor account rolls for Bedale in the second quarter of the fifteenth century mention 30 buildings, all of which had timber frames on stone footings, walls infilled with wattle-and-daub, and thatched or stone-slated roofs. Contemporary houses in the same district, or even the same village, varied considerably in their quality. At Snape, two or three miles south of Bedale, house walls were constructed entirely of wattling and rendered with mud. The great castles and manor houses completely overshadowed the humble dwellings of the majority of the population.

Monasteries and friaries

During the thirteenth and fourteenth centuries Yorkshire's abbeys and priories achieved the splendid forms that we can still recognise in their present ruined condition. They too sometimes obtained licences to crenellate their walls and towers – St Mary's Abbey, York (where more walling survives than in any other monastery) in 1318, Guisborough Priory 1344, Drax Priory 1362, Selby Abbey 1375, and Bridlington Priory 1388. Each of the three Benedictine abbeys was greatly enlarged. Selby Abbey's huge church was extended in the thirteenth and fourteenth centuries, St Mary's Abbey, York, was provided with spectacular Gothic architecture, starting in 1271 at the east end of the 360 feet long church, and at Whitby Abbey Abbot Roger began a building programme in the 1220s that lasted for a hundred years, more than doubling the size of the Norman church. There, the gables with three tiers of lancets in the north transept and at the east end remain an arresting sight high on the cliff-top above the town and harbour.

The Cistercians began to build with a flamboyance that would have outraged their predecessors. The sombre style of Kirkstall was rejected in favour of soaring Gothic. At Rievaulx Abbey the contrast between the lavish presbytery, which was rebuilt for the monks in the early thirteenth century, and the simplicity of the earlier architecture of the lay brothers' part of the church shows how far the Cistercians had moved from their original ideals. In the fourteenth century the order abandoned the vegetarian diet and monks were sometimes provided with small apartments in place of the communal dormitory. At Fountains Abbey, too, the contrast between the old and the new is apparent as one walks through the church from the Norman nave to the Chapel of the Nine Altars at the east end. Byland Abbey suffered badly at the Dissolution, but foundation stones show that, at 330 feet, it once had the longest Cistercian church of a single build in the country. The ornate west front was completed in the first quarter of the thirteenth century with a great rose window that would never have been allowed a few decades earlier.

The Augustinians built with the same enthusiasm. At Bolton Priory the transepts and most of the eastern part of the church were redesigned at the close of the thirteenth century. Kirkham Priory has mostly gone, but a gatehouse in the Decorated style of the last quarter of the thirteenth century provides a glimpse of the former quality of the architecture. When the canons of Guisborough Priory decided to rebuild their monastery they hired master masons and accommodated them and their families in the town. After a disastrous fire in 1289 building was restarted to a new Decorated design; when it was complete, the church was 352 feet long and the 56 feet high and 23 feet wide east window was one of the largest of its time. The enormous scale of the thirteenth-century nave of Bridlington Priory, preserved as the parish church, was judged to be fitting for one of the wealthiest Augustinian houses in England. Yorkshire's nunneries were much poorer than these famous institutions, but the Benedictines of Nun Monkton were able to erect a high-quality

The shell of the former Benedictine abbey at Whitby seen from the north-east. It was built in the first half of the thirteenth century and completed in the fourteenth, by which time it was over 300 feet long.

church in two stages, with fine lancet windows in the Early English style of *c.*
1240 rising above a Norman doorway that was 60 years older. The demolished
Cistercian church at Nun Appleton was 150 feet long and the other nunnery
buildings were extensive.

By the late thirteenth century, many Cistercian monasteries, including
Fountains and Kirkstall, were heavily in debt. In 1291 the situation at Rievaulx
had got so bad that the abbot dispersed the monks temporarily to other
Cistercian houses in order to reduce running costs. Wool of excellent quality
from the sheep runs of the Dales and the North York Moors was the mainstay
of the economy of Yorkshire's wealthiest Cistercian houses. They raised credit
through advance sales of wool to Florentine merchants for up to 20 years, but
they became dangerously vulnerable to outbreaks of scab, such as that which
affected the Rievaulx flocks in 1280. The costs of building, feeding the monks
and their workforce, hospitality, charity, and taxation could not be matched by
income. Fountains Abbey's debts spiralled out of control from £900 in 1274 to
£6,373 in 1291. After the battle of Bannockburn in 1314, the marauding Scottish
army added to monastic gloom by plundering their estates and burning their
granges. For a time, Bolton Priory had to be abandoned.

After the Black Death, monasteries recruited fewer monks and even less lay
brothers, but the new, austere order of the Carthusians established two houses
in Yorkshire, at Hull (from 1377) and at Mount Grace (from 1398), where,
uniquely in England, sufficient of the ruined priory survives to demonstrate the
physical arrangements. The early fifteenth-century church occupies a central

St Mary's Abbey, York. This major Benedictine abbey was founded by William II in 1088–89, on the site of an earlier monastery, just outside the city walls. The extensive grounds were enclosed by a substantial wall, much of which survives. The ruins of the abbey church date from the late thirteenth century, and the plan of the earlier church is marked on the ground. The rebuilding was started at the east end in 1271, using magnesian limestone brought from Tadcaster. The abbey was dissolved in 1539.
PHOTOGRAPH: CARNEGIE, 2005

left Mount Grace Priory is the best preserved of the ten Carthusian charter-houses in England. It was founded in 1398 as the last of Yorkshire's medieval monasteries. Each monk occupied his own two-storeyed cell around three sides of the Great Cloister. The one in the background is a reconstruction, furnished with replica furniture based on contemporary illustrations; that in the foreground is now marked by low walls and foundations. Carthusian monks withdrew from the world to practise an austere life, living in silence and spending most of their times in meditation alone in their cells.
PHOTOGRAPH: CARNEGIE, 2005

right The Presbytery, Rievaulx Abbey. The most substantial remains of the abbey church are at the east end, where the original Norman building was replaced in the thirteenth century in a glorious Early English style, complete with confident, slender flying buttresses. This is where the monks maintained a daily round of seven services. The new presbytery was begun in the 1220s and when complete was three storeys high and seven bays long. Five chapels occupied the east end.
PHOTOGRAPH: CARNEGIE, 2005

Bridlington Priory. Founded in 1113 by Walter de Gant, Bridlington Priory was the first in northern England to be established for the Augustinian order. Once it had acquired the whole of Bridlington and lands and churches elsewhere in Yorkshire and Lincolnshire, the priory became one of the wealthiest monasteries in the county. It also gained a wide reputation for its learning and spirituality and the tomb of St John of Bridlington became a major pilgrimage shrine. After its dissolution in 1537 the monastic buildings were demolished and the church was reduced to under half its size, the former nave being adapted as a parish church. The towers at the west end were heightened and given their present appearance in the 1870s by Sir George Gilbert Scott.

position and beyond the cloisters the monks' two-storeyed cells (one of which has been reconstructed) were set out in line, each with its own little garden. The cells were spacious but austere and the reclusive monks received their food through hatches. They had taken a vow of silence and rarely met their fellow brethren.

In reaction to those monks who deliberately sought to be free of society in rural isolation, the friars were based in the towns so that they could preach to lay audiences and maintain themselves by begging. The friars did not accumulate property other than their churches and conventual buildings. They arrived in Yorkshire in the late 1220s and their numbers grew quickly until enthusiasm began to wane by the early fourteenth century. Nearly every Yorkshire town attracted at least one of the four orders. The friars were well-received and supported by the burgesses and were rarely a threat to the existing monasteries. They did, however, arouse hostility from parish priests, who saw their main source of funds diverted from their churches.

In 1221 the Dominicans (Black Friars) became the first preaching order to reach England and six years later they had become established in York, where they eventually had 60 members. Foundation dates are sometimes difficult to fix, but other Dominican friaries were established at Beverley (by 1240), Scarborough (by 1252), Pontefract (1256) and Yarm (by 1266). The Franciscans (Grey Friars, who were dedicated to absolute poverty) had also arrived in York by about 1230 and were soon active at Beverley, Doncaster, Hull, Richmond and Scarborough. The Carmelites (White Friars) came soon after and were based at York (1253), Hull (1289), Scarborough (1320), Doncaster (by 1346) and Northallerton (1356). The Augustinian order (Austin Friars) were also found in York (by 1240), Tickhill (c.1256) and Hull (1317); their friary at Tickhill had between 18 and 24 members in the early fourteenth century, but by the Dissolution numbers had shrunk to a prior and seven friars. Finally, the Crutched Friars and the Friars of the Sack also gained temporary footholds, but did not flourish.

Greyfriars' Tower, Richmond. This Franciscan friary was built just outside the town walls of Richmond upon land donated by its founder Radulph Fitz-Radulph in 1258. The slender tower, which rose between the nave and chancel of the friary church, survives much as is seen here in an engraving of 1819, set within what is now a small public garden. It dates from the fifteenth century and is crowned in the distinctive style of Yorkshire's finest contemporary churches.
BY COURTESY OF GROVE RARE BOOKS, BOLTON ABBEY

York's great collection of medieval religious buildings included friaries of all four of the main orders. Scarborough hosted three friaries – Franciscans, Dominicans and Carmelites – and the continued popularity of the brethren is revealed by bequests in 127 of the 210 wills that survive from the borough between 1349 and 1500. At Doncaster the image of the Virgin at the Carmelite friary attracted pilgrims from far and wide, for miracles were reputed to happen before the shrine. Yet, despite their undoubted size and importance, the remains of the county's friaries are insubstantial, for after the Dissolution their prime sites were vulnerable to redevelopment. Those at Doncaster, Hull, Northallerton, Pontefract, Scarborough and Yarm have gone completely. The only important ruin is the fifteenth-century Greyfriars' Tower, the centrepiece of the friary that the Franciscans built just beyond the town walls at Richmond, on land donated in 1258 by Radulph fitz Radulph. No complete friary survives anywhere in Britain.

Medieval hospitals were another form of

religious institution that were associated principally with towns. Seventy-two of the 90 known Yorkshire sites were urban. Most hospitals were small and many did not last very long, so they are poorly recorded. They were staffed by a master, brothers and sisters, and servants and were devoted to the welfare of the sick and infirm. York had 19 hospitals at different times and Beverley had ten, but few of Yorkshire's medieval hospitals have left any standing remains. St Leonard's, York, is the outstanding example, as it was in its hey-day, and the hospitals of St Anne and St Mary Magdalene survive as ruins in Ripon. At Tickhill, St Leonard's hospital now serves as the parish room; the ground floor of this timber-framed building of ten bays was built about 1470, but the upper floor is a complete rebuilding of 1851. Doncaster had three hospitals in the Middle Ages, only one of which can be identified with certainty. Scarborough, too, had three hospitals, as well as its three friaries and the grand parish church of St Mary's.

Churches

Whereas the parish churches that the Normans erected in the towns were rebuilt in later centuries to accommodate the growing population and to demonstrate

left Perched high on top of the crumbling East Cliff, Whitby Abbey is one of the country's most picturesque monastic ruins. The monastery founded by St Hilda in the seventh century had been destroyed by the Vikings, but in 1078 it was refounded as a well-endowed Benedictine abbey. Rebuilding in the Early English and Decorated Gothic styles took place over the thirteenth and early fourteenth centuries. The monastery had only 22 monks when it was dissolved in 1539.

The photograph shows work underway on the new visitors' centre. At the bottom right is St Mary's, Whitby's famous Norman and Georgian parish church, approached from the old town around the harbour by a steady climb of 199 steps.

NATIONAL MONUMENT RECORD

increased wealth, in the countryside many parishes found that their twelfth-century churches remained adequate for their needs. In most cases, the adoption of the Early English Gothic style at parish church level is evident only in minor architectural features such as an inserted lancet window, yet Skelton has the most perfect small Early English church in the country. The church was built in the middle years of the thirteenth century in a style so redolent of recent work at York Minster that it is likely that Roger Haget, the York treasurer, was largely responsible for it. The two-bay nave and its narrow aisles share the steeply sloping roof, which rises to a bellcote marking the division between nave and chancel. The deeply moulded arches were carved with the latest stiff leaf and dog tooth designs. Other good examples of Early English work can be found in parish churches in the East Riding at Filey and Hedon and in the North Riding at Bossall.

Yorkshire's three great collegiate churches were also rebuilt in the thirteenth century in various Gothic styles. At different times in the Middle Ages Yorkshire had 21 secular colleges of priests who were not bound to any particular monastic rule. The major ones were founded within the diocese of

right The west front, Ripon Cathedral, is entirely Early English in style, with some Victorian restoration of the original thirteenth-century work. It is filled with lancets, many of them blank, in a straightforward, rather severe way. The spires which originally topped the two towers were taken down in 1664.

St Giles's Church, Skelton. This small church, just north of York, is an unusually complete example of Early English work of the thirteenth century. Churches are rarely of one style, and those that are had a rich patron. Skelton church was built in the 1240s at the cost of Robert Haget, treasurer of York Minster.

below Ruined Chapter House and Chancel, St Peter's Church, Howden. The great collegiate church known as Howden Minster served the ancient territory of Howdenshire. In 1080 William the Conqueror gave both the manor and the church to the Bishop of Durham. The large manor house of the medieval bishops stood south-east of the church-yard, but little of it remains. From 1267 the church was served by a college of five priests or secular canons, so called because they did belong to a religious order and did not live communally. The college was dissolved in 1547, together with other colleges and chantry chapels, and the new tithe owners refused to keep the choir and chapter house (seen here) in repair. Howden was now served only by curates.

The lofty tower that Bishop Skirlaw financed was still incomplete when he died in 1406. The thirteenth-century nave continues in use as the parish church, but the roof and the upper walls of the choir collapsed in 1696 and the chapter house lost its roof in 1750. The roof has been restored since this photograph was taken.

The chapter house was built in the late fourteenth century as the business or administrative centre for the collegiate church, and Bishop Skirlaw again helped to finance it.

PHOTOGRAPH: AUTHOR

York long before the Norman Conquest at Beverley, Ripon and Southwell (Nottinghamshire) and afterwards at Howden. Each of these four lay at the centre of an ancient multiple estate alongside a market town that grew rich as the early medieval economy expanded. Wilfrid's seventh-century monastery at Ripon had been refounded as a collegiate church after its destruction by fire in

left The nave of Ripon Cathedral. The rebuilding of Ripon Cathedral in stages meant that the chancel and nave are not perfectly aligned and some of the piers in the crossing tower are those of the earlier building, producing a rather lopsided effect, and suggesting that the masons were uneasy about the ability of the tower. The nave is in the Perpendicular style, with surviving earlier fragments. The wooden ceiling dates from 1868. This medieval collegiate church, on the site of a seventh-century monastery, was raised to cathedral status in 1836.

PHOTOGRAPH: CARNEGIE, 2005

The font at Beverley Minster. The Norman font in the south aisle of the nave is made of black Frosterley marble from Weardale, County Durham. It was made about 1170, well before the church was rebuilt in Gothic style.

PHOTOGRAPH: CARNEGIE, 2005

The Great East Window, Beverley Minster. The east end of the minster is dominated by this huge window of nine lights, dating from the second decade of the fifteenth century. The surviving stained glass, which adorned the church in the Middle Ages, was reassembled in this window during the seventeenth and eighteenth centuries and has been restored on several occasions. The pieces date from the thirteenth to the fifteenth century and include (in the apex) a representation of St John of Beverley and the symbols of the four evangelists.

PHOTOGRAPH: CARNEGIE, 2005

The south transept of Beverley Minster. The Early English work of the south transept dates from the middle decades of the thirteenth century. The perfectly proportioned tiers of lancets in the gable end, the use of dark Purbeck marble shafts in each of the three storeys, and the tall arches leading into aisles at both sides of the transept demonstrate why Sir George Gilbert Scott, the great Victorian ecclesiastical architect, thought that Beverley Minster was 'the finest Gothic church in the world'.

PHOTOGRAPH: CARNEGIE 2005

Chapter house, York Minster, completed *c.*1285. At this time chapter houses were designed as polygons, creating good acoustics and allowing architectural display. The external view – seen best from the city walls – is composed of large Geometric windows, sturdy buttresses and an ingenious pyramidical roof. The interior is enriched by naturalistic carvings and Purbeck marble shafts.

950, but the famous west front is of the 1220s; Ripon achieved cathedral status in 1836. A similar story can be told of Beverley, where the early eighth-century minster was refounded as a collegiate church about 935 by King Athelstan; by the thirteenth century it resembled a cathedral in its proportions, with some of the best Early English architecture in Yorkshire. The county's third great collegiate church at Howden belonged to the Bishop of Durham and was made collegiate in 1267. First the transcripts were rebuilt, followed by the choir and nave, then the west front, which was completed in the first decade of the fourteenth century, and finally the crossing tower, which was finished almost 100 years later. After the college was dissolved and the market declined, this fine church could no longer be maintained. In 1696 the roof and upper walls of the choir collapsed, in the mid eighteenth century the roof of the chapter house fell in, and over time the bishop's manor house became ruinous.

Once the master masons at York Minster had completed the north transept about 1260 they started work on the octagonal chapter house, the meeting place of the Dean and Chapter. This masterpiece of the new style, with Purbeck marble shafts, an abundance of carved foliage, and a pyramidal roof supported by a wooden vault, was the largest of its kind in England. Seventy years of work on a new nave began in 1291, featuring Ivo de Raghton's great

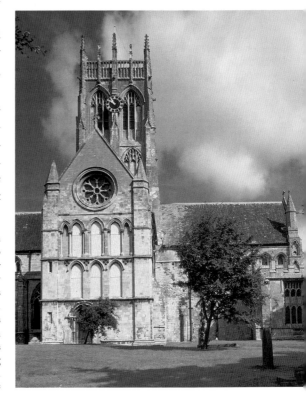

St Augustine's Church, Hedon. In the Middle Ages Hedon was a flourishing port and borough until trade was lost to Kingston-upon-Hull, and the creek leading to the Humber silted up. The town shrank and St Augustine's was the only one of the three churches to survive. The quality of its Gothic architecture reflects the town's medieval prosperity. The south transept, boarded up in this 2005 photograph, is Early English in style, but the rose window dates from Street's restoration of 1868–76. The large belfry windows and delicate pinnacles which crown the impressive crossing tower completed the design in Perpendicular style.

St Patrick's Church, Patrington. This famous and beautiful church was built in the Decorated style of the late thirteenth to the middle of the fourteenth century, when Patrington was a busy port and market town and the Archbishop of York was lord of the manor. It is a landmark for miles around and would have been a welcome sight to sailors returning from the North Sea up the Humber estuary. The spire of the crossing tower is 189 feet high, if we include the weather cock, and the church is 150 feet long externally. The cathedral-like proportions are emphasised by the double aisles of both nave and transepts, an unusual feature in a mere parish church. The builders are likely to have been members of a local family who went on to gain national repute in the later fourteenth and fifteenth centuries. Robert of Patrington, senior, was master mason of York Minster in 1369, where some of his carved capitals and bosses resemble those of the church of his native parish.

west window, which was completed in 1338. But the new Gothic styles that were adopted elsewhere in Yorkshire during the later thirteenth century were based more on Selby Abbey's beautiful seven-bay choir of 1280–1340, which has the entire range of Decorated tracery types, most famously in the east window. The East Riding, which was the most prosperous part of the county at the time, has a wonderful collection of great parish churches that were rebuilt in the late thirteenth and fourteenth centuries, particularly St Augustine's at Hedon, Holy Trinity at Hull, and, best of all, St Patrick's at Patrington, names that are famous throughout the country. The parish churches of Cottingham and Skipwith also have Decorated features of high quality and a complete example of a church built in this style during the second quarter of the fourteenth century is to be seen at Bainton. The North Riding does not have much high-

Yorkshire's pride and chief glory, York Minster is built at 45 degrees across the Roman military headquarters and upon the foundations of earlier churches. The church built by King Edwin of Northumbria in the early seventh century is believed to have been close by, although it was not discovered when the minster foundations were excavated. Thomas of Bayeux, who became Archbishop of York in 1070, built a huge Norman cathedral before his death in 1100, but nearly everything which survives of his building is now beneath the minster, within the crypt.

The earliest surviving Gothic architecture is found in the transepts, from the time of Archbishop Walter de Gray (1216–55). The chapter house was begun on the north side in 1260; work on the new nave was started in 1291 and completed seventy years later, when work began on a new east end. This was finished when the great east window was unveiled in 1405. The final stage of this Gothic masterpiece was the building of the three towers. These had acquired their present form by 1472 when the minster was reconsecrated. Just to the bottom left of the Minster in this view is the church of St Michael-le-Belfry.

WWW.WEBBAVIATION.CO.UK

quality architecture from this period and in the West Riding the great age of church rebuilding lay in the future. Nevertheless, a few parishes on the magnesian limestone or further east in the lowlands, notably Barnby Dun, Fishlake, Owston, South Anston, Thorpe Salvin and Wadworth, extended or redesigned their churches at this time. The Decorated style fell out of favour in the late 1350s upon the completion of the east windows at Fishlake and at Welwick (Holderness), where the tracery has a hint of the new fashion for

The impressive rose window, set high in the gable of the south transept, dates from *c.*1515 and combines pairs of white and red roses to commemorate the union of the Houses of York and Lancaster in 1486.

right In 1291 work began on a new nave to replace the Norman building. It took almost half a century to complete and a succession of master masons were involved. The west front was designed by Ivo de Raghton, from Raughton in Cumberland, by far the richest mason in the city and an exceptionally gifted designer who was instrumental in introducing the flowing Curvilinear style, seen here in the 75-feet high central window. Contracts show that this window and those at the end of the aisles were ready for glazing in 1338. Archbishop William Melton paid for this work. The two western towers were erected between 1432 and 1472 to designs of another master mason, William Waddeswyk.

Perpendicular Gothic, which was adopted throughout England for the next two centuries.

The master masons of York Minster once again led the way with a fresh style. William Hoton the younger, who had succeeded his father in 1351, used new designs in the presbytery but made sure they harmonised with the work that had just been finished in the nave. The presbytery which Hoton and his successor, Robert Patrington, built between 1361 and 1373 contains some of the earliest Perpendicular work in the north of England. Meanwhile, the golden age of East Riding church building continued well into the Perpendicular period. Walter Skirlaw, Bishop of Durham from 1388 to his death in 1405, was an important patron of the first phase of the Perpendicular style. He paid for William Thornton's great east window at York Minster, for the chancel, the lower part of the crossing tower, the choir transepts, a small chantry chapel, and the chapter house at Howden, and, in 1401, for St Augustine's church in his native parish of Skirlaugh, which was designed like a

St Mary's Church, Tickhill. The lower part of the tower dates from the end of the twelfth century, when this new church was built at the edge of Castle Green. The upper part of the tower, together with the nave and its aisles, were constructed in early Perpendicular Gothic style in the late fourteenth and early fifteenth centuries, and finished with the help of a bequest from a local landowner in 1429.
PHOTOGRAPH: AUTHOR

college chapel. Other early examples are St Mary, Cottingham, where the chancel was completed in Perpendicular Gothic by 1384 before work began on a crossing tower, and Holy Trinity, Hull, where the Decorated chancel was succeeded by a Perpendicular nave that was built between 1389 and 1418.

In South Yorkshire two churches within the honour of Tickhill were the first to be rebuilt in the new style. St Mary's, Tickhill, displays the arms of John of Gaunt, Fitzwilliam, Eastfield, Sandford and White, thus dating the work to between 1373 and 1399, the merchant, Richard Raynerson, bequeathed 100 shillings in 1390, and the will of John Sandford reveals that the crown of the tower was added in 1429. The nave was reconstructed with ogee arches, heightened and given a range of clerestory windows, and provided with a fine east window above the chancel arch. As lord of the honour, within the Duchy of Lancaster, John of Gaunt was instrumental in rebuilding All Saints, Laughton-en-le-Morthen, whose aisle windows are adorned with the likenesses of Edward III and Richard II and their queens, though it is intriguing to note that the great church builder, William of Wykeham, was prebend of the peculiar jurisdiction of Laughton from 1377. During the following century the Perpendicular style was to sweep all before it.

Towns

Throughout the Middle Ages York remained the leading city in the North, ranking with Bristol and Norwich as the most populous place in the provinces, though nowhere near the population levels that were achieved in London. During the thirteenth and early fourteenth centuries the city was enclosed by 2¾ miles of walls that were erected above their Roman, Anglo-Scandinavian and Norman predecessors. By the time they were complete, the walls had four great bars, six posterns and 44 towers. At the same time, the bars were given their present appearance and Monk Bar was placed at a new north-eastern exit, replacing that which had been used since Roman times. Continuous walls were not needed on the eastern side of the city, which was controlled by the two Norman castles that stood on opposite banks of the Ouse. By 1268 Baile Hill was no longer in use, but between 1245 and 1270 York Castle was greatly improved by the building of Clifford's Tower and by the damming of the Foss to create a lake and fishpond. The citizens of York have maintained their walls better than anywhere else in the country and much original masonry survives amongst later work. The city was a busy commercial and administrative centre, with crowded market places and much coming and going along the river and highways. The medieval street plan within the walls is recognisable today, though only two bridges spanned the Ouse and the Foss. Beyond the walls, suburbs stretched along the main thoroughfares and beyond lay the common pastures that are still known as Heworth Moor, Hob Moor and Knavesmire.

King and Parliament were based in York on five occasions between 1298 and 1338, during the wars against Scotland, and once again in 1392. During the

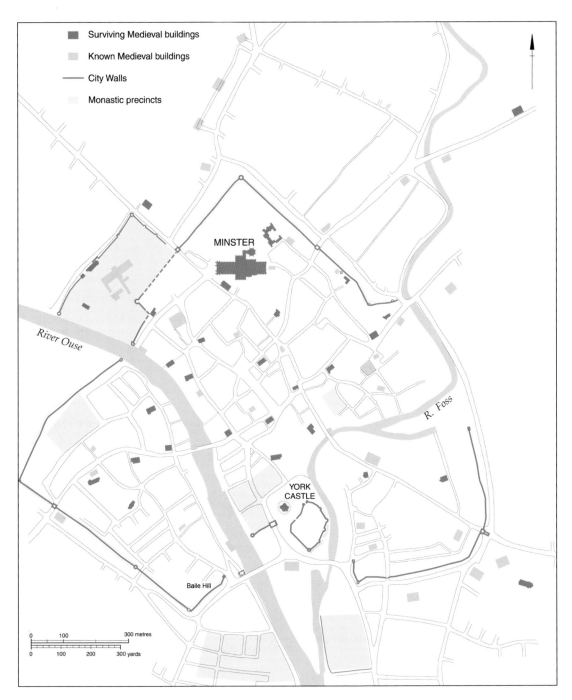

Surviving Medieval buildings

Known Medieval buildings

City Walls

Monastic precincts

MINSTER

River Ouse

R. Foss

YORK CASTLE

Baile Hill

0   100   300 metres

0   100   200   300 yards

thirteenth and fourteenth centuries, and for much of the fifteenth, York's
prestige was at its height. Not only was it a great centre of both ecclesiastical
and secular administration and a flourishing inland port and market town,
through which lead and wool were exported from the Pennines and food and
luxury goods were imported from the Mediterranean and across the North Sea,
but a place where skilled craftsmen such as pewterers, bell-founders and glaziers

lived and worked. Royal charters of 1393 and 1396 elevated York to the status of county borough and the trade guilds had assumed great importance in the town's economic, social and religious life. From the middle years of the fourteenth century the Merchant Adventurers found new European markets for their wool and in the 1370s they exported 1,600 of the 2,700 sacks that were shipped from Hull. York's expanding economy attracted immigrants and by 1377 the city's population exceeded 10,000, a 50 per cent increase since before the Black Death. By the end of the century the population was even larger, the cloth-making industry had recovered, and York merchants handled more than half of wool and cloth exports through Hull and about a third of the imports.

England's most thriving medieval towns were either ports or centres of the cloth trade. The lay subsidy of 1334 demonstrates that just two Yorkshire districts were comparable in wealth with the prosperous southeast at that time, namely that around York and that between Beverley and Hull. London paid £11,000 in tax in that year, Bristol £2,200 and York £1,620. Beverley paid £500 and ranked 20th in the country. By that time, Beverley had long enjoyed a reputation as a producer of good-quality cloth and its trade in the export of raw wool to the cloth towns of the Low Countries was almost at its peak. The Beverley Beck, which flowed into the navigable river Hull, was vital to the wellbeing of these trades and was regularly scoured. The flourishing community which developed around the beck head became the town's most

prosperous suburb, its wealth rivalling that of the central wards. Beverley was unusual in that the whole town and its environs were included in one of the major sanctuaries of the Middle Ages. The minster clergy continued to play a dominant role, especially in the rich pageantry of Cross Monday, when the relics of St John of Beverley were paraded around the town.

The town that had been established at the confluence of the Hull and the Humber during the third quarter of the twelfth century by the Cistercian monks of Meaux Abbey was known simply as Wyke, but when Edward I bought the manor in 1293 'to increase the fitness of the port for ships and traffic' its name was changed to Kingston-upon-Hull. The king enlarged the quay, built a water-powered mill, ordered the construction of new approach roads from Beverley and York, extended the markets and fairs, and established a mint. In 1299 he granted the townsmen a borough charter with freedom from tolls throughout the kingdom and from 1304 the town returned two members of Parliament. Sustained royal interest stimulated Hull's growth and by 1296 50 new burgage plots had been laid out beyond the old settlement, fronting the streets that stretch to the west of Holy Trinity church. In 1321 and 1327 the burgesses obtained licences to build massive town walls and towers as England's first public work undertaken in brick and in 1331 they achieved complete independence from the crown. From the early fourteenth century to the end of the fifteenth Holy Trinity church was also rebuilt in brick and by the time its tower was completed it was the largest church by area in the country. Even so, until 1661 it remained a chapel-of-ease within the parish of Hessle (from which Hull had been carved), and in Lowgate St Mary's formed part of the parish of North Ferriby.

Hull was the home of the Richard and William de la Pole, England's wealthiest wool merchants and money-lenders. The brothers were recorded as burgesses in 1316 and as the chamberlains in charge of the town's finances in 1321–24, when Hull was fortified in fear of the Scots. Richard acted as the king's agent in Hull until 1328, when he moved to London, where he soon became an alderman of Bishopgate. William stayed in Hull, where he became an in-dispensable financial and political operator for the crown. He was able to purchase a large estate and the remarkable rise of the family was marked in 1385 when his son, Michael, was created Earl of Suffolk.

Scarborough was the fourth wealthiest town in Yorkshire in the late fourteenth century, well below York but not far behind Hull and Beverley and ahead of Pontefract and Doncaster. It was different from other towns for its fortunes depended upon the landing of fish in a harbour nestling below the castle and upon serving an enormous hinterland. Scarborough fair, which was established in 1253 on the shore, was exceptional in lasting 45 days between the Assumption of the Blessed Virgin Mary (15 August) and Michaelmas (29 September). As in most medieval towns, wealth was concentrated in the hands of a few patrician families.

The strangest port of all, however, was that of Ravenser Odd on a headland at the mouth of the Humber. At the end of the thirteenth century Ravenser, Old Ravenser and Ravenser Odd were three separate places, but it is impossible to locate them as all three have been eroded away. About 1235 sand and stones swept down the coast by the North Sea were deposited at the tip of the Spurn peninsula. Fishermen began to dry their nets here and an enterprising man used the timbers of a wrecked ship to build a hut from where he sold meat and drink to passing seafarers. In the following decade the Count of Aumale founded a borough on the headland and by the 1260s over 100 burgesses, trading mostly in herrings and other fish, had settled here. The chronicler of Meaux Abbey described it as 'distant from the mainland a mile or more. For access it had a sandy road no broader than an arrow's flight yet wonderfully maintained by the tides and the ebb and flow of the Humber'. But the causeway was breached by the sea (perhaps in the great storm of 1256) and Ravenser Odd became an island. The borough thrived nonetheless and in 1300 and 1337 returned members of Parliament, but between 1334 and 1346 about 200 houses, or two-thirds of the town, was washed away by the sea. In the words of the Meaux Abbey chronicler,

> All men daily removing their possessions, the town was swiftly swallowed up and irreparably destroyed by the merciless floods and tempests. This was an exceedingly famous borough devoted to merchandise and very much occupied with fishing; having more ships and burgesses than any on this coast.

The small boroughs that had been founded along the lower reaches of the Ouse and the Humber during the thirteenth century at Drax, Airmyn and Brough survived but failed to prosper in face of fierce competition from Hull. Neither could Hedon and Patrington compete. Hedon's creek silted up, and although Patrington had a haven for light craft and the Archbishop of York as lord of the manor to sponsor a Tuesday market, it was not sited favourably for river traffic. Meanwhile, the West Riding towns that eventually overtook the old urban centres of the East Riding had not yet acquired their industrial strength.

The countryside

Medieval towns were very small by modern standards and the great majority of the population lived in the countryside as customary tenants of manorial lords. Most families maintained themselves by farming 10–15 acres of arable land, with grazing their livestock on the fallows of the open fields and on commons, though of course some peasants were wealthier and the number of cottagers with even less land increased as the population grew and new fields were cleared from the wastes. By the late thirteenth century large numbers of cottagers were farming less than five acres of land in many different parts of Yorkshire, for example at Kirkbymoorside and Thoralby on the edge of the North York Moors, in the Vale of York at Buttercrambe, Riccall and Stillington,

Ravenser Odd is '… distant from the mainland a mile or more. For access it had a sandy road no broader than an arrow's flight yet wonderfully maintained by the tides and the ebb and flow of the Humber'

CHRONICLER OF MEAUX

and at Cottingham in the Hull valley. Here, as in most other parts of England, about 40 per cent of manorial tenants were cottagers. Somewhere between 1½ million and 2½ million English people struggled to obtain a living at this level. Some men practised crafts or were able to find industrial employment to increase their earnings, but such work was often irregular. One relief for tenants in the northern half of England was that the demands made by manorial lords were less burdensome than in the southern half of the country. Labour services had traditionally been light in Yorkshire and during the twelfth and thirteenth centuries they were usually converted to money rents.

Peasant farmers spent nearly all their time working on their family farms, growing their own cereals and tending their livestock. The national population was small by today's standards, but large acreages of land were needed to

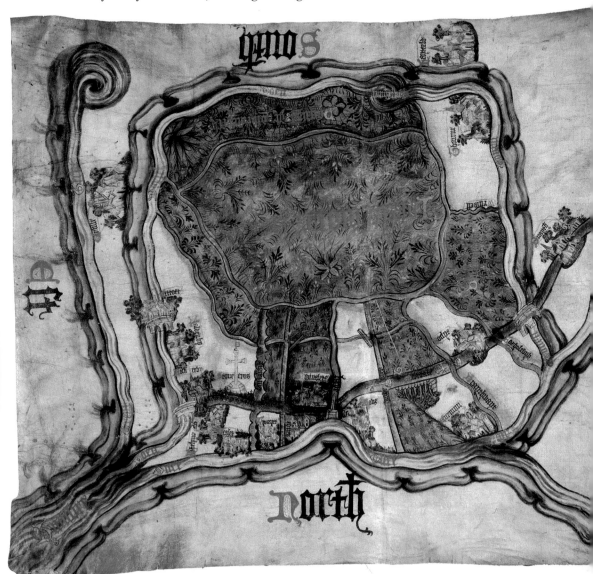

provide sufficient food, for yields were low. The farmers were hampered by poor-quality seed, the lightness of the ploughs, inadequate drainage on the heavy clays, a shortage of manure, and the time-consuming task of getting rid of weeds. Livestock farming was no more productive. Medieval farmers expected a cow to give 120–150 gallons of milk a year – about one-sixth of present-day expectations – and the average dairy cow at Bolton Priory produced only 72 lbs of butter and cheese. A herd of 25 cows at Harewood produced an average of 17 calves a year in the 1260s and 1270s, but this modest achievement was better than the one calf per two cows at Bolton Priory. During the last years of the thirteenth century, estates in many parts of England were recording lower levels of productivity and some of the newly won lands that had been cleared of wood or heather were losing their fertility.

The clearing of land to feed the expanding population gathered pace during the thirteenth century until many of the valleys that dissected the North York Moors supported large populations. The new farmsteads were sited at the tops of the 'intakes', with moorland stretching above, the arable running down the slopes, and the meadows occupying the valley bottoms. In Farndale clearings were made under the supervision of the manorial lord, who was keen to profit from the high rents that he could charge. At Goathland the bailiffs of the Forest of Pickering cleared about 500 acres of woodland to let to the tenants, and in Danby 42 cottagers were farming small closes by 1336. Huge stretches of moorland formed part of manorial and monastic estates and were set aside for cattle farms, sheep runs and deer parks. The monasteries owned about a third of the land on and around the North York Moors and exploited it through their granges. The clearing of land in the moorland valleys by peasant farmers was on a much smaller scale, but in remote Hartoft Dale 32 men cleared over 100 acres between 1312 and 1334, an average of three acres each. Further inroads into the North York Moors were made by the freeholders of the surrounding villages, especially on the northern edges, and sometimes this led to the formation of new hamlets. A survey of the Forest of Pickering in 1334 reveals the unsatisfactory nature of many of the 1,400 acres of land that had been cleared over several generations. Few intakes were sown both in winter and spring, many more were sown just with oats or with a mixture of oats and hay, but most could support crops only for a few years before they were rested as

Map of Inclesmoor, 1406–7. This remarkable map – the oldest regional map held by the National Archives – depicts a vast tract of moorland and other lands bounded by the rivers Aire, Ouse, Humber, Don, Old Don and the Trent more than two centuries before Vermuyden's drainage scheme. Inclesmoor – a name which has long since been abandoned – was a rich source of peat for domestic and industrial fires. Cart and boat loads of 20,000 to 40,000 turves, sometimes much more, were commonly taken to Doncaster, Hull, Selby, York, Wakefield, Leeds, Gainsborough and Lincoln. After the Earl of Lincoln granted generous turbary rights to religious houses and other outsiders in the early fourteenth century, great advances were made into the moor. Property rights in this waste area had never been well defined and so boundary disputes now became common. Contention between the Duchy of Lancaster and St Mary's Abbey, York led to the production of this map during the winter of 1406–7. A large stone cross acts as a boundary point in a contentious area between Whitgift and Haldenby. Churches dominate the villages and Thorne has a stone tower on top of the motte known as Peel Hill. The houses of the peasants are timber-framed and one house at Hatfield appears to be reared on crucks.
THE NATIONAL ARCHIVES, MAPS AND PLANS, MPC 1/56

pastures. They were soon abandoned when population pressures eased in the fourteenth century.

From Norman times to the middle of the fourteenth century peasant farmers extended cultivation on to the slopes of the Pennine foothills. In the limestone dales, particularly in Wharfedale and Wensleydale, the outline of terraced fields known as lynchets form steps on the steep hillsides where farmers brought extra land under the plough. In south-west Yorkshire the taking in of new land is well documented in the thirteenth century but the process was probably just as active in the poorly recorded twelfth century. The woodland and moorland clearances on the edges of the Pennines and on the coal-measure sandstones were normally enclosed by a ditch and a hedge, for stone walls were then a much rarer feature of the landscape than they are today. Their usual names were royd, intack or stubbing. Royd is a dialectical form of Old English rod, which was not much used north of the Wharfe or south of the Don, or beyond the county boundary, and was often combined with the personal name of the farmer who had laboured to make the clearing. Hundreds of farmsteads, hamlets and fields pre-serve this word and many of the West Riding's most distinctive surnames, such as Ackroyd, Boothroyd, Holroyd and Murgatroyd are derived from them.

The stewards of the manor of Wakefield, which extended high on to the Pennines, encouraged their tenants to bring new land into cultivation, because of the extra entry fines and rents that they brought. Lax supervision meant that many clearances went undetected until 1316, when large numbers of tenants were henceforth made to pay. The average size of intakes within the manor was between one and two acres in the period between 1274 and 1320, but increased demand then led to a fall in size to about half an acre and the cost of a licence rose sharply as the manorial stewards charged what the market would bear. In Sowerby the cultivated area doubled in size during the first half of the fourteenth century and at Scammonden, on the western edge of the parish of Huddersfield, an entire valley was settled for the first time, especially in the 1330s and 1340s. The first farm that was created beyond the old boundary of settlement was The Hey, an eighteen-acre, 'hedged enclosure' which is still demarcated by a long bank and a ditch and by two streams in the valleys below. Some of the farm names go back to the fourteenth century and the surnames of the tenants show that the settlers were local people, perhaps younger sons taking advantage of new opportunities. The pattern of farmsteads and field boundaries that was established before the Black Death is largely preserved in the present landscape, though the farmhouses and outbuildings have been replaced in stone and walls now follow the lines of the original hedges.

Medieval farmers grew cereals on the edges of the Pennines, but high rainfall and thin soils meant that the usual crop was oats, which was sown in spring and harvested late, perhaps after a winter-sown crop of rye. Scammonden was exceptional in not having a communal 'townfield' amongst its extensive pastures. In south-west Yorkshire townfields can be identified in most hamlets, though in many cases the documentary evidence is post-medieval. At

Roughbirchworth in the parish of Penistone the old strip pattern is preserved by the walls that were erected in the early modern period when communal farming was abandoned. In some places, the corn-growing fields were occasionally enlarged for a while, then the extensions were given several years to recuperate while other marginal land was cultivated. These outer fields were often known as foreland, a term that has been found in West Yorkshire at Stanbury, near Haworth (1422), and in central and eastern districts at Barwick (1258), Addingham (1313), Otley (early fourteenth century), Leeds (1357), Methley (1376) and Lofthouse (1425).

The lords of the manor of Wakefield used the moorland fringes in the Upper Calder Valley for rearing cattle. By the end of the thirteenth century they had six vaccaries in Sowerbyshire, each of which had 24–30 acres of fenced grazing land that supported over 40 head of cattle all the year round. The principal aim of the vaccaries was to rear oxen, which were then moved along the 'Wakefield gate' to be sold as draught beasts. Further north, the canons of Bolton Priory were also engaged in a market economy. In 1297 their 400-strong herd of cattle, under the control of a single stockman, included 189 cows, which were kept for their calves and dairy produce. Other moorland pastures on the Pennines were used as vast monastic or manorial sheep-runs. The lords of Hallamshire, for example, had sheep runs at Agden and Ewden, vaccaries at Fulwood Booth and Old Booth and cattle heys at Howden, beyond their extensive hunting chases in the Loxley and Rivelin valleys.

The carboniferous limestone soils of the north-west Pennines also supported extensive pastures. In the reign of King John William Mowbray and Adam of Staveley agreed on the terms by which the Forest of Menwith was to be grazed. The rights of Adam and his tenants in Ingleton and High and Low Bentham included grazing for beasts during daytime, pannage for pigs and the collection of wood for building and burning. The Bentham men had the additional privilege of grazing 20 mares and their foals at all times. William and his men of Burton-in-Lonsdale were permitted to graze their cattle within the bounds of the forest and William was allowed to make lodges and vaccaries for breeding cattle. Adam had three further vaccaries on Whernside, Souther Scales and Birbladewith. Other evidence comes from the manor court at Malham, which agreed in 1264 that each tenant of a standard oxgang of land could pasture on the commons up to six oxen, six cows with their young of less than three years, four mares with their young, 200 sheep, five she-goats, one sow with her young of one year, and five geese.

On the coal-measure sandstones to the east of the Pennines the active taking-in of new land made lords aware that their surviving woods must be carefully managed and enclosed within a ditch and a bank, surmounted with a fence, to prevent livestock from eating young shoots. The four tenants of Wakefield manor who bought trees in the Westwood of Crigglestone in 1307 agreed to 'cut the wood as close to the ground as possible, and to clear the place of twigs, so as not to impede the fresh growth of the wood'. A number of trees were

nurtured to provide timber, while the underwood was coppiced at regular, short intervals. Those woods that were subject to common grazing rights for cattle and pigs had grassy clearings, or launds, within them and temporary fences to protect new growth. Amongst the plants and fungi that indicate the antiquity of Hallamshire's Beeley Wood, cow wheat can still be found growing in the grassy parts, thus supporting the documentary evidence that in 1442 the lord received 20 shillings 'from the grass of the pasture in Bylleywode'. Further north, the common wood of the townspeople of Wakefield, known as Outwood, or 'the outer wood of Wakefield' as it was described in 1391, covered most of the north section of Stanley township and part of the adjoining township of Alverthorpe. But other woods were felled and their trees stubbed up in the continuous search for new land. On the hills south of Holmfirth the name of Copthurst farm is a reminder of a vanished 'wood of pollarded trees' that was recorded as Coppedhirst in 1307.

Many parishes in the Vale of York still had plenty of woodland. In the middle of the twelfth century 140 pigs could be found grazing in the 260-acre wood at Escrick, where the tenants of the manor each had common for 10 pigs, 10 cattle, and 20 sheep. Once forest law was removed from the Ouse–Derwent district in 1234, and two years later the Statute of Merton allowed manorial lords to clear land for their own use provided 'sufficient' commons were left, many new 'riddings' and 'thwaites' were cleared. The old planned village of Wheldrake had 16 households, but by the time the Black Death arrived the number had grown to 84. The arable area was expanded beyond the old turf dyke in order to feed the growing number of villagers and at first the new clearances were subject to common grazing rights once the crops had been

The Hey, Scammonden. The predecessors of the white building (Hey Laithe) and the building to the left were marked on a map of 1607 within an eighteen-acre enclosure known as The Hey, a 'hedged enclosure' which is still defined by a long bank and ditch and the streams in the two valleys. It was the first of several local farms that were created in this moorland district in the first half of the fourteenth century, when the population was still expanding. The author's surname is derived from this spot.

PHOTOGRAPH: AUTHOR

harvested. After the removal of the forest laws Fountains Abbey, which had a grange in the parish, led the way in bringing fresh land into cultivation. Many of the new clearances were incorporated within the open fields, which were reorganised into four units during the fourteenth century. Beyond the arable area, numerous individual closes and large meadows, or 'ings' stretched towards the River Derwent and the sandy North Moor and Roxhall Moor and the ill-drained areas known as the Horse Marsh and the Moss formed the common pastures. The open-field systems of the Vale of York gradually came to resemble those of the English midlands, whereby winter- and then spring-sown crops were succeeded by a fallow. The villagers' livestock grazed the fallow and the stubble of the other fields after harvest. The parishes on the fertile lands of the magnesian limestone adapted this system at an early date. At Warmsworth, for instance, the strips of the three open fields stretched to the parish boundary by the time of the earliest local deeds in the late thirteenth century.

Aerial photographs of the High Wolds have identified extensive ridge-and-furrow patterns with the characteristic headlands, balks and reverse-S-shape strips of open-field agriculture which was abandoned here after the Black Death. The remoter parts were left to sheep and rabbits, but most Wolds farmers followed a sheep-and-corn system of husbandry, where barley was the major crop and sheep manured the arable. In some parishes the arable lands climbed so high on to the Wolds that the sheepwalks had to be protected by legal agreements. When Bridlington Priory was granted grazing rights for 500 sheep on the pastures of Willerby, the donor's son confirmed that he would not plough any land which had not been tilled previously and that he would stop others from so doing. The granges of Bridlington Priory at Burton

Hornsea Mere. Holderness was known for its numerous meres in the Middle Ages, but this is the only substantial one to survive. The village grew up by the mere and around St Nicholas's church, about a mile inland from the coast, where a seaside resort grew in the nineteenth century.
PHOTOGRAPH: CARNEGIE, 2005

Fleming and Speeton, of Meaux Abbey at Dalton, Octon and Wharram, and of Malton Priory at Mowthorpe were concerned with cereals as well as sheep. In 1299 the arable fields of Burton Fleming extended to the boundaries of six neighbouring villages. The limits of cultivation on the Wolds had already been reached.

By the thirteenth century the fields of Holderness yielded fine barley and wheat and by the mid fourteenth century about a fifth of the land was used for growing peas and beans, one of the highest proportions in the whole of England. Considerable amounts of hay were needed for the winter feed of oxen, cows, horses and particularly sheep and much of the peas and oats was consumed by draught animals. Landlords invested capital in expensive schemes of draining and reclamation to create new sheep pastures and in building walls along the banks of the Humber so that marsh and silt could be converted to pasture and arable. In 1287, for example, St Leonard's Hospital, York, owned 358 acres of good-quality arable land and 68 acres of the best pasture at Broomfleet with a further 32 acres of salt pasture beyond the banks. Back from the coast, the Counts of Aumale and the Abbots of Meaux ordered the construction of channels that were deep and wide enough to take boats. In the 1160s and 1170s Ashdyke was built to connect Meaux Abbey to the river Hull and by the early thirteenth century Monkdike, Skernedike and Forthdike were in regular use. The dykes in the Hull valley drained the land, separated the arable fields from the marshes and woods, and served as parish boundaries. New settlements were formed at Newland, Sculcoates and Stoneferry, but then the sea began to rise again, tides reached up the valley to Cottingham, and by the middle of the thirteenth century Sutton and Drypool were seriously flooded. Much of the marshland that had been converted into meadows and pastures was reclaimed by the sea, but by that time the population had been much reduced by the Black Death and the pressure on available resources had slackened.

The meres and rivers of Holderness were fished for bream, pickerel, pike and enormous quantities of eels. The 4,000 eels a year that the Sutton family sent to the Count of Aumale as rent for their lands at Sutton-on-Hull was a typical feudal payment. Domesday Book records annual renders of 7,000 eels from the fishery at Beverley and 6,400 eels from eleven fisheries at Leconfield. Further west, each of the 20 fisheries at Tudworth, within Hatfield Chase, provided the lord of Conisbrough with 1,000 eels each year. Fish formed a major part of the medieval diet, especially during Lent and other religious festivals, but prices were high. Monasteries built complex breeding tanks to provide a regular supply to their own communities and manorial lords constructed fishponds near their castles or manor houses, sometimes within their deer parks. They also erected weirs across the lower reaches of rivers so that fish could be caught in baskets or nets; in 1279, for instance, Peter de Mauley had a fishery at his mill in Rossington and another in the marsh at Doncaster, close to Fisher Gate. Meanwhile, North Sea fishermen provided the market towns with herring, haddock, cod and skate.

Pestilence, war and famine

The rapid growth of the national population came to an abrupt end in the early fourteenth century with plague, famine and war. The series of harvest failures and livestock disasters between 1315 and 1322 were unprecedented in recorded English history. The poor summer of 1314 was followed by an exceptionally wet one the following year, when heavy, persistent rain from May till autumn ruined the hay and corn harvests and weakened people's resistance to disease. A chronicler at Lanercost Priory (Cumberland) observed that 1316 saw 'such a mortality of men in England and Scotland through famine and pestilence as had not been heard of in our time. In some of the northern parts of England, the quarter of wheat sold for 40 shillings', eight times the previous average national price. Then, in the winter of 1319–20,

> the plague and murrain of cattle which had lasted through the two preceding years in the southern districts, broke out in the northern district among oxen and cows, which after a short sickness generally died; and few animals of that kind were left, so that men had to plough that year with horses.

As the climate worsened, the North Sea lashed the Yorkshire coast and destroyed the protective banks. Near Easington 33 acres of grassland at Orwythfleet and a 90-acre grange at Tharlesthorpe disappeared into the Humber. The 26 acres that Meaux Abbey held at Hornsea Burton were reduced to a single acre by the end of the century. The whole of Hoton and Hyth townships were lost to the sea and in the fifteenth century the parish churches of Hollym, Skeffling and Withernsea had to be rebuilt on safer sites further inland. The eroded material was swept along the North Sea and Humber coast-lines and deposited by gales and tidal waves on the constantly changing shape of the sandy headland of Spurn Point.

Meanwhile, encouraged by their victory at Bannockburn in 1314, Scottish armies were plundering northern England, deep into the heart of Yorkshire. In 1318 Northallerton was ransacked, all but 20 of Knaresborough's 160 houses were burned, and the inhabitants of Ripon and the monks of Fountains Abbey escaped only by paying fines. In the following year the Scots got as far south as Pontefract. The economy of the Bolton Priory estate in Craven collapsed under the combined onslaught of the Scots and natural disasters. Persistent rains during the summers of 1315 and 1316 ruined the harvests and halved the estate's total income from rents and tithes. Sales of wool – the priory's chief cash crop – fell as the flock of sheep on the sodden pastures was reduced from more than 3,000 to 913 and wheat had to be bought in at five times the usual price. When the marauding Scots arrived in 1318, the canons and their tenants fled with their livestock and personal belongings but left their corn stock at Halton Grange to be stolen or burnt. The Scots left Yorkshire with cattle and hostages, but returned the following year to defeat Archbishop Melton's army at Myton-on-Swale and renew their plunderings; all the 43 oxen at Halton

Grange may have been taken. In 1319–20 the severe outbreak of cattle murrain that had devastated farms in southern England spread to Yorkshire. The remaining stock of oxen on the Bolton Priory estate fell from 139 to 53 and the 225 head of other cattle were reduced to 31. The canons abandoned the priory and sought refuge in other monasteries, but five years later they were strong enough to return and they soon began to rebuild their church in the new Decorated style of Gothic architecture.

We can now see that 1315, 1316 and 1321 were the worst years of harvest failure in Yorkshire, that 1313–17 was the period of sheep murrain and that 1319–21 was the time of cattle plague. Not since the harrying of the North had the county experienced so much misery. The massive tax reliefs for townships in the six northern counties confirm the scale of the troubles. In the North Riding many communities had their tax assessments lowered by 50 per cent or more and few churches were rebuilt in the Decorated style of the first half of the fourteenth century; only Thornton Dale is of much interest. Many places had not fully recovered by 1341–42, when the tax known as the Inquisition of the Ninth was collected; more than 80 North Riding settlements still had waste and uncultivated land and outlying settlements had been abandoned. In Cleveland deanery all but four parishes recorded waste and in Bulmer deanery eleven parishes claimed that some land which had been tilled at the time of a previous tax assessment in 1291 now lay uncultivated. At Alne 200 acres were unploughed and worthless, while another 1,000 acres were valued at only 2d. each; at Easingwold 200 acres were uncultivated because of the lack of a plough team; at Danby a third of the arable lay waste; a similar tale came from Bowes, Brignall, Marske and Ronaldkirk. The returns for the East Riding do not survive, but some early fourteenth-century manorial surveys note vacant holdings and uncultivated land in the High Wolds. The West Riding fared better, but it is clear that even in districts that lay well to the south of the Scottish invasion routes the rural economy had contracted. At Almondbury in 1332 it was noted that herds of cattle had been reduced by murrain and by the troubles brought about by the Earl of Lancaster's revolt; ten years later an inquisition held at Sheffield found that all 240 acres of the lord's arable land lay uncultivated. In 1341 the townships on the grits and sandstones of south-west Yorkshire were commonly assessed at only two-thirds of the tax that they paid in 1291 and in some places at less than half; a major share of the arable at Penistone and Hoyland lay waste and 340 acres of arable at Silkstone had not been ploughed.

Aerial view of Wharram Percy. The earthworks of England's most famous deserted medieval village are picked out clearly by the shadows of the oblique sun. The ruined church of St Martin and a short row of nineteenth-century labourers' cottages stand in the valley bottom. The outlines of the twelfth-century manor house and of peasant farmsteads and their tofts stretch up the hillside. Sunken tracks provide access. The ridge-and-furrow patterns of part of the former open arable fields are seen to the left. This is the landscape that was abandoned in medieval times, but underneath it are even older features, stretching back into the Saxon, Roman and prehistoric periods long before the deserted village seen here was laid out.

NATIONAL MONUMENT RECORD

The Black Death

The Black Death arrived in Yorkshire in the spring of 1349 and was virulent during the summer months, when eleven churchyards, eight of them in the North Riding, were specially dedicated for the burial of plague victims. During the twentieth century it became accepted that this disease was bubonic plague, spread by fleas on the backs of black rats, but this theory is now discredited, for contemporaries made no remarks about rats and studies of epidemics of bubonic plague in other parts of the world have shown that mortality rates were always much lower than in 1349 and that the patterns of development were different. The plague that was endemic in England from the 1340s to the 1660s must have been caused by an unknown, but deadly virus that disappeared as mysteriously as it arrived. What cannot be doubted is that it killed at least a third and possibly a half of the English population and that it had equally devastating effects in much of the rest of western Europe.

Mortality rates varied across the country and some places escaped altogether. The crowded towns suffered worst, but even in the Forest of Knaresborough death rates appear to have reached 40–45 per cent and in both lower Nidderdale and the upper Calder Valley about 40–45 per cent of holdings were left empty

upon the death of tenants (including those who died of more normal causes) in 1349–50. We have to rely on unconnected scraps of evidence, such as that at Meaux Abbey only ten of the 42 monks and seven lay brothers survived. Death rates amongst beneficed clergy ranged from 21 per cent in the moorland deanery of Cleveland to 45 per cent in the archdeaconry of York and 61 per cent in the Wolds deanery of Dickering. At Middleton-on-the-Wolds in 1350 about 60 acres were said to be 'lying waste and untilled ... owing to the great mortality'. Boynton, Easton and Gatton had also suffered and in 1354 Dickering villages had their tax assessments reduced substantially, some by over two-thirds. At the foot of the Wolds, Rotmanby paid no tax at all in that year, so it seems to have been one of the few villages that was depopulated at a stroke by the Black Death; it was never recorded again and the characteristic earth-works of a deserted medieval village can be seen near the hall. Barthorpe, near Aclam, may also have been destroyed the plague, but gradual decay was more common. Villages with shrunken populations often began a journey of steady decline, but others survived as hamlets and some eventually recovered.

A major epidemic that struck the young in 1361–62 became known as the children's plague. Perhaps this was a mutant form of the disease or perhaps many adults had acquired immunity during earlier attacks? Even so, one-third of the beneficed clergy of the deaneries of Richmond and Catterick died in that year. Another major epidemic spread through Yorkshire in 1374 and plague remained endemic with repeated local outbreaks throughout the fifteenth century. The evidence is patchy and we have no firm figures on how many people died, but the cumulative effect was to reduce the national population level dramatically. In the parish of Wheldrake, for example, the number of households fell from 84 in 1348 to 73 in 1361 and to 56 in 1394 and the hamlet of Waterhouses alongside the river Derwent was abandoned. Everywhere in England, land was no longer in short supply and the lucky survivors stopped scratching a living from unsuitable soils at the edges of woods, moors, fens or marshes.

The Black Death stopped further expansion into the Pennine valleys, but at Scammonden the farms that had been created during the 1330s and 1340s soon attracted tenants in place of those who had died. The surnames recorded there in the poll tax returns of 1379 suggest that the new farmers came from nearby settlements; perhaps they were younger sons or men who had previously been cottagers in neighbouring townships? At Saltonstall, a few miles further north within the same manor, the rents were reduced by a third in 1351 because they could not be let at the former rate. So there were opportunities for families to improve their standard of living and for the wealthier peasants to buy up more property and found dynasties of yeomen and minor gentlemen. The richer ones were constrained only by the higher wages they had to pay their labourers and by the lower rents which they could charge their sub-tenants. The average size of farms rose during the fifteenth century and the great majority of country people enjoyed an improved standard of living. The labourers, too, were better off, for demand outran supply and in the early 1360s the Yorkshire sessions of the peace found it difficult, if not impossible, to enforce the Statute of Labourers (1351), which tried to regulate wages.

Plague weakened village communities and sometimes forced them to abandon the old methods of communal agriculture, but they usually lingered on for several generations. Auburn's tax quota was reduced by 55 per cent in 1354, but it survived as a 'very beggarly village' until Elizabethan times. The number of deserted villages began to rise in the middle years of the fifteenth century, a hundred years or so after the Black Death. Lords saw the commercial advantage of enclosing the open fields and converting the arable lands to cattle or sheep pastures, and the necessity of doing so where they were unable to find enough tenants to work the land. Large profits could be made from wool and fewer mouths to feed meant less demand for corn. The more ambitious, fortunate or grasping men prospered not only by farming more land of their own but by leasing the demesne land of absentee landlords. Many of England's yeomen and minor gentry families emerged from the ranks of manorial tenants during the fifteenth century.

Over 3,000 medieval English villages were eventually deserted, with at least 375 in Yorkshire. The North Riding suffered worst, with 171 losses, particularly in the Vales of York, Mowbray and Pickering and on the Howardian Hills. Most of the 129 deserted villages in the East Riding lay on the Wolds or in neighbouring parts of Holderness. The West Riding lost only 75 villages, but here settlements were scattered throughout the countryside and an unknown number of small hamlets and isolated farmsteads were abandoned. Vast though these numbers are, they do not tell the full story, for the number of shrunken sites is thought to have been far greater than the number of deserted ones. Some of the villages that decayed had once been populous. For example, in 1379, a generation after the Black Death, 117 inhabitants of the fenland settlement of Haldenby paid tax, but the site is now deserted. A more typical story comes from Cowlam, on the Wolds, where 54 people paid the poll tax; the village had once been larger, for in 1352–54 its tax quota was reduced by more then half, but by the early eighteenth century only two shepherds lived there and church services had to be held in the ruined chancel, which was the only part of the church that was still standing. The villages that were most vulnerable were those that had inferior soils and which were small even before the Black Death, but not all succumbed.

The fullest picture comes from the four decades of summer excavations at Wharram Percy, the most famous deserted medieval village in the country. The parish covered 9,500 acres, comprising five separate medieval settlements on the Wolds, each of which had its own open fields; a deed of 1384 shows that the arable lands in the Raisthorpe fields were arranged by the sun-division method. Wharram village, too, had a planned element, dating from the twelfth century when houses were built on the bank high above the original nucleus around the church, but the basic framework of settlement had been determined long before by the layout of the Romano-British fields. Wharram was badly affected by the Black Death and over 60 per cent of its tax quota was remitted in 1354, but the last villagers did not leave until some time in the late fifteenth century. The national enquiry of 1517 into enclosures that had been made during the previous 30 years reported that the lord of Wharram had 'put down four ploughs and allowed four houses to decay'. Three of the parish's other four townships also decayed and their lands were converted to sheep pastures. Only the township of Thixendale survived and until 1879 its inhabitants had to walk or ride three miles over the Wolds for services in the lonely parish church, which by then was much reduced in size.

Village markets and communications

As the national population and economy expanded during the thirteenth century the wealthiest or better-connected lords obtained royal licences to hold weekly markets and annual fairs in their villages. Before the Black Death, England probably had three or four times as many market places than we have today, but in many cases all the evidence that survives is a foundation charter and perhaps the stump of a cross. In Emley, for example, William of Woodall is known to have obtained a charter in 1253 for a Thursday market and a four-day May fair and the base of the old market cross still stands at a road junction. In the same year the lord of Hooton Pagnell paid for a charter for a Thursday market and a three-day fair at the feast of St Lawrence, the patron saint of the local church, and the cross that marked the site is still mounted on steps in the village street.

Some places prospered and grew into market towns, among them Bedale, Driffield, Easingwold and Wetherby, but other speculative ventures never really got off the ground or withered during the late-medieval recession. The East Riding wapentake of Dickering provides a reasonably typical example of the mixed fortunes of market centres within a particular district. Bridlington had a market long before a charter confirmed its privileges in 1200; Burton Agnes a Tuesday market and annual fair from 1257; Carnaby a Thursday market and two six-day fairs from 1299; Filey a Friday market from 1221; Flamborough an undated market and fair; Hunmanby a market by 1231; Kilham a thirteenth-century market and fair that was 'of little note' by 1778; Lowthorpe a Friday market and fair from 1304; Nafferton a Thursday market and fair from the same year; Thwing a mid thirteenth-century Wednesday market and fair; and finally Bempton may have had similar privileges at some unknown date, for in 1767 one of its open fields was known as Market Dale. These markets may not all have been going at the same time and we cannot say how long they continued, though it is clear that plague and the consequent decay of the national economy brought many of them to an end. The example of Campsall, on the magnesian limestone may be typical. In 1291 Henry de Laci, lord of the great honour of Pontefract, obtained market and fair charters for Pontefract, Bradford,

Almondbury and Campsall. The Campsall market day was Thursday and the four-day fair was held each July during the festival of St Mary Magdalene, the patron saint of the parish church. We hear nothing more until 1627, when a survey noted that all was 'now decayed and lost by discontinuance'. No market cross survives, but a map of about 1740 marks 'Market Flatt' at a road junction just north of the village. In other settlements, the former market place can still be traced in outline though the market stalls have long since disappeared. For example, the original village of South Cave was clustered around the church but when a market place was laid out on the former Roman road from Brough to York it attracted a new settlement which grew larger than the old one.

The creation of so many markets shows that medieval peasants, as well as great landowners, were sometimes able to produce a surplus for sale and that medieval people were more mobile than was once believed. Much of this mobility was limited to a 10- or 20-mile radius around the market towns, but longer journeys were undertaken regularly by tradesmen or members of great households, albeit slowly and often with difficulty. In the fourteenth century the carriage of goods from Westminster to York took ten to 14 days. Water transport was much cheaper than land transport, so wherever possible, heavy, bulky goods were taken by river and along the coast, but the 'ways' and 'gates' that headed for the market and religious centres and the local lanes which linked farmsteads, hamlets and villages formed a complicated network of routes whose pattern has endured into modern times. The packmen and carriers who became so numerous in the seventeenth century were already characteristic figures. Adam the Bagger (badger) of Shelley (1308) and John Jagger of Stainland

(1427) were two whose occupations gave rise to North Country surnames and who made regular journeys within the districts that they thought of as their 'country'. Others travelled longer distances to sell their wares, especially the packmen who brought salt from the Cheshire salt works at Northwich, Middlewich and Nantwich or from the North Sea coast to market towns throughout Yorkshire. A distinctive group of minor place-names – some still in use, others found in medieval and later records or marked on old maps – record the journeys of the salters. On their way to Rotherham, for example, they crossed Saltersbrook, climbed Salter Hill, grazed their animals at Salter Close and approached the town's medieval bridge along Salter Lane.

Family names

Medieval people often moved from the parish where they were born, but on the whole they did not go far. They stayed within the district that they knew as their 'country', bounded by the nearest market towns. These 'countries' were sometimes the old multiple estates such as Hallamshire or Howdenshire, sometimes natural regions such as the Vale of Pickering or the Wolds, and sometimes places like Swaledale which fitted both categories. People did not yet

Saltersbrook, the boundary stream between Yorkshire and Cheshire, takes its name from the packmen who brought salt from the Cheshire 'wiches' to the market towns of Barnsley, Doncaster, Rotherham and Wakefield. This ancient highway was a turnpike road from 1741 to 1828, when the present Woodhead road replaced it.

think of themselves as Yorkshiremen and women, for they had little concept of the 'countries' that lay beyond. Their speech, customs and surnames were peculiarly their own.

Southern visitors failed to distinguish local Yorkshire dialects and accents from those of the rest of northern England. In 1387 John of Trevisa, echoing the pronouncement of William of Malmesbury about 1125, declared:

> All the language of the Northumbrians, and specially at York, is so sharp, cutting, and abrasive, and ugly, that we southern men may scarcely understand that language. I believe that this is because they are near to strange men and aliens, that speak strangely, and also because the kings of England always live far from that country; for they are more disposed to the south country, and if they go to the north country they go with great help and strength.

Northerners, too, were well aware that they spoke differently from people who lived south of the Trent. When the first shepherd in the Wakefield mystery plays said, 'But Mak, is that truth? Now take out that southern tooth', his meaning must have been clear to his audience.

During the thirteenth and fourteenth centuries most English people acquired hereditary surnames, a fashion that had been introduced into this country by Norman barons and which had spread slowly down the social scale. Surnames were derived from either a parent's personal name, a nickname, an occupation, or the name of the place where a person lived or from where he had recently moved. In areas of scattered settlement about half of the names came from farmsteads and hamlets, so the West Riding came to have some of the most distinctive family names in the land. Very many of them are still concentrated within the 'countries' where they originated in the Middle Ages and help to give these districts their special character. This type of 'locative' surname is far less common in those parts of Yorkshire where the typical form of settlement was the village, so the East Riding has fewer distinctive names.

The farmsteads of the Upper Calder Valley have given us family names such as Ackroyd, Bairstow, Barraclough, Gledhill, Haley, Midgley and Murgatroyd, all of which were confined in the valley until they began to multiply in the sixteenth and seventeenth centuries. They are mentioned in the earliest records of the huge manor of Wakefield or in the poll tax returns of 1379, our first reasonably comprehensive list of inhabitants in the West Riding. The Hugh de Suthclif, who was living at Hipperholme in 1274, was probably the ancestor of all the Sutcliffes, for many of these distinctive surnames have a single-family origin; the name came from the 'south cliff', now known as Sutcliff Wood. His neighbour, Richard de Prestlay, was the forerunner of the Priestleys, whose name is commemorated locally by Priestley Green. Further up the valley, the Gaukrogers took their name from a prominent rock, the Greenwoods from a farm known as Greenwood Lee in Heptonstall, the Horsfalls from a 'horse clearing' and the Shackletons from a cattle-rearing farm in Sowerby. Further north, the Armisteads took their name from a farmstead in Giggleswick, the

Binns family were once at High Binns in Oxenhope, near Haworth, and the Hebblethwaites came from a small place near Sedbergh. One of the most distinctive names from the Huddersfield district is Armitage, which was derived from a hermitage in South Crosland at a place now known as Armitage Bridge. In the Holme Valley the Hinchcliffes and the Littlewoods took their surnames from minor place-names, and in Penistone parish farmsteads on the edge of the moors were the original homes of the Biltcliffs, Bulluses and Reaneys. Across the Little Don in Hallamshire, other farmsteads have produced local names such as Broomhead, Creswick, Dungworth, Housley and Staniforth. The home of a family name can be difficult to locate if the farmstead has disappeared or has been renamed. The house by the crab-apple tree in Sowerby township, where a John de Crabtre was recorded in 1391, cannot be identified, the small place called Thackray in the parish of Fewston, which has given us at least ten forms of the surname Thackeray, is now under a reservoir, the Micklethwaite or 'large clearing' that gave rise to a family name near Cawthorne is now occupied by Banks Hall, and the 'stony ford' of the Staniforths became Low Wincobank.

Other surnames, such as Askwith, Barnsley, Scargill, and Selby, were derived from towns and villages which families left in search of better fortunes at the time when surnames were being formed. Most families stayed in Yorkshire, but Pickering and Wakefield were unusually prolific sources of names that spread far and wide. Names that were derived in other ways were equally confined to the district around their place of origin. It seems, for example, that all the present-day Oddys share a common descent from someone bearing the Old Scandinavian personal name, *Oddi*, who lived in the Ribblesdale township of Rimington. In the north of England surnames were often formed by adding -son to a father's name (and occasionally to a mother's). This method has produced many common names, but others have a narrower distribution. The Aldersons live mainly in Swaledale, the Hansons originated in Rastrick, the Hopkinsons came from Sowerbyshire, and most of the Moxons are still found in south-west Yorkshire. Recent DNA analysis which has shown that 85 per cent of the Dysons share the same Y-chromosome supports the suggestion that the name was first used in the fourteenth century by the son of Dionisia of Linthwaite. Nicknames have produced such family names as Beever, Roebuck and Senior, all of which are found particularly in townships close to Huddersfield, and some occupational names have

J. B. Priestley. Shown here at his typewriter in Moscow in 1945, Priestley was a popular war-time broadcaster. He had previously made his reputation as a novelist, playwright and essayist. Born in Bradford in 1894, as a young man he worked as a junior clerk at a wool firm and wrote articles for the *Bradford Pioneer*. He refused a knighthood and peerage, but accepted the Order of Merit in 1977.

an equally striking distribution. The rare name Frobisher, a polisher of armour, came from the Wakefield district, the Scorers originated in Cawthorne, and the original Jagger was a packman from Stainland, where the family probably gave their name to Jagger Green. Very many more West Riding surnames – such as Ambler, Appleyard, Boothroyd, Lockwood, Marsden, Pickles, Scholey, Waterhouse and Wimpenny – have similar origins and distribution patterns that have lasted to this day. A high proportion of the present inhabitants of Yorkshire, particularly those in the West Riding, have firm roots that go back well into the Middle Ages and no doubt to long before the beginning of recorded history.

Old St Thomas's Church, Heptonstall. Part of the tower collapsed in a storm in 1847, after years of neglect. A public subscription was raised to build a new church between 1850 and 1854, when the rest of the old church was dismantled, with the shell left as a ruin. The churchyard is paved with gravestones upon which are inscribed distinctive local surnames, such as those of John and Martha Greenwood, seen here on the left.

PHOTOGRAPH: CARNEGIE, 2005

The Late Middle Ages | CHAPTER 5

The Wars of the Roses

The Duchy of Lancaster passed back to the crown when John of Gaunt's son was crowned Henry IV in 1399 and the Duke of York's estates were incorporated into crown lands when Edward IV became king in 1461. By 1500 the crown had united the two duchies and had become lord of more than half of Yorkshire. But in many parts of the county, notably in Pennine districts such as Craven, there was hardly any crown land at all.

The long drawn-out series of plots, rebellions and battles between the Lancaster and York dynasties, known to us as the War of the Roses, began in 1455 with the Battle of St Albans and ended 30 years later with Henry VII's triumph at Bosworth Field. The leading families in the East and West Riding supported the house of Lancaster overwhelmingly, but in the North Riding loyalty was divided. The Nevilles of Sheriff Hutton and Middleham, the Scropes of Bolton, the Latimers of Danby and Snape, and the Mowbrays of Thirsk and Burton-in-Lonsdale supported the house of York. The Nevilles' great rivals, the Percies, together with the Cliffords of Skipton, Ros of Helmsley, Greystock of Hinderskelfe, Stafford of Holderness, and Talbot of Sheffield fought for the Lancastrians. Two of the major battles in the wars were fought in Yorkshire. On 30 December 1460 Richard, Duke of York and many of his supporters were killed at the battle of Wakefield after leaving the security of Sandal castle to fight a much larger Lancastrian army. The Duke's head was severed, crowned in mockery with gold paper, attached to a pole, and set above Micklegate Bar, York.

In a snowstorm on Palm Sunday, 29 March 1461 the Yorkists won a decisive battle at Towton, when Edward, Richard of York's heir, marched north from London and defeated Henry VI's forces. The battle is thought to have been the largest ever fought on British soil, with well over 50,000 combatants, including most of the English nobility. An enormous number were killed and their bodies left on the battlefield but, later, Richard III ordered their burial either in Saxton churchyard or by a new chapel that he built at Towton in 1483, now the site of Towton Hall. The grisly heads of the Yorkist leaders were removed from the bars of York and replaced by those of their enemies and the Duke of York was crowned as Edward IV. The struggle resumed in 1470 when the 'kingmaker',

Richard Neville, Earl of Warwick changed sides and released Henry VI from prison. Edward fled to Holland but returned next year via Ravenser and the Humber and though the citizens of Hull refused him entry he obtained the support of Beverley and York and went on to kill Warwick at the battle of Barnet and to murder Henry VI after the battle of Tewkesbury. From 1475 Edward's brother, Richard, Duke of Gloucester, the youngest son of Richard of York and Cecily Neville, began to concentrate his land holdings in the North and used his castles at Middleham and Sheriff Hutton as his power base, though he acted as much in his brother's interest as his own before his triumphal, stage-managed entry into the city of York in 1483 as King Richard III.

In the fifteenth and sixteenth centuries northern lords continued to wield enormous power on their own estates and, more widely, as representatives of the crown. A sumptuous feast that was held over several days at Cawood Castle in September 1465, ostensibly to celebrate George Neville's appointment as Archbishop of York, demonstrated the leading role of the Neville family in the North of England. The guests included seven bishops, ten abbots, 28 peers, numerous great ladies, 59 knights and various lawyers, clergy, aldermen and esquires, with their attendants from all over England. The 2,500 or so people who came ate their way through 113 oxen, six bulls, 1,000 sheep, 2,000 each of geese, pigs and chickens, 12 porpoises and 4,000 cold venison pasties. Throughout the Tudor period the life-style of the English nobility resembled that of their medieval ancestors. In 1521 Lord Darcy had a household of 80 people, including the sons of gentry and yeomen as well as menial servants, and his contemporary, Henry Percy, 'the magnificent' fifth Earl of Northumberland, celebrated Christmas and the New Year at Leconfield and Wressle with a Lord of Misrule, visits from the boy-bishops of York and Beverley and their entourages, and entertainments that included nativity plays, minstrels and trumpeters and performing bears.

Upon his death in 1527 Henry Percy held at least 333 Yorkshire manors, but during the next decade his son, mentally incapable of responsibility, gave much away to favourites and had to sell other estates to pay his debts. In the West Riding the family that rose to pre-eminence in the early sixteenth century was that of Clifford of Skipton Castle. Henry Lord Clifford was made first Earl of Cumberland in 1525 and by his death in 1542 he was the greatest landowner in Craven, having purchased the Percy fee and the main part of the Bolton Priory estate. He was a man who did not hesitate to use violence and to defy the law when it suited him. In the south of the county John Talbot, whose military exploits in Ireland and France led to his ennoblement in 1442 as Earl of Shrewsbury, had married the heiress of the lordship of Hallamshire, which his sixteenth-century descendants came to regard as their chief estate. In the 1520s and 1530s George, the fourth earl, converted the old hunting lodge in the park into a country house and upon the dissolution of the monasteries he bought the neighbouring manor of Rotherham and estates in Derbyshire and Nottinghamshire.

The massive gatehouse of Skipton Castle faces the town and leads into the outer bailey. It was built for Robert de Clifford between 1310 and 1314. The upper part, crowned with the motto 'Desormais', was rebuilt by Lady Anne Clifford in the mid seventeenth century.

Barden Tower, Wharfedale. The original tower was built in a picturesque setting by Lord Clifford, during the reign of Henry VIII, but it had been derelict for over half a century when Lady Anne Clifford restored it in 1658–59, about the same time that she was restoring Skipton Castle. She added a large chapel and the adjoining cottages.

The great majority of resident lay landowners in late-medieval Yorkshire were not nobles but gentry who ranged in wealth and status from knights down to mere 'gentlemen'. On the whole, the knights and prominent esquires of the West Riding were not as wealthy as their counterparts in southern England. Many of them were lords of manors that were dependent on the large lordships or honours, which they often served as stewards or bailiffs. In the later part of Henry VIII's reign the two richest men in the West Riding were Sir Henry Savile and Sir William Gascoigne, followed by Sir William Maleverer of Wothersome, Sir William Middleton of Middleton and Stockeld, and Sir George Darcy of Aston. With estates as far apart as Gawthorpe, Thorp Arch and Burghwallis, as well as some manors in the East Riding, Sir William Gascoigne was as rich as many nobles. The eight suits that were brought against him in the Court of Star Chamber between 1499 and 1535 portray him as a man who imposed his will on lesser men by threats or force, if necessary. The Star Chamber records also tell of a long drawn-out conflict between Sir Richard Tempest of Bolling and Sir Henry Savile of Thornhill. Sir Richard was steward of Wakefield manor and constable of Sandal Castle, positions that were inherited by his son, Sir John. The Saviles were a gentry family of Norman origin who added to their original estates in Golcar and Rushworth by a series of marriages to heiresses. In this way they acquired the manors of Elland,

Nappa Hall, near Askrigg, Wensleydale. One of Yorkshire's best examples of a fortified late-medieval house, Nappa Hall was built by Thomas Metcalfe in the 1450s, with a pele tower, a low central hall, and a smaller tower containing a kitchen and other service rooms. The pele tower is four storeys high and is crowned with battlements. Tiny windows were inserted into its thick walls. The Metcalfes were wardens of the royal forest of Wensleydale and stewards of the abbots of Jervaulx. They were here until 1756.

PHOTOGRAPH: CARNEGIE, 2005

Soothill, Tankersley and Thornhill, which became their principal seat. In 1537 Sir Henry Savile, replaced Lord Darcy as steward and constable of the honour of Pontefract. The (largely fictitious) sixteenth-century ballad, *The Eland Feud*, which recounted murders by outlaw gangs 200 years earlier, was designed to warn Savile and Tempest and other Yorkshire gentry of the grave consequences of their bitter quarrels.

The Robin Hood tales, which were first told in aristocratic and knightly households, speak of the corruption of the legal and administrative system. The earliest ballads were set in thirteenth-century Barnsdale, which was well known as a dangerous place for travellers where the Great North Road divided into two branches, heading for Pontefract, Wetherby and Boroughbridge or for York via Wentbridge and Sherburn-in-Elmet. One of the earliest ballads, *A Lyttell Geste of Robyn Hode*, which was written in the first half of the fifteenth century, mentions Doncaster, Kirklees Priory, Wentbridge and a minor place-name, 'the Saylis', which can be identified with Sayles Plantation 500 yards east of Wentbridge, where Little John kept watch on the valley below. The 'stone of Robin Hood', which was mentioned in a Monk Bretton Priory charter of 1422, was probably a boundary stone or guide post that stood less than a mile south west of Barnsdale bar. The area is now marked by 'Robin Hood's Well', an early eighteenth-century monument that was designed by Sir John Vanburgh. The Nottinghamshire tales, centred on Sherwood Forest, seem to come from a separate, later tradition.

Tower houses

The tower houses of the northern Pennines and the Scottish borders show how security was uppermost in the minds of the late-medieval gentry. The rooms were placed on top of each other, as in a Norman castle, rather than arranged side by side. In Wensleydale, about 1460, Thomas Metcalfe built Nappa Hall with a west tower as the main unit, a lower east tower which contained the service rooms, and a central hall. In Craven, the three-storeyed solar wing that was added to the early fourteenth-century Farnhill Hall was virtually a separate tower house. Mortham Tower, the medieval seat of the Rokebys in Teesdale, began as a fourteenth-century pele tower but in the fifteenth century it was converted into a picturesque courtyard manor and the tower was strengthened with a gateway, new upper walls and battlements. Thomas Rokeby's domestic arrangements included a great chamber, which was remodelled in the seventeenth century, and a hall that has been considerably altered and which at one time served as a barn, though it still retains two of its original roof trusses. Other examples that survive from the fifteenth century include Ayton Castle near Scarborough, Sir Richard Conyer's castle, which stands all alone on a hill above the contemporary church at South Cowton, and Lawrence Hammerton's Hellifield Peel on the Pennines. The towers of Aske Hall, Bolling Hall and Bolton-on-Swale Old Hall now form part of much larger houses. All these

Scargill Tomb, Whitkirk.
A branch of the family at
Scargill Castle migrated
south during the Middle
Ages. Their tombs can be
found in the parish
churches at Darrington
and Whitkirk. Here at St
Mary's, Whitkirk is the
monument of Sir Robert
Scargill (died 1531-32) and
his wife (died 1546-47),
presumably erected soon
after her death. Mourners
are represented below.
The whole monument is
made of fashionable
alabaster and would have
been coloured originally.

examples were built of stone, but the manor house by the Ouse at Riccall has a three-storeyed brick tower built about 1480 with a lookout room on the top of a turret. Another brick tower house, near the sands of the Humber at Paull Holme, which dates from the same time, had a portcullis and was surrounded by a moat. Other fifteenth-century houses that were built with defence in mind were arranged around a courtyard, as at Barforth Hall and Scargill Castle just south of the Tees. In South Yorkshire Denaby Old Hall was 'built partly of lath and plaister, on three sides of a square court'. These courtyard manor houses were smaller and more humble versions of the fourteenth-century castles at Bolton, Sheriff Hutton and Wressle.

Government

During the late Middle Ages Yorkshire people were governed through numerous different authorities, ranging from townships and manors up to the county court at York Castle, which was presided over by the high sheriff and served by a coroner and many minor officers. The Council of the North grew out of the Council of the Duke of Richmond, which from 1525 met either at Pontefract Castle or at Sheriff Hutton but by 1545 was known as the Council at York, with jurisdiction over the whole of Yorkshire. York also remained the centre of ecclesiastical administration and jurisdiction for the northern

left In 1348 Matilda, the widow of John Marmion, obtained a royal licence to 'crenellate' or fortify her castle alongside the parish church at West Tanfield, overlooking the River Ure. A similar licence had been granted in 1314. All that remains of the castle is the later gateway, which is adorned with a fifteenth-century oriel window (*right*). By that time, status symbols were more important than defence.
PHOTOGRAPH: AUTHOR

province. In 1396 the city of York was given county status with its own sheriff and the authority of the mayor and corporation stretched beyond the city over the whole of the wapentake of Ainsty. Kingston-upon-Hull was granted county status in 1440 and Beverley and Ripon were made special liberties with their own JPs. In 1467 Edward IV made Doncaster a fully incorporated borough whose ruling body consisted of a mayor, twelve aldermen and 24 common councilmen, and the mayor and corporation soon became lords of the soke of Doncaster, which included several of the surrounding rural settlements. Pontefract was incorporated by Richard III in 1484 and Scarborough in the following year, but the other places that were referred to as boroughs in sixteenth-century records were still partly dependent on the lord's manor court. The burgesses of Sheffield, for instance, held a charter of 1297 that confirmed their privileges but they never went against the wishes of the great earls at Sheffield Castle.

As Yorkshire was such a large county, powers and responsibilities were devolved to the three ridings. The quarter sessions met on rotation at convenient market towns and the JPs were local gentry who sat at the bench only at sessions that were held in their own wapentakes. Although they had lost their judicial powers, the wapentakes long continued as the bodies that were responsible for assessing and collecting taxes and raising musters. Below them,

Kildwick Hall. Set high in the Aire Valley, north-west of Keighley, Kildwick Hall bears the date 1663 on a rainwater head. This seems to be the date when the house was finished after a decade or more's work. A tall building, three storeys high above a basement, with a central hall and projecting wings, it was built of rubble limestone by the Currer family. The attractive, arch-headed windows in the central part of the top storey are typical of the Craven style of the period.
PHOTOGRAPH: AUTHOR

the smallest unit of local government was the township. Sometimes a township covered the same area as an ecclesiastical parish, but large moorland parishes were each divided into several townships and many average-sized parishes consisted of two or three. By the end of the Middle Ages the West Riding had about 170 parishes and 600 or so townships. The manorial courts formed a separate system that dealt with tenures, dues, land transactions, farming practices and petty law and order. Manorial boundaries, particularly in the highland districts, rarely coincided with those of the township or parish.

Churches

Many of Yorkshire's parish churches were rebuilt on a larger scale in the fifteenth and early sixteenth centuries, when the flowing tracery of the Decorated period gave way to the last phase of English Gothic, the Perpendicular, which inspired church builders for over 200 years. Unlike previous styles, it was not introduced from France and was a purely native development. Whereas in earlier times, wealthy people had made grants of property to monasteries, now their successors paid to improve a parish church or to build a private chantry chapel at the end of an aisle or alongside the chancel and to employ a priest there to sing masses for departed souls. More than three out of every four of the Yorkshire chantries that were recorded at their dissolution in 1547 were founded after the Black Death, particularly in the late fifteenth and the early sixteenth centuries. The monuments assembled in a

Mortham Tower. This picturesque fortified house in Teesdale was the medieval seat of the Rokeby family. It began as a mid fourteenth-century pele tower and was extended in the fifteenth century into a courtyard manor house with the tower in the north-west corner. The gateway, walls and battlements and the upper part of the tower date from the fifteenth century. Thomas Rokeby's new quarters include a Great Chamber (remodelled in the seventeenth century) and a Great Hall to the right of the tower. The hall has been much altered and at one time served as a barn, but it still has two original roof trusses. In the eighteenth century Sir Thomas Robinson built his Palladian Rokeby Hall nearby.
AUTHOR COLLECTION

chantry chapel or in the chancel demonstrate the local importance of many a gentry family. In the East Riding, for example, the monuments of the Griffiths and the Boyntons are displayed prominently in St Martin's church at Burton Agnes and the memorials of the St Quintin family are contained in the north chapel of Harpham church, starting with the alabaster tomb-chest of William de St Quintin, who died in 1349, and including a high-quality brass memorial to Sir Thomas and his wife, who died in 1418. In the West Riding Barnburgh has an effigy of Sir Thomas Cressacre, from the 1340s, carved out of oak, with the knight in plate armour holding his heart in his hands, his crossed legs resting on a lion, Harewood has six medieval alabaster tomb-chests with recumbent figures commemorating local lords, including the Gascoignes, and Worsbrough has a wooden monument that depicts young Roger Rockley, who died in 1534, by his skeleton lying underneath his living image.

Beverley not only has its Minster Church but a beautiful example of the Perpendicular Gothic style in St Mary's, set between the Saturday Market and the North Bar of the town. Although there is earlier work from the Norman period onwards, the church – particularly when viewed from outside – is almost uniform in style. Work progressed through much of the fifteenth century and the tower was not completed until about 1530. The interior is nationally famous for the outstanding series of misericords in the choir, dating from the second quarter of the fifteenth century, and for the much restored ceiling paintings of 40 English kings, ending with Henry VI. Altogether, this is one of the nation's outstanding medieval parish churches.

Alabaster tomb, All Saints' Church, Harewood. Harewood church has several outstanding tombs, carved in alabaster from the Trent valley, the fashionable material for such memorials from the late fourteenth to the early seventeenth century. This one depicts Sir William Gascoigne, who died in 1419, and his wife, their feet resting on heraldic animals. He is shown wearing his judge's robes. Angels stand holding shields on all four sides of the tomb chest.

PHOTOGRAPH: CARNEGIE, 2005

Memorials of the Griffith Family, St Martin's Church, Burton Agnes. The Griffiths were lords of the manor of Burton Agnes for 300 years. Here in the north chapel of the parish church the reclining figures, carved in alabaster, represent Sir Walter Griffith, who died in 1481, and his wife. Such figures were once colourfully painted. The Renaissance monument fixed to the wall commemorates Sir Henry Griffith, who died in 1645, and his two wives, symbolised by three black coffins. At the base, skulls and bones are assembled haphazardly. The curtains and black columns add to the macabre effect. The monument is topped by obelisks and the Griffith coat of arms.

PHOTOGRAPH: AUTHOR

The cost of rebuilding a parish church in the new Perpendicular style was sometimes borne entirely by the local gentry family. In 1412, for example, Katherine de Burgh and her son John gave the mason Richard Crakehall 170 marks and a gown to demolish the old church of St Anne, Catterick, and to erect the present chancel, nave, aisles and tower on a fresh site nearby. In 1458 the new church of St Michael, Cowthorpe, was completed and a memorial brass to Brian Ronclyff and his wife was designed to show the couple holding a large model of the church they had commissioned. But in most parishes the cost of building and maintenance was shared between all the inhabitants, both through private donations and special fund-raising events such as Church ales and May games.

The lack of funds delayed work on the new choir of York Minster until 1390, but the five bays that Hugh Hedon designed in the Perpendicular style were finished by 1405. King Richard II contributed 100 marks in 1395, and ten years later Bishop Skirlaw of Durham, a Yorkshireman who hoped to be the next archbishop, paid for the immense east window, 76 feet high and 32 feet wide, and containing 1,680 square feet of stained glass. This masterpiece of John Thornton, the Coventry glazier, is rightly considered a major monument of European glass painting. The minster was now entirely Gothic in style above ground level and the only remaining Norman work was in the crypt. The dean and chapter then resolved to erect a massive central tower, designed by William Colchester and paid for by

The great east window, York Minster, was designed by John Thornton, master glazier, and paid for by Walter Skirlaw, a Yorkshireman who was Bishop of Durham. It was built and glazed between 1405 and 1408. The glass in the apex depicts God enthroned, with Old Testament figures and the nine orders of angels. The glass below illustrates Old Testament stories and the Revelations of St John.

Bishop Skirlaw. Masons' marks on the stonework suggest that most of the central lantern was built before 1450, but an ambitious plan to crown the tower with a spire had to be abandoned when it was feared that the extra weight might cause the whole structure to collapse. By 1430 the decision had been made to concentrate funds and energies instead on building the two western towers to designs of William Waddeswyk. The south-western tower was finished by about 1450 and its twin was completed during the next two decades. After the interior of the crossing had been painted York Minster was reconsecrated on 3 July 1472.

With the completion of the west front by the middle of the fifteenth century Beverley Minster had become, in Sir George Gilbert Scott's opinion, the finest Gothic church in the world. In St Mary's, at the edge of the old town, Beverley also possesses one of England's most beautiful parish churches. Its rebuilding in Perpendicular style began about 1400 and did not end until the splendid tower, topped with battlements and pinnacles, was completed in the 1520s. Both the minster and the parish church have an outstanding collection of carved misericords that are famous nationwide. The distinctive openwork parapet that

St Mary's Church, Thirsk. St Mary's is the finest church in the North Riding. It stands proud and aloof from the market place for its site had been chosen for worship before the market was founded in the early Middle Ages. It is approached from the centre of the town along the gentle curves of Kirkgate, and the first view of it leaves an abiding memory. Rebuilding began in the 1430s with the tower, followed by the nave and its aisles and finally the chancel, which was completed about 1460. St Mary's is therefore a remarkably complete example of the mid fifteenth century Perpendicular style of Gothic architecture. The openwork parapet and pinnacles give it an air of distinction. This is a feature copied from York Minster and the Greyfriars' Tower at Richmond.
PHOTOGRAPH: CARNEGIE, 2005

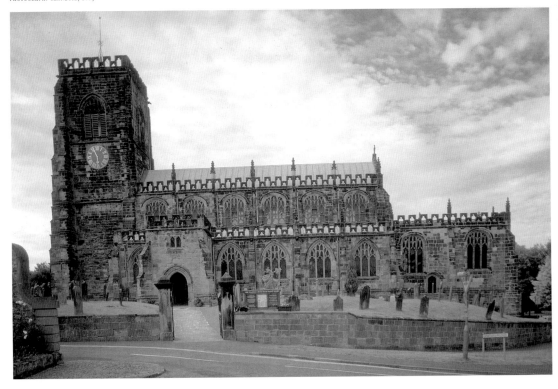

All Saints Church, Rotherham. This fine town church also served several rural settlements in a large parish. Rebuilding in Perpendicular style began in 1409 and was completed in 1483, partly through the gifts of Thomas Rotherham, a native of the town who became Archbishop of York and Chancellor of England under Edward IV.

PHOTOGRAPH: CARNEGIE, 2005

crowns St Mary's is paralleled in slightly different forms in distant parts of Yorkshire, from Richmond and Thirsk to Coxwold and Tickhill. In York the design was used for the eastern part of the minster and in All Saints Pavement and St Martin le Grand. At St Mary's, Thirsk, the finest church in the North Riding, where the open parapet runs all way round the building, reconstruction in the Perpendicular style began in the 1430s and was finished by about 1460. At St Augustine's, Hedon, the church was completed with the addition of a crossing tower during the first half of the fifteenth century and, elsewhere in the East Riding, fine towers in the Perpendicular style were erected at Great Driffield, Holme-upon-Spalding Moor, and Pocklington. Spires were less in favour in Yorkshire, except where they could be built of magnesian limestone, but a beautiful example at Laughton-en-le-Morthen is one of the county's medieval glories and Heming-borough's spire is an amazing sight, rising 126 feet above the tower to a full height of 189 feet.

During the late fifteenth and early sixteenth centuries those parts of the West Riding that became prosperous through the textile and metalware trades were able to build parish churches that matched the best in the East Riding in both scale and style. At Rotherham an ambitious programme of rebuilding started in 1409 when the Archbishop of York granted an indulgence to all those parishioners who contributed towards the cost of a new tower and by the 1480s Rotherham had one of the finest town churches in Yorkshire. The arms of several local families from the rural parts of the extensive parish were recorded at a visitation in 1585, but the most notable benefactor was Archbishop Thomas Rotherham, a native of the town, who built the south chancel chapel in 1480 and shortly afterwards founded the nearby College of Jesus. The parishioners of Bradford, Doncaster, Halifax, Sheffield and Wakefield and of the more prosperous rural districts were also rebuilding in the second half of the fifteenth century. In the lowlands to the east of Doncaster the Norman masons had been forced to use the cobbles and boulders that they had gathered locally, but by the late Middle Ages the parishioners were sufficiently wealthy to import ashlar blocks from the magnesian limestone quarries that were worked several miles away to the west. The badge of Edward IV that is displayed on the tower of

The old Norman nave of Beverley Minster was gradually replaced from 1308 onwards, after the eastern end was finished. Care was taken to harmonise the new nave with the Early English architecture of the choir.

PHOTOGRAPH: CARNEGIE, 2005

St Michael's Church, Coxwold. Designed in one piece in fifteenth-century Perpendicular Gothic, the church is distinguished by the openwork battlements and finials which pierce the skyline and by the unusual octagonal tower. The chancel was rebuilt in 1774. The church is the successor to an eighth-century monastery and, appropriately for a hill-top site, is dedicated to St Michael. Lawrence Sterne, author of *Tristram Shandy* and *A Sentimental Journey*, was the minister here from 1760 to his death in 1768.

PHOTOGRAPH: CARNEGIE, 2005

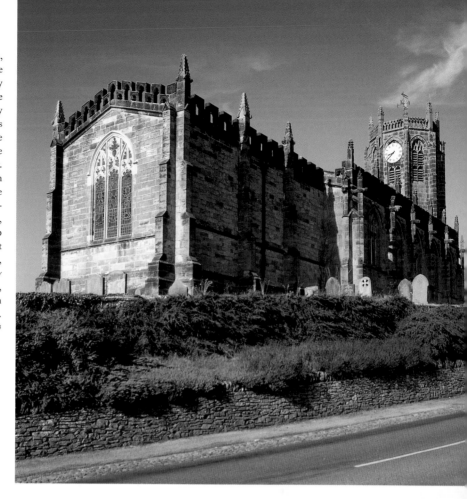

Carved musicians, Beverley Minster. Work on the new nave was resumed in 1308 in the Decorated style of Gothic architecture and continued for many years. On the north wall are a large number of beautifully carved musicians, who incidentally provide us with much information about medieval music making.

PHOTOGRAPHS: CARNEGIE, 2005

St Cuthbert, Fishlake dates the structure to 1461–83, and in the neighbouring parish of Hatfield the shield of Sir Edward Savage, keeper of Hatfield park and master of the game within the chase, shows that the tower of St Lawrence's church was going up in the reign of Henry VII. On the magnesian limestone belt further west the belfry stage of the tower at Sprotborough was said to have been of new construction when William Fitzwilliam made his will in 1474 and belfries of a strikingly similar design at nearby Conisbrough and Wadworth were probably built by the same team of masons.

The ways in which new designs were copied by neighbouring parishes are evident in other districts. In the central parts of the West Riding, notably at Bardsey, Batley and Methley, the churches have corbel tables below the parapets on the tower and at Dent, Kirkby Malham, Sedbergh, Skipton and elsewhere in Craven the fashion was for long, low buildings with straight-headed windows and rather short towers. In the North Riding some sturdy towers were perhaps designed with the threat of further Scottish invasions in mind; the most famous example is at St Gregory, Bedale, where portcullis grooves can be seen at the foot of the tower stair and the upper chamber has a fireplace and a garderobe.

The finest churches on the edges of the Pennines are in south-west Yorkshire, where much rebuilding in the Perpendicular style took place from about 1480 to the 1520s. An indulgence for the repair of All Hallows, Almondbury was granted in 1486 and an inscription on the ceiling of the nave says the work was completed in 1522. At Silkstone the crossing tower was demolished in 1479 because of its unstable condition and the new tower that was erected at the western end was completed by 1495. The tower at Penistone is so similar that it must have been built soon afterwards, perhaps before the same team of masons moved on to Darton and Royston, where their marks are identical to the ones on the new tower at Silkstone. An inscription on a wall-plate in the chancel of All Saints, Darton, informs us that the east end was completed in 1517 by 'Thomas Tykyll, prior of Monk Bretton and patron of this church'; the nave and tower were, of course, the joint responsibility of the parishioners. The three churches of Hallamshire – Bradfield, Ecclesfield and Sheffield – were also remodelled in fine Perpendicular Gothic style. The Carthusian monks of St Anne's Priory, Coventry (who had succeeded the abbey of St Wandrille in Normandy) collaborated with the parishioners of Ecclesfield from about 1480 to 1520 to erect a building that was worthy of a town church. Roger Dodsworth, the seventeenth-century Yorkshire antiquary, thought it was 'the fairest church for stone, wood and glass' that he had seen in a rural parish. By the reigns of the early Tudors the West Riding had churches that could rank with those in the eastern part of Yorkshire.

The interiors of medieval churches had a very different appearance from today for they were a blaze of colour depicting Christ, the Virgin, Saints, biblical stories and religious beliefs. York has a magnificent collection of stained glass in its minster and in All Saints, North Street, where John Thornton

The stalls in the chancel of Ripon Cathedral are dated 1489 on a misericord and 1494 on a bench end. They are similar in style to those at Beverley Minster and St Mary's church and form an outstanding collection. This one, showing a rabbit being chased down a hole by a griffin, has become a tourist attraction as a possible source of inspiration for Charles Dodgson, alias Lewis Carroll, whose father was a canon here.
PHOTOGRAPH: CARNEGIE, 2005

St Gregory's Church, Bedale. St Gregory's occupies a prominent position at the top of the principal street of the Georgian market town. A church was recorded here in the Domesday Book and a castle once stood nearby. A weekly market and annual fair were founded in 1251. Externally the church is in the Decorated and Perpendicular Gothic styles of the later Middle Ages, but the nave is Norman. In times of danger in the fourteenth century, the church tower served the same purpose as a pele tower by providing security against marauding Scots. A portcullis groove can be seen at the foot of the stairs and a fireplace and a garderobe in the first floor room of the tower. The portcullis was rediscovered in the 1830s after a flash of lightning brought it down with a crash.
PHOTOGRAPH: AUTHOR

designed a window incorporating the 15 signs of the end of the world, taken from Richard Rolle's *Pricke of Conscience*, a moralising summary of contemporary theology with an emphasis on death and retribution. Rolle had acquired a national reputation in the fourteenth century as the author of mystical works even though he remained in Yorkshire all his life, living as a hermit alongside the Cistercian nunnery at Hampole. More of his manuscripts survive than of any other contemporary English writer. The finest collection of medieval wall paintings in the country are at Pickering, where they were re-discovered in Victorian times. They date from the mid fifteenth century and depict the coronation, annunciation and burial of the Virgin, seven scenes from the Passion and seven acts of mercy, St George and the dragon, St Christopher carrying the Christ child over the water, St Catherine with her wheel, the martyrdoms of St Edmund and St Thomas Becket, the display of St John the Baptist's head at Herod's feast, the Descent into Hell and the Resurrection. Paintings and carvings were not always explicitly Christian, for some were pagan images presented in a Christian light. The 23 misericords at St Mary, Beverley, include green men and a variety of animals as well as kings and knights, and the 68 at

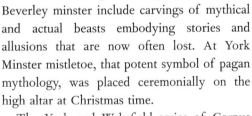

Beverley minster include carvings of mythical and actual beasts embodying stories and allusions that are now often lost. At York Minster mistletoe, that potent symbol of pagan mythology, was placed ceremonially on the high altar at Christmas time.

The York and Wakefield series of Corpus Christi plays throw a direct and vivid light on medieval popular beliefs. Known as 'the mystery plays' because they were performed by the various 'mysteries' or guilds, the texts of the York series are the best preserved nationally. Each of the 56 short plays was performed on pageant waggons at regular stops in the streets in progression. The actors had to rely on verbal effects such as alliteration, rhymes and punchy rhythms rather than scenery and movement. Collectively, the plays told the Biblical story from the Creation to the Day of Judgement. Sometimes, as when the fishermen and mariners performed the story of the flood, the play was appropriate to the guild. The performers moved slowly round the streets from dawn to dusk at

Medieval wall paintings, Pickering. The medieval paintings on the walls of the nave of the church of St Peter and St Paul, Pickering, are the most complete set in Britain. They date from the 1450s and were covered over about a century later during the changes of the Reformation. They were rediscovered in 1862, when the plaster was removed. For a time they were then whitewashed over, as the vicar denounced them as being full of 'Popish superstitions' and a distraction from his sermons. They were, however, restored to their former splendour in 1876.

The upper painting depicts the Coronation of the Virgin and, below, Herod's feast where the head of St John the Baptist was brought in on a charger.

The lower painting depicts the martyrdom of St Edmund, the Christian King of East Anglia, who in 870 was defeated in battle by the Vikings. He refused to renounce his religion and become a dependent ruler, and so was stripped of his clothes, tied to a tree, shot with arrows and then beheaded. The inscription on the right states that heavenly bliss was the reward for his good deed. He became England's most popular native saint and has many churches named after him.

PHOTOGRAPHS: CARNEGIE, 2005

Corpus Christi, a moveable feast that falls between 21 May and 24 June. Mystery plays were once performed in all the major towns and helped to give each community a firm sense of belonging. The York plays were suppressed by Archbishop Grindal in 1570.

The Dissolution of the Monasteries

During a short five-year period between 1536 and 1540 all the 650 monasteries in England and Wales were closed and their possessions confiscated by the crown. By Christmas 1539 monastic life in Yorkshire had been obliterated. About a third of English abbeys, priories, friaries and nunneries have left no trace above ground and the physical remains of another third are insubstantial. In Yorkshire 28 abbeys, 26 priories, 23 nunneries, 30 friaries and 13 cells were dissolved, a total of 120 religious institutions of all kinds. Some of these had a long history from the early years of the Norman occupation and most had been founded by the twelfth century. Yet Henry VIII was able to destroy them almost without a struggle. More than any other event, the dissolution of the monasteries marks the end of the period that we know as the Middle Ages.

Long before the end of this remarkable tradition much of the old fervour had gone and the monasteries struggled to recruit people who were prepared

Wakefield Bridge and chantry chapel. Philip Reinagle painted this scene in 1793, well before the nineteenth-century restoration of the chapel. The medieval bridge over the River Calder has nine pointed arches with chamfered ribs on the underside. The chapel of St Mary-on-the-Bridge occupies a tiny island in the river. A licence to build it was granted in 1357. Travellers said a prayer for their safe journey and donated money for the upkeep of the bridge. Profusely decorated, the chapel was the best of the handful that survived the dissolution of chantries in 1547, but it was already 'much defaced' when William Camden saw it a generation later. In 1847 Sir George Gilbert Scott was put in charge of the restoration of the chapel and was persuaded by a local mason to rebuild the façade entirely. The replica itself weathered badly and had to be restored in 1932.
WAKEFIELD ART GALLERY

to take the vows. By the end of the fifteenth century total numbers in England had dropped to about 10,000 monks and 2,000 nuns. Some monasteries maintained their high standards, but they no longer attracted endowments on the old scale. The crown's valuation of ecclesiastical property in 1536 demonstrated a large gap between a few rich establishments and the rest, for only 4 per cent had incomes of over £1,000 per annum whereas nearly 80 per cent had to be content with less than £300 a year. At St Mary's (York), Fountains, Selby and Guisborough Yorkshire had some of the richest abbeys and priories in England and as mitred abbots the heads of St Mary's, Selby and Whitby had the same status as bishops. Throughout the kingdom monks were landlords, farmers, industrialists, tithe-owners and builders, but after the Black Death they often leased their estates and towards the end this policy was normal practice. The presence of the religious was nowhere more apparent than in the city of York and its suburbs, with the minster and its dependent buildings, 40 parish churches, four monasteries, a nunnery, four friaries and numerous hospitals, maisons dieu and chapels. Here, the impact of the Reformation was particularly traumatic.

'the abbeys in the north parts ... one of the beauties of this realm to all men and strangers passing through.'

ROBERT ASKE, 1536

Henry VIII did not start with the clear intention of destroying all the monasteries. His government first dissolved those institutions (except the Gilbertines) which had fewer than a dozen monks or nuns and an annual endowment of under £200. Some of the smaller ones escaped the first round of destruction because Yorkshire's great monasteries were unable to house those who would have been displaced. Nevertheless, the suppressions added to fears and rumours that parish churches were to be dissolved, church goods confiscated and a tax imposed on baptisms. Widespread resentment at a remote central government quickly turned into a spontaneous and popular rebellion known as the Pilgrimage of Grace. Beginning in Lincolnshire on 2 October 1536, within a week the rebellion was supported in Beverley, from where it spread rapidly into the Wolds and Holderness, Howdenshire and the marshland around the lower Ouse. The rebels forced their local gentry to swear allegiance to their cause and to lead them into battle. Their commander was Robert Aske, a lawyer from Aughton in the Derwent flood plain, where his ancestors had lived in a motte-and-bailey castle and a moated manor house and had been buried in nearby All Saints church. Aske had written a defence of 'the abbeys in the north parts', praising their hospitality and alms, their masses for the souls of the dead, the places they provided for the younger sons of gentlemen, and their contribution to the maintenance of roads, bridges and fen dykes, concluding that they were 'one of the beauties of this realm to all men and strangers passing through'.

On 16 October Aske's Pilgrims arrived in York, where the mayor judged that the city was too divided to withstand a seige. They were welcomed by many citizens who wished to see the restoration of the dissolved houses of St Clement and Holy Trinity and the nearby Healaugh Priory. The Archbishop of York, other senior clerics and many Yorkshire gentry sought refuge in Pontefract Castle, which was in the custody of the elderly Thomas, Lord Darcy, but when the rebels advanced south Darcy readily surrendered the castle and agreed to become one of the Pilgrims' leaders. A second, independent rising that had broken out in Riponshire and Richmondshire joined forces with Aske's men at Pontefract and advanced on Doncaster and by the end of October the rebels controlled virtually the whole of the North between the Don and the Scottish border. Few of Yorkshire's leading families remained loyal to the king, but George Talbot, fourth Earl of Shrewsbury and lord of Hallamshire barred the way and the Duke of Norfolk, on the king's behalf, recognised the weakness of the crown's position and adopted the tactic of negotiation and false promises to delay the advance of the Pilgrims. On Doncaster bridge Aske was promised that a Parliament would be held in York to discuss the rebels' grievances and that a free pardon would be granted to all who disarmed. The rebels tore off the badges that symbolised the Five Wounds of the Crucified Christ and returned to their homes. Within a few months many of them, including Aske and Darcy, were executed.

A fresh revolt gave Henry the excuse to renege on what had been promised. On 16 January 1537 Sir Francis Bigod of Settrington raised a muster in Buckrose wapentake to march on Hull and Scarborough in the false hope that the Percies would support him. The new twist to the story reveals the complex and sometimes contradictory nature of the rebels' motives. Bigod had been a member of a group of Protestants gathered around Thomas Cromwell in London and he mistakenly saw the Pilgrimage of Grace as an opportunity to implement his plans for church reform. He had written a book that attacked the monasteries which received the great tithes of parishes but gave little in return, pointing out that nearly two-thirds of Yorkshire's 622 parish churches had been appropriated by monasteries or other religious institutions and that over 100 of them were served merely by curates. On 10 February Bigod was captured in Cumberland and on 2 June he was executed at Tyburn. Many of those implicated in the earlier revolt were arrested and killed. Aske was dragged through the streets of York on a hurdle and hanged from the top of the castle and Sir Robert Constable received the same punishment at Hull; he was 'so trimmed with chains', gloated the Duke of Norfolk, 'that I think his bones will hang there this hundred years'. Lord Darcy, Sir Thomas Percy, the abbots of Fountains, Jervaulx and Rievaulx, and the priors of Bridlington, Guisborough and Doncaster's Carmelite friary were amongst the prominent men who were sentenced to death. 'Adam Sedber Abbas Jorvall 1537', scratched on a wall in the Tower of London, is a poignant reminder of the savage treatment of the Pilgrims. Sedber was particularly unfortunate, for when the rebels arrived at Jervaulx to demand his leadership he fled to Witton Fell and then sought shelter with Lord Scrope at Barnard Castle, but one of his monks charged him with treason. When Jervaulx Abbey was dissolved that year the monks were ejected without pensions.

The king's pressing need for yet more money to finance his wars made him turn a greedy eye on the estates and treasures of the greater monasteries. The

Jervaulx Abbey. This Cistercian abbey was founded in 1156 from Fors, a daughter house of Byland Abbey. Jervaulx is the Norman French version of Ure-Vale. The last abbot, Adam Sedbar, was executed in 1537 for his role in the Pilgrimage of Grace. The ruins are among the most romantic in Yorkshire, largely because they are in private hands and are not neatly trimmed like the properties in the care of English Heritage. The upper view from the church shows the east range of the cloister. The round-headed arch to the left marks the position of the chapter house. The second arch was the entrance to the monks' day stairs, and the small arch beyond leads to the undercroft of the monks' frater (refectory).
PHOTOGRAPH: AUTHOR

left The west wall of the monks' dorter, or dormitory, lit by nine lancet windows, is the most substantial surviving fragment at Jervaulx. The small, square holes mark the wooden partitions between the private bedrooms. At the far end, night stairs provided access to the cloister and so to the church for services. Below the dormitory stood a vaulted undercroft.
PHOTOGRAPH: CARNEGIE, 2005

commissioners who were sent to induce surrenders with offers of fair pensions met with only muted opposition, cowed by the brutal punishments that had been meted out to the Pilgrims. At Kirkstall Abbey the lead roofs were stripped and the bells were recast as cannon. At Roche Abbey the choir stalls were burned to melt the lead roof, the best-quality stone was plundered and the timber was sold to local families. Michael Sherbrook, rector of Wickersley and the son of an eye-witness, wrote: 'All things of price [were] either spoiled, carped away, or defaced to the uttermost ... it seemeth that every person bent himself to filch and spoil what he could ... nothing was spared but the oxhouses and swinecoates and such other houses of office, that stood without the walls'.

On 26 November 1539 the abbot and 31 monks at Fountains were forced to leave the abbey and their 1,976 horned cattle, 1,146 sheep, 86 horses, 79 swine and 221 quarters of grain were sold to Sir Richard Gresham. Later in the

West doorway, Bolton Priory Church. The original priory church, built in the twelfth and thirteenth centuries, now serves the parishioners. The western tower was begun in 1520 by the last prior, Richard Mone, but was not completed by the time of the dissolution in 1539. Here we see the ornate base of the tower, with niches and shields between the doorway and the great window.

PHOTOGRAPH: CARNEGIE, 2005

The ruined transepts at Roche Abbey survive almost to their full height. They date from the 1170s and are among the earliest surviving examples in the country of the new Gothic style of architecture.

PHOTOGRAPH: AUTHOR

century Fountains Hall was built as a gentleman's residence at the edge of the monastic site and the outlying granges of the abbey were converted into farmhouses and minor halls. Henry VIII soon sold the estates that he had confiscated to noblemen, gentlemen, courtiers, lawyers and merchants. Many a family that did not scruple to grab a share of the spoils was able to increase its fortunes substantially, sometimes with lasting consequences to this day. A few monastic churches, including such well-known ones as Bolton, Malton and Selby, survived as parish churches, but most were despoiled and the monks were rarely heard of again. The Monk Bretton group who bought 148 books when their library was auctioned and who lived together for at least 20 years in a nearby house at Worsbrough were unusual survivors. The friars fared even worse, for when they were driven out in 1538 they received no pensions.

The Reformation

Henry's successful suppression of the Pilgrimage of Grace made the English Reformation possible. York Minster lost much of its treasure, the archbishop was forced to make unfavourable exchanges of property with the crown, and in 1541 the archdeaconry of Richmond became part of the new diocese of Chester. Sweeping changes during the reign of Edward VI had a profound affect on the city of York, which lost about 100 chantries and nearly all its religious guilds. The colleges of St William and St Sepulchre were suppressed by the crown and 13 of the smaller parish churches were closed by the corporation. Throughout England the physical appearance of churches was altered radically and services were reformed upon orders issued by the Privy Council. In 1548 the major ceremonies of the Catholic church were denounced as superstitious and images were

right Rotherham bridge chapel. When John Leland passed through Rotherham about 1540 he crossed the River Don by 'a fair Stone Bridge of iiij [4] Arches', on which was 'a Chapel of Stone well wrought'. It can be dated approximately by the will of the local grammar school master, John Bokyng, who in 1483 left 3s. 4d. 'to the fabric of the Chapel to be built on Rotherham Bridge'. It was served by a priest until chantry chapels were dissolved at the Reformation, in 1547. One of the best-preserved medieval bridge chapels in the country, it survived because it was adapted at various times as an almshouse, a town gaol, and a tobacconist's shop. In 1924 it was restored as a chapel and provided with new windows, based on the original design, as the old ones had been blocked in during the chapel's time as a gaol. Weekly services are held and it is possible to descend to the bed rock by the river, upon which the chapel is built.

PHOTOGRAPH: CARNEGIE, 2004

The first school at Gigglewick. One of Yorkshire's early grammar schools, it was typical in being founded by a cleric. In 1507 James Carr, priest of the Rood chantry, leased land on which to build a school. When the chantry was dissolved in 1547, his nephew Richard Carr, was the priest and schoolmaster. The school was re-founded in 1553 at the petition of the vicar and other inhabitants of the town and parish. Somehow, it gained a generous endowment of lands from former chantries in the East Riding, which paid for a master and an usher. The school had eight governors, including the vicar, and it developed close connections with Christ's College, Cambridge. A new school was built in 1790.

GIGGLESWICK SCHOOL

destroyed and in 1550 altars were replaced by communion tables. The fearful churchwardens of Yorkshire's parish churches offered little resistance. At St Michael, Spurriergate, York, a churchwarden's account of 1547 noted that twopence was paid to a labourer when the images of saints were taken down and at All Saints, Rotherham, handwritten copies of the Edwardian service books were used until printed copies were available. Robert Parkyn, the curate of Adwick-le-Street, was dismayed by the changes, but his narrative of events, written in Mary Tudor's reign, provides no hint of resistance.

Before the dissolution of the chantries, colleges and hospitals the West Riding had nearly 900 clergymen, but by the end of Henry VIII's reign their number had been reduced to between 500 and 550 and by the time that Mary came to the throne in 1553 only 250 were left. Early in Mary's reign, a Pontefract man claimed that the town had once had an abbey, two colleges, a friary, an ancress, a hermit, four chantry priests and a guild priest but now they were left with an unlearned vicar who hired two curates to serve a living that was worth under £3 a year. The parish priests of the late Middle Ages were mostly men of simple faith, low incomes and limited learning. The Protestant reformers came from the ranks of the better educated who had taken advantage of the growing number of schools and colleges which shared a common constitution, curriculum, aims and facilities. By the end of the fifteenth century, in addition to the provision at York, the West Riding had at least 18 schools, the North Riding nine and the East Riding eight and by 1550 this number had risen to 40 in the West Riding, 16 in the North Riding and ten in the East Riding. They varied in range from small schools which were taught by a chaplain, sometimes in his chantry chapel, to well-endowed colleges. One of the best was the College of Jesus that Thomas Rotherham, Archbishop of York and Chancellor of England, had founded in 1482–83 in his native town. This college was served by a provost who was responsible for theology and three fellows who taught grammar, singing, and writing and arithmetic and it provided accommodation for six choristers and five chantry priests from the parish church. A few years before its dissolution John Leland described it as a very fair college sumptuously built of brick. In the late Middle Ages able Yorkshire boys, notably Thomas Rotherham, John Wyclif and Roger Ascham, grasped the educational opportunities to rise to national fame.

Towns

The decay of the national economy and the dramatic collapse of the English population from the high level that had been achieved before the Black Death

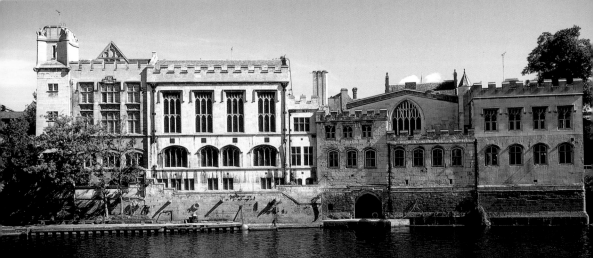

left Skipton Castle is perched on a sheer cliff rising from the Eller Beck on a site chosen by the Norman lord, Robert de Rumily, in the late eleventh century. It served his new honour of Skipton, which stretched from Airedale into Wharfedale. Its present appearance, including the mighty towers, dates largely from 1310–14, when Robert de Clifford was lord, but it was altered by his descendants during the reign of Henry VIII and again in the seventeenth century. A parish church dedicated to Holy Trinity was erected alongside the castle and, beyond, a wide market place stretched down the hill to the right of the picture, as Skipton's High Street. Under the patronage of the castle, Skipton became a successful Norman borough. The stretch of water which can be seen around the western side of the Castle is not a moat, but the Springs Branch of the Leeds and Liverpool Canal which was built in the 1780s to receive limestone which had been quarried at the How Bank quarries at Embsay and transported here via a tramway and inclined plane, parts of which can still be seen from the towpath.

naturally affected towns and villages alike. By the second half of the fifteenth century York, Beverley, Hull, Richmond, Ripon, Scarborough and Tickhill, and no doubt many other Yorkshire towns, were smaller and less buoyant than they had been two centuries earlier. Some of the most successful towns of the early Middle Ages felt the chill wind of recession. A similar tale could be told throughout western Europe. Smaller numbers of people meant less demand for goods from urban merchants and craftsmen.

York suffered particularly badly. In 1400 it had ranked as the first provincial city in the land, with a population of more than 12,000, but by the 1520s it had slipped to sixth position and had fewer than 8,000 people. The city's population had begun to drop in the 1420s, when the wealthiest merchants stopped making huge profits from foreign trade and the inhabitants began to dress in cloth made in the West Riding countryside rather than in the city. By the third quarter of

right This two-storeyed building attached to the south aisle of the nave of York Minster was erected in 1418–20 as the Minster Library and now serves, appropriately, as the bookshop.

left The Guildhall, York, has been well restored after it was badly damaged by bombing during the Second World War. The main hall was built between 1449 and 1459, the cost being shared by the Corporation and the guild of St Christopher. The low arch on the bank of the River Ouse is the entrance to a vaulted passage, known as Common Hall Lane, along which goods could be taken from the staith up to St Helen's Square in the heart of the city. It passes below the inner chamber, which also dates from the mid fifteenth century.

PAYNLY CROFT

the fifteenth century York was in the depths of recession and in 1487 the corporation admitted to Henry VII that fewer than half the number of good men who
had been citizens in the past were now living within the city walls or the
suburbs. The decay of overseas trade and the urban cloth industry is evident
from the corporation's records, which reveal falling incomes from house rents
and a sharp drop in the number of admissions of freemen. One mayor thought
that the Halifax, Leeds and Wakefield clothiers had proved too competitive for
the merchants and manufacturers of York because they had the advantage of
water-powered mills for fulling and a workforce of spinners, carders and
weavers who were able to keep a few animals on their smallholdings and who
had little expense in maintaining themselves, unlike the people of York, whose
provisions were dear and hard to come by. Nevertheless, York's economy did
not collapse and as late as 1475 the city remained pre-eminent in the clothing
industry. The city's fortunes did not reach their nadir until the reign of
Henry VIII.

In the early sixteenth century York was still the secular and ecclesiastical

Thomas Jeffreys' map of
York, 1771–72, shows the
city of York largely
confined within its
medieval walls, with small
suburbs around its bars.
The River Ouse divides
the settlement, as it did in
Roman times. The Viking
street pattern is well
preserved. The monastic
buildings are in ruins or
are built over and the
number of parish churches
has been reduced, but the
plan of the city is still that
of a great medieval city.
AUTHOR COLLECTION

capital of northern England, the seat of the archbishop, the high sheriff and the body that became known as the King's Council in Northern Parts, and the only place outside London to have a royal mint. Though it was small by European standards, it was still one of only a handful of English provincial cities that foreigners thought worth visiting, for it was famed for its buildings, ranging from the minster and St Mary's Abbey to the numerous parish churches and small chapels, hospitals and colleges. St William's College had been founded in the 1460s with the generous support of George Neville (the future Archbishop of York) and his brother, the Earl of Warwick, on a site close to the east end of the minster, in order to house the cathedral's chantry priests. The building is arranged in a quadrangle around a narrow, rectangular courtyard, housing a chapel, a library and chambers for the priests. It was by far the largest college for chantry priests in England's cathedral cities and at its dissolution in 1547 it housed a provost and 28 priests. The 36 vicars-choral,

St William's College, York. The college was founded in the 1460s with the generous support of George Neville (later Archbishop of York) and his brother, the Earl of Warwick, on a site close to the east end of the minster, in order to house the chantry priests of the minster. The building is arranged in a quadrangle around a narrow, rectangular courtyard. It incorporated a chapel, a library and chambers for the priests. The ground floor is constructed of magnesian limestone obtained from the Huddleston quarries and the jettied first floor is timber-framed. St William's was by far the largest college for chantry priests in England's cathedral cities. At the Dissolution in 1547 it housed 28 priests and a provost. It has been altered considerably since the Dissolution. Seventeenth-century work can be seen in the courtyard and the façade has eighteenth-century bow windows and dormers and a recent Gothic doorway. The building has been well restored in modern times. This part is now a restaurant.

The Merchant Taylors'
Hall, York. This fine
timber-framed hall was
erected just inside the
medieval city walls at
Aldwark about 1400 for
the Merchant Taylors, one
of York's leading craft
guilds, and the religious
fraternity of St John the
Baptist. The hall is entered
via a screen's passage and
is open to the roof. The
tie-beams were inserted to
strengthen the roof in the
Elizabethan period. The
building was encased with
brick walls in the late
seventeenth or early
eighteenth century.

PHOTOGRAPH: CARNEGIE, 2005

St Anthony's Guildhall,
Peasholme Green, York.
Built as a meeting house
for a religious fraternity in
the mid fifteenth century,
with the usual arrange-
ment of chapel and
hospital on the ground
floor and two halls on the
timber-framed upper floor,
it was used by the city's
smaller guilds after the
Reformation. In recent
times it housed the
Borthwick Institute of
Historical Research.

PHOTOGRAPH: CARNEGIE, 2005

The Merchant Adventurers' Hall, Fossgate, York. Standing low, by the banks of the River Foss, the Merchant Adventurers' Hall dates back to the mid fourteenth century, when it belonged to the Guild of Our Lord and the Blessed Virgin. In the early fifteenth century this guild was absorbed by the Guild of Mercers and Merchants, who became the Merchant Adventurers about 1580. The brick and stone walls of the undercroft mask a timber-framed interior, which is divided into two 'naves' by a central arcade. It contained the hospital and a chapel, for guilds were charitable and religious institutions as well as commercial ones. The chapel was extended beyond the south end and was licensed in 1411. The upper floor contains the spacious hall, which too is divided into 'naves'. Its roof truss is a particularly complicated and ingenious piece of craftsmanship. The large windows in the side walls are eighteenth-century insertions.
PHOTOGRAPH: CARNEGIE, 2005

Interior of the Merchant Adventurers' Hall, York. The outstanding timber-framing of the Great Hall, erected between 1357 and 1361.
PHOTOGRAPH: CARNEGIE, 2005

who deputised for the cathedral canons, had been a largely self-governing body since 1252 and they were formally incorporated as a college in 1421. Their accommodation at the Bedern, some 150 yards east of the minster, was in separate chambers with a common dining hall and a chapel. Now partly restored, the Bedern was the first such institution to be established in any English secular cathedral.

York merchants traded with other British ports and with Spain, France, Belgium, Holland, Germany, Poland and Scandinavia. They exported wool, cloth, hides, butter, and lead, and imported salt, fish, wine, spices, dried fruit, iron and medicines. The various guilds of York began as fraternities with common business interests and religious, social and charitable aims. They issued trade regulations, employed searchers to maintain standards, bound apprentices and admitted freemen. The Guildhall, or Common Hall, was built in stone by the corporation on the northern bank of the Ouse in the late 1440s for two guilds; it has been restored since it was badly damaged in the Second World War. The fraternity that honoured Jesus Christ and the Blessed Virgin Mary, and which became incorporated as the mercers' guild in 1430, built their timber-framed hall by the Foss in 1357–61. In 1581 it became the hall of the Company of the Merchant Adventurers, York's main trading body. On the upper level the great hall, which acted as the business and social centre of the guild, is framed with massive oak beams that support a roof which is celebrated for its early carpentry techniques. Below, the undercroft is built of brick, the oldest known use of this material in York since the Romans left. It was used as a hospital, with a chapel, which was rebuilt in 1411, at the far end. The other two medieval guildhalls stand just inside the northern city wall. The timber-framed part of the Merchant Taylors' Hall at Aldwark dates from about 1400, and from 1552 it served the amalgamated drapers' and tailors' guild. St Anthony's Guildhall at Peasholme Green was constructed in 1446–53 as the meeting house of a large fraternity, with a stone and brick ground floor used as the chapel and hospital and an upper, timber-framed floor divided into two large halls. After the Reformation, the corporation gave it to the smaller guilds to use as a common hall.

Wealthy merchants with extensive links through marriage dominated the affairs of late-medieval York, Beverley and Hull. Most of them had migrated from the Vale of York and the East Riding or from only slightly further afield, yet their knowledge of London and the northern European ports set them apart from their neighbours. York and Hull were incorporated cities with county status and though Beverley remained a seigneurial borough of the Archbishop of York its leading townsmen were not intimidated by great landowners, neither lay nor ecclesiastical. The political longevity of merchant families in Beverley – the Coppendales, Holmes and Tirwhits – was exceptional, for relatively few merchant families survived more than one or two generations in the male line. A steady flow of newcomers replenished the merchant groups and each generation largely made its own wealth by adapting to fresh business opportunities.

When the economy boomed, fortunes could be won from international wholesale trade. Wool and cloth were exported and wine and an amazing variety of Atlantic-coast and Baltic Sea commodities were imported. But in the harder times of the late fifteenth and early sixteenth centuries many merchants lost all. Only Hull survived the international recession with some shreds of its overseas trade intact.

About 1540 John Leland noted that Beverley was a large town, with well-built wooden houses and brick bars at the entrances. He observed the great channel that had been cut to the river Hull and the vessels that came up it to the edge of the town, but he was told that the once-flourishing cloth-making industry was now much decayed. The fortunes of Kingston-upon-Hull were also in decline, despite a charter of incorporation from Henry VI in 1440, for the merchants of the Hanseatic League had obtained a monopoly of the Baltic Sea trade. By 1460 Hull's wool exports had fallen to less than a quarter of their value at the beginning of the century. In 1462 only about 50 ships entered the port of Hull from overseas and they were mostly foreign-owned vessels from Antwerp and Calais. By 1465 the rents of the most expensive properties in High Street had fallen. Worse times lay ahead as trade continued to decay and population levels fell. By 1527–28 most rents had dropped to at least half the level recorded in 1465.

Yorkshire was not alone in its troubles. Some of England's most famous provincial towns withered during the late fifteenth and early sixteenth centuries and suffered badly during a decade of unprecedented economic hardship in the 1520s. Ripon remained the largest town in the West Riding, with about 2,000 people in 1532 and a wide reputation for its annual horse fairs, but a few years later John Leland saw a great number of abandoned tenters by the riverside and found that 'idleness was sore increased' by the collapse of the woollen cloth industry. His observation is confirmed by an estate account of 1532 which noted that several tenters were vacant for lack of tenants.

The declining fortunes of smaller towns is not as well recorded, but Northallerton's experience was shared by many others. Its economy was sluggish throughout the decades between 1470 and 1540, especially during the last years of the fifteenth century. The Wednesday markets and annual fairs that served the Allertonshire district continued in a modest way in the single street of the town, tapering south from the parish church with the bishop's palace standing aloof to the west, but the population had declined from its peak of about 750 in the late fourteenth century. The town remained a closely regulated, stable society, but it was very small by later standards.

Yorkshire's smaller ports had mixed fortunes. In the first half of the fifteenth century about 35 Scarborough fishermen owned a fleet of 70–100 vessels, though most of these were boats and cobbles. The most substantial men went on long voyages to fish herring, often sailing as far as Iceland, but a century later, Leland found that the pier at Scarborough was 'sore decayed'. In contrast, a new quay and port were under construction at Whitby at the time of his visit

The interior of St Michael-le-Belfry, York. Completely rebuilt in Perpendicular style between 1525 and 1536 under the direction of John Forman, master mason at the Minster close by, the church has no division between nave and chancel. The reredos was designed by local architect William Etty in 1712. Guy Fawkes was baptised here. Many of York's churches have become redundant but St Michael's has a thriving congregation.

PHOTOGRAPH: CARNEGIE, 2005

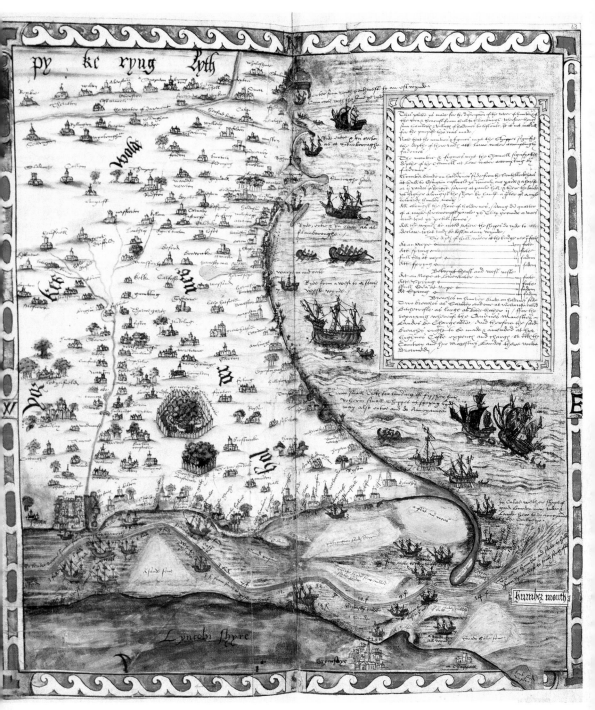

Lord Burghley's chart of the River Humber and North Sea coast, *c.*1560. Queen Elizabeth I's chief minister, concerned about the defence of the realm, ordered this chart to show the shifting and treacherous lower reaches of the Humber, downstream from Hull, and the East Riding coast, which had no harbours south of Bridlington. It marks the course of the River Hull and the sites of settlements on the Wolds and in Holderness, particularly those that were clustered along the north bank of the Humber and which had once been rivals to Hull. The North and South Parks at Burstwick, which had been royal deer parks until 1558, are displayed prominently.

and Robin Hood's Bay had a dock a mile long for its 20 boatmen. On his journey up the Humber, Leland noted that Hedon had been 'a fair haven town', but that some places where the ships had once anchored were now overgrown with flags and reed, so that the haven was 'very sorely decayed'. He concluded that the truth of the matter was that when Hull began to flourish, Hedon declined.

Leland visited many other towns that fared no better than Hedon. He thought that Bawtry was a very bare and poor market town and the wharf on the Idle that served South Yorkshire and north Derbyshire did not attract his attention. Yet while some towns declined their neighbours remained vibrant. Tickhill was very bare but Rotherham was flourishing, Aberford was a poor thoroughfare place but Tadcaster was doing much better, Boroughbridge was 'but a bare thing', Wensley 'a little poor market' and Catterick 'a very poor town', but the markets at Middleham, Masham and Knaresborough were thriving. Malton too had a good market and Pontefract was 'a fair, large market town'. In 1534 Robert Goldsborough, a fishmonger, said in evidence that every market day he 'conveyed fresh fish from the sea to Pontefract and brought it into the market place to sell', or on rainy days 'in an open shop opening towards the market place'. Communications were slow by modern standards, but a network of routes linked all the market towns.

North Bar, Beverley. This entrance to the northern part of the town was built in 1409 with 125,000 hand-made bricks, produced locally. The bricks are rarely more than 2 inches thick but up to 10 inches long, with plenty of mortar to make the courses regular. Beverley and Hull were among the first places in the country to erect their public buildings in brick.
PHOTOGRAPH: CARNEGIE, 2005

The sturdy bridges over the Don at Doncaster, Rotherham and Sheffield were erected to take wheeled vehicles and accounts of labour services at Sheffield Castle in the 1440s show that wains were commonly used even in the most hilly districts. But the combined population gains of the successful towns did not match the huge losses of the great cities and other declining urban centres in the late-medieval period.

West and south-west Yorkshire fared much better than the other parts of the county in the late fifteenth century. While cloth-making declined in York, Beverley, Ripon and the Vale of York, it began to flourish in the huge parish of Halifax and adjacent districts. Leland found that Wakefield was a busy and large market town, where sea and river fish were on sale and all food was so cheap that 'a right honest man shall fare well for twopence a meal'. Its fortunes rested on the success of its cloth trade. He told similar stories about Bradford and Leeds.

Rural industries

Cheap woollen kerseys, at first used particularly for hose and stockings, had long been manufactured in a modest way on the edges of the Pennines, but the poll tax returns of 1379 suggest that the cloth trade of the Halifax–Bradford district was then of minor importance. By 1473–75, however, the parish of Halifax was second only to York in the number of woollen cloths that were counted by the ulnage collectors and during the sixteenth century kerseys were exported from Halifax all over western Europe. The upper Calder Valley had become the largest producer of kerseys in England. The population of the town of Halifax soared from a mere 313 in 1439 to about 2,600 in 1566, at a time when most places were declining. The population of the extensive parish grew even faster, from about 1,000 people in 1439 to around 8,500 in 1548. The preamble to the famous 'Halifax Act' of 1555, which allowed exemption from the ban on middlemen, argued that the inhabitants of the parish 'being planted in the great waste and moors, where the fertility of ground is not apt to bring forth any corn nor good grass, but in rare places … by exceeding and great industry' lived entirely by cloth making. The majority of the inhabitants being unable 'to keep a horse to carry wool, nor yet to buy much wool at once, had ever used only to repair to the town of Halifax … and there to buy from the wool driver some a stone, some two, and some three or four, according to their ability, and to carry the same to their houses some three, four, five or six miles off, upon their heads and backs, and so to make and convert the same either into yarn or cloth, and to sell the same and so to buy more wool'.

The growth of the rural textile industry in the second half of the fifteenth century and the first half of the sixteenth is obvious from the increased number of fulling mills in the Leeds–Wakefield–Halifax triangle. In 1425 Leeds had only one fulling mill, by 1548 it had four. By the middle of the sixteenth century at least 25 fulling mills were at work in the three wapentakes of Agbrigg, Morley and Skyrack. They and the corn mills were the only buildings in the river valleys at that time, for it was not until the Industrial Revolution that settlements were built alongside the mills. The stewards of the manor of Wakefield encouraged entrepreneurs such as the Kayes of Woodsome to construct fulling mills by charging only the normal customary rents. By the middle of the sixteenth century West Riding clothiers were selling cloths in Blackwell Hall, London.

The dual economy of farming and weaving that was pursued by the small-holders and cottagers in the farmsteads, hamlets and villages on the hillsides

41–45 Goodramgate, York. This three-storeyed, jettied house dates from the late fifteenth or the early sixteenth century. Before the fifteenth century most houses in York were only one or two storeys high. Here, the top storey was originally open to the rafters. This substantial property, three bays wide, may have combined domestic accommodation with commercial use on the ground floor. The windows are later insertions.

PHOTOGRAPH: CARNEGIE, 2005

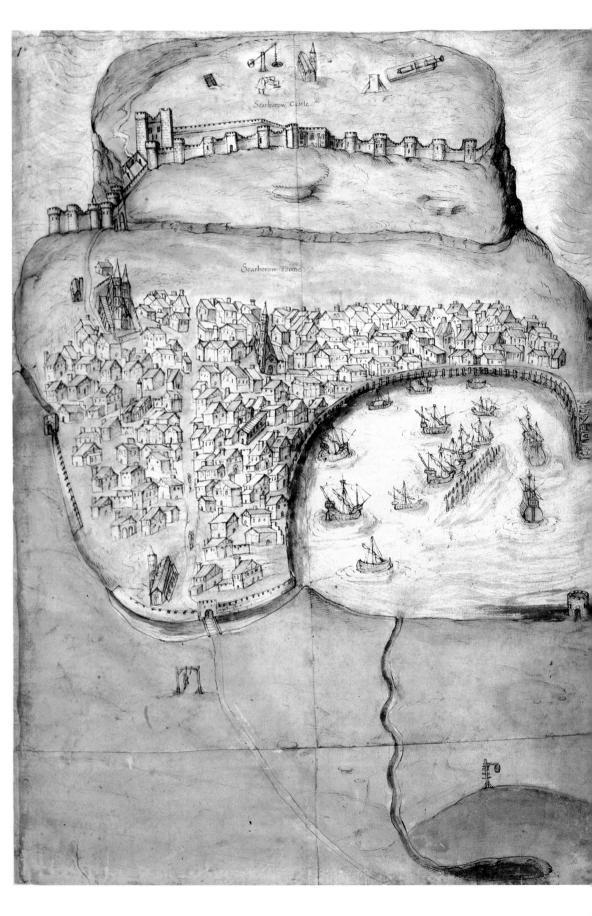

Scarborow Castle

Scarborow Towne

above the Pennine valleys flourished in districts that had light manorial burdens and which were free of the restrictions imposed by urban guilds. Taxation records show that the rural textile districts had high proportions of householders who were assessed on small amounts of land, people who made sufficient profits to invest in looms and other necessary equipment. Natural resources are only part of the explanation of why the Calder Valley became pre-eminent in the cloth business. Most of the wool was imported and the industry did not flourish in every area which had plentiful supplies of fuel. It developed in Agbrigg and Morley wapentakes rather than in Nidderdale, for example, a district which had a similar topography and an commercial outlet nearby at Ripon. Social structure and relative freedom were important ingredients for success.

The metalworkers of Hallamshire had a similar lifestyle to the inhabitants of the parish of Halifax. A reference to a Sheffield knife in Chaucer's *The Reeve's Tale* shows that Hallamshire cutlery was widely known by the late fourteenth century. John Leland found many smiths and cutlers in Hallamshire and very good smiths for cutting tools in Rotherham. The Tankersley seam of ironstone was used for forging blades, but steel for the cutting edges had to be imported from abroad. The Earls of Shrewsbury took a paternal interest in the local trades and Hallamshire had the inestimable advantage of coal for cutlers' smithies, suitable stones for grinding sharp edges, and swiftly descending streams to drive them. Medieval Sheffield had a distinctive character as a market town where cutlery was made and the surrounding rural parishes were beginning to specialise in the manufacture of scythes, sickles or nails, but the great expansion of the metal trades took place in the second half of the sixteenth century.

The smelting of lead and iron required levels of investments that could be provided only by great landowners, including the monasteries, but in the later Middle Ages sites were usually leased to 'farmers' who employed a small, specialist workforce. The finished products were taken down the rivers and sometimes exported abroad. Coal, on the other hand, was mined mainly for domestic fuel. At Rotherham, for instance, John Leland found that the people burnt a great deal of coal because it was 'plentifully found there and sold good cheap'. Few men were described in contemporary records as miners and those that were usually had a smallholding, like most rural workers.

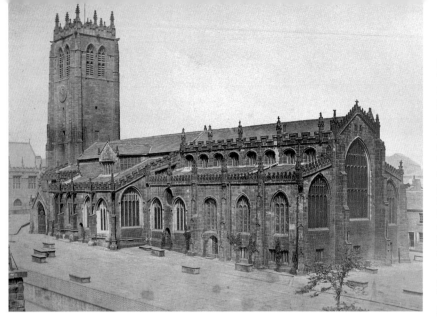

St John's Church, Halifax.
The medieval parish of
Halifax was the largest in
England, covering 124
square miles, so it was
divided into several
chapelries. St John's
Church stands in a
curious, almost lonely
position below the central
streets of the town. A few
traces of an earlier church
can be found, but the
building is over-
whelmingly in the
Perpendicular Gothic style
of the fifteenth century.
This is a large church,
paid for out of the profits
of the trade in woollen
cloth. Both the nave and
the chancel have aisles and
the nave has chapels on
both the south and north
sides of its aisles. The
skyline is pierced by
pinnacles and battlements.
When the tower was
finished about 1475 the
rebuilding was complete.
BY COURTESY OF THE YORKSHIRE
ARCHAEOLOGICAL SOCIETY

The countryside

The decay of urban life in the late Middle Ages was matched in those parts of
the countryside that had no industry and which were totally reliant on farming.
Village markets were no longer held and in some districts villages disappeared
entirely. The classic site is on the Wolds at Wharram Percy, where the layout
of the village is frozen in time after it had been abandoned about 1500. Aerial
photographs, field surveys and excavations have shown that the village was
planned as a very elongated triangle around a green cut through by a road,
with two long rows of dwellings and one much shorter row. Each house plot
was 18 metres wide, the width of two field strips, but the fields were shaped by
an existing framework of Roman and earlier boundaries. Had Wharram not
been abandoned, its carefully planned origins might have been obscured by later
activities. In some villages clear evidence of an early medieval plan has endured
in the landscape or is shown on early maps, but elsewhere the picture is blurred
by subsequent developments.

Another classic site that is well marked by the tell-tale grassy mounds and
holloways of former houses and lanes is that of East Tanfield, an abandoned
village which once stood on the banks of the Ure between Ripon and Masham
in the northern Vale of York. In 1301 East Tanfield contained 17 families and
at the peak of its prosperity it probably had 22. Manorial records show that the
village had started to shrink by the 1440s and in 1517 a government enquiry
into the effects of enclosure noted that 400 acres had been enclosed in the last
30 years, that eight houses had been demolished and that 32 people had been
evicted from their homes. The enquiry was concerned only with what had
happened since 1488, by which time the main period of conversion to sheep
and cattle farming had passed, nevertheless it provided a great deal of evidence
about what was happening all over the Yorkshire countryside. The commission
noted 29 cases involving the enclosure of 3,660 acres in the West Riding, 30

cases concerning 2,628 acres in the North Riding, and 25 cases relating to 1,560 acres in the East Riding. In Yorkshire as a whole this amounted to a total of 84 cases in which 7,848 acres of land were enclosed and 232 houses or cottages had been demolished.

The 1517 enquiry noted a number of cases where arable lands had been enclosed to create or extend manorial parks. Many a great house owes its privacy and uninterrupted view to the decay or removal of a village. Allerton Mauleverer, Harewood, Norton Conyers and Ribston are examples that immediately spring to mind. At Cridling, which had 22 families in 1425, the entire site of the village was enclosed within a park by Henry Vavasour and at Thrybergh, in South Yorkshire, Richard Reresby enclosed 60 acres of pasture and wood and 26 acres of arable land into the park that now forms a golf course. At Steeton-in-Ainsty 45 people paid poll tax in 1377 but by 1514 the village had shrunk to just four houses besides the mansion of the Fairfaxes. At Temple Newsam the 1517 enquiry heard that the remaining four dwellings had been recently demolished and 80 acres enclosed by the lord of the manor, whose estate also absorbed the nearby settlements of Skelton and Colton. In the East Riding the creation of parks was said to have been the reason for enclosures at Holme-upon-Spalding Moor, Leconfield and Scorborough. Other deserted village sites in Yorkshire are marked now not by a hall but by an isolated church, such as the early fourteenth-century chapel which stands alone in a flat landscape at Lead, or the medieval church at Frickley where the surrounding fields now once more support fine crops of wheat and barley. At least seven of the parks that are shown on Saxton's map of the West Riding in 1577 were in places where there had once been a village – Allerton Mauleverer, Cridling, Gawthorpe, Ribston, Temple Newsam, Wilstrop and Wothersome. At Risby, near Beverley, the Ellerkers enclosed a new park in the first half of the sixteenth century and extended it several times, but they were going against the prevailing fashion, for the popularity of deer parks declined in the fifteenth and sixteenth centuries and many of the existing parks were abandoned, particular those that were on former monastic estates.

In those upland parts of Yorkshire that had flourishing rural industries the population grew steadily, while in many lowland districts it continued to decline. In 1540 as many as 380 acres of the demesne land at Snaith had reverted to waste for lack of tenants and other parts of the lord's estate had been enclosed within Phippin Park. At Foulby and Wragby (which now form a single township) 21 cottages were unoccupied in 1541 because of recent pestilence. The late Middle Ages was a time when many families grasped their opportunities to rise to the ranks of the yeomen and even to the minor gentry. It is often difficult to identify the individuals who changed their family's fortunes and in many cases the advances were made slowly over the generations, but in Hallamshire the descendants of ordinary farming families were more often than not the ones who built the gabled halls of the seventeenth century. The Shirecliffes, whose surname was derived from a minor place-name to the north

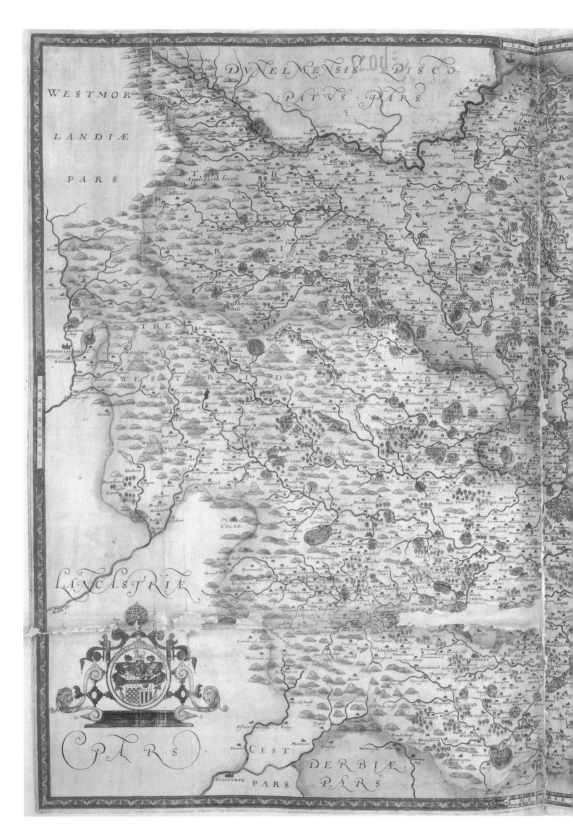

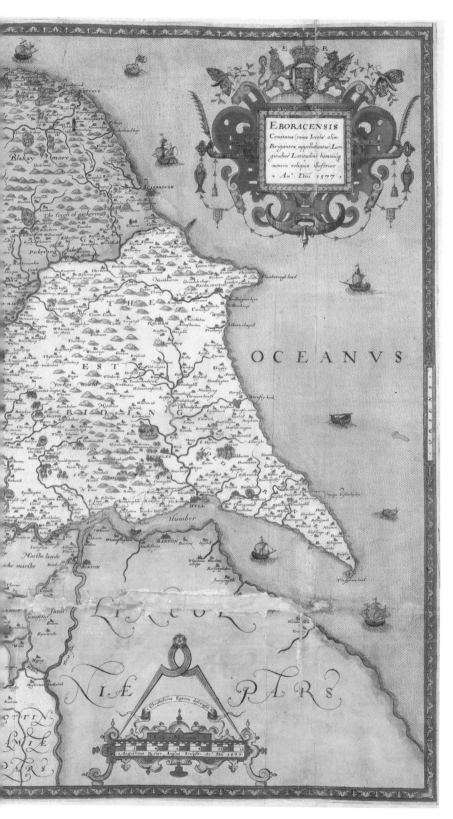

Christopher Saxton, the greatest mapmaker of the Elizabethan age, came from Dunningley, near Dewsbury. His survey of all the counties of England and Wales, was commissioned by Thomas Seckford, master of the Court of Requests, and supported enthusiastically by William Cecil, Lord Burghley, Elizabeth's first minister. Saxton began work in 1574 and finished his project five years later. His national atlas and accompanying wall map were unparalleled in Europe at that time and long provided the framework for other English mapmakers, notably John Speed, who published a new series of county maps between 1605 and 1610. Saxton's map of Yorkshire is dated 1577. It marks the ridings and the city of York with the Ainsty, towns, parks, rivers and hills and is a remarkable improvement on medieval maps in its accuracy. His wall map of England and Wales (1584) proudly marks the hamlet of Dunningley. In later life, Saxton was widely employed, especially in Yorkshire, to produce local estate maps. These are listed and described in Ifor. M. Evans and Heather Lawrence, *Christopher Saxton: Elizabethan Map-Maker* (Wakefield Historical Publications, 1979).

of Sheffield, were small farmers in the fourteenth century who were taxed at the lowest rate in 1379. Their fortunes began to improve in the third quarter of the fifteenth century, when John Shirecliffe took a lease of the Ecclesfield Priory estate and by Henry VIII's reign they had a share in the profitable business of collecting the tithes of Ecclesfield's large parish. Meanwhile, Thomas Shirecliffe had become master of game in the lord of Hallamshire's chases and park and the family were involved in numerous land transactions at the manor court. By 1510 William Shirecliffe of Ecclesfield Hall was being described as 'gentleman', though the family did not gain a coat-of-arms and a crest until 1614, and Thomas's descendants built Whitley Hall, which at the time was the finest residence in the parish. Many junior branches of the family, however, had to earn their livings as cutlers and husbandmen.

Making a profit from a lease of the lord's demesne or a monastic grange was a sure way of rising in society. Such men were in a good position to buy former monastic lands which came on the market. In 1540, William Ramsden, the head of a small yeoman family near Halifax, inherited a portion of his father-in-law's estate at Longley, near Almondbury, and with this wealth he was able to make small purchases and to acquire the leases of watermills on the crown's estates. The dissolution of the monasteries provided him with the opportunity to make many successful property speculations through the Court of Augmentations and his descendants became lords of both Huddersfield (1599) and Almondbury (1627). Another time-honoured way of building up an estate was to invest the profits that had been made from business. Between 1519 and 1538 John Wirrall, a prominent merchant and mayor of Doncaster in 1524, bought the neighbouring manors of Loversall and Stancil and some property in Tickhill. After his death in 1544, his son, Hugh, extended the family estate by buying former monastic lands.

Most farming families stayed close to the places where their surnames had originated, often working the same land as their ancestors for generation after generation. The Wilkinson family were at Crowder House in Hallamshire from 1402 to 1859. Such people formed the stable core of local societies and their distinctive surnames are still found most commonly in the 'countries' that they

All Saints Church, Frickley. Frickley is a deserted medieval village, where the church stands alone amidst the corn fields. The village had gone by the seventeenth century, but the church survived because it served the neighbouring settlement of Clayton. It was restored by the squire of Frickley Hall in Victorian times. although it remains basically Norman in character.

Even before the Black Death Frickley was only a small place, but in 1379 its poll tax payers still comprised six married couples and eleven single persons over the age of sixteen. A rental of 1426 names three open-fields, one of which was Kirkfield, 'the field by the church'. All traces of the village disappeared during eighteenth-century landscaping. The Victorian squires made sure that the miners of Frickley Colliery were housed beyond the parish boundary, out of sight of the hall and the church.

PHOTOGRAPH: AUTHOR

inhabited in the Middle Ages. They had more opportunities than earlier generations, for population pressure on the land had eased and industrial by-employments sometimes provided extra income, so unless they were lured by the fame of London they tended to move no further than the nearest town or to another farm within a few miles of their birthplaces.

Farming practices were adapted to the great variety of soils and landscapes that were found in Yorkshire. When John Leland visited the North late in the reign of Henry VIII he travelled between Bawtry and Doncaster 'by a great plain and sandy ground' and observed very good meadows, cornfields and some woods. Heading for Thorne, he saw a great mere a mile or so wide that was full of fish and wildfowl, then as he passed along the Great North Road towards Pontefract he observed that much of the countryside was well wooded and enclosed but that all parishes had fruitful arable lands and pastures. Within a day's journey a traveller in Yorkshire could ride through very different types of countryside. Between York and Leconfield Leland found little wood but good crops of corn and grass, but beyond lay large woods and then low ground used as meadows and pastures. Between Hull and Beverley he passed through five miles of low pasture and marshland and another mile of enclosed and rather woody ground. Good-quality cornfields surrounded Walkington but between North Cave and Scalby lay low marsh and meadows. Walling Fen was 16 miles in circumference with many small settlements in and around it.

When Leland crossed the North York Moors from Scarborough to Pickering he saw a landscape that is still familiar to us, with corn and grass growing in the dales but hardly any trees. In the Yorkshire Dales little corn was grown and the emphasis was on feeding cattle. He saw little wood in the Forest of Knaresborough except on the banks of the river and found no woods worth mentioning throughout the northern Vale of York, except in a part of the Forest of Galtres which otherwise consisted of poor scrub land, common pasture or low-lying meadows and carrs. South of Sutton-on-the-Forest Leland moved into a great plain that was used to graze beasts and dig turf, then as he approached York he marvelled at the crops of corn. Between Myton and Helperby he found some woodland amongst the cornfields, pastures and

Ecclesfield Priory and Hall. The thirteenth-century priory (*right*) was built for the Benedictine monks of the Abbey of St Wandrille in Normandy, the owners of the tithes and a large estate in Ecclesfield. After the Dissolution of the Monasteries in the sixteenth century, it was converted into a Tudor Hall. The Georgian extension was built in 1736.

meadows and approaching Northallerton he discovered fine cereals and a long stretch of low pasture and moor. The soils of the northern Vale of York and the Vale of Mowbray varied from light sands to quite heavy clays and farming practices varied accordingly.

In some parts of Yorkshire the enclosure of the communal open fields was well under way by the middle of the sixteenth century. Many of the small 'townfields' that surrounded the hamlets and villages on the edges of the Pennines were put down to grass as money earned from pastoral farming and rural industry enabled families to buy their bread or meal from local markets or travelling badgers. A survey made in the reign of Henry VIII shows that most of the open fields in the township of Dent had been enclosed. The piecemeal nature of the process can be observed at Kippax from 1515 onwards when seven tenants paid for licences to enclose small parcels that amounted in all to six acres of arable land and nine acres of meadow.

Upland districts which were once set aside for hunting were sometimes converted to pastoral farming by the lord or his steward. In 1449 Richard, Duke of York ordered that his park at Erringden, in Sowerbyshire, which covered some 3,000 acres of very barren ground, be broken up and leased out in enclosed parcels to tenants. At first, only eight families set up home there but by 1545 the settlers numbered about 50 households, far more than are found there at the present time. The taking in of new land from the edges of the moors gathered pace in the 1490s in Sowerby and Warley townships. The lord of the manor benefited from the new rents and entry fines and the farmers had sufficient land, pasture rights on the commons and opportunities to weave cloth to enable them to earn a living. The moorland edges also attracted squatters who enclosed a few acres around a cottage. Landlords were often slow to take action against them, but from time to time a determined effort would be made to enforce the payment of rent. In 1557, for instance, the Earl of Cumberland held an enquiry on his manor of Silsden, in Craven, which produced a long list of minor encroachments that had been made without licence over the previous ten years.

Mirfield Old Rectory. Designed to a simple, rectangular plan, with a ground floor of local sandstone, the Old Rectory has an eye-catching display of timbers in the upper storey. The struts of the gable end are arranged in herringbone patterns, similar to those of the nearby Hopton Old Hall; the long sides have simple close studding. Perhaps they once reached down to the sill? The building stands to the west of the parish church. It may once have been open to the rafters. An external staircase provided access to the upper rooms once the central hall, kitchen and parlour were reduced by ceilings.
PHOTOGRAPH: AUTHOR

Hopton Old Hall. Next to the church at Upper Hopton, the Old Hall was built mostly of the local coal-measure sandstone, but its wings are displayed in the old-fashioned, West Riding vernacular style of timber-framing. Their gabled roofs are supported by king-posts rising from sturdy tie-beams and the struts are arranged diagonally, at right angles to the rafters, for visual effect. The black-and-white appearance dates only from late-Victorian times.

PHOTOGRAPH: AUTHOR

Yorkshire's woods supplied timber for building and underwood for fuel, poles, handles, fencing and numerous other purposes. In the late Middle Ages they also often had clearings and 'launds' where livestock could find sheltered grazing, especially in winter time. Increasingly, the 'springwoods' had to be managed carefully to preserve resources, for many parishes had no woodland at all. The golden age of coppicing came later, but sufficient evidence survives to suggest that late-medieval woodwards were dividing their woods into sections which were felled on a rotation basis. For example, in the 1530s Hampole Priory owned a 120-acre wood 'in which are 18 coppices called haggs, viz. 1 of the age of 18 years another of the age of 17 years and so in succession from year to year'. At the same time, Esholt Priory's woods included the 16-acre Nunwood, where 300 great oaks had been left to grow for 200 years, another wood of 30 acres on Bastone Cliff, where 200 oaks of 40 years' growth reared above underwood that had last been felled 12 years ago, a three-acre close with 40 oaks aged 40 years and underwood of 10 years, and a one-acre wood containing 20 oaks of 40 years growth and underwood that had sprung up a year ago. Upon the dissolution of the monasteries, the woods of Roche Abbey contained 800 oaks and ashes of 60 and 80 years growth, which were either pollarded for browsing or cultivated as timber for repairing houses and making ploughs, carts and stakes for hedges, while the coppices were felled in short rotations lasting up to 15 years. The production of charcoal was an ancient activity in the woods on the coal-measure sandstones, the Pennine foothills and parts of the North York Moors, in order to meet the demands of industries and of cottage housewives trying to light damp sticks in their humble grates.

Peasant houses

Most of Yorkshire's surviving timber-framed buildings are not immediately recognisable from the outside, for they have been encased in stone or brick at a later date. Ordinary farming families lived in one-storey houses that were framed by pairs of crucks that rested on stone footings. In midland and south-western England a few surviving cruck frames date back to the thirteenth century, but in the North such early survivors are rare. The dating technique known as dendrochronology confirms the documentary evidence which first mentions cruck buildings in the fifteenth century. For instance, in 1432 a house at Holdworth Ing in Ovenden township, high in the Calder Valley, was framed with eight crucks and roofed with slatestones and in 1495 the abbot of Whitby repaired his house at Goathland 'after the manner of the country' with 'three pairs of forks', a typical alternative name for crucks. By the reign of Henry VIII cruck frames were used in most, if not all, parts of Yorkshire for farmhouses, cottages and outbuildings. An Elizabethan survey of the manor of Cracoe, in Wharfedale, noted that nearly all the houses and barns were constructed in this way. In south-west Yorkshire dendronchronlogy techniques have dated a cruck-framed house in Stannington to 1539, a demolished building near Fulwood to the 1540s, a barn in Stannington barn to 1588 and a demolished cruck at Waleswood to the 1630s, and upon his death in 1638 Hugh Mellor of Shiregreen left his son two pairs of crucks that were already broken and other timber with which to build a cutler's smithy. The majority of surviving cruck-framed buildings in Yorkshire date from the fifteenth to the seventeenth centuries, but in some places this method of construction was still considered adequate for barns and other outbuildings well into the eighteenth century. The farmhouses, cottages and barns that have survived with their cruck frames at least partly intact were later encased in stone, or sometimes in brick, when the original walls were in need of repair. On the hills above Stocksbridge, in south-west Yorkshire, the names of William and Sara Couldwell and the date 1688 are carved on the walls of a six-bay barn, but the cruck-frame that supports the building is much older. The Pennine fringes of south-west Yorkshire, the North York Moors and their neighbouring districts have the largest numbers of cruck-framed buildings in the country, but in many other parts of Yorkshire the physical evidence has gone completely.

Yorkshire's more substantial post-and-truss buildings overlap with crucks both in time and space, though on the whole they were built by families that enjoyed a higher standard of living. At Shore Hall and Dean Head in the parish of Penistone two aisled barns with collar-rafter roofs date from the late fourteenth or fifteenth centuries and a similar but unaisled barn at Nether Haugh, north of Rotherham, is also late medieval. Roofs constructed in this manner were not confined to the lowland zone of England, as was once thought, but were found even on the edges of the Pennines. South-west Yorkshire was open to influences from all directions and so contains examples of different building types. Netherfold farmhouse at Thorpe Common, which has been dated by dendrochronology to 1495, resembles the hipped-roofed structures of the Vale of York and typical West Riding king-post roofs can be found in barns such as the fine example at East Riddlesden Hall, though they tend to be later, and many are post-medieval.

The 60 or so timber-framed houses that have been surveyed in the Vale of York date from the middle of the fifteenth century to as late as 1680 and they

right A simple, one-bay cruck barn at Dyke Side, Langsett, south-west Yorkshire. The oak frame was revealed when the later walls and roof were removed during the demolition of the barn. Many other timber frames are hidden from view because of later encasing with stone.
AUTHOR COLLECTION

right The barn at Shore Hall, Penistone (now demolished) had sturdy roof trusses dating from the late fifteenth century. This was a superior building to those framed with crucks.
AUTHOR COLLECTION

Helmsley Rectory, an Elizabethan timber-framed house, standing close to the parish church on the north side of the market place. It has lost one of its wings. It dates from the 1580s and was one of the first in that part of Yorkshire to have a chamber built above the hall, instead of the medieval tradition of a hall open to the rafters. It was occupied by the Crosland family, agents to the Duke of Rutland before it became the rectory. The panelling was decorated by diagonal struts, but the 'black-and-white' appearance is Victorian in date.

PHOTOGRAPH: CARNEGIE, 2005

Shibden Hall, Halifax. This fine timber-framed house was built by William Otes in the early fifteenth century in the typical West Riding fashion of the times, using king-posts and diagonal struts. It was owned later by the wealthy Savile and Waterhouse families. Part of the south front was encased in stone and given mullioned windows in the seventeenth century. The tower was built by Anne Lister in the early nineteenth century.

left This timber-framed, thatched farmhouse at Carlton Husthwaite consists of 3½ bays, one room deep, but originally with an aisle running all way along the rear. It probably once had aisles at each end as well. It was built open to a common rafter roof but was adapted later to provide upstairs rooms. A smoke-hood standing free of the frame funnelled the smoke to the chimney. The timber wall studs of the exterior are all nailed on to the earlier frame. The house was thoroughly restored in 1967, when the rear aisle was demolished. The plan and style are typical of the late-medieval and Tudor farmhouses of the Vale of York.

have a wide variety of plans. Their typical features include collar-rafter roofs, walls with posts set close together, and usually an aisle or an outshut to the rear or at one end. The earliest examples were open to the rafters, but the later ones have upstairs chambers. The skilled carpentry techniques of the crown-post roof that were common in southern England were used in York, particularly in the Shambles, and less frequently in other medieval towns such as Beverley, Ripon, Scarborough and Tickhill. Crown-post roofs are rarely found in the Yorkshire countryside, but good examples dating from the late fourteenth and early fifteenth centuries survive at Housley Hall in Ecclesfield parish and at Woodall on Yorkshire's southern boundary. York was open to wider influences and so possesses a variety of late-medieval building styles, usually with jettied upper storeys; for instance, a building just off Goodramgate has the typical features of the 'Wealden houses' that are so common in Kent. The county has a far larger and more varied collection of medieval buildings than was realised until recent years. They refute the old idea that the whole of late-medieval Yorkshire was part of a 'backward North'.

Towards the end of the Middle Ages some West Riding families acquired sufficient wealth from farming and industry to rebuild their homes on a scale that was comparable with those of the best in south-east England. These houses had king-post roofs with ridge-poles and purlins that were sturdy enough to support heavy, stone-slates, and close-studded walls that were decorated with diagonal patterns, especially in the gable ends. Gentry houses such as Elland New Hall, Shibden Hall and Thornhill Lees Hall each had a central hall that was open to the roof and cross-wings that were divided into two storeys. In the parish of Sheffield the Wickersley family built Broom Hall, a typical example of this type of structure which has been dated by dendronchronlogy to within a few years of 1507. The standard of carpentry in these gentry houses was very high; indeed the two roofs at Calverley Hall were given a display of hammer beams, a technique that was rarely employed in the north of England.

The collection of houses that were built by the yeomen-clothiers of the Halifax district are of even greater interest than the dwellings of the gentry, for they form a unique group with no parallels elsewhere in England. More than 20 examples from the second half of the fifteenth century or the first quarter of the sixteenth have been recorded. As some of them are in clusters of two or three in a village or a hamlet such as Boothtown, the owners obviously did not acquire their wealth solely from the land, so no doubt most of their money came from the textile trades. The few houses of this type that have been identified further south around Huddersfield and at Shelley Woodhouse and Barnby Hall are much thinner on the ground than those in the huge medieval parish of Halifax. The most distinctive feature of these houses is the use of aisles, usually in the form of a single aisle to the rear of the hall.

Thornhill Lees Hall. This timber-framed house was built by the Nettleton family in the early sixteenth century with a king-post roof in the West Riding tradition. The door where the woman is standing leads into a cross passage, to the right of which the hall is open to the rafters. The building once had another wing extending on the right hand side. The photograph shows how this fine building had declined over the centuries through age and neglect.

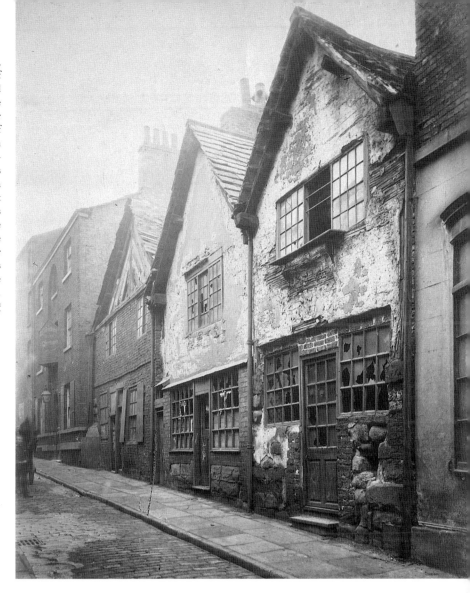

Though they are arranged in the normal manner with a central hall, cross passage, service wing and solar wing, all under one roof, they are not easy to recognise from outside, for they have been clad in stone and are heavily disguised. Their halls were open to king-post roofs, but instead of an open hearth in the centre the fire was contained within a timber and plaster smokehood at one end. These Halifax houses were built at the same time as the fine Perpendicular Gothic churches of the West Riding and together they offer valuable visual evidence of the growing prosperity of the cloth-manufacturing district in contrast to the stagnating economy of places, particularly those in the East Riding, which had once been the wealthiest in Yorkshire. The fashion soon began to spread so that by the end of the Middle Ages Yorkshire yeomen were no longer living in smoke-filled rooms. Their social inferiors often had to wait until the seventeenth century before they enjoyed similar benefits.

From Reformation to Civil War, 1550–1660

Religion and rebellion

The Reformation was not a popular movement that triumphed quickly but a long drawn-out process that was imposed from above. The corporation of York obeyed the orders of the Elizabethan settlement of 1559 reluctantly, but many of its citizens continued to use Catholic phrases in their wills throughout the 1560s. No-one in Yorkshire was killed for his or her religion during Mary Tudor's brief reign (1553–58), though 45 were punished for heresy, but 20 Catholics were martyred at York in the 1580s. The most famous was Margaret Clitherow, a butcher's wife in the Shambles, who was pressed to death in 1586 for refusing to plead to a charge of harbouring priests. Many other martyrs were also natives of the city or its hinterland, but the stronghold of Catholicism was the Yorkshire Dales. Nearly all the leading families in Nidderdale and half those in Richmondshire were Catholic. In the last two decades of Elizabeth's reign, 35 North Riding men are known to have been trained as priests in continental seminaries and the number of Catholics in this part of Yorkshire actually increased, despite the severe penalties threatened by the law. Guy Fawkes, of course, came from York. In James I's reign Catholics were seen as less of a threat to the state, though crippling fines were often imposed upon them. Two out of every three of the 300 or so Yorkshire households that remained staunchly Catholic throughout Elizabeth's reign were of gentry status. Rural squires, who were related through marriage, such as the Ingilbys, Yorkes, Trappes, Plomptons, Middletons and Tankards, saw Catholicism through its most dangerous years. and in north-western parts of the county numbers rose during the reigns of the early Stuarts. In most parts of Yorkshire, however, Catholics formed an insignificant minority.

Neither the Wakefield plot of 1541 nor the Seamer rising of 1549 caused the government much concern, but the rising of the northern earls in County Durham and North Yorkshire in 1569–70 was a serious rebellion led by the Earls of Northumberland (Percy), Westmorland (Neville) and Cumberland (Clifford), the heads of old feudal families who resented their loss of power to the Tudors. The plot championed the Catholic cause but it failed to attract the

same response as the Pilgrimage of Grace had done a generation earlier. The rebels marched from Durham to Ripon, burning communion tables, English bibles and service books, but they failed to take York and were forced to retreat. Neville fled to Flanders and in 1572 Percy was beheaded in York Pavement and his head displayed on Micklegate Bar. The failure of the revolt marked the end of the Middle Ages as surely as did the dissolution of the monasteries and the events of the Reformation. Elizabeth appointed trusted men to key positions; Edmund Grindall became Archbishop of York and Henry, Earl of Huntingdon, was made Lord President of the Council of the North. Strong Tudor government brought its rewards, for the prosperity of England rose markedly from the middle years of Elizabeth's reign onwards.

George, the sixth Earl of Shrewsbury, was given the unenviable task of keeping Mary, Queen of Scots, prisoner after she had fled to England. Between 1569 and 1584 she moved from one of the earl's properties to another but was held mostly at Sheffield, where the old hunting lodge had been converted into a great country house. George was the mightiest lord north of the River Trent

Pontefract Castle. This painting purports to show the castle and All Saints church about 1640, just before the Civil War. This view was based on an Elizabethan survey and is of uncertain accuracy. The castle was undoubtedly one of the most important in the North until it was sleighted by Parliament in the late 1640s after it had been actively occupied by Royalist troops. It was built on a rocky outcrop and a Norman new town was laid out beside it. All Saints was a large church that was severely damaged during Civil War seige. In 1789 it was replaced as the parish church by St Giles.

ẽ Talbot earle of Shrewsbury

and a firm Protestant, a man who could be relied upon to support the crown in the North, just as his ancestors had.

The great landowners

When Elizabeth came to the throne in 1558 six noblemen and 557 gentlemen had seats in Yorkshire. On the eve of the Civil War in 1642 the number of gentry had risen to 679, of whom 195 lived in the North Riding, 142 in the East Riding, 320 in the West Riding and 22 in York. Many could trace their descent from medieval knights and at least 270 had ancestors who had lived in Yorkshire since 1500. James I knighted 60 Yorkshiremen, raised 35 to the new order of baronetcy and ten to the peerage, but many other gentry families fell upon hard times through bad management and costly suits at law or by living beyond their means.

The signatories to a petition for a new university at York in 1641 confessed that 'we have been looked upon as rude and barbarous people', yet at that time 172 heads of gentry families had been educated at university – mainly at Cambridge – and more than 100 had travelled on the continent. Elizabethan families with cultured interests, such as the Fairfaxes and Saviles, were the first to have a sense of being Yorkshire folk, distinct from other Northerners. Sir William Fairfax decorated his great chamber at Gilling Castle with a splendid collection of the arms of the Yorkshire gentry. Outsiders recognised the

left Turret House, Sheffield Manor Lodge. During the sixteenth century the Earls of Shrewsbury converted the old hunting lodge in their deer park into a splendid country house. Most of the house was dismantled in the early eighteenth century, but the turret house, which stood at the entrance to the grounds, still stands in much the same state as when it was built in the 1570s and 1580s.

right George, Sixth Earl of Shrewsbury (c.1528–90). George was the richest nobleman north of the Trent. His many properties included Sheffield Castle and the Manor Lodge, where he held Mary, Queen of Scots, in custody.

SHEFFIELD LIBRARIES, ARCHIVES AND INFORMATION: LOCAL STUDIES

peculiarities of Yorkshire speech and character. In 1549 William Thomas remarked that the difference between a Yorkshireman and a Londoner was as pronounced as that between a Florentine and a Venetian and nearly 40 years later Edwin Sandys, Archbishop of York, was moved to say that he had never met or heard of such a 'stiff-necked, wilful, or obstinate people'. A character in a *Brief Discourse between Yorkshiremen & Scottish-men* (1650) declared that he was 'a Yorkshireman born and bred, I care not who knows it; I hope true York-shire never denies his county'. Most people in seventeenth-century Yorkshire did not think of themselves in this way, however, for their mental horizons were limited to the 'countries' or neighbourhoods with which they were familiar. Dalesmen had nothing much in common with the farmers of Holderness, while the cutlers of Hallamshire had little contact with the textile workers to the north of the Don and Dearne, let alone the inhabitants of the other two ridings.

The satirical ballad, *The Dragon of Wantley*, which denounced the ruthless way that the Wortley family extended their chase at Wharncliffe, attacked the selfish interests of hard-headed gentry. The Constables, Fairfaxes, Gascoignes, Saviles, Tempests and others were as powerful in their own districts as their medieval predecessors had been. They tackled their loss of revenue from inflation with such vigour that on most Yorkshire estates rents rose higher than prices in the century leading up to the Civil War. The Saviles of Thornhill managed to increase the rents on their 12 Yorkshire manors by 400 per cent between 1619 and 1651. Landlords and tenants were often engaged in long and bitter struggles, though a few examples of a more conciliatory approach can be found, as when Henry Tempest of Tong advised his son in 1648 that he would be blessed and his descendants would prosper if he did not oppress his tenants and allowed them to live comfortably.

Recovery and growth

During the reign of Elizabeth the population of England recovered from its long decline to a level that had not been reached since 1300. This recovery had begun by the late 1530s, when the earliest parish registers regularly record more baptisms than burials. Growth was particularly vigorous in the western parts of Yorkshire where land was cleared from the wastes again. Between 1377 and 1563 the population of the West Riding rose from about 75,000 to 100,000, with the fastest rates of growth in Swaledale (about 900 to 2,600) and Richmond (620 to 1,615). In the Forest of Knaresborough the number of cottagers on the edges of the commons attracted the bailiff's attention in the 1520s and caused increasing concern in the second half of the century. The whole of western Europe witnessed moderate growth at this time and England's population almost doubled from about 2.75 million to about 5 million between 1541 and 1640. The old problem of how to sustain more people was solved by new industries and improved farming practices which provided enough food in all but the worst years of harvest failure.

Yet people were still likely to succumb to sudden outbreaks of disease. In August 1551 all but six of the 49 people who were buried at Halifax had died of the 'sweating sickness', seemingly a variant of influenza. In 1555 and 1556 harvests were ruined by heavy, persistent rains and in the following two years the sickness killed 8 or 9 per cent of England's population. In 1557 and 1558 the parish registers of the West Riding woollen district recorded more burials than baptisms and in the Kirkburton register the words 'plague time' appear against the months of July, August and September 1558. Parts of Yorkshire were visited by both plague and 'sweat' in 1551–52 and by the 'new ague' in 1558–59. During these years, York's population was reduced by at least a third to unprecedented low levels. The city was thereafter immune to epidemics for 45 years, prompting a local gentleman to say in 1598 that the city rarely suffered from any infectious disease. Other Yorkshire towns that succumbed to virulent plagues included Doncaster, where 747 people died in an outbreak that lasted from September 1582 to December 1583, and Richmond, where plague killed two-thirds of the inhabitants between August 1597 and December 1598; the parish register recorded 1,050 deaths by 'pestilence' and others were buried in

Aerial view of Richmond Castle, with the town beyond. Holy Trinity church stands in the Market Place and the curving row of buildings follow the line of the medieval walls. Richmond recovered from the severe outbreak of plague to become a prosperous Georgian market town. It is interesting to compare this modern view with Speed's map on page 89.

The tomb of George, Sixth Earl of Shrewsbury, Sheffield Cathedral. George is depicted as a knight in armour, with his head resting on a rolled-up mat, as was usual then, and his feet on a talbot. A huge monument, inscribed with his virtues, honours and connections, rises above him. His wife, Bess of Hardwick, is buried in Derby Cathedral.

PHOTOGRAPH: CARNEGIE, 2004

unconsecrated ground in Castle Yard and Clarke's Green. An inscription in Penrith church claims that 2,200 people in the deanery of Richmond died at that time.

In more settled times, the outer bailey of Richmond castle was converted into a market place around Holy Trinity chapel. The parish church lay on the outskirts of the town, probably on the site of an earlier church that served the pre-Conquest settlement. In the fourteenth century the bailey defences were enclosed with town walls, whose curving lines are now followed by shop frontages. By the time of Speed's map, some of the old market stalls had been replaced by permanent buildings and the livestock market had become so congested that it had been removed to the edge of the town. Extramural development along Frenchgate, Bargate and Newbiggen occurred early in the medieval period as the town began to prosper. In 1258 the Franciscans founded a friary to the north of the town.

Local populations recovered from such epidemics because of younger marriages and higher birth rates, but plague continued to strike randomly. York's immunity came to a dreadful end in 1604 when 3,512 people, that is 30 per cent of the inhabitants, were killed in the city's last major visitation of the disease. In 1631 plague broke out at Bingley, Halifax, Heptonstall and Mirfield and ten years later at Brighouse, Clifton, Dewsbury, Hipperholme and Shelf. After another four years, however, Yorkshire was to be free of plague. The stringent controls on movement that were imposed by the JPs and the prohibition of trade with London meant that the county did not suffer in 1665–66 during England's last outbreak of this mysterious disease.

Fears of famine remained very real in Elizabethan England. After the disastrous harvests of 1586 and 1587 the number of burials rose significantly in Richmond and the woollen district of the West Riding. New high levels of burials were recorded in Hatfield in 1592 and at Sheffield in 1597. A series of harvest failures weakened human resistance to another outbreak of plague in Richmondshire in 1597–98 and caused some people elsewhere to die of hunger. Deaths through starvation were recorded in Yorkshire as late as 1623 but the county did not fare as badly as Cumbria, Northumberland and upland parts of Lancashire. In 1622–23 the high cost of food and the depressed state of the woollen industry caused many deaths in Leeds and Halifax. The textile district suffered again in 1643 and 1645 but by the middle of the seventeenth century widespread starvation, like the plague, ceased to be a major worry.

Towns

The recovery of the national economy was marked by the revived export trade. By the middle of the sixteenth century Hull was exporting Yorkshire and Derbyshire lead to London and West Riding cloths and other goods to the Low Countries and, increasingly, to the Baltic ports. In the 20 years after 1565 the number of cheap northern kerseys sent from Hull to the Baltic rose six-fold, then doubled or trebled again to a peak in the mid 1590s. Ships returned across

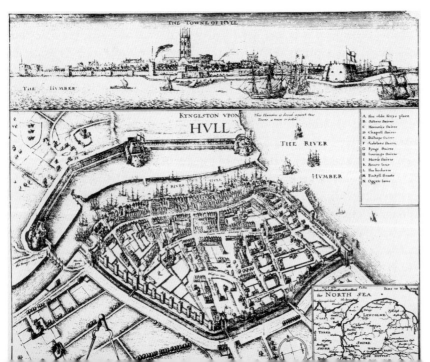

Wenceslaus Hollar's *View of Hull*, c.1640. The town of Kingston-upon-Hull was still contained within its fourteenth-century walls when this view was taken on the eve of the Civil War. Plenty of space was still available for development within the old confines, though by the end of the seventeenth century Hull was badly congested. New streets were not laid out beyond the walls until the later eighteenth century when the first docks were constructed.

Hollar's view shows ships anchored in the River Hull near its confluence with the Humber and several stairs leading down to the quayside. The planned layout of the medieval town is evident and the massive brick walls and towers are intact. Hull stood firm for the parliamentarian cause and famously refused to allow Charles I to enter in the summer of 1642. For a time it was the only place in Yorkshire not under Royalist control.

the North Sea ladened with flax for the linen weavers and corn from Poland. The port also supplied cheap, bulky goods to a large hinterland that was reached by the tributaries of the Ouse and the Trent and each year 50 or 60 small vessels sailed along the coast and up the Humber with a variety of goods, including coals from Newcastle.

York had lost forever its leading position as a manufacturer of woollen cloth, but by the 1580s the city's merchants and tradesmen were benefiting from the general revival of trade throughout western Europe and were actively engaged in the home and overseas markets. By the close of the sixteenth century York was England's third largest provincial city, with a population of 11,500. Young immigrants from Cumberland, Westmorland and the Yorkshire Dales came in search of work as tradesmen, craftsmen, shopkeepers and labourers. York was not only the most important seat of ecclesiastical and secular government in the North but still the largest social and commercial centre in Yorkshire. The freemen pewterers, silversmiths, builders and other tradesmen lived within the walls of the city but the wealthy, professional people mostly lived and worked in the liberties outside the corporation's jurisdiction, in and around the minster, the castle and the King's Manor.

York's markets flourished once more. The Tuesday, Thursday and Saturday markets brought local villagers into the city and the annual fairs attracted buyers and sellers from places many miles away. General markets were held in Pavement and the space known as the Thursday Market, the malt market was sited by St Martin's, Coney Street, and the leather sellers assembled in the Common Hall. Fish was sold on the two bridges over the Ouse, pigs were haggled over in Swinegate and on Peasholme Green and cattle were herded for sale on Toft Green. In 1546 a new cloth market was opened in the Common Hall and from 1590 a horse and cattle fair was held every fortnight between Lent and Advent. The purchasers of corn from the surrounding countryside and malt from as far as Pocklington and Barnby Dun (where no doubt it had come up river from Lincolnshire) included badgers who had travelled from Skipton and other places up to 30 or 40 miles to the west. The city's two major fairs had long been held at Whitsuntide and the feast of Sts Peter and Paul (29 June) but from 1586–87 the Whitsun fair expanded into the Thursday Market. Meanwhile, the older and more important Lammas fair of the Archbishop of York was held in Bootham. By a charter of Richard I the freemen of York were free from tolls throughout England, so by the 1560s York goldsmiths and drapers were attending the great Stourbridge fair outside Cambridge and by the end of the century Howden fair had become the regular business venue for the merchants of York and London. Though York was linked to the capital by a regular carrying service, river traffic remained more important than land carriage. Baltic iron, pitch, tar, linen, boards, wainscotting, salt, grain, oil, wine, sea fish and eels came up the Ouse to be distributed far and wide and the boats returned ladened with Richmondshire and Craven lead which had been weighed at the common crane in Skeldergate.

Bootham Bar, York, 1880s. Myles Birket Foster's painting shows the Minster dominating the city. Bootham Bar was one of the four entrances through the medieval walls. Until 1832 the Norman archway was entered through a barbican, like the one which survives at Walmgate Bar. In the left foreground is Queen Margaret's Arch of 1503, forming the north-eastern corner of the walls surrounding St Mary's Abbey.

Pontefract Old Hall. The hall was built for Edward Talbot, the younger son of George, sixth Earl of Shrewsbury, the year after his father's death. The central porch of the main front (to the right of the photograph) has a 1591 datestone. It was designed in similar style to Old Hardwick Hall, which Edward's stepmother, Bess, had started to build after her estrangement from her fourth and last husband. Like Old Hardwick, Pontefract Old Hall is a tall, compact, symmetrical building, with prominent towers, great mullioned windows and level parapets. Abandoned in the eighteenth century, it survived as a ruin until the 1960s.

Bawtry had lost its medieval borough status but began to thrive again with the recovery of trade. South Yorkshire metalware and Derbyshire lead and millstones were taken by catches and keels down the Idle to Stockwith, on the Trent, and groceries, continental steel for the cutlers, and London hides for the tanners were brought the other way. George, the sixth Earl of Shrewsbury, the largest lead smelter in the country, took a lease of Bawtry manor from the crown and by 1585 was exporting over 100 tons of lead per annum from his wharf and forcing everyone to weigh their lead at his beam and pay for storage and

below View of Hull, looking down the Humber, by Francis Place (1647–1728), showing Holy Trinity church rising above the medieval town walls.

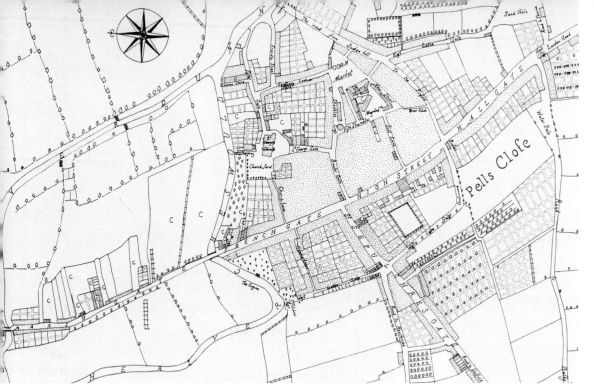

Map of Doncaster, 1767. The medieval plan of the borough was still evident on the ground in Georgian times. The River Cheswold (the old course of the Don before it was diverted to feed the town's mills) formed the boundary in the north (*left*) and the rest of the town was mostly confined by the earthen rampart and water-filled ditch that had been constructed by 1215. Doncaster never had town walls, but it was entered through four substantial stone gates at St Mary's Bridge, Gillot Bar (St Sepulchre Gate), Hall Gate (leading into High Street) and Sun Bar (into the market place). The ditch was filled up in 1734, but its line can still be followed.

St George's church stands on the site of the Roman fort and Norman castle. The original parish church was St Mary Magdalene's in the heart of the market place. The triangular shape of the market place can be seen on the map, though by 1767 it was congested with shops, stalls and shambles. It was sited conveniently close to the River Don, which was navigable up to this point for much of the year. The Great North Road formed the central street of the town, part of which bore the significant name, Frenchgate.

passage. Merchants prospered as the Derbyshire lead field became the most productive in Europe. In 1641, for instance, Stephen and John Bright of Sheffield shipped 2,416 pigs of lead from Bawtry to Hull or directly to Amsterdam. Their wealth enabled them to add a stone wing to the timber-framed Carbrook Hall and to make it the finest gentry house in Hallamshire.

Yorkshire's other market towns also prospered in the later Elizabethan period. Doncaster was not only a regional market centre, with two weekly markets and two annual fairs, but a river port and thoroughfare

Carbrook Hall, Sheffield, drawn by Edward Blore in 1819. The Bright family prospered from the lead trade and rose from yeomen to gentry status. In 1623 Stephen Bright added a stone wing to the medieval timber-framed house.

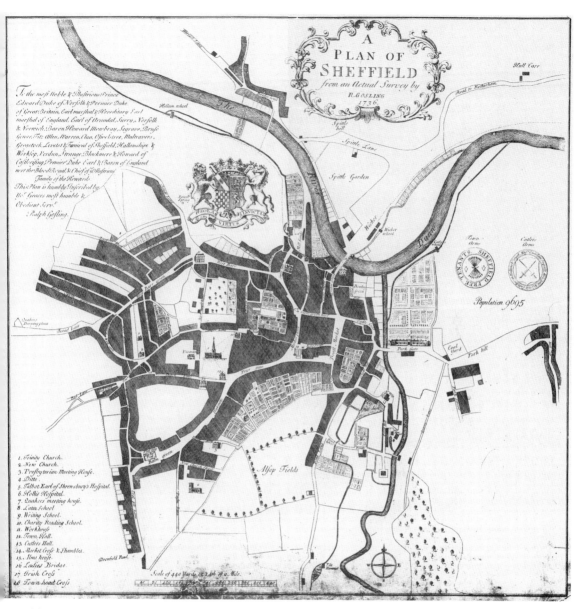

Ralph Gosling's map of Sheffield, 1736. Drawn by the master of the local Writing School, this is the earliest surviving map of Sheffield. It shows the town as it began to expand beyond its medieval limits, but still largely bounded by the rivers Don and Sheaf. The castle at the confluence of the rivers had long since gone, but the medieval market place still lay at the heart of the town. The long gardens to the south of Prior Gate (High Street) preserve the burgage plots of the leading inhabitants. The central street plan and names such as Fargate and West Bar are medieval in origin. In the east, the name of the new mining settlement at Park Hill commemorates the huge medieval deer park.

SHEFFIELD LIBRARIES, ARCHIVES AND INFORMATION; LOCAL STUDIES

town on the Great North Road. By the early seventeenth century trading activities had spilled over into the streets beyond the medieval market place. In 1605 the corporation agreed to hold the horse fair in Hallgate, between the pinfold and Hall cross, the beast fair in the market place, the sheep fair between the butchers' cross and the pinfold, and the swine fair in St Sepulchre Gate. Seven years later, the horse fair was removed to Waterdale, just outside the town.

Corn Exchange, Wakefield. The Corn Exchange in Westgate was erected in 1837 to the Grecian designs of a Doncaster architect, W. L. Moffat. Pevsner thought it was the best building in Wakefield. Fifteen years earlier, Baines' *Directory* had noted that 'Friday is the market day at Wakefield, and a great deal of business is done in corn and wool'. Fortnightly cattle markets added to Wakefield's reputation as a flourishing market town rather than a centre of woollen manufacture. The corn trade had been greatly improved by the Aire and Calder navigation.

BY COURTESY OF THE YORKSHIRE ARCHAEOLOGICAL SOCIETY

Within the old market place, part of it now encroached upon by shops in narrow streets such as Meal Lane and Roper Row, the butchers, fishmongers, drapers, shoemakers, and dealers in corn or wool sold their wares. Customers were attracted from both near and far by the corn and beast markets and sometimes a many as 6,000 fleeces were sold in the wool market each Saturday during the summer, principally to the West Riding clothiers. Doncaster had a guild of weavers, walkers and shearmen, another guild of linen drapers, dyers and upholsterers, and numerous poor stocking knitters. For much of the year the market place could be approached by river as well as by road and many people made a good living as middlemen or inn-keepers. In 1631 the town had no fewer than 135 alehouse keepers.

Meanwhile, Pontefract had gained a reputation for an unusual product: the growing of liquorice on the banks below the castle walls. George, the sixth Earl of Shrewsbury, may have been the man who introduced the crop here in the 1560s and on another of his estates at Worksop, for he was one of the 'Commonwealth' men at the heart of government who were concerned to stimulate industries. In 1638 *Barnabees Journal* claimed that 'the choicest Licorice' was found in Pontefract: 'Here Liquorice grows upon their mellowed banks, Decking the Spring with her delicious plants'. The crop needed plenty of dung, and as it took three summers for the roots to grow to a satisfactory size, vegetables such as onions and lettuce were cultivated on the same plots in the meantime. When Celia Fiennes visited Pontefract at the end of the seventeenth century she saw gardens full of liquorice.

Some West Riding market towns had acquired a decidedly industrial character. During Elizabeth's reign Sheffield became the leading provincial centre for the manufacture of cutlery as it captured the cheap end of the national market. London remained pre-eminent in the trade but Hallamshire saw off rivals such as Salisbury and Thaxted. The Earls of Shrewsbury took an active interest and the fast-flowing Pennine streams and local sandstone quarries gave Sheffield a competitive edge in grinding. After the death of Gilbert, the seventh Earl of Shrewsbury, in 1616 the cutlers had to fend for themselves but in 1624 they were strong enough to obtain an Act of Parliament incorporating them as the Company of Cutlers in Hallamshire. In the year of his death, Gilbert ordered a survey of Sheffield before endowing a hospital for 20 poor persons. The survey found that in the central, urban township 725, or about a third of the 2,207 inhabitants, were 'not able to live without the charity of their neighbours'. A further 160 householders did not contribute towards the poor rates, for they were 'not able to abide the storm of one fortnight's sickness, but would be thereby driven to beggary'. Only 100 householders paid for the relief of the poor and even they were 'but poor artificers; among them is not one which can keep a team on his own land, and not above ten who have grounds of their own that will keep a cow'. The greater part of the workmen and their children were 'constrained to work sore, to provide them necessaries'. Some allowance has to be made for special pleading and perhaps for the harsh winter of 1615–16 when this report was drawn up, but no doubt most of Yorkshire's other towns could have told a similar tale at that time. The growth of the cutlery industry was Sheffield's salvation. By the middle of the seventeenth century well over half the workforce were directly involved in the manufacture of knives and scissors and some of the surrounding rural communities were specialising in such products as scythes or sickles.

Leeds set the pace for Yorkshire's towns. The population of the parish had doubled to 6,000 by the reign of James I and most of the growth had been in the central urban township. When the whole of the parish was incorporated in 1626 the timber-framed houses of the town were still packed tightly in the medieval streets around the market place. The market flourished but Leeds was becoming known as the place where broad cloths were expertly finished by dressers, croppers and dyers. Among the manufacturers who provided work for craftsmen and labourers was John Harrison, who equipped Leeds with St John's church, a grammar school, an almshouse and a street of buildings. Leeds was the West Riding's chief cloth market, Wakefield the principal weekly market for wool; in 1628 it was claimed that Wakefield was the greatest market and principal place of resort of all sorts of clothiers, drapers, and other dealers. Wool was also bought at the great fairs of Doncaster, Pontefract and Ripon or directly from the sheep masters. In 1615 it was claimed that the West Riding clothiers bought wool as far afield as Lincolnshire, Leicestershire, Rutland, Warwickshire, Oxfordshire and Buckinghamshire. The wool drivers and chapmen also carried the finished pieces of cloth to Hull to be exported overseas or made regular journeys to London to the weekly market at Blackwell

Even those who did pay poor rates were 'but poor artificers; among them is not one which can keep a team on his own land, and not above ten who have grounds of their own that will keep a cow'

SURVEY OF SHEFFIELD, 1616

Hall and to the great annual cloth fair near Smithfield. A report of 1595 noted that at Wakefield, Leeds, and some of the nearby villages, about 120 pieces of coloured broad cloth were made every week.

But the wonder of the age was Halifax, where a market town with a cloth hall and wool shops had grown up the slope from the medieval parish church. By 1560 the town contained 520 houses and the surrounding rural population was expanding in an equally remarkable way. 'There is nothing so admirable in this town', declared William Camden, the great Elizabethan antiquary, 'as the industry of the inhabitants, who, notwithstanding an unprofitable soil, not fit to live in, have so flourished by the cloth trade (which within these last seventy years they fell to), that they are both very rich, and have gained a great reputation for it above their neighbours'. Other commentators also praised the local clothiers' willingness to respond to changing fashions. The narrow kerseys of Halifax parish and the broad cloths that were made further east were made into cheap garments. Like the Hallamshire cutlers, the West Riding clothiers first catered for the bottom end of the market before they turned to the manufacture of better-quality goods. Both had the inestimable advantage of water power for an essential process. At the edges of the textile district even cheaper cloths such as Penistones and Keighley whites were offered for sale in Blackwell Hall by the beginning of Elizabeth's reign. In the countryside most families aimed to produce one piece of cloth per week, with the children and women preparing and spinning the yarn and the men doing the weaving. Little capital was needed to start up in the trade, which could easily be combined with farming a smallholding. Fulling mills were erected in the river valleys by local gentry families, who were quick to exploit any opportunity to increase their wealth through industrial and agricultural improvements, and the skilled processes of dressing and dyeing were performed in the towns. Elizabethan observers found the growth of industry and population on and just off the Pennines a matter of wonder and inspiration, but though the West Riding cloth trade was a great success story it was not one of uninterrupted progress. During the second decade of the seventeenth century, for instance, many complaints of bad trade were heard and in the winter of 1622 a list of poor people in the parish of Huddersfield numbered 700, including 419 children. But on the whole clothmaking provided steady employment for numerous townsmen, small-holders and cottagers and enabled fullers and middlemen to prosper.

> 'There is nothing so admirable in this town as the industry of the inhabitants [of Halifax], who ... have so flourished by the cloth trade ... that they are both very rich, and have gained a great reputation for it above their neighbours.'
>
> WILLIAM CAMDEN

The countryside

Most Yorkshire people had no crafts and earned their living purely through agriculture. Their way of life and their farming practices depended on the nature of their environment. In Holderness most townships still had two enormous common fields that stretched for hundreds of acres over the boulder clays, but in some places the farmers had agreed to convert these fields into private enclosures or had turned some of the arable lands into grass leys. Before

Brandesburton was enclosed in 1630 the East Field covered 1,174 acres and the West Field 1,321 acres and each year one was allowed to lie fallow. Patrington had large open fields, meadows and saltmarsh pastures, but in 1649 a jury at Hornsea found that in the previous 100 years the sea had washed away 38 houses and their closes and had eroded a mile-long and 240 yards-broad stretch of a common field. Effective drainage schemes enabled Holderness to prosper as a corn-and-cattle district. Wheat and barley surpluses were sold in the East Riding market towns or exported from Hull and Bridlington and livestock grazed in the pastures, carrs and meadows in summer time and were fed on hay, beans and peas in winter. The available technology was inadequate when faced with the regular flooding of the Hull valley; in 1657 much of the ground in Flaxfleet and South Cave was said to be overrun with rushes, sedge and coarse grass 'for want of scouring the drains'. Here, improvement still lay a long way ahead.

The low-lying townships in the eastern and southern parts of the Vale of York were also badly drained and meadows, pastures and large common wastes covered far more ground than the communal arable fields on the drier lands around the villages. Most farms were small, so generous common rights were essential and fishing, fowling and the digging of turf for winter fuel were necessary by-employments. In summer time the marshlands of the Humberhead Levels offered good grazing and valuable layers of turf. By far the most ambitious drainage scheme was that attempted on Hatfield Chase in the late 1620s, when Charles I offered a Dutch and Flemish company organised by Cornelius Vermuyden a third of the reclaimed lands and the chance to buy the crown's share; the remaining third was divided amongst the local inhabitants in compensation for their loss of common rights. Vermuyden blocked the meandering southern branch of the Don and diverted the whole river into the straight channel that had been cut from the northern branch at some unknown date by the early Middle Ages, but in so doing he flooded lands in Fishlake and Sykehouse that had not previously been at risk. In 1630 Richard Bridges of Sykehouse wrote as 'a woeful spectator of the lamentable destruction of my native soil and country'. The drainers were assaulted and a few were killed before the problem was solved. The scheme brought about the decay of Tudworth on the disused southern branch of the Don, but it benefited the small river port and market town of Thorne and the Flemish settlers in Hatfield Levels. It did not transform the local economy, for the villagers continued to farm their lands in the old manner and the wettest tracts could not be drained effectively until steam engines were employed in the nineteenth century.

On the Low Wolds huge common arable fields sometimes stretched to the parish boundaries. Even the steep slopes of dry valleys and escarpments had been brought under the plough by flights of lynchets. The farmers of the neighbouring townships of Fimber, Fridaythorpe and Wetwang concentrated almost entirely on cereals and the deserted medieval village of Holme Archiepiscopi had been absorbed into the Wetwang common fields. At Flamborough the corn-

growing land was divided into four fields and the 'ancient custom' was for only one of them to lie fallow. Even some of the thin soils on the bleak tops of the High Wolds were tilled from time to time; in 1611 the infield at Bishop Wilton was worked on a two- or three-year rotation and was valued at more than three times the outfield on the chalk scarp. Most of the High Wolds, however, was fit only for sheepwalks and rabbit warrens. On the lower levels farmers concentrated on sheep and barley and to a lesser extent on cattle and wheat. Each night sheep were brought down from the hills and put within folds to manure the fallow cornfields. Deserted village sites became vast sheep runs; for example, in 1540 John Constable kept a flock of 400 sheep in the former common arable fields of Caythorpe and three years later John Thorpe pastured 460 ewes, 300 wethers and 360 hogs at Wharram Percy. In other parishes, such as Sewerby, the common arable fields were converted to pasture after enclosure. Elsewhere, as at Thwing, grass leys were intermingled with the arable strips throughout the common fields or, as at Settrington, the meadows and pastures were enclosed by agreement but the common arable fields remained intact until the age of parliamentary enclosure.

Many Wolds parishes were dominated by a squire such as Henry Best, whose house still stands at Elmswell, near Driffield. In 1641 Best drew on a lifetime's experience to write an unusually detailed account of his farming practices, particularly those regarding sheep. He tried new ideas to improve his crops and livestock and saw the benefits of enclosure which enabled him to charge his tenants three times the previous rents. He usually sold his wool to buyers who made regular visits to his home between clipping time and Michaelmas, but sometimes his men carried it to the fairs at Beverley, Halifax and Wakefield. He sold his cereals at Beverley, Malton and Pocklington or to the ship masters at Bridlington quay and rarely sent fewer than eight horse loads to market at a time, with two men to guide them. He knew where to get the highest prices for his goods and how best to use the East Riding markets and fairs. He bought seed peas at

Bridlington Quay. Bridlington was originally two settlements; the Old Town around the Augustinian priory, a mile inland, and the Quay, where the Gypsey Race flows into the bay sheltered by Flamborough Head. In stormy conditions sailing ships and fleets of colliers sought a haven here. A fishing industry developed after the coming of the railway. In this view some visitors to the new seaside resort brave the elements by strolling along the north pier, which was designed to protect the harbour.

Aerial view of Rosedale Abbey. This small settlement grew up around the Cistercian nunnery which was founded here in 1158 and dissolved in 1535. The fields in the valley bottom were cleared in the Middle Ages, but the valley slopes and the moors above were used for grazing sheep and cattle. It is now surprising to find that the dale was once the home to various industries. Rosedale had a late sixteenth-century glassworks and the mining of ironstone and coal was developed from small beginnings into considerable enterprises. As these industries came to an end, so the population fell dramatically. In the whole of the dale it dropped from 1,396 in 1901 to just 273 in 1981, thereby creating the peaceful surroundings of today.

Driffield or Kilham, butter at Beverley, Malton or Frodingham, and more unusual items at Beverley. He knew that on calm Tuesdays and Fridays Lincolnshiremen would cross the Humber to Hull in search of oatmeal. Corn from Norfolk or abroad came up the Humber and strong Holland cloth was sold to linen drapers and by them to country pedlars. Best himself occasionally sold yarn to the weavers of Malton. His other contact with the North Riding was through the itinerant 'moor-folk' who came to work for him at harvest time.

Linen weaving helped to raise the incomes of the farming families of the North York Moors who otherwise pursued their traditional way of life. In 1649 the manor of Rosedale was said to consist of huge common wastes and turbaries and small enclosures on very bad ground. The small amount of wood within the manor was mostly old rotten trees and underwood fit only for the fire. In the Vale of Pickering much of the corn-growing land had been converted to pasture and the characteristic holding was a small dairy farm. Further west, the Forest of Galtres ceased to be subject to forest law in the reign of Charles I and even the landless cottagers were granted four acres of good land in the share-out. In villages such as Huby and Easingwold the allotments were increased to six or seven acres 'in pity and commisseration'.

By the middle of the seventeenth century about 70 per cent of the townships in the northern Vale of York and the Vale of Mowbray had been fully enclosed and the communities that kept their common fields intact provided extra grazing by turning arable strips into grass leys. The township meadows, which had often been divided annually by lot, were usually the first to be fenced into closes. The arable fields at Aldborough were partly enclosed in 1628, Healaugh's three fields were wholly enclosed within the next eight years, and 1,500 acres of commons and fields at Sutton-on-the-Forest were enclosed by the agreement of 26 farmers in the mid 1650s. The present pattern of long, narrow closes at Allerthorpe, some of which have the classic reversed-S shape of medieval strips and furlongs, dates from a farmers' agreement of 1640. Generally speaking, cereals and livestock were of equal importance in these northern vales, but the nature of the soils created much local diversity. The townships around Ripon, for example, had already acquired a national reputation for rearing fine horses and colts.

The fertile lands of the magnesian limestone district saw the same trend towards enclosure for pasture and the conversion of strips to grass leys. Villages such as Frickley and Wildthorpe that had decayed in the late Middle Ages now disappeared off the map and other settlements were turned into small estate villages. A few parishes went against the general trend; for example, at Loversall in the 1630s the lord's demesne lands were said to be 'of great tillage' and the decayed market centre of Braithwell still had enough freeholders to work the common arable fields. Elsewhere, however, open fields were divided up long before the age of parliamentary enclosure and restrictions had to be placed on the number of animals each farmer could graze on the common pastures. Hooton Pagnell had such an agreement by 1570 and the best pastures at Braithwell were stinted by 1652.

In the Dales the common arable fields had virtually disappeared by the end of Elizabeth's reign, except in the lower reaches, and much of the best meadow and pasture land had been divided into small closes. A little oats and barley (known by the northern names of haver and bigg) and some winter-sown wheat and rye (or a mixture known as maslin) were grown, but the typical Dales farmer with 15–20 customary acres and generous common rights spent most of his time with his cattle and sheep. Oxen were used for ploughing and horses for riding and pulling sleds, wains and carts (with iron-bound wheels). Grazing rights were vital to each family's livelihood and though the moor edges had been nibbled away by intakes enormous common pastures remained. The roughest grazing was left to the sheep, but better-quality cow pastures were carefully controlled and stinted. In winter time the cattle were fed on hay in the lower closes and sheep were allowed to wander down from the moors to the better pastures; when snow lay deep on the ground the sheep were fed on holly. Gentry families kept flocks of over a thousand sheep. In 1567 Thomas Rokeby of Mortham had nearly 1,200 sheep on the fells, in 1579 Sir William Ingleby of Ripley's flock numbered 1,465, and in 1617 Sir Henry Bellasis of Newburgh Priory kept about 1,700. When Charles Dransfield, esquire, of Garrestone in Hauxwell died in 1552 he had nearly 1,000 sheep, 258 cattle (of which 201 were dairy cows and their young) and 51 horses. At certain times of the year great herds of beasts driven by Scottish drovers fed on the roadside pastures on their way to lowland grazing grounds near the market towns.

In an inflationary age the men who had bought the great monastic estates in the Dales were keen to make as much profit as they could from their tenants by raising rents and entry fines. As the owner of the lordship of Richmond, the Forest of Knaresborough and other properties the crown too was involved in a protracted struggle with its tenants. The crucial questions that were brought before the law courts were whether the tenants enjoyed security of tenure for life and the right of their heirs to inherit, whether rents or entry fines were fixed or variable, and whether a tenant could sell or sub-let his

The Wensleydale Knitters.
Stocking knitting was one
of the most successful
projects of the Elizabethan
Age. By the 1590s
Richmond, Barnard
Castle, Askrigg and
Doncaster were
recognised centres of the
craft. When George
Walker produced his
Costume of Yorkshire in
1814 families in the Dales
still used every spare
moment to earn extra
income by knitting. He
wrote: 'Simplicity and
industry characterise the
manners and occupations
of the various humble
inhabitants of Wensley
Dale. Their wants, it is
true, are few; but to
supply these almost
constant labour is
required. In any business
where the assistance of the
hands is not necessary,
they universally resort to
knitting. Young and old,
male and female, are all
adepts in this art.
Shepherds attending their
flocks, men driving cattle,
women going to market,
are all thus industriously
and doubly employed.'

The landscape near
Gunnerside, Swaledale.
Gunnerside, anciently
Gunnersett, was originally
Gunnar's *saetr* or summer
pasture. This classic Dales
landscape of drystone
walls and field barns once
formed part of a medieval
park. The township's
former common pastures
rise above the valley
bottom.

PHOTOGRAPH: CARNEGIE, 2005

holding. In 1562 the customary tenants of the Forest of Knaresborough won complete security of tenure and inheritance. Nine years later, customary tenure was abolished in the lordship of Richmond in exchange for 40-year leases. On the former Fountains estates tenants were forced into paying higher rents and by the end of the sixteenth century the crown had successfully converted the manor of Grinton to 21-year leases. The introduction of leases on some manors meant that the widespread system of sharing a father's property between all his sons was replaced by one that favoured the eldest.

The growing population needed extra land and space for housing. During Elizabeth's reign the court of the Forest of Knaresborough repeatedly issued warnings against illegal encroachments and unauthorised cottages. In 1563, for example, Brian Lawson was fined 15 shillings for claiming common rights of pasture and turbary around his newly erected cottage at Menwith Hill. But this may simply have been a roundabout way of getting money in lieu of rent. After 1595 small intakes that were admitted in the lord's court were allowed upon payment of an entry fine and a yearly rent. In 1651 a survey listed 159 cottages in the forest. Elsewhere, the rising population was accommodated by sub-dividing houses and by converting outbuildings. The poorest families had to make do with just one room.

The Dales cottagers and farmers earned extra income from various textile crafts. Lists of the personal estate of 207 Nidderdale people who died between 1551 and 1610 included 86 which recorded wool, yarn, spinning wheels, looms or tenters. The smallholdings of the farmer-weavers were similar in size to those who relied solely on agriculture. By the end of the sixteenth century weaving was a widespread craft in Nidderdale and linen was beginning to overtake woollen cloth as the main product. Most Swaledale inventories record small quantities of wool, some of it dyed, carded and spun locally and much of it used in the knitting industry that had been established around Richmond as one of the Elizabethan government's projects to foster rural industries. Richmond hosiers provided the raw materials, collected finished stockings from Swaledale, Teesdale and Wensleydale and saw to their export to London and Holland. By 1644 over 2,000 dozen pairs per annum were being shipped from Stockton-on-Tees. Each member of a Dales family did a share of the knitting to meet the normal target of three dozen pairs a week. In 1634 an enquiry held in Dentdale and Garsdale was told that the farms were 'so small in quantity that many of them are not above three or four acres apiece, and generally not above eight or nine acres so that they could not maintain their families were it not by their industry in knitting coarse stockings'. Four years later, Richard Brathwait's comment on Askrigg in *Barnabees Journal* was 'Here poor people live by knitting'.

The other alternative source of income in the Dales was, of course, lead. On his visit to Grinton Leland had found that the market for corn and linen cloth was much used by the Swaledale lead miners. The typical enterprise remained a small partnership between miner-farmers who worked the lead rakes above the water table on the commons, but in the early seventeenth century John Sayer of Great Worsall sunk and drained the Marrick mines in Swaledale and Sir Stephen Proctor of Fountains Hall smelted the lead from the Greenhow field and allowed his workers to erect cottages haphazardly on Greenhow Hill and to create smallholdings from the wastes. This new community lived at a much higher altitude than the earlier miners, at about 1,250–1,300 feet above sea level alongside the road from Pateley Bridge to Grassington. Gentry families such as the Proctors made substantial profits from investing in smelting. In 1565 William Humphray had introduced a water-powered bellows and a shaft furnace for smelting in Derbyshire. His method replaced the medieval bole hills on the windswept gritstone edges of the Peak District and soon spread into the northern lead fields. The lonely ruins of abandoned smelt mills remain a characteristic feature of the Swaledale landscape.

The decline of the great medieval lordships and the break-up of the monastic estates also affected the lives of moorland farmers further south. James I tried to raise ready money by offering the tenants of Wakefield manor the chance to become freeholders. A series of enquiries between 1604 and 1608 showed how tenures varied from township to township. The small size of many of the Pennine farms came about not only from piecemeal intaking of new land but through inheritance customs. In the upper Calder Valley the usual practice was to divide farms between the sons and to give daughters a lump sum or an annuity. Many of the smallest farms were rented by subtenants. Smallholders were dependent on their common rights to pasture animals on the wastes and had to seek extra income from weaving. In Scammonden the court rolls record the occasional sub-division of the medieval farms and the increasing tendency for men to be described as clothier rather than husbandman. By 1607 the 11 original farms that had been created in the first half of the fourteenth century supported 24 houses or cottages.

Many of the Pennine townfields were enclosed privately by numerous separate agreements and converted into permanent or temporary pastures. Enclosure was often a long-drawn out process. At Heptonstall, for example, the South Field was enclosed gradually in the sixteenth century but the North Field remained open until 1783. In many cases, groups of strips were not rearranged into closes but were fossilised in the landscape by the building of drystone walls around their boundaries. In 1633 two JPs from Agbrigg and Morley wapentakes reported that 'generally where enclosures are made with us houses are erected upon them'.

On the coal-measure sandstones the common fields of townships such as Shafton and Worsbrough were enclosed by agreement, but other places retained their arable strips until the era of parliamentary enclosure. In 1613 Wath-upon-Dearne had three fields known as Over Field, Sandygate Field and Brampton Sike Field, which were separated from Wath Wood by a new ditch two yards broad and 2½ yards deep. In 1649 Barnsley had a large common pasture or waste and four open fields, which were grazed in common, without restriction, after harvest. Elsewhere, the grazing rights on the best common pastures were stinted; in 1637, for instance, the manor court of Barwick-in-Elmet ordered that no-one should put more animals on the commons in summer time than they could keep in winter. A ruthless landlord could enforce enclosure of the best pastures if it suited him. In the 1630s, for example, Sir Francis Foljambe enclosed three-quarters of the common between Rawmarsh and Kilnhurst, threatening to ruin opponents by costly litigation. But many West Riding manors still provided a framework for the farming year based on church festivals; thus in 1574 the jurors of the manor court of Greasbrough and Barbot Hall ordered that swine should be ringed from the feast of St Bartholomew until the feast of the Purification of the Blessed Virgin Mary and yoked from Candlemas until harvest was over. Such by-laws were the sensible, practical decisions of experienced farmers who were concerned with the day-to-day arrangements of communal agriculture. The Greasbrough jurors ordered the fencing of the corn fields to keep out the livestock and forbade the ploughing of common headlands and balks, the grazing of cattle in the common meadows, the felling of timber and holly (for their leaves and bark provided winter fodder) and the putting of diseased animals on the common pastures.

Industry

During the sixteenth and seventeenth centuries the character and economy of many of West Riding settlements became markedly different from the towns and villages in other parts of Yorkshire. Communities that had once been the smallest and poorest were now the most thriving. Though the inhabitants of the eastern townships of the West Riding remained dependent entirely on farming, in the west smallholders commonly had a dual occupation. Weaver-farmers, metalworker-farmers, collier-farmers, tanners, leather workers, charcoal burners and other craftsmen were found in growing numbers in villages, hamlets and isolated farmsteads and cottages on the coal-measure sandstones and the Pennine fringes, where they were free from tight manorial control and regulation. Immigrants and innovators found few barriers in such open communities as these, where an insufficient livelihood could be gained by agriculture alone, but where industrial wealth increased the incomes of all classes of society.

The new stocking-knitting industry that had taken off in such a big way around Richmond and Doncaster was just one of the projects inspired by the 'Commonwealth men' at the centre of government, whose aim was to make England much less dependent upon foreign exports. New crafts were intro-duced into places with little or no previous expertise and established industries were changed by new techniques and ideas that were often brought in from abroad. Another successful Yorkshire project began in 1611 with the opening of alum works on the cliffs of the North Sea coast at Mulgrave, Asholme and Sandsend; within half a century alum was sold not only to English dyers and tanners but to the continent of Europe, the East Indies and the New World. Another successful project was pin-making; Leland had found 'many pinners' at Sherburn-in-Elmet in the 1540s and a century later Richard Brathwait's *Barnabees Journal* reads, 'Thence to Sherburne, dearley loved / And for Pinners well approved'. Barnabee moved on to Aberford, 'whose beginning came from buying drink with pinning', but he observed, 'Poor they are, and very needy / Yet of liquor too too greedy'.

In south-west Yorkshire the Tankersley seam of ironstone was mined in shallow bell-pits and for much of the sixteenth century the ore was smelted in large working units known as bloomeries or smithies. One of the few sites to have been excavated is that at Rockley, where three water wheels, a bloom hearth, a string hearth, a reheating hearth and a possible fourth hearth of unknown purpose were worked from about 1500 to 1640. The revolutionary

Wortley Top Forge. According to a datestone, this water-powered forge on a bend in the River Don was rebuilt in 1713. It occupies a site which had been used as a bloomery from at least 1600 and as a forge from 1638. It formed part of a partnership led by the Spencer family of Cannon Hall, Cawthorne, who dominated the South Yorkshire iron industry in the charcoal era. It was adapted to new processes in the eighteenth and nineteenth centuries and worked until 1912. It is being restored by volunteers and has open days for visitors.
AUTHOR COLLECTION

Shepherd Wheel on the Porter Brook is the best-preserved of Sheffield's numerous former cutlery grinding wheels and is now a museum. The site has been used since Elizabethan times. The present buildings date from the late eighteenth century, when a Mr Shepherd was tenant. In 1794 they housed ten grinders' troughs.
PHOTOGRAPH: CARNEGIE, 2004

new technique of the charcoal blast furnace was introduced into the Sussex Weald by ironworkers from Lorraine in the reign of Henry VIII. Whereas the old bloomeries produced 20–30 tons each year, the new furnaces could cast up to 200 tons per annum to be reworked at a forge into 130–150 tons of bar iron. During the winter of 1573–74 charcoal blast furnaces were constructed on the Earl of Shrewsbury's South Yorkshire estates at Kimberworth and Wadsley and associated forges were built on the Don at Attercliffe, with the aid of 20–30 workmen descended from the French immigrants who had settled in the Weald. Men with strange names, such as Vintin, Perigoe, Dippray, Maryon and Valliance, appear in local records about this time. The new technology soon spread into many parts of the West Riding coalfield. Wire mills and slitting mills were built near some of the forges to supply wire drawers and nailers, but for a time old bloomeries continued to make bar and rod iron by traditional methods. After the death of Gilbert Talbot in 1616 the Shrewsbury furnaces and forges, charcoal woods, and ironstone and coal pits were leased by Lionel Copley of Rotherham and Wadworth. By the mid seventeenth century the average output for Copley's improved furnaces was about 400 tons of pig iron per annum. The Copleys and other gentry families controlled the iron trade until new men began to challenge them in the middle years of the eighteenth century.

Local iron was of sufficient quality for blacksmiths, founders, nailers and wire drawers but it could not produce the sharp edges that were needed for knives and tools. In 1614 the Sheffield manor court insisted that steel should be used for all cutting edges – steel which had to be imported from the continent. In 1574 the bailiff of Hallamshire noted the safe arrival of six barrels of Spanish steel from Bawtry; other records show that steel also came via the Rhine or the Baltic Sea. The first mention of a steelworks in South Yorkshire comes from a letter of Charles Tooker of Rotherham, written in 1642, in which he complained that his furnace had been destroyed by Parliamentarian troops. The Hallamshire cutlery industry flourished not only in Sheffield but in the rural townships, especially Attercliffe. In 1637 a survey of the manor claimed that 400–500 members of the Cutlers' Company used the lord's grinding wheels on a regular basis. By 1660 at least 49 sites on the Don, Sheaf, Porter, Loxley and Rivelin, and others on the Blackburn Brook and Moss Beck, were used for grinding cutlery, milling corn, smelting lead and other industrial purposes; two out of every three of these water wheels were geared to the grinding of cutlery and edge-tools.

As the population grew, so did the demand for fuel in the form of coal or turf. In York it was said in 1597 that turves were 'now the greatest part of our fuel'. They were brought up the Ouse from Thorne and the other villages around Inclesmoor, as were coals from Newcastle. Coal was also brought by wains from West Riding mines, whose output increased during the last quarter of the sixteenth century, but the Yorkshire coalfield was too landlocked to compete with Northumberland and Durham in national markets. Punchwood for pit props was supplied from local coppice woods; in 1642 a survey of

Sheffield manor noted that Burngreave was 'now felling for punch wood' and that within the previous three years Wilkinson Spring and Cook Wood had been cut for similar and other purposes. Some Sheffield woods had not been cut for over 30 years and the whole of the 371-acre Greno Wood had been felled in one operation. The main buyers of underwood were local ironmasters who needed charcoal. In 1637 Sheffield manor contained an estimated 2,000 acres of wood and timber (not including the trees in Sheffield Park), comprising 1,600 acres of spring woods and a great store of old trees that were fit for no other purpose than the making of charcoal. The surveyor also noted the 'very stately' timber belonging to the lord, especially in Haw Park, where it grew tall and straight; strangers had commented that they had not seen such timber on their travels through Christendom. Woods were felled on rotation in the old manner where a charcoal ironworks was no more than 20 miles away, but in more distant parts woodland management was not as profitable. When nearly 1,600 trees were felled at Settrington, on the Wolds escarpment, in the 1590s it was proposed that the former 'haggs and springs' should be converted to pasture. At Holme-upon-Spalding Moor the 80 acres of woods that were recorded in 1586 had been turned into arable and pasture land by 1620.

The tanners had a keen interest in woods for they needed a regular supply of oak bark. In the towns the tanneries were placed on the outskirts – in Fishergate in Doncaster and by the Ponds in Sheffield, for instance – because of their offensive smell and the flies that they attracted, but tan pits were also found in the countryside. Leather was used for making garments and footwear, harness, horse collars, saddles, straps, bags and bottles, and in Hallamshire for bellows, grinders' belting and sheaths for knives. By the late 1620s West Riding tanners were importing about 4,000 hides a year from London as back-carriage on boats that sailed up the Humber and the navigable rivers. When Thomas Pickles, a Kirkheaton tanner, died in the 1640s, he owned £16 worth of tanned leather, £20 worth of bark, the hides of 20 country steers and of 50 cows valued at £50, 2,240 hides bought at London for £220, and another 120 hides bought at London for £150 but 'not yet at Hull'.

The substantial growth of all these trades meant that many more horses and vehicles used the roads. In 1555 the government had ordered a new system of maintenance and repair based on parishes or townships and supervised by the JPs at the quarter sessions. Every able-bodied householder was made to work four (later, six) days a year on the roads and unpaid parish overseers of the highways were elected each year with power to raise money from local taxes. The 'most considerable bridges' were paid for out of county rates. Traffic headed to and from the industrial sites, the market towns and the inland ports, for water transport was much cheaper than land transport for heavy, bulky goods. By late Elizabethan times the towns of Yorkshire were connected to London by regular carrier services. In 1588 Doncaster corporation employed three men to run a postal service to and from the capital and in 1617 that the highway from Rotherham to Mansfield via Mile Oaks and Whiston was said to be the London way for carriers. Twenty years later, a London publication, John Taylor's *Carriers' Cosmographie*, showed that all parts of England were connected to the capital city by weekly carrying services. The growth of internal trade also meant more inns and alehouses; a national census of inns taken in 1577 recorded 239 inns and nearly 3,700 alehouses in Yorkshire. Most of the inns were in the market towns but the JPs struggled to regulate the number of alehouses by a licensing system. Trying to prevent the spread of plague in 1638, they stopped people selling ale and beer on the Great North Road between Doncaster and Wentbridge who, they claimed, 'entertain and discourse with all manner of passengers and travellers, wanderers and idle beggars'. In the summer months a great deal of traffic was to be seen on the highways and, on the whole, the parish repair system worked reasonably well.

Houses

The Elizabethan Great Chamber at Gilling Castle was designed by Barnard Dinninghof for Sir William Fairfax as a withdrawing room on the principal upper floor. Here in the corner of the plaster frieze we see three male and three female musicians, suggesting one of the pleasant uses to which the room was put.

York was beginning to recover from the prolonged recession of the late Middle Ages. It remained the political, judicial and ecclesiastical capital of the North and now it was the seat of the Council of the North. Successive presidents of the Council took over the late fifteenth-century house of the abbot of St Mary and gradually converted it into the King's Manor. In the 1560s and 1570s the house was turned to face the minster and the Huntingdon room was completed with a plaster frieze and a striking fireplace. In 1565–68 Sir Thomas Eynns, the secretary of the Council, built Heslington Hall in brick in the new symmetrical style with a classical doorway, dormer gables and large mullioned and transomed windows. The hall was built to traditional proportions but decorated with Renaissance plaster work. When Thomas Cecil, son of the great Lord

The King's Manor, York. Upon the dissolution of St Mary's Abbey, the abbot's house became the seat of the King's Council in Northern Parts. The house was extensively altered in the 1560s and given a new front facing Bootham Bar and the Minster. During further extensions early in the reign of Charles I under the president of the council, Sir Thomas Wentworth, Earl of Strafford, the royal coat of arms was displayed above the main door.
PHOTOGRAPH: CARNEGIE, 2005

Burghley, rebuilt Snape Castle in 1587 he gave it four sturdy corner towers like those of the 200-year old Bolton Castle further up the dale. Towers no longer had a military purpose, but they provided comforting feelings of authority and security. The striking grid patterns of the glittering windows of the Tudor Gothic style were concerned more with display than defence. Burton Constable Hall, in Holderness, built for Sir John Constable or his son Sir Henry in Elizabeth's reign, has battlemented towers and large, regularly spaced windows. So did Howley Hall, a grand Elizabethan building now demolished that Sir Robert Savile and his son John built in the heart of the West Riding in the 1580s.

The symmetrical façades disguised the traditional arrangement of the interiors around a large central hall that was open to the rafters. A through passage, dividing the hall from the service rooms and lesser chambers, passed behind a screen which helped to keep out draughts and kitchen smells. The carved oak and plaster screen, replete with symbolism below the musicians' gallery at Burton Agnes, is particularly eye-catching. Behind the dais end of a hall were the parlours and the principal private room known as the great chamber and in the most ambitious 'prodigy' houses a long gallery stretched all way along the upper floor. The great chamber which Barnard Dinninghof, the German glass painter, designed for Sir William Fairfax at Gilling Castle in the 1570s as a showpiece of

Burton Constable Hall, Holderness. The Elizabethan home of the Constable family was built, with stone dressings, by either Sir John or his son, Sir Henry. The projecting wings of 1600–10 partly hide the embattled corner towers, and the turret with the flag was one of a pair with an ogee cap. In 1759–60 the house was heightened by the addition of a top storey and the huge coat of arms under a pediment was placed over the central doorway that had replaced the original entrance through a screens passage. The Elizabethan mullioned and transomed windows were retained, however. The grounds were landscaped by 'Capability' Brown in the mid eighteenth century.
PHOTOGRAPH: CARNEGIE, 2005

Thorpe Salvin Hall. Hercy Sandford, the last of a long line of local gentry, built an impressive manor house near Yorkshire's southern border in the middle years of Queen Elizabeth's reign. He died in 1582. It was one of a number of tall houses in the West Riding and the East Midlands whose source of inspiration was Bess of Hardwick's house at Chatsworth. It was abandoned in the 1690s when the owner, Thomas Osborne, Duke of Leeds, built a new house at Kiveton Park in the next parish.

The Sandford arms adorn the gateway, which is topped by a stepped gable in the Dutch style. The south façade of the hall retains its sturdy chimney stacks and round corner towers, but the chimney pots that once pierced the skyline have fallen. The large windows in the top storeys suggest that here were a great chamber and long gallery. The building was once a rectangular structure, arranged perhaps around a small courtyard. The hall was still intact in 1828, when a drawing of it was included in Joseph Hunter's *South Yorkshire*, vol. 1.

PHOTOGRAPH: AUTHOR

Burton Agnes Hall. The great Elizabethan architect Robert Smythson designed this house for Sir Henry Griffith, who came here from Staffordshire on becoming a member of the Council of the North in 1599. Datestones show that it was built during the first decade of the seventeenth century. The glittering bay windows must have had a sensational impact. Smythson was fond of building tall houses with an irregular and dramatic skyline and a symmetrical façade. The external design masks a traditional interior with a great hall, screen and cross-passage. A long gallery ran all the way along the top storey in the front, providing a view right out to the North Sea. The only significant change to the façade has been the replacement of some mullioned and transomed windows with sashes in the eighteenth century. The grounds are enclosed by a high brick wall and a Jacobean gatehouse.

PHOTOGRAPH: CARNEGIE, 2005

contemporary art is the finest surviving example in England. The heraldic theme of the stained glass windows is continued in the plaster frieze that depicts the coats of arms of almost all the Yorkshire gentry, while in the corner of the frieze the images of six musicians are a pleasing indication of how the room was sometimes used. The ribs and hanging pendants of the plaster ceiling, the marquetry panelling of the walls, and the carved oak chimneypiece that frames the Fairfax coat of arms complete a memorable display.

The dramatic skylines, enormous windows, formal entrances and strapwork designs of the great houses of the leading families in late Elizabethan England oozed power and money. The richest and most powerful figure in the North was George Talbot, sixth Earl of Shrewsbury, Earl Marshal of England, and husband of that great builder, Bess of Hardwick. The houses and old castles of the Talbots and Cavendishes, scattered throughout the north midlands and south-west Yorkshire, inspired less wealthy men to copy their tall, compact shapes, with chimneys and turrets silhouetted against the skyline and a long gallery running along the top storey above a traditional hall. The ruined façade of Hercy Sandford's Thorpe Salvin Hall provides a striking example.

Robert Smythson, who designed several houses for the Talbots and Cavendishes and other leading families, was the architect of Burton Agnes Hall and possibly also Fountains Hall. Burton Agnes had been the residence of a powerful lord since Norman times. Sir Henry Griffith moved here from Staffordshire about 1599 when he became a member of the Council of the North and soon began to build. Datestones show that the hall and the gatehouse were erected between 1601 and 1610. The symmetrical façade is adorned with glittering bay windows, gables, finials, battlements, chimney stacks and Flemish-style strapwork designs, which disguise a traditional interior arranged around a small internal courtyard. The gatehouse resembled the Elizabethan turret house at Sheffield and Sir Mauger Vavasour's banqueting house at Weston Hall in lower Wharfedale, but the hall was decidedly modern in having a long gallery with a plaster ceiling and wood carvings, wainscotting, plaster ceilings and alabaster work inspired by the Renaissance. Fountains Hall was built by Stephen Proctor, the son of a lead smelter, with stones from the ruined abbey. A zealous Calvinist who had obtained the lucrative post of Collector of Fines on Penal Statutes in the year after the Gunpowder Plot, Proctor persecuted his Catholic neighbours and engaged them in costly lawsuits over land, minerals and common rights. His house was five storeys high at the front but not very deep, for it was built against a steep bank for dramatic effect. The servants were kept out of sight in the basement.

The lesser gentry were often content to refashion their timber-framed houses

The gatehouse at Burton Agnes Hall has a 1610 datestone and the coat of arms of Sir Henry Griffith, flanked by two allegorical figures.
PHOTOGRAPH: CARNEGIE, 2005

within a new stone shell and perhaps to add new features from time to time, sometimes spread out over more than one generation. Woodsome Hall, near Almondbury, was a timber-framed building arranged in a traditional manner until Arthur and Beatrix Kaye built a fireplace in the open hall and decorated it with their names in large, flowing letters sometime before 1562. Then they placed a similar chimney in the low parlour, glazed the windows and decorated the ceilings with plasterwork. Their son John added more chimneys and rooms, wainscotted the interior so as to be fashionable and to keep out draughts, and paved the hall floor and the courtyard. By about 1580 the work was finished and the house had been encased in stone, but John had kept some old-fashioned features and had built a new drawbridge across the moat. When John's son, Robert, added a north wing he expressed his modernity with a colonnade of Tuscan columns. Robert was of sufficient standing to become a JP and his grandson was made a baronet.

The timber frame of an old house that had been remodelled and encased in stone had a lasting effect on the arrangement of the rooms. The initials of John Batt and the date 1583 are carved in the stonework over the entrance to Oakwell Hall and the only external clue to the antiquity of the interior is provided by the 30 lights of the great seventeenth-century window which illuminate two storeys. The porch leads into a cross-passage which separates the service rooms from the medieval open-hall behind the screen and the parlour wing beyond. Likewise, all the details of the symmetrical stone façade of Guiseley Rectory date from 1601, when it was completed by Robert Moore, but behind it we find a medieval aisled hall whose timber posts separate the main rooms from a smaller range at the rear. Elsewhere, builders used familiar styles even when they faced no restrictions. The Nunnery at Arthington, which was built for the Briggs family in 1585, made a dramatic visual impact but was rooted firmly in the vernacular tradition.

The Jacobean gentry continued to build in the Elizabethan style but

Fountains Hall was built in the early seventeenth century for Sir Stephen Proctor, who had bought the former abbey estate in 1597. Proctor's fortune was based on smelting lead and iron and he profited from his position as Collector of Fines on Penal Statues, harassing his Catholic neighbours after the Gunpowder Plot. The hall has Tudor Gothic windows, finials and battlements, mixed with Renaissance columns, arches and niches. It rises five storeys, but is not very deep, being deliberately set on the steep slope of a valley for dramatic effect. It is similar in style to Robert Smythson's great houses in the East Midlands for the Cavendishes and Talbots. The building stone came from the ruined abbey.

PHOTOGRAPHS: CARNEGIE, 2005

Oakwell Hall. The 1583 datestone on the door lintel has been re-cut, but seems to be trustworthy as the initials are those of John Batt, who had inherited the property eleven years earlier. When he rebuilt his father's house, Batt simply encased the old timber-framed building in stone. The door leads into a traditional cross-passage behind the screen that divides the two-storeyed central hall, lit by a great window, from the service end, seen here on the right. A parlour range containing the best rooms at the front and several small rooms at the rear extends beyond the line of the hall to the left. Oakwell Hall, which is open to the public, is an outstanding example of how a minor gentleman converted an old house to the new standards of the late-Elizabethan and Stuart age, with much contemporary furniture on display. It is also a literary shrine, as the model for 'Fieldhead' in Charlotte Bronte's novel, *Shirley*.

introduced new fashions in the details. When Sir William Bamburgh built Howsham Hall about 1619 he chose to fill the whole of the south front with a display of glass, but created an attractive skyline with rounded battlements (known as merlons) and ball finials. Several Yorkshiremen were appointed to lucrative offices by the early Stuart kings and so were able to build on a grand scale. Sir Richard Hutton, a judge of the Court of Common Pleas, built Goldsborough Hall about 1620, William Pennyman, one of the six Clerks of

below The Nunnery at Arthington was erected a generation after the dissolution of the Cluniac priory on this site, a mile or so to the east of the village of Arthington, on the road to Harewood. Carved above the doorway is the date 1585 and the initials TB, suggesting that it was built by a member of the Briggs family, perhaps re-using stones from the nunnery. The house is unusual for this social level in the Elizabethan age in being three storeys high and having no gables or projecting wings. Instead, ranges of small, mullioned windows were preferred, with oriels over the entrance into a cross-passage that separated a parlour (*left*) from the hall and another parlour beyond. The chimney stack and a spiral staircase were set into the thickness of the dividing wall. The service rooms were contained in a continuous lean-to or outshutt at the rear.

Chancery, erected Marske Hall five years later, and Sir George Calvert, a principal secretary of state, began Kiplin Hall in 1622; as Lord Baltimore he later founded the colony of Maryland. Sir Richard Graham rose from humble origins in the service of the Duke of Buckingham and Charles I and after his acquisition of Norton Conyers through marriage in 1624 he adorned the medieval hall with a row of Dutch gables; his descendants still live there.

The most powerful Yorkshiremen in the early decades of the seventeenth century were Sir Arthur Ingram and Sir Thomas Wentworth, first Earl of Strafford. Ingram's financial schemes kept James I and Charles I independent of Parliament and he grew enormously rich from the spoils of office, with estates in four counties, a splendid town house behind York Minster, and a fine brick lodge at Sheriff Hutton. His principal residence was near his native Rothwell at Temple Newsam, where he converted the brick house that the Darcys had erected on former Knights' Templar property into a major building in the same severe style as the north front of Robert Cecil's Hatfield House in Hertfordshire.

When Sir Thomas Wentworth became Charles I's chief adviser he began to build on a similar scale, starting with his ancestral home at Wentworth Woodhouse where he presided over a household of 64 people. As President of the Council in the North he extended the King's Manor in York and he was probably responsible for enlarging Ledston Hall, a former grange of Pontefract Priory that had been converted into domestic accommodation by the Witham family. The front of the house was adorned with angle turrets capped with ogee-shaped domes, similar to those at Hatfield House and Blickling Hall (Norfolk), and with curious rows of Dutch gables with flat tops carrying pediments, just like the ones that John Smythson, Robert's son, had seen in London in 1619 and then imitated at Bolsover Castle (Derbyshire) and Welbeck Abbey (Nottinghamshire). New styles spread into the provinces when rich families copied the buildings they had visited during the London season. In 1640, for example, Sir Henry Slingsby of Scriven was 'much taken' by Lord Holland's Kensington home and thereupon 'took a conceit' to rebuild Red House at Moor Monkton.

The most distinctive houses of the second and third quarters of the

Porch of High Sunderland Hall. The grand house that Abraham Sunderland began at High Sunderland, Halifax in 1629 has unfortunately been demolished. It was one of the first and most influential of the 'Halifax houses' which were built by minor gentlemen and wealthy clothiers in this prosperous period. These combined traditional vernacular elements with Renaissance ideas imported from outside. The Ionic columns and sculptured figures framing the door must have seemed sensational at the time.
FROM L. AMBLER, *The Old Halls and Manor Houses of Yorkshire* (1913).

seventeenth century were built by the gentlemen and wealthy clothiers of the Halifax district. The internal arrangements were traditional but the decorative details that were applied to the exteriors were an astonishing mixture of Gothic and Renaissance forms. It all began with the (demolished) Methley Hall, a fifteenth-century building that was enlarged between 1588 and 1611 by Sir John Savile and his son, Sir Henry. This was the first house in the West Riding to have an enormous hall window divided by numerous mullions and transoms. The master masons who worked here were probably those members of the Ackroyd family whose names appear in the contemporary Methley parish register. John, Abraham and Martin Ackroyd also built the first houses with windows that were shaped like a rose or a Catherine wheel, though the original source of

Wood Lane Hall, Sowerby. An outstanding example of a seventeenth-century 'Halifax house', Wood Lane Hall was built in 1649 for John Dearden. It has all the architectural details that were so admired by the wealthy clothiers of this parish. The skyline is pierced by Gothic battlements and pinnacles and from the sides project a series of extraordinary gargoyles. The porch has the usual classical columns and a strange lintel that is modelled on a 1633 example at Warley. Above is a rose-window that is identical in design to one at Elland New Hall. The great hall window is also similar to the one at Elland in being divided by mullions and transoms into 27 lights. As with some other 'Halifax houses' the parlour end projects slightly to balance the porch. Despite these similarities with its neighbours, Wood Lane Hall has a character all of its own. It is built in a distinctive vernacular style that is confined to this part of the West Riding.
AUTHOR COLLECTION

South porch, East Riddlesden Hall. The 'Halifax houses' of the second and third quarters of the seventeenth century are characterised by elaborate porches built in an extraordinary mixture of Gothic and Classical styles. They owe their inspiration to the great Elizabethan architect, Robert Smythson, and to the work experience gained at Oxford by local masons, the Ackroyds and Bentleys. The ornamental porches on both sides of East Riddlesden Hall are topped with battlements and finials above a rose window, which are all decidedly medieval in spirit, but they are supported with newly fashionable Corinthian columns. The hall is one of a group of six local houses, all built within a few years of each other, which have windows of a similar design. The porch leads into a traditional cross-passage through the house.

PHOTOGRAPH: AUTHOR

inspiration may have been a design of Robert Smythson's. The (demolished) Bradley Hall at Stainland, which the Ackroyds built for Sir John Savile, had a rose-window that was used as a model at Barkisland Hall a generation later. Through the patronage of the Saviles, Halifax masons were also introduced to the classical columns and entablatures that they used in the porches below their rose-windows, for it was Sir John's younger brother, Sir Henry, the celebrated mathematician, Greek scholar and Warden of Merton College, who invited the Ackroyds and Bentleys to Oxford to extend the Merton Fellows' Quad and to build the Tower of the Five Orders at the Bodleian Library.

The (demolished) hall that Abraham Sunderland built at High Sunderland in 1629 was the first 'Halifax house' to have classical columns. Together with the unusual curvilinear designs of the pilasters on the garden gateways, these must have attracted much comment in the locality. But this new house was constructed around a previous timber-frame and the low proportions, battlements and pinnacles, string courses, and mullioned and transomed windows were decidedly from the vernacular tradition. This combination of classical and medieval features in an elaborate display inspired Sunderland's neighbours.

An outstanding example of the fully developed style, which copied the best features of other local houses, is Wood Lane Hall at Sowerby, which was built for John Dearden in 1649. The finials on top of the battlements resemble those at Kershaw House, Luddenden; the great hall window, the battlements and the rose-window of the porch are modelled on those of Elland New Hall; the design of the doorway lintel is similar to an earlier one at Warley; the balanced projection of the porch and the parlour wing is taken from the plan of Barkisland Hall and some other outstanding local houses; the stepped windows in the gables have several local parallels; and the plaster ceiling is comparable with that at Howroyd. Yet Wood Lane Hall is triumphantly individual in its appearance and decidedly Gothic in flavour. No two 'Halifax houses' are alike and some seem to go out of their way to be different. The porch of the (demolished) Horton Hall at Bradford was a particularly eccentric feature, rising above its rose-window into a tower or observatory, where the owner, Abraham Sharpe, indulged his interest in astronomy. The remarkable East Riddlesden Hall was the home of James Murgatroyd of Warley, a wealthy clothier who moved there in 1638 and finished the building ten years later; he also built two smaller houses nearby at Long Can, Ovenden and Oats Royd, Luddenden. Some of the owners of these halls aspired to the status of minor gentry, but most were content to inscribe their lintels merely with their initials and the date. John Gledhill had his coat of arms and the date 1638 carved over his porch at Barkisland Hall, but the owners of Hawksworth Hall, Elland Hall and Lower Hall at Norland decorated their rooms with the royal arms as they had none of their own.

The continuity of building traditions from the late Elizabethan period into

The Folly, Settle. Settle seems an unlikely setting for such an extravagant building. Although it was built to a traditional plan, with a central hall and slightly projecting cross wings, the unusual character of its architectural details soon earned it the nickname of The Folly. It was built for Thomas Preston in 1679. The windows on the ground floor are arranged in long, low ranges and are given semi-circular heads. On the first floor windows are carried on around the corner and the central ones have a distinctive arch. At the rear, the main staircase is contained in a tower. Most striking of all are the strange pair of columns which flank the principal doorway. Preston's Folly came at the end of a West Riding vernacular tradition which applied fanciful details for striking effect. Pevsner thought them 'capricious and wilful'.

PHOTOGRAPH: CARNEGIE, 2005

the second half of the seventeenth century makes it difficult to date houses for which there is no firm evidence. Even at the same social level owners sometimes chose to build in the accepted manner two generations later. Gawthorpe Hall, Bingley, which has many characteristic features of the style, has a datestone from 1596, but Thomas Netherwood's Giles House at Lightcliffe and Sylvanus Rich's Bullhouse Hall near Penistone are both dated 1655. The characteristic gabled halls of the West Riding cannot be dated by assuming that complicated buildings are later than simple ones. The most distinctive external features of the old halls and manor houses of Yorkshire were the windows and drip moulds. Large windows divided into numerous lights by mullions and transoms illuminated halls, kitchens and parlours and sometimes chambers as well. Some other parts of England shared the fashion for carrying up the centre lights of gable windows, but none shared the West Riding's enthusiasm. Friars Head at Winterburn is a perfect example, with the stepped arrangement displayed in four small, symmetrical gables adorned with finials. In Craven a common variation framed triple lights in an ogee-shaped arch and in the neighbourhood of Settle door heads were shaped in a variety of crazy curves, especially at the house that Thomas Preston built in 1679 and which soon got the nickname of The Folly.

Meanwhile, the general standard of ordinary farmhouses had improved considerably, either through modification or by complete rebuilding. Ceilings were inserted to create upstairs chambers and if enough money was available parlours and service rooms were provided with wainscotting and boarded floors and fitted with fireplaces and glass windows. The 'iron chimneys' that replaced the old open hearths often got a proud mention in yeomen and husbandmen's wills in the middle years of the sixteenth century. Whereas in earlier times houses were furnished meanly with tables, benches, stools and beds and the minimum essential cooking pots, plates and mugs, by the late Elizabethan and early Stuart period the better Yorkshire farmhouses had a greater range of furniture and household goods, such as pewter drinking vessels and cooking pots made of iron, copper or brass. Food was now more plentiful and varied and people were better-dressed. But many small farmers and cottagers did not share this improved standard of living. Sixteenth-century farmhouses in Swaledale remained one-storeyed cruck constructions that were little different from their medieval predecessors. Very few inventories of personal estate mentioned separate rooms and the sparse collections of household goods were valued at only a few shillings.

During the seventeenth century many old buildings were encased with stone walls and roofed with stone slates. In York thatch had long been banned because of the risk of fire and the city's timber-framed houses were roofed with tiles. But some owners still valued timber for its decorative effect, even when they used stone for their lower walls. In south-west Yorkshire, Godfrey Bosville's mid sixteenth-century Gunthwaite barn and his (demolished) lodge at Oxspring displayed timbers only at the upper level and while the upper storey of

Wormald's Hall, Almondbury appears to date from the sixteenth century the ground floor was rebuilt in stone in 1631. In most parts of Yorkshire yeomen, husbandmen and craftsmen did not begin to rebuild their homes in stone or brick until well into the seventeenth century. By the time of the Civil War, however, only the humblest structures were still being built of wood. Old timber-framed town houses were often given a coat of plaster and a colour wash; for instance, when James I stopped at York on his way down from Scotland in 1603, the inhabitants were ordered by the corporation to 'paint the outside of their houses with some colours to the street forwards'. The first house in York to be built completely in brick was not erected until 1610, but even in the mid sixteenth century Yorkers were protesting against 'the great destruction of wood' within 16 miles of the city and Thorganby, eight miles away, had insufficient wood to repair its own buildings. The owners of West Riding woods may have found it more profitable to coppice underwood than to grow standards for timber, but changing fashion and fear of fire in populous places were probably as important as the shortage of timber in the general adoption of stone or brick as the normal building materials. The timber-framed tradition survived longer in the countryside. For example, when Edward Tailor added a new wing to his house in Oulton in 1611 he designed it with king-posts, struts, braces and finials to match the older parts of the building.

The surviving timber-framed houses in the Vale of York that were erected in the decades before the Civil War are mostly well-built, two-storeyed houses that are now encased with brick or stone and are thus hard to recognise. A detailed survey of the Ingilby possessions in Ripley and its hamlets in 1635 described the houses of 40 tenants. Five houses or cottages (and many of the outbuildings) were framed with crucks and the other 35 were framed with posts.

Timber-framed house, Oulton. It is not often that we get such firm dating evidence for a timber-framed building in the countryside. Edward Tailor proudly announces the completion of his work on 10 April 1611. 'I.T.' presumably commemorates his wife in more modest style. The building is framed in the traditional style of the yeomen houses of the West Riding, with king posts, struts, finials and close studding. However, datestones do not always tell the whole story. An internal investigation of the house reveals that Edward Tailor merely added a wing to an earlier structure.

AUTHOR COLLECTION

The six largest farmhouses were four to seven bays wide, 20 others that were framed with posts had three bays, and the remaining nine had just one or two bays. As 29 houses had at least one chamber, they must have been substantially built, yet all these tenants were smallholders; 31 had less than 10 acres of land and only four families had more than 20 acres. Even at this level of society living conditions were improving significantly. On the other hand, between 1550 and 1699 one in four farmers at Swillington (a large arable township with extensive open fields) lived in old-fashioned houses that had a 'low end' for storing seeds, crops and tools, and for housing cattle in winter.

The poor

The cottages of the poorest inhabitants of sixteenth- and seventeenth-century Yorkshire do not survive, which says something about their humble nature, but we can learn a little about them from scattered documentary evidence. For example, in 1578 the Sheffield manor court noted a few encroachments at Owlerton, where Robert Shawe had built 'a little house of the lord's waste there containing one bay' and Widow Alfrey had built a two-bay cottage with a garden. In 1616 Nicholas Shooter rented '1 small cottage 1 bay thatched' near the centre of Sheffield, High Milnes lived in a similar one-bay, thatched cottage in Church Lane, and Alex Hydes had a two-bay house with a slate roof in Castle Green with an old barn just one bay long and a thatched lean-to. In many different parts of Yorkshire, especially in the west, poor people were building homes on the wastes or commons. In 1652 a survey of the magnesian-limestone village of Braithwell found 'four poor houses built on the lord's waste'. A survey of Cawthorne, taken 14 years earlier, had noted that nine men and two women 'being very poor people and standing need of relief have within the compass of fifty years last past erected poor cottages upon the wastes' and some of the freeholders had built cottages for their coal miners. Parishes such as this, where industrial jobs were available, were particularly attractive to immigrant squatters.

The dissolution of religious houses, especially the hospitals, had left the old and the needy with little hope of charity. The problem of the poor worsened as the national population grew and the corporation of York were especially troubled by vagabonds who were drawn to the city from the shrunken and deserted villages of the countryside. The late Elizabethan government made each parish responsible for its own poor; unpaid overseers of the poor were elected at Easter vestry meetings and empowered to raise local rates in order to set the poor on work, apprentice poor children and relieve the 'lame, impotent, old, blind and such other among them being poor and not able to work'. Begging was forbidden and those who were caught attempting it were whipped. When a small group of 'rogues and vagabonds' were brought before

the Richmond quarter sessions in 1610 the JPs ordered that the women should be whipped and the men branded with the letter R. Two years later, the West Riding JPs were alarmed about the 'great abundance of wandering rogues and concourse of beggars and strangers'. Their decision to build a House of Correction at Wakefield 'much suppressed the number of sturdy and incorrigible beggars and rogues and other dissolute and disordered persons', but in 1631 the JPs at the Wetherby sessions found that their orders concerning beggars had been 'greatly neglected' by parish officers, who were severe on immigrant paupers but generally supportive of their own 'deserving' poor.

When the chantries were dissolved in 1547 some parishes managed to keep their properties to pay for the poor and other public purposes under the management of 'feoffees'. The Ecclesfield feoffees, for example, administered 65 acres of former chantry land for the benefit

of the church, the poor and the local highways; in 1638 their income, topped up by the poor rates, enabled the parishioners to build a workhouse. In neighbouring Sheffield the lands that had belonged to the medieval burgery were divided in 1554 between two new bodies that still operate as the church burgesses and the town trustees and in 1632 the rents were used to build the town's first workhouse. Rotherham's feoffees, who took responsibility for the lands of a medieval guild, helped the poor and eventually provided a school for local children. The donations of these public bodies were supplemented by private acts of charity, large and small, from the late sixteenth century onwards. An outstanding example of an Elizabethan almshouse survives at Beamsley. Built in 1593 and 'finished more profusely' in 1651 by Lady Anne Clifford, a low range of rooms are approached through a central arch adorned with a coat of arms, and beyond stands a circular building, topped by a central lantern and tall chimney stacks and containing further rooms and a chapel. A contemporary almshouse at Freeston, founded in 1595, is built around a central dining hall, lit by mullioned and transomed windows.

Schools

Most of Yorkshire's medieval grammar schools seem to have survived the dissolution of the chantries, even though many of them were the successors to earlier schools that had been held inside churches and taught by clergymen. School buildings that survive from the Elizabethan or Jacobean period are commonly sited close to the parish church and that at Felkirk was placed within the churchyard. Worsbrough Grammar School was founded on a piece of waste ground immediately north of the churchyard in 1560 with the endowments of the former chantry school; the present building was erected in 1632 when John Rayney, a local man who had made his fortune in London, left a bequest for a well-qualified master to teach 'learning, cyphering [and] the grounds of religion'. Rayney was a Puritan who also provided a lecturer to preach regularly in St Mary's church. He was typical of men who had prospered in the capital or a provincial city and who remembered their birthplace when they

'… being very poor people and standing need of relief have within the compass of fifty years last past erected poor cottages upon the wastes.'

CAWTHORNE, 1638

Burnsall School. Built next to the parish church in this picturesque Wharfedale village, the school was founded in 1602 by Sir William Craven, a native of the parish who had become a wealthy merchant and Lord Mayor of London. He is commemorated by an inscription over the porch. The schoolroom occupied the range to the right of the porch and the master had a downstairs room and two bedrooms to the left. It is built of local stone in the vernacular style of the yeoman farmhouses in the vicinity. It was extended to the rear in 1960 and still serves as a school.

PHOTOGRAPH: CARNEGIE, 2005

came to make a will. The almshouses and schools that they founded were often adorned with inscriptions to their generosity and perhaps a coat of arms. One of the most attractive small schools that is still in use in Yorkshire is that erected in 1602 next to the church at Burnsall by Sir William Craven, former Lord Mayor of London, with a house for the master and dormitories for boarders. Like the slightly later school beyond the churchyard at Laughton-en-le-Morthen, it is built in the local style of the domestic houses of the period. Town schools, notably the former Otley Grammar School (1611), were also built in the vernacular style and many owed their foundations to Puritans. George Savile and his son were benefactors of Wakefield Grammar School (1591) and Dr John Favour, the vicar of Halifax, was the driving force behind the establishment of Halifax Grammar School (1600).

Religion and politics

The Calvinists within the Church of England who disliked the compromise of the Elizabethan settlement were a minority at the beginning of James I's reign, but their influence was beginning to grow. In 1604 only three of the 60 parishes of the Deanery of Doncaster had ministers who were wholly devoted to the Puritan cause, though another was sympathetic in some matters and 13 were 'seeming weary of the ceremonies'. Of the 80 clergymen who served these parishes, 42 did not preach, 26 were 'insufficient' and 12 were 'painful', that is painstaking or Puritan. Some found parts of Yorkshire that were congenial to their beliefs, but the most determined decided to move far away. One of the leaders of those who crossed the Atlantic to Plymouth Rock on the *Mayflower* was William Bradford of Austerfield, the governor of the colony for most of the time from 1621 until his death in 1657.

During the first half of the seventeenth century Beverley, Hull and York, the emerging West Riding industrial towns of Bradford, Halifax, Leeds, Sheffield and Wakefield, and the chapelries that stretched over the Pennines became Puritan strongholds. Some of the most eminent and fervent Puritans were ministers in the 12 chapels-of-ease of Halifax parish and in the chapelries of Morley and Woodkirk between Leeds and Dewsbury, which were dominated by the Puritan Saviles of Howley Hall. The leadership of the Puritan gentry in these districts was as decisive as that of the Catholic squires in the Dales. Some built chapels on their own land and appointed 'godly preachers'. The simple interiors of these plain, box-shaped buildings were focused on the pulpit. The best surviving examples are the chapels that Robert Dyneley built at Bramhope in 1649 and Sir Edward Rodes erected at Great Houghton in the following year. The chapels-of-ease that Puritan gentlemen built at Attercliffe and Ecclesall in the large parish of Sheffield survived the Civil War, but whereas Ecclesall eventually acquired a new church and became a separate parish the old building at Attercliffe was reduced in size in 1909 and now stands forlorn amongst modern development.

In 1632 Archbishop Richard Neile started a purge of the Puritans inside the diocese of York. Ministers such as Thomas Toller, the vicar of Sheffield from 1598 to 1635, were forced out and parish churches were re-furnished for the performance of ceremonies. The number of Puritan clergy in Yorkshire, which had grown from 38 in 1603 to 96 in 1633, fell to 65 by 1640. An outstanding church from this period was built in Leeds to accommodate the greatly increased population. Dedicated to St John, it was paid for by John Harrison, a wealthy alderman, and built in a Gothic survival style with a memorable display of woodwork and interior decoration, far removed in spirit from the plain, preaching boxes that were favoured by the Puritans.

Despite this setback, the Puritan movement attracted increasing support amongst the gentry. Whereas in 1570 only 25 Yorkshire gentlemen were committed Puritans, by the 1630s the number had increased to 138, or one in five of the 679 gentry families. In the East Riding wapentakes of Dickering and Buckrose nearly half the gentry were Puritans, but in the North Riding, where the Catholic tradition was strong, only 11 per cent favoured the Puritan cause. Many of Yorkshire's ancient gentry families were now Puritan, including nine baronets and 25 knights, but the movement also attracted a substantial number of professional and commercial men in the towns. When the Civil War broke out, 64 Puritan gentlemen enlisted in the Parliamentary army, compared with 24 who favoured the Royalists, but many other families were neutral or divided in their allegiance. In some cases the head of the family fought on one side while his heir fought on the other. Wealth played little part in the choice of sides and both armies attracted men from rising or declining families. The Royalist cause was based in York, the seat of the Council of the North, but Sir Thomas Wentworth, the Earl of Strafford, had antagonised some powerful Yorkshire families by his arrogance and his policies. Lord Fairfax, Sir Hugh Cholmley, Sir Arthur Ingram and Henry Bellasis were on the House of Commons committee that drew up the indictment that led to Wentworth's execution in 1641.

Soon after he raised his standard at Nottingham on 22 August 1642, Charles I came to York and troops and supplies were brought by sea to Scarborough, but he was denied entry to the crucial port of Hull. Several years of misery were about to begin, in which buildings were destroyed, churches vandalised, trade greatly disrupted, and troops were billeted upon ordinary householders without recompense. Minor battles and skirmishes and the unruly behaviour of soldiers, who stole horses, bedding and food, made life unpleasant and sometimes unbearable in the many parts of Yorkshire which were subject to repeated plundering. The Scottish allies of the Parliamentary troops terrorised large parts of the North Riding. Harsh taxes were levied, markets closed, rents and bills went unpaid. York, Hull, Pontefract, Bradford and Skipton had to endure long sieges and Scarborough changed hands no fewer than seven times between 1642 and 1648, with two prolonged and costly sieges in 1645 and 1648.

The Parliamentarians, led by Ferdinando, Lord Fairfax and his son, Sir Thomas, marched into the West Riding clothing towns, where they were

Skipton Castle Conduit Court. Ten years after its partial destruction in 1649, at the end of the Civil War, Skipton Castle was lovingly restored by Lady Anne Clifford, Countess of Pembroke, the descendant of Robert de Clifford who had acquired the honour of Skipton in 1310. By 1672, when it was taxed on 60 hearths, the castle was the largest dwelling in the West Riding. Lady Anne also restored Barden Tower, which had been built in Wharfedale by her ancestor in the reign of Henry VIII. The view shows Conduit Court, named after the well. The mullioned bay windows and the tree in the centre of the courtyard make this the most picturesque part of the castle interior. The Clifford coat of arms is placed centrally above the door. The staircase on the left led to the Great Hall in the north range.

confident of support, but they were defeated by the forces of William Cavendish, the Earl of Newcastle, at Adwalton Moor and forced to leave Leeds and Bradford. The whole of Yorkshire, except for Hull, quickly came under Royalist control and several medieval castles were garrisoned, but when Newcastle had to deal with the threat of a Scottish invasion Sir William Constable led his troops out of Hull to a victory on the Wolds and to the capture of Bridlington and Whitby. Royalist counter-attacks led by John Bellasis were twice stopped at Bradford and in April 1644 Bellasis' army was decisively beaten by Sir Thomas Fairfax's troops at Selby. Newcastle was forced to return to York Castle, where he was besieged by the joint forces of the Scots and the Parliamentarians. Prince Rupert's army advanced through the Welsh Marches and Lancashire to his aid, collecting recruits on their way through Skipton and Knaresborough. The stage was set for one of the most decisive battles that was ever fought on Yorkshire soil. On 2 July 1644 at Marston Moor Oliver Cromwell's cavalry routed Prince Rupert's horsemen then destroyed Newcastle's infantry in the centre: 'God made them as stubble to our swords', he said. During the next few months the remaining Royalist garrisons in the North were taken one at a time and at the end of the war many of the old castles were dismantled so that they could never be fortified again. Those at Pontefract and Sheffield were razed to the ground. Fifteen Yorkshiremen were amongst the judges at Charles I's trial in 1649 and six were present at his execution. Puritan preachers replaced those ministers who conformed to the Church of England and a Commonwealth was proclaimed. It soon degenerated into the dictatorship of Oliver Cromwell.

Towards an Industrial Society, 1660–1780

CHAPTER 7

Growing numbers of people

From the restoration of the monarchy in 1660 to the middle of the eighteenth century the population of England increased only slowly, from about 5.2 million to perhaps 5.7 million. This was a slower rate of growth than in the previous 100 years and it gave no hint of the population explosion that was to come, except that London and some industrial towns were growing quickly as people left the countryside in search of work. For example, it has been estimated that between 1664 and 1743 some 3,000 people moved away from the rural parishes of mid Wharfedale and that substantial numbers of countryfolk left the Bainton Beacon division of Harthill wapentake in the East Riding. Other parts of Yorkshire that were also dependent entirely on farming fared no better, for this was the time when many villages that had shrunk in the late Middle Ages were finally deserted. In both Wharfedale and Harthill the parish registers reveal a surplus of baptisms over burials, so the loss of population can be explained only by emigration. But these two agricultural districts were not typical of the whole of Yorkshire. The communities of the Calder Valley and other textile districts flourished as never before and the thriving metal trades of Hallamshire supported population growth in the south-western corner of the county. The 210 nailmakers who in 1733 signed an agreement at Ecclesfield to enforce the old regulations complained that youngsters who had abandoned their apprenticeships 'do frequently marry very young and inconsiderately and by that means have often a great charge of children to maintain before they scarce know how to maintain themselves'. Economic opportunities in the industrial districts were allowing earlier marriages and thus more children.

Most Yorkshire people were prepared to move from the place of their birth, but on the whole they remained within their own neighbourhood, bounded by the nearest market towns. The great exception to the rule that most mobility was over short distances was the capital city, for London was a magnet that attracted youngsters in droves. In 1680 Sir John Reresby of Thrybergh observed that London 'drained all England of its people'. Most of the immigrants into the growing industrial towns of the West Riding travelled only short distances. The apprenticeship registers of the Hallamshire Cutlers' Company from 1624 to 1799 show that two out of every three boys came from places that lay within 21 miles of the centre of Sheffield and that fewer than one in ten came from places more than 41 miles away. The labour force was overwhelmingly local in origin and remained so after as the population grew rapidly. Men and women chose their marriage partners from within the same district and the most common surnames were those that had been formed locally three or four centuries ago. Early in the eighteenth century Daniel Defoe referred to 'the country called Hallamshire', a district that was distinguished by the lordship centred on Sheffield Castle, its topography, the overwhelming importance of the cutlery and allied trades, the dialect of the inhabitants and their network of family ties and friendships. The Broomheads, Creswicks, Dungworths, Housleys and Staniforths rarely ventured north into other parts of Yorkshire. They probably never came into contact with the distinctive families of other 'countries', such as the Aldersons of Swaledale, the Armisteads of Ribblesdale, the Stansfields of the upper Calder Valley, or the Littlewoods of the Holme Valley. In each 'country' local names had ramified during the sixteenth and seventeenth centuries and had become more characteristic of their native districts than ever before. The sense of belonging to both a particular place – a town or a rural parish – and to a wider district was stronger than it is now and most people lived in a world of limited horizons. The cutlers of Hallamshire had little in common with the weavers of the West Riding textile district and knew nothing about the farmers of the Vale of York. The inhabitants of Holderness farmed their lands in a very different manner from the smallholders of the Yorkshire Dales. The whole way of life for ordinary families was peculiar to their particular 'countries'. Although Yorkshire's gentry families were sometimes linked by marriage at the county level, ordinary people were not. The distribution patterns of Yorkshire surnames suggest that before the Industrial Revolution most people felt that they belonged to a town or parish and to their 'country', but not to the county.

The sense of being Yorkshire folk came later and at first was more apparent to outsiders than to the natives. In the seventeenth century John Aubrey wrote, 'The indigence of Yorkshire are strong, tall, and long legg'd, they call 'em opprobriously long-legd tyke', the common name for a snarling, obstinate dog. Another unflattering description came from a contemporary phrase, 'To put Yorkshire of a man', meaning to cheat or deceive him. John Dryden wrote, less aggressively, of a girl who was 'Like a fair Shepherdess in her Country Russet, talking in a Yorkshire tone' and Aubrey noted that Ben Jonson took his 'hint for clownery' when writing *The Tale of a Tub* from the Yorkshire words and proverbs spoken by John Lacy, a player of the King's House who had come to London from Doncaster in 1631. Scholars began to take an interest in the peculiarities of local speech in the late seventeenth century. The first dialect dictionary was John Ray's *Collection of English Words* (1674), which had a list of East Riding words added to it in 1691 by Francis Brokesby, rector of

The indigence of Yorkshire are strong, tall, and long legg'd, they call 'em opprobriously long-legd tyke.'

JOHN AUBREY

Rowley, then in 1703 a catalogue of words spoken in the Leeds area was made by the antiquary, Ralph Thoresby. An unknown author published his *Yorkshire Dialogue between an Awd Wife, a Lass and a Butcher* at York in 1693 and four years later George Meriton's *The Praise of Yorkshire Ale* included a section entitled: 'A Yorkshire Dialogue in its pure Natural Dialect as it is now commonly spoken in the North parts of Yorkshire', followed by 'Some Observations concerning the Dialect and various Pronunciations of words in the East Riding'. Most of the early dialect writing in Yorkshire came from the North and East Ridings, perhaps because the speech of those areas differed from the standard language more than did the West Riding vernacular.

According to estimates based on the numbers of householders who were taxed on their hearths in 1672, the West Riding was the most populous and prosperous part of Yorkshire, with about half of the county's 350,000 to 430,000 inhabitants. Throughout England, the population was still overwhelmingly rural. Three out of every four people were countryfolk and many others lived in small market towns which were not much larger than villages. York had only 12,000 inhabitants in the 1660s and by the end of the century Yorkshire's second largest town, Leeds, had about half that number. Some industrial towns and villages continued to grow throughout the seventeenth century, but it was not until after 1700 that the pace quickened. The population in the central urban township of Sheffield rose four and a half times between 1616, when it was 2,207, and 1736, when it was counted at 10,121, but most of this rise took place in the early eighteenth century.

York Minster, 1840 attributed to F. Mackenzie. In fact the surroundings were never as spacious as this. In the Middle Ages the present space on the north side of the Minster was occupied by the archbishop's palace and in the seventeenth century by a large town house belonging to Sir Arthur Ingram.

The growth of the population in the industrial and commercial districts was checked in the 1720s by the last of the great epidemics that swept the country in the wake of disastrous harvests. In his *History of Hull* Thomas Gent remembered that during the 1720s 'in our Distress we were supplied with ship loads (of corn) from Italy, Flanders, Poland and other distant parts' and in 1729 a Vale of York vicar noted in his burial register: 'The greatest mortality that ever can be remembered, or made out to be in the parish of Arksey'. Arthur Jessop of Holmfirth completed his diary for 1730 with the words: 'conclusion of another year and many hath been taken away ... reduced to great straits ... forced to live upon coarse mean fare such as is not usual for man to eat but life was preserved to turn our scarcity into plenty and a plentiful crop the last year ... another plentiful crop this year'. During various years between 1723 and 1729 many parishes recorded more burials than baptisms in their registers.

Between July and October 1715 the Sheffield parish registers noted 224 burials, more than twice the normal rate; 185 of these were children and in August of that year only one of the 54 recorded deaths was that of an adult. In the spring of 1723 another epidemic ravaged Sheffield, when the burial total soared to 638, which was more than that of the two previous years put together, and further epidemics broke out in 1726 and 1728–30. Contemporary doctors noted that several diseases were rampant at this time. England had to import large quantities of grain in 1727 and 1728 in the wake of two disastrous harvests. In 1727 William Hillary, a Ripon doctor, noted that 'many of the labouring and poor people, who used a low diet, and were much exposed to the injuries and

Old Ouse Bridge, York, 1763. William Marlow's painting shows the only bridge in the city that crossed the Ouse and the highest point of navigation. Here were the corporation's staith – or quay – and the common crane. Houses, shops and public buildings lined the bridge, which was replaced by the present structure in the second decade of the nineteenth century.

changes of the weather, died; many of whom probably wanted the necessary assistance of diet and medicines'. After the severe winter of 1728–29 John Hobson of Dodworth Green recorded that people had been 'reduced to great straits' and that they had been 'forced to live upon coarse mean fare such as is not usual for man to eat'.

From the 1740s onwards the growth of the population of England and Wales was dramatic. By 1801 it had soared to 9.2 million. This unprecedented rise was accompanied by an enormous shift in the distribution of the national population. The agricultural counties of southern and eastern England lost their dominance, one person in every three now lived in a town, and industrial Lancashire, Staffordshire, Warwickshire and the West Riding of Yorkshire had risen to greater national importance. Beyond the capital city, Manchester, Liverpool and Birmingham were now the most populous towns in the land and of the old provincial centres only Bristol remained in the top six. Two out of every three Yorkshiremen now lived in the West Riding, that is 564,593 compared with 158,955 in the North Riding, 111,192 in the East Riding and 24,393 in York and its dependent wapentake, the Ainsty. A great shift in emphasis had occurred since the late Middle Ages. Leeds was now the largest town in Yorkshire and Sheffield came next. York was no longer the undisputed capital of the North.

Towns

Before this great change occurred, York retained its traditional role as the major political, ecclesiastical, judicial, commercial and social centre in the North of

Beverley Market Cross. The Saturday Market was laid out in the twelfth century to provide extra space for commercial activities once the Wednesday Market by the Minster became overcrowded. The late medieval tower of St Mary's Church is seen in the background. The elaborate market cross was erected in 1714 at the joint expense of Sir Charles Hotham and Sir Michael Warton, Beverley's two Members of Parliament.

BY COURTESY OF THE YORKSHIRE ARCHAEOLOGICAL SOCIETY

England. At the time of a War Office enquiry in 1686 it had 483 guest beds and stabling facilities for 800 horses, far more than the 294 beds and 454 stalls at Leeds, the second largest town. The River Ouse was still a major thoroughfare and the city's markets and fairs were as busy as ever. Celia Fiennes found the narrow streets and low houses a poor contrast to the modern layout of Nottingham, but a little later Daniel Defoe enthused over 'a pleasant and beautiful city', where he found 'abundance of good company'; he thought that, 'no other city in England is better furnished with provisions of every kind, nor any so cheap'. During the eighteenth century country gentry families such as the Bourchiers of Beningborough Hall built town houses in Micklegate or in other fashionable streets, assembly rooms were designed by the Earl of Burlington, and the Knavesmire racecourse acquired a grandstand designed by John Carr. Most of the city's workforce were employed in service industries and skilled craftsmen made jewellery, stained glass, books and other objects that were sought by the county gentry.

The War Office returns of 1686 show the continuing importance of old towns and the growing importance of the industrial parts of the West Riding. Yorkshire's top 11 towns with over 100 beds available in their inns were York, Leeds, Wakefield, Doncaster, Malton, Hull, Beverley, Halifax, Sheffield, Ripon and Thirsk. The next rank, with 50–99 beds, comprised Richmond, Pontefract, Northallerton, Scarborough, Skipton, Howden, Barnsley, Rotherham, Selby, Bawtry, Bedale, Tadcaster and Boroughbridge. York and Hull were the only Yorkshire towns that managed to elect members of Parliament free of aristocratic interference. The county returned two MPs and 14 boroughs each had the right to elect two members. Six other boroughs had lost their rights since the Middle Ages and Leeds and Halifax no longer had the privilege of electing one member each, which they had enjoyed briefly under Cromwell. The growing industrial towns such as Bradford, Sheffield and Wakefield had no members, yet 'pocket boroughs' like Knaresborough (which was controlled by the Duke of Devonshire) or Aldborough and Boroughbridge (both dominated by the Duke of Newcastle) returned two members each.

Travellers were generally pleased with Yorkshire's larger market towns. Celia Fiennes thought that Beverley was better than any that she had visited except Nottingham and Defoe found that the 'very neat, pleasant, well-built town' of Ripon had 'the finest and most beautiful square that is to be seen of its kind in England'. The Beverley Saturday Market was adorned with a splendid cross, erected in 1714 by the local MPs, and Ripon was famous for its horse fair, two great cloth fairs and a wool fair, and its leather market. Many of Yorkshire's old towns, such as Bedale, Beverley, Stokesley or Yarm, were rebuilt in brick during the eighteenth century and retain much of their Georgian character. Richmond is of national importance, but Doncaster is no longer 'one of the most clean, airy and elegant towns in the British dominions'. Both of these ancient towns remained great regional trading centres. In 1749 Richmond had 'one of the best corn markets in the north of England' and its

Beverley Beck. The beck was a vital waterway that linked the town to the River Hull and so to the Humber. It was made navigable for boats by the twelfth century. Together with the railway, it fostered Beverley's industries in the Victorian age and is still well used.

cheap provisions included sea-fish imported from Hartlepool and Redcar, flax, iron, tar, timber, salt and groceries which had come via Yarm or Stockton, and coal from County Durham. The growing industrial towns too were centred on their market places. During the seventeenth century the market place by the church at Wakefield was filled with the booths of the bakers and leather workers and surrounded by numerous inns; old names such as Shambles, The Cross, Bull Ring, Hog Market and Market Place survived at the heart of the town. In the early eighteenth century Defoe observed that Wakefield was 'a clean, large, well-built town, very populous and very rich ... and yet is no corporation town'; the Friday cloth market was held 'after the manner of that

Clothmakers and packhorses. This watercolour of 'Cloth-makers' in George Walker's *The Costume of Yorkshire* (1814) shows men on their weekly journey from their homes in the countryside, with pieces of cloth for sale in the Piece Halls of the leading West Riding textile towns. Walker thought, 'these men have a decided provincial character; and their galloways also, which are always overloaded, have a manner of going peculiarly their own'.

BY COURTESY OF THE YORKSHIRE ARCHAEOLOGICAL SOCIETY

Aerial view of Halifax. The rectangular Piece Hall, which dominates this scene, was built between 1775 and 1778 as a venue for the sale of woollen cloth and was seen as one of the wonders of its age. Clothiers rented one or more of the 315 rooms, which were arranged in three galleries around a spacious courtyard. It was placed between the main streets of the town (*left*) and the medieval parish church (*top right*). The spire which rises 235 feet on the lower, eastern side of the Piece Hall is that of Square Congregational Church, designed in 1857 in Gothic style by Joseph James, a London architect, as the largest Nonconformist church in the country. The tower and spire were paid for by Sir Francis Crossley, the carpet manufacturer. The church was largely demolished after a disastrous fire in 1970.

WWW.WEBBAVIATION.CO.UK

of Leeds, tho' not so great'. The congestion at the heart of the town was eased when an Improvement Commission was appointed in 1771 to deal with the 'very ruinous condition of the streets' and by the end of the century Wakefield had an attractive Georgian square of brick terraces arranged around the new St John's church.

During the seventeenth century many Yorkshire towns still traded in woollen cloth. York remained a prominent marketing centre, Doncaster woolstaplers brought in good-quality wools from beyond the county, and cloth fairs were held at Ripon, Pontefract and Barnsley. But the cloth markets at Leeds and Wakefield were now pre-eminent. At Leeds, Defoe heard that clothiers set off in the early hours of the morning to be in Briggate by 6 a.m. in the summer and 7 a.m. in the winter and that business was finished by 8.30 a.m. During the eighteenth century the West Riding textile towns built cloth halls to protect their markets from inclement weather. The one built in Halifax in 1708 was replaced in 1779 by the surviving Piece Hall, the major monument from the era of domestic economy before the factory age, with 315 rooms arranged around a central courtyard. The cloth hall built in Wakefield in 1710 caused the Leeds merchants to erect their own in the following year; later, Leeds built a large White Cloth Hall in 1755 and another large hall in 1774, and in 1776 Wakefield merchants built their Tammy Hall. At the southern edge of the textile region the small cloth market established at Penistone in 1743 was transferred to a new cloth hall 20 years later and at Huddersfield, where kerseys had been exposed for sale on a churchyard wall every Tuesday since the granting of a market in 1671, a cloth hall was built in 1766 at the expense of Sir John Ramsden. In 1775 Gomersal men tried to draw away some of the Leeds trade by erecting a cloth hall and in 1773 Bradford acquired its Piece Hall. Bradford was still only a small place with about 4,200 people in 1780 and the town was not yet firmly established as the centre of the worsted trade.

In the later seventeenth century nearly 10,000 people lived in the borough of Leeds, which extended over the 21,000 acres of the medieval parish. Two out of every three inhabitants lived in the urban township that covered no more than half a square mile. There the houses of the rich and poor were intermingled with workshops. Briggate had the most substantial dwellings and the poorest houses were found among the dyehouses and fulling mills in the eastern district stretching form Mabgate to Marsh Lane. The hearth-tax returns of 1664–72 show that Leeds had relatively few people who were too poor to pay the tax and that about two in five of the inhabitants had a single hearth, a similar-sized group had two or three hearths and one in five households had more. In 1698 Celia Fiennes observed that 'Leeds is a large town, severall large streets clean and well pitch'd and good houses all built of stone, some have good gardens and steps up to their houses and walls before them; this is esteemed the wealthyest town of its bigness in the Country … they have provision so plentifull that they may live with very little expense and get much variety'. She also noted that the town was 'full of Dissenters'; the Presbyterians built a chapel in Mill Hill in 1674 and by the 1690s the Congregationalists and Quakers too had their meeting places.

The opening of the Aire and Calder navigation in 1700 was a great stimulus to the commercial and industrial development of Leeds. In the eighteenth century the town grew more rapidly than any other place in Yorkshire, both by the natural increase of the population and by the immigration of apprentices and journeymen labourers. By 1775 the town had 17,121 inhabitants, all of whom lived and worked within the old confines of the medieval settlement, and the typical workplace remained a small craft shop. Leeds' success was not based

Sheffield file cutters. File cutting was still a hand craft in the heart of Sheffield when this scene was drawn in 1866, but it was already losing the battle with mechanisation. By the end of the century file cutting by hand was confined to the surrounding villages. The handle of the file cutter's hammer was angled to allow a wristy motion. When one side of a file had been cut, it was turned over and placed on a lead block so that the cuts underneath would not be damaged. The boy on the left is pouring molten lead into moulds for this purpose.

Sheffield grinders. A group of men sit astride their 'horsing' and grind table knives on rotating sandstone wheels. For centuries, the wheels had been driven by water power, but by the time that this view was taken in 1866 steam had become the principal source of power. Grinding had become a notoriously dangerous occupation in these conditions, with many men dying young because of the damage to their lungs.

on a single trade, however, for the proportion of the workforce involved in textiles declined after 1740, as the number of firms engaged in other trades rose rapidly. These included long-established industries involving coal, bricks and wood or building, dressmaking, tailoring, shoemaking and printing and new industries such as the manufacture of pottery, linen, chemicals, soap-boiling and sugar-refining.

In the first half of the eighteenth century Sheffield was largely rebuilt in brick and by 1764 it had become 'a town of considerable note for its manufactures'. Though it was still arranged around its medieval market place, Sheffield was no longer dominated by its manorial lords, the absentee Dukes of Norfolk. The castle had been demolished, the manor lodge was in ruins, the deer had been removed from the park and chases, and the cutlers organised their trade through their own company. Beyond the Market Place and the High Street the typical house had a cutler's smithy attached to it or one standing to the rear. In 1672 the urban township had 224 smithies, one to every 2.2 houses, while other cutlers worked in their chambers at the skilled job of finishing. High-quality cutlery was now produced for a wide market and the growing fashion for forks encouraged a new craft, alongside other specialisations such as file making. Between 1660 and 1740 the number of water-powered sites on the local streams and rivers rose from 49 to 90, about two-thirds of which were used for grinding cutlery, and the number of wheels at each unit rose appreciably. No other place in England used so much water power. The first steam-powered cutlery factory was not opened until 1823 and the small workshop worked by a 'little mester' with an apprentice and perhaps a journeyman or two remained the typical unit of production. Sheffield was still a cutlery town rather than a place where steel was made. A number of South Yorkshire gentry families

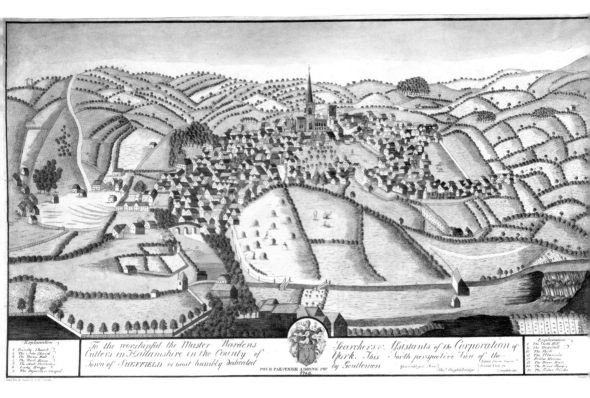

Thomas Oughtibridge's view of Sheffield from the north, high above the River Don, was drawn in 1737. It shows a town of 10,121 people, just as it was beginning to expand beyond its medieval limits. The parish church dominates the view, for the castle had been demolished in the late 1640s. Although the town seems tiny by modern standards, Daniel Defoe thought it 'populous and large'.
SHEFFIELD GALLERIES & MUSEUMS TRUST

below left An Old Sheffield Plate basket, made by John Hoyland in 1768. This new trade developed quickly after Thomas Boulsover's invention in 1743.
SHEFFIELD GALLERIES & MUSEUMS TRUST

right The last remaining cementation furnace. Sheffield once had about 260 cementation steel furnaces, but only one survives intact, in the middle of a car park. It once formed part of Daniel Doncaster's works in Hoyle Street, and was probably erected in the 1830s.
PHOTOGRAPH: CARNEGIE, 2004

KINGSTON UPON HULL.
Published by T. Malton N° 34 Rathbone Place Nov° 1° 1780.

Kingston upon Hull, 1780. Thomas Malton, junior's view of the Market Place, looking north, shows the heart of the old town near the confluence of the rivers Hull and Humber. The late-medieval tower of Holy Trinity church rises majestically beyond. The gilded statue of William III by Peter Scheemakers was erected in 1734 to celebrate (somewhat belatedly) the Glorious Revolution of 1688. Merchants' houses line the street. This was then the opulent part of the town.

Whalebone scrapers. Painted by George Walker for his *The Costume of Yorkshire* (1814), a group of men are employed in cleaning and scraping whalebone, which has just been brought to land. Hull and Whitby were Yorkshire's major ports for this arduous trade. Walker recognised the variety of specialist occupations related to whale fishing and concluded, 'it is an excellent nursery for seamen, employs a quantity of shipping, and the preparation of the Oil and Whalebone provides work for another class of people at home'.

invested their wealth in cementation steel furnaces in the later seventeenth century but the first furnaces to be be erected in Sheffield by Samuel Shore and Thomas Parkin date from the early years of the eighteenth century. The dramatic change came a generation later, when Benjamin Huntsman moved to Handsworth in 1742 to begin his experiments with crucible steel. His success was the foundation upon which Sheffield eventually became the steel capital of the world and the high quality of his product enabled Hallamshire cutlers and new edge-tool businesses to capture international markets and overtake London as the leading centre of manufacture. About the same time, in 1743, Thomas Boulsover, a Norfolk Street cutler, invented Old Sheffield Plate, whereby silver and copper were fused together and worked as one metal. Boulsover, Joseph Hancock, John Hoyland, and Tudor & Leader soon developed an important industry whose products were sold throughout the British Empire as a cheaper version of silver goods. The platers quickly became the wealthiest men in town.

Industrial growth in the West Riding stimulated the expansion of Hull into the country's fourth largest port, after London, Liverpool and Bristol. Wenceslaus Hollar's view of Hull, taken just before the Civil War, shows much open ground within the medieval walls and no suburban development, but by the end of the century the town was badly congested and the population of Hull and its suburb of Sculcoates had risen to about 7,500. Defoe found the town 'exceeding close built ... 'tis extraordinary populous, even to an inconvenience', with the merchants still living above their counting houses in High Street. A series of Improvement Acts after 1755 dealt with the building, traffic, sanitation, lighting and repair problems of the growing town, and the remaining medieval walls were destroyed by the three docks that were constructed between 1774 and 1829. The first dock, which covered nearly ten acres and sheltered more than 100 ships, was the largest that had then been built in England. Hull's volume of shipping rose from 11,000 tons per annum in the first quarter of the eighteenth century to 135,000 tons in 1792. Two or three dozen merchant houses, led by those of Crowle, Thornton, Maister, Sykes, Mowld, Somerscale and Broadley, dominated the export and coastal trades. Whaling was a spectacular but relatively minor business. Oil obtained from Dutch whalers had been prized for lighting since Tudor times, but British seamen rarely ventured to Greenland or the Davis Straits until the 1730s. Hull was the major British whaling port, but great blubber houses were also built at Whitby, alongside the inner harbour. Whitby was a busier port than Scarborough, and Filey and Bridlington were mere fishing settlements in comparison.

The eighteenth century was a time of urban renaissance for many towns as civic pride led to new public buildings and rows of Georgian houses arranged around squares. Public amenities, such as theatres, concert halls, assembly rooms, approached by paved footpaths and streets lit with oil lamps, came with increased wealth, the growth of leisure and learning, and new tastes in polite architecture. Leeds led the way with a weekly newspaper, the *Leeds Mercury*

'[Hull is] exceeding close built ... 'tis extraordinary populous, even to an inconvenience.'

DANIEL DEFOE

(1718) and a town history, Ralph Thoresby's *Ducatus Leodiensis: or, the Topography of Leeds and the Parts adjacent* (1715), which was followed by Thomas Gent's *The Ancient and Modern History of the Famous City of York* (1730), the same author's *History of Kingston-upon-Hull* (1735), Francis Drake's *Eboracum: or the History and Antiquities of the City of York* (1736) and later the Revd John Watson's *History of Halifax* (1775).

A new type of town, the spa, which offered health cures based on the supposed healing properties of sulphur and chalybeate springs, emerged during the seventeenth century. The fashion spread from the Low Countries and Germany to Bath, Epsom, Wells, Tunbridge Wells and the northern resorts of Buxton, Harrogate and Scarborough. The chalybeate Tewit Well at Harrogate had been recommended by Yorkshire doctors in Elizabeth's reign, then in the seventeenth century three mineral springs were discovered on the commons at High Harrogate. 'It's all marshy and wett', wrote Celia Fiennes, and at first visitors stayed in nearby Knaresborough, but once they began to drink from the springs and bathe in tubs of heated sulphur water nearby accommodation became necessary. At Scarborough, where medicinal springs had been discovered on the sands in 1626, buildings were not erected nearby until about 1700. Sea-bathing was an added attraction and Scarborough was probably the first place in England where it became popular. The poorer end of the town, in and around Newborough, was transformed into a fashionable resort, with inns, coffee shops and places of entertainment for the gentry of northern England and Scotland who came there during the season. Fishing remained an important activity and in 1702 it was claimed that about 160 sail or collier ships sought shelter in the port during winter time. Defoe thought that the harbour was 'one of the most commodious of this kingdom, yet scarce able to hold the ships belonging to the place', but though Scarborough men traded with the Netherlands and Norway the lack of a navigable river prevented the town's development into an important distribution centre.

Some of Yorkshire's smaller market towns also attracted favourable comments from visitors. Celia Fiennes thought Tadcaster 'a very good little town for travellers, mostly Inns and little tradesmen's houses' and Defoe noted that Northallerton was 'remarkable for the vast quantity of black cattle sold there' at the fortnightly summer fairs to graziers who fattened them in the Lincolnshire fens or the Isle of Ely before selling them in London. But in 1751 Wetherby struck Dr Pococke as 'a poor town very pleasantly situated' and a generation later Viscount Torrington thought it small, gloomy and ill-built. Wetherby had suffered from cattle plague and agricultural depression in the mid eighteenth century and over half of its 70 or 80 properties had been destroyed by fire in 1723. In 1776 the population was only 912, but Wetherby was nevertheless distinguished from its rural neighbours by the 15 innkeepers in the High Street, Market Place and the adjoining Chapel Yard, its eight professional families, its provision dealers and craftsmen, and its brewery, tannery and mills for grinding corn and crushing rape seed. Otley was another typical minor market town,

Bridge and New Dock, Hull, 1802. Robert Thew's view of the dock gate and office, looking westward, shows the first stage in the expansion of Hull's facilities. This new dock, started in 1774, provided anchorage for over 100 ships. At the time it was England's largest. The street lamps, here and in the town, were lit by whale-oil. The windmill adds to the impression that this could be a Dutch landscape.

Scarborough holiday makers, 1770. T. Ramsey's painting shows how Scarborough first attracted genteel visitors who came for the beneficial effects of the spa waters and bathing. Horse-drawn bathing machines allowed bathers to undress discreetly and to be conveyed to the sea. The visitors seem to be overdressed by today's standards. The view is taken from near the spa at the southern end of the South Bay.

South Bay, Scarborough, 1791. Francis Nicholson's view shows the Georgian town largely confined within its medieval limits below the castle and St Mary's church. It was still possible to drive a coach and horses over the sands and only a few bathing machines are to be seen. During the following century the railways were to change all that.

where a market for corn and provisions was held every Tuesday and fairs for horned cattle and household goods were organised twice a year on 1 August and 15 November. In the later seventeenth century Yorkshire had over 60 market towns. Ancient rights to hold markets had lapsed at Frodingham, Hornsea, Hunmanby, Kilham and elsewhere, but Thorne (1659), Huddersfield (1671) and Penistone (1699) had acquired new charters for weekly markets and annual fairs and several short fairs had been established in the countryside; by 1770 fairs were held in 97 different places. Some villages had their own range of shops. At the close of the seventeenth century Abraham de la Pryme wrote that although Hatfield 'be not dignify'd either with a market or fair, yet it stands so conveniently that it is not far off any', having Doncaster, Thorne and Bawtry nearby, but indeed it was 'so well furnished with one or two of almost every trade, as butchers, mercers, chandlers, joyners, cutlers, chirurgians, etc, that other places stands in more need of them than the latter of the former'.

Farming

By the seventeenth century the market system was so effective that farmers were able to concentrate upon what they could do best. Pennine farmers spent their time in dairying, rearing and industrial by-employments, which paid for their imported malt and bread corn that came via the navigable rivers, the market towns and carrying services provided by local badgers. In the North Riding the great landowners and gentlemen-farmers reared horses for the coach and saddle and many of the tenant farmers specialised in dairying, selling their best butter to London or to continental factors and their cheaper produce to the inhabitants of the northern industrial towns. In Charles II's reign nearly 42,000 firkins of butter per annum were carted up to 30 miles to Yarm, Stockton or Whitby for export along the coast or across the North Sea.

Farmers in many parts of Yorkshire were willing to try new ideas to improve the quality of both crops and livestock. In 1664 a committee of enquiry was told that farmers in the liberty of Ripon pared, dried and burned their pastures and worst sorts of ground to yield three or four good crops, then they spread lime, dung, or marl mixed with dung to make good pastures. The practice of spreading lime on acid soils was widely adopted when it was brought as back carriage to be burned in kilns at the head of navigable rivers and canals. One of the most successful farming innovations was the Rotherham plough, which was patented in 1730 by Joesph Foljambe of Eastwood, yeoman, and Disney Staniforth of Firbeck, esquire; it became popular over a wide area and the basis for many metal ploughs in the nineteenth century. Turnips or clover were grown on suitable soils from the late seventeenth century, so that by the 1720s, for example, clover had replaced peas, and turnips had partly replaced rye, in the rotations of the townfields of Hatfield. Potatoes had been introduced as a field crop into Lancashire and Cumberland in the mid seventeenth century and had become a common sight in the western parts of the Lancashire Plain, especially in the reclaimed mosslands. Small plots were cultivated in Masham and Nidderdale by 1712–13 and at Cowick in the southern Vale of York by the 1730s, but it was not until the mid eighteenth century that they were widespread on the rich loams and warpings of Holderness and Howdenshire. A Board of Agriculture report of 1800 stated that in the North Riding potatoes had become an object of field husbandry (as distinct from a garden crop) not more than 40 years previously, but by then they were universal. An older crop that became popular was rape, which was grown in Holderness, the Vale of Pickering and other lowland areas as fodder for sheep and as a valuable supply of vegetable oil, much of which was exported

The Rotherham plough was patented by Disney Staniforth and Joesph Foljambe in 1730 and soon became popular in many parts of Yorkshire and the Midlands. It was probably based on the Dutch ploughs that had been introduced into the Hatfield Levels in the seventeenth century and was the forerunner of nineteenth-century metal ploughs. In this mezzotint of 1801 it is shown being pulled by oxen.

to Holland. Amongst the newer crops were the hops which were cultivated around Doncaster.

This progressive spirit was far from universal. In 1729 the steward of the manor of Bilbrough in the northern Vale of York failed to get his tenants to grow less corn and to concentrate upon dairying and wrote in disgust that they were 'like Old Cart Horses, one can't thrust 'em out of their old beaten track'. Later in the century William Marshall, the agricultural writer from Pickering, observed that 'poverty and ignorance are the ordinary inhabitants of small farms'. Family farms in most parts of Yorkshire was often less than 30 acres. In 1788 Marshall found that over half the land in the Vale of Pickering was laid out in farms that were rented at less than £20 per annum and perhaps three-quarters were let at under £50. He wrote that leases were unknown on most of the larger estates, where farms were let at will on a yearly tenancy, though in practice they had been passed down from father to son through successive generations. The Board of Agriculture reporter made the same point about the North Riding generally and thought that few parts of England could produce a tenantry 'who, and whose ancestry have lived an equal number of years uninterruptedly on their farms'. The reporter for the East Riding found that tenants were just as secure without leases and that 'estates, in general, throughout the district, are let on very fair, and many even on moderate terms, and many of them have been occupied by the progenitors of the present tenants during two, three or four generations'. Tenure was just as secure for the farmers of the West Riding, where the reporter remarked upon 'the astonishing number of freeholders' and others with sound copyhold. The West Riding was one of the strongholds of small freeholders with less than 20 acres of land, for many of them had an additional source of income from industry.

Nearly all the Pennine farmers within the Graveship of Holme were copyhold tenants of the huge manor of Wakefield. The right to graze animals on the commons and extra income from cloth making were essential to the family economy. As the population grew farms were sub-divided and new ones created on the moorland edges. Similar trends are evident in the Yorkshire Dales, where the arable townfields had mostly disappeared by the end of the seventeenth century. Inventories of the personal estate of Wensleydale farmers taken between 1670 and 1700 show that only one in seven farmers in the lower parts and as few as one in 20 in the upper dale grew any crops. Small meadows and pastures lined the dale bottoms and large, stinted pastures covered the fell sides. Though many weaver-farmers kept to the old life-style, farms had generally dwindled in size and numerous cottagers earned most of their living from a craft; linen weaving rather than the manufacture of woollen cloth was now the mainstay. In Swaledale smallholders turned to lead mining for extra income and by the late eighteenth century they were more properly described as miners who were part-time farmers.

In the later seventeenth century farmers in many other Yorkshire townships agreed to abandon communal agriculture by enclosing their open fields and

sometimes also their commons. Few open-field systems survived in the northern Vale of York as late as the era of parliamentary enclosure and throughout the county adaptations to allow new crops or to convert strips into grass leys meant that the fields of one township might be organised in a very different manner from those of their neighbours. In the lower Dearne Valley, for instance, Wath's common fields survived until their division by Act of Parliament in 1814, but at neighbouring Adwick two-thirds of the land had been enclosed by 1737 and though the remaining common fields were still divided into strips they were held in compact blocks by the lord's tenants. North of the river, Bolton retained 1,715 acres of common arable fields, ings, pastures and wastes until 1761, but Mexborough had 300 acres of 'old enclosures' alongside 700 acres of common fields, 160 acres of common ings and 90 acres of common pastures. Neighbouring townships with similar soils and field systems could have a very different history of enclosure, for the patterns of landownership and tenure and human decisions were as important as the physical factors. In Holderness, for example, the long lands of the ancient two-field system remained intact in some townships, but not in those

Hatfield. A farmstead and its outbuildings and the tower of a disused windmill are built in brick, but in the distance we see the late-medieval tower of the parish church, built of imported magnesian limestone. The prohibitive cost of transporting stone meant that it could not be used for vernacular buildings, so when the old clay and timber-framed houses and cottages were replaced from the seventeenth century onwards, local bricks were used and the roofs were covered with pantiles, or 'Dutch tiles' as they were first known.
PHOTOGRAPH: AUTHOR

where the farmers decided upon enclosure and the conversion of strips into temporary or permanent grass leys. Holderness was a corn-and-cattle district with wheat and beans the principal crops and an average head of 15 cattle per farm that was the highest in Yorkshire. Much land remained unenclosed there until the later eighteenth century.

Parliamentary enclosure was the method that was resorted to when the full agreement of the landowners could not be obtained. If the owners of about three-quarters of the value of the land agreed upon the desirability of enclosure, their wishes could be enforced by private Act of Parliament. Between 1750 and 1850 over six million acres of land in England and Wales were enclosed by about 4,000 private Acts. Scattered strips were re-arranged into closes and those who had rights (such as grazing and turf-digging) upon the commons and wastes were compensated with new allotments. As these rights were related to the size of the farms, the largest allotments were given to the biggest free-holders. The small cottager who previously had the right to graze a few animals often found that his compensation was inadequate and expensive to fence. Though parliamentary enclosure was carried out with a scrupulous regard for the law, in practice the poorer sections of society fared badly.

The fields of Hepworth. The curving walls follow the lines of former strips in Far Field, one of the open-fields of Hepworth township. Elsewhere, most of the fields have the geometric patterns that were created in 1834 when commissioners appointed by Act of Parliament completed the enclosure of the common pastures and moors of the Graveship of Holme. The village of Hepworth can be seen in the background.
PHOTOGRAPH: AUTHOR

In the West Riding the process began in 1729 with an Act to enclose the remaining open fields of Thurnscoe. The South Field had been enclosed in 1675 and the common wastes were divided by local agreements in 1738 and 1825, for the expensive method of enclosing by private Act of Parliament was used only as a last resort. Four West Riding Acts were passed before 1755, then another 95 Acts were obtained between 1756 and 1785. In the North Riding 97 Acts were passed between the 1740s and 1780 and another 157 by 1820. In 1731 the Holderness township of Cowick was the first in the East Riding to use parliamentary enclosure and by 1850 162 Acts had reached the statute book. The Wolds were particularly affected, for about 206,000 acres had been divided in this way by 1810. New compact farms with symmetrical brick houses and outbuildings were planted in the countryside, dew ponds were dug out for livestock, plantations provided shelter, and hawthorn hedges transformed the Wolds landscape into large, rectangular fields. This physical transformation was accompanied by a striking change in farming practice, as old pasture was converted to tillage and even the sheepwalks and rabbit warrens were ploughed up. By 1812 two-thirds of the Wolds were farmed as arable with a four-course rotation of turnips, barley, clover or grass, and wheat, or with local variations adapted to different soils. New crops meant that store cattle could now be fed through winter, but flocks of sheep remained an essential part of this farming economy, for they were folded in the valleys by night for their manure.

Houses

Yorkshire has no timber-framed houses that are later than 1680, for by then stone and brick were the favoured building materials in all but the most humble outbuildings. In some areas, notably the Wolds and the magnesian limestone belt, the rebuilding of villages was so thorough that few traces of former timber-framing survive, but in other parts of the county older frames are still concealed behind stone or brick shells. In his description of Hatfield at the close of the seventeenth century Abraham de la Pryme remarked that,

> The manner of building that it formerly had were all of wood, clay and plaster, but now that way of building is quite left of, for every one now from the richest to the poorest, will not build except with bricks; so that now from about 80 years ago (at which time bricks were first seen, used and made in this parish), they have been wholy used, and now there scarce is one house in the town that does not, if not wholy, yet for the most part, consist of that lasting and genteel sort of building; many of which are also built according to the late model with cut brick and covered over with Holland tyle, which gives a brisk and pleasant air to the town, and tho' many of the houses be little and despicable without, yet they are neat, well furnished, and most of them ceiled with the whitest plaster within.

Gypsum plaster was 'digged up in great Quantity and plenty' in the Isle of Axholme and the different nature of the local clays and the varying methods used in the firing process produced bricks of diverse colours and textures. Brick now became the usual building material in lowland Yorkshire, but in western parts the first brick buildings were so distinctive that they were commonly given the name of Red House. Nevertheless, by the middle years of the eighteenth century brick was widely used in the West Riding industrial towns. The Sheffield baptism and burial registers of 1698–1703 name only one brickmaker amongst the 1,149 men whose occupations are recorded, but by 1764 the curate could report that 'The buildings are in general of brick'.

Brick houses were normally roofed with pantiles, the 'Holland tyle' of Pryme's account. In 1694 Ralph Thoresby described Stapleton in the southern

Vale of York as 'a pretty village, where the Dutch tiles are much used'. They were imported through Yarm from the Low Countries during the 1670s and were soon manufactured locally, but it was well into the eighteenth or even the nineteenth century before they were generally accepted. At Swainsby, for example, in 1807 almost all the houses were thatched but by the 1840s they had all been roofed with pantiles. Converting roofs was a straightforward job, for the pitch did not have to be altered, but pantiles were easily lifted by the wind and they often allowed rain to percolate the interior rubble of the walls, so a bottom course of stone slates was commonly provided. Though Norwegian softwoods were imported via the Humber and Tees in the eighteenth century and trusses were increasingly copied from pattern books, simple traditional roof designs were used well into the nineteenth century, especially in cottages and outbuildings. Another change, widely adopted in brick buildings, was the replacement of mullions by sash windows. Sliding-sashes were an innovation of the 1680s that combined practical value with aesthetic appeal. Vertical sashes were soon a feature of such gentry houses as Middlethorpe Hall on the southern outskirts of York, but they did not appear at vernacular level until after 1700. Many a farmer preferred the sideways-sliding type known as Yorkshire sashes that appeared about the same time. In stone houses, however, mullions continued in fashion much later and can be found in nineteenth-century buildings such as weavers' cottages.

Yorkshire has a wide range of vernacular houses that date from the seventeenth and eighteenth centuries. Former houses of yeomen-clothiers survive in their hundreds in the upper Calder Valley. Built of solid millstone grit to a two-unit, three-unit, or cross-wings plan with a workshop at the lower end, they confirm the evidence of the hearth tax returns of Charles II's reign that this was the richest part of rural Yorkshire. Three main types of house-plans in North Yorkshire and Cleveland from this period are widespread, regardless of building materials. The hearth-passage plan seems to have developed from the medieval gentry hall, where a screens passage separated the main rooms from the service end, and from the more lowly longhouse, where a cross-passage divided domestic accommodation from the cow byre. Such houses had three rooms on the ground floor, were one room deep, and were normally two-storeyed. The passage ran behind the chimney stack and divided the building into two unequal parts. Sometimes the low end contained two small service rooms of unequal size, but more often the whole space was taken for a kitchen. If an extra chimney were not provided at the low end, the cooking was done in the 'firehouse' or 'house', the main living room. Craven houses were often provided with handsome, stone-arched fireplaces, but elsewhere the fashion was to have a funnel-shaped timber and plaster firehood resting on a wooden beam. Beyond the 'house' lay the parlour, which was a retiring room and commonly the best bedroom, and sometimes part of the top end was used as a small dairy. The chambers served as extra bedrooms, lumber rooms, and occasionally as work rooms. The second type of plan – the lobby-entrance –

Ilkley Manor House. The only part of the medieval manor house that can be seen from outside is the doorway leading into the cross passage. The house was completely remodelled in the late Elizabethan period, with the usual range of gables, topped by finials, and rows of mullioned and transomed windows. The lower wing was rebuilt in the middle years of the seventeenth century, by whom is not known.
PHOTOGRAPH: CARNEGIE, 2005

Vernacular architecture, Austwick. This Craven village has several small houses which were built in local limestone for the leading farming families in the last decades of the seventeenth century and the early years of the eighteenth. They are characterised by the curious decorations of the lintel-stones above the doorway and by the stepped arrangement of the attic window, following the designs of upper windows in local gentry halls at Friars Head and Kildwick.
PHOTOGRAPH: AUTHOR

was somewhat similar except that the chimney stack stood immediately behind the door, blocking the passage and providing heat to the rooms on either side. It was the dominant type in the Vale of York, Craven and the southern Dales, but was rare in north-eastern parts of the county and apparently unknown north of the Yorkshire border. A third type, with the chimney stack at one end and a central door leading directly into the house, was also popular and widespread. Extra service rooms were sometimes added in the form of a wing or outshut to the rear, or sometimes the back of the parlour end was partitioned off for this purpose. This simple plan continued in use in the nineteenth century, especially at the level of labourers' cottages.

The quality and dates of the houses vary considerably from one part of

Yorkshire to another. Datestones indicate different peaks of building between 1630 and 1719 and renewed activity between 1740 and 1770, though rebuilding in the East Riding was generally even later. The poorest and most backward areas were the North York Moors and adjacent parts of the coastal belt and the Vale of Pickering. In 1664 Goathland had only one house taxed on more than one hearth and that belonged to a gentleman with two. Fir Tree House, otherwise known as Beck Hole, dated 1728, is the earliest house of two full storeys on these moors. The pattern in the northern Vale of York is of a few large farmhouses scattered amongst the much greater number of middling and small buildings of the nucleated villages and market towns. Farmers in the southern Vale of York, especially those in the riverside parishes, generally had a higher level of prosperity which was reflected in the large upper storeys and kitchens of their farmhouses. As in medieval times, however, the quality of housing varied a great deal from village to village. Another wealthy area was Craven, which has some of the most picturesque old farmhouses in the county, built with a conscious element of display in a superb setting; in 1673 35 per cent of Craven houses had more than two fire hearths. Further north, the Dales smallholders lived in compact, unpretentious houses that were remarkably uniform in plan, structure and decoration, but on the whole they were well furnished, even on the upper floor.

Yorkshire still has a great number of seventeenth- and eighteenth-century gentry halls and some of the finest noblemen's seats in the country. The later Stuart age saw the beginnings of great changes in architectural styles and fashions of living. In 1682 Sir John Reresby celebrated Christmas in the lavish manner of his ancestors, 'with great mirth and ceremony'. On nine separate

Beningborough Hall. One of the National Trust's most attractive Yorkshire houses, Beningborough Hall stands near the River Ouse in the flat lands north-west of York. The initials of John and Mary Bourchier and the date 1716 above the main entrance and on the great staircase provide a completion date. The builder was William Thornton, a 'Joyner and Architect' of York, who had worked at Castle Howard and other Yorkshire houses under the leading architects of the day. He not only drew up the plans and elevations, but was responsible for the magnificent woodcarvings. The house, seen here from the gardens, stands two storeys high, above a basement, and has an attic storey for the servants. Stone quoins and large wooden brackets supporting the eaves relieve the otherwise plain, brick exterior; decoration was applied only to the door surrounds. Upon passing through the door, however, we discover an elaborate Baroque interior.

occasions between Christmas Eve and Epiphany he invited a total of 144 tenants, 61 gentlemen and their wives, and 12 clergy and noted contentedly that 'For musick I had two violins and a base from Doncaster that wore my livery, that plaid well for the country; two bagpipes for the common people; a trompeter and drummer. The expense of liquor, both of wine and others, was considerable, as well as of other provisions, and my guests appeared well satisfied'.

A lord of the manor's household no longer contained as many servants as it had in the past and this style of entertaining was generally regarded as old-fashioned. The designers of newer houses abandoned the medieval concept of a great hall separated from the service rooms by a screens passage; the servants now had their meals in their own quarters near the kitchen and went about their chores via their own staircase, discreetly placed at the rear of the building. This new type of accommodation had been introduced into southern England by Royalist exiles returning from France and the Low Countries after the restoration of Charles II. The fashion spread to the North when provincial nobles and gentlemen, who resided for much of the year in the capital, approved the new designs and copied them at home. 'Restoration houses' were compact in plan, comfortable and warm to live in, and satisfying in their proportions. Gables were eliminated in favour of a double-pile house with a hipped roof and central lead flat and though the buildings were normally only of two full storeys, they often had a small attic floor and a basement. They were no longer vernacular in style but readily let themselves to classical shapes and details. Whereas the houses of the minor gentry usually had a plain, symmetrical elevation, the grander buildings had a flight of steps and a pediment adorned with the owner's coat of arms. The hall was now a grand entrance room with a great parlour beyond and smaller rooms to the side; above the parlour was the saloon, the successor to the great chamber as the most splendid room in the house.

Yorkshire's best 'Restoration houses' date from the last quarter of the seventeenth century and are found particularly in the Vale of York, notably Bell Hall at Naburn, Middlethorpe Hall, Newby Hall, Nun Monkton Hall and Slade Hooton Hall. One of the earliest is the 15-bay brick hall at Ribston on the banks of the river Nidd, erected about 1674 for Sir Henry Goodrick, who subsequently helped the Earl of Danby to secure York for William of Orange and was rewarded with the post of Lieutenant-General of the Ordnance and a seat on the Privy Council. On a similar scale is Beningborough Hall, completed in 1716 for John Bourchier to the designs of William Thornton. Both the Goodrick and Bourchier families had resided on their estates since the sixteenth century, but fine houses were built for newcomers like Sir John Hewley, a lawyer and MP for York and owner of Bell Hall, and Sir Edward Blackett, MP for Ripon and the son of a Newcastle coal-owner, who erected Newby Hall.

The Parliamentary victory in the Civil War did not bring about great changes in landownership, for although heavy penalties were imposed on the losing side, many Royalist families were able to repurchase their forfeited estates. Nor did the Restoration seriously affect the fortunes of former Parliamentarians. For half a century or so after the outbreak of Civil War very few great houses were built in Yorkshire, but during the period of stability ushered in by the 1688 revolution stately homes that were sometimes as grand as palaces were erected all over England. The latter decades of the seventeenth century saw the emergence of great estates in Yorkshire; a consolidation of property brought about by purchases, exchanges, enclosures, and above all by inheritance and marriage. Professional services offered by the growing number of stewards, agents and attorneys enabled landowners to secure their estates and legal schemes were an effective aid in ensuring the transfer of property intact. Great landowners took pride in the family's past achievements and in their own standing in society and they took their duty to future generations seriously. A failure of male heirs leading to indirect successions did not weaken this sense of obligation, but personal behaviour influenced dynastic fortunes. The importance of national office and court sinecures as extra sources of wealth was decisive to families aiming for the top. During the seventeenth and eighteenth centuries Yorkshiremen held some of the most powerful positions in the country and were able to amass great estates on which they built splendid houses and created landscaped parks. Some of the finest architects in the country were active in Yorkshire, designing houses in the English Baroque style, a development on a much larger scale of the rectangular, double-piled houses that had come into fashion after the Restoration. But Yorkshire also had some gifted native craftsmen such as William Thornton and the Ettys of York and talented gentlemen-architects like Lord Bingley and William Wakefield, who between them produced some of the county's finest buildings.

Those Yorkshiremen who played a prominent part in the 1688 revolution that placed William III on the throne soon received their reward, none more so than Sir Thomas Osborne, who as Earl of Danby had been the greatest public figure after the monarch during the 1670s. Danby was appointed Lord President of the Council and created Duke of Leeds. The enormous wealth that he had obtained from public office enabled him to engage William Talman, who was then busy at Chatsworth, to design a new brick house at Kiveton Park (demolished in 1811) and to employ Laguerre and Thornhill for the interior decorations. Talman was approached by Charles Howard, the third Earl of Carlisle, to design a new house at Henderskelfe, to be called Castle Howard, but he quarrelled with his patron and lost the commission to Sir John Vanbrugh and Nicholas Hawksmoor. This astonishing building, the likes of which had never been seen before, was Vanbrugh's first serious attempt at architecture and was remarkably successful in setting the style for the provincial palaces of the nation's leading figures. The earl was on two occasions the First Lord of the Treasury, the office soon to be equated with that of prime minister. His visitors were left in no doubt that they were at the home of a great man, long before they reached the state rooms or audience chambers. The Carmire Gate, mock

Castle Howard, south front. In 1699 Charles Howard, third Earl of Carlisle, commissioned Sir John Vanbrugh to design a country house in Baroque style to replace the burnt ruin of Hinderskelfe Castle. It was Vanbrugh's first building and nothing had been seen like it before. His assistant, Nicholas Hawksmoor, played a crucial role in implementing Vanbrugh's ideas. Nearly 200 men began work in 1700 and by 1714 the central block, dome, and east wing were finished. The west wing was never built as Vanbrugh intended; instead, it was erected in the 1750s to a Palladian design of Sir Thomas Robinson's, the brother-in-law of the fourth Earl.
PHOTOGRAPH: AUTHOR

military structures on the crest of the hill, and a 100 feet-high obelisk mark the entrance to the 1,000-acre park, which is tastefully adorned with a lake, waterfalls, terrace, statues and some wonderful landscape buildings modelled on Italian structures seen on the Grand Tour. The Temple of the four Winds, for example, was based on the Villa Rotonda at Vicenza.

Robert Benson had been to Italy to study architecture and with the large fortune he had inherited from his father he was able to purchase an uncultivated estate at Bramham in 1699 to build a house and lay out formal gardens in the French style with high, clipped yews, long, straight vistas and intersecting

Castle Howard is famous for the striking monuments in its landscaped grounds. Vanbrugh's Temple of the Four Winds (1724–26) was modelled on Palladio's Villa Rotonda at Vicenza. It stands on a knoll at the corner of Ray Wood and was used as a summer house or belvedere from which to view the scenery. Young aristocrats who had been on the Grand Tour aspired to recreate classical Italian landscapes in the English countryside, despite the differences in weather.
PHOTOGRAPH: AUTHOR

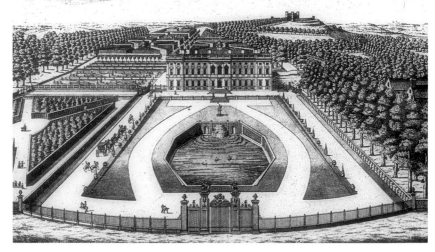

rides, water-works, temples and other eye-catchers. The gardens remain wonderfully intact, an outstanding example of the style of the period. Benson was MP for York, a favourite of Queen Anne, and from 1711 Chancellor of the Exchequer; in 1713 he was created Lord Bingley. At the height of his power and influence he supervised the building of Yorkshire's next great Baroque mansion, at Stainborough. Here, in the early 1670s, Sir Gervase Cutler had erected one of the county's earliest classical buildings (now the north range), but he was a spendthrift and in 1708 his son was forced to sell the estate to Thomas Wentworth, Lord Raby, the British ambassador in Berlin. Wentworth was a Tory who acquired a fortune as he rose in the army and diplomatic service under Queen Anne. The great nephew of his famous namesake, he was determined to outshine his Whig cousins who had inherited the ancestral estate at Wentworth Woodhouse. In Berlin he persuaded Johannes von Bodt, a leading continental architect, to design a new Baroque range with a long gallery running all along the top floor. Upon the death of Queen Anne he was forced to retire to his estates where he concentrated upon completing his house and gardens and upon a romantic scheme to build a mock castle on the site of the fort from which Stainborough's name was derived. By 1731 the estate was known as Wentworth Castle.

The challenge was taken up by Thomas Watson-Wentworth, the future Marquis of Rockingham, who inherited Wentworth Woodhouse from his father in 1723. He immediately set about building a Baroque range to face the village, but when this was finished in the late 1720s he found that the design was considered old-fashioned and imperfect. The strict Palladianism of the Earl of Burlington's circle was now the new orthodoxy. In 1715 Colen Campbell had championed this style in the first volume of *Vitruvius Brittanicus* and in 1721 had designed Yorkshire's first Palladian villa, Baldersby Park, for Sir William Robinson, MP for York. Watson-Wentworth determined to build a vast east range, modelled on Campbell's Wanstead House in Essex, with the largest front of any country house in England, as a deliberate statement of his wealth, power and privilege. Meanwhile, the surroundings of the house were altered dramatically by Humphrey Repton and others. By the middle of the eighteenth

Wentworth Woodhouse, the house with the longest front of any stately home in England, is shown here in J.P. Neale's view of 1847. It was built for Thomas Watson-Wentworth, first Marquis of Rockingham, who had inherited the property in 1723 and who had immediately begun to build a fine Baroque house looking towards the village. Unfortunately, by the time it was completed between 1725 and 1728 this style had gone out of fashion, especially for an aspiring Whig politician. The new rage was the strict Palladianism of the Earl of Burlington and his circle of architects. Watson-Wentworth began to build anew in the opposite direction.

The model for the Palladian range was Wanstead House, north-east of London. In their central portions, crowned at Wentworth by the motto, '*Mea Gloria Fides*', My Faith is My Glory, the two houses were identical. The new plans were approved by the Earl of Burlington, who recommended that Henry Flitcroft should be put in charge. Flitcroft designed the marble saloon on the first floor as a larger version of Inigo Jones' Queen's House at Greenwich. Work on the interior continued for decades and the final version of the house, including the wings designed by John Carr, was not completed until 1806. By then, the front extended for 606 feet.

century the park had been so enlarged that it was over nine miles in circumference and by 1800 the Wentworth estate had been doubled in size to 17,200 acres. The grounds were provided with a terrace, ha-ha and ponds, an enormous stable block was erected behind the house and lodges and the grandiose follies known as Needle's Eye, Hoober Stand, Keppel's Column and the Mausoleum were sited on prominent points. Wentworth Woodhouse was a Whig palace dominating a large part of South Yorkshire. The second Marquis became leader of the Whig party and for two short periods Prime Minister.

The Earl of Burlington, the dominant aristocratic figure in the Palladian movement, spent most of his time in the capital but his ancestral estate was at Londesborough in the East Riding. The Earl designed the York assembly rooms and his Bridlington protégé, William Kent, became an architect and designer of national repute. Prominent amateur architects in Burlington's Yorkshire circle included Sir Thomas Robinson, who designed his own hall at Rokeby on the banks of the Tees, and Colonel James Moyser of Beverley, who provided designs for Bretton Hall and Nostell Priory. Nostell was built for Sir Rowland Winn, who had married the wealthy daughter of a former Lord Mayor of London upon his return from a lengthy Grand Tour on the continent and particularly in Italy. The design was modelled on Palladio's drawings for *Four Books of Architecture* and the internal decoration was the work of the young James Paine, Antonio Zucchi and Joseph Rose, and subsequently Robert Adam; the furniture was created by Thomas Chippendale of Otley. Paine went on to

right This print by J.P. Neale (1847) shows Bretton Hall, which was built for Sir William Wentworth about 1720, with the extensive alterations that were made at the end of the Napoleonic War. The architect was Wentworth's friend, Colonel James Moyser of Beverley, a prominent member of the Yorkshire circle gathered around the Earl of Burlington, the most influential figure in the Palladian movement. The nineteenth-century extensions, including the large bow window, were designed by Jeffrey Wyatt, known later as Wyatville, for Colonel Beaumont. The house was set amidst landscaped grounds, with an artificial lake, in the fashion of the time.

Nostell Priory. J. P. Neale's view of 1847 shows the house which was built for Sir Rowland Winn after he had returned from the Grand Tour in 1729 to marry the daughter of a former Lord Mayor of London. The architect was Colonel James Moyser, who had recently been responsible for Bretton Hall. Moyser based his plan on a design of an Italian villa by Andrea Palladio. The principal rooms on the first floor were approached by a flight of steps leading to the giant Ionic columns that supported a pediment bearing the baronet's coat of arms. The original design had four corner pavilions, but only the two shown here were built, and the foremost of these has since been demolished. Work began in 1735–36, under the supervision of the 19-year-old local man, James Paine.

In 1776 Robert Adam designed the new wing to the right, but the plan to balance this with a similar wing on the left was never implemented. The house (which now belongs to the National Trust) takes its name from the former Augustinian priory on the site. A few medieval remains can be found in the outbuildings.

acquire a national reputation and to design several other Yorkshire houses, including Heath House, Wakefield, the Mansion House, Doncaster, the garden front of Cusworth Hall, Wadworth Hall, Cowick Hall and the Earl of Scarbrough's villa at Sandbeck Park.

The style of a nobleman's house and the size of his estate reflected his political power and standing in local society. Eighteenth-century English aristocrats took their responsibilities seriously. Many of them tried to live like the senators and philosophers of the ancient world and regarded classical art,

The approach to Fountains Abbey. This picturesque view of the east front and tower of the abbey church was created by the owners of the neighbouring estate of Studley Royal, John Aislabie and his son William. John began his water gardens and landscaping scheme in the early eighteenth century, with a view of the abbey designed as the culmination of a guided tour for visitors. William inherited Studley Royal in 1742 and soon purchased the abbey estate in order to extend the landscaped area in the current picturesque style. The National Trust has restored the walk along the banks of the Skell to its former glory. From W. Westall's *Views of Fountains Abbey and Studley Park*.
BY COURTESY OF GROVE RARE BOOKS, BOLTON ABBEY

left The Temple of Piety, Studley Park.

architecture and literature as ideals to be sought after. At Newby Hall, William Weddell, a renowned collector of art treasures, commissioned Robert Adam to design a gallery to display his classical sculptures. At Studley Park John Aislabie created a superb approach to the ruined Fountains Abbey with such features as the moon pool, complete with a statue of Neptune, and a Temple of Piety. And high above the remains of Rievaulx Abbey Thomas Duncombe constructed a terrace with a Tuscan temple at one end and an Ionic temple at the other. The great houses and parks of the eighteenth-century Yorkshire aristocracy must be seen not just in a national but a European context.

The price of land was driven up by noblemen from remoter parts of the realm who wished to purchase an estate nearer the capital and by those who had made their fortunes in commerce and who decided to consolidate their position in the accepted way. In South Yorkshire, for instance, the manor of Edlington was bought in 1708 by Viscount Molesworth, an Irish peer who proceeded to build a suitable house, and a few years later the Scottish Earl of Kinnoul made Brodsworth his principal English seat. At Sledmere, tucked away in the Wolds, the

Gothic temple, Bramham Park. The formal gardens at Bramham Park were created in the French and Dutch style by Robert Benson, Lord Bingley, in the first quarter of the eighteenth century. Benson was a self-made man who rose in the service of Queen Anne and was appointed Chancellor of the Exchequer in 1711. His gardens are amongst the best preserved from this period, for they were never landscaped when their formal designs fell out of fashion. However, some new buildings were erected as eye-catchers in the grounds in the second half of the eighteenth century, including this Gothic Temple beyond the pond.
PHOTOGRAPH: AUTHOR

Sykes family dramatically transformed the landscape. This dynasty of Leeds and Hull merchants had been founded in the mid sixteenth century by a younger son of a Cumberland yeoman. The family acquired Sledmere in 1718 but it was not until Richard Sykes inherited the property in 1748 that great projects were put in hand. During the next half century Richard and Sir Christopher Sykes built a house close by the parish church and removed the village to a new site on the Malton–Driffield road beyond the park. The mere that gave the place its name was drained, roads were blocked, the park extended, and the house and church left in seclusion. Likewise, at Harewood Edwin Lascelles altered the landscape out of all recognition and began to build a new house after he had inherited the estate from his father in 1759. Henry Lascelles was a director of the East India Company, whose wealth, acquired through the ribbon trade and collecting customs in Barbados, enabled him to purchase the Harewood–Gawthorpe estate. In the Middle Ages Harewood had been a flourishing market village protected by a castle but by the sixteenth century it had decayed. Edwin Lascelles removed all except the church, which now stands hidden in the trees, and demolished Gawthorpe Hall to make way for his new house and landscaped park. His architect, John Carr, also designed a new village at the gates of the park, tastefully assembled to provide a widening vista of the entrance. Robert Adam and Thomas Chippendale were commissioned to decorate and furnish the interior of the house, which was partly remodelled by Sir Charles Barry in the 1840s.

Walton Hall. A Georgian house, built in 1767–68, Walton Hall has a plain exterior with a pediment resting on four Tuscan pilasters over a Tuscan-columned porch. It is surrounded by a lake, which is crossed by a cast-iron bridge. In the nineteenth century it was the home of Charles Waterton, traveller and naturalist, who transformed the lake and the park into the world's first wild fowl sanctuary. He enclosed his estate with a high wall, erected a water gate for nesting birds, and built a grotto. The hotel has been restored and is now the Waterton Park Hotel.

Churches and chapels

The restoration of Charles II led to the re-establishment of the former practices of the Church of England and to the ejection of those ministers who refused

St Mary's Church, Whitby, has the best-preserved Georgian interior of any English parish church. It escaped the attentions of the Victorian High Church movement which removed the clutter of box pews and galleries in favour of a more dignified appearance. By the eighteenth century, the church which the Normans built on the cliff top close to St Hilda's Abbey could no longer accommodate the growing population. White-painted galleries with numbered seats were fitted high above the box pews that had taken up every space in the nave, and external staircases were built to provide access. The settlements of each quarter of the parish were designated a particular part of the church. When full, the church seated 2,000 people. The Cholmleys, lords of the manor, had a special pew, supported by four 'barley sugar' columns and adorned with their coat of arms. Like its predecessor, the medieval rood screen, it blocked the view into the chancel. The Cholmleys faced the rest of the congregation and breathed down the necks of the minister in the three-decker pulpit and the parish clerk below him. The church was heated by a stove, whose flue reaches up through the ceiling; it was lit by a baroque brass chandelier and other candles. Commandment boards are displayed on the walls and the pointed windows were divided into lancets in the revived Gothick style. The church is reached by the famous climb of 199 steps from the old town around the harbour.

NATIONAL MONUMENT RECORD

to conform to the Act of Uniformity of 1662. The Anglican church entered a long period of stability and eventually of slumber. During the late seventeenth and eighteenth centuries church buildings were refashioned at such places as Boynton, Fewston, Thorganby, Wentworth, Wortley and Yarm and new chapels-of-ease served the growing towns of Leeds and Sheffield, but few of these buildings had much architectural distinction. In the countryside the personal tastes of a squire produced structures as different in style as the neo-Norman church at Allerton Mauleverer and John Carr's Gothick design at Ravenfield. The modest classical church of St James at Tong was built in the 1720s by the Tempest family who lived in the smart, new brick hall nearby; the church is still furnished with box pews (including the squire's pew with its small fireplace), three-decker pulpit, west gallery and all the other accoutrements of a 'prayer-book' church untouched by the reforming zeal of the Victorian High Church movement. Other Yorkshire churches still arranged in this way include the small buildings at Lead, Midhope, Slaidburn and Holy Trinity, York. The seating arrangements of such churches formalised the social structure of the parish, for the pews could not be alienated from the various farms and cottages to which they belonged.

The nation's most famous example of a church which preserves its Georgian

'Are not more bodies lost than souls saved through going to church in winter time?'

TOBIAS SMOLLETT, 1771

interior intact is perched on the cliff by the ruined abbey, high above the port of Whitby. Here, between the late seventeenth and early nineteenth centuries the old Norman church of St Mary was gradually transformed into a building that could seat 2,000 people. Transepts were added in Gothick style and fitted with white-painted galleries reached by external staircases and every space in the nave was crammed with dark-brown pews, three-decker pulpit, baroque brass chandelier, and a stove whose flue disappears through the roof. But that is not all. The Cholmleys had their own peculiar seating arrangement in an elaborate pew adorned with garlands and cherubs' heads and supported by four 'barley-sugar' columns, built across the chancel arch where the medieval rood screen had once been, so that during service time the squire and his family faced the congregation and breathed down the necks of the preacher. Keeping out the winter cold was a constant consideration and the floors of Yorkshire churches were commonly covered with rushes. Tobias Smollett wrote satirically in *Humphry Clinker* (1771), 'Are not more bodies lost than souls saved through going to church in winter time?'

Rural gentlemen and urban tradesmen helped to preserve Nonconformity during the years of repression between 1662 and 1689. Many ejected ministers served tiny congregations in a discreet manner, particularly in remote countryside where patrons provided meeting places and offered some protection from the law. In contrast, dissent was easily suppressed in estate

Interior of Holy Trinity Church, Goodramgate, York. The church was founded before the Norman Conquest, but the present building dates from the thirteenth to the fifteenth century. The charm of this simple building lies in its seventeenth- and eighteenth-century fittings, for it was never 'restored' by the Victorians. They include an early eighteenth-century communion rail, a reredos (1721), two-decker pulpit (1785), and box pews. The east window contains late fifteenth-century stained glass.

PHOTOGRAPH: CARNEGIE, 2005

High on the nave wall at All Saints Church, Pocklington, this homely inscription commemorates the exemplary career of John Dobson, third generation of parish clerks.

PHOTOGRAPH: AUTHOR

View of Sprotborough, 1708. This bird's-eye view of the seat of Sir Godfrey Copley was included in *Britannia Illustrata*, published in 1708 by the Dutch artists, Kip and Knyff. Copley's hall was built from about 1685 in the new French style that he had seen on government service in France. Sir Godfrey was a leading intellectual, whose name is commemorated by the annual Copley Medal of the Royal Society. The grounds of his estate were also laid out in the French style, high above the River Don. The medieval parish church appears almost as an outbuilding of the estate. The houses of the tenants are clustered in the village street. Two rows of tenter frames, where woollen cloth was stretched and dried after its return from the fulling mill, are seen in the foreground. Sprotborough Hall was demolished in the 1920s and the grounds now form a housing estate.

AUTHOR COLLECTION

villages where resident lords such as the Fountaynes and Montagus of High Melton or the Copleys of Sprotbrough ensured that their communities remained dependent upon the estate for tenancies and employment.

The Compton ecclesiastical census of 1676 shows that only four per cent of the nation's communicants were dissenters, but that some places had many more than the average. In Doncaster, where only eight of an estimated 3,000 communicants were Nonconformists, the mayor and corporation claimed five years later that, 'We can truly say without boasting that we have neither in our town nor corporation one dissenter from the present government in church and state', but a few miles away the industrial town of Sheffield had about 300 dissenters among its 3,000 or so communicants. Wakefield had 300 dissenters amongst 2,400 communicants, but Barnsley had only seven out of 638, despite the fact that it had a flourishing market and a wire-drawing industry and was merely a chapel-of-ease of Silkstone parish. Economic and topographical considerations favoured the spread of dissent but did not automatically produce it and it is the lack of any

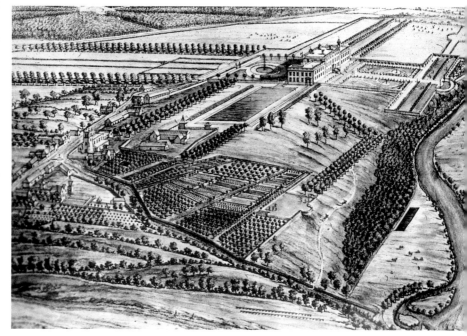

The former meeting house in Quaker Lane, Warmsworth, was built in 1706 by a local yeoman, Thomas Aldham. George Fox had preached in Warmsworth and neighbouring Balby, which became the quarterly meeting place for the South Yorkshire Quakers. The Anglican squires of Warmsworth owned 75 per cent of the village, but the Aldhams were freeholders who were sufficiently independent to build on their own land. A branch of the family were tanners in Sheffield, where they were prominent members of the Quaker meeting house in Hartshead. Family links were the glue that provided the strength and continuity of Nonconformity.

PHOTOGRAPH: AUTHOR

urban pattern that is striking at this time. In the countryside, however, the moorland chapelries and those large lowland parishes that had links with Hull remained well disposed towards the dissenting cause. The same geographical pattern is evident in John Evans' 'List of Dissenting Congregations' in 1715; Nonconformity flourished in its urban and rural strongholds but attracted little support beyond. The 1,163 people who attended services in the Upper Chapel at Sheffield formed the largest dissenting congregation in Yorkshire and included some of the most important people in the town. The 200 people who gathered at the chapel that Elkanah Rich had built in his grounds by Bullhouse Hall included some from beyond the parish boundary. The Rich family dominated their meeting houses as effectively as an Anglican squire controlled the church of his estate village.

Though dissenters were a minority group in the country at large, their influence in certain places remained strong. The most widespread of the old dissenting sects were the Quakers, whose initial appeal was to the poor, but they soon attracted richer converts, notably some of the gentry ironmasters of the West Riding. Briggflatts meeting house, erected in 1675 in a remote corner of the Pennines, preserves the original arrangements of its interior and High Flatts meeting house, on the edge of the parish of Penistone, remains the focal point of a hamlet where all the farmhouses were once occupied by Friends. Endowed by the Jacksons, the yeomen-clothiers of Totties Hall, High Flatts served as a centre for a wide area and in 1764 'many came out of different parishes' to swell the congregation to about 100. These and other meetings remained strong when others withered away as toleration, respectability and wealth lessened their spiritual zeal. By the mid eighteenth century Quaker membership was on the decline and the Presbyterians and Independents had lost much of their force as some congregations drifted into Unitarianism, whose rational approach attracted ministers and merchants but had little appeal to the

'We can truly say without boasting that we have neither in our town nor corporation one dissenter from the present government in church and state.'

DONCASTER CORPORATION, 1676

poor. Neither the Established Church nor the old dissenting sects had the 'enthusiasm' to attract the growing masses in the towns and industrial villages. 'No other preaching will do for Yorkshire', wrote John Nelson to John Wesley, 'but the old sort that comes like a thunderclap upon the conscience. Fine preaching does more harm than good here'. The Methodists set out to remedy this situation.

On their first visits to Yorkshire the Wesley brothers and George Whitefield sought rural farms and hamlets for their headquarters in the old dissenting areas, both in the lowland parishes within a few miles of Epworth and in the semi-industrial areas further west. They met with violent opposition when they first preached in the towns: 'Hell from beneath was moved to oppose us', wrote Charles Wesley in 1742, after his first visit to Sheffield. A local man reported in 1760 that. 'We have also preached at Barnsley, where they were very angry, cast rotten eggs at us, and gave us heavy curses'. The early Methodists co-operated with the Moravian groups led by the Revd Benjamin Ingham of Halifax, who in 1744 established a colony at Fulneck, near Pudsey. In time, Fulneck became a self-sufficient community with houses, schools and workshops arranged around a chapel. The West Riding had 17 'Ingham Societies' in 1745, with a total membership of 856. The visits of famous preachers were highlights that encouraged local people to continue their efforts, but progress was slow and in many places preaching was abandoned. The vicar of Ecclesfield was convinced that the Methodists would 'not be of any long continuance' and the hostility of the Established Church was expressed by the vicar of High Hoyland in 1764 (referring, presumably to the new industrial settlement of Clayton West at the edge of his parish): 'Some

The Moravian Chapel, Fulneck. The Fulneck Moravian Settlement near Pudsey was established in 1744, when the Revd Benjamin Ingham moved his followers from Halifax. The Moravians originated in Germany in the early eighteenth century, under the leadership of Count Zinzendorf, but their teachings go back to the fifteenth-century martyr, Jan Hus. In England, the Moravians had links with the early Methodists. Fulneck was the first of seven Moravian villages that were built in England and Ireland between 1744 and the 1780s.

The Settlement was constructed as a self-contained community, with the chapel as the focal point of houses, workshops and schools, arranged in a long terrace. The scheme took many years to complete. The vestibule and cupola were added to the chapel in 1770. The elders of the Settlement enforced a strict moral code at their monthly meetings.

PHOTOGRAPH: AUTHOR

Interlopers from Places infected with Methodism are endeavouring to propagate their Notions, but gain few Proselytes. There is no licensed or other Meeting House, except a few private Houses may be called so; where the Above Crazy Visionaries sometimes assemble'. It was chiefly in the traditional dissenting districts that Methodism first flourished. Even so, by 1773 the Sheffield circuit (which included north Derbyshire and most of South Yorkshire except the eastern parishes) contained only 910 members. Methodism had not yet achieved the success that was to come its way in the nineteenth century.

The poor

During the later seventeenth and eighteenth centuries rural squires and other wealthy people continued the well-established tradition of building and endowing almshouses and schools. Surviving examples of former almshouses include the Fauconberg hospital at Coxwold (1662), the Fountains hospital at Linton (1721) and Mary Wandesford's hospital for 'ten poor maiden gentle-women' in the York suburb of Bootham (1743). Ledsham has two foundations; in 1670 Sir John Lewis of Ledston Hall erected a range of 11 almshouses and in 1721 his grand-daughter, Lady Betty Hastings, built an orphanage. But these are modest structures compared with the grandiose Turner schemes at Kirkleatham, where Sir William Turner, a former Lord Mayor of London, and his great-nephew, Cholmley Turner, built a house, school and impressive hospital and provided the church with new fittings and their family monuments.

The hearth tax returns of the 1660s and 1670s show that some townships

left Heptonstall Methodist Church. Built in 1764 on the slope below Westgate, at the edge of the village, this octagonal building is thought to be the oldest Methodist chapel in continuous use to the present day. It was partly rebuilt in 1802.
PHOTOGRAPH: CARNEGIE, 2005

right The interior of Heptonstall Methodist Church. Nonconformist chapels were built to hear the Preaching of the Word. The pews on the ground floor and in the galleries are therefore arranged to focus on the pulpit.
PHOTOGRAPH: CARNEGIE, 2005

The Fauconberg Hospital, Coxwold. The Bellasis family, who acquired Newburgh Priory at the dissolution of the monasteries, became Earls of Fauconberg. Coxwold was their estate village, close to the former priory, so here in 1662 they built a hospital or almshouses halfway down the village street, opposite the village pub, The Fauconberg Arms. All of the buildings in the village are of local stone.

PHOTOGRAPH: CARNEGIE, 2005

had large numbers of poor people but that many others, especially those with a flourishing local industry, had well below the national average. Except in times of dearth and depression, the effects of poverty were felt less acutely in Yorkshire than in most other English counties. In normal times able-bodied men and women could find work, even if much of it was part-time or seasonal. The wages offered by industry meant that farmers had to pay their labourers more than the abysmally low levels of southern and eastern England; even the labourers in the agricultural East and North Ridings benefited in this way. The old, the sick, the infirm and dependent youngsters who together constituted the

Ledsham orphanage. This substantial, charitable institution (now a private house) was erected in 1721 by Lady Betty Hastings, the granddaughter of Sir John Lewis, the East India merchant who had become the squire of Ledston Hall, and the daughter of the Earl of Huntingdon. She inherited the Ledston estate in 1708. Her marble monument inside the parish church at Ledsham was designed by Peter Scheemakers in 1739. She was a noted beauty, intellectual and philanthropist, and a supporter of the young John Wesley.

The orphanage is built in local magnesian limestone and is three storeys high, crowned by octagonal chimney stacks.

PHOTOGRAPH: AUTHOR

'genuine poor' were on the whole treated sympathetically by their neighbours, but idlers and the poor of other parishes met with a hard-headed response.

Throughout England the later years of the seventeenth century saw a substantial decline in long-distance subsistence migration. Beggar bands no longer roamed the countryside in a desperate search for a living. As population growth slowed down and agricultural output increased, towns brought their social problems under control and in rural communities old traditions of neighbourly help and paternalism flourished once more. At the same time, new settlement laws and attempts to licence itinerant traders hindered migration; even before the passing of the 1662 Act of Settlement some local authorities took a firm stance on wandering paupers for whom they were not responsible. At meetings of the quarter sessions JPs found themselves increasingly occupied with settlement cases as contending parishes engaged lawyers to prove that paupers were legally settled elsewhere. The JPs heard tales of great hardship when trade was bad. When the population began to rise again in the eighteenth century many places built workhouses to accommodate and employ the poor.

Attitudes towards the poor hardened during the second half of the eighteenth century as local rates began to rise and more squatters encroached upon the commons. In the North Riding expenditure on the poor rose from an average £5,581 per annum in 1748–50 to £12,702 in 1775–76 and to £18,866 in 1783–85; nevertheless, only nine of England's 42 counties spent less on their poor and 30 North Riding villages had no poor at all. By 1776 at least 35 workhouses, capable of housing 964 people, had been built by donation or subscription in the North Riding. The problem of how to provide for the poor worsened towards the end of the eighteenth century.

Communications

Packhorses carrying a load of about 240 lbs were still the most economical form of land transport. Long-distance carriers such as the men who took cloth to London or to the great Stourbridge fair near Cambridge used large teams of packhorses. Joseph Naylor of Rothwell had as many as 101 horses in 1718, but a more typical figure was Abraham Pilling, the leading Doncaster carrier, who had 16 packhorses in 1695. If waggons were to be used profitably, roads had to be passable in winter as well as summer and demand for carriage and backcarriage had to be substantial and regular. The West Riding landscape retains many features from the packhorse era in the form of causeys, bridges and guide stoops that now seem old and quaint but which mark the efforts to improve local highways and byways in response to the growing demands of an increased volume of traffic. Between 1660 and 1740 stone packhorse bridges replaced the old wooden ones and in 1733 the West Riding JPs ordered the erection of guide stoops 'for the better convenience of travellers', particularly upon 'large moors and commons where intelligence is difficult to be had'. A few guide stoops still mark the ancient crossings of the North York Moors; otherwise only

New Mill packhorse bridge. A bridge over the Ewden Beck by the new corn mill was recorded in a charter which pre-dates 1270. This was a wooden bridge that was replaced in 1734 by the one shown here. A local mason, Benjamin Milnes, was employed by the inhabitants of Bolsterstone township to demolish the old bridge and build a stone one. This new structure was part of a scheme to improve the route from Bradfield to Silkstone, and so on to Barnsley and Wakefield; guide stoops and another bridge along this old highway date from the same time. Packhorse bridges survive on minor or abandoned routes that never became turnpike roads. This bridge was re-erected in Glen Howe Park, Wharncliffe Side when the Ewden reservoir was constructed.

AUTHOR COLLECTION

Derbyshire has a similar set of waymarkers from the era before roads were turnpiked.

Carts and wains were commonly used over shorter distances and a great deal of carrying was done on a part-time basis by farmers during slack spells, especially in the summer months. A 1752 survey lists a large number of West Riding bridges that were paid for out of county rates and which were sufficiently wide to take wheeled vehicles. Leeds bridge had recently been widened to 17 feet and was the broadest in the riding; the smallest county bridges were only 11–12 feet wide. By the early eighteenth century stage-waggon services were operating weekly from southern parts of Yorkshire to London. Stage-coaches had offered quick connections with the capital via the Great North Road since the mid seventeenth century and in 1658 Bawtry could be reached from London in just three days. The road maps published by John Ogilby in 1675 indicated the routes of the two major highways that came into Yorkshire from the south; the Great North Road and a more westerly line via Mansfield, Rotherham, Barnsley, Huddersfield and Halifax all the way to Richmond. John Warburton's map of Yorkshire (1718–20), which marks the highways that connected the various market towns, shows that the turnpike roads that were created a generation or two later made only minor deviations from routes that had been used from time immemorial. Thomas Jeffreys' much more detailed map of 1767–72 also depicts a pattern of lanes and tracks that is still familiar today. Along such lanes pedlars, badgers and hawkers travelled to even the remotest hamlets and farmsteads. These packmen grew significantly in number during the decades after the Civil War and helped to integrate Yorkshire even more closely into the national economy.

Wherever possible, heavy industrial goods were taken down the navigable rivers. South Yorkshire metalware and Derbyshire lead and millstones were exported from Bawtry down the river Idle to the Trent, while good-quality

left A guide stoop on the North York Moors. The North York Moors have a few guide stoops of early eighteenth-century date which are similar in style to the far more numerous collection in the West Riding. Part of their charm is derived from the phonetic spellings of the directions. Here, a hand points the way to Kirkbymoorside. Guide stoops were an invaluable aid to travellers across the moors in the immediate pre-turnpike era.
PHOTOGRAPH: AUTHOR

right A causey at Goathland. Surviving causeys are impossible to date accurately, for they consist of simple stone slabs laid down to provide a solid surface for travellers. Documentary sources suggest that they are mostly eighteenth- or nineteenth-century in date, although the word is Norman French in origin and causeys of various kinds were constructed in the Middle Ages. Some were built by private landowners, but most were paid for out of parish rates.

William Marshall, the great agricultural writer from Pickering, observed in 1808 that 'these flag pavements were formed for horse paths, not foot paths.' They were used by 'pack horses and travellers on horseback, in the winter season; when clayey lanes were otherwise impassable.'
PHOTOGRAPH: AUTHOR

continental iron and steel, Norwegian deals and groceries came the other way. Daniel Defoe was much impressed by the bustle at Bawtry wharf and its trading position on the Great North Road in the days before it was by-passed by the Don navigation and the Chesterfield canal. During the seventeenth and eighteenth centuries the River Ouse remained a vital waterway, with numerous minor shipping points such as Cawood, Wistow, Stillingfleet, Naburn and Bishopthorpe, as well as important quays serving a large hinterland at York and Selby. In 1698 the mariners and watermen on the Ouse possessed 'several vessels of good burthen which are constantly employed in carrying great quantities of woollen manufactures, lead, butter, corn, rape-seed, tallow and

several other commodities ... to Hull, London, Newcastle and several parts beyond the seas, from whence they bring all sorts of merchandise and sea-coals for supplying the city of York and the adjacent counties'. The typical Ouse vessel was the all-purpose 'Yorkshire' or 'Humber' keel. About £5,000 was spent on the Ouse in the late 1720s and early 1730s and the Naburn lock, dam and weir were constructed in 1757.

Improved waterways were an essential aid to economic progress. By 1730 about 1,160 miles of English rivers were navigable for light craft and major efforts had been made in Yorkshire to improve not only the Ouse, but the rivers Aire, Calder, Derwent, Don and Hull. An Act to improve the river Derwent was obtained in 1702, but far more important were the determined efforts to make rivers navigable into the heart of the industrial West Riding. A major step was taken in 1699 with the implementation of a scheme to extend the Aire navigation beyond its tidal limit at Knottingley to Leeds and along the Calder to Wakefield. Many improvements were made subsequently by means of cuts, locks and deeper beds. Previously, much of the produce of the textile district had been taken overland to Selby, along the Hambleton causey, but now the bulk of the export trade went down the river to join the Ouse at Airmyn. For two generations Selby languished, but by the later eighteenth century the Aire and Calder navigation could no longer cope adequately with the growing volume of traffic. In 1778–81 a canal was constructed from the navigation at West Haddlesey to Selby, which once again became the West Riding's chief port. After men and installations had been moved from Airmyn, a third of Selby's population was employed in building and repairing ships and in transferring goods from canal barges to the 200-ton vessels which sailed down the Ouse.

The river Don was tidal as far as Wilsick House in the parish of Barnby Dun and navigable up to Doncaster for nine months of the year. Under two

Bingley Five Rise Locks on the Leeds and Liverpool Canal. Work on building the canal began from both ends in 1770 but the canal as a whole was not completed until 1816. The canal rises 500 feet along its 127-mile journey journey across the Pennines. This flight of locks at Bingley climbs 59 feet.

PHOTOGRAPH: CARNEGIE, 2005

Acts passed in 1726–27 Doncaster corporation improved the river down to Wilsick House and the Hallamshire Cutlers' Company assumed responsibility for the much more difficult stretch west of Doncaster. By 1740 a wharf had been constructed at Rotherham and in 1751 the scheme was completed all the way to Tinsley on the eastern boundary of Hallamshire. The Duke of Norfolk feared that the water supply to his iron works and grinding wheels would be affected by a further extension and so the navigation did not reach Sheffield basin until 1819. Meanwhile, in 1758 John Smeaton had begun the extension of the Aire and Calder navigation up the Calder and Hebble to Halifax and 20 years later Sir John Ramsden constructed a small, private canal from this new waterway to Huddersfield. The next, ambitious step was to connect the industrial towns of the West Riding with those of Lancashire across the formidable barrier of the Pennines. Three ingenious and costly schemes eventually came to fruition. The first to cross the summit but the last to be completed was the Leeds and Liverpool Canal. Work began in the mid 1770s at the Aire and Calder terminus at Leeds, but was not finished until 1816.

Up to the middle of the eighteenth century the energies of the Hallamshire Cutlers' Company were directed towards improving their waterway. They showed far less interest in land carriage, for they had no trouble in selling their wares at fairs and markets. The West Riding lagged behind Lancashire in providing turnpike roads. In the 1730s Manchester merchants improved their moorland highways as far as the county boundary, but the 1732 turnpike road to Saltersbrook was not extended to the Don navigation at Rotherham and Doncaster until 1741 and the 1735 road over Stanedge was not continued to Huddersfield and Wakefield until 1759. The early turnpike trusts aimed not to replace existing highways but to maintain and improve them. Roads which proved unsuitable for wheeled traffic were eventually abandoned in favour of easier routes, but at first only minor detours were made to avoid the steepest hills. New routes along the valley bottoms, such as the Wadsley–Langsett turnpike road of 1805 via Deepcar and Stocksbridge, came later. At first, efforts

'Great Quantities of manufactured Goods, Cheese, Salt, and Potatoes, are carried from Manchester, Barnsley and Parts adjacent to Doncaster, on Horses, and return loaded with Hemp, Flax and German Yarn.'

TURNPIKE PETITION

Stone breakers on the road. George Walker included this watercolour in his *The Costume of Yorkshire* (1814) to depict the primitive methods of repairing and maintaining both the turnpike roads and the local highways that were the responsibility of parishes or townships. He explained that stone was 'brought in large pieces from the quarry, and thrown from the carts on the road side, at convenient distances, where repair is necessary.' Men were then employed to break and spread the stones. Walker expressed surprise that no machines for this purpose had yet been invented.

were concentrated on the Pennine crossings and the roads heading for the ports. The earliest Yorkshire turnpike road was the 1735 improvement to the Rochdale–Halifax route via Blackstone Edge. In 1741 six schemes dealt with links between Manchester or Rochdale in the west and Halifax, Bradford, Leeds, Wakefield, Selby and Doncaster in the east. All the petitions to Parliament emphasised the great amount of traffic that used these highways; the petition to improve the Saltersbrook route, for example, claimed that 'great Quantities of manufactured Goods, Cheese, Salt, and Potatoes, are carried from Manchester, Barnsley and Parts adjacent to Doncaster, on Horses, and return loaded with Hemp, Flax and German Yarn'; and the Act for the Selby, Leeds, Bradford and Halifax turnpike observed that the road was 'much used and frequented for Carriage and Conveyance of Wooll, Woollen Manufactures, Dying Ware, etc'. Other important early schemes included the 1744–45 turnpiking of the roads leading to Hull.

Turnpike trusts were concerned with the major thoroughfares, for 'the Benefit of Trade'. Minutes of individual trusts show that the most active trustees were usually merchants. Between 1751 and 1772 five Pennine routes were turnpiked and people began to speak of 'turnpike mania'. The heroic figure of John Metcalf – 'Blind Jack of Knaresborough' – who was responsible for many West Riding and Lancashire roads, represents the optimism of the age, but the lack of adequate technology and of experienced road builders meant that the early trusts had to be content with old methods of repair applied more thoroughly and regularly than before. A great deal of money was spent laying stones and gravel (and in some cases furnace cinders), on levelling and draining, and on maintaining an adequate surface at least 20 feet wide, but the primitive nature of many a moorland turnpike road is evident in the surviving stretches that were abandoned before major improvements had taken place. Travellers' descriptions, even when an element of exaggeration is allowed for, leave no doubt about major highways, even after they had been turnpiked.

When Arthur Young travelled from Rotherham to Sheffield in 1769 he found that the road was 'execrably bad, very stony, and excessively full of holes'.

Minor routes which joined the turnpike roads and connected minor settlements remained the responsibility of the parish repair system. Those which crossed commons and wastes were improved by enclosure commissioners. The most noticeable improvements made by the turnpike trusts were the great savings in time on long journeys and the widening of bridges so that wheeled vehicles could pass at all seasons of the year. In 1758 a House of Commons Committee was told by a Halifax merchant that broad-wheeled waggons drawn by eight horses were able to carry 30 packs, each weighing 240 lbs, from Halifax to London. The load was 3.75 times heavier than the equivalent number of horses could carry on their backs. Turnpike roads widened the range of choice, whether of destination, of season, or of speed, expense and quality of travel. Their success can be judged by the fact that old roads which were not turnpiked, like the Pontefract–Hemsworth–Rotherham road, quickly declined in status.

Industrial progress

Until the late eighteenth century coal miners were usually part-time farmers and were not regarded as a separate group. The first townships with a high proportion of miners included those on the Rockingham estate at Greasbrough, where wooden railways of the type used in Northumberland and Durham connected the pits to the Don navigation. John Hirst laid a track from his colliery at Ginnhouse in 1735 and by 1763 three large collieries near Greasbrough, belonging to Messrs Hirst, Bowden and Fenton, moved their coal along 'Newcastle roads'. In 1779–80 the Marquis of Rockingham employed William Jessop to make the Greasbrough cut to the Don, with four broad locks and a reservoir. West Riding coal miners received better wages than most craftsmen and labourers. In 1770 Arthur Young reported that miners near Rotherham relieved 7–9 shillings a week and that those in the Wakefield district received 10–12 shillings. The scale of operations was still small in most mines, but in 1773 the large Middleton colliery at Leeds employed 50 men underground and 27 on the surface. The improved waterways provided access to markets in the North and East Ridings and in Lincolnshire, but despite the network of navigable rivers West Riding coal was not shipped down the coast to London until well into the nineteenth century.

When John Foster, a Woolley yeoman, died in 1721 he had £260 worth of coals 'sold to York, Lincolnshire & severall other places' and coals valued at £110 upon the 'stennard', an island in the Calder, at Wakefield. Foster also had local sales worth £70, coals at Bimshaw pits worth £30, and a £110 valuation placed upon his mine and coals at Darton. He had installed two horse-gins at Bimshaw and his 24 picks, 22 baskets and 17 sledges suggests a considerable enterprise for that time. Further east, in 1718 Richard Bingley of Goldthorpe had a winding gin and a horse gin with chains, worth in all £60, with coals valued at another £60. The first Thomas Newcomen atmospheric engine that was used to pump water out of a West Riding colliery was built about 1714 on Brown Moor, Austhorpe, five miles east of Leeds, but it was not a success and lasted only four years. A second engine was installed in the 1730s at Rothwell Haigh, the first large concern of the Fentons, 'coal kings' of the West Riding, who soon had other major collieries at Wakefield Outwood and Greasbrough. The Fentons had been yeomen or gentlemen-farmers on the south side of Hunslet since at least the sixteenth century and one of their number, William Fenton, had been mayor of Leeds in 1658–59. They were also the owners of one of Yorkshire's largest glassworks at Rothwell Haigh and their varied interests included copper smelting in Cornwall and South Wales. Other colliery owners also invested in Newcomen pumping engines. In 1735 John Hirst installed one to drain Ginnhouse colliery and before 1750 the West Riding had eight.

Low Mill Furnace, Silkstone. This coke-fuelled iron smelt may have been rebuilt from a charcoal blast furnace at the end of the eighteenth century. It was worked by Cockshutt & Co. in the early 1820s. The hearth and shaft of the brick furnace can be seen behind the stone cladding. The wheelpit is found beyond. It stands on private land, close to the former mineral railway, which ran from Silkstone to Barnby Basin, the terminus of the Barnsley branch of the Dearne and Dove canal.
PHOTOGRAPH: AUTHOR

During the seventeenth century the English glass industry moved from the woods to the coalfields. The Rosedale furnace, which has been reconstructed in the Ryedale folk museum, is thought to have been worked during the last quarter of the sixteenth century on similar lines to sites built by immigrants from Lorraine in the Weald. One of the first furnaces to be built on the Yorkshire coalfield was that on Sir Thomas Wentworth's estate at Glasshouse Green, Wentworth, in 1632, but it lasted for only a few years and had no connection with later enterprises, which were owned or managed by immigrants. The Pilmays, who had built a glass furnace at Silkstone by 1658, were connected by marriage to other Lorrainers. Their technology was remarkably sophisticated. When Abigail Pilmay died in 1698 the Silkstone glasshouse was making not only green bottles, but crystal and flint glass. Very high-quality sand from Brierley in Staffordshire and red lead were used for the crystal glass; rape ashes provided a source of alkali for green bottles; blue

Catcliffe glassworks. The glassworks at Catcliffe, near Rotherham, was founded in 1740 by William Fenny, a descendant of a Huguenot family who were famous glassworkers at various sites in Yorkshire and Lancashire. He became manager of the Bolsterstone glassworks (in modern Stocksbridge) upon his marriage in 1718 to Mary Fox, daughter of the owners. His mother-in-law threatened to cut his children from her will if he went ahead with his plan to open another glassworks within 10 miles of Bolsterstone. Catcliffe lies 10½ miles away. The cone was one of a pair and is the oldest surviving building of its type in Europe. Glass was made here until the early twentieth century.

PHOTOGRAPH: AUTHOR

powder and manganese were the main colouring agents; and salt petre was used to avoid amber coloration in window glass and to convert any iron into a less-colouring state. Another prominent immigrant family were the Fenneys. Henry Fenney leased Glass Houghton, Joshua was at Rothwell Haigh, other members of the family worked at Thatto Heath in Lancashire, and in 1718 William married Mary Fox and became the manager of Bolsterstone glasshouse. In 1727 the Bolsterstone works used not only salt petre but starch, a chemical reducing agent that allowed the production of amber glass to be controlled precisely. Thirteen years later, William Fenney erected the Catcliffe glasshouse, whose cone is the oldest surviving structure of its kind in western Europe.

Many of these old glasshouses ceased production in the later eighteenth or early nineteenth centuries and some were turned for a time into potteries; Silkstone was converted about 1750, Rothwell Haigh in 1768, Bolsterstone in 1778 and Gawber in 1821. Before the middle of the eighteenth century Yorkshire potteries were small local concerns, but the improved waterways offered opportunities for larger businesses where suitable clays and coals were available. The Leeds Old Pottery, established about 1755, was the first to operate on a large commercial scale, establishing a wide reputation for cream-coloured earthenware. The Green family, who helped to found this enterprise, were associated with other famous West Riding potteries, notably those at Swinton, the Don works and Castleford. The surviving cone at Swinton is another important and interesting piece of industrial archaeology. The pottery was established in 1745 but it achieved its greatest fame after 1826.

The Tankersley seam of ironstone was smelted in charcoal blast furnaces and reduced to rod and bar iron at the forges and slitting mills owned by a group of gentry ironmasters led by the Spencers of Cannon Hall. Much of it was sold to the 100 or so nailers who in 1672 worked in villages, hamlets and

Cannon Hall, Cawthorne, was the home of the Spencer family, the leading West Riding ironmasters, who came from the Welsh Borders in the mid seventeenth century. The architect of their new house is unknown, but the house was shown without its wings in a sketch by Samuel Buck, c.1720. John Carr, the famous Yorkshire architect, designed two wings in 1765 to serve as a dining room and library, but these were just one storey high. Carr also redesigned the interior, especially the entrance hall and the dining room, in 1778. The wings were given an additional storey in 1804–5, so the house was complete by the time J.P. Neale made this drawing in 1821.

In 1760 John Spencer employed Richard Woods of Chertsey (Surrey) to lay out a park and gardens. Cannon Hall and Cusworth Hall are the only examples of the work of this famous landscape gardener north of Trent. Three lakes were constructed in 1762–64 and great numbers of trees and flowering shrubs were planted. The house and gardens are now maintained by Barnsley Metropolitan District Council as a museum and country park.

AUTHOR COLLECTION

isolated farmsteads immediately beyond the cutlery district. Nailmaking was essentially a rural craft that required little capital or technical knowledge and which was normally combined with farming until the rapid increase of the population destroyed this old way of life. In 1739 William Murgatroyd of Wortley forge observed that between March and August clasp nails were made for the London market, during harvest time nailmaking stopped, in the autumn flat points were made for Virginia until Martinmas, then sharp points were made for the Leeward Isles and Jamaica. Local chapmen supplied the nailers from the slitting mills and saw to sales in distant fairs and markets, but from the 1730s onwards the Spencers became directly involved in exporting nails down the rivers and along the coast to Deptford, where London merchants collected them for redistribution in southern England and America. The local nailing industry was second only to that of the Black Country. The humble nailing craft not only helped to sustain population growth by offering employment, it provided much of the capital and leadership needed to launch an industrial revolution. Samuel and Aaron Walker, who became the leading ironmasters in the North,

Fruit basket and stand, Don Pottery. The Don Pottery was one of Yorkshire's largest potteries in the nineteenth century. Established in 1801 by the master potter John Green, who had been a partner in both the Leeds and Swinton (Rockingham) potteries, the Don Pottery made some of Yorkshire's finest earthenwares. The site lay between Swinton and Mexborough on the South Yorkshire coalfield and was close to the Don Navigation and the Dearne and Dove canal. The firm's flint mill lay further down the river at Sprotborough.

John Griffin has researched the history of the Don Pottery and has identified its products, with the help of a surviving design book. He comments that this delicate creamware basket and stand was also frequently seen in pearlware with blue underglaze transfer printed patterns and that the enamelled border decoration is typical of the type used by most potteries in the early years of the nineteenth century.

The jugs and mugs of the early years of the Don Pottery can be identified by their decoration and shape, particularly of some of their handles. This one was made for Sarah Wightman of Lincoln in 1828. At that time, about 300 men were employed at the pottery. The firm continued in production under the Barkers until 1893.

Meanwhile, the Leeds Pottery (1770–1881), founded at Hunslet under the direction of John Green, achieved even greater fame. By 1851 it was employing 400 people and was probably Yorkshire's largest factory pottery. The majority of its wares were exported to Europe, stretching from the Baltic Sea to the Mediterranean, and also to North and South America.

started their careers as typical nailer-farmers and the new iron and steel works which they established at Masborough in 1746–48 was financed by John Booth, the leading nailchapman in South Yorkshire.

Tankersley ironstone was good enough for the local nailers, wiredrawers and panmakers, but was of insufficient quality to provide the cutting edges needed by the cutlers and tool-makers, who had long relied upon continental imports. By the later seventeenth century Swedish iron from the Dannemora district was being brought via Oregrund and Hull and the navigable rivers. Sheffield's fame as the world's greatest centre of quality steel production still lay in the distant

The charcoal blast furnace at Rockley, south of Barnsley, was built for Samuel Shore, a Sheffield merchant and industrialist, and William Westby Cotton, gentleman-ironmaster of Haigh Hall, in 1723. It survives almost to its full height, although the hearth and most of the dressed stone on the outer faces have gone. It was charged through the top of the stack, blown by bellows which were worked by a water wheel, and tapped at the bottom. It produced about 400 tons of pig iron a year, an average output for that era. It went out of production in the middle years of the eighteenth century, but was adapted for new purposes briefly during the Napoleonic wars.

PHOTOGRAPH: AUTHOR

future, long after 1742 when Benjamin Huntsman began to recast cementation steel in fireclay crucibles, using coke fires and a natural draught. His melted steel was much more uniform and pure, ideal not only for his watch springs but for the fine cutting edges required in the cutlery and tool making trades.

During the seventeenth and eighteenth centuries the English woollen industry was carried on in the same regions as it had been in the late Middle Ages; all counties had some weavers but East Anglia, the West Country and the West Riding were pre-eminent. The progress of the West Riding industry was steady but unspectacular for most of the seventeenth century, when its main export outlet was through Holland and Germany, for expansion was hindered by keen foreign competition and the Dutch wars. After the opening of the Aire

Earle's cement factory, Hull. George and Thomas Earle started their business in 1811 and became celebrated Portland Cement manufacturers on the river front at Wilmington. Their products were 'esteemed among engineers, contractors, and builders in every quarter of the modern world'. The view shows their 14-acre site, served by eight river jetties, seven railway-waggon entrances and seven steam and hydraulic cranes for rapid loading. Their raw material came from 23 acres of nearby clay beds. The firm had space to store 20,000 tons of stock ready for dispatch on short notice. They quickly acquired a world-wide reputation.

CARNEGIE COLLECTION

G. & T. EARLE'S CEMENT WORKS, HULL, COVERING AN AREA
OF 13 ACRES. 3 ROODS. 16 PERCHES. WITH 7 RIVER JETTIES & 2 PRIVATE SIDINGS.

and Calder navigation in 1700, however, Leeds merchants were able to penetrate home and overseas markets that had been previously dominated by London, Norwich and Exeter merchants, particularly the south European trade and from the late 1750s the American trade. The West Riding had outstripped its competitors long before the great changes that transformed the woollen cloth industry from the 1770s onwards. Its production of broad cloths in 1770 was nearly 3½ times that of 1727 and the number of its narrow cloths in 1785 was more than double the output for 1740. Yorkshire's share of the total English production grew from less than 20 per cent in 1700 to about 60 per cent a century later. Meanwhile, the growth of the West Riding worsted industry had been nothing less than sensational. Worsteds had been made here during the Middle Ages but during the sixteenth century the weavers had turned instead to kerseys and dozens. After the Restoration worsted manufacture was re-introduced and once the Aire and Calder navigation had substantially reduced the cost of importing long wools from Lincolnshire and Leicestershire the industry expanded enormously. By 1770 output in the West Riding had reached the same level as that of Norwich, the traditional leading centre of worsted manufacture in England.

It was a source of strength for the West Riding to have this unique combination of woollen and worsted industries in close proximity. By 1700 Halifax was not only the leading centre of kersey manufacture but also of worsted shalloons. Worsteds were made in the upper valleys of the Calder and Aire as far north as Haworth and Keighley and as far east as Bradford (the later centre) and even Wakefield and Leeds. Kerseys and other narrow woollen cloths were manufactured in Pennine districts stretching south of Halifax to Huddersfield (the later centre of fancy woollens) and Penistone. Broad cloths were made in the district bounded by Leeds, Wakefield, Huddersfield, Halifax and Bradford, with Leeds as the finishing and marketing centre, white or undyed cloths were produced in the Calder Valley, and coloured cloths were made in the parish of Leeds and in the villages to the west and south. Daniel Defoe passed through some of these populous villages on his journey from Halifax to Leeds and thought they presented, 'A noble scene of industry and application'.

As early as 1627 the inhabitants of Leeds, Wakefield and Halifax had declared that 'there is not the quantitie of cloth made in these three towns and their precincts as is made in the severall and dispersed towns and villages about us'. Villages such as Armley, Beeston, Churwell, Haworth, Holbeck, Hunslet, Morley and Woodhouse grew steadily as the cloth industry expanded. In his account of Mirfield in 1755 the Revd J. Ismay noted that the parish contained over 400 houses and 2,000 people, of whom 400 were employed in carding, spinning and preparing wool for the looms and 200 in making broad cloth for Leeds market. The hamlets within the parish included

> the dwellings at or about Hopton Hall [which] are increased in less than forty years from three to eleven, and the inhabitants form seventeen to eighty …

'A noble scene of industry and application.'

DANIEL DEFOE

Thomas Jeffreys' map of Yorkshire, 1771–72 (detail). This section of Jeffreys' map shows the rural setting of many of the industrial sites of South Yorkshire in the early years of the Industrial Revolution. They include cutlers' grinding wheels, forges and tilt hammers on Sheffield's rivers, the glassworks at Catcliffe, early steel furnaces (not marked here) at Ballifield, Richmond and Darnall, and the coal mine drained by a Newcomen-type 'Fire Engine' on Attercliffe Common. Benjamin Huntsman had perfected his method of making crucible steel at Handsworth in the 1740s before moving to Attercliffe. Coppice woods and extensive commons still covered much of the landscape.

AUTHOR COLLECTION

There are forty pairs of looms for weaving of white broad cloth in the hamlet. [Not far away] about two years ago only three families lived on the north side of Lee Green, but now the number amounts to twenty-three and more new buildings are about to be erected.

Lee Green had three pubs, a workhouse and a new Moravian chapel. Few cottages were without a piece of land, for the West Riding was one of the strongholds of a dual economy that emphasised both farming and a craft. When John Nobles, a Kirkburton kersey clothier, made his will in 1715 he instructed his supervisors to 'chuse such a master for my son where he may learn both the clothier trade and husbandry'. An analysis of 3,300 probate inventories for the West Riding cloth area has shown that 77.6 per cent of clothiers had agricultural goods worth £1 or more and that in the rural parts of Halifax parish the proportion was as high as 86 per cent. Only in the towns and in the villages near Leeds was weaving divorced from farming.

Contemporaries believed that the West Riding's success was due to the peculiar structure of its industry, which provided opportunities for men of enterprise and initiative. Certainly, the textile district had no advantage in terms of wool supplies or export markets and the differences in labour costs were minimal. The West Riding was a much more complex and forward-looking industrial area than its competitors, whose cloth manufacturing took place in an otherwise agricultural setting, and the variety of woollens and worsteds that were produced meant that manufacturers could switch relatively easily from

'... chuse such a master for my son where he may learn both the clothier trade and husbandry.'

CLOTHIER'S WILL, 1715

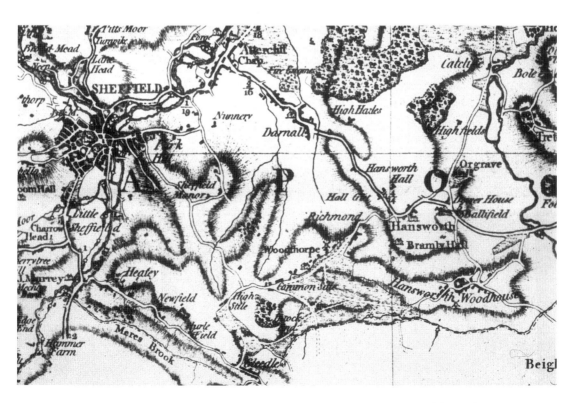

product to product as occasion demanded. When Dr Pococke visited Keighley in 1750 he found a place where 'woosted, calimancoes, shaloons and stockins' and 'the small wares of Manchester' were manufactured. The West Riding concentrated upon the cheap end of the market with cloths of excellent value which were bought eagerly by the rising population both at home and abroad. The parallels with the cutlers of Hallamshire are clear.

The most notable feature of the West Riding textile industry was the domestic system of organisation. Whereas the trade in East Anglia and the West Country was dominated by wealthy merchants and clothiers who employed numerous outworkers in return for wages, the characteristic West Riding enterprise was the independent family unit which produced one piece of cloth each week for the local market. Only a small amount of capital was needed for such a venture, which was often profitably combined with the running of a smallholding. This type of organisation enabled the industry to expand enormously, though some large-scale employers did emerge and in Leeds the merchants dominated the trade. The worsted industry had been organised on a capitalistic basis from the start and the masters had many workers at their command. Samuel King of Making Place, Soyland, was such an employer. Letters written early in 1738 show that he sold almost 1,000 pieces of worsted cloth in less than three weeks, which implies a workforce of at least 200 weavers and many more spinners. As the population rose, cottagers were increasingly obliged to work for an employer on a piece-rate basis at a specialist occupation such as weaving, spinning or combing, but those families with smallholdings continued to work to the old system well into the Victorian period.

Most of the early woollen mills were erected not by wealthy merchants but by small manufacturers who had previously been involved in the trade. At first, the domestic industry welcomed the new machinery from Lancashire. Kay's flying shuttle was in general use in the West Riding by 1770 and when Hargreaves' spinning jenny was introduced into Holmfirth about 1776 it was 'hailed as a prodigy'. In upland villages and hamlets small manufacturers installed a few hand-looms and jennies in their 'warehouses' and employed others to spin and weave at home. Machines based on Arkwright's carder appeared in the mid Calder Valley, the old centre of the cardmaking trade, in the 1770s, but in the early years they were operated by hand or by a horse-drawn gin. Soon, however, the preparatory processes of carding and scribbling were adapted to water-power and later to steam. The West Riding was about to be transformed by the population explosion and the Industrial Revolution.

CHAPTER 8

The Spectacular Growth of Industry, 1780–1850

The rise of the West Riding

When the first census of England and Wales was taken in 1801 two out of every three Yorkshire people lived in the West Riding, that is 564,593 compared with 158,955 in the North Riding, 111,192 in the East Riding and 24,393 in York and its dependent wapentake, the Ainsty. The trend became even more marked during the next 50 years, during which Yorkshire's population more than doubled from 859,133 to 1,797,995. The rate of growth was astonishing and unprecedented. By 1851 the West Riding had 1,315,885 inhabitants, the East Riding 220,983, the North Riding 215,225 and York and the Ainsty 45,902. Yorkshire's population was now 1,797,995, of whom 73 per cent lived in the

What was to become Yorkshire's industrial heartland – the southern part of the West Riding. Cary's map of 1787.

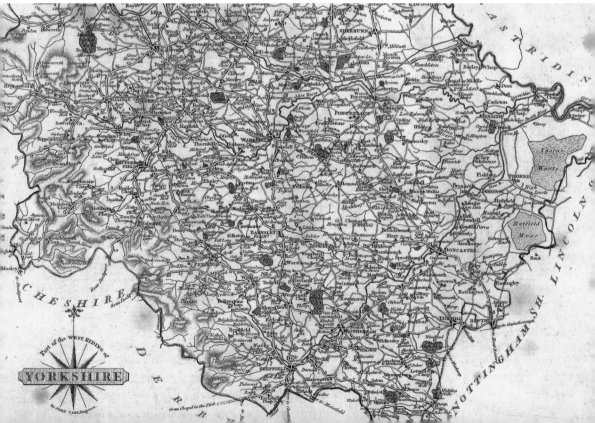

West Riding, that is nearly three out of every four. The North Riding and the East Riding, beyond Hull, had grown much more modestly, in a similar fashion to the counties of southern England. The West Riding was like Lancashire and Staffordshire, where farming was now secondary to industry and where hamlets, villages and small towns were transformed into sprawling industrial communities.

In 1801 York had 17,238 inhabitants, but it was no longer the most populous place in the county. Comparisons between urban populations are not easy to make, for many settlements included large rural hinterlands within the boundaries of their ancient parishes, the units which eventually became boroughs. The central, urban township of Leeds had 30,669 inhabitants in 1801 but the whole borough had 53,162. Sheffield had 31,314 people in its central township but 45,755 in its parish (which was made a borough in 1843); in 1851 the inhabitants of the new borough numbered 135,310. Bradford and Hull were the next largest towns. In 1780 Bradford township had only 4,506 inhabitants and the other three townships of the future borough had a combined total of 4,019, but after the Napoleonic wars Bradford grew rapidly as it became a world centre for the manufacture of worsted cloth. Its population growth exceeded 50 per cent during every decade between 1811 and 1851, and during the ten years between 1821 and 1831 it grew by a sensational 65.5 per cent. By 1851 the borough's population was 103,778. Beyond the West Riding, the only large town was Hull, which in 1801 had 29,516 people confined within its medieval limits.

By 1851 Yorkshire had 12 towns with over 10,000 inhabitants. All but three – Hull, York and Scarborough – lay in the West Riding. If the definition of town is limited to the central township and no allowance is made for the outlying parts of boroughs, then the ranking was: Leeds 101,343, Sheffield

Warehouses in Peel Place, Bradford. In the nineteenth century Bradford flourished as the centre of the worsted industry. From the 1840s onwards, and particularly between 1860 and 1873, warehouses for this trade were designed in an Italianate style, imitating the palaces of medieval Florentine merchants, particularly in the streets that became known as Little Germany. The ground floor and staircase hall were richly decorated to impress buyers. The cloth was brought through large entrances to the rear and hoisted to the upper floors. This view of new warehouses in Peel Place, designed by Eli Milnes in 1862 and now demolished, was published in *The Builder*. A statue of Sir Robert Peel commemorates his repeal of the corn laws.

NEW WAREHOUSES, PEEL PLACE, BRADFORD, YORKSHIRE.— Mr. E. Milnes, Architect.

83,447, Bradford 52,493, Hull 50,670, York 36,622, Huddersfield 30,880, Scarborough 25,830, Halifax 25,159, Wakefield 16,989, Barnsley 14,913, Dewsbury 14,049, and Doncaster 12,052. Rapid population growth and economic development was also evident in the industrial villages of the West Riding. Between 1801 and 1851 the population of the huge parish of Halifax rose from 64,434 to 140,257, that of Birstall from 14,657 to 36,222, and that of Keighley from 5,745 to 18,259. The parish of Birstall, which lay at the heart of the textile district, had no urban centre but it included within its boundaries the spreading settlements of Cleckheaton, Drighlington, Gomersal, Heckmond-wike, Liversedge, Tong and Wiske, whose combined population increased 4.6 times during the course of the nineteenth century.

The textile industry

The factory system that gradually transformed the West Riding textile industry was introduced into the cotton and worsted branches from Lancashire. Keighley acquired several cotton mills in the 1790s, notably Ponden mill (1791) and Turkey mill at Goose Eye (1797). In Leeds, Richard Paley, soap boiler, ironfounder, potash manufacturer and property developer, built two steam-powered cotton mills at the Bank in 1790, though later he went bankrupt and the Leeds cotton industry failed. In Sheffield the silk mill that had been erected about 1760 and which had been the largest employer in town was converted into a cotton mill by 1789 and soon afterwards was converted to steam power, but a couple of disastrous fires ruined the business. Cotton manufacture took hold particularly in the Craven district, which had 44 cotton mills by 1835, most of them powered by water, with the largest businesses at Skipton, Barnoldswick and Settle. Further south, Saddleworth shared Lancashire's interest in fustians, linens and cottons as well as having a domestic woollen industry.

The most successful cotton business was that started at Todmorden in 1782 by Joshua Fielden, who came from a long line of farmer-weavers. His five capable sons built up the firm as partners, especially after the opening of the Rochdale canal in 1804. Their business expanded greatly after the Napoleonic wars. By 1827 their Waterside mill had ten power looms and numerous spinners and weavers had moved across the border from Lancashire to gain employment as outworkers. By 1832 Fielden's was a major enterprise with 39,048 spindles, 684 power looms and more than 1,000 dependent handloom weavers who produced 2,000 to 3,000 pieces of cloth each week. The partners also bought raw cotton and sold finished cloth on weekly visits to Manchester. The railway provided a fresh stimulus to trade, so that by the 1850s about 100,000 spindles and 1,600 looms were in production and 1,925 outworkers were employed as weavers. At least 20 per cent of Todmorden's population was dependent directly or indirectly on Fielden Brothers, who accumulated more capital in business than any other cotton firm in Britain before the watershed of the American Civil War. The family were Unitarians who remained patriarchs of

left Scalegill cotton mill, Kirkby Malham. An old corn mill on this site was converted for cotton spinning by Roger Hartley in 1792. Three years later, he erected the building shown here, which was described as: 'All that new erected cotton mill called Scalegill Mill situate about four miles from Airton aforesaid, with a very convenient dwelling house, outhouses, and other appurtenances adjoining to the mill … it has a constant and powerful supply of water, and in a situation where wages are low'. Between 1818 and 1820 John Dewhirst & Co. of Skipton took over the mill and installed new machinery.

right Woodhouse Cotton Mill, Langfield, Todmorden. This steam-powered mill was built for cotton spinning in 1832 by Richard Ingham on the side of the Rochdale canal. Five storeys high, its blackened exterior is the result of a disastrous fire.

PHOTOGRAPHS BY COURTESY OF GEORGE INGLE

the town to the fourth generation, but they provided little in the way of public facilities.

The West Riding's first worsted-spinning mill with Arkwright's machines was opened at Addingham in 1787 to produce yarn for Bradford weavers. Five years later a similar mill was constructed at Mytholmroyd by Thomas Edmondson, one of the partners of Britain's earliest worsted-spinning mill at Dolphinholme, near Lancaster. By 1800 the West Riding had 22 worsted mills. During the second half of the eighteenth century market forces had gradually persuaded the inhabitants of the Pennine settlements west of Bradford, including those in the great parish of Halifax, to abandon the manufacture of kerseys in favour of worsteds. As the population of this district rose to new high levels, families were unable to find a smallholding to supplement the wages from their craft and were forced to work full-time for an employer on piece-rates, albeit in their own homes until it became apparent that worsted yarn could be spun by water power equally well as cotton. Except in the combing process, where the technical problems were formidable, the transition to factory production was far more rapid in the worsted than in the woollen trade. The longer stapled wools of the worsted manufacturer were more suited to machines than were those of the woollen clothier, who was unable to introduce powered spinning for another two or three decades. By the 1820s the worsted-spinning mills were organised in a similar manner to the cotton factories, with women

Halifax from the south east, 1775. Although Halifax was one of the first places to grow dramatically with the Industrial Revolution, it still looked like a market town in 1775, with fields and moors all around. The town stretched up the hill from the ancient parish church and tenter frames stood in the fields. Yet Halifax was spreading beyond its ancient bounds. The buildings in the foreground and to the left look like recent additions.

and children providing most of the labour, but water power was only just becoming applied to the weaving of worsteds. The relatively high wages of the combers and weavers attracted thousands of the rising population into the worsted trade, including many from agricultural districts. An estimated 20,000 weavers and combers were working in the Bradford area in 1825 on the eve of

High in Calderdale, right on the Lancashire border, Todmorden grew at an astonishing rate in the nineteenth century and became a borough in 1896. A turnpike road, a canal and a railway provided links to the West Riding and Lancashire textile towns. Todmorden's spectacular rise was the result of the success of the cotton business, founded by John Fielden (1784–1849) and developed by his sons. The Town Hall, which dominates this view at the top of Fielden Square, was built at the expense of the Fielden brothers between 1870 and 1875. The architect, John Gibson, designed a hall that was lavishly decorated and arranged like a Classical temple supported by giant Corinthian columns.

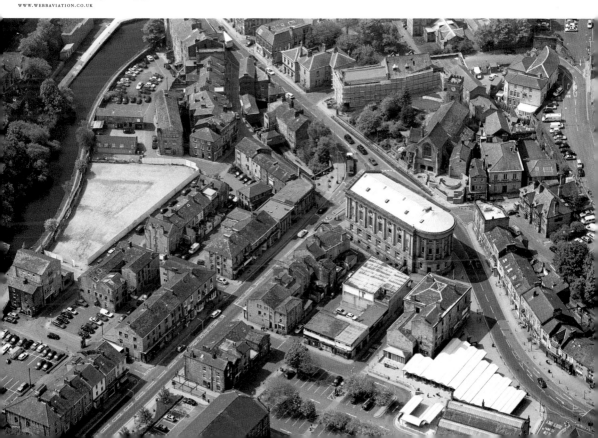

a bitter 23-week strike, which ended in total defeat for the workforce. The woolcombers who had once been privileged artisans had descended to the humble status of out-worker.

In most industries progress was gradual rather than revolutionary, with few significant changes before the 1790s. The 73 woollen cloth firms that were based in Leeds in 1781 varied considerably in size; two-thirds of the cloth trade was organised by the 24 largest firms, but even they had at most 30 dressers and a few packers, pressers and clerks. Leeds merchants were mostly descended from substantial yeomen or smaller landed families, such as the Wades and Sykeses, rather than from clothiers. They were closely connected through marriage and dominated the town's political and social life as well as economic affairs, but few of these family concerns continued for more than half a century. During the 1790s Leeds acquired two enormous water-powered factories that became celebrated throughout the land as wonders of the age. In 1792 John Marshall, who three years earlier had installed Cartwright power looms at Scotland mill in the parish of Adel, built the largest flax-spinning mill in England at Holbeck and established Leeds as an important centre of the linen trade alongside Knaresborough and Barnsley; by 1804 the mill operated 4,000 spindles. Even more impressive was the Bean Ing woollen mill which Benjamin Gott of the Leeds cloth merchant house of Wormald and Fountaine erected on the banks of the Aire. Bean Ing was the first mill in the West Riding to have a Boulton and Watt steam engine. By 1797 Gott's 12,000 workers were making 4,000 broad cloths per annum, mainly cheap clothing and blankets for the army in the French wars. In 1800 Gott constructed a second mill and a mansion at Armley and soon became a noted philanthropist. He had few imitators at first and the nineteenth century was well advanced before the West Riding had many large woollen mills. Even at the beginning of Victoria's reign it was unusual for a business to employ more than 400 workers.

Most of the early woollen mills were built not by wealthy merchants but by small manufacturers who had previously been involved in the trade. Until the 1820s domestic production of woollen cloth remained far more important than factory output and small mills and workshops were always more typical than the large concerns. Newcomen-type steam engines manufactured by local foundries were used to pump water back into the dams so that the water wheels had a regular supply. Boulton and Watt engines were expensive and so were adopted slowly, but they allowed mills to be sited away from the rivers. Gradually, the skylines of the West Riding mill towns and villages were pierced by a growing number of tall chimneys. A typical small-scale development occurred in a moorland clough near Meltham, where in the 1780s a scribbling mill and then a fulling mill were erected near the old manorial corn mill and where a new settlement known as Meltham Mills soon flourished. Three miles away, the changes in the Holmfirth district were on a much larger scale. Until the late eighteenth century nearly all the inhabitants of the Graveship of Holme, as the district was known, had lived on the hillsides. The valley bottom that is now occupied by the town of Holmfirth had few buildings apart from the manorial corn and fulling mills until 1784, when John Fallas, a woollen clothier, acquired these properties and added a scribbling mill. Workers' houses were soon scattered haphazardly along the banks of the river and on the slopes of the hills. Thomas Jeffreys' map of 1772 marked 18 mills on the local rivers and streams and new valley settlements grew up not only at Holmfirth but at Holmbridge, Hinchliffe Mill and at New Mill, the site of the new manorial corn mill of the early fourteenth century. Holy Trinity church, completed by 1787 at the bottom of the valley, served these new communities but Holmfirth did not become an independent parish until 1858. The rows of two- or three-storeyed terraced houses that characterised these new settlements were very different in scale and plan from the previous detached cottages. They were soon to become the normal type of accommodation for industrial workers in the West Riding mill towns.

Factory machine spinning was introduced into the woollen industry in the 1820s but the weavers stayed in the hills and their craft long remained a domestic occupation. Villages and hamlets as well as towns took part in the tremendous expansion of the textile trades. Houses were clustered in folds or arranged along the streets with an upper range of mullioned windows extending all along the front so as to catch the maximum amount of light on the looms. The traditional economy of the weaver-farmer, whose workplace was his home, flourished well into the Victorian period, but with the great rise in population weavers were increasingly a wage-earning class, whose cottages were rented from the manufacturers. Many weaving villages were linked with newer settlements in the valleys, where the yarn was prepared and spun; Skelmanthorpe, for instance, was a typical upland community with warehouses and weavers' cottages, whereas the scribbling and spinning mills were down in the river valley at Scissett and Denby Dale. By the middle years of the nineteenth century the worsted industry was dominated by factories, but the woollen trade still employed numerous domestic workers.

The exploitation of female and child labour, the long hours, and the hard working conditions that became such familiar features of the factory system had long been characteristic of the old domestic industry, but workers in the textile mills now had the additional burdens of strict discipline and the tyranny of the clock. When many skilled craftsmen were replaced by new machines, the Luddites won widespread public sympathy, including that of many 'respectable inhabitants' who were appalled at a system that threatened to destroy the old social order. Machine-breaking began in 1811 in Nottinghamshire, Leicestershire and south Derbyshire, where framework knitting was rapidly becoming a depressed craft. In the spring of 1812 the knitters' example was followed by West Riding croppers and shearmen, those skilled, well-paid craftsmen who 'finished' the cloth and who now found their livelihoods threatened by the gig mill and shearing frame. Between 1806 and 1817 the number of gig mills in Yorkshire rose from 5 to 72 and the number

'those magazines of British infantile slavery – the worsted mills of the town and neighbourhood of Bradford.'

RICHARD OASTLER, 1830

of shears worked by machinery increased from 100 to 1,462. As a result, 1,170 of the 3,378 shearmen were thrown out of work and 1,445 received only part-time employment. Unskilled men and children were able to work the machines. The attacks began in Leeds, then in Huddersfield and the Spen Valley, where the greatest number of machines had been installed.

In April 1812, six or seven weeks after the first acts of destruction, the Luddites turned to more desperate measures. On 9 April an estimated 300 men set fire to Joseph Foster's mill at Horbury and destroyed all the machines. Two days later, 150 Luddites, led by George Mellor, a young cropper from Longroyd Bridge, attacked William Cartwright's Rawfolds mill in the Spen Valley, but were met by a a hail of musket fire. Expected reinforcements from Halifax failed to arrive and the Luddites were forced into retreat, leaving two members dead and five wounded. William Horsfall of Ottiwells near Huddersfield was equally determined to defend his mill and was as loud as Cartwright in his condem-nation of Luddism. On 28 April, on his return from Huddersfield market, he was shot dead by George Mellor from behind a wall on Crosland Moor. The assassination was a turning point, for public sympathy changed and Luddite groups were broken up by arrests, threats, betrayals and disillusion. In January 1813 Mellor and 16 other Luddites were executed at York and seven others were transported to Australia.

The West Riding textile industry entered its most prosperous era during the middle decades of the nineteenth century. By then it had easily outstripped its rivals in East Anglia and the Cotswolds. Great shifts of population had trans-formed the ancient pattern of settlement as the mills attracted new and populous communities in the deep river valleys. All the way down the Calder Valley mill towns crammed every available space around the factories. The contrast between the old and the new is perfectly illustrated at Heptonstall and Hebden Bridge, a few miles into the Pennines west of Halifax. On the lofty summit of a bleak hill stands Heptonstall, a weaving village full of dark vernacular houses and cottages clustered together, a sturdy Pennine community that remains a wonderfully preserved period piece from the days of the old domestic economy. The village continued to thrive in Victoria's reign but its inhabitants must have been astonished at the youthful vigour and spectacular growth of the settlement down below at Hebden Bridge. Before the nineteenth century a few houses had gathered near the old bridge over the River Hebden just above its confluence with the Calder but now they were engulfed by rows of houses perched on the steep bank sides in places which earlier settlers had avoided instinctively. The

A section of Aikin's map of the West Riding, published in 1795 as part of his *Decription of the Country From Thirty to Forty Miles Around Manchester*. The map marks parks, early turnpikes and some minor roads, and shows the sizes of the towns as they began to expand (Heptonstall on the top left, for example, is still marked as much more significant that the tiny settlement of Hebden down in the valley). Aikin shared the contemporary fascination with canal building, and although parlia-mentary approval had only just been received and work had barely begun, he was keen to mark the routes of all of the great new trans-Pennine links – the Rochdale (completed 1804), the Huddersfield (1811), and the Leeds and Liverpool (begun 1770 at both ends and only finally completed in 1816).

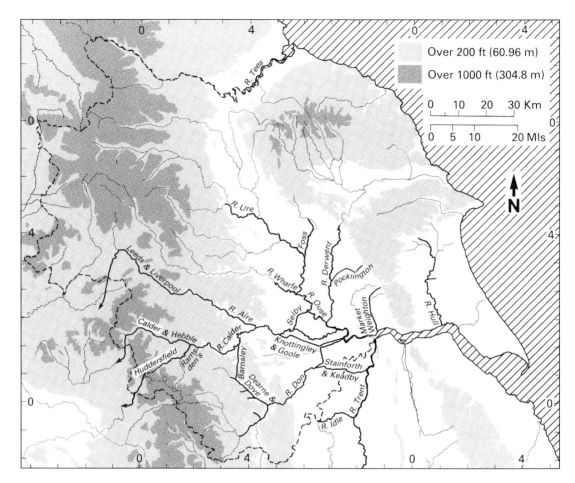

above Navigable rivers and canals.

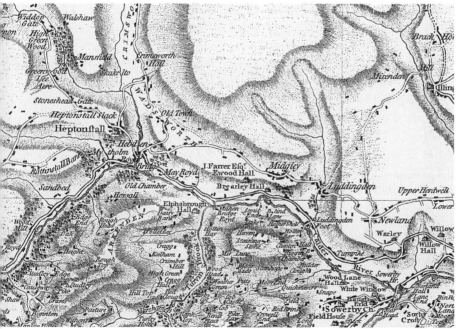

A section of Jeffreys' map of Yorkshire, 1771, showing the area around Heptonstall and Hebden Bridge.

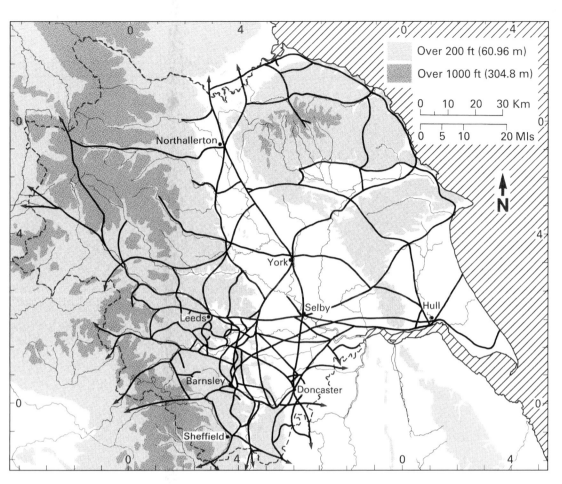

Over 200 ft (60.96 m)

Over 1000 ft (304.8 m)

0   10   20   30 Km

0   5   10   20 Mls

N

Northallerton

York

Leeds

Selby

Hull

Barnsley

Doncaster

Sheffield

above Yorkshire's railways.

opening of the Rochdale canal and then the Lancashire and Yorkshire railway encouraged the expansion of new communities in the Calder Valley, especially when Hebden Bridge, Mytholmroyd and Sowerby Bridge were provided with railway stations. White's 1853 directory noted that Sowerby Bridge had 'extensive cotton worsted, and corn mills, commodious wharfs, and several chemical works, iron foundries, etc.' By then Sowerby Bridge was more populous than the old village of Sowerby, Mytholmroyd had outgrown Midgley, and further down the valley the former hamlet of Brighouse had become larger than neighbouring Rastrick. A similar story could be told about developments in the Colne and Holme valleys and about the towns that sprawled along the banks of the Aire.

The hill villages did not decline in absolute terms, for weaving long remained at the domestic stage of manufacture and mining, quarrying and the usual range of village crafts provided other employment. The old dual economy of the smallholder-craftsmen lingered on late into the Victorian era. Baines reported that even in 1859 as many woollen workers were employed outside the factories as within. Nevertheless, by the time of the Great Exhibition of 1851 it was clear that within another generation or so the changeover to the factory system would

right Holy Trinity Church, Holmfirth. The territory known as the Graveship of Holme or 'the forest of Holmfirth' comprised several Pennine townships within the huge manor of Wakefield. For ecclesiastical purposes, those townships which lay north of the River Holme were within Almondbury parish, while those to the south and east were within the parish of Kirkburton. A medieval chapel of ease that served the whole graveship was erected next to the corn mill on the River Holme in what is now the town of Holmfirth. It was apparently ruinous by 1360 and was rebuilt in 1472. The present church, which dates from 1777–87, was designed by John Jagger. In the late twentieth century several parts of Yorkshire have become well known nationally as the locations for TV series. The centre of Holmfirth has become a tourist attraction as the setting for many of the scenes in *Last of the Summer Wine*.

PHOTOGRAPH: CARNEGIE, 2004

be complete. The number of West Riding woollen mills rose from 129 in 1833 to 606 in 1838 and to 880 by 1850 and steam engines rather than water wheels were now the major source of power. Meanwhile, in the worsted industry hand-weaving declined rapidly, while between 1838 and 1850 employment in factories more than doubled. New combinations of alpaca and mohair with cotton warps enabled the worsted trade to compete with cotton in the market for cheap, light fabrics. By 1838 the West Riding produced about 85 per cent of the nation's worsted goods and 12 years later its share had risen to 90 per cent.

By the 1830s widespread unease at the regimented working conditions in the *left* Holmfirth. In the Middle Ages, Holmfirth was the name of a district on the moorland edge of the great manor of Wakefield. It was known alternatively as the Graveship of Holme and was divided into several townships, each consisting of villages or scattered farmsteads high on the hills. This ancient pattern of settlement was changed by the Industrial Revolution, when scribbling and spinning mills were erected on the River Holme and its tributaries, alongside the ancient corn or fulling mills. Workers' houses were then built along the valley bottoms and wherever land was available on the steep hillsides. New roads and a railway were constructed to serve them. The name Holmfirth was no longer associated with the whole district but was applied to the major settlement in the valley. In 1842 it acquired a Town Hall.

PHOTOGRAPH: AUTHOR

textile mills, which had broken the ancient link between home and place of work, burst into an indignant revulsion for the new system. This disgust was expressed by Richard Oastler of Fixby Hall in a famous letter to the *Leeds Mercury* on 16 October 1830 in which he condemned 'those magazines of British infantile slavery – the worsted mills of the town and neighbourhood of Bradford'. Child labour in these mills, wrote Oastler, was worse than negro slavery in America. Recalling his early days in Pudsey, where he was born in 1821, Joseph Lawson remembered that large numbers of women and girls were burlers of cloth who picked out specks with mall irons after the scouring process and that the slubbers who drew out the cardings and wound them ready for the spinners earned twice as much as the weavers. Children, however, were paid a pittance of only 3s. or 3s. 6d. for standing at their work sometimes 90 hours a week. Oastler was typical of many small West Riding squires whose sympathies lay with the mill-workers rather than the owners. They were Tory paternalists concerned with restoring the old social order rather than Radicals who dreamed of a new one. John Fielden of Todmorden, John Wood of Bradford and Michael Sadler, the Tory MP joined Oastler in the Ten Hours Movement to limit the daily hours of work in the textile mills. They met furious opposition from the mill owners, particularly the Ackroyds of Halifax, who at a meeting on 5 March 1831 drew up 'fourteen points' against Oastler. Many of the local Church of England clergy spoke out on behalf of the masters, but in 1832 the philanthropists got their way with the establishment of a royal commission, whose sympathetic questioners elicited damning evidence of the abuse of child labour. As a result of the commission an Act was passed in 1833 which prohibited the employment of children under the age of nine in textile mills; those aged 9–13 were limited to a 48 hour week; those aged 13–18 were allowed to work 60 hours a week but could not be employed on night shifts.

Heptonstall Cloth Hall. Now a house in Towngate, this building was erected in the 1540s or 1550s as a cloth hall, but was eventually unable to compete with the great cloth market at Halifax. It was converted into cottages in 1613.

PHOTOGRAPH: CARNEGIE, 2005

Hebden Bridge. Deep in the gorge where Hebden Water flows into the River Calder, the settlement takes its name from a wooden bridge that was recorded in 1327 and the stone successor of 1510. Hebden Bridge is a classic example of a West Riding textile town which grew up alongside the mills that were located in the valley bottom to make use of water power from the river there. Through the valley came a turnpike road (1772), the Rochdale Canal (1794 onwards) and the Manchester–Leeds railway (1841), all great technical and civil engineering achievements of the Industrial Revolution. These further stimulated economic growth and encouraged the building of steam-powered mills and terraces of workers' houses stretching up the steep slopes of the valley.

The Act also established the important principle that government inspectors should ensure that the law was applied strictly. In 1847 Oastler's campaign achieved its objective with the passing of the Ten Hours Act.

Textile towns

In Leeds the textile industries, particularly the manufacture, dyeing, finishing and marketing of woollen cloth, remained pre-eminent throughout the first half of the nineteenth century. In 1855 the borough had twice as many workers in the woollen and worsted industries than in the 37 flax mills which employed 9,500 people. Leeds also had a significant trade in carpets, cotton yarn, and silk, and the textile trades provided an important market for the machines and steam engines that were produced in local engineering works. Founding and engineering had become major Leeds industries during the first half of the nineteenth century. By 1850 Leeds was a town of many trades, including a dozen extensive tanneries and skin works. The rapidly rising population was densely packed into yards and folds that lacked running water and sanitation facilities. At the beginning of Victoria's reign 341 people were crowded into 57 rooms in the notorious Boot and Shoe yard. An official report in 1842 noted

A PLAN
of
LEEDS.

SCALE of Chains.

Jeffreys' town plan of Leeds, 1771, shows the importance of the Aire as a navigable river and as a source of power for the mills. The main streets are those of the medieval borough to the west of the old settlement around St Peter's church. The seventeenth-century St John's church still marked the northern limit of the town and the cloth hall and infirmary stood in open ground to the west. Leeds had not yet burst beyond its medieval limits.

that in a typical irish weaver's cottage in Leeds 'the kitchen is not only appropriated to culinary purposes, but is the house, the sleeping-room, the hen-house, and the piggery; whilst upstairs are three or four looms, all but touching each other; and perhaps, in a corner, a bed on the floor for one of the owners of these looms'. Beyond the old town centre, alongside the main highways, were row after unvaried row of brick, back-to-back houses. Piecemeal, unplanned development began in 1787 when Richard Paley acquired land to build speculative housing or to sell in lots to developers. Paley built 275 houses before he went bankrupt in 1803 and 290 houses that had been erected by other builders on his plots. The long, narrow fields that adjoined the town were ideal for the back-to-back method of construction and by 1850 Leeds had 360 streets of them. In the southern townships of Holbeck and Hunslet three times as many houses were built during the first half of the nineteenth century than in the northern townships of Headingley, Potter Newton and Chapel Allerton.

Crowded folds and back-to-back terraces vied for space with great flax mills, foundries, gasworks, railway sidings and brickyards. In Leeds at least 700 people died of cholera in 1832 and over 2,000 died in the outbreak of 1848–49.

Unlike Leeds, Bradford was not an important town before the Industrial Revolution, but merely a small market centre for a large, thinly settled parish. In 1780 the compact medieval origins of the central township were still obvious around the junction of Ivegate, Westgate and Kirkgate. The availability of coal for steam power and the construction of the Leeds and Liverpool Canal were crucial to Bradford's industrial development. The first Boulton and Watt steam-powered textile mill in Yorkshire was erected at Baildon in 1796 by Cockshott and Halliday, but by 1810 Bradford had only five spinning mills. Until the 1820s much of the spinning and all of the weaving was done under the domestic system. In 1851 Bradford still had 1,117 handloom weavers and large numbers continued to work in the old manner in the surrounding villages. By then, however, Bradford had become the 'worstedopolis' that had overtaken Halifax as the leading centre of worsted manufacture in the North. After 1830, some of the most prominent manufacturers came from Germany, men with names like Behrens, Flersheim, Furst, Gumpal, Hertz, Mayer, Schlesinger and Sichel, who like their counterparts in the Manchester cotton industry gave a cultural as well as business lead to the town. Youthful immigrants flocked to the

Leeds from Rope Hill, c.1840. This watercolour by Alphonse Dousseau shows the smoky, industrial town spreading out into the fields. By then the central township of Leeds had 88,741 inhabitants, while the population of the borough had reached 152,054. A report of 1842 criticised the smoke emitted by the town's 362 steam engines and the pollution caused by the dye works, whose low chimneys 'pour out their dense volumes of unconsumed carbon, which traverses the streets and fills the houses' of the poor inhabitants who lived alongside.

borough, whose population rose from 8,525 in 1780 to 103,778 in 1851. Half the inhabitants were under the age of 20 at the time of the 1841 census; ten years later only one in four had been born in the borough.

The staggering rate of growth brought immense problems of housing, sanitation, water supply and atmospheric pollution. One of the Health of Towns Commissioners described Bradford as 'the dirtiest, filthiest and worst regulated town in the kingdom'. Its infant mortality rates were amongst the highest recorded and the average age at death was only 20 years, the lowest in Yorkshire. Drainage was provided by open sewers which saturated the surrounding soil and ran down to the Bradford canal, a major health hazard known locally as the 'River Stink'. The prosperous middle classes lived in pleasant villas in Manningham Lane but the town-centre slums were amongst the worst in the country, particularly in the Wapping and White Abbey districts where woolcombers lived and worked in crowded cellars. During the 1830s and 40s Bradford gained a radical reputation as its youthful and oppressed society rioted against the Poor Law (1837), took part in the plug-drawing riots (1842) and enthusiastically supported the Chartists (1839 and 1848). The borough was also noted for its religious nonconformity and in 1837 was the first town to have a Temperance Hall. Early attempts to tackle the massive public health problems were hampered by the chaotic local government structure before Bradford

'the dirtiest, filthiest and worst regulated town in the kingdom.'

BRADFORD, BY A HEALTH COMMISSIONER

achieved its borough status in 1847. The lord of the manor held his courts leet and baron and controlled the markets, fairs, slaughter houses and weights and measures; the ratepayers met as a vestry at Easter to elect churchwardens, constables, surveyors of the highways and overseers of the poor, until the establishment of a board of guardians in 1837 and a board of surveyors in 1843; the justices of the peace supervised the vestry officials and served as local magistrates; and from 1803 the 58 Improvement Commissioners, appointed by a local Act of Parliament, were in charge of cleansing, lighting and watching the town centre streets and the removal of nuisances and obstructions. Even those who were involved in administration were unsure of the exact scope of their rights and responsibilities and no body had adequate powers to cope with disease and social disorder.

Huddersfield was another textile town that grew quickly during the first half of the nineteenth century. It had been a small market town since 1671 and was now the centre of the fancy trade, whereby figured silk and wool or worsted yarns were woven into patterns to make flowered waistcoats and other fancy goods. The trade had developed during the later eighteenth century under the stimulus of the Lancashire cotton industry. In 1822 Baines' *Directory* listed 102 'Manufacturers of Fancy Goods who attended Huddersfield Market, with their places of abode and Inns or Warehouses' in cluttered yards near the cloth hall. The trade was at the mercy of changing fashion but it expanded considerably in the mid Victorian era. Fancy weavers also worked in their chambers in the villages to the east and south of Huddersfield, at Kirkheaton, Dalton, Almondbury, Lepton, Honley, Shepley, Cumberworth, Skelmanthorpe, Denby Dale and Thurlstone. A manufacturer paid £5 of the cost of a loom and £2 was paid by the weaver out of his wages. Huddersfield attracted conflicting opinions from visitors. One outsider in 1849 thought it 'by no means a well-built town' with three-quarters of the working-class

A detail of an 1850 map of the Huddersfield estate of Sir John William Ramsden, baronet, showing the new streets of the town centre near the oval cloth hall. The Ramsden family owned most of the land, and were largely responsible for the town's development.

districts consisting of back-to-back houses, but five years earlier Friedrich Engels had written that 'Huddersfield is the handsomest by far of all the factory towns of Yorkshire and Lancashire, by reason of its charming situation and modern architecture'. The paternal influence of the Ramsden family and the powers granted by Improvement Acts in 1820 and 1848 ensured an orderly layout with proper drainage facilities when the town expanded beyond its old limits around the church, market square and cloth hall. The streets were given ample widths with a grid pattern and decent two-storeyed houses and public buildings. When John Wesley 'rode over the mountains to Huddersfield' in 1757 he noted, 'A wilder people I never saw in England. The men, women and children filled the streets and seemed just ready to devour us'. Evangelical religion channelled this energy to more constructive uses, however, and 1836 saw the foundation of a choral society that was to become world famous.

Halifax was now not only the commercial hub of its large parish but a major manufacturing centre, with spacious new factory and warehouse accommodation, progressive banking and insurance facilities and access to turnpike, waterway and railway networks. It was incorporated as a borough in 1848. Between 1750 and 1850 the population of the central township grew from around 5,000 to 25,159, while that of the parish as a whole rose at almost the same rate from around 31,000 to 149,257. The families who left the domestic economy of the rural townships to work in the new urban factories were accompanied by large numbers of outsiders, many of them Irish. The well-established woollen and worsted industries catered for a growing domestic market, clothed British armies in the colonial conflicts of the late eighteenth century, and exported cloths to Spain, Portugal, the Levant and Guinea. By the second decade of the nineteenth century Halifax had lost its leadership of the West Riding worsted industry to Bradford, but the trade continued to grow and by 1835 half the textile workers in Halifax were engaged in worsted production. Meanwhile, new textile industries, notably cotton and silk, had been introduced into the parish, but the transition to factory-based production was a gradual process. It took more than 60 years for the woollen and worsted industries to become fully mechanised. By 1851 the number of textile mills in Halifax parish had risen to 254, including 18 new spinning mills in the borough. At that time, 22 per cent of adult males in the Halifax registration district were employed in worsted manufacture, compared with 9 per cent in woollens and nearly 4 per cent in cottons. The manufacture of carpets at Dean Clough Mills was begun in 1802 by John Crossley and by the time of his death in 1837 the business had 150 looms and about 300 employees. His sons John, Joseph and

Dean Clough Mills shortly after it opened, *c*.1803.

WEST YORKSHIRE ARCHIVE SERVICE, CALDERDALE

Francis continued to expand the business, which by 1849 employed about 1,500 workers. The opulence of the most successful merchants and manufacturers in the late eighteenth century is evident from the fine Georgian mansions they commissioned on the southern edge of the town. During the first half of the nineteenth century many more manufacturers who had risen from obscure beginnings built town houses and mansions in Halifax. An outstanding example were the Akroyds, wealthy worsted manufacturers who originated as yeomen-clothiers high in the Calder Valley. In 1849 Edward Akroyd, shocked by the violence of the plug riots of 1842, commenced his first model industrial community at Copley; in 1859 he started his more ambitious housing scheme at Akroydon.

Other textile towns and large industrial villages flourished in the years after the Napoleonic wars. Baines' 1822 *Directory* noted that Keighley was a considerable market town, that worsteds and cotton goods were made there and at Bingley, and that Dewsbury had many extensive establishments for the manufacture of blankets, woollen cloths, and carpets, which were exported via the Aire and Calder navigation and the canal to Huddersfield and so to Manchester and the western sea. Mirfield was a centre of woollen manufacture, Heckmondwike had very extensive blanket and carpet manufactories, and Brighouse, Haworth, Horbury, Morley and Pudsey were populous clothing villages. Pudsey was a chapel-of-ease of the parish of Calverley with only 4,422

Ebor Mill, near Haworth. Hiram Craven and his sons, Thomas and Hiram, built this worsted spinning mill in 1819, perhaps on the site of a former mill. A beck was dammed to work a water wheel and the spun yarn was put out to handloom weavers. The mill was greatly enlarged in the second half of the nineteenth century as part of the business of the firm of Merralls, one of Yorkshire's largest worsted spinning concerns. The tall chimney reveals the use of steam to power weavers' looms.

inhabitants in 1801 but a thriving community of 18,469 people in 1901. Joseph Lawson recalled that in his childhood in the 1820s the houses were mostly scattered, for people built their homes to suit their personal whims regardless of taste, order or sanitary conditions. Narrow local prejudices existed between neighbouring villages and even between clans in different parts of the same village. Strangers were regarded with suspicion and pelted with stones. On the other hand, the Moravian colony at nearby Fulneck 'had a kind of charm for us, and we remember thinking and saying that it always looked like Sunday there, all being so quiet and clean, and most of the people well dressed'. The villages of the West Riding were as varied in their individual characters as were the great industrial towns.

The iron and steel industries

The signs of a new industrial age were plentiful to see. The old charcoal iron industry had given way to a technology based on coal and to operations on a much larger scale. In the middle of the eighteenth century the Walker brothers – Samuel, Aaron and Jonathan – had taken over the site of the Masbrough slitting mill, Rotherham, so as to be near the navigable river Don, after the success of their experiments with an 'Air Furnace in the old nailor's smithy, on the backside of Saml. Walker's cottage at Grenoside', and later John Cockshutt had adapted Wortley forge to the new techniques of coke-fuelling, puddling and rolling. Meanwhile, Richard Swallow, the heir to the Fells of Attercliffe, had converted Chapel furnace and Attercliffe forge to the coke-fuelled production of iron and steel. By 1806 his son and namesake was making 3,737 tons of metal per annum, compared with the average 450 tons of the old Chapel

These bell pits at Bentley Grange, Emley, were used for mining ironstone in the seventeenth and eighteenth centuries. The mounds are the spoil heaps thrown up the shaft by the miners. When a pit became difficult to work, the miners dug another alongside it. The hollows at the top of the mounds were formed when the shaft was abandoned. These pits were once thought to be medieval, on the basis that Bentley Grange belonged to the Cistercian monks of Byland Abbey, who had a forge there. However, it is now clear that they are post-medieval, supplying ironstone to Bank Furnace, a nearby charcoal blast furnace.

PHOTOGRAPH: AUTHOR

furnace. In 1793 George Newton and Thomas Chambers moved from Sheffield
to begin a lease of Earl Fitzwilliam's iron and coal mines at Thorncliffe, just
up the valley from Swallow's Chapeltown works, and to build a foundry. By
1806 their output was 2,500 tons a year and they employed some 300 miners,
furnacemen, foundrymen and labourers. At Masbrough the Walkers founded a
dynasty of iron and steel masters who lived in fine Georgian houses around
the town and built an Independent chapel near their works. They made steam
engines and other machinery castings, bridges, and cannon, and became the
leading ironmasters in northern England.

Further north, the iron industry was concentrated not only near ironstone
deposits but where coal was of suitable quality for coking. In the Bradford
district, for example, Emmet's ironworks was established at Birkenshaw in 1782,
six years later the Bowling ironworks began manufacturing pig iron and such
cast-iron domestic goods as fire-grates, fire-irons and frying pans, and in 1789
the Low Moor Iron Company, the best known of all, started production. The
Low Moor works were founded by John Hardy, a Bradford solicitor, John
Jarratt, a draper, Richard Hind, a woolstapler, and the Revd Joseph Dawson,
a Nonconformist minister. As none of the partners had any previous
ironworking experience, the technical side of the business was left to the
engineer, Edward Smalley. The French Revolutionary Wars stimulated the iron
trade through lucrative government contracts for armaments and during the
course of the nineteenth century the West Riding became an important centre
for the engineering industry.

In 1736 the population of the parish of Sheffield was 14,531; by 1851 the
same area (incorporated as a borough in 1843) contained 135,310 inhabitants.
The first planned development beyond the old limits of the town took place
in the later eighteenth century on the Duke of Norfolk's Alsop Fields estate
on the south-eastern edge of the town, where both houses and industrial

premises were laid out on a grid plan of new streets. Then the wedge-shaped common of Little Sheffield (now the shopping district known as The Moor) was enclosed and given over to building. In the early nineteenth century working-class suburbs on the eastern and northern edges of the town grew up at Park Hill, Wicker and Bridgehouses and by the 1820s the town was expanding in a north-westerly direction as industry and housing crept up the Don valley. A grid pattern of streets was laid out to the west of the town on Earl Fitzwilliam's estate and, after the construction of the turnpike road to Glossop and Manchester over the Snake Pass in 1821, middle-class suburbs developed in Broomhill and on the Broom Hall estate, away from the smoke of the metal industries.

In 1841 the Revd J. C. Symons wrote that Sheffield was 'one of the dirtiest and most smoky towns I ever saw'. Thanks to crucible steel, Sheffield had now overtaken London as England's pre-eminent cutlery centre. Hallamshire cutlers had become increasingly specialised as forgers, grinders or finishers, or as the manufacturers of particular products, such as razors or surgical instruments. The 'little mester' with his apprentice and a journeyman remained a typical figure but small partnerships were now common and a few larger firms had been formed. By 1789 journeymen were said to outnumber freemen by as many as ten or 12 to one and the authority of the Cutlers' Company collapsed under the sheer weight of numbers. The break with the past was far from complete, however, for handicraft skills remained the traditional ones and most working units were small. By the late eighteenth century the River Don had an average of three water-powered sites per mile, the Loxley and Sheaf had four, the Porter five and the Rivelin six. Many of these sites had also been enlarged to accommodate more grinders; dams had been widened; and new water wheels had been designed for greater efficiency. By the late eighteenth century almost every available site on the rivers was occupied. Sheffield's industrial development was firmly based on water power and its concentration of water-powered sites was without parallel in the rest of Britain. By the late eighteenth century London

'All the way along from Leeds to Sheffield it is coal and iron and iron and coal'

WILLIAM COBBETT

Marsh Brothers, Ponds Works, Shude Lane, Sheffield, mid-1840s. This old cutlery firm moved here in 1828 to make a range of tools, cutlery and razors from their own steel, especially for the American market. The rectangular chimney stacks on the central range of buildings serve the crucible furnaces, while the conical chimneys to the right are the cementation furnaces. A range of small forges can also be seen across the yard. The main building houses the offices and small work chambers. The tall chimney expelled the fumes from the boiler fire.

SHEFFIELD LIBRARIES, ARCHIVES AND INFORMATION: LOCAL STUDIES

and overseas markets had become even more important than before. Some Sheffield firms had warehouses in London and salesmen in America, and by 1800 much of the world's cutlery trade, especially that of America and the British Empire, was dominated by Sheffield. The Sheaf Works, which was built about 1823 by Messrs Greaves by the new canal basin, is regarded as Sheffield's

William Ibbitt, *South-east View of the Town of Sheffield*, 1854. A view of the new borough from Park Hill, looking across the gloomy Ponds district to the market area and the spires of St Peter's, St Marie's, and St Paul's. The western limits of the town are marked by St George's and St Philip's. Industry has spread along the Don Valley but the hills are not yet covered with housing. On the right, a train pulls out of the Victoria station on the newly completed railway line from Manchester. Greaves' Sheaf Works and the Duke of Norfolk's Park colliery are sited close to the canal basin. Sheffield was beginning to acquire an industrial East End.
SHEFFIELD GALLERIES & MUSEUMS TRUST

first self-contained factory, by far the largest business in the town at that time. The workers converted and melted cementation steel, made their own tools, and then produced razors, penknives and other cutlery wares, especially for the American market. Small works in the back streets remained the typical units of production, but by 1850 four other firms that had international reputations for the quality and design of their knives employed hundreds of workers: Joseph Rodgers & Son's Norfolk Works, George Wostenholm's Washington Works, Mappin Bros' Queen Cutlery Works, and James Dixon's Cornish Place Works. Even in these firms, however, the manufacture of cutlery remained a series of handicrafts, some of which were performed by outworkers.

Meanwhile, Benjamin Huntsman's invention had made Sheffield internationally famous for the manufacture of steel. The industry had grown so quickly that by the mid nineteenth century the Sheffield district made 90 per cent of British steel and nearly half the European output. The larger cementation ('blister') steel furnaces had the capacity to produce over 40 tons in each operation and about 260 of them now ejected smoke into the Sheffield atmosphere. The production of high-quality crucible ('cast') steel was on a much smaller scale. The water-powered scythe works at Abbeydale Industrial Museum provides a good idea of the modest size of the typical crucible-steel furnace. By the 1780s the largest steel firms, notably that of John Marshall of Millsands, had both types of furnaces. The Sheffield tool industry also grew rapidly with the use of crucible steel for cutting edges. A directory of 1787 named 12 edge-tool makers in the town and six more just beyond. The best surviving example of a firm that grew in size during the prosperous 1840s and 50s is the brick-built, steam-powered Butcher's Wheel in Arundel Street, where William and Samuel Butcher, who had inherited a cutlery business that went back to 1725, made steel, files, razors, chisels, planes and high-quality cutlery, pocket knives and Bowie knives for the American market.

Meanwhile, the foundations of a new Sheffield industry had been laid by a local cutler. In 1743 Thomas Boulsover discovered that when silver and copper were fused together they could be worked as one metal to look like solid silver.

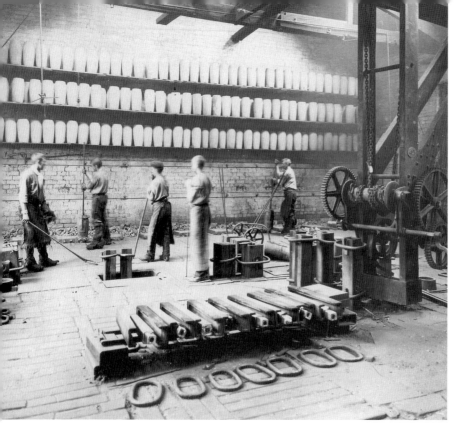

He was quick to recognise the commercial possibilities of his discovery and soon acquired a fortune from making plated buttons and other wares. Old Sheffield Plate added much to Sheffield's growing reputation as a place where high-quality wares were made. Other men, in both Sheffield and Birmingham, took up his invention to make not just buttons, buckles and knife handles, but snuff boxes, candlesticks, saucepans and coffee pots and then solid silver artefacts as well. Joseph Hancock, rather than Boulsover, became 'the Father of the Old Sheffield Plate Trade'. Joseph Hoyland & Co., Tudor, Sherburn & Leader, and Roberts, Cadman & Co. also became well-known firms. The silver platers became some of the richest men in town and they paid high wages to their skilled workmen. By 1825 Sheffield had about 28 firms of platers.

At the opposite end of the county, Middlesbrough was growing in a remarkable way. In 1801 the settlement consisted of four houses with 25 inhabitants; in 1831 the tiny population stood at 154; but ten years later it had risen to 5,463 and by 1901 it had soared to 91,302. The development of the site began in 1829 when a group of Quaker industrialists led by Joseph Pease of Darlington extended the Stockton to Darlington railway into the bleak salt marshes on the southern bank of the Tees where they constructed large wharves to export coal. Two years later, Pease laid out a new town on a symmetrical plan behind the wharves, around a market square, church and town hall, and a pottery, foundry and rolling mill provided extra employment for the immigrants who began to pour into Middlesbrough. By 1840 1.5 million tons of coal were exported every year from the new port, but the development of a national rail network meant that the sea-borne coal trade soon declined sharply. This setback was more than compensated for by the spectacular growth of the local iron industry. The man most responsible for Middlesbrough's change of course and continued growth was Henry Bolckow, who came from Mecklenburg to Newcastle in 1827 at the age of 21 and who 14 years later established an ironworks on the banks of the Tees. His partner, John Vaughan, had previously worked at the Dowlais ironworks and at Carlisle and Newcastle. For several years their business was a small concern dependent upon imported ore, but during the 1850s they began to exploit the ironstone deposits in the nearby Cleveland hills at Eston, which had previously been considered of poor quality. Middlesbrough's spectacular growth came in the second half of the nineteenth century, but the foundations for that success were secure by 1850.

Canals and railways

The success of the improved river navigations and the new canals encouraged others to extend the waterways system in the early years of the nineteenth century. In 1804 the Rochdale canal to Halifax provided a second crossing of the Pennines. The third crossing was the most difficult of all, for it involved the construction of the Stanedge tunnel, at 5,456 yards the longest on any English canal. This was the Huddersfield canal, which was opened in 1811 from Ashton-under-Lyne (where the Peak Forest canal led to other waterways in and around Manchester) to link with Sir John Ramsden's canal and the Calder and

Hebble navigation at Cooper bridge. The East Riding's three canals linked the market towns of Driffield, Pocklington and Market Weighton to navigable rivers, but their effect was less dramatic than in the industrial west. A new settlement called Newport grew up where the Hull road crossed the Market Weighton canal and by 1823 the seven manufacturers there were producing an estimated 2 million bricks and 1.7 million tiles per annum; the population had grown to 777 by 1851. Another lowland canal, the Stainforth and Keadby (1793–1802), provided access from the Don to the Trent via Thorne for craft up to 200 tons, but the most important project in the Vale of York was the Knottingley and Goole canal, which opened in 1826 as the Aire and Calder navigation company's final scheme to improve the route to the Ouse. The place-name Goole, first recorded in 1362, means a drain. A small, straggling settlement had grown up at the mouth of the Dutch river, but in 1821 the township contained only 450 persons. After 1826, however, when the navigation company put their enormous resources into developing a town and docks, Goole became the latest of a group of canal ports that included Runcorn, Stourport and Ellesmere Port, which 'mushroomed' within a very few years into a thriving settlement.

Almost all the goods that were imported and exported through Hull spent part of their journey on navigable rivers and canals. Hull's commercial prosperity benefited hugely from the growth of industry in the West Riding. Its main exports were woollen and worsted cloth and Sheffield metalware. Its imports came mainly from Norway (wood), Sweden (iron) and Russia, Poland and Prussia (wood, hemp, flax, iron). Trade boomed during the 1780s until Hull became England's third largest port, albeit a long way behind London and Liverpool. The great merchant houses, led by Joseph Pease & Sons, also traded along the east coast and the link to London was vital; back carriage included goods from the East and West Indies. The whaling industry was 50 years old in 1804, when 40 ships brought 4,018 tons of oil into the port, and it continued to grow until the 1820s. The dockland area was also noted for its shipbuilding and processing industries such as sugar-refining, tobacco and brewing, but Hull remained predominantly a commercial town. The dock that Henry Berry built between 1775 and 1778 was the largest yet constructed and its success encouraged the merchants to ask John Rennie to design a second one.

The new era of steam transport had begun in 1802 when Richard Trevithick experimented with a locomotive at Coalbrookdale. The technical problems were not overcome until 1812, when John Blenkinsop and Matthew Murray built *Prince Regent* and *Salamanca* to move coal from the Middleton colliery along the old waggonway across Hunslet Moor to the staithes on the Aire and Calder navigation. Each locomotive could pull 20 loaded waggons at a time and they attracted great interest throughout the world. One of the men who came to see them was George Stephenson, who was soon to make major advances in the designs of locomotives and the construction of railways. Leeds businessmen and Hull merchants (who feared the rise of Goole) commissioned Stephenson

Waterside at Knaresborough, 1890. John Buxton Knight's romantic view shows the distant ruins of the medieval castle high on the sandstone cliffs above the Nidd Gorge, overlooking Knaresborough. The scene is dominated by the spectacular, castellated railway viaduct which crosses the river into the heart of the town. The first viaduct on this line between Harrogate and York had collapsed shortly after construction in March 1848 because of poor workmanship and shoddy materials. The new viaduct was designed by Thomas Grainger and was opened in 1851.
HARROGATE MUSEUMS AND ARTS, MERCER ART GALLERY

and Joseph Locke of Barnsley to construct a railway that would link the industrial heart of the West Riding with the county's major port. In 1834 the line was opened from Leeds to Selby and six years later it was extended to Hull. Meanwhile in 1836 Leeds had also backed an early scheme to cross the Pennines to Manchester under the supervision of Stephenson and James Walker. About 1,000 navvies completed the Littleborough tunnel by 1840 and in Yorkshire the route followed the Calder Valley all the way from Todmorden to Normanton so as to connect with Stephenson's York and North Midland railway of 1836–38, which was part of a wider scheme to link the capital with the North. By 1841 it was possible to travel all the way from London via Derby, Rotherham, York and Darlington and seven years later a more direct route via Doncaster and Selby to York made for an even quicker and more economical journey.

Such early successes led to the 'railway mania' of the mid 1840s, an era personified by George Hudson, twice Lord Mayor of York and the most ebullient of the first railway magnates. Hudson's reign as 'railway king' ended in shame in 1849 when his financial chicanery was exposed and he eventually left England in disgrace, but his contribution to the development of the national railway system was nonetheless of permanent value. Above all, he realised that as the small private companies which had built the early lines had insufficient resources amalgamation was the key to progress. He pioneered the way with his Midland Railway Company of 1844 and at the height of his powers five years later he had financial control of almost all the railway system of Northumberland, Durham and the North and East Ridings; his Midland company had a monopoly in Nottinghamshire, Leicestershire and Derbyshire; and his was the dominant interest in East Anglia. Under Hudson, York's fortunes were restored as it became a great railway administrative centre with accompanying waggon and coachbuilding works.

Other important amalgamations created the Manchester, Sheffield and Lincolnshire Railway Company in 1846–47 and the North Eastern Railway Company in 1854. The North Eastern owned about 1,700 miles of line and worked another 300. By the mid 1850s nearly all the major English railway lines had been completed or were under construction. The most ambitious railway engineering project undertaken in Yorkshire was the Woodhead tunnel, which provided a link through the Pennines between Sheffield and Manchester. Begun in 1839, it took six years to complete and at 3 miles 13 yards was by far the longest tunnel in Britain at that time. At the height of the operation over 1,500 navvies worked night and day, including Sundays, tunnelling from 12 different rock faces at once. The tunnel crossed the moors at about 1,000 feet above sea-level and the longest ventilation shaft was sunk to a depth of 579 feet. All but 1,000 yards of the tunnel had to be lined with masonry to prevent falls from the roof. The work was dangerous and unpleasant. It involved standing ankle-deep, and sometimes knee-deep, in mud and if the parched men drank the water which ran down the walls they soon suffered from chronic diarrhoea. In an infamous reply to a question at a parliamentary enquiry in 1846, Wellington Purdon, the assistant engineer to Joesph Locke, agreed that perhaps the safety fuse was a better way of conducting explosions than the one he employed, 'but it is attended with such a loss of time, and the difference is so very small, I would not recommend the loss of time for the sake of all the extra lives it would save'. At least 32 men were killed while building the tunnel and (incomplete) records detail 23 cases of compound fractures, 74 simple fractures, and 140 serious cases involving burns, contusions, lacerations and dislocations. As Edwin Chadwick remarked, the 3 per cent killed and 14 per cent wounded nearly equalled the proportionate casualties of a military campaign or a severe battle.

The navvies lived with their wives, mistresses and children in stone huts at the Yorkshire end at Dunford Bridge and in worse conditions at Woodhead. They were attracted by high wages and when they were paid every 9–13 weeks they invariably went on a drunken rampage. Stories of their wild, dissolute, heathen life alarmed the respectable inhabitants of the towns and villages a few miles away. Public concern over Woodhead led to the establishment of a parliamentary enquiry into the employment of railway labourers in 1846. A second bore was constructed alongside the original tunnel in 1847–52 and this time

The safety fuse '... is attended with such a loss of time, and the difference is so very small, I would not recommend the loss of time for the sake of all the extra lives it would save.'

ASSISTANT ENGINEER,
WOODHEAD TUNNEL PROJECT

working conditions were better and fewer men died; an outbreak of cholera killed 28 navvies at Woodhead, however, in 1849.

The impact of the railway age is nowhere more evident than at Doncaster, where the Great Northern railway from London arrived in 1848. Four years later a major railway engineering works known as the Plant was established on the west side of the town for the construction and repair of locomotives, coaches and waggons; here were built the famous locomotives designed by Sturrock, Stirling and Gresley that became known throughout the world. By the end of 1853 the Plant employed 949 workers; by the early 1890s, when it extended over two miles, its workforce had risen to about 3,500. The workers came mostly from the countryside to live in monotonous streets of little brick and slate houses, separated by corner shops, pubs and places of worship, in Hexthorpe and Balby, next to the works. They formed a very different type of community from those of the small, agricultural villages which had previously surrounded Doncaster. Edward Baines had described Doncaster in 1822 as 'one of the most clean, airy and elegant towns in the British dominions', but now it was transformed into a bustling Victorian town. After a disastrous fire in 1853 the noble parish church of St George was rebuilt to a grand design of Sir George Gilbert Scott.

One of the benefits of the railways was that they allowed ordinary families to visit the seaside. Scarborough had pioneered sea bathing during the eighteenth century. Five bathing houses were shown on Buck's prospect of the town in 1745 and by 1787 the resort had 26. Purpose-built, rented lodging houses were erected from the 1760s, beginning with a terrace known as New

Buildings. The population had reached 5,000 by 1745, but then it levelled out and even as late as 1845, when the railway station was opened, Scarborough's built-up area was not much bigger than it had been before the Black Death. Meanwhile, Bridlington had attracted its first bathers about 1770, but its development alongside the quay away from the old priory church and market town was modest until a railway reached the town in 1846.

Coal mining

West Riding collieries were at the forefront of improved winding and haulage technology. After the Duke of Norfolk had taken his Sheffield collieries under direct management in 1781, John Curr, his engineer from County Durham, installed underground waggonways and designed large corves which could be hauled fully loaded up the shafts. He also replaced the 1¾ mile wooden tramway from the collieries to the town with a new one built of cast-iron plates. The special rows of colliers' houses that were built elsewhere from the 1790s were often close to existing settlements; only occasionally were new rows such as Belle Isle at Middleton erected in isolation near the pit shafts. Eventually, successful collieries fostered new communities, with rows developing into villages. The first planned colliery village in Yorkshire seems to have been

Coal pit, Threshfield Moor. Coal has been mined in shallow pits on Threshfield Moor since at least 1607, when Lancelot Johnson sank a pit here. The last owner, John Delaney, built a washery at the pit head to improve the quality of the coal which fuelled his new lime works in Threshfield. The coal seam was exhausted by 1905, when the colliery was abandoned.

The Collier. George Walker's famous representation of a Yorkshire coal miner in 1814. He is represented 'as returning from his labours in his usual costume'. In the background is Middleton colliery, the largest coal mine in Yorkshire at that time. The locomotive is either the *Prince Regent* or the *Salamanca*, which were designed in 1812 by John Blenkinsop and Matthew Murray to move coal along a waggonway across Hunslet Moor to the Aire and Calder navigation.

Waterloo, built on the banks of the Aire for the Fentons on the boundary between Rothwell and Thorpe Stapleton; by 1821 it consisted of two rows and a school. The scale of operations remained small in most mines, but the large Middleton colliery at Leeds employed 50 men underground and 27 on the surface in 1773 and a total of 230 men 20 years later; by 1820 the labour force at Middleton had risen to 380. No women or girls were employed in the larger West Riding collieries until the nineteenth century and even then (apart from at Silkstone) only in small numbers. The recorded death of a woman in a Handsworth pit in 1799 is the earliest reference to female labour in Yorkshire mines.

The Duke of Norfolk was not the only aristocrat to invest in coal mining. William, the fourth Earl Fitzwilliam (1748–1833) was one of the greatest landowners in England.

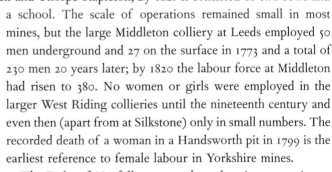

Despite the 1787 date on a lintel, this Newcomen-type beam engine was built in 1794–95 to pump water out of Earl Fitzwilliam's Elsecar New Colliery. A new cylinder (1801), an extra boiler (1803–4), a new wooden beam (1811–12), replaced by an iron beam (1836) enabled the engine to keep working until , when electrical pumps were installed.

In 1756 he succeeded to a large estate at Milton, near Peterborough, and to more than 80,000 acres in Ireland; then in 1782 he inherited the Wentworth Woodhouse and Malton estates of his uncle, the second Marquis of Rockingham, together with a London town house in Grosvenor Square. He and his son, Charles, the fifth earl (1786–1857), shared a paternalistic concern for those dependent upon them for home and employment and a conviction that the ruling classes should recognise their responsibilities and work to promote God's kingdom on Earth. These beliefs cost Charles his posts of Lord Lieutenant of the West Riding and of Ireland when he spoke out against the massacre of Peterloo. In comparison with most coal owners at that time the Fitzwilliams were outstanding employers. They were fortunate to be well served by Joshua Biram and his son, Benjamin, two remarkable mining engineers and viewers, and they exploited their coal reserves at Elsecar, Park Gate and Stubbin so successfully that eventually their mineral income greatly exceeded their revenue from agriculture.

In 1794–95 Earl Fitzwilliam, sunk his Elsecar New Colliery to the Barnsley seam and installed the only Newcomen-type engine that still stands on its original site anywhere in the country. The earl commissioned John Carr of York, who had extended the great house and built the enormous stable block at Wentworth Woodhouse, to design colliers' houses at Elsecar, which compared most favourably with contemporary farm labourers' cottages or the typical one-storeyed miners' cottages that were found elsewhere. Meanwhile, John and William Darwin leased ironstone and coal mining rights and built the first Elsecar furnace; a second furnace followed in 1800 and the firm prospered till about 1812 making pig iron, domestic ranges, spoutings and rails for colliery tramways. The heyday of the Elsecar ironworks came after 1850 when George and William Dawes from Birmingham ran the business until its closure in 1884. Less than a mile away, at the end of the eighteenth century the Walkers of Masborough established the Milton ironworks. The reputation of the works was enhanced in 1824 when William and Robert Graham came from London to

56–64 Fitzwilliam Street, Elsecar. The Fitzwilliams were paternalistic employers who housed their miners and ironworkers in decent accommodation. Their industrial village at Elsecar was developed from the 1790s and was served by a branch of the Dearne and Dove canal. This group of five houses in Fitzwilliam Street were built in the 1850s or 1860s in good-quality ashlar stone.
PHOTOGRAPH: AUTHOR

manufacture pig, rod, hoop and sheet iron, castings, steam engines and boilers, suspension and other bridges, iron boats and general millwork. Lime kilns, coke kilns and a tar distillery followed the opening of a branch of the Dearne and Dove canal in 1799 and a major boost to production came in 1850 when the South Yorkshire railway provided access to the London market via Doncaster.

Elsecar grew rapidly from a hamlet to a model industrial village. Between 1796 and 1801 Station Row and Old Row were built, the long, curving terrace of Reform Row was added in 1837 and the Miners' Lodging House in Fitzwilliam Street was opened in 1854 for 'young colliers' at the Simon Wood colliery. The new community, which continued to be extended along Cobnar Lane and Fitzwilliam Street in the 1860s, was provided with a Wesleyan Methodist chapel (1842), Holy Trinity church (1843) and a Church of England school (1852), which replaced the 1836 National School. All these buildings, together with the flour mill (1842) and the earl's private railway station (1870), survive in a designated conservation area.

In 1851 an estimated 8 million tons of coal were mined in the Yorkshire and north Midland coalfield, stretching from Leeds to Nottingham. Old agricultural villages on the exposed coalfield such as Featherstone and Hemsworth were transformed into pit villages and the ancient market towns of Wakefield and Barnsley acquired a new character. Few great estate owners other than the Fitzwilliams or the Lister-Kayes were directly involved in exploiting their mineral resources as well as benefiting from royalties and mineral rents. Most coalmasters were a new breed who came from a minor landowner, professional or business background. The most successful were the Charlesworths of Chapelthorpe Hall, the successors to the Fentons. Joseph Charlesworth began mining at Crigglestone in 1799 and his son, John, expanded the family's interests considerably in West and South Yorkshire. The Charlesworths prospered by using advanced technology and commercial methods and by cultivating good industrial relations. In Victoria's reign they were able to join the ranks of the West Riding gentry.

In the days of shallow pits mining had normally been safe occupation, but the large-scale development of the Yorkshire coalfield in the railway age brought all sorts of hazards and hardships. The dust at the coal face wore away a hewer's lungs and the work was exhausting, Few major accidents occurred before deeper mines were sunk to the fiery Barnsley seam. In 1803 30 men were killed in an explosion at Barnby and during the next two generations the death toll rose appallingly. In 1847 an explosion at the Oaks colliery killed 73 men and two years later 75 died in a disaster at Darley Main. Greater calamities occurred in the following decades. The nation had been appalled earlier by a different kind of accident, in which 26 children were drowned after a sudden storm flooded the Husker pit near Silkstone. One of the boys was only seven years old; five children were aged eight; and the average age of all children was ten. It was normal at that time for children to be at work and boys were employed throughout the coalfield, but most Yorkshire pits did not employ girls and R. C. Clarke's

Yorkshire collieries in 1855 (after G. D. B. Gray, fig. 2.2, in J. Benton and R. G. Neville (eds), *Studies in the Yorkshire Coal Industry*, Manchester University press, 1976, p. 36).

Silkstone mines were unusual, though not alone, in having so many. The youngest children sat by themselves in the dark and opened the ventilation trap doors whenever a corve came along. In some parts of the coalfield the youngest trappers were only five or six years old. The older children worked as hurriers, pushing the loaded corves along rails from the coal face to the bottom of the shaft. The normal day's work involved 20 journeys with an aggregate distance of 3¾ miles. On the western edge of the coalfield, on the thin seams between Huddersfield and Stocksbridge, the hurriers had the hardest task of all. At Foster Place colliery near Hepworth no rails were installed, so the hurriers were attached by belt and chain to loaded sledges. J. C. Symons, the commissioner appointed by Parliament in 1841 to investigate child labour in Yorkshire mines in the wake of the Silkstone disaster, reported, 'One of the most disgusting sights I have ever seen was that of young females, dressed like boys in trousers, crawling on all fours, with belts round their waists, and chains passing between their legs, at day pits at Hunshelf Bank and in many small pits near Holmfirth and New Mill'. An Act passed in 1842 prohibited the employment of females in mines and forbade the use of boys under the age of ten.

It was about this time that the miners made a united effort to increase their wages. In 1842 the Miners' Association was formed at Halifax and on 20

'One of the most disgusting sights I have ever seen was that of young females, dressed like boys in trousers, crawling on all fours, with belts round their waists, and chains passing between their legs, at day pits at Hunshelf Bank and in many small pits near Holmfirth and New Mill.'

PARLIAMENTARY COMMISSIONER, 1841

February 1844 nearly 4,000 men attended a demonstration at Hood Hill near Chapeltown. This impressive display of solidarity caused the employers to gather at Wakefield to discuss the 'unsettled disposition of the colliers'. The masters resolved to lock out any employee who joined the union and they declared their intention not to raise wages. Their announcement provoked a series of strikes all over the coalfield and on 12 May 1844 most of the West Riding colliers stopped work. R. C. Clarke was one of the owners who were determined to crush the strike at all costs, even by ejecting the strikers from their homes. A large and hostile crowd watched the ejections and made a collection on behalf of the homeless families. The miners were defeated and it was not until 1858 that their union was revived, but the events of 1844 were a foretaste of many bitter conflicts to come.

Rural Yorkshire

The market towns that serviced the agricultural parts of the county grew modestly and proceeded unhurriedly in their time-honoured ways. The population of Pocklington, for example, rose from 1,502 in 1801 to 2,546 in 1851, but this rate of growth was slow compared with that of the West Riding industrial towns. Pocklington remained a retail and service centre for a small rural hinterland with numerous shopkeepers and craftsmen and a social elite dominated by a few solicitors, doctors and wealthy tradesmen. This enclosed and in many ways unprogressive world was very different from that of the Victorian borough but it was an environment that was familiar to tens of thousands of Yorkshiremen and one that remained profoundly characteristic of

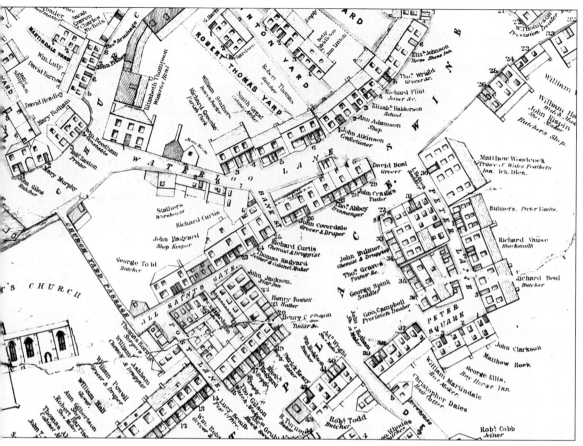

A detail of William Watson's plan of Pocklington, 1855. William Watson's detailed plan of this East Riding market town at the foot of the Wolds includes elevations of all the buildings and the names (sometimes with the occupations) of the householders. It is a remarkably valuable source for local and family historians, particularly as it can be linked to the census enumerators' returns of 1851 and 1861.

This detail shows part of the old market place and swine market, stretching away from the parish church. An impressive range of services were on offer in the shops and inns, some of which have encroached on the market space. Pocklington was almost certainly a market centre long before it received a grant of a four-day fair in 1245; the burgesses who were recorded in Domesday Book would have been traders. By the seventeenth century Pocklington held seven annual fairs and a weekly market each Saturday.

the age. Driffield followed a similar path of development when turnpike roads were succeeded by a canal in 1770 and a railway in 1846. The town's population grew markedly after 1780 and rose from 1,411 in 1801 to 3,963 in 1851. By 1840 Driffield was 'a brisk and well-built market town' with several corn mills and 'commodious wharfs and warehouses, and two mills employed in crushing bones for manure' at the canal head, together with an iron foundry, tannery, and a few looms for weaving carpets, linen and sacking.

Most Victorian market towns had some small-scale industries, perhaps a brewery or an ironworks, a tannery or a corn-milling business, but the local economy was based firmly on the varied activities of numerous skilled craftsmen, who created and sold their goods on their own premises and who sometimes hawked them around the countryside. Typically, these craftsmen

An eighteenth-century lime kiln, Coverdale. Sited close to the medieval St Simon's Well, near Coverham, the kiln has faint traces of a date that seems to read 1786. It is typical of the field kilns where limestone was burned, then slaked with water, before being spread on acidic soils such as reclaimed moorland in order to improve the grassland. Slaked lime was also used in making mortar. In other parts of Yorkshire lime kilns were often erected at canal basins, using imported lime.

turned their hand to a variety of work, for demand was rarely sufficient to enable them to specialise. For example, in the 1850s Tadcaster's 2,500 inhabitants included nearly 300 small masters, journeymen and apprentices; a third of whom were tailors, shoemakers and dressmakers, while another third were employed in the building trades. In a society dependent upon horse transport the six wheelwrights, ten saddlers and the ten men who worked in the three blacksmiths' smithies fulfilled an essential role. Market towns also provided professional and trade services and on market day they created a sense of excitement and pleasure as well as business.

By the beginning of Victoria's reign the long-term effects of parliamentary enclosure were being felt in those agricultural regions where the movement had been most active. On the Wolds new compact farms with functional brick houses and outbuildings were planted in the countryside, dew ponds were dug out for livestock, plantations provided shelter, and hawthorn hedges transformed the landscape into large, rectangular fields. This physical transformation was accompanied by a striking change in farming practice, as old pasture was converted into tillage and even the rabbit warrens were ploughed up. By 1812 two-thirds of the Wolds were farmed as arable with a four-course rotation of turnips, barley, clover or grass, and wheat, or with local variations adapted to different soils. New crops meant that store cattle could now be fed through winter, but flocks of sheep remained an essential part of this farming economy, for they were folded off the Wolds at night for their manure. More wheat was grown on the Wolds and turnips were introduced into crop rotations so that sheep might be fattened; here farmers had to be men with capital who were responsive to new ideas, for farms of 800–1,000 acres were in greater demand than those of only 300 acres. In Holderness the old two-course crop rotations that had been suited to the arrangement of the open fields were replaced by four courses (including a bare fallow) and small farms were engrossed into larger arable ones. Most of the 18 agricultural societies that had been founded in Yorkshire by 1835 were in the East Riding or the Vale of York. The Yorkshire

Blackshaw Head. High above the later industrial towns of Todmorden and Hebden Bridge is a contemporary rural landscape. Blackshaw Head is recorded as a topographical name from 1539, but most of the housing seen here consists of nineteenth-century weavers' cottages and the fields have the distinctive, geometrical shapes of parliamentary enclosure.

PHOTOGRAPH: CARNEGIE, 2005

Agricultural Society was founded in 1837 and held its first show the following year in York.

Moorland areas were also changed radically by parliamentary enclosure. Miles upon miles of dry gritstone walls gradually gave a new regularity to thousands of acres of former commons and wastes, old lanes were straightened and new ones created to standard widths of 30 feet or more. On the Pennines in particular the modern road system owes much more to parliamentary

Mantley Field Laithe. This field barn near Malham bears the date 1755 and the initials IH on the lintel over the small door. The central porch allowed access for a loaded hay cart. The barn provided shelter for cattle during winter, then in spring the manure was spread on the adjoining meadows. *Laithe* was a Viking word for a barn that passed into Northern speech.

YDNPA, HISTORIC ENVIRONMENT RECORD

Fields at Malham. The
limestone walls were built
after the enclosure of
Malham Moors in
1847–49, following the
rectangular shapes drawn
by the surveyors and
commissioners, but an
older pattern, marked by
earthen banks or lynchets,
can be discerned under the
modern one. These were
arable fields in the Middle
Ages.

PHOTOGRAPH: AUTHOR

enclosure than to the turnpikes. Farmsteads and field barns were erected
amongst the new fields, rough land was brought under the plough for the first
time, and the trim, green appearance of the new meadows and pastures
provided a vivid contrast with the unreclaimed moorlands beyond. Thousands
of acres of waste that could never be tamed remained as vast sheep runs or
now became private grouse-moors, with public access rights obliterated. But it
was not just the large freeholders who favoured enclosure; small freeholders
shared their concern at the rising number of squatters who nibbled away the
moorland edges. Parliamentary enclosure brought to an end this centuries-old
tradition.

In the Yorkshire Dales, the two-storeyed field barn standing alone amongst
the rectangular-shaped fields was a characteristic product of parliamentary
enclosure. These barns were built into the slope so that hay could be pitched
straight into the loft while the lower part was used as shelter for young cattle.
South of Craven, in the hilly country bordering the industrial West Riding, a
distinctive type of building known to historians as the laithe-house combined
farmhouse, barn and byre under a single roof. Much favoured by smallholders
who pursued the traditional dual occupations, the laithe-house is unique
amongst English buildings in remaining unchanged over nearly 250 years. The
earliest known example is Bank House, Luddenden, dated 1650, but the style
was the standard form of building on the reclaimed moors in the era of parliamentary enclosure and until the late Victorian period. The house part consisted
of two-up, two-down accommodation with a central chimney stack and a
separate entrance. Very few laithe-houses have internal communication
between the domestic and farm sections, and their most prominent external

Parliamentary enclosure in the Pennines. Much of the Pennine landscape was transformed by the parliamentary enclosure of the commons and wastes in the late eighteenth and early nineteenth centuries. Here, between 1812 and 1816 outlying parts of the township of Thurlstone were brought under cultivation for the first time and new, straight lanes were designed to a standard width of 30 feet. This is a landscape created on the drawing board. The farm in the centre of the photograph was given the name of Bella Vista.

AUTHOR COLLECTION

feature is the high, arched entry which allowed a loaded hay cart or sledge to enter the barn. All these buildings were constructed of local stone and given a stone-slate roof.

Enclosure brought other changes. Some parishes took the opportunity long before the Tithe Commutation Act of 1836 to make a deal with tithe-owners and in the industrial parts of the West Riding former common land was used for new housing. In low-lying agricultural areas enclosure was often the prelude to massive drainage schemes. The 4,000 acres of Potteric Carr, for instance, were enclosed in 1765–71 and drained in 1810–11 and the 5,000 or so acres of Wallingfen were enclosed in 1781 and drained by cuts leading into the Market Weighton canal. One of the most impressive drains was constructed in 1798 to take water 15 miles along the western side of the Hull valley from Hempholme to Hull; the eastern bank was drained in 1832. Much of the Vale of Pickering was also drained after enclosure, but the heavy soils of many a lowland parish were not improved significantly until tile drainage was carried out on a large scale in the Victorian period.

During the second half of the eighteenth century and the first part of the nineteenth the number of Englishmen employed as farm labourers rose substantially. The great increase in the size of the national population not only swelled the ranks of the industrial workers but provided cheap labour on the farms, so that long before Victoria's reign rural society in many non-industrial districts was divided into three classes: landlords, tenant farmers and labourers. In 1851 the agricultural labour force of England and Wales reached a peak of 1.88 million; thereafter it declined in both relative and absolute terms. The poor law commissioners of 1834 reported that labourers in Yorkshire were often employed on piece-work rather than on a permanent basis and that little work was available for women and children. In Campsall and Norton vagrancy was regarded as a threat to the social order: 'the neighbourhood swarms with vagrants. Gangs of gypsies infest the country and frighten the farmers and overseers by threatening to fix their settlement with them'. Elsewhere, farmers in the East Riding were dependent, as of old, on the seasonal migration of labourers from the moors and dales to help with gathering the harvest and the landlords of 'close' villages needed the services of labourers from surrounding 'open' villages on a more regular basis.

During the nineteenth century many old crafts and rural industries declined and sometimes disappeared. In the North Riding the woollen knitware trade and the alum industry, two successful projects of the Elizabethan and early Stuart era, collapsed before Victoria came to the throne and the scattered linen industry withered soon afterwards in face of Irish and continental competition. The lead fields remained in production, however, despite prolonged periods of depression in 1816–18 and 1824–33, and its miners farmed moorland intakes in the manner of their ancestors. Production reached new peaks in the middle years of the nineteenth century but afterwards the lead fields became exhausted.

The vernacular tradition of building in rural districts survived well into the nineteenth century and local building materials were used until the railways reduced the transport costs of Welsh blue-slates and machine-made bricks. The cottages of the labourers were the last domestic buildings to be influenced by outside styles. In 1800 Tuke, the Board of Agriculture reporter for the North Riding, wrote, 'The cottages of the labourers are generally small and low, consisting only of one room, and very rarely, of two, both of which are level with the ground, and sometimes a step within it'. Strickland, the reporter for the East Riding, thought that the cottages there were more comfortable than in many other parts of England, being mostly of the two-up, two-down kind. He went on to say that, 'The houses and farmeries of the tenantry are in general good, except upon the Wolds, where (chiefly in consequence of the nature of the materials of which they are constructed) they are miserably bad'. The old buildings on the Wolds were 'in general, composed of chalkstone, with mud instead of lime-mortar, and covered with thatch', but most East Riding buildings were by then made of bricks and pantiles and many were designed

'The houses and farmeries of the tenantry are in general good, except upon the Wolds, where (chiefly in consequence of the nature of the materials of which they are constructed) they are miserably bad.'

BOARD OF AGRICULTURE REPORT, 1800

above Harewood House. Turner's view – from *Loidis and Elmete* (1816) – shows the south façade of the eighteenth-century house before it was remodelled in the 1840s by Sir Charles Barry. The Harewood–Gawthorpe estate had been bought by Henry Lascelles, a wealthy merchant and director of the East India Company. His son Edwin inherited the estate in 1759 and immediately began to build a new house and to remove all other buildings except the medieval parish church (whose tower can be seen peeping over the trees) in order to create a landscaped park with an ornamental lake in the fashion of the times. A new village was created beyond the park gates. His architect was John Carr, but Robert Adam was responsible for decorating the interior, and Thomas Chippendale made the furniture.

as Georgian farmhouses with a central hall-way and sometimes as double-depth houses in styles that had become popular throughout England.

J. R. Mortimer, the Victorian archaeologist, recalled life in the Wolds village of Fimber in the 1830s, where both farmers and their servants dressed in fustian jackets and long smocks and ate oatmeal dumplings and bread for breakfast and supper and plain food such as bacon, salted beef and their own cheese for their main meal. Water was obtained from two stagnant meres until wells were sunk and fuel was often so scarce that dried cow dung had to be burnt. The poorest families lived in thatched, cruck-framed cottages, open to the roof, whose single room with mud floor was entered down three steps. He saw a considerable improvement in housing standards during his boyhood when labourers built cottages with chalk walls.

The wealthy owners of substantial houses built in a Grecian style or with the gables and mullioned-and-transomed windows of the Tudor and Jacobean age. Anthony Salvin's Moreby Hall in the East Riding or the hall built at Broomhead on the edge of the Pennines for James Rimington, a Sheffield barrister, were conscious revivals of a style that had gone out of fashion nearly 200 years earlier. In south-west Yorkshire Thrybergh Park and Sir Jeffry Wyatville's Banner Cross Hall are rare eighteenth-century examples of the castellated or Gothic mode of building that was to be revived so vigorously in the following century. In the West Riding the Grecian style gave way to the Italian at Grimston Park, the home of Lord Howden and his wife, a Russian princess, and then to the unrestrained display of Sir Charles Barry's alterations at Harewood House.

By the beginning of the nineteenth century many parts of the West Riding had been deeply affected by industrial change and Leeds and Sheffield were well on their way to becoming two of the leading cities in the land, but an older, more traditional way of life was found everywhere alongside the new. Farming parishes in eastern parts of the West Riding proceeded in their own unhurried way and estate villages remained immune to social change. An 1806 list of men liable for militia service in Staincross wapentake identifies estate villages such as Stainborough, West Bretton, Woolley and Wortley by their occupational structure and reveals how some crafts had recently become concentrated in certain districts. The linen weaving trade had spread from Barnsley to the surrounding villages of Ardsley, Barugh, Dodworth, Monk Bretton and Worsbrough Common, whereas the weaving of woollen cloth was performed mainly in Denby Dale and Thurlstone, at the southern edge of the textile district. The nailmakers were found in Mapplewell and Staincross, two of the hamlets of Darton parish, and coal mining as yet employed only 115 miners, with 32 in Cawthorne, just 23 in Barnsley and 11 in Silkstone. A variety of small crafts and family businesses, such as basket weaving, glass making, pottery manufacture and tanning, wood working and shoemaking, were scattered across the wapentake and farming remained the main occupation with 36 per cent of the workforce. Even on the exposed coalfield farming was still the major provider of livelihoods.

left The south front of Harewood House by Sir Charles Barry, 1843–49. In the fashion of the times, the formal gardens contain several ornate fountains and statues (*below*).
PHOTOGRAPHS: CARNEGIE, 2005

The poor

On his national tour in 1797 Sir Frederick Eden arrived at Great Driffield and noted, 'There are only 3 inmates in the Poor-house, many receive relief at home, which appears to be more convenient for them and not disadvantageous to the parish', and at Market Weighton, 'Very few paupers have ever been in the house, as they could be maintained at a cheaper rate on weekly pensions'. In the West Riding the 34 paupers in the Southowram workhouse were chiefly old people and children who appeared to be comfortable and well fed. The general impression from his report is that throughout Yorkshire the problem of poverty was under control for most of the time, though great hardship was endured in years of harvest failure and trade depression. The diet of the labourer was often monotonous but it was better than in other parts of the country. Eden observed that in Settle, 'The food used by the labouring Poor is oatmeal, tea, milk, butter, potatoes and butcher's meat', at Stokesley 'bread, milk and tea, potatoes, and meat sparingly', and at Great Driffield 'barley bread, potatoes and perhaps 2 lbs of butcher's meat once a week, when they can afford it'. At Halifax he noted that, 'Butcher's meat is very generally used by labourers', and at Leeds, 'Wheaten bread is generally used. Some is made partly of rye and a few persons use oatmeal. Animal food forms a considerable part of the diet of labouring people. Tea is now the ordinary breakfast, especially among women of every description, and the food of both men and women is more expensive than that consumed by persons in the same station of life in the more northern parts'.

After 1770 Britain became a net importer of cereals in order to feed the growing population. The inhabitants of the West Riding towns and industrial villages were amongst the first to suffer in times of dearth for they were dependent upon the corn markets. Food riots, which tried to force retailers to charge 'a fair price' and which stopped movements of corn to places where higher profits could be obtained, were a common popular response when dealers tried to gain financially from short supplies. The worst crises came in 1795–96 and 1800–1, when harvests were poor, industry was depressed and trade with the continent of Europe was blocked during the Napoleonic wars. In the summer of 1795 riots broke out in several parts of the West Riding. During these hard times many more people died than usual, but a combination of public and private relief and self-help societies enabled the country to cope far better than during the old subsistence crises of previous centuries.

The years of depression after the Napoleonic wars, especially those of 1815–22 and 1828–32, saw widespread unemployment. Wages fell and many farm labourers were forced to leave the countryside in the hope of work in the industrial towns or to search for a new life in Canada and the United States. At this time, more people left the North Riding than any other English or Welsh county; the rural settlements on the North York Moors and the decaying lead-mining communities of the Yorkshire Dales were particularly affected. Local

> 'Very few paupers have ever been in the house, as they could be maintained at a cheaper rate on weekly pensions.'
>
> MARKET WEIGHTON, 1797

friendly societies and a general sympathy amongst ratepayers for the genuine poor of their parishes provided relief from the worst effects of poverty and when trade recovered industrial wages forced up the levels of those earned by farm labourers. Yorkshire was free from the serious social tension that afflicted the countryside in much of southern and eastern England. The burden of poverty was harsh enough for thousands of Yorkshire families in times of depression, but it did not weigh as heavily as in many other parts of the land.

Expenditure on the poor rose considerably in the late eighteenth and early nineteenth centuries as the national population grew to new high levels. In the parish of Ecclesfield, for instance, it shot up from £676 a year in 1783–85 to £3,550 in 1803 and more was now spent on the 100 inmates of the workhouse than had been spent on all the poor 20 years ago. The oldest and youngest age groups accounted for most of the poor, but two out of every five were able-bodied. Yet, although 516 people were receiving some form of relief in 1803, this was only one person in ten, a similar proportion to previous years. By 1818 the expenditure on Ecclesfield's poor had risen again to £5,955. The same thing was happening all over the country, except in the 'close' parishes dominated by a squire or a few farmers who kept the poor out of their villages and employed labourers from neighbouring 'open' settlements. The system of parish relief that had worked reasonably well since Elizabethan times was in need of an overhaul.

In 1834 the Poor Law Amendment Act inaugurated a new system of relief based on unions of parishes and the workhouse, but when assistant commissioners were sent north to organise unions in 1837–38 they were greeted with riots in Bradford, Dewsbury and Todmorden. An Anti-Poor Law movement was organised in the West Riding and Lancashire by Oastler, Fielden and Stephens, who felt that in the North the old system had worked in both a humane and economic way. They said that workhouses were irrelevant in industrial areas, for few able-bodied paupers were to be found when trade was good and the unemployed masses were too numerous to be accommodated in workhouses when trade was bad. Their point was eventually conceded; the workhouse test was never enforced in the West Riding and Lancashire and outdoor relief was granted in the old manner. The poor relief system reduced the possibility of death from starvation. Despite the population explosion, the death rate in England during the first half of the nineteenth century was on the whole a great deal lower than that of countries far less urbanised and industrialised.

Beliefs and attitudes

The national census of church attendance on 29 March 1851 – the only one that has ever been taken in this country – revealed that just 40.5 per cent of the population of England and Wales attended any service at all. Worshippers formed about 35 per cent of the West Riding's population and in the large towns

Haworth Parsonage. Built about 1800, the parsonage stands just beyond the churchyard wall at the western edge of the old village. Patrick Bronte was the curate here from 1820 to 1861, when Haworth was still a parochial chapelry of Bradford. It has long been Yorkshire's greatest literary tourist attraction, as the place where Charlotte, Emily and Anne wrote their novels and poems.

PHOTOGRAPH: CARNEGIE, 2005

such as Sheffield fewer than one person in ten attended either church or chapel; the urban working classes were largely absent. Of those who did attend nationwide, 48 per cent preferred a chapel to the established church. In the West Riding the proportion of Nonconformists was considerably higher than that. In Leeds a new vicar observed in 1837 that 'The *de facto* established religion is Methodism'. There the Anglicans had lost control over the borough's Improvement Commission by 1829 and the town council after 1835. Dissenters also wrested control of the vestry, which set the church rate and managed the financial affairs of the parish and by 1833 they formed a majority of the church-wardens there.

The situation in 1851 was very different from what it had been in the late seventeenth century when dissenters formed only 4 per cent of the nation. The Unitarians and Quakers were unmoved by the Evangelical Revival but the other old dissenting sects – the Independents (Congregationalists) and Baptists – joined in the religious fervour. The new Independency was a product of indus-trial areas and it appealed chiefly to the better-off. But now Wesleyan Methodism was easily the strongest Nonconformist sect in England and Wales. The triumph of Methodism was not limited to the older strongholds of dissent, but had spread both in the towns and the countryside. Whereas the old dissent had been largely the concern of the respectable classes, Methodism attracted people of all social backgrounds in almost every type of community. It was particularly successful in industrial towns and villages, especially in outlying settlements that lay well away from the parish church. The hill-top village of High Hoyland had only its established church, but in the valley below the new textile settlement of Clayton West had chapels for its Wesleyans, Independents, Particular Baptists, Methodist New Connection and Primitive Methodists and the Wesleyan Reform movement gathered 150 people in Aaron Peace's warehouse. Only those estate villages that remained under the firm grip of an Anglican squire still resisted dissent.

Up till then, Wesleyan Methodism's greatest building period had been in the 1830s. Like some of the old dissenting sects, it was now firmly established and its members had become respectable. The industrial poor turned increasingly

'The de facto established religion is Methodism.'

LEEDS, 1837

to the Methodist New Connection (founded 1797) or to the Primitive Methodists (who broke away in 1812). By 1851 the Primitives (or 'Ranters') were the second strongest Nonconformist sect. In the towns they could attract large numbers, such as the 1,550 who attended evening service at the Sheffield Bethel, but in the countryside their meetings were small affairs, like the group of 12 who met in a cottage in the limestone-quarrying community of Levitt Hagg. Their main period of strength was still to come.

The Church of England had woken from its eighteenth-century slumber and had begun to tackle the problems caused by the population explosion. In Sheffield ten new churches were erected under the terms of the Million Act between 1825 and 1850 and in 1846 the medieval parish was divided into 25 new units; in 1851 large congregations met in the borough's Anglian churches, but even so the combined numbers of worshippers at the Established Church did not match those of the numerous dissenting sects. In 1851 the Church of England was stronger in Leeds than it was in Sheffield or Bradford. The Revd Walter Farquhar Hook, vicar from 1837 to 1959, led a spirited counter-attack, emphasising a deep social as well as a spiritual concern; unlike most Anglican clergymen in the West Riding at the time he was a High Churchman.

Relief sculpture on a plinth which once carried a statue to Peel, showing the distribution of bread to the poor and celebrating the success of the Anti-Corn Law League. The plinth is now in the grounds of the Tolson Museum in Huddersfield.
PHOTOGRAPH: CARNEGIE, 2005

The Sunday School movement that was started by Robert Raikes in Gloucester in 1785 spread rapidly throughout the country amongst both Anglicans and Nonconformists. By 1851 it was providing a basic education to nearly 2.5 million children, that is nearly two-thirds of the 5 to 14 age range. From this movement sprang the day schools – the National Schools of the Church of England and the British Schools of the Nonconformists – but they were unable to cope with the growing number of children. In 1840 an official enquiry thought that not more than half the children in Sheffield attended school regularly and that only one-third were able to read 'fairly'. A national enquiry in 1843 estimated that two-thirds of the male population and nearly half the females were illiterate.

The enormous population growth and industrial developments of the nineteenth century turned Victorian towns into great arenas for political struggles. The first working-class political organisations, such as the Sheffield Society for Constitutional Information (1791), were formed in towns during the initial excitement of the French Revolution. At that time the populous manufacturing towns of Yorkshire had no Members of Parliament. The election of John Marshall, the Leeds fax-spinner, as MP for Yorkshire in 1826 announced the arrival of a new urban elite in county politics and the beginning of a protracted conflict between the Liberal and Dissenting merchants and manufacturers and the old Tory and Church of England establishment. A partial and pragmatic attack upon grievances turned in the 1840s into a major assault upon the established church. Towns were the natural venues for the great political campaigns of the day, notably that of the Anti-Corn Law League. Ebenezer Elliott's *Corn Law Rhymes* (1831) made him Yorkshire's popular champion of this cause and in 1854 Sheffield workmen paid for a bronze statue of him to be erected in the market place. Huge Chartist meetings demanding the right to vote and other constitutional reforms were held in the towns when the voice of the working classes was first heard on a national scale during the 1830s and 40s. Chartism gathered support in all parts of the country, but its greatest strength lay in the manufacturing districts, where it was a protest movement that provided a vigorous outlet for diverse hopes and demands. Industrialisation had produced a working-class culture that was radically different from that of the labouring poor of previous centuries.

Yet people's concerns and loyalties were still expressed mainly at a local level. They still thought of themselves as belonging to a parish and to the wider 'country' beyond. Even in the industrial towns the workforce was drawn overwhelmingly from the traditional hinterland. Yorkshire had not yet experienced large-scale immigration. The pattern throughout rural England remained the ancient one of considerable movement between neighbouring parishes, but relatively little migration beyond the nearest market towns. Surname distribution patterns remained similar to those of previous centuries and local societies were markedly different from each other in their customs, speech and employment. 'The County of York', observed George Walker, 'offers perhaps a greater variety and peculiarity of manners and dress than any other in the kingdom'. The 'humble individuals' who attracted his attention were depicted in his *Costume of Yorkshire* (1814) in 'their simple and sometimes squalid garb' in an attempt at a true portrayal of ordinary Yorkshire people. 'These men', he said of the West Riding cloth-makers, 'have a decided provincial character'. Though gentry families had begun to speak a standardised English by the end of Elizabeth's reign, marked regional differences in speech were evident at other social levels. The differences between the various 'countries' of Yorkshire were more obvious than the similarities. Most ordinary people did not acquire the gentry's sense of belonging to the county of Yorkshire until organised sport began to attract their loyalties. This began when cricket was actively encouraged by those who saw it as a peaceful, enjoyable and manly alternative to cruel sports and violent activities. The first organised games were professional challenge matches, such as the one held in 1771 between Sheffield and Nottingham and the oldest clubs in the north, at York and Hallam (Sheffield), can trace a continuous history back to 1804, but the Yorkshire County Cricket Club was not founded, at Sheffield, until 1863.

CHAPTER 9

Workshop of the World, 1850–1914

The Victorian population

During the reign of Queen Victoria the industrial districts of Yorkshire grew so rapidly that by 1901 the population of the West Riding was nearly 3½ times the combined total of the rest of the county. It was now hard to believe that the East and North Ridings had for centuries been the more populous and wealthy parts. Between 1851 and 1901 the population of England and Wales grew from 17.9 million to 36.1 million and between 1881 and 1911 the proportion of people who lived in towns rose from two in every three to four out of every five. Only London, Lancashire and the West Midlands saw a more rapid rate of population growth and increased urbanisation than the West Riding. During the 50 years between 1851 and 1901 the population of Yorkshire doubled from 1,797,995 to 3,584,675; that of the West Riding rose from

Marygate, Wakefield. Like those of many Yorkshire towns, the central streets of Wakefield were still characterised by family-run shops, warehouses and small businesses in Victorian times. Here in Marygate, it was possible to buy flour, corn for your horse, baskets, barrels and other cooper wares, or a variety of dyes.

BY COURTESY OF THE YORKSHIRE ARCHAEOLOGICAL SOCIETY

right Bradford Town Hall.
The West Riding's most
picturesque Victorian town
hall was designed by
Lockwood & Mawson, the
winners of an open
competition in 1873, at a
cost of £100,000. Based on
the early thirteenth-
century French Gothic
style, it is full of intricate
detail. The 200 feet tall
tower was based on the
campanile of the Palazzo
Vecchio, Florence. Other
elements were borrowed
from Italy to emphasise
cultural and commercial
links through the wool
trade. The opening was
marked by a three-mile
long procession that
demonstrated the town's
trades. This was
Bradford's answer to
Leeds.

1,315,885 to 2,733,688; the East Riding from 220,983 to 392,392; the North Riding from 215,225 to 391,011; and York and the Ainsty from 45,902 to 67,584. The most spectacular rates of growth came in the West Riding boroughs. Leeds grew from 172,023 to 428,572, Sheffield from 135,310 to 380,793 and Bradford from 149,543 to 290,297; elsewhere, only Hull could compete, with a rise from 56,613 to 159,194.

When county councils were created in 1888 Wakefield, Beverley and Northallerton became the administrative centres of the three ridings, with county halls, offices and prisons. The rise of the West Riding was recognised by the new status accorded to its leading towns, so that by the end of the nineteenth century it had 20 county and municipal boroughs compared with only four each in the other two ridings. In 1888 Wakefield was made a cathedral city at the head of a new diocese, five years later Leeds and Sheffield were given city status, and in 1897 Bradford and Hull were elevated to the same rank.

Most of this growth came from the natural increase of the native population, but immigrants from other parts of Britain flocked to the new town of

The Dock Offices, Hull. Built in 1867–71 to the Italianate design of Christopher Wray, the offices were contemporary with the Albert Dock of 1869. Hull was the third port in England, after London and Liverpool, and its trade with the Baltic sea ports was flourishing. The offices occupy a prominent position in Queen Victoria Square, near the later City Hall. It cost about £90,000.

Middlesbrough or to the coalfield and agricultural labourers moved north to work in the Sheffield steelworks or at Doncaster Plant. The 1901 census recorded 39,145 people in Yorkshire who had been born in Ireland, 6,443 of whom had settled in Leeds. Migrants stuck together in the poorest parts of towns, such as the Irish quarter in Walmgate, York. Poor Jews who had fled from the Russian Empire arrived in the last quarter of the nineteenth century. The Leylands district of Leeds was already 85 per cent Jewish by the late 1880s and Leeds had about 20,000 Jews by 1911. Marks & Spencer trace their origins to the Penny Bazaar that Michael Marks, the most successful of these Jewish immigrants, opened in the covered market at Leeds in 1884.

Most migrants did not move much further than their ancestors had. On the whole, people remained loyal to their 'country', the neighbourhood bounded by the nearest market towns where they had friends and relations and work that was familiar to them. The cutlers and steelmakers of Hallamshire rarely came into contact with the spinners and weavers of the textile district and their only contacts with the other two ridings were through trade with Hull or railway

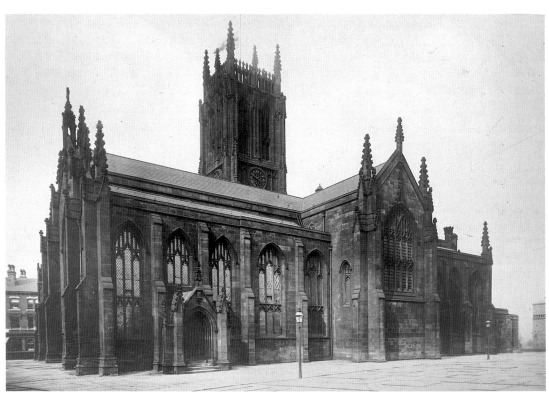

Crawstone Hall, Greetland, near Elland. The three gabled bays were erected for John Ramsden in 1631; the wing to the right was added *c.*1700 and its windows altered later. The 1631 house has mullioned windows on the ground floor, but larger mullioned and transomed windows upstairs, suggesting that the chambers were the better rooms. This is a large house, two rooms deep. Like many old properties, by the late nineteenth century it had been sub-divided.

BY COURTESY OF THE YORKSHIRE ARCHAEOLOGICAL SOCIETY

St Peter's, the parish church of Leeds, was entirely rebuilt between 1838 and 1841 at the instigation of Dean Hook, the new vicar. It stands in Kirkgate, whose ancient name provides a clue that a medieval predecessor stood on this site. In 1869 a railway cut it off from the heart of the town. The church was designed in neo-Gothic style and soon became blackened in the smoky atmosphere of Victorian Leeds.

BY COURTESY OF THE YORKSHIRE ARCHAEOLOGICAL SOCIETY

journeys to the seaside. Life remained intensely local in its experiences and attachments. Maps of surname distributions at the time of the 1881 census show that most of the family names that had originated in particular localities several centuries earlier were still found in or close to the same neighbourhoods. In particular, the West Riding textile district remained the home of the Barracloughs, Beevers, Dysons, Greenwoods, Mallinsons, Sutcliffes and very many others. Names such as these helped to give local communities their distinctive character.

Victorian England was still a horse-drawn society and many places remained remote. The bicycle was only just becoming popular and as yet few cars travelled along the unmetalled roads. In the towns electric trams did not begin to replace horse-drawn omnibuses until the closing years of the nineteenth century and Ordnance Survey maps show that even the new cities of Sheffield and Leeds were still surrounded by small settlements, fields and woods. The suburbs had not yet spread far into the countryside. While the industrial towns grew out of recognition, the ancient market centres in the East and North Ridings developed at a slower pace. Their enclosed and in many ways un-progressive world was very different from that of the industrial boroughs but it was an environment that was familiar to tens of thousands of Yorkshire people and one that remained profoundly characteristic of the age. In his *Little Guides* to the three ridings, published between 1904 and 1911, Joseph Morris described Bedale as 'a very small, very sleepy old market town', Great Driffield as 'an old-fashioned red-brick market town', Easingwold as 'a quiet old town, with a number of respectable houses', Hawes as 'a rough little mountain town, with houses that confront one another at every sort of angle', Howden as 'a dull and depressing little town', Northallerton as 'a dull old town, consisting chiefly of one long, broad street, with cobbled pavements, and a number of old-fashioned houses' and Tadcaster as 'a small, old-fashioned town, dominated, whether seen from far or near, by the chimneys of its enormous breweries'.

Railways

The notion of progress and the spectacular transformation of the landscape by civil engineering skills were nowhere more evident in the towns and the countryside than in the viaducts, embankments, cuttings and tunnels of the railways. The 32 tall, narrow arches of the Lockwood viaduct leading to the classical monumentality of Huddersfield's railway station is an early example from 1846 to 1848. The 13-mile line from Penistone to Huddersfield, which was opened in 1850, starts with a viaduct of 29 arches over the river Don and continues over the 21 huge arches at Denby Dale and through numerous cuttings and tunnels. The Settle & Carlisle railway, which was opened in 1875–76, is the most spectacular in England, with 13 tunnels and 21 viaducts. The largest viaduct on this line, which J. S. Crossley designed at Ribblehead,

The Ribblehead viaduct. One of the great engineering achievements of the Victorian era, J.S. Crossley's viaduct on the Midland Railway's Settle to Carlisle line was opened in 1875. Its 28 arches rise to 104 feet and span 440 yards. The 72-mile line crosses some of the wildest terrain in England and for much of its length is above the 1,000 feet contour, before descending to sea level. It needed 13 tunnels and 21 viaducts, four of them over 100 feet high.

R. WHITE, YORKSHIRE DALES NATIONAL PARK AUTHORITY

is 104 feet high with 28 arches and a total length of 440 yards. These striking additions to the landscape must have seemed brash at the time but they have mellowed over the years and are now an essential part of the physical character of the West Riding.

The railways provided an enormous stimulus to industry and opened up the Yorkshire coalfield, allowing it to compete with Northumberland and Durham in a national market. Doncaster retained its role as a regional market centre, with a large new Corn Exchange opened in 1873, but it was now one of Britain's great railway towns. When the engineering works known as 'the Plant' were opened in 1853 the local population rose by nearly 3,000. The Great Northern Railway built two schools and a church for the families that were housed in new rows of terraced houses to the west of the town at Balby and Hexthorpe. By the end of the century the works stretched over 200 acres, had 60 miles of sidings and employed 4,500 men. Other railways connected Doncaster to Sheffield and Hull and the trade in coal was immense.

Oxenhope Station. The terminus on the Keighley and Worth Valley Railway, which linked the new mill settlements. Here the boilers of the locomotives took in fresh water. An Act was obtained in 1862 and the railway was opened five years later, serving six stations.

PHOTOGRAPH: CARNEGIE, 2005

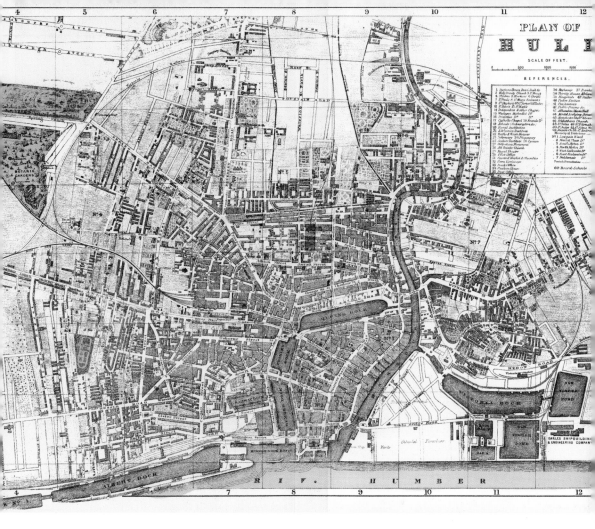

Hull in the late nineteenth century. The Old Town on the right bank of the River Hull, by its confluence with the Humber, was now enclosed with docks. Beyond, more docks had been constructed along the banks of the Humber. Railway lines converged on the two passenger stations and rows of terraced houses extended the suburbs in all directions. The key names the numerous public buildings, including the 60 new Board schools.

CARNEGIE COLLECTION

The railways strengthened Hull's competitive position as England's third port. Hull's overseas trade was still mostly with north-east Europe and its major imports were Baltic iron, timber, grain, flax, linseed and rape-seed. Seed crushing was a well-established dockside industry by the 1860s and it was soon followed by flour milling and ancillary trades associated with fishing, such as the curing of herrings. After much argument, the docks were extended and ornate offices were erected in an Italianate style. The Victoria Dock of 1850 and the Albert Dock of 1869 were soon overshadowed by the St Andrew Dock of 1883 (the largest fish dock in the world) and the Alexandria Dock of 1885, which enclosed 46 acres of water at a depth of 33 feet. Finally, in 1907 the Riverside Quay between Albert Dock and the Humber provided docking facilities for large ships at any state of the tide. Hull thrived and its population rose rapidly. In 1870 the local shipping industry was run by a number of small firms but by the end of the First World War it was dominated by the Wilson Line. Trading links had been extended beyond Europe to the river Plate, Bombay and Alexandria, but on the eve of the First World War nearly two thirds of the total tonnage entering Hull's docks still came from Russia, Scandinavia, Denmark, Germany, Holland, Belgium and France.

J. R. Smith's drawing of Halifax from Haley Hill in the 1860s, shows the North Bridge crossing the Bowling Dyke before its replacement with a cast-iron one in 1868. The valley is crowded with industrial buildings and tall chimneys belching out smoke. Northgate winds its way to the right and he tower of the medieval parish church can be seen in the distance.

The textile district

The woollen and worsted industries were now as concentrated in the West Riding as cotton was in Lancashire. By the end of Victoria's reign the West Riding textile district had grown to such an extent that it contained six county boroughs and seven municipal boroughs. In 1870 J. M. Wilson's *Imperial Gazetteer* thought that Dewsbury, incorporated nine years earlier, 'presents now a modern appearance' and that although Batley was 'remarkable only as a seat of manufacture' it 'evinces much public spirit'. Queenshead, which straddled the boundary between Bradford and Halifax parishes, had grown rapidly from a small village into a small town and had recently changed its name to Queensbury. The *Imperial Gazetteer* noted the 'extensive alpaca, mohair, and worsted-spinning manufacture, with employment of about 3,0900 hands'. The village of Pudsey, a chapel-of-ease of the parish of Calverley, had grown at such a spectacular rate that it had achieved the coveted status of municipal borough. It had only 4,422 inhabitants in 1801, but 18,469 people 100 years later.

The West Riding textile district readily adapted to changes in fashion. The economies of mill towns such as Halifax – 'a town of 100 trades' – had become increasingly diversified during the second half of the nineteenth century, though the woollen and worsted industries remained dominant. In 1851 one-third of Halifax's male workforce were directly involved in textile manufacture. Mills had grown considerably both in size and number as steam replaced water as the source of power. By 1901 a dozen leading firms employed 40 per cent of Halifax's textile employees and for the past 30 years Crossley's had provided jobs for 5,000 people. In the mills throughout the West Riding textile district women and girls outnumbered men and boys. In 1901 Halifax's textile trades employed 19,342 adults and children, of whom 11,668 were females and 7,674 males. The borough had also become noted for the development of its financial services, particularly those associated with the growth of building societies, which had grown out of the old friendly societies and the Nonconformist virtue of thrift. The Halifax Permanent Building Society was founded in 1853, at a time when several West Riding towns were starting similar societies with a broader social appeal than the old banks. By 1885 the Halifax Permanent had larger reserves than any other Yorkshire society and by 1902 it had about 50 branches in neighbouring towns and villages. On the eve of the First World War its assets exceeded £3 million, the highest of any society in Britain. The Halifax Equitable Building Society, founded in 1887, soon became the second largest; the two societies merged in 1927.

In the Huddersfield district the range, type and quality of woollen cloth was wider than in any other area of the Yorkshire woollen trade. Most goods were made for the home market, but local specialisms found ready sales in Europe, North America and the colonies. A notable development, mainly in the Colne Valley but also in the mills of Huddersfield, was the tweed trade for the working classes, which grew out of the fancy trade and the increasing use of recovered wool, known as shoddy and mungo. By the 1870s over one quarter of all clean wool used in the British wool textile industry was recovered wool, a proportion that rose to over one-third by the early twentieth century. Dewsbury and Batley were the main centres of shoddy production from old woollen rags; the word had not then acquired its present meaning of poor-quality. By the 1870s Huddersfield was also famous for its worsted coatings, especially plain twills, a trade that became dependent on the American market. Versatility and adaptability were keywords and a wide range of products, including some made of silk and cotton, were made. The traditional manufacture of fancy woollen cloth, often with very intricate designs and weaves, continued through the second half of the nineteenth century and handloom weavers were employed until at least the 1890s, but by the mid nineteenth century the woollen industry was fully mechanised in its principal processes. Power looms were adopted rapidly after 1850 and businesses became increasingly integrated. Fewer than 4,000 power looms had been installed in Yorkshire's woollen mills before 1850 and only 20 per cent of these mills were integrated, but by 1874 over 30,000 power looms were working and 56 per cent of Yorkshire woollen mills were integrated in both spinning and weaving. In the third quarter of the nineteenth century many new mills, often five or six storeys high, were erected in the expanding industrial suburbs around Huddersfield.

Huddersfield was made a borough in 1868 and during the 1880s Sir John William Ramsden's Kirkgate and Westgate schemes and the rearrangement of the street layout near the railway station turned the town into a considerable retailing centre. The borough included the industrial villages of Dalton, Lindley, Lockwood and Moldgreen, which lay beyond the old township of Huddersfield. The wealthiest families lived in Edgerton, to the north, and the lower middle classes favoured Hillhouse. The poorest households, including the Irish, were packed in the courts and yards that were sandwiched between the main streets in the town centre.

St Peter's Church, Huddersfield. The parish church was rebuilt in 1834–36, but the old box pews and three-decker pulpit were not removed until 1873 Three rows of galleries (*left*) were inserted in the nave aisles. The altar canopy (*below*), supported by four Tuscan columns, and the stained glass in the east window were both designed by Sir Ninian Comper in 1921. Comper's work can be seen in several Yorkshire churches.

PHOTOGRAPHS: CARNEGIE, 2005

Boar Lane, Leeds, 1881. John Atkinson Grimshaw's view of the new shops in one of the central streets of the town. In 1868 the Boar Lane Improvement Scheme had widened the street from 21 to 66 feet. Here were built Leeds' finest and most fashionable shops for the middle classes, including 'Mr Richard Boston's great Fruit, Game and Fish Market' opposite Holy Trinity Church, whose 1839 tower rises gracefully above the Georgian church designed by William Etty in the 1720s.

ON LOAN TO LEEDS MUSEUMS AND GALLERIES (CITY ART GALLERY) UK WWW.BRIDGEMAN.CO.UK

left The fine Tudor house known as 'Six Chimneys' in Kirkgate, Wakefield bore the date 1566 on the tie-beam of its southern gable, but by Victorian times it had been converted into shops, like so many houses in the central streets of our towns. The cooper's barrels and baskets are displayed proudly.

BY COURTESY OF THE YORKSHIRE ARCHAEOLOGICAL SOCIETY

Wakefield had taken a different turn. It was much more a commercial centre for the neighbouring manufacturing districts than a mill town. Although it had 17 worsted mills employing 1,195 spinners and a single mill for both spinning and weaving by the middle of the nineteenth century, this was a relatively small number compared with those in the towns further west. Even after the coalfield was developed on a large scale, Wakefield did not become an industrial centre. The Town Hall that was built in 1877–80, the West Riding County Offices that were erected between 1894 and 1898, and the spire of the medieval church that had been raised to cathedral status in 1888 gave Wakefield a distinctive skyline that was not dominated by mill chimneys. The old market place still lay at the heart of the town.

Leeds too had a different character to the towns that were so dependent on textiles. Here the manufacture of cloth declined in importance between 1851 and 1914 and the production of flax almost ceased in the face of Belfast and foreign competition. As the textile industries declined, the engineering, leather and chemical industries expanded and new trades arose in clothing, footwear and printing, so that by the First World War Leeds had a much more diverse economy. The engineering industry grew rapidly in the 1840s and 50s. John Fowler, the most famous name, began to manufacture traction engines and steam ploughs in 1850, but Leeds' early specialisation in steam engines and

Leeds Town Hall. Designed by Cuthbert Brodrick, a young architect from Hull, and built in millstone grit between 1853 and 1858, Leeds Town Hall was immediately hailed as a great success. Influenced by the monumental buildings he had seen in France and Italy, Brodrick designed a Baroque dome and cupola to rise above a giant colonnade. Leeds Town Hall led the way in the expression of provincial civic pride and dignity. When Queen Victoria opened the hall in 1858, 18,000 children sang the national anthem. The four lions in Portland stone were added in 1867.

textile machinery became only part of a great metalworking tradition that was based on local iron and coal. The production of wrought iron in local foundries fell towards the end of the Victorian era as local ores became exhausted, but engineering firms used Cleveland and Sheffield steels and continued to prosper. By 1893 engineering was the core trade and it was Bradford rather than Leeds that dominated the West Riding textile industry. Leeds engineers made railway locomotives and rolling stock, road rollers, traction and ploughing engines, and they supplied specialist machinery to the mills and factories. Joshua Tetley & Son, founded in 1822, were a major brewing company and tanning, the making of boots and shoes, and tailoring were other important trades. The labour force in the clothing trade was provided by Jewish immigrants and by the thousands of women and girls who had previously worked in the flax industry. Sewing machines had been introduced into the city's workshops about 1855 and the band-saw, which could cut many thicknesses of cloth simultaneously, was first used about a decade later. Many of the small workshops in Leeds were

A Fowler traction engine. John Fowler (Leeds) Ltd were the leading British manufacturer of portable steam threshing engines and steam ploughs from the mid nineteenth century up to the First World War. The firm was established in Leathley Road, Hunslet, between 1859 and 1864, close to the Airedale Foundry. Their records show that they were heavily dependent on their export trade. Traction engines such as this are now a popular features of agricultural shows and similar events.
WWW.STEAM-UP.CO.UK

'Leeds like all great manufacturing cities in England is a dirty, smoky, disagreeable town ... perhaps the ugliest and least attractive town in all England.'

J.D. KOHL, 1884

overcrowded and unhygienic and rates of pay for long hours were abysmally small; the city had a great many 'sweatshops' towards the end of the century. By 1914 Leeds had about 100 wholesale clothiers with perhaps 80 factories and over 300 small workshops crammed in whatever space was available. The most famous business to rise from this background was Montague Burton and Company. Leeds also became the leading provincial printing centre, specialising in quality colour printing, mostly for the local market, and by 1911 about 8,000 people were employed in this trade. Leeds had a strong and diverse industrial base and was indisputably the most important commercial centre in Yorkshire.

In 1884 J. D. Kohl thought that 'Leeds like all great manufacturing cities in England is a dirty, smoky, disagreeable town ... perhaps the ugliest and least attractive town in all England'. In the central township the pace of growth began to slacken in the 1870s when some residential streets were given over to retail shops, warehouses, banking, insurance and commerce, and transport improvements encouraged the middle classes to move north away from the smoke and the noise. Horse-drawn omnibuses ran daily to Headingley and Roundhay from 1858 onwards and the first horse-drawn tram service to Headingley began in 1871. Great wealth could be earned in Leeds but it was also a city of filth and squalor. The most ambitious project was the grandiose town hall of 1853–58, designed by the young Hull architect, Cuthbert Brodrick. When Queen Victoria came to open it she was welcomed by a record crowd of 32,110 Sunday school children on Woodhouse Moor, which remained Leeds' principal recreational area until the purchase of the Roundhay estate in 1872 provided the city with the finest park in England. Leeds took part in a national and even an international culture as wealthy families, notably the Gotts, toured the Continent and collected art objects for local galleries and museums. The first Leeds music festival was held in 1858, the reference and central libraries were opened in 1871–72, the art gallery in 1888, and the Yorkshire College in 1874 (the forerunner of the university 30 years later). In the later nineteenth century the central shopping area was developed by widening Briggate and Boar Lane and by creating shopping arcades and a new market, with the middle-class shopper in mind.

Victorian Bradford brimmed with confidence as the chief rival of Leeds. After 1847 the corporation tackled the problems of water supply, drainage and building regulations and became one of the first provincial towns to have a police force. Civic pride asserted itself in the building of St George's Hall in 1851–53, with a concert hall, restaurant, gallery and accommodation for 3,100 people. Bradford developed a strong choral tradition, had regular visits from the Hallé orchestra, and in time acquired two theatres and two music halls. Lockwood and Mawson, the local architects who designed St George's Hall, built the other major public buildings, including the Exchange (1864), Victoria Hotel (1867), Town Hall (1873), Independent College (1874), Markets (1877) and Bradford Club (1877). They were also commissioned by Titus Salt to design his model village at Saltaire after he had moved his alpaca and mohair mills out into the countryside near Shipley. Salt was Bradford's mayor in 1848 and its MP in 1859; ten years later he was made a baronet. His new mill was opened with great celebrations in 1853 and by the following year 150 houses were ready for his workforce; eventually 820 houses were completed in rectangular blocks of 16 properties arranged in a grid pattern. Each house had a parlour, kitchen, two or three bedrooms and a back yard, though no garden. The public buildings included Congregational and Methodist churches, school and institute, and a bridge leading into an attractive park. Salt wanted his estate to combine 'every improvement that modern art and science had brought to light', including the banning of public houses. This Congregationalist businessman imposed his ideals on his new community as effectively as an Anglican squire dominated his estate village. Saltaire attracted enormous interest, though it was overshadowed later by the garden villages of other enlightened, paternalist employers.

Though Leeds, Bradford, Halifax, Huddersfield and Wakefield had much in common, their buildings and topography, their economic and social structures

Salt's Mill, Saltaire. Having made his fortune out of alpaca wool, Titus Salt (1803–76) opened his new mill in the countryside near Shipley with great ceremony on his 50th birthday. The architects were the Bradford firm of Lockwood & Mawson. Fourteen boilers and four beam engines powered 1,200 looms that were capable of manufacturing 30,000 yards of cloth each day. He built a model village for his workers on the banks of the River Aire and was a generous philanthropist. Saltaire became a World Heritage site in 2001. After the mill was closed in 1986 it was purchased by Jonathan Silver and redeveloped as an industrial and leisure complex, starring a David Hockney gallery. It has been a great success.

BY COURTESY OF THE YORKSHIRE ARCHAEOLOGICAL SOCIETY

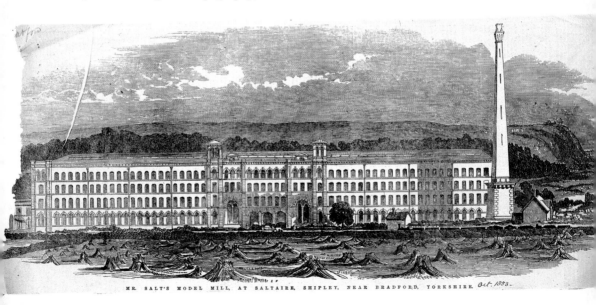

MR. SALT'S MODEL MILL, AT SALTAIRE, SHIPLEY, NEAR BRADFORD, YORKSHIRE. Oct. 1853.

Congregational Church, Saltaire. Sir Titus Salt was a Congregationalist, so the church which served his family and workforce in his model village was of this denomination. It was built in 1858–59 by Lockwood and Mawson, the Bradford architects. The family mausoleum is attached to the north side.
PHOTOGRAPH: CARNEGIE, 2005

left Salt's first mill at Saltaire lies right alongside the Leeds and Liverpool canal and the later railway.
PHOTOGRAPH: CARNEGIE, 2005

right Mechanised spinning. This Edwardian photograph shows a young woman operating the machine invented by W. H. Arnold-Foster, which enabled one person to 'doff' hundreds of bobbins at a time.
BRADFORD INDUSTRIAL MUSEUM

Sorting wool in a Bradford Mill at the beginning of the twentieth century. The sorters are separating the wool into its various grades. Not only do the individual fleeces differ, but the wool in each fleece is itself of several qualities.
BRADFORD INDUSTRIAL MUSEUM

Drying wool. The drier was made by Taylor Wordsworth & Co., Leeds.
BRADFORD INDUSTRIAL MUSEUM

Re-packing mohair in a Bradford Mill in the Edwardian age. Mohair was imported from Turkey and the Cape and was used in the manufacture of bright goods such as 'Alpacas'.
BRADFORD INDUSTRIAL MUSEUM

and their responses to their problems were all different from each other. They each prided themselves on their independence and their particular character and so did the smaller communities of the woollen and worsted conurbation. Despite their proximity and similarities, their rivalries were intense.

The steel and iron districts

In 1853 Henry Bolckow, the ironmaster who had been largely responsible for the spectacular growth of Middlesbrough, became the new borough's first mayor and five years later he was elected unopposed as the first MP. A staunch Liberal and Wesleyan, he was a noted philanthropist, the leading subscriber to every good cause and a benefactor who provided schools and a public park. Other ironmasters such as the Bells, and Wilson, Pease & Company, followed in the wake of Bolckow and Vaughan. By 1873 the north-eastern iron field was producing over 2 million tons of pig iron per annum, that is about one-third of the total British output. The Teesside furnaces were larger and more efficient than the older plant elsewhere in the country and the high wages enjoyed during the boom years of the later 1860s gave workers as well as masters a shared sense of prosperity. Local Cleveland ores still produced 84 per cent of Teesside requirements in 1883, but from then onwards the area became increasingly dependent on overseas ores, so that by 1913 local supplies accounted for only 60 per cent of consumption. A change of emphasis from iron to steel came in the mid 1870s under the leadership of Arthur Dorman and Albert de Lande Long. Teesside became a major centre for the production of Bessemer steel, then that of the open-hearth process and of sheet steel for ship plates. By 1913 the North-East produced over 2 million tons of steel per annum, or nearly half the national output.

Middlesbrough attracted immigrants from far afield. The 1871 census revealed that nearly half its population were born outside Yorkshire, including a large Irish contingent of 3,622 people, 1,531 from Wales, 1,368 from Scotland, 1,169 from the west midlands and about 600 who were born overseas. The various buildings that were erected to cater for immigrant religious beliefs included a Jewish synagogue and a Roman Catholic cathedral that served a new bishopric. Middlesbrough's population rose quickly during the second half of the nineteenth century from 7,431 in 1851 to 91,302 in 1901. The growing town burst beyond the original grid pattern and in the 1880s a new centre was laid out on the other side of the railway line around the grand town hall of 1883 and other public buildings of that period. The working-class houses that were built as near to the place of work as possible until an electric tram system was installed in 1898 were as overcrowded as those of any other industrial town. Middlesbrough was an undistinguished place, but in 1911 it could boast of one major feat of engineering when the Transporter Bridge was built by the Cleveland Bridge and Engineering Company; at 850 feet long and 215 feet high, it was the largest bridge that had been built on the gantry principle anywhere in the world at the time.

The railway age inaugurated a new era in the Sheffield steel industry. The firms that had set up business in the Don Valley to the east of Sheffield – Cammell, Vickers, Firth, Brown, Jessop – responded quickly to the international demand for steel for railway rolling stock and machine tools. The local cutlers were no longer the main customers for the steelmakers and during the second half of the nineteenth century steel overtook cutlery as Sheffield's major industry. From the 1860s bulk steel was made by new methods, starting with the Bessemer converter and then the Siemens open-hearth process. Henry Bessemer moved from London to open a works in Carlisle Street in 1858 and his new neighbours soon started to take out licences to install their own converters. By 1870 more steel was made in converters than in crucibles, but the old method continued to

Bessemer converter, Kelham Island Industrial Museum, Sheffield. Henry Bessemer's invention of the converter in 1856 was quickly taken up by the steel-masters in Sheffield's east end. Steel could now be produced quickly and in large quantities. The converter at the museum entrance is one of the last pair to be used in Britain – at Workington, where production ceased in 1975.

PHOTOGRAPH: CARNEGIE, 2004

produce high-quality steel. The wrought iron industry was the one that suffered from the success of the new process. By 1873 the Sheffield district was making about a quarter of a million tons of rail per annum and America, in particular, was a major importer of Sheffield steel. Brown's and Cammell's alone exported to the United States about three times the whole domestic American output. But the boom in railway building in Britain finished in that year and by 1876 the export trade in rails to America had collapsed as new methods of production allowed the exploitation of America's vast reserves of iron ore. Sheffield's steelmasters turned increasingly to the manufacture of armaments, which had begun about 1860. Brown's and Cammell's became the major British manufacturers of armour-plate; Firth's led the way in making projectiles and guns; in 1880 Hadfield's began the large-scale manufacture of shells; and soon Vickers' became the leading supplier of all types of ordnance. These Sheffield firms became national names in the middle and late Victorian period and were amongst the largest in the country. The arms race up to the First World War filled the order books of Sheffield firms. Although both America and Germany had overtaken Britain as bulk producers of steel by 1890, Sheffield remained the leading international centre for special steels. Most of the major alloy steels were discovered there before the First World War as Sheffield steelmakers turned increasingly to science instead of the old rule-of-thumb methods. The two outstanding discoveries were those of manganese steel by Robert Hadfield

J. Pennell, *Fog, Steam and Smoke on the River Don* (*c.*1909). This was 'Smoky Sheffield' at its worst. It is impossible to recognise any buildings other than the central churches, whose spires are lit by the only shaft of sunlight that penetrated this grim scene.

in 1882 and stainless steel by Harry Brearley in 1912, but there were many others.

The working-class east end of Sheffield was entered from the town centre through the dramatic Wicker Arches leading from the Victoria railway station. Many steelworkers lived in the Wicker, which was within walking distance of the works, but rows of terraced houses sprang up on the northern side of the Don Valley and later in Attercliffe and Darnall. The steelmasters did not build houses for their workers and made no attempt at social control. They lived in the western suburbs, away from the smoke and the grime. John Brown and Mark Firth commissioned grand Italianate mansions at Endcliffe and Oakbrook and the growing professional and managerial classes chose to live in Collegiate Crescent and the attractive Broomhall estate, where no commercial development was allowed.

New steelworks were also founded beyond the boundaries of Sheffield, particularly in the Rotherham district and further up the Don Valley at Stocksbridge, where Samuel Fox had a wiredrawing business in a disused cotton mill. In 1848 Fox began to make umbrellas and six years later he started to melt his own crucible steel, but his business was transformed in 1862 when he bought a licence to use the Bessemer process in order to make rails, billets, springs and rods for the railways. Immigrants flocked to work in the new steel town and by 1881 Stocksbridge's population had mushroomed to 4,660, a five-fold increase since the mid nineteenth century. By 1911 it had reached 7,090.

Meanwhile, Sheffield was still the world's major producer of cutlery and tools. By the end of the nineteenth century virtually all the makers of knives in the United Kingdom worked in Sheffield. The largest and most famous cutlery works in the world was that of Joseph Rodgers & Sons, who employed 1,200 workmen and had offices and warehouses in London, New York, Montreal, Toronto, New Orleans, Havana, Bombay and Calcutta. Nearly as

Samuel Fox's steelworks dominates the valley of the Little Don, the ancient boundary between Hallamshire and the Honour of Pontefract. When John Stocks' bridge crossed the river in the early eighteenth century, only a fulling mill stood nearby. A cotton mill was erected in 1794–95 and ten years later a new turnpike road opened up the valley. Samuel Fox came here in the 1840s as a wiredrawer, then an umbrella manufacturer. He started making crucible steel in 1854, then in 1862 he began to convert steel by the new Bessemer method. Many of his workers were housed in stone-built terraces alongside the works. By 1911 the population of Stocksbridge had reached 7,090.
SHEFFIELD LIBRARIES, ARCHIVES AND INFORMATION; LOCAL STUDIES

well known in America as a manufacturer of high-quality knives was George Wolstenholme, who shortened his firm's name to Wostenholm. He crossed the Atlantic 30 times in pursuit of orders and travelled as far west as San Francisco. The factory that he built in Wellington Street in 1848 was named Washington Works because of his American connections and the middle-class Kenwood estate that he created at Sharrow was named after and modelled on country estates that he had seen in upstate New York.

The third largest cutlery business was the Queen's Cutlery Works of Mappin Bros. The owners were descended from a foreign immigrant who had settled in Sheffield in the 1590s. John Newton Mappin made his fortune as a brewer and bequeathed his art collection and the Mappin Art Gallery to the borough. His nephew, Frederick Thorpe Mappin (1821–1910) had a large business in knives, razors and plated wares. A director of the Midland Railway, Liberal MP for East Retford and then for Hallamshire, and Lord Mayor of the city in 1877, he was created a baronet in 1886 and Sheffield's first honorary freeman in 1900. He founded the Technical School and helped to establish the University, where he was the first senior pro-chancellor. When he died in 1910 he left a fortune of nearly £1 million, far more than any Sheffielder had left before, and 80 pictures to the Mappin Art Gallery. Meanwhile, his younger brother, John Newton Mappin (1835–1913) had started his own electro-plating and cutlery business with his brother-in-law, George Webb. The emphasis was on quality and artistic design and Mappin & Webb soon became a household name. Walker & Hall, James Dixon & Sons, and William Hutton & Sons also flourished in the same line of business.

Sheffield had well over 250 tool firms by the 1870s, most of them operating on a small scale, though several larger firms employed 200–400 men. File making led the way, but the manufacture of saws and joiners' tools were also important. By 1880 Spear & Jackson employed over 800 workers who made saws, files and edge tools from the firm's own steel. Thomas Turton & Sons, David Flather & Sons, and William Marples & Sons were other prominent integrated businesses. Tyzack's made scythes at their Little London Works and at Abbeydale, Skelton's made shovels and garden tools at Heeley, and

One of the forges at Abbeydale Industrial Hamlet, now open to the public as part of Sheffield's industrial museums.
PHOTOGRAPH: CARNEGIE, 2004

Chesterman's made measuring equipment. Tool making was the important third branch of the metalware industry that accounted for Sheffield's astonishing growth. In 1851 the borough's population had reached 135,310, by 1901 the new city had 380,793 inhabitants, or well over 400,000 if newly incorporated areas are added.

Coal mining

Britain's industrial success in the Victorian era was based on its large deposits of coal. The workforce in the nation's mines rose from *c.*50,000 in 1800 to over

This photograph was taken about 1910 at an unidentified coal mine. It captures the 'pick-and-shovel' nature of the work, even where the hewers had plenty of space to work at a large seam. Hewers earned higher wages than the men who saw to the removal of the coal from the face along 'gates' to the bottom of the pit shaft, such as the man who is stacking a truck to the right. The rails for the trucks came right up to the face.
NATIONAL COAL MINING MUSEUM FOR ENGLAND

1 million by the First World War and most of this increase occurred in the second half of the nineteenth century. Whereas the Yorkshire and North Midland coalfield produced an estimated 8 million tons per annum in 1851, by 1913 its annual output was 73 million tons. The 1901 census recorded 94,110 coal miners in the West Riding, many of whom lived in new settlements such as Fitzwilliam or at places like Grimethorpe which had been mere hamlets before. Old villages such as South Kirkby and Wath-upon-Dearne acquired a new character and from the 1870s onwards colliery muck stacks became a dominant feature of the landscape throughout the coalfield.

The Lundhill Disaster Memorial. This monument was erected in a quiet part of Darfield churchyard to commemorate the 189 men and boys who died in a gas explosion at Lundhill colliery, Wombwell, on 19 February 1857. The majority of the victims were buried close by. The new, deep mines of the South Yorkshire Coalfield were prone to this type of dreadful accident in the Victorian age.

PHOTOGRAPH: AUTHOR

In the Dearne Valley the population of the old parish of Darfield almost doubled between 1861 and 1881. This growth occurred particularly in the township of Wombwell and at Snape Hill and Low Valley near Darfield village. At first, the majority of the miners at Snape Hill came from the West Riding, whereas those who found homes at Low Valley had often travelled long distances and nearly one-third of the population of Wombwell Main came from beyond Yorkshire, mainly from Nottinghamshire and Derbyshire. The 1871 census returns noted that over half of Low Valley's population had been born outside Yorkshire, especially in Staffordshire and other west midland counties and that Snape Hill was now also attracting migrants from the west midlands. The population grew more quickly when the collieries of Mitchell Main, Houghton Main and Cortonwood were opened during the 1870s and the 1881 census revealed that many of the newcomers came from the Black Country, where mines were closing. The typical migrant was a member of a young family who had kinship or friendship links with his neighbours in the new settlements and most of the single men knew the people with whom they lodged long before they moved. Having arrived, the migrants stayed put and the new communities within the parish of Darfield soon acquired distinctive characters.

As mines got deeper the chances of a gas explosion increased. The South Yorkshire coalfield suffered much worse than the one in West Yorkshire. In the Dearne Valley 189 miners were killed at Lundhill in 1857; seven years later 59 died a mile or two away at Edmunds Main; then, in 1866, in the worst calamity of all, 361 men were killed in a second disaster at the Oaks colliery. The recommendations which had been made after the explosion there in 1847 had not been put into effect and too much reliance had been placed upon safety lamps for detecting gas, rather than upon improving the ventilation system. The blast on 12 December 1866 was heard three miles away and only six of the 340 miners who were working at the time survived. Tragically, the following day a second explosion killed 27 rescue workers. National opinion was horrified and £48,747 was collected by the Lord Mayor of London's Fund. The Oaks disaster was the worst in the country at the time. Later disasters included the deaths of 143 miners at Swaithe Main in 1875, only a short distance from the Oaks colliery, and the explosion at Cadeby in 1912 which killed 90 men.

The Yorkshire pits which worked the Barnsley seam were often given the distinctive name of Main, a usage that was almost without parallel in Britain's other coalfields. When a new pit was opened in 1868 at the eastern end of the exposed coalfield, the name Denaby Main was also applied to the village that was founded alongside it. It was very different from the older settlements such as Wombwell or Wath, which had more amenities and alternative sources of employment. In 1861 the small village of Denaby had only one coalminer, but ten years later the new pit village of Denaby Main, sited on the parish boundary, housed 166 colliers, only ten of whom were born in Yorkshire; more came from Derbyshire (56), Nottinghamshire (17), Staffordshire (16), Ireland (14) and Durham (12) than from their adopted county. Other miners lived nearby in Old Denaby, Conisbrough and Mexborough. The 1871 census showed that Mexborough had 258 miners and that the 74 who had been born in Yorkshire were outnumbered by those from Cheshire (34), Staffordshire (33), Lancashire (27), and Derbyshire (14). The pit at Denaby Main employed 473 men and was the largest in Yorkshire. It was sunk by a partnership of West Yorkshire coal owners who accommodated their miners in two-up, two-down brick cottages with no bath and only an outside WC. The company owned all the houses and provided the public buildings. This was a new 'frontier' community that was very different from earlier Yorkshire pit villages which had developed from an older nucleus. The owners were hard-headed men who had taken considerable commercial risks and the miners were immigrants welded by their shared working experience into a close-knit and militant community. Conflict broke out as early as 1869 when notice was served on those who had joined the miners' union. The 350 miners who went on strike at the beginning of March were evicted from their homes, but on 16 September the owners had to admit defeat. Further major strikes occurred there in 1877, 1885 and 1902–3.

By the end of the nineteenth century coal mining had come to be dominated by powerful employers, whose heavily capitalised firms and companies worked several collieries and employed large numbers of men. The Miners' Federation of Great Britain, founded in 1889, faced its first major test in 1893, when 300,000 workers in the central coalfields were locked out after refusing to take a 25 per cent reduction in wages to help offset a 35 per cent fall in prices. The dispute was largely peaceful, but in some West Riding pit villages such as Hoyland and Orgreave the militia were called out to quell disturbances. The Riot Act was read at Featherstone on 7 September and two men were killed and 16 wounded when the militia opened fire. On 17 November the miners returned to work victorious. In 1912, a dispute over guaranteed minimum wages led to the first national miners' strike, involving over 1 million men. A national ballot showed that the strike was supported by 4:1 and that in Yorkshire the proportion was as high as 6:1. The miners in the Yorkshire coalfield had acquired a reputation for militancy.

In the late Victorian and Edwardian era deep mines were sunk on the concealed coalfield under and beyond the magnesian limestone and many of the old farming parishes of the Doncaster district were altered beyond recognition. Only the squires of trim estate villages managed to preserve their rural setting whilst benefiting from royalties earned from the mining of coal below their land. These squires were far from being remote county gentry with limited horizons. William Aldam of Frickley Hall (1814–90), for example, was a successful businessman who invested in canals and railways. But the names of new collieries, such as Frickley, Brodsworth Main and Hickleton Main, were deceptive for the squires took care to preserve their own environment and to insist that the mines were sunk beyond their parish boundaries and that new pit villages should be built out of sight from their halls. The Frickley miners were housed in South Kirkby and South Elmsall, the Hickleton men in Thurnscoe and Goldthorpe, while the estate villages continued in their old, sedate manner. So new, sprawling colliery towns now existed alongside pretty estate villages and industrial districts spread far into the countryside. In an age before the motor car and the radio people still lived in local worlds, whose general character and living standards varied considerably one from another.

The pit villages of the later nineteenth century were built to high densities in unimaginative layouts. They soon acquired shops, pubs, churches and other public buildings, but they were slow to adopt water closets and before pithead baths were built miners had to wash in the family's tin bath in front of the fire. But one Edwardian pit village was as exceptional as Elsecar had been in a previous era. When Brodsworth Main pit was sunk to the Barnsley seam in 1905–8 in a joint operation between Hickleton Main Colliery Company and Staveley Coal and Iron Company, no coal miners settled in Brodsworth village. Instead, in 1907, Arthur Markham, Liberal MP and one of the owners of Hickleton Main, persuaded the company to commission Percy Houfton of Chesterfield to design a new model village immediately north of the grounds of 'Woodlands' house in the neighbouring parish of Adwick-le-Street. The plan of the estate and the original miners' houses, set amidst large greens, are well preserved. All the houses had at least three bedrooms, a bathroom and hot water

Woodlands was designed as a model village for the miners of Brodsworth Main pit and their families. Designed in 1907 by Percy Houfton, the houses were spacious and well equipped by the standards of the times and each one had easy access to green, recreational areas.

AUTHOR COLLECTION

and the density of building was kept as low as six houses per acre. A full-time social worker helped to run the various clubs and societies and two Methodist chapels opened immediately, followed in 1913 by All Saints church. Woodlands was perhaps the most ambitious mining village ever built in Britain, a planned community that was completely different from the terraced houses of the normal pit village at that time. It set the standard for the council estates that were built after the First World War and was followed in 1920 by a development known as Woodlands East and in the late 1920s by another estate to the north, but neither were as spacious as the original village.

Pit villages such as New Edlington remained more common than Woodlands, however. The construction of the South Yorkshire Joint Railway in 1909 had encouraged the further development of the concealed coalfield. While the Yorkshire Main colliery was being sunk between 1909 and 1911 by the Staveley Coal and Iron Company, the sinkers lived in huts and gained a notorious reputation for gambling, drinking and fighting. An investment company meanwhile started to build the village. For a time the new settlement was known as Staveley Street but it was eventually named in comparison with the village of Old Edlington, centred on its Norman church at the top of the hill. The roads were like a quagmire as bricks were brought by traction engines from Conisbrough and Balby. The houses were erected in units of four or six, with large flower and vegetable gardens to the rear. On the ground floor was a living room with a Yorkshire range and small side-boiler, a scullery with a sink and copper to heat water for washing clothes and for bathing in a portable zinc bath, a small pantry, a sitting room and two outshutts serving as WC and coal-place. Upstairs were two bedrooms and a box room. The manager's house was a large brick villa set in its own grounds and the other officials lived in semi-detached houses. For a year or so a few mobile carts and travelling shopkeepers came on regular visits, but the nearest shops, schools, post office and pubs were at Warmsworth and Balby. The miners came chiefly from Derbyshire and Nottinghamshire, where their own pits had been worked out. A temporary 'tin tabernacle' doubled as chapel and social hall until better facilities could be provided. By 1914 New Edlington had a church, school, co-operative store, pub and concert-cum-dance hall.

As coal-mining villages grew, so Yorkshire's other mining industries declined when seams became exhausted or foreign competition proved too powerful. Cleveland's iron ores still provided 84 per cent of Teesside's requirements in 1883 but by 1913 the proportion had dropped to 60 per cent because of foreign imports. The number of lead miners fell dramatically in the second half of the nineteenth century. Grassington's population declined by 123 in the 1850s and then by a further 400 between 1861 and 1881. In 1851 nearly half of Swaledale's workforce had been employed in the lead industry, but within 40 years the proportion had fallen to a fifth. Muker lost a quarter of its inhabitants in the 1850s, some going to the industrial parts of the West Riding or Lancashire, others emigrating to the United States or Canada. But the main exodus occurred during

Settle Market place, 1838. Painted by an unknown artist, this view shows a stage-coach arriving in the Market Square at the heart of the town. The Town Hall had been built six years earlier in the Elizabethan style, to the designs of George Webster. To the left of the market cross can be seen two of the six open arches of the seventeenth-century Shambles. In late Victorian times this was given an upper storey.

Thorne, 1908. This postcard view of Edwardian Thorne looks down Finkle Street towards The Green. At that time, children could still play in the central streets without fear of traffic, apart from the occasional horse and cart. Yet Thorne was not a sleepy village, but a busy little town that came alive on market day.

Wakefield Cattle Market, 1920. In 1765 the medieval cattle market had been moved from the heart of the town to the Ings to the south. At first it was held every fortnight, but in 1849 it became a weekly market on Wednesdays. Although it was known as the cattle market, it always included sheep as well. In 1868 a total of 50,289 cattle and 360,112 sheep were penned; the figures for 1901 were 73,465 cattle, 190,662 sheep, and 5,145 pigs. The market continued to prosper well into the twentieth century.

BY COURTESY OF THE YORKSHIRE ARCHAEOLOGICAL SOCIETY

the 1880–82 depression, when many mines were abandoned. During the year ending October 1882 Reeth school lost more than half the children on the register; the township of Melbeck lost nearly half it population in the 1880s; and Arkengarthdale lost 44 per cent when its mines failed in the 1890s. Between 1871 and 1891 the population of Swaledale declined by nearly 50 per cent. The characteristic Dales farms of today are often amalgamations of even smaller holdings that were vacated when the lead industry declined.

Rural Yorkshire

Old market centres such as Ripon and Thirsk acquired much of their present character in the Victorian and Edwardian period and many a small market town was able to take advantage of improved communications and to prosper in a modest way. In Tadcaster the breweries were the town's major employer. When John Smith died in 1879 his brother Samuel developed the old brewery while another brother, William, continued the trade name at a new site in the town. In 1874 John Murray described Thorne as 'an active market town, carrying on considerable trade in corn, coal, and timber ... the Quay called the Waterside [is] resorted to by sailing-vessels, and when the tide permits, by steamers from Hull'. Ships were built at Thorne and the port flourished during the second half of the nineteenth century when the peat-cutting trade grew in response to the enormous demand for bedding material for horses. Dutchmen came to provide technical skills and capital and by 1889 about 100 immigrants lived in a Dutch colony at Thorne Moorends. In 1896 five companies amalgamated to form the British Peat Moss Litter Company which worked the peat moors between Hatfield and Goole. Demand for peat declined sharply after the First World War when motor transport began to replace the horse.

Market towns provided professional and trade services and on market day they created a sense of excitement and pleasure as well as of business. Fred Kitchen remembered 'the smell of tarpaulin, leather, cow-cake, apples, calves, pigs and poultry' and 'the biggest babel of dialects since the time of Noah' when he went to the hiring fair at Doncaster in a carrier's cart. Country carriers had adapted well to the age of the railways; many of them had other occupations for the rest of the week, but on market day they brought passengers, goods, shopping lists and messages to town and returned in the evening with purchases and many a fine tale to tell. By the 1880s or 1890s the great annual livestock fairs were a thing of the past. The railways had hastened their decline and their absorption into the weekly market system, but they were retained in a few places for the annual hiring of servants and for merrymaking. However, even the growing numbers of village shops did not replace the thought of market day in some nearby local town as an event to look forward to.

During the nineteenth century rural society was polarised more than ever before between the rich and the poor. At the bottom of the social hierarchy the ranks of the farm labourer had been swollen by the population explosion and at the top gentry families had become more exclusive as younger sons no longer took their place among the middling farmers but served in the army, the church or the professions. In the country as a whole landed estates and their tenants farmed about 85 or 90 per cent of the available land, leaving only a small proportion for owner-occupiers, and the landlord–tenant relationship had a customary, almost feudal air about it. In 1873 the 11 East Riding landowners who had over 10,000 acres together owned about 28 per cent of the land, another 24 great landlords with 3,000 to 10,000 acres each owned a further 18 per cent, and 58 men with 1,000 to 3,000 acres each owned 13 per cent. The Crown was by far the largest corporate owner with 12,230 acres, but this estate was nowhere near as large as those of Sykes (34,010 acres), Londesborough (33,006 acres), Cholmley/Strickland (20,503 acres) and several other private owners who employed London or provincial firms as professional land agents.

On the North York Moors the Revd J. C. Atkinson, the scholarly Vicar of Danby, witnessed much improvement during his long incumbency. Danby was a parish of small farms; 'in all, there may be now six or eight farms of more than 100 acres; all the rest, in number if at all under seventy, and exclusive of small holdings or cow-keepings, scarcely average seventy-five acres each'. These farms, however, were larger than in earlier times for their total number had been reduced by 25 per cent during the last 200 years. The quality of the livestock had improved in the late nineteenth century but the system of crop management had remained unaltered in every particular. Atkinson had seen much moral improvement – rowdyism had declined and drunkenness carried a stigma – and he felt quiet satisfaction at the achievements of church, chapels and schools, regretting only that education had led to 'the decay of the old pure Yorkshire speech'. Contemporaries who shared his concern to record dialects included Samuel Dyer, whose *Dialect of the West Riding of Yorkshire* appeared in 1891 and another Yorkshireman, Joseph Wright, whose monumental *English Dialect Dictionary* was published in six volumes between 1898 and 1905.

Atkinson was fascinated by the survival of a former culture and knew that 'still there is a singular amount of old and unchanged custom, habit, feeling, among us'. When he had arrived in Danby in 1847 most of the moorfolk believed in fairies, beneficial or otherwise, small people like the Hart Hall Hob in Glaisdale who dwelt in the prehistoric burial mounds scattered on the moors. Burial parties clung steadfastly to hallowed routes or church-ways, for fear that if they took a short-cut the ghost of the deceased would rise to haunt them. Superstitious beliefs were widely accepted and were similar to those that J. R. Mortimer remembered on the Wolds. Both men wrote, for example, about bee-customs that secured the future prosperity of the hive upon an owner's death; Mortimer recalled that hives were decked with strips of black crepe and the bees were given ale on a plate or saucer before their dead owner was taken to his grave. Every rural area supposedly had its resident witch whose evil powers could sometimes be countered by witch-wood (rowan or mountain ash) or other magical charms or by visiting a wise-man with a reputation for remedying misfortunes. John Wrightson, the wise man of Stokesley, performed the role of a primitive vet and herbalist; he was a semi-magical figure who reassured those who feared they were bewitched and who frightened thieves into returning lost property. As such he was a valuable member of the community.

The major rural festivals of the nineteenth century were the parish feasts and the Martinmas hiring fairs. At Darrington the annual feast was the occasion for all to make merry: 'everybody kept open house; friends and relations who had left the village came back to it, sometimes from far distances, and there was a great reunion of families'. The hiring or 'statis' (statute) fairs in Edwardian Doncaster attracted farmers and labourers from South Yorkshire, north Lincolnshire and parts of Nottinghamshire and Derbyshire. Bargains were clinched by a 'fastening-penny', which varied in value according to the generosity of the farmer; a head-waggoner usually got five shillings, a seconder half-a-crown, and lads a shilling. To Fred Kitchen it always seemed a wretched business, especially for a lad of 13 or 14 to be taken like a sheep or calf to market and sold to the highest bidder. But Martinmas did provide a welcome week's holiday for a farmworker.

Though traditional tools and farming methods survived, especially on small hill farms, much progress was made elsewhere in Yorkshire. At the start of Victoria's reign few machines were used on English farms, but by the end of the century the same farms were the most mechanised in Europe. By then, Fowlers of Leeds and other agricultural engineers supplied steam engines and a range of machinery far beyond the capacity of the old country workshops which turned out ploughs and cultivating implements. In the 1860s and 70s wire fencing became common, dairy farmers started to use oilcakes and other cattle feeds, chemical fertilisers were accepted and farmers responded to the needs of the growing urban population by producing more meat, vegetables, dairy produce and hay for the townsmen's horses. Incomes, rents and wages all rose during the prosperous years of high farming, particularly during the 1860s, and the amount of arable land farmed in England and Wales rose from 12 to 15 million acres. One of the agricultural improvements that was widely advocated was the under-draining of land that was naturally heavy and wet. About 30 per cent of the Earl of Scarbrough's South Yorkshire estate, for example, was drained during the second half of the nineteenth century. Between 1848 and 1893 Yorkshire lost 774 acres to coastal erosion, some of which was deposited on Spurn Point, so that by 1851 this stretch of sand was 2,530 yards longer that it had been in 1676. At the same time, however, 2,178 acres were reclaimed within the Humber estuary and warping (the process by which fine, muddy deposits were left by the tides) was encouraged in the Humberhead Levels by the construction of dikes and embanked fields in which potatoes and other root crops were grown.

From the late 1870s to the mid 1890s so much corn was imported from the prairies and steppes that home prices came tumbling down. Wheat prices fell by a half and those of barley and oats by about a third. The corn-growing districts such as Holderness and the Wolds were hit very badly and the distress of the arable farmers was made worse by the atrocious weather of 1878–82. The Wolds farmers suffered further because wool prices fell sharply in face of Australian competition. Many were the tales of personal hardship and tragedy. But the story was not one of uninterrupted gloom. Although refrigerated meat and dairy imports caused English prices to fall by 15–20 per cent, the superior quality of English beef and mutton helped to maintain sales. During the 1880s beef and dairy cattle became the mainstays of many farmers. Those who concentrated on meat and milk, potatoes, hay, poultry, eggs and fresh vegetables managed to survive the worst years of the depression and some were able to prosper.

In 1851 the agricultural labour force in England and Wales had reached a peak of 1.88 million, but thereafter it declined both in relative and absolute terms. A shift in emphasis from arable to pasture meant that fewer hands were needed and demand for manual labour was reduced further by the adoption of seed drills, horse hoes, mowers and reaping machines in the 1850s and 60s, followed by self-binding reapers in the 1880s. Women left the fields first and they more than the men swelled the ranks of those searching for work in the towns and industrial villages. Without this migration rural areas would have suffered widespread unemployment. The poor quality of cottage accommodation increased the determination of some country families to move to the towns, though the standard of rural building improved in the 1880s, particularly in estate villages where squires were anxious not to see their workers leave. In some estate villages the population rose again during the last quarter of the nineteenth century while that of neighbouring 'open' villages declined. By 1900, after a quarter of a century of agricultural depression, all the extra land that had been brought under the plough had again been put down to grass.

Housing and public health

The housing conditions of the working classes undoubtedly improved in the later part of the nineteenth century. Higher wages and the trend towards smaller families meant more comfort and space for many, though overcrowded slums remained a disgrace until after the First World War. Municipal corporations responded quickly to the Public Health Acts by providing sewage farms and water works and by issuing local by-laws, modelled on those of the Local Government Board in 1877, which insisted on sound building construction and lower densities. No two boroughs acted in the same way. Sheffield was typical of the industrial towns that had not coped with the public health problems posed by its unprecedented population growth. In the 1850s the disposal of sewage had become a major problem when houses were built in low-lying, ill-drained areas that previous generations had shunned. Throughout the second half of the nineteenth century death rates in Sheffield from contagious and infectious diseases were amongst the highest in England. By 1864, when a corporation by-law banned such buildings, Sheffield had 38,000 back-to-back brick houses, usually arranged in terraces that had been erected as speculative ventures by local tradesmen. As the number of industrial and domestic chimneys multiplied, Sheffield's smoke problem worsened. John Murray's *Hand-book for Travellers in Yorkshire* (1867) judged that: 'Sheffield, with the exception of Leeds, the largest and most important town in Yorkshire, is beyond all question the blackest, dirtiest, and least agreeable. It is indeed impossible to walk through the streets without suffering from the dense clouds of smoke constantly pouring from great open furnaces in and around the town'. As in other towns, a considerable improvement in the environment came with the provision of open spaces in the form of public parks and recreation grounds, through donations by wealthy families and municipal purchases.

The municipal corporations were also active in building hospitals. Sheffield's

'What struck every observant delegate was the utter blankness of the faces [in Sheffield] ... Stooped shoulders, hollow chests, ash-coloured faces, lightless eyes, and ghastliest of all, loose-set mouths with bloodless gums and only here and there a useful tooth.

TORONTO GLOBE, 1909

Crowded courts in Sheffield. The Medical Officer of Health has measured these Sheffield slums prior to compulsory purchase and demolition in the 1920s.

SHEFFIELD LIBRARIES, ARCHIVES AND INFORMATION; LOCAL STUDIES

General Infirmary and Royal Hospital were reinforced by specialist hospitals for women, children and the mentally ill and by isolation hospitals. In 1900 an imaginative housing scheme was begun at High Wincobank, Sheffield's first working-class garden suburb and a pioneering example of municipal reform; 617 houses were built there by 1919. But as yet, the industrial cities and boroughs had neither the resources nor the authority to clear their slums. In 1914 nearly 17,000 Sheffield families still lived in back-to-backs and another 8,000 families lived in houses which required some attention to make them fit for human habitation. About 11,000 privy middens still served 16,600 of Sheffield's 107,000 houses, a higher number than anywhere else in Britain.

The rapid growth of population presented all towns with similar problems. The ancient cathedral city of York now had heavy and light industries in the form of railways and confectionery and its poor districts, such as Walmgate, were as bad as those in the new industrial boroughs. In 1901 Seebohm Rowntree published *Poverty: A Study of Town Life*, the result of a thorough survey of 11,560 families living in 388 of the city's streets, covering 46,754 of York's 75,812 inhabitants. Rowntree concluded that 27.84 per cent of York families lived in poverty, which he defined in two categories. The primary poverty of 9.91 per cent of the city's population was endured when the four basic requirements of food, fuel, shelter and clothing were not met from income, no matter how carefully family budgets were managed. Another 17.93 per cent of the population drifted into secondary poverty when they did not have the money to meet irregular but essential expenditure, such as medicine. Rowntree's most important finding was that poverty arrived at three points in the life cycle: during childhood; when a newly married couple had to raise young children;

Leeds Infirmary. Designed by Sir George Gilbert Scott, the General Infirmary was built on Great George Street in 1863–67 as a replacement for the overcrowded building which had been erected in 1770. Built of polychromatic brick and carved stone, it resembles the St Pancras Hotel in London, which Scott was designing at the same time. Scott thought that 'some form of Architecture formed on the Mediaeval styles but freely treated would meet the requirements of such a building better than any other'. The Infirmary was one of the first Gothic buildings in the West Riding to challenge the prevailing Italianate style. To the right of the photograph are George Corson's extensions of 1891–92 in the same style as Scott's.

and when people were old and sick. His investigators found that many slum dwellings had only two or three rooms, in houses that had been built before the Public Health Acts or local by-laws had imposed better standards. Some of the worst dwellings were in narrow alleys paved with cobbles, others were packed in confined yards with little sunlight or air. Rowntree's team found a few houses that were clean and tidy but that the general air of dilapidation was the result of apathy and carelessness. Most of these slum houses were dark, dirty, damp and overcrowded, with broken windows stuffed with rags or pasted over with brown paper. In the back yards, ashpits overflowed, the shared earth closets were inadequate and insanitary, a single tap sufficed for a large number of houses, and offensive smells wafted over from nearby slaughter houses. As a positive response to the report, the Rowntrees built a model village, or industrial garden suburb, for their workers at New Earswick, close to their chocolate factory on the northern edge of York. The houses were designed in a rustic vernacular style, with steeply pitched tiled roofs and simple, often whitewashed walls containing fairly large windows. Wide frontages enabled the living rooms to take full advantage of the sunlight and each house had a utility room.

Ten years after Seebohm Rowntree's report, Lady Florence Bell organised a team of social workers to do a similar survey of the working-class houses of Middlesbrough. They visited over a thousand homes and concluded that most houses had a kitchen or living room that opened straight from the street, with a parlour or bedroom behind and a little scullery at the back, and two bedrooms upstairs. They judged these houses to have sufficient space for a family consisting of parents and two or three children but thought that they were totally inadequate for larger families, some of which had ten or 12 children. Most building was speculative and cheap and even the newest houses were packed together.

Technological advances made many homes more comfortable towards the end of the nineteenth century. The greatest benefit was the rapid spread of gas cooking and lighting, especially after slot meters were widely installed in houses from the 1890s onwards. Gas lights replaced sooty paraffin lamps and gas

New Earswick. This group of houses form part of the model village that was built on the northern edge of York in the early twentieth century for workers at Rowntree's chocolate factory. Raymond Unwin's designs incorporated Arts and Crafts ideas to make this industrial garden suburb resemble a village in the countryside. His houses were given steeply pitched tile roofs, whitewashed walls and large windows to allow the rooms to be well lit.

PHOTOGRAPH: CARNEGIE, 2005

Hickleton Hall. Built about 1740 for Godfrey Wentworth in local magnesian limestone, Hickleton Hall and its outbuildings stand apart from the village that stretches down the hill on both sides of the busy main road from Doncaster to Barnsley. It was probably designed by the master mason, George Platt, who was also responsible for the first stage of the nearby Cusworth Hall. In 1829 the Hickleton estate was bought by Sir Francis Wood, who proceeded to rebuild his tenants' houses in the vernacular style of the Elizabethan and Stuart age. Hickleton Hall remained with the family until 1947, when it was sold by Edward Wood, Earl of Halifax and leading politician. It was soon converted into a Sue Ryder home.
PHOTOGRAPH: AUTHOR

Joseph Paxton's glass-house, opened in 1836 and restored recently, forms the main attraction in the Botanical Gardens which Robert Marnock designed in west Sheffield.
PHOTOGRAPH: CARNEGIE, 2004

cookers took over from open fires. Although street lamps powered by electricity had been erected from the 1860s and Bradford had built the first municipal power station in 1889, electricity did not become widely used at home or at work until the 1930s. Another major improvement was the supply of piped water, though most women still had to heat it in pans on the fire or in a fixed container in the kitchen or scullery known as a set pot or copper, which had a coal fire underneath. By 1914 most houses in the larger towns had their own supply of piped water and their own water closets, but some families in the countryside still had neither amenity.

In the Victorian era the middle classes moved out of town into new residential suburbs. The most carefully planned middle-class development in Sheffield was that at Nether Edge, where George Wolstenholme, a leading cutlery manufacturer, commissioned Robert Marnock, who had designed Sheffield's Botanical Gardens, to design curving, tree-lined avenues with a variety of stone-built houses. The new residents had to sign covenants which prohibited the use of their premises for industrial or commercial purposes. The

detached houses in the better streets were provided with large gardens and semi-detached houses of various sizes were built in smaller plots in Kenwood Park Road, Thornsett Road and Steade Road. Wolstenholme then joined forces with a builder, Thomas Steade, to form the Montgomery Land Society for developing the rest of the Upper and Nether Edge estates.

The middle classes of Bradford moved up Manningham Lane, where detached and semi-detached villas were built above the smoky town. There too a freehold land society erected good-quality houses for those a little further down the social scale. The lower middle classes of Leeds moved into small villas and terraces at Headingley and other northern suburbs and after the 774 acres of Roundhay Park were sold to the corporation in 1871 part of it was developed for large villas set amongst tree-lined avenues and arranged in quiet cul-de-sacs at a density of about three per acre. Huddersfield's middle-class suburb at Edgerton had a similar picturesque appearance. The wealthier Victorians had an eclectic choice of style, ranging from the Classical to the Gothic and the Tudor to the Italianate and even the Scottish baronial, but far more typical were the middle-class terraces that were built in every West Riding town.

The tough, coarse sandstones that were quarried on the edges of the Pennines gave the towns and villages a strong visual character that was completely at one with the natural landscape. Mills, churches, chapels, public buildings and even the rows of nineteenth-century working-class houses were roofed with stone slates and the streets paved with flags. Halifax, Huddersfield and Bradford and the Pennine villages were built largely, if not entirely, of stone from local quarries. The hardness and durability of York stone (a somewhat misleading term as the county capital chose magnesian limestone) did not allow much carved decoration but gave the buildings a monumental quality. The sparkle of large quartz grains amongst the varied browns, buffs and greys softened the rugged appearance of the buildings until the smoke turned them completely black. Off the Pennines, however, the inhabitants of Leeds and Wakefield and often even those of Sheffield preferred brick to stone except for their public buildings. Leeds went for brighter colours in terra-cotta dressings and coloured glazed tiles for its commercial buildings, largely because of the development of faience on an estate of 150 acres at Burmantofts, which exported its products to all parts of the Empire.

The Victorian aristocracy and gentry adapted their eighteenth-century country houses to modern technology and added conservatories and other features but built relatively few new properties. Striking examples of Victorian country houses include Allerton Park, a Gothic mansion for Lord Stourton, that was finished in 1852, the extravagant additions to Carlton Towers in 1873–75 for Lord Beaumont, and Brodsworth Hall, a remarkable house of the 1860s that was designed in an Italianate style by Casentini of Lucca for Charles Sabine Augustus Thellusson and surrounded by formal gardens. The Thellussons and other wealthy families spent only part of the year in their country houses, but such places continued to dominate many parts of rural Yorkshire up to the First World War, especially during the shooting season. The success of a day's shooting was measured by the number of grouse that were brought down by gunfire from the butts that gamekeepers had built on the moors. The highest bag in a single day was recorded in August 1913, when nine guns shot 2,843 grouse on Broomhead Moor in the northern part of the Peak District.

The parsonage was another important Victorian building in the countryside and in estate villages such as Hooton Pagnell or Wortley the incumbent lived in comfortable style in a house that was second only to that of the lord of the manor. When Sir Joseph William Copley of Sprotborough Hall rebuilt Sprotborough and Cadeby villages in the late 1840s, the parsonage and steward's house stood a little apart from the cottages in the village street. The Revd John Fardell, the incumbent, thought the cottages were 'replete with the comfort and necessaries of that station of life ... so that the poor now enjoy houses not to be excelled by the poor of any parish around'. About the same time, Sir Francis Wood rebuilt the homes of his Hickleton tenants in the vernacular style of the Elizabethan and Stuart age, with magnesian limestone walls and pantile roofs, all tastefully assembled beyond the grounds of the hall. The 'close' villages of a great landowner provided a strong visual as well as a social contrast with the more numerous 'open' villages which no single landlord could dominate. When the agricultural depression began to bite later in the century, squires had to provide better houses to stop their tenants from migrating to the towns, but although the labourers in the estate villages had superior accommodation others preferred a less deferential life away from the control of 'the family in the big house'.

'... the poor now enjoy houses not to be excelled by the poor of any parish around.'

SPROTBOROUGH, 1840s

Religion and education

Many new churches were needed in the towns to serve the spiritual needs of the rapidly expanding population. In the countryside ancient parish churches were ruthlessly restored or completely rebuilt. Victorian zeal saved many a crumbling edifice but the enthusiasm for stripping walls of their plaster and for removing the galleries, box-pews and other fittings so familiar to their Georgian ancestors eventually provoked an outcry against what was being done in the name of restoration and improvement. Though the archaeological study of ancient churches reached new scholarly levels, much that was old and worthy was undoubtedly lost. The destruction of the historic church of All Saints, Dewsbury, is particularly lamented. The East Riding churches were the ones that were most badly treated, but the new buildings that were erected there were among the very best. St Helen, Escrick, by F. C. Penrose (1856–57) and St Mary, South Dalton (1858–61) by J. L. Pearson are the most memorable. Sir Tatton Sykes (1826–1913) built a dozen churches on his Sledmere estates and restored another eight. In the West Riding Earl Fitzwilliam commissioned

St Helen's Church, Escrick. At first glance this fine church in an estate village to the south of York looks medieval, but in fact it was designed in the Decorated style of *c*.1300 by F. C. Penrose in 1856. It was built at the expense of the incumbent, the Rev. and Hon. Stephen Willoughby Lawley, the second Lord Wenlock. Among the Lawley monuments inside the church is one commemorating the benefactor, designed by Eric Gill. Immediate clues that this is not a medieval building are provided by the polygonal apse and the positioning of the tower on the north side of the church, both seen here.

PHOTOGRAPH: AUTHOR

Pearson to build Wentworth Holy Trinity on a scale befitting the great estate at Wentworth Woodhouse, to replace the modest chapel-of-ease that survives in a ruined state further down the hill. Such churches stood alone, often at the end of the drive to a great house, and they served as landmarks for miles around. The new ritualism of the High Church movement was well accommodated in Scott's church at Doncaster (1854–58) and Norman Shaw's church at Bingley (1866–68). Most of the great Victorian architects were active in Yorkshire. Butterfield was particularly busy in the North Riding and at Baldersby he not only designed St James' church (1856–58) on a lavish scale for Viscount Downe at Baldersby Park, but also built the vicarage, a school and brick cottages for the tenants. Meanwhile, in 1847 the Mill Hill Unitarians in Leeds had built the first West Riding chapel in the Gothic style that had been so enthusiastically resurrected by the Anglicans. Soon the West Riding had pompous and showy chapels, like Cleckheaton Central Methodist (1875–79) and Heckmondwike Upper Independent (1890), that were far removed in spirit from the simple boxes of earlier times or the 'tin tabernacles' of the poorer sects.

In 1851 Halifax had 25 churches and chapels, by 1900 it had four times as many. The Sunday School Jubilee Sing at the Piece Hall in 1890 attracted 30,985 participants from 93 Nonconformist Sunday schools within Halifax's huge parish. In Sheffield the congregations of the Church of England more than doubled in the 30 years after 1851, but this figure has to be considered against the enormous rise in the total population. By 1881 Sheffield had 50 Anglican churches, all of them evangelistic or low church in outlook, but the growth of Nonconformity was greater and Sheffield was now regarded as a Methodist borough whose affairs were dominated by a web of Wesleyan, New Connection and Free Methodist families. The Nonconformists flourished in all the West Riding towns and the chapel culture became a pervading influence. In politics it was a driving force behind the Liberal Party and many of the leading citizens were linked by shared membership of one or other Nonconformist

Springfield Board School, Sheffield. One of the finest of the schools that were erected by the local Education Board, it was designed in 1875 by C. J. Innocent and Thomas Brown. The school was enlarged in 1891–92 – to include a playground on the roof – and again in 1897. The architects called their style 'English Domestic Gothic'. Innocent's son was the author of *The Development of English Building Construction* (1916), a famous, pioneering study of vernacular architecture.

PHOTOGRAPH: CARNEGIE, 2004

denominations. Many Nonconformist families were involved in philanthropic causes and were influential in promoting the 'respectability' of the Victorian artisans, with an emphasis on regular work, education, thrift and temperate drinking. The Tories were increasingly the party of industrial businessmen as well as landlords and they based their elective strength on the middle classes. In Sheffield the semi-independent cutlers who had the vote supported the Liberals, whereas the unskilled immigrants in the east end steel industry formed a new type of working class, bound together by trade unionism, which had become a powerful force for the improvement of wages and working conditions. The Independent Labour Party was founded at Bradford in 1893 but it made slow progress before the extension of the franchise in 1918.

The provision of elementary education improved considerably under the influence of the Evangelical movement. From the 1840s and 50s scores of schools were erected in Victorian Yorkshire, both in the towns and the countryside. By 1858 Leeds had over 130 schools which provided places for about 35,000 pupils. A Mechanics Institute for working men had been founded in 1824, but despite all this voluntary activity educational provision for the masses remained inadequate before the building of board schools, paid for out of local rates, after 1870. The state provision of education took away the need for Sunday Schools to teach reading and writing and allowed them to concentrate on religious instruction. The churches and chapels continued to build schools throughout the 1870s, but were eventually unable to compete with the new board schools. By 1892 Sheffield had 23 board schools, each with over 1,000 pupils, which remain some of Sheffield's finest Victorian public buildings. In rural Yorkshire squires of estate villages were quick to build church schools that they could control rather than have a board school run by elected ratepayers.

Victorian working-class children had little chance of progressing beyond the elementary stage of education, but in the later years of the nineteenth century some local boards, especially those in the industrial towns, founded higher-grade schools, which were secondary schools in all but name. The government provided grants for technical education and the old grammar schools widened their curriculum and some began to admit girls. In a major reorganisation of 1902 board schools were replaced by the council schools of local educational authorities. The leaving age was raised, from 1906 school dinners were provided free of charge, and in the following year local authorities were made responsible for the health of schoolchildren. As yet, however, only a very small proportion of the pupils went on to higher education.

Leisure and shopping

Holidays were revolutionised by the coming of the railways, which provided opportunities for day-trips to the seaside and longer stays for those who could afford it. Bridlington became popular with holiday-makers from Hull, the West Riding and the north-east midlands. The opening of a railway prompted the growth of Filey as a seaside resort and a grid of new streets which was laid out from the 1850s to 1890. Scarborough catered for the rich as well as for the working classes, with cliff-top villas and hotels beyond the ancient limits of the town, notably Cuthbert Brodrick's Grand Hotel, which rises 13 storeys on the side facing the sea. The railways also enabled Yorkshire families to visit Cleethorpes and places on the Lancashire coast or to get to Harrogate, England's smartest inland spa, which was replanned and rebuilt as a superior Victorian resort with spectacular rooms behind sober façades. The Royal Baths, which opened in 1897, had numerous hydropathic bathing and treatment rooms decorated with marbles, mosaics, ornate wood and plasterwork. The Majestic Hotel, the Grand Opera House, the Royal Hall and other pleasure buildings and shops were opened in the next few years and visitors took healthy walks along The Stray or the Valley Gardens. Harrogate had become one of the most fashionable places in the North.

Ilkley was a smaller version of Harrogate. It had become a flourishing resort and an expanding dormitory for Leeds and Bradford businessmen by the 1840s, well before the railway was opened in 1865. The first substantial spa building was the Ben Rhydding Hydropathic Establishment (now demolished), which was built in 1843–44 in the Scottish baronial style. Then in 1858 Cuthbert Brodrick designed Wells House, a towered hotel that provided both accommodation and hydropathic treatment. Ilkley offered a wide variety of comfortable suburban villas in a rural setting. Many of its grandest buildings and shops date from the late Victorian or Edwardian period. Meanwhile, smaller spa centres such as Askern attracted a local clientele. In 1870 J. M. Wilson's *Imperial Gazetteer* noted that Askern was 'not long ago, a paltry hamlet, but is

The Crescent, Filey. Before the railways from York and Hull arrived in 1846 and 1847 Filey was an old fishing village, divided from its parish church by a wooded ravine. The new resort was developed as a grid of streets by a Birmingham solicitor, J. W. Unett. The first block of stuccoed houses in The Crescent (which never achieved a full crescent shape) was built in a late classical style by 1850 and other blocks were soon added. The scheme was not completed until 1890. The public gardens in front of The Crescent stretch to the cliffs which rise 100 feet above the sands.

BY COURTESY OF THE YORKSHIRE ARCHAEOLOGICAL SOCIETY

now a pretty place, with hotels and lodging-houses, much frequented by invalids and others seeking cures for rheumatism and scorbatic diseases'.

Improved communications helped to turn towns into entertainment centres, with racecourses, sports grounds, concert halls, theatres and music halls. With the coming of the railways Doncaster races became an event of national importance. It was said in 1874 that the town was 'best known to the world for its Races, which take place annually in September, and last four days. They are among the most celebrated in England, attracting a vast assemblage of persons, and contributing not a little to the prosperity of the town'.

The railways, and later the trams, helped to transport the thousands of people who began to watch organised sport. The opening of the cricket ground at Bramall Lane, Sheffield, in 1854, which replaced earlier venues at Darnall and Hyde Park, led to the formation of the Yorkshire County Cricket Club there in 1863. The club did not fare particularly well until its reorganisation 30 years later and the ending of Sheffield's dominance. Under Lord Hawke (a Yorkshireman by ancestry though not by birth) the team became county champions in 1893, 1896 and 1898, then between 1900 and 1902 they lost only two of their 80 matches. They were champions again in 1905, 1908 and 1912 and were never far from the top. A new tradition had been born that enabled Yorkshiremen to identify themselves with their county and to adopt the white rose of the medieval House of York. The players were all Yorkshire-born and the best of them, George Hirst and Wilfred Rhodes, were the greatest players in the game. The Roses match with Lancashire (who had adopted the red rose of the House of Lancaster) attracted 79,000 people in 1904.

Meanwhile, the ancient, popular game of football had also been organised on a regular, competitive basis and had attracted wide support amongst the working classes. Sheffield Football Club, founded in 1857, is the oldest surviving football club in the world. The National Football Association, formed in 1863, and its FA Cup of 1871 were the products of the public school interest in the game, whereas the Football League, established in 1888 (with two divisions from 1892) reflected the desire of working-class supporters for regular enter-

'Not long ago, a paltry hamlet, but is now a pretty place, with hotels and lodging-houses, much frequented by invalids and others seeking cures for rheumatism and scorbatic diseases.'

ASKERN IN 1870

A single cow grazes on the Stray, Harrogate. The large building, centre left, is the White Hart Hotel, with the Crown Hotel to its right.
BY COURTESY OF THE YORKSHIRE ARCHAEOLOGICAL SOCIETY

tainment. Numerous local leagues were also created and teams were sponsored by bodies as diverse as churches, chapels and pubs. Sheffield's two Football League teams grew out of organised cricket. In 1867 the Wednesday Cricket Club decided to keep its members together during the winter months by playing football and in 1889 the United Cricket Club gave birth to a football team that was soon one of the most successful in the land. Between 1897 and 1901 they won the league championship once, were runners up twice, won the FA cup once and were also beaten finalists. Barnsley FC won the FA Cup in 1912 and then Sheffield United's achievement was bettered by

Huddersfield Town (founded 1907), who dominated the football scene in the 1920s. Huddersfield was also the home of another type of organised football,

The Free Well, Harrogate. This cartoon by H. B. Templar gently mocks the various types of people who came to sample the spa water at the Free Well in Low Harrogate.
HARROGATE MUSEUMS AND ARTS, MERCER ART GALLERY

The Royal Baths at Harrogate, built in 1897 to the designs of the London firm of Baggalay & Bristowe, enhanced the town's character as a wealthy resort.
HARROGATE MUSEUMS AND ARTS, MERCER ART GALLERY

for it was here at the George Hotel that representatives of 20 clubs met in 1895 to form the Northern Rugby Union, which from 1922 has been known as the Rugby League. On the eve of the First World War Huddersfield's team were the finest in the industrial North.

As the Victorian middle classes moved into the suburbs the streets in the centres of the larger towns and cities became retail and entertainment districts. Sheffield's central streets were widened to twice their medieval width to allow the passage of the new electric trams and to accommodate the large shops and department stores, notably that which John Walsh opened in 1900, whose steel and glass construction was exposed on the ground floor but masked by stone on the upper storeys. In Halifax Simpson & Sons' five-storey showroom, all linked by elevator, offered furniture for every room in a house and the Borough Market that was opened in 1896 contained 43 shops and over 100 stalls under its glass and iron dome, with another 19 shops and a pub arranged around its perimeter; the fish market under the same roof had a further 22 shops. Firms trading under the names of their founders helped to give each town its

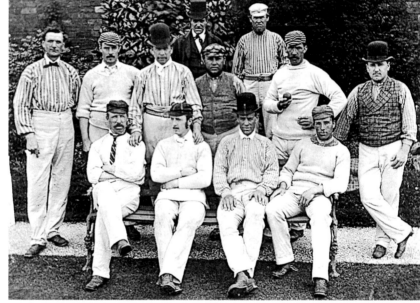

The Yorkshire County cricket team (1875). This is the earliest known photograph of the county cricket team. It was taken before a game with Surrey at Bramall Lane, Sheffield, in June 1875. The Yorkshire C.C.C. had been founded at a meeting in Sheffield in 1863. Bramall Lane had replaced earlier cricket grounds at Darnall and Hyde Park.

SHEFFIELD LIBRARIES, ARCHIVES AND INFORMATION: LOCAL STUDIES

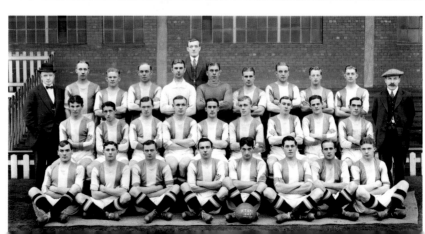

Huddersfield Town Football Club, 1914–15. Founded in 1907, within a few years the club had a squad of 26 players. Huddersfield Town dominated the game in the 1920s, winning the League Championship three years in succession.

PHOTOGRAPH COURTESY OF KIRKLESS COMMUNITY HISTORY SERVICE

individual character. Sheffielders drank Ward's beer, while Leeds men preferred their own Tetley's. In Halifax, in 1890, John and Violet Mackintosh began to sell a novel blend of traditional English butterscotch toffee and American caramel and in Sheffield, in 1899, George Bassett's confectionery business started to make Liquorice Allsorts.

Leeds had become the leading shopping centre in the North and its central streets were thronged with traffic. Between 8.20 and 8.30 a.m. on a day in January 1898, 2,306 pedestrians, 3 omnibuses, 10 tramcars, 3 four-wheeled cabs, 6 hansom cabs and 2 post mail carts were counted passing along Briggate. The borough's first department store was Alexander Montieth's Grand Pygmalion, which in the 1880s employed 200 assistants on four floors. Shops catering for the middle classes were grouped together in special arcades, named Thornton's (1878), Queen's (1888–89), Grand (1896–98), Victoria (1898), County Arcade and Cross Arcade (1898–1903). The Leeds City Markets of 1902–4 had 18 shops fronting the main roads, small shops and stalls on the ground floor and a hotel, a restaurant and billiard, coffee and club rooms in the upper storeys. In 1909 the *Leeds Shopping Guide* claimed that, 'No City in England can boast a more wonderful transformation than that witnessed in Leeds during the past two or three decades'.

The working classes too had more money to spend and increased leisure as average weekly working hours fell from 60 or 70 in the early years of Victoria's reign to 53 by 1910. Many branded foods and what are now regarded as traditional English meals, such as egg-and-bacon breakfasts and fish-and-chip dinners or suppers, became common in the late nineteenth century. Working-class co-operatives were often well established by the 1860s and by the end of

Cross Square, Wakefield, 1884. Among the advertisements at Brooke & Sons 'posting station' for local shops and traders are posters for Roberts Victoria Circus Tour to be held at Boar Lane, Leeds, 'a grand tournament on the American principle', as well as posters for forthcoming football and rugby matches.

the century the Leeds Industrial Co-operative Society had 70 shops, most of them in the working-class industrial suburbs. Nevertheless, small family shops still shared 80 per cent of Britain's retail trade before the First World War. In the manufacturing towns, in particular, the little corner shop flourished in the late Victorian and Edwardian period.

New traditions that were forged in the towns and industrial villages improved the quality of life, especially in the field of music. By the mid Victorian period many a home had its piano and most places in the West Riding had a brass band. Nonconformity brought discipline and religious fervour to communal singing at a time when German oratorios had almost replaced the traditional anthems in popularity. The towns provided the large number of performers that were needed and buildings big enough to accommodate them. The biggest towns had civic libraries and their own newspapers, such as the *Yorkshire Post*, which appeared as a daily from 1866 in succession to the weekly *Leeds Intelligencer*. The towns were also focal points for various historical, literary, philosophical and scientific societies that enlivened nineteenth-century provincial England. The Yorkshire Archaeological Society grew out of meetings begun in Huddersfield in 1863, six years later it published the first of its annual journals and in 1885 began to print its invaluable record series. The North Yorkshire Record Society produced its first volume in 1884. The Thoresby Society at Leeds began to publish its transactions in 1889 and the Hunter Society at Sheffield followed in 1914. Meanwhile, a number of good local histories had appeared, often written by parsons or prominent townsmen and the books that are now regarded as the classic pioneering studies of the nation's vernacular architecture were written by Addy, Innocent and Ambler.

The late Victorian and Edwardian era was a time of rapid progress, yet it was also a time when traditional crafts flourished as never before. The railways had opened up the market for Whitby fish, but the techniques used by the fishermen and their families remained largely traditional ones. The fisherfolk who were captured in the beautiful photographs of Frank Meadow Sutcliffe have a strikingly distinctive appearance. The complex technical knowledge that the men had acquired about the winds and tides, the behaviour of the sea, and the habits of fish was passed on in an oral culture and like most occupational groups they had their own specialised language which was virtually incomprehensible to the outsider. Their houses were clustered near the waterfont around Whitby harbour and in the neighbouring coastal villages of Robin Hood's Bay, Runswick and Staithes. Lacking baths, water closets and piped water, these dwellings were also workplaces where much of the gear was made and where the women and girls shelled mussels and limpets, cleaned and baited the fishing lines, and mended the nets. Their craft skills and lifestyles were a world apart from those of the Hallamshire cutlers, the Dearne Valley coalminers, or the Dales farmers. On the eve of the First World War Yorkshire remained a county of numerous and diverse local societies.

F. M. Sutcliffe's photograph shows a group of young women skaning mussels on Tate Hill, Whitby. Women and girls had the tedious, repetitive job of preparing the lines for the fishermen and skaning thousands of mussels daily as bait. They used a knife to remove any hair and bits that had become entangled before prising the mussel open and cutting away the soft parts. With practice, this became a mechanical process that took only a few seconds.

CHAPTER 10

The First World War to the Present

The First World War

Thousands of Yorkshiremen were amongst those who volunteered for action in the First World War. On the first two days of the public enlistment of volunteers, for instance, 900 men were accepted into the Sheffield City Battalion. Yorkshire families were as involved as much as those of any other region of Britain; indeed, a disproportionate number of soldiers came from the northern industrial cities and from Scotland and Ireland. Yorkshiremen enlisted in many regiments, but particularly in the York & Lancaster, the West Yorkshire, the East Yorkshire, the Yorkshire, the Duke of Wellington, and the King's Own Yorkshire Light Infantry.

The harsh reality of the war was soon made obvious by the enormous casualties and the introduction of conscription in 1916. The figure of 8,814 members of the York & Lancaster Regiment who were killed during the war was typical. Of the 770 men of the 16th Battalion, The Prince of Wales Own West Yorkshire Regiment who went 'over the top' on 1 July 1916 at the battle of the Somme 515 were reported killed, seriously wounded or missing by the third day; the 18th Battalion's casualties were also over 70 per cent. During the four years of the war 5,139 Sheffielders and over 10,000 of the 82,000 men who were recruited in Leeds were killed and many others were wounded. Halifax had 2,226 casualties and war memorials in every town and village in the land speak of the appalling carnage. In the whole of the British Empire nearly 1 million men and women were killed and over 2 million were wounded.

During the war the economy was at full stretch and women did jobs which had been thought of as male occupations. Factories in Leeds contributed to the war effort by making guns, shells, tanks and aircraft and an enormous range of clothing. Important new munitions factories were opened at Armley, Barnbow, Hunslet and Newlay, where women and girls formed the majority of the workforce. The Sheffield armaments and tool steel firms expanded to an even greater size than before and installed electric-arc furnaces, so that by 1915 up to 25,000 tons of steel a week left Sheffield for use by the Allied forces. Women were recruited in large numbers in the east end steel works, especially in the

The Guildhall, Hull. Designed by A. G. Street in 1906 and completed just before the First World War, this grand imperial building dominates the northern edge of the old town. Pevsner thought that it 'would look convincing in an Italian city', where similar buildings were erected in the Victor Emmanuel style. Despite its name, which harks back to an earlier era, its function is that of a town hall.

PHOTOGRAPH: CARNEGIE, 2005

Lieut.-Col. S. C. Taylor, Major L. M. Howard, Officers and Recruiting Staff, with Mr. J. B. Hamilton, Mr. J. Wardle, and Dr. White about to start with the Recruiting Car, through which passed over 800 Recruits. June, 1915. Leeds.

workshops where millions of shells were produced; Firth's Templeborough Works, for example, employed 5,000 women. The reality of foreign war was brought home to British people for the first time and was witnessed at first hand by some when the Zeppelin raids began and when Scarborough was shelled by two German ships. The bombings provided for a foretaste of what was to happen in 1940 and 1941.

The Depression years

The soldiers who returned from the war were promised 'a land fit for heroes', but the post-war economic boom collapsed in 1921. British industry had lost much of its competitive edge and the rest of the twentieth century saw a gradual decline in Yorkshire's importance in the national economy as the old manufacturing industries contracted in face of international competition. The world-wide depression of 1929–31 brought unprecedented levels of unemployment. After hovering at about 10 per cent in the 1920s, the national unemployment rate shot up to 21 per cent in 1931. By the following year Britain had nearly 3 million people, or 23 per cent of its labour force, out of work. The industrial districts of the North and the Midlands were hit hardest of all, with unemployment levels well above the national average. For many families, the inter-war years were a time of dreary struggle to make ends meet.

Before the First World War British steel production had fallen behind that of the United States and Germany, but urgent wartime demand for ships, shells and armour plating and the brief boom that followed the war had revitalised the industry. Investment in new plant at Redcar and elsewhere on Teesside enabled north-eastern England to claim nearly one-third of British pig-iron production by 1920 and about one-fifth of the output of British steel. During that year 69 north-eastern furnaces, using both Cleveland and foreign ores, were in blast. Most of these furnaces were small, however, and their equipment was elderly. In this they were typical of much of the British steel industry. Though the major part of national output was controlled by a relatively small number of companies, the industry was still characterised by numerous family firms.

The collapse of the post-war boom in 1921 meant that national crude steel production fell from 9 million tons a year to less than 4 million tons. Both home and foreign demand dropped sharply as steel's main customers in the heavy engineering and shipbuilding industries were hit disastrously by their loss of trade. Production levels improved in 1923–24, though prices did not rise, and they picked up again in the late 1920s, but then came the world-wide depression that followed the Wall Street Crash of 1929. In the early 1930s steel output was halved and by 1932 unemployment in Sheffield had risen to a new peak of 34.1 per cent of the registered workforce. Most of the unemployed were steel workers and many stayed out of work until the late 1930s. During these years of depression a series of amalgamations produced giant companies whose wide-spread interests lay not just in steel, but in coal, shipbuilding and heavy engineering. In 1918 the Sheffield firm of Steel, Peech & Tozer, whose new Templeborough works had 14 open-hearth furnaces, two billet mills, a nearby rod mill, and bar and strip mills, amalgamated with Samuel Fox of Stocksbridge, the Workington Iron & Steel Co., the Frodingham Iron & Steel Co. and the Rother Vale collieries to form the United Steel Companies, which controlled coal mines and ore fields as well as all stages of iron and steel production. On Teesside, Dorman Long amalgamated with Bolckow Vaughan in 1919, with the South Durham Iron and Steel Co. four years later, and with Bowesfield Steel at Stockton in 1936. Further amalgamations in the Sheffield–Rotherham district during the 1930s saw John Brown merged with Mark Firth and Vickers Armstrong joining forces with Cammell Laird to form the English Steel Corporation. By the Second World War the only giant steel firm not to have merged with a partner was Hadfield's. These big companies employed thousands of workers and concentrated on making heavy forgings and castings, the mass production of alloy steels for engineering, and armaments. The smaller, private firms often remained family businesses that made tool steel and high-grade alloys and castings. The most successful new firms in the inter-war years were the Neepsend Steel & Tool Corporation, which was developed by (Sir) Stuart Goodwin, and Tinsley Wire, which was founded in 1933 by Leon Bekaert, a Belgian. Production techniques in the steelworks of the Sheffield–Rotherham district were a curious combination of the latest technology from the research and development departments and the old methods employed in the making of crucible steel, which survived until the 1960s. The steel industry began to recover in 1936, when the Government ordered a national rearmament programme to meet the threat of Nazi Germany.

In the 1920s and 1930s the typical firms in the Sheffield tool trade remained small- or medium-sized and, though they made an enormous variety of high-quality products, they were essentially Victorian in outlook and organisation. So too were the large number of small cutlery firms that failed to modernise. At the outbreak of the Second World War nearly 200 firms manufactured cutlery in the city and the basic structure of the industry was similar to what it had been a century earlier. Although the workforce stayed at about 10,000 in the inter-war years, output did not rise. The cutlers did, however, recognise the value of stainless steel and after the First World War millions of knives marked 'Firth Stainless' were manufactured by mass-production techniques.

The world-wide depression brought hardship and bitterness to the coalfields. On the eve of the First World War Britain's share in the world export trade in coal had amounted to 55.2 per cent but a quarter of a century later it had fallen to 37.6 per cent. The number of men employed in the nation's coal mines dropped sharply, from 1,227,000 in 1920 to 827,000 in 1932. Britain's peak year for the production of coal had been 1913, when 287.4 million tons were mined, but the South Yorkshire coalfield, which in that year was responsible for 27 million tons, reached its peak much later, producing 33.5 million tons or 13 per cent of Britain's total in 1929. The South Yorkshire coalfield had grown much larger than the West Yorkshire one and by 1935 Doncaster had emerged as the most important mining centre in Yorkshire. The concealed coalfield, east of the magnesian limestone escarpment, was now being fully exploited and the most distant mine had been sunk in 1925 at Thorne, some 10 miles north-east of Doncaster. Many South Yorkshire collieries also had coke ovens and by-product plants and some, including Newton Chambers at Chapeltown and Manvers Main near Wath-upon-Dearne, had blast furnaces, steelworks and brickyards. Surplus gas, which was fed into the South Yorkshire coke-oven gas grid that had been created in 1930, supplied local industry and public utilities.

As the mining industry contracted because of falling exports in the post-war slump, the owners lowered the miners' wages. The miners' refusal to accept these cuts led to a lock-out on 1 April 1921, but by the beginning of July the men returned to work demoralised, hardship having forced them to accept the new conditions. Five years later, as the depression worsened, the owners proposed not only to cut wages but to increase the working hours from seven to eight each day. Led by their inflexible president, a Yorkshireman, Herbert Smith, the miners responded with the slogan 'Not a penny off the pay, not a minute on the day' and a long, grim battle began. Widespread sympathy for the miners' cause brought British industry to a standstill on 4 May 1926. For nine days the country experienced the only General Strike in its history, but then other trade unions withdrew their support. The miners stayed out for a further seven months before they submitted and the bitterness of their struggle long remained fresh in the memories of the mining communities and helped to create their unity, defiance, pride and insularity. Yorkshire's typical mining settlements were towns in terms of size but villages in most of their facilities

The 1926 General Strike. On 4 May 1926 Britain's workers came out on strike in support of the coal miners, who were faced with a pay cut and longer working hours at a time of economic depression. The General Strike – the only one in the country's history – lasted for nine days, after which the other trade unions withdrew their support. The miners stayed on strike for another seven months before they returned to work defeated and demoralised. Here, miners at Cudworth in the South Yorkshire coalfield gather to receive their weekly strike pay from the local branch of the National Union of Mineworkers. They all seem to have been of stocky build and to have worn the same style of clothes and caps

and characteristics. Shared experiences bound the mining families tightly together and the social cohesiveness of the pit villages became legendary.

The output of the West Riding textile industries also declined considerably during the inter-war years, though unlike the experience of the Lancashire cotton industry this was not due to the effects of international competition. Rather, it simply reflected the general fall in the amount of world trade, particularly after 1929. The West Riding woollen and worsted firms relied less on exports than did the cotton industry and more on the home market and their quality trade remained unchallenged. Nevertheless, unemployment levels rose steadily and were well above the national average.

'Not a penny off the pay, not a minute on the day.'

<small>MINERS' SLOGAN, 1926</small>

The slump of 1921 threw 60,000 Bradford people out of work and in Halifax the Chamber of Commerce reported that 'the trade of the town and district came practically to a standstill'. The summer of 1925 saw the largest strike and lock-out in the history of the West Riding woollen and worsted industries. It was supported by nearly 12,000 workers in Halifax and by large numbers in Bradford until a court of inquiry settled the dispute in favour of the workers. In 1929 the rate of unemployment in Halifax reached 20 per cent of the workforce. Then the West Yorkshire textile and engineering industries were badly affected by the collapse of world markets following the Wall Street Crash. In Halifax 400 textile firms closed between 1928 and 1932. Bradford and its satellite towns and villages, such as Saltaire and Shelf, where the mill was often the only source of employment, were particularly vulnerable. However, the introduction of government duties on foreign imports in 1931 enabled West Yorkshire worsted manufacturers to compete in the domestic market and by 1937 the losses of the depression years had been largely made up.

The knock-on effects of the decline of Yorkshire's staple industries were felt in Hull, where half of the city's 8,240 dockers were out of work in 1931. For the long-term unemployed these were grim years. During the depression, the

The decline of Hull's docks began in the depression years between the two World Wars. In the late twentieth century, as old trades and industries disappeared, one response of Yorkshire's cities and towns has been to cater for leisure activities. Hull Marina now occupies former docks, and not far away, on the opposite bank of the River Hull, The Deep – 'the world's only subarium' – has become a major tourist attraction.

PHOTOGRAPH: CARNEGIE, 2005

Leeds engineering industry was hit hard and its workforce fell from an all-time peak of 36,000 in 1921 to 15,000 in 1926. The story is not one of unrelieved gloom, however. Unemployment in Leeds remained significantly lower than in any other major northern city and the clothing industry was spectacularly successful. The mass-production bespoke tailoring industry grew enormously under the leadership of Montague Burton, a Jewish refugee from Lithuania, who in 1909 acquired his first Leeds tailoring factory and soon afterwards a chain of tailors' shops. Made-to-measure suits were ready within a week. By 1925 his new clothing factory at Hudson Road was the largest in Europe and by 1939 he had 595 shops nationwide. Other Leeds tailoring firms which became household names included John Collier, Jackson the Tailor, Price, and Hepworth. By 1927 the clothing industry employed 30,000 workers, most of whom were female. The Leeds printing industry also grew between the wars. E. J. Arnold produced school exercise and text books and supplied all kinds of equipment, while Waddington's printed cigarette and playing cards and new games such as jigsaws and Monopoly. The diversity of industries, ranging from food processing to newspapers, enabled Leeds to do better than other northern towns and to employ an increasing number of women in the commercial, financial, professional and service sectors. Many of the shops in the central streets were rebuilt in the inter-war period.

The countryside

The loss of people from the countryside continued well into the twentieth century, when the mass-ownership of motor cars reversed the trend. Farming remained depressed between the wars and the disappearance of rural industries meant fewer job opportunities for the countryman. Arable farmers could not compete with mass-production techniques from overseas, but others found a living from milk and beef cows and from growing vegetables. Between 1902 and 1939 the number of cattle on Yorkshire farms increased 20 per cent and the number of sheep rose 12 per cent. Farming remained a laborious occupation that offered little financial reward. It reached its lowest point of profitability during the 1930s when capital improvements were virtually at a standstill. The James Herriott books and films captured this hard way of life perfectly.

The East Riding was no longer a relatively prosperous part of rural England. Its total dependence on farming and its isolated position, away from the industrial districts and major through roads, preserved a slower approach to life that was far removed from the bustle of the West Riding. Well into the twentieth century, most East Riding boys were still hired out for a year at a time as farm servants. They received board and lodging on the farm as part of their wages and they had very little time for anything other than work with the horses. The married labourers who lived in cottages in villages also worked long and hard. But the inter-war depression years can now be seen as a watershed when this system came to an end. By 1950 the East Riding was clearly a different place from what it had been before the First World War.

Throughout Yorkshire, the horse-and-cart era was rapidly coming to a close, though it survived on small family farms in upland districts until the 1960s. Long after the Second World War the rural districts were quiet, remote places, utterly dark at night time and served by unmetalled lanes. The cooking was still done over the fire and many farmhouses and cottages were without gas,

Horse and cart at the Springs, Wakefield. Motor vehicles and tractors began to replace this ancient method of transport between the two World Wars, but in some rural parts of Yorkshire it survived until the 1960s.

electricity or water closets. The National Farm Survey of 1941–43 found that many farms were little different from what they had been in Victorian times. Country people did not travel far to work, although sometimes buses were now available to take them a few miles. Near relations and distant cousins were mostly to be found within walking distance in the traditional 'countries', bordered by the nearest market towns, with which people were familiar.

In many parishes, however, an important change took place after the First World War. The power of an aristocratic family in their country house or the squire in his hall was weakened by the long years of agricultural depression, and in some cases it vanished altogether. A considerable number of aristocratic and gentry estates were sold in the immediate post-war years. Land was no longer the sound investment that it had once been and in the coalfield parishes the gentry moved away from the pollution and the grime to spend their royalties elsewhere. After the Copleys had left Sprotborough in 1925 and the Cookes had sold their Wheatley estate to Doncaster Corporation, their halls were demolished and Wheatley became an industrial estate. Other gentry families struggled on until after the Second World War, but their halls became increasingly dilapidated. The votes of the farming families nevertheless ensured that the rural districts of Yorkshire remained solidly Conservative at election times.

Town planning, housing and public health

In urban districts the Labour Party made spectacular advances after the widening of the franchise in 1918 to all men and to women over 30. Before the First World War Yorkshire had only six Labour MPs and few seats on local councils, but in the 1919 local elections Labour made big gains in Leeds, Sheffield and other industrial towns and for a year or so the party had a slender majority in Bradford, the home of the Independent Labour Party. The number of Yorkshire Labour MPs rose from 21 in 1922 to 40 in 1929 but fell to seven in the debacle of the 1931 election, at the depth of the depression. Numbers rose again to 27 in 1935 and to 44 in 1945 when the Parliamentary Labour Party was able to form its first majority government. Meanwhile, Labour had taken control of some important local authorities, notably Sheffield, which in 1926 became the first council in Britain to have a Labour majority. Leeds and Hull also fell to Labour for a time in the late 1920s. In Halifax, as in many other West Yorkshire towns and cities, an anti-socialist alliance operated in municipal politics during the inter-war years, when it was common for a Labour candidate to be opposed by only one of the other parties. This alliance was maintained in Halifax throughout the 1920s and 1930s and the Liberals remained the largest group on the council, but in Leeds the Liberal vote collapsed and for most of the twentieth century control of the council swung between the Conservatives and Labour. In Huddersfield the Liberals kept an overall majority from 1868 to 1945. As in other matters, the West Yorkshire textile towns went their separate ways and their political history des not conform to a simple, general pattern.

After the First World War the city and borough councils were made responsible for planning and improving their towns. Leeds council were quick to grasp the powers that they were granted under the 1919 Town Planning Act. Several

Barnsley Town Hall. Most West Riding towns have Victorian town halls in a Gothic or Renaissance style, but Barnsley's dates from 1932–33. It was built of Portland stone and designed by Briggs & Thornely in a late revival of the Classical style. Sir Nikolaus Pevsner thought that the tower was 'of a bleak cubic kind which betrays a knowledge of the twentieth-century style but a lack of courage to adopt it'. It is, nevertheless, a striking landmark on Market Hill and can be seen from the M1 motorway.

new roads were created in the 1920s, including a ring road scheme and the grand redesigning of the Headrow to relieve traffic congestion. In 1928 Leeds became the first town in England to install traffic lights. The city long relied upon the corporation's trams to move people around, for they were cheap, clean and efficient. The Leeds Civic Hall, which was opened in 1933, provided a splendid new administrative headquarters. About the same time, Barnsley opened a new Town Hall, built in a Classical revival style, and Sheffield acquired a City Hall and a Central Library with the Graves Art Gallery on its upper floor.

The main concern of local government after the war was housing. Though the 1906–11 Liberal government had alleviated much of the poverty described in Rowntree's survey of York, during the early 1930s many families still lived below the poverty line. Another survey of York, taken in 1936, found that 6.8 per cent of the city's working classes were living in primary poverty according to the Rowntree definition and 31.1 per cent of the working classes (or 17.7 per cent of the total population of York) were living in either primary or secondary poverty. The problem was partly resolved by the dramatic slowing down of the growth of the population. Throughout Britain, the trend was towards smaller families and the shift of population from town centres to the suburbs. But the legacy of crumbling nineteenth-century houses, blackened with smoke, lacking basic facilities and crammed into every available yard of space near the works or mills posed formidable problems for the planners. In 1921 the percentage of families living in overcrowded conditions, that is with more than two persons per room, ranged from 10.7 per cent in Bradford and 12.0 per cent in Leeds to 13.2 per cent in Halifax and 13.6 per cent in Huddersfield. Determined efforts to clear the slums and to erect council houses reduced these figures, so that by 1931 the percentage of families living in overcrowded conditions had fallen in Huddersfield to 7.8 per cent, Bradford to 6.9 per cent and Leeds to 8.2 per cent, leaving Halifax with the highest figure at 10.0 per cent. Within another five years the Halifax figure had been reduced to 5.2 per cent, that for Huddersfield to 4.6 per cent and that for Bradford to as low as 2.4 per cent, so considerable progress was made during these years.

Housing schemes that had been started before the First World War, such as the 603 new houses built in Garden Village, Hull, between 1907 and 1916, set the standards for later building. By 1935 Hull had 74,000 houses, 19,000 of which had been built since the war, and 8,600 of these were the responsibility of the corporation. In 1907 Bradford's worst slums in Westgate had been replaced by the city's first council tenements at Longlands, followed shortly afterwards by conventional council housing in Faxfleet Street, Bankfoot. Addison's Housing Act of 1919 gave financial encouragement to municipal corporations that provided homes for working-class families to rent. The borough of Halifax built 1,029 council houses by 1929 and 3,061 by 1939. The Wheatley Housing Act of 1924 encouraged Bradford council to demolish the slums of White Abbey and to erect 5,000 new houses within five years. Further housing legislation in the 1930s supported the large-scale clearance of slums and the improvement of substandard properties by the addition of water closets and sculleries. By 1938 Bradford had refurbished 2,000 houses in this way. Between 1919 and 1939 Bradford council built 10,000 houses, most of which were semi-detached with hot water, electricity, bathrooms, two or three bedrooms, a living-room and kitchen, all surrounded by a garden. The amount of land that was needed meant that many of these estates had to be built on vacant land on the outskirts of the city, at Ravencliffe, Swain House and Wibsey. Private building schemes were also encouraged by government subsidies between the wars. In this way Bradford acquired 13,000 new homes on middle-class estates at Moorhead (Shipley), Charlestown (Baildon), Heaton (Bradford) and in the rural villages of the Aire and Wharfe valleys, such as Wilsden and Burley.

The lives of most of the urban working classes were spent in streets packed with back-to-back houses that were cheap to rent and easy to heat. The persistence of local and family identities even among an urban sprawl was observed by Richard Hoggart in Leeds:

> To a visitor they are understandably depressing, these massed proletarian areas; street after regular street of shoddily uniform houses ... But to the insider, these are small worlds, each as homogeneous and well-defined as a village ... they know it as a group of tribal areas ... This is an extremely local life in which everything is remarkably near.

People were conscious of a multitude of fine-gradings of status. Families from certain streets, chapels or pubs thought themselves superior to their neighbours and at work a clear hierarchy of working-class occupations was evident.

When a Labour council was returned by a narrow majority in 1933, some 75,000 back-to-backs still stood within the city's bounds and little attempt had been made at slum clearance. The Revd Charles Jenkinson, the charismatic Vicar of Holbeck and new chairman of the Housing Committee, had a practical knowledge of housing conditions. He saw to the appointment of R. A. H. Livett as Leeds' first City Architect and embarked on a massive programme of slum clearance and rehousing in huge suburban estates. By 1937 the council had built 15,000 houses, cottages and flats in 24 estates, ranging in size from 33 to 3,500 houses. Whereas in 1914 about 80 per cent of the population of Leeds had lived within two miles of the city centre, large numbers of working-class families were now housed in spacious, low-density garden suburbs at affordable rents. The downside was that close-knit communities were broken up and many found that the absence of shops, industrial premises and other activities had a deadening effect. The most ambitious housing scheme between the wars was that undertaken by Leeds City Council on Quarry Hill, the site of one of the worst slums. Over 3,000 people were re-housed in 938 high-rise flats, accompanied by a shopping parade, a communal laundry and other amenities, all constructed in a modernistic style. Between 1935 and 1941 Quarry Hill grew into the largest council estate in England and attracted international attention, but it was demolished 40 years later. Meanwhile, the middle classes moved out to Headingley, Gledhow, Moortown, Alwoodley, Roundhay, Oakwood, Weetwood and Adel.

In Sheffield the council took advantage of government subsidies to build 25,000 houses between the wars. Most of these were erected by the public works department that was created when Labour came to power in 1926. The most ambitious early project was the 'garden city' Manor estate that was built to high standards and a low density on a geometrical pattern within the medieval deer park of the lord of the manor. In the 1930s this estate was extended as far as Wybourn in the north and Arbourthorne in the south and, under another scheme, Sheffield spread in a northerly direction over Woodside and the Brushes estate and across Southey Green and Parson Cross. All these new houses were semi-detached, with gardens at both the front and the back. Between 1934 and the outbreak of the Second World War an average of 2,400 council houses were built each year. By 1938 about 24,000 slums had been cleared and 44 per cent of them had been replaced by new dwellings, but although the council erected houses at twice the national rate almost three-quarters of the central area's housing was still condemned as unfit for human habitation. At the same time, large numbers of privately owned houses were constructed in the western parts of Sheffield, well away from the smoke and

Howden Dam. The group of reservoirs in the Upper Derwent Valley, which formed the moorland boundary between Yorkshire and Derbyshire, were constructed to supply water to Sheffield and the East Midlands. Howden Dam (seen here) and Derwent Dam are majestic structures with castellated dams. This one was begun in 1906 and completed six years later. In the foreground, an ancient holloway descends from the moors. Many of these were the routes by which farmers brought down the peat that they had cut for winter fuel.

PHOTOGRAPH: AUTHOR

From Victorian times onwards Whit Monday was a public holiday when the local Sunday Schools gathered together to pray, sing hymns and listen to sermons. The tradition was particularly strong in northern industrial towns. In some places, the Catholics paraded separately on the following Friday. The occasion was one for new clothes and the return of relatives and old friends. A brass band led the parade, with the scholars of each Sunday School and their parents walking behind a banner carried by strong young men. Here we see a gathering near the Newton-Chambers ironworks at Thorncliffe in South Yorkshire. Afterwards, the scholars returned to their churches or chapels for a tea and competitive games. The Whitsuntide processions remained a highlight of the communal year until the 1960s.

grime of industry. The middle classes spread into the countryside to make Fulwood, Dore and Totley the new desirable residential areas. Cheap land and regular tram and bus services facilitated the move out of town and between the wars Sheffield became even more polarised between its east and west ends.

The first half of the twentieth century was the heyday of local government. Housing and planning, highways and transport, public health, the supply of electricity, gas and water, education, poverty, policing, the fire service, markets, baths, parks, libraries and art galleries all came under their remit. By 1930 the killer diseases of Victorian England, such as measles, typhoid and tuberculosis were in retreat, death rates fell and life expectancy improved. The increased use of gas and electricity for both manufacturing and domestic purposes helped to clear up the towns and cities, though smoke everywhere polluted the atmosphere. When George Orwell visited Sheffield in the mid 1930s, he 'halted in the street and counted the factory chimneys I could see; there were thirty-three of them, but there would have been far more if the air had not been obscured by smoke'. He observed that, 'If at rare moments you stop smelling sulphur it is because you have begun smelling gas. Even the shallow river that runs through the town is usually bright yellow with some chemical or other'. One of the greatest achievements of the municipal councils was the provision of an abundant supply of water through major reservoir schemes. Sheffield, for instance, obtained its water from Victorian and twentieth-century reservoirs in the hills north-west of the city centre and from joint projects in the Derwent

Valley, where work at Ladybower was allowed to go ahead during the Second World War.

Leisure

In the inter-war years the chapel culture was still strong in the West Riding. The Wesleyans and the Primitive Methodists, in particular, experienced a further spurt of growth in the 1920s. The Whitsuntide processions were still major events in the northern calendar and Sunday school unions could arrange events that were attended by thousands. One of the most memorable in Halifax was the gathering on 28 June 1919 of children and teachers from 120 Sunday schools at Thrum Hall Rugby League ground in an act of thanksgiving after the signing of the Treaty of Versailles. The churches and chapels were often the focus of social life as well as religious observance, but during the 1920s the old attachments weakened as alternative leisure activities beckoned.

In spite of mass unemployment the inter-war period was a prosperous era for those who kept in work. They saw a steady rise in their standard of living in terms of more spacious housing and comfortable furniture, improved diet and better health, and enjoyable recreational activities as participants or spectators. Sports events attracted huge crowds as the Yorkshire County Cricket Club continued to dominate the county championship and local football teams, especially Huddersfield Town and Sheffield Wednesday, did well in the inter-war years. Meanwhile, local amateur leagues and cup competitions flourished as never before and rambling and cycling clubs explored the countryside.

The cinema provided a new form of mass entertainment, even in the small towns. Hull was typical of the larger towns and cities in having 30 cinemas with a total of 40,000 seats, a repertory theatre and three variety theatres with the exotic names of Alexandra, Tivoli and Palace; together they attracted 200,000 customers a week. Village halls provided venues for dancing, whist drives and occasional entertainments and trips to the seaside were organised by Sunday schools and other organisations. At home, some leisure time could be spent on reading daily newspapers or listening to the radio or a gramophone, activities that were not available to previous generations and which made people more aware of the wider world beyond that of their local community.

'I counted the factory chimneys I could see; there were thirty-three of them, but there would have been far more if the air had not been obscured by smoke.'

GEORGE ORWELL ON SHEFFIELD, 1930S

The Second World War

Although the casualties in the Second World War were dreadful, they were not on the same heavy scale as those in the First World War. This time, however, the civilian population were involved in those cities that bore the brunt of the German attacks. The devastation caused by bombs, especially in Hull, whose coastal position made it particularly vulnerable, multiplied the problems faced by councils that were trying to clear their slums. The worst raids on Hull came on 13 and 18 March 1941. By the end of the war over 5,000 houses had been destroyed there, together with half the central shopping area, over 3 million square feet of factory space, 27 churches and 14 schools or hospitals. Sheffield's steel works were another prime target, but the Luftwaffe failed to find them. Instead, they blitzed Sheffield city centre on 12/13 December 1940 and attacked again three days later. Terrible damage was inflicted on the city centre. Altogether, 2,906 houses and shops were destroyed or damaged beyond repair, 82,413 buildings were affected, 589 people were killed and 488 were seriously injured. The towns in the textile conurbation suffered too, but not to the same extent.

Population changes

Since the First World War every decennial census has noted an increase in the population of each of the three Ridings, though the phenomenal growth rates of the nineteenth century have not been maintained. Yorkshire's population growth in recent decades has in fact been lower than that of the national average. Between 1911 and 1971 the population of the West Riding rose from 3,131,357 to 3,785,015, that of the North Riding from 483,957 to 725,658, and that of the East Riding and York from 432,759 to 543,316. During those 60 years the population of the whole of Yorkshire increased from 4,048,073 to 5,053,989, reaching nearly as many as the total population of Scotland. The trend towards urban living continued, so that by 1971 the population of Sheffield was counted at 520,327, that of Leeds at 496,009, Bradford 294,177, Hull 285,970, Huddersfield 131,190 and York 104,782. By then, 16 Yorkshire boroughs had over 40,000 inhabitants each. Changing boundaries make comparisons between different authorities difficult, but during the 1920s and 1930s population growth had been most noticeable in the smaller towns and after the Second World War the suburban estates that were built either by a council or by private developers were the new growth areas. Yorkshire's Victorian cities have shared the familiar national experience of declining numbers as migrants moved from the old urban centres into the suburbs or the surrounding countryside.

A typical story is that of the County Borough of Halifax, whose population declined by 2.4 per cent from 101,594 in 1911 to 98,115 by 1931. Whereas in 1881 only one-fifth of Halifax's population were aged over 45, by 1921 the proportion was more than one-third. By 1981 the borough's population had fallen to 87,488, largely because of outward migration. By then Halifax formed part of the metropolitan borough of Calderdale, which had also experienced a decline in population, despite an influx of immigrants from the New Commonwealth who came to live in the St John's and Town wards of west central Halifax; by 1991 these immigrants formed 4.6 per cent of the local population. So the ethnic composition of the borough has changed and the age profile has moved towards the elderly.

After the Second World War the recovery of the worsted trade was restricted by a severe shortage of labour, particularly of women, as millowners found that they had to compete with newer and faster-growing industries which paid higher wages and provided better conditions and greater security. The main solution was to employ immigrants, firstly from Central and Eastern Europe, then from Pakistan and India, who were prepared to work at cheaper rates. Polish, Ukrainian and Hungarian refugees from the Soviet bloc, together with a new influx of Irish people, arrived in Yorkshire during the 1940s and 50s to work in the textile mills and the coal mines. Bradford had the largest proportion of Poles among its inhabitants than any other British town, but these European immigrants formed relatively small groups and were easily absorbed into existing communities.

Immigration of a totally different kind began in the late 1950s and continued on a large scale until the 1970s. Thousands of families from the New Commonwealth countries – from Pakistan, India, the West Indies and former British territories in Africa – arrived in search of work and an improved standard of living or to escape from persecution. They flocked to the large towns, particularly the West Riding mill towns, where they were prepared to take on menial jobs and work unsocial hours. Some immigrants found jobs on public transport or in the hospitals, but most made good the labour shortage in the staple industries, working on the night shift. In the early 1950s it was still rare to meet a coloured person in Yorkshire, but two decades later Asian or West Indian immigrants had taken over many of the old quarters of the Victorian cities. Their distinctive appearances, languages, religions and cultures made them a bewildering phenomenon to their neighbours. Over 80 per cent of the coloured immigrants in Yorkshire settled in the West Yorkshire conurbation. Though the West Riding had far fewer New Commonwealth immigrants than London or the Midlands, some of its towns attracted large numbers. Bradford had the third highest total of immigrants in the country and Leeds and Huddersfield were both among the first ten. These three towns accounted for nearly 90 per cent of those who came to live in the textile district. Further south, by 1968 Sheffield had about 5,000 West Indians and a similar number of Asians.

Sikh taxi drivers wait for customers in Huddersfield town centre. The West Riding textile towns now have large communities of New Commonwealth immigrants or their descendants.
PHOTOGRAPH: CARNEGIE, 2005

By 1966 the West Yorkshire conurbation had an estimated 53,000 New Commonwealth immigrants, of whom 25,500 were Pakistanis, 14,000 West Indians and 12,000 Indians. Bradford had 21,000 of these, Leeds 12,000, Huddersfield 12,000, and Dewsbury and Batley 2,000 each. By 1991 coloured immigrants formed 15.6 per cent of the population of Bradford Metropolitan Borough, 10.7 per cent of Kirklees, and 5.8 per cent of Leeds. The immigrants from Pakistan lived mostly in Bradford, Halifax, Dewsbury and Keighley, the Indians had settled in Bradford and Leeds, and to a lesser extent Batley and Dewsbury, and the West Indians had found homes in Leeds and Huddersfield and sometimes in Bradford. In Leeds, many of the Caribbean and Asian immigrants settled in Chapeltown and Harehills and parts of Burley and Hyde Park. In Bradford the new families settled in the inner wards, so that by 1966 Listerhills and Exchange had probably the highest proportions of immigrants of any local electoral area in the country; 1,275 of the 1,417 lodging houses known to the council were owned or occupied by Indians and Pakistanis. These lodgings were mostly large houses formerly occupied by middle-class families and much sub-divided after their original owners had moved out of the inner city. By the mid 1960s the transition from a migrant labour force to an ethnic community was well under way, so that by the time of the 1971 census returns the estimated number of New Commonwealth citizens living in Bradford was 30,000 (10 per cent). Within such towns, immigrants from particular districts in their original countries tended to flock together and, as with Irish

left Humber Bridge. At the time of its construction, this was the longest single-span suspension bridge in the world and the first to use towers of reinforced concrete rather than steel. Designed by Freeman, Fox & Partners, consulting engineers of London, the bridge was opened in 1981, having taken nine years to build.
PHOTOGRAPH: CARNEGIE, 2005

right The deep cutting and large embankment on the M62 just west of Huddersfield, with Scammonden reservoir just visible on the right.
PHOTOGRAPH: CARNEGIE, 2005

immigration a century before, many of them settled in ghettos in the inner city. By 1971 66 per cent of Bradford Asians lived in four wards of the city centre. The Bangladeshi Asians tended to settle between Manningham Lane and Midland Road, the Sikh community largely settled in Bradford Moor, while Mirpuri Pakistanis were widespread but were found principally in the Manchester Road area of Bowling. As families grew in size, the total numbers continued to grow long after the restrictions on immigration posed by the Commonwealth Immigration Act of 1962 and later legislation. By 1987 Bradford contained 64,000 South Asians, of whom 43,600 were from Pakistan and 15,800 from India. The widespread rioting and looting by young, unemployed, alienated Asians at Manningham in 1995 became a matter of national concern, but in other places, notably Huddersfield, race relations were good at the end of the twentieth century. In other parts of Yorkshire, many local communities still have no inhabitants of New Commonwealth descent.

The decline of manufacturing

The Second World War had re-emphasised the value of the traditional manufacturing base and after 1945 the mining, metallurgical and textile industries remained dominant in Yorkshire. A new era of full employment seemed assured, but the full force of foreign competition was soon to be felt. During the 1960s and 70s many old-established firms went out of business and major enterprises were forced to reduce their scale of operations. Another traditional source of employment to disappear at this time was the Hull fishing industry, which received a death blow in 1978 when Iceland imposed a ban on fishing for cod within 200 miles of its shores. Hull remained Britain's third largest port and the long-dreamed of Humber Bridge was completed, but the docks handled

Old warehouses now stand derelict in Quebec Street, only about a quarter of a mile from Bradford Town Hall, after the collapse of much of the textile industry.
PHOTOGRAPH: CARNEGIE, 2005

far less trade than London or Liverpool. Meanwhile, throughout Britain new technology replaced many traditional crafts and greatly reduced the need for unskilled labour. The economic and demographic trends were away from the old northern industrial centres to London and south-eastern England.

Traditionally the British woollen and worsted industry contained numerous small family units of production. The bubble burst in 1950–51 when Australian farmers began to charge higher prices for their wool. Many small businesses collapsed and others were forced to merge. The brief recovery at the end of the 1960s was followed by the international oil crisis of 1974. Between 1978 and 1981 23,000 manufacturing jobs were lost in Bradford, 16,000 of them in textiles and engineering, and the great Victorian mills at Saltaire and Manningham were closed. When the staple industry suffered such losses, other local firms were forced out of business.

As manufacturing declined the service sector of the economy began to grow, particularly after 1971. Manufacturing had provided 70 per cent of the jobs in Calderdale in 1951, but 40 years later it employed only 38 per cent. In the meantime, jobs in the services had grown from 24 per cent to 57 per cent. A fundamental shift had taken place in the economy. Within the manufacturing sector the decline of the textile industry was dramatic, for whereas it had employed almost 36 per cent of the total workforce in 1951, it provided jobs for a mere 5 per cent in 1991. The associated clothing industry saw its workforce fall almost 75 per cent during the same period and engineering jobs fell by 25 per cent. The diversity of small industries in Calderdale made the decline of manufacturing more protracted than in other parts of West Yorkshire, but unemployment still reached 13 per cent there in 1983. A major blow was the closure of Crossley's carpet mills at Dean Clough in 1984.

The workforce in the steel and cutlery industries were fully employed throughout the 1950s and 60s. In 1951 the city of Sheffield was unusual in having 57.5 per cent of its workforce employed in manufacturing, 44 per cent of them in the traditional heavy and light trades. At that time, women formed 32 per cent of the gainfully employed labour force in Sheffield and employment in the service sector had risen to 29.6 per cent. No other city in Britain was so dependent upon the fortunes of its staple industries. The ethos and structure of the cutlery industry remained Victorian and it was soon undercut by the cheap products of the Far East. By the early 1990s the number of Sheffield cutlers had fallen from 10,000 to 2–3,000 and just a few firms remained in business. The tool industry experienced the same difficulties and many of the numerous small family firms collapsed, the old hand skills disappeared, and by 1989 the workforce was reduced to 3,650. Meanwhile, the steel industry was faced with a world glut as other counties built their own furnaces and rolling mills. A calamitous decline in demand for steel in the late 1970s and 1980s cost thousands of jobs. The steel industry's problems were not the result of complacency, for about £150 million had been spent on post-war modernisation. The most impressive developments were United Steel's new Templeborough Electric Melting Shop, which opened in 1963 with a capacity of over 1.25 million tons per annum, and the English Steel Corporation's new £26 million Tinsley Park Works, which opened in the same year. In 1964 the ESC employed 14,140 workers, Steel, Peech & Tozer had 9,315, Samuel Fox 7,679, Firth-Brown 7,500, Park Gate 6,200, Hadfield's 4,000, Balfour Darwin 3,500, Brown Bayley's 3,500, Osborn 3,000, Arthur Lee 2,700, Jessop-Saville 2,550, Edgar Allen 2,000 and Saunderson Kayser 1,900. These were major enterprises by any standard at the time. But by the 1970s Sheffield no longer produced as much alloy steel as did countries as diverse as Brazil, Italy, Spain and Sweden. The world market had a surplus of steel and the local industry was forced into re-structuring. When British Steel Stainless was created in 1976 its Shepcote Lane site was developed into the biggest purpose-built stainless steel plant in Europe.

From 1979 Sheffield's manufacturing base shrank dramatically. Massive redundancies were announced and some famous steel and engineering works ceased production. The national steel strike that was called in 1981 ended in failure. Soon afterwards, the English Steel Corporation's Tinsley Park Works closed and production was concentrated at Stocksbridge. By 1987 the unemployment rate had reached a peak of 16.3 per cent of the registered workforce and in parts of Sheffield a very much higher proportion were out of work. The number of steel workers in the Sheffield–Rotherham district fell from 60,000 in 1971 to 16,000 in 1987 and to below 10,000 by the mid 1990s. Meanwhile, a similar tale was unfolding on Teesside. By the end of the twentieth century two-thirds of the jobs in Sheffield were in the service sector and only one-quarter of the workforce found employment in manufacturing. The leading employers were all in the service sector: the City Council, the Sheffield Health Authority and the two Universities. The Meadowhall shopping centre, which was built on the site of Hadfield's East Hecla works, employed 7,000 workers, but many of the new jobs went to women, for less pay, and often on a part-time basis. Even so, the local steel industry is still of inter-national importance. Sheffield and Rotherham have some of the most advanced and productive steel-melting facilities in the world and almost all of Britain's special engineering and stainless steels are made here. Modern technology has destroyed jobs, but more steel is now made in Sheffield than during the Second World War.

The coal industry also underwent major changes after the war. On 1 January 1947 the newly established National Coal Board took over a workforce of 704,000 men who mined 184 million tons of coal a year in 958 pits. By then, open-cast mining had become a large-scale business, with 10 million tons, or about one-third of national output, mined in Yorkshire during the 3¾ years leading up to nationalisation. The most productive sites were around Wentworth, where the Barnsley seam was over 10 feet thick. The National Coal Board operated in a seller's market until 1956–57 when the effects of cheap imported crude oil were first felt. Uneconomic pits were closed and machines replaced men until by 1976 only 247,100 worked in the nation's mines. As the

This view of the Barrrow Colliery and coke ovens, south of Barnsley, was taken from Blacker in 1969, almost 100 years after the pit was sunk and a new mining community was established at the southern edge of Worsbrough township. Most of the old farming parishes in the Dearne Valley were transformed in this way during the Victorian period. Now all the pits are closed and a regeneration programme is gradually transforming the district. The Barrow colliery has been levelled, large numbers of trees have been planted on the site, and the railway has been converted into part of the Trans-Pennine trail. In the neighbouring parish of Wombwell the RSPB and other bodies are managing the low-lying wetlands for public recreational uses. Much of the Dearne Valley is becoming green again. Meanwhile, a new road, linked to the M1, and other government and European Union initiatives are helping the former mining settlements to adapt to the new services-led economy.

older pits became exhausted or were declared uneconomic, the centre of the Yorkshire coalfield moved further east. All the pits on the Silkstone seam and many that worked the Barnsley seam were closed. When the era of cheap oil came to an end in the early 1970s the bargaining power of the National Union of Miners was strengthened and successful strikes restored the colliers to their premier position as industrial wage-earners. The Yorkshire coalfield was one of the most militant in Britain and it was here that the national 1984–85 strike was sparked off by the threatened closure of Cortonwood colliery. It was this militancy as much as the area's central position that had encouraged the NUM to move its headquarters from London to Sheffield. In the aftermath of the failure of the strike most of the Yorkshire pits were closed. A mighty industry was brought to its knees, with disastrous consequences for those who lived in the pit villages that had sprung up in Victorian times. At the beginning of the twentieth century coal mining had been the nation's largest single occupation; at the close of the century only a few thousand were left. In parishes where the landscape has reverted to its former character, now that colliery muck stacks have been levelled or disguised by grass and trees, it is hard to believe that coal mining was once the major occupation. The so-called 'traditional' pit villages are not in fact very old when placed in the context of Yorkshire's ancient settlements, but they can now be viewed as an historic phenomenon that transformed the nature of the West Riding during the Victorian and Edwardian era but came to an end in the late twentieth century. A major reclamation scheme is providing the Dearne Valley with a new economy and character, but most of the former pit villages are struggling to acquire a different identity, and unemployment rates remain high.

Regeneration

The desirability of attracting new industries and of reducing the dependence on a few forms of employment was evident to all, but the legacy of industrial dereliction – of colliery muck stacks, vast acres of despoiled land, decaying buildings and rusting machinery, pollution and an all-pervading grime – made the old manufacturing districts uninviting to investors. In recent years reclamation schemes and financial inducements to start new businesses in depressed areas have made an impact, but official surveys of consumer trends consistently show that most Yorkshire families are well below the national average in terms of purchasing power. Regions such as the West Riding which relied heavily on traditional industries fell behind in relative terms even though their inhabitants have shared in the unprecedented rise in national standards of living since the 1950s.

The Town and Country Planning Act of 1947 required local authorities to prepare development plans for their districts. These included zones for the location of industry and light industrial estates, other areas set aside for new housing estates, and plans for ring roads and other methods of relieving traffic congestion. Private development was forbidden unless the consent of the local authority had been given. Councils acquired powers of compulsory land purchase and were awarded large government grants to demolish slums, preserve buildings of historic and architectural interest, designate green belts, build new bus stations and multi-storey car parks, and convert streets into pedestrian precincts. The 1950s saw the beginnings of a wholesale redevelopment of city centres. Within a couple of decades the local identities of the West Ridings boroughs had been lessened in a new environment of glass and concrete, with national or multinational department stores, supermarkets, multi-storey car parks and ring roads. The old urban centres had long ceased to be residential areas and reliable public transport and the growing number of

Although Bradford retains many of its fine Victorian buildings, much has been replaced by concrete-and-glass structures that have no local identity. The individual character of the West Riding's textile towns is less evident than in the past.

PHOTOGRAPH: CARNEGIE, 2005

The rise of superstores
and new uses for old
buildings: Morrison's car
park at Skipton looks out
towards converted mill
buildings.
PHOTOGRAPH: CARNEGIE, 2005

family cars hastened the movement to the outer suburbs and beyond. Many an old rural community was engulfed in the urban sprawl and environmental groups sprang up to defend the countryside by successfully advocating the creation of national parks and of green belts around the towns. The Peak District National Park, the first to be opened in 1951, included the Pennine parts of south-west Yorkshire, and the Yorkshire Dales and North York Moors parks followed soon afterwards. But the most astonishing and welcome change of all was the transformation of the grimy Victorian towns and cities by the vigorous application of the 1956 Clean Air Act and the later use of government grants to clean public buildings.

In the rush to modernise between 1955 and 1965 much that would now be regarded of considerable architectural value was lost. Some of Bradford's finest Victorian buildings were sacrificed when parts of the historic core of the city were replaced by drab, grey buildings in the standard designs of the developers. The disappearance of many of the mill chimneys and Nonconformist chapels, which were such dominant visual features at the beginning of the twentieth century, took away much of the character of the textile towns. Some industrial buildings were preserved because they were divided into smaller units for new, small firms, often those which specialised in information technology, but many other properties simply became derelict eyesores. On the other hand, some new enterprises were spectacularly successful. The Leeds and Bradford airport at Yeadon (which had been requisitioned for the war effort as soon as it was completed in 1939) was opened as a joint municipal enterprise in 1959. Bradford's Ken Morrison became a multi-millionaire owner of a supermarket chain; Jonathan Silver transformed Saltaire mill into a vibrant retail and tourist centre; and Ernest Hall revitalised the Dean Clough mills.

As the textile industry declined, Halifax turned itself into a financial services centre. The Halifax Building Society opened its new administrative head-quarters in the town in 1973 and 20 years later it was by far the largest private employer in Calderdale, with a workforce of 3,134 people. Attracting tourists was another option in the regeneration programme. The Piece Hall survived a demolition threat and upon its restoration it was re-opened in 1976 with a market and a variety of small retail outlets. By 1982 Shibden Hall and Bankfield

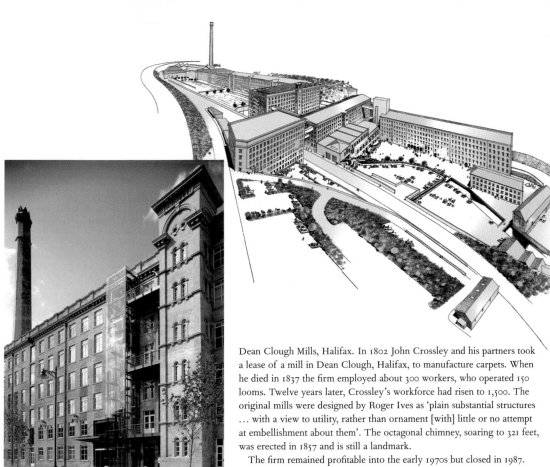

Dean Clough Mills, Halifax. In 1802 John Crossley and his partners took a lease of a mill in Dean Clough, Halifax, to manufacture carpets. When he died in 1837 the firm employed about 300 workers, who operated 150 looms. Twelve years later, Crossley's workforce had risen to 1,500. The original mills were designed by Roger Ives as 'plain substantial structures ... with a view to utility, rather than ornament [with] little or no attempt at embellishment about them'. The octagonal chimney, soaring to 321 feet, was erected in 1857 and is still a landmark.

The firm remained profitable into the early 1970s but closed in 1987. Since then, the complex of buildings has been put to other uses in a remarkable regeneration scheme led by Ernest Hall.

DEAN CLOUGH LTD

Museum were each getting 50,000 visitors a year and the opening of the Eureka children's museum was another success story. By 1998 day-trippers to Halifax were spending an estimated £12 million a year and overnight visitors added another £3 million to the local economy. Halifax's shops continued to serve the neighbourhood, but by the 1990s the competition of out-of-town shopping centres and supermarkets was causing concern. As in all other towns, the streets were congested with the greatly increased volume of traffic and drastic schemes to relieve the problem had to be implemented. Halifax's answer was the opening in 1973 of Burdock Way, a ring road with a massive concrete flyover.

In 1951 half of the registered workforce in Leeds were employed in manufacturing industries, especially tailoring, engineering and textiles, but already well over two-fifths were now in the service sector. The decline in manufacturing continued apace during the second half of the twentieth century, but Leeds had low levels of unemployment until the mid 1970s. During the 1980s the number of Leeds people who worked in manufacturing industries dropped to 60,000, while employment in the financial sector, for example, grew by two-thirds, reaching 45,000 jobs by 1991. A strong institutional base was provided by the headquarters of two of the country's leading building societies – the Leeds

Halifax Building Society Offices. The new administrative headquarters of Britain's leading building society was designed by the Building Design Partnership and constructed by John Laing Construction Ltd in 1972–73. Rising over its neighbours in Commercial Street at one end of the town, its domineering bulk has aroused controversy. It has all the confidence of the Victorian millowners who shaped the West Riding textile towns, but the stark, arrogant design can also be overwhelming.

COURTESY OF HALIFAX PLC

Permanent and the Leeds & Holbeck – and by the Yorkshire Bank and a branch of the Bank of England. A rapid growth of jobs in accountancy and legal practices added to Leeds' reputation as a city that moved with the times. By the end of the century, six of the United Kingdom's top legal firms were based in Leeds and 16 of the largest accountancy practices had offices there.

By 1990 the largest employers in the city were the public service organisations and the privatised public utilities: Leeds City Council employed 35,000 workers, the Area Health Authority 14,000, the University of Leeds 4,500, the Post Office 3,900, Leeds Metropolitan University 2,400, British Gas 2,200, British Telecom 2,000, Central Benefits Agency and the Departments of Health and Social Security 2,000, Yorkshire Electricity 1,800, and so on. Leeds had also become a media centre, with television studios and soap-opera filming at nearby locations. At the end of the century the city's success was marked by the decision of the fashionable London business, Harvey Nicholls, to open a shop there.

Sheffield's city centre had to be redesigned after the destruction of the blitz and its appearance was changed for the better by the vigorous application of the Clean Air Act of 1956. The Town Hall was cleaned in 1959, the cathedral in 1964, and buildings blackened by soot and grime became a thing of the past.

Sheffield Town Hall (*right*) was the first public building in the city to have its decades of grime removed. The Cathedral (*left*) was cleaned a few years later. The wires that frame the picture are those of the Supertram system, which has provided first-class public transport since the mid 1990s.

PHOTOGRAPHS: CARNEGIE, 2004

Soon, the whole of the urban parts of the West Riding were transformed in this way. Sheffield was no longer 'the foulest town in England' but the cleanest industrial city in western Europe, set in some of the most attractive countryside in Britain. The arrival of the M1 motorway and the prolific office building of the 1960s and 70s brought major economic benefits. New shops, sports centres, discos and clubs, the Crucible theatre, the University and the Polytechnic, and the new Hallamshire Hospital exuded confidence before the catastrophic downturn in the fortunes of local industry. By 1980 a group of left-wing councillors, led by David Blunkett, were dominant in the Labour-controlled council and loud in their opposition to the Conservative government, but in the mid 1980s a new mood of realism prevailed and the council began to cooperate with private enterprise to regenerate the east end of the city. In 1988 the Sheffield Development Corporation was given a £50 million government grant and full control of planning from the Wicker Arches and the old canal basin by the city centre as far as the M1. A new Don Valley Link Road cost £30 million and the rest of the money was spent on infrastructure and landscaping, offices, and business and retail parks, placed in attractive sites with ample parking. In 1990 the Meadowhall shopping centre, a huge enterprise that provided totally enclosed shopping with free parking for 11,000 vehicles and 1.2 million square feet of shops, was opened on the site of Hadfield's East Hecla steel works, by the M1 motorway, with train and bus stops nearby. It has been a huge success. Sheffield's hosting of the 1991 World Student Games, held in new venues such as the Don Valley Stadium and the Ponds Forge swimming and diving pool, was a psychological turning point, though a costly one. The supertrams that began to run in the mid 1990s, the refurbishment of the Lyceum theatre, the conversion of the Polytechnic into Sheffield Hallam University, the opening of the Millennium Gallery and the Winter Gardens, and the re-designing of the Peace Gardens as a public space all helped to give the city a more modern appearance.

Park Hill Flats, Sheffield, in 1985. When these flats were built in the 1950s and 1960s, they seemed the answer to the city's housing problem. Rising dramatically on the skyline across the River Sheaf from the city centre, the scheme provided houses, shops, schools and pubs for 3,500 people. It attracted international attention but by the 1980s high-rise flats had become unpopular.

Housing

The two Metropolitan County Councils of South Yorkshire and West Yorkshire, which were created in 1974, lasted only 12 years. All powers were then transferred to the single-tier Metropolitan District Councils that had been formed at the same time. Improved housing remained the leading priority for local authorities. The 1951 census had found that 85,000 of Sheffield's households did not have a fixed bath and a national housing survey of 1956 revealed that, together with east Lancashire and the Durham coalfield, the West Yorkshire conurbation had the largest proportion of obsolescent housing in England and Wales. One in every eight houses – twice the national average – was considered unfit for people to live in. After the Second World War the policy of building suburban housing was continued on the Buttershaw, Woodside and Allerton estates around Bradford, where a total of 3,381 houses were built alongside shopping and recreational centres. Between 1950 and 1962 a further 10,139 houses and flats were built by the corporation on more suburban estates at Thorpe Edge, Bierley, Holme Wood and Netherlands Avenue. By 1962 Bradford had managed to demolish 20,000 of its worst 30,000 houses, but in the smaller towns the pace of renewal was slower. The drive to clear the slums seemed never ending. The physical limits of the city of Leeds were greatly enlarged as suburbs spread into the countryside. The city of 21,593 acres in 1900 was turned into the Leeds Metropolitan District of 134,916 acres in 1974. In 1912 the townships of Roundhay, Seacroft, Shadwell and part of Cross Gates were brought within the city's bounds, in 1919 Middleton was annexed,

One of the pair of Lister's Mills at Manningham in Bradford in the early stages of refurbishment. These enormous mills were designed in Italianate style by Lockwood & Mowson, Bradford's leading architects, and opened in 1873. One of the great industrial monuments of the Victorian era, the mills have long stood empty, but are now being restored and converted for residential and commercial uses by a leading company in this field, Urban Splash. Elsewhere, too, mills have been successfully converted into apartments.

PHOTOGRAPH: CARNEGIE, 2005

East Riddlesden Hall, *c.*1920. E. Riley's painting captures the rural setting of one of the West Riding's finest vernacular houses of the mid seventeenth century. It was built for a wealthy clothier, James Murgatroyd of nearby Warley, who bought the property in 1638 and soon began to extend the old house. His first phase was completed in 1642, just before the outbreak of the Civil War, and his Royalist sentiments were expressed by a carving of the king's head and the inscription: 'Vive le Roi 1642'. The fireplace in the south room has a puzzling inscription: 'They Maides of Coign. in A 1648'. The view is across the lake from the gateway at the northern entrance to the property (which now belongs to the National Trust).

followed by Adel-cum-Eccup in 1925, and Woolley, Temple Newsam, Eccup and part of Austhorpe in 1927. Despite strong resistance from neighbouring authorities, further expansion occurred in 1937.

Sheffield's failure to secure land in neighbouring authorities forced the council to build at relatively high densities on difficult and sloping sites. In 1952 they obtained compulsory purchase orders for land within their boundaries at Gleadless, Stannington, Bradway, Totley and Foxhill and in the following year work began on major slum-clearance schemes in or close to the centre of the city. Houses were cleared for new dwellings at Park Hill, Woodside, Netherthorpe, Burngreave and Norfolk Park and work began on new sites at Gleadless, Greenhill, Norton and Woodhouse. By 1960 12,500 council houses had been completed and many private houses had been erected on the fringes of the city. The housing estate that provided 4,000 dwellings in the Gleadless Valley by the mid 1960s was one of the most successful and popular, for it was carefully designed to merge into the existing landscape, a fine setting with mature trees and extensive views. But the council's next scheme was much more ambitious and controversial. In the late 1950s and early 1960s 3,500 dwellings were constructed in high-rise blocks of reinforced concrete at Park Hill and Hyde Park, close to the city centre and places of work. Inspired by Le Corbusier's concept of 'street decks' or 'streets in the sky' and by Quarry Hill Flats in Leeds, they rose dramatically on the skyline to the east of the city centre. At Park Hill former neighbours were re-housed together and provided with shops, schools and pubs, so as to maintain a sense of community. Other high-rise estates were soon built elsewhere in the inner city, notably the even higher Hyde Park flats nearby, which were opened in 1966. The Park Hill housing scheme attracted international attention, but by the 1980s high-rise flats were deeply unpopular and many have now been demolished. When Sheffield's working-class suburb of Darnall was rebuilt in the 1970s and 80s the modern design was fitted into traditional terraces to try to keep the old community spirit. Everything had to be done within tight government cost controls. The housing programme supplied 2,5000 dwellings each year by the mid 1960s, but this was still insufficient to meet demand. A breakthrough came in 1967, when the city's boundaries were extended southwards into the Derbyshire countryside and Mosborough was chosen as the site for Sheffield's 'new town'.

Rural Yorkshire

Many of Yorkshire's villages have also grown considerably since the 1960s. Only the old estate villages and those now designated as conservation areas are confined within their old limits. Within the last few decades the provision of electricity, gas, piped water, water closets, telephones, radio and television has dramatically improved rural standards of living and has reduced the isolation of country life. But the motor car has proved a mixed blessing as villagers can now shop in distant supermarkets, so forcing the closure of local shops and the withdrawal of services such as regular buses, and because properties have been bought by outsiders as weekend cottages or holiday homes. The rural population has become elderly as young couples find it difficult to afford the rising prices of homes in their native villages and have to move out to the towns and cities. But some rural communities have benefited from the enthusiasms of new residents who have restored houses and have taken an active part in village social life.

In the upland parts of Yorkshire farmers still follow the traditional concerns of the past 300 years. The Dales farmer, for instance, keeps dairy cattle on the lower slopes and sheep on the higher land, though since 1956 all Wensleydale cheese has been made in factories rather than on the farm. Here, and on the Pennine foothills further south, farms remain small, family businesses and often the farmer has to take another job to earn a sufficient living. The National Trust and Yorkshire's three National Parks, together with effective conservation groups, led by the Council for the Preservation of Rural England, have done a great deal to preserve historic landscapes in these upland districts. On the North York Moors the biggest change has occurred since the 1920s, when the afforestation programme began; by 1959 about 23,000 acres were covered with trees. Elsewhere, the management of deciduous woodland declined after the First World War when demand for traditional products fell. It is in the arable parts of the countryside that the greatest changes have taken place over the last 50 years, as hedges have been destroyed to create huge fields and as silos and other modern outbuildings have replaced the old barns and stables. The mechanisation of cultivation and harvesting continued apace as central government and European Union subsidies made farming a profitable business. In the lowland vales the mixture of livestock and corn is much the same as before, except that more barley is now grown and more emphasis is placed on cash root crops such as potatoes, sugar beet and carrots; the bright yellow fields of early summer show how much oil rapeseed is grown in response to generous subsidies. In Holderness more than 60 per cent of the land is under the plough at any one time, for corn yields well, but dairy cows remain important as Hull is so near. Corn and sheep are still the mainstays on the Wolds, where an arterial grid supplies water to the farmsteads and fields. But as the twentieth century drew to a close it became apparent that farming had become less profitable and that too much land was under the plough. The closing of access to the countryside upon the outbreak of foot-and-mouth disease made it obvious that rural areas were increasingly dependent upon tourism and leisure activities to make a living and that farming alone was often no longer a viable option.

Yorkshire has become a major tourist attraction, with millions of visitors flocking each year to York and other historic towns, to the Cistercian abbeys of Fountains and Rievaulx, and to the great houses in the countryside. Castle Howard, Burton Agnes, Burton Constable, Bramham Park and Newby Hall have to attract summer tourists to remain family homes; the National Trust has taken over Beningborough Hall, Nostell Priory and some smaller houses such as Nunnington and East Riddlesden; English Heritage has restored Brodsworth Hall and is responsible for some of the county's medieval castles; and local authorities accepted responsibility for Temple Newsam, Bolling Hall, Cusworth Hall, Cannon Hall and other, smaller houses and converted the halls at Bretton, High Melton, Wentworth Woodhouse, Wentworth Castle, Woolley and Wortley into educational establishments. Elsewhere, gentry houses, such as those at Heckmondwike, Kildwick and Middlethorpe, have been turned into restaurants and inns. An interest and pride in historic buildings has blossomed and many old halls and manor houses that had declined to mere farmhouses or had been converted into cottages have been restored with all the added advantages of modern comforts.

The great changes which have occurred in all aspects of life since the Second World War and particularly since the late 1950s are a national rather than a regional story. In such matters as social attitudes, education, religion and leisure activities Yorkshire has conformed to national trends. The plight of the poor was improved radically after the war by the establishment of the Welfare State and by an international rise in the standard of living experienced by all western democracies. The late twentieth century saw a consumer revolution brought about by the mass-production of cheap, high-quality goods and an un-precedented rise in the purchasing power of ordinary families. Sports facilities, garden centres and DIY stores have sprouted everywhere. The advent of quick communications, cheap travel and mass culture has weakened regional identities and has reduced the influence of the provinces on the great social and political issues of the day. Yet despite the local government boundary changes of 1974 Yorkshire remains a recognisable entity, not only to its residents but to outsiders, whether or not they approve of distinctive Yorkshire characteristics and well-known personalities. In the second half of the twentieth century the novels and plays of Alan Bennett, John Braine, Stan Barstow, Barry Hines, David Storey and Keith Waterhouse brought national acclaim for a group of West Riding authors. Local roots have also been important for Henry Moore, Barbara Hepworth and David Hockney who achieved international distinction in the arts, for Ted Hughes, the Poet Laureate, and for many who have been successful in other fields, notably Henry Asquith and Harold Wilson, two West Riding men who became Prime Ministers. Yorkshire remains firmly in the public mind even if it no longer survives as an administrative unit and many of its inhabitants still bear the distinctive surnames that were formed within the county several hundred years ago.

Select bibliography

K. J. Allison, *The East Riding of Yorkshire Landscape* (London: Hodder & Stoughton, 1976)

M. Allison, *History of Appleton-le-Moors* (Easingwold: privately published, 2003)

L. Ambler, *Old Halls and Manor Houses of Yorkshire* (Holmfirth: Toll House reprints, 1987)

J. C. Atkinson, *Forty Years in a Moorland Parish* (London: Macmillan, 1891)

G. E. Aylmer and R. Cant (eds), *A History of York Minster* (Oxford University Press, 1977)

R. N. Bailey, *Viking Age Sculpture* (London: Collins, 1980)

K. C. Barraclough, *Steelmaking Before Bessemer*, 2 vols (London: The Metals Society, 1984)

M. W. Beresford, 'The Lost Villages of Yorkshire', part II, *Yorkshire Archaeological Journal*, 38 (1955), 215–40

M. W. Beresford, *New Towns of the Middle Ages* (London, Lutterworth Press, 1967)

M. W. Beresford, *East End, West End: The Face of Leeds During Urbanisation, 1684–1842* (Leeds: Thoresby Society, 1988)

M. W. Beresford and H. P. R. Finberg, *English Medieval Boroughs: A Handlist* (Newton Abbot: David & Charles, 1973)

M. W. Beresford and J. K. St Joseph, *Medieval England: An Aerial Survey* (Cambridge University Press, second edition, 1979)

C. Binfield *et al.*, *The History of the City of Sheffield, 1843–1993*, 3 vols (Sheffield Academic Press, 1993)

J. Binns, *A Place of Great Importance: Scarborough in the Civil Wars, 1640–1660* (Preston: Carnegie, 1996)

J. Binns, *The History of Scarborough* (Pickering: Blackthorn Press, 2001)

D. W. Black, I. H. Goodall and I. R. Pattison, *Houses of the North York Moors* (London: HMSO, 1987)

R. Brown *et al.*, *A General View of the Agriculture of the West Riding* (London, 1799)

A. Burl, 'The Devil's Arrows', *Yorkshire Archaeological Journal*, 63 (1991), 1–24

S. Burt and K. Grady, *The Illustrated History of Leeds* (Derby: Breedon Books, 1994)

J. Burton, *The Monastic Order in Yorkshire, 1069–1215* (Cambridge University Press, 1999)

J. Burton, *The Yorkshire Nunneries in the Twelfth and Thirteenth Centuries* (York: Borthwick Papers, 56, 1979)

L. Caffyn, *Workers' Housing in West Yorkshire, 1750–1920* (London: HMSO, 1986)

S. Caunce, *Amongst Farm Horses: The Horselads of East Yorkshire* (Stroud: Sutton, 1991)

J. Chartres and K. Honeyman (eds), *Leeds City Businesses* (Leeds University Press, 1993)

M. Clarke, *The Leeds and Liverpool Canal: A History and Guide* (Lancaster, Carnegie, 1994, 2003)

J. T. Cliffe, *The Yorkshire Gentry from the Reformation to the Civil War* (London, Athlone Press, 1969)

G. Coppack, *Fountains Abbey* (English Heritage, 1993)

D. Crouch and T. Pearson (eds), *Medieval Scarborough: Studies in Trade and Civic Life* (Yorkshire Archaeological Society, 2001)

W. B. Crump and G. Ghorbal, *History of the Huddersfield Woollen Industry* (Huddersfield: Tolson Museum, 1935)

H. C. Darby and I. S. Maxwell, *The Domesday Geography of Northern England* (Cambridge University Press, 1962)

R. Davis, *The Trade and Shipping of Hull, 1500–1700* (York: East Riding Local History Series, 17, 1964)

D. Defoe, *A Tour through the Whole Island of Great Britain* (London: Everyman edition, 1962)

A. G. Dickens, *Lollards and Protestants in the Diocese of York, 1509–58* (Oxford University Press, 1959)

R. B. Dobson, *The Jews of Medieval York and the Massacre of March 1190* (York: Borthwick Papers, 45, 1974)

B. F. Duckham, *The Yorkshire Ouse: The History of a River Navigation* (Newton Abbot: David & Charles, 1967)

B. English, *The Lords of Holderness, 1086–1260* (Oxford University Press, 1979)

M. L. Faull and S. A. Moorhouse (eds), *West Yorkshire: An Archaeological Survey to AD 1500*, 3 vols (Wakefield: West Yorkshire County Council, 1981)

G. Fellows-Jensen, 'Place-names and Settlement in the North Riding of Yorkshire', *Northern History*, XVIII (1978), 19–46

G. Fellows-Jensen, *Scandinavian Personal Names in Lincolnshire and Yorkshire* (Copenhagen: Akademisk Forlag, 1968)

G. Fellows-Jensen, *Scandinavian Settlement Names in Yorkshire* (Copenhagen: Akademisk Forlag, 1972)

C. Fenton-Thomas, *The Forgotten Landscapes of the Yorkshire Wolds* (Stroud: Tempus, 2005)

R. Fieldhouse and B. Jennings (eds), *A History of Richmond and Swaledale* (Chichester: Phillimore, 1978)

G. Firth, *A History of Bradford* (Chichester: Phillimore, 1997)

A. Fleming, *Swaledale: Valley of the Wild River* (Edinburgh University Press, 1998)

P. Frank, *Yorkshire Fisherfolk* (Chichester: Phillimore, 2002)

D. Fraser (ed.), *A History of Modern Leeds* (Manchester University Press, 1980)

H. Geake and J. Kenny (eds), *Early Deira: Archaeological Studies of the East Riding of Yorkshire in the Fourth to the Ninth Centuries AD* (Oxford: Oxbow, 2000)

C. Giles, *Rural Houses of West Yorkshire, 1400–1830* (London: HMSO, 1986)

C. Giles and I. H. Goodall, *Yorkshire Textile Mills, 1770–1930* (London: HMSO, 1992)

E. Gillett and K. A. MacMahon, *A History of Hull* (Oxford University Press, 1980)

J. Goodchild, *The Coal Kings of Yorkshire* (Wakefield Historical Society, 1978)

J. A. Green, *The Aristocracy of Norman England* (Cambridge University Press, 1997)

W. Greenwell, 'Early Iron Age Burials in Yorkshire', *Archaeologia*, 60 (1907), 251–324

D. Hadley, *The Northern Danelaw: Its Social Structure, c.800–1100* (London and New York: Leicester University Press, 2000)

H. Haigh (ed.), *Huddersfield: A Most Handsome Town* (Huddersfield: Kirklees Cultural Services, 1992)

I. Hall (ed.), *Samuel Buck's Yorkshire Sketchbook* (Wakefield Historical Publications, 1979)

R. A. Hall, *Viking Age York* (London: English Heritage/Batsford, 1994)

C. Hallas, *Rural Responses to Industrialisation: The North Yorkshire Pennines, 1790–1914* (Bern: Lang, 1999)

A. Harding, 'Prehistoric and Early Medieval Activity on Danby Rigg', *Archaeological Journal* 151 (1994), 16–97

J. A. Hargreaves, *Halifax* (Lancaster: Carnegie, 1999, 2003)

B. J. D. Harrison and B. Hutton, *Vernacular Houses in North Yorkshire and Cleveland* (Edinburgh University Press, 1984)

S. Harrison, *The History of Driffield* (Pickering: Blackthorn Press, 2002)

M. Hartley and J. Ingilby, *Life and Tradition in the Yorkshire Dales* (Otley: Smith Settle, 1997)

M. Hartley and J. Ingilby, *Life and Tradition in the Moorlands of North-East Yorkshire* (Otley: Smith Settle, 1990)

J. C. Harvey, 'Common Field and Enclosure in the Lower Dearne Valley', *Yorkshire Archaeological Journal*, 46 (1974), 110–27

M. Harvey, 'Planned Field Systems in Eastern Yorkshire: Some Thoughts on their Origin', *Agricultural History Review*, 31 (1983), 91–103

C. Haselgrove et al., 'Stanwick, North Yorkshire', *Archaeological Journal*, 147 (1990), 1–15

R. P. Hastings, *Poverty and the Poor Law in the North Riding of Yorkshire, c.1780–1837* (York: Borthwick Papers, 61, 1982)

H. Heaton, *The Yorkshire Woollen and Worsted Industries from the Earliest Times up to the Industrial Revolution* (Oxford University Press, second edition, 1965)

D. Hey, *A History of Penistone and District* (Barnsley: Wharncliffe Books, 2002)

D. Hey, *A History of Sheffield* (Lancaster: Carnegie, 1998, 2005)

D. Hey, *Historic Hallamshire* (Ashbourne: Landmark, 2002)

D. Hey, *Medieval South Yorkshire* (Ashbourne: Landmark, 2003)

D. Hey, *Packmen, Carriers and Packhorse Roads* (Ashbourne: Landmark, 2001)

D. Hey, 'Yorkshire's Southern Boundary', *Northern History*, XXXVII (2000), 31–48

J. D. Hicks (ed.), *A Victorian Boyhood on the Wolds: The Recollections of J. R. Mortimer* (York: East Yorkshire Local History Series, 34, 1978)

R. Hoggart, *The Uses of Literacy* (Harmondsworth: Penguin, 1957)

R. Horrox, *The de la Poles of Hull* (York: East Yorkshire Local History Series, 38, 1983)

R. W. Hoyle, *The Pilgrimage of Grace and the Politics of the 1530s* (Oxford University Press, 2001)

G. Ingle, *The Yorkshire Cotton Industry, 1780–1835* (Lancaster: Carnegie, 1997)

G. Jackson, *Hull in the Eighteenth Century* (Oxford University Press, 1972)

B. Jennings, *Yorkshire Monasteries: Cloister, Land and People* (Otley: Smith Settle, 1999)

B. Jennings (ed.), *A History of Nidderdale* (Huddersfield: Advertiser Press, 1967)

B. Jennings (ed.), *A History of Harrogate and Knaresborough* (Huddersfield: Advertiser Press, 1970)

B. Jennings (ed.), *Pennine Valley: A History of Upper Calderdale* (Otley: Smith Settle, 1992)

J. Kermode, *Medieval Merchants: York, Beverley and Hull in the Later Middle Ages* (Cambridge University Press, 1998)

I. Kershaw, *Bolton Priory: The Economy of a Northern Monastery, 1286–1325* (Oxford University Press, 1973)

I. Kinnes et al., 'Duggleby Howe Reconsidered', *Archaeological Journal*, 140 (1983), 83–108

F. Kitchen, *Brother to the Ox* (Harmondsworth: Penguin, 1983)

B. R. Law, *Fieldens of Todmorden: A Nineteenth-Century Business Dynasty* (Littleborough: Kelsall, 1995)

H. E. J. le Patourel, *The Moated Sites of Yorkshire* (London: Society for Medieval Archaeology monograph series, 5, 1973)

H. E. J. le Patourel. M. H. Long and M. F. Pickles (eds), *Yorkshire Boundaries* (Yorkshire Archaeological Society, 1993)

D. Linstrum, *West Yorkshire Architects and Architecture* (London: Lund Humphries, 1978)

W. H. Long, *A Survey of the Agriculture of Yorkshire* (London: Royal Agricultural Society, 1969)

J. McDonnell (ed.), *A History of Helmsley, Rievaulx and District* (York: Stonegate Press, 1963)

T. Manby, S. Moorhouse and P. Ottaway (eds), *The Archaeology of Yorkshire: An Assessment at the Beginning of the 21st Century* (Yorkshire Archaeological Society, 2003)

W. Marshall, *The Rural Economy of Yorkshire* (London, 1788)

G. Mee, *Aristocratic Enterprise: The Fitzwilliam Industrial Undertakings, 1795–1857* (Glasgow and London: Blackie, 1975)

P. Mellars and P. Dark, *Starr Carr in Context* (McDonald Institute for Archaeological Research and Oxbow Books, 1998)

R. Morris, *Churches in the Landscape* (London, Dent, 1989)

R. Muir, *The Dales of Yorkshire: A Portrait* (London: Macmillan, 1991)

R. Muir, *Landscape Detective: Discovering a Countryside* (Bollington: Windgather Press, 2001)

R. Muir, *The Yorkshire Countryside: A Landscape History* (Keele University Press, 1997)

C. M. Newman, *Late Medieval Northallerton* (Stamford: Shaun Tyas, 1999)

R. van de Noort, *The Humber Wetlands* (Bollington: Windgather, 2004)

D. M. Palliser, *Tudor York* (Oxford: Oxford University Press, 1979)

Sir N. Pevsner, *The Buildings of England: The West Riding* (Harmondsworth: Penguin, 1959); *The Buildings of England: The North Riding* (1966)

Sir N. Pevsner and D. Neave, *The Buildings of England: York and the East Riding* (London: Penguin, 1995)

S. Pollard, *A History of Labour in Sheffield* (Liverpool University Press, 1959)

A. Raistrick and E. Allen, 'The South Yorkshire Ironmasters, 1690–1750', *Economic History Review*, old series, IX (1939), 168–85

G. Redmonds, *Yorkshire: West Riding; English Surnames Series* (Chichester: Phillimore, 1973)

G. Redmonds, *Surnames and Genealogy: a New Approach* (Birmingham: Federation of Family History Societies, 2002)

P. Roebuck, *Yorkshire Baronets, 1640–1760* (Oxford University Press, 1980)

B. S. Rowntree, *Poverty: A Study of Town Life* (London: Macmillan, 1901)

Royal Commission on the Historical Monuments of England, *York*, 5 vols (London: HMSO, 1962–81)

P. F. Ryder, *Medieval Buildings of Yorkshire* (Ashbourne: Moorland, 1982)

J. Sheppard, 'Metrological Analysis of Village Plans in Yorkshire', *Agricultural History Review*, XXII (1974), 118–35

A. H. Smith, *The Place-Names of the North Riding of Yorkshire* (Cambridge University Press, for the English Place-Name Society, 1928)

A. H. Smith, *The Place-Names of the West Riding of Yorkshire*, vols I–VII (Cambridge University Press, for the English Place-Name Society, 1961–62)

L. T. Smith (ed.), *Leland's Itinerary* (London: Centaur Press, 1964)

R. B. Smith, *Land and Politics in the England of Henry VII: The West Riding of Yorkshire, 1530–1546* (Oxford University Press, 1970)

D. Spratt and B. J. D. Harrison (eds), *The North York Moors Landscape Heritage* (North York Moors National Park, 1989)

I. Stead, *The Arras Culture* (Yorkshire Philosophical Society, 1979)

H. E. Strickland, *A General View of the Agriculture of the East Riding of Yorkshire* (London, 1812)

C. Stoertz, *Ancient Landscapes of the Yorkshire Wolds* (London: HMSO, 1997)

H. M. and J. Taylor, *Anglo-Saxon Architecture*, 3 vols (Cambridge University Press, 1980 and 1978)

N. Thomas, 'The Thornborough Circles', *Yorkshire Archaeological Journal*, 38 (1955), 425–45

E. P. Thompson, *The Making of the English Working Class* (London: Gollancz, 1963)

J. Tuke, *A General View of the Agriculture of the North Riding of Yorkshire* (London, 1800)

G. Tweedale, *Steel City: Entrepreneurship, Strategy and Technology in Sheffield, 1743–1993* (Oxford: Clarendon Press, 1995)

The Victoria History of the Counties of England: East Riding of Yorkshire, 7 vols (1969–2002) *The Victoria History of the Counties of England: The City of York* (1961)

B. Waites, *Monasteries and Landscape in North-East England* (Oakham: Multum in Parvo Press, 1997)

G. Walker, *The Costume of Yorkshire* (London, 1814)

T. D. Whitaker, *A History of Richmondshire in the North Riding of the County of York* (London, 1823)

T. D. Whitaker, *Loidis and Elmete; or an Attempt to Illustrate the District … of Aredale and Wharfdale* (London, 1816)

R. White, *The Yorkshire Dales: A Landscape through Time* (Scarborough: Great Northern Books, 2002)

W. E. Wightman, 'The significance of "waste" in the Yorkshire Domesday', *Northern History*, X (1975), 55–71

R. G. Wilson, *Gentlemen Merchants: The Merchant Community in Leeds, 1700–1830* (Manchester University Press, 1971)

A. J. L. Winchester, *The Harvest of the Hills: Rural Life in Northern England and the Scottish Borders, 1400–1700* (Edinburgh University Press, 2000)

A. Young, *Tour through the North of England*, I (London, 1771)

Index

Index entries in *italic* type refer to illustrations or their accompanying captions

Acknowledgements

During the picture research for this project, the publishers have received considerable help and advice from a number of sources. Martin Foreman at Hull and East Riding Museum was very helpful in providing images and information about the Wetwang Slack burials. Christine Kyriacou of York Archaeological Trust supplied a selection of useful images. The staff of English Heritage (National Monument Record) kindly searched their archives for the eight aerial images from their collections which are reproduced in the book. Mike Spick of Sheffield Local Studies Library kindly allowed us to reproduce a selection of images from the 'Picture Sheffield' collection. Catherine Mullins of Sheffield Galleries and Museums Trust gave permission for us to use several images. Jim Bright on behalf of Leeds Museums and Galleries kindly allowed us to reproduce images from their collections. Laura Turner of Ferens Art Gallery kindly gave permission for us to use several images of Hull. Jemma Street and Ursula Oldenburg of the Bridgeman Art Library were both extremely helpful and supplied a number of images from their extensive collection. Harrogate Museums and Arts very kindly provided a selection of images, and we would like to thank Jane Sellers in particular for her help. Melanie Baldwin of York Museums Trust was helpful and knowledgeable about illustrations from their collection. *Out of Oblivion*, part of the Yorkshire Dales National Park Authority, kindly supplied a number of archaeological images and aerial photographs, and we would particularly like to thank Robert White for his help and advice. Sebastian Fattorini very kindly supplied and allowed us to use his excellent photographs of Skipton Castle. Dominic Powlesland of the Landscape Research Centre and Malton Museum kindly supplied images of the West Heslerton excavations. Karl Noble of Clifton Park Museum gave permission to reproduce images relating to the archaeological finds discovered at Templeborough. Eugene Nicholson of Bradford Industrial Museum was very knowledgeable about images of the woollen industry from their collection. Mary Matthews of Wakefield Art Gallery was very helpful and allowed us to reproduce two beautiful illustrations of Pontefract Castle and Wakefield bridge and chantry chapel. Scarborough Art Gallery supplied a selection of images for us to choose from, and Louise Marr was particularly helpful. Andrew Sharpe of Grove Rare Books, Bolton Abbey, provided help and advice and kindly allowed us to photograph items from his extensive collection of rare Yorkshire books. Yorkshire Archaeological Society kindly allowed us to photograph items from their extensive archives, and we would particularly like to thank Robert Frost for his invaluable help.

Thanks are also due to Webb Aviation aerial photography for several excellent modern aerial photographs. These were taken by Jonathan C.K. Webb, a pilot who has been in the UK aerial photography business since 1991. Much of his work is industrial aerial photography, but he also runs the Webb Aviation aerial photography Picture Library, where anyone can browse for an aerial photograph of their house or street (see www.webb-aviation.co.uk). Numerous others provided crucial illustrations and we would like to thank them all for their help and advice. It is much appreciated. The author thanks Richard Bird, Malcolm Dolby, Sheila Edwards, Peter Ryder and Meridian Airmaps Ltd for some of the photographs in his collection.

Most of the modern photographs were taken by Alistair Hodge on wide-ranging motorcycle tours of the county during the summers of 2004 and 2005. Very many local people helped give directions to sites that were hard to locate, and gave permission for photographs to be taken.

The publishers have made every effort to trace copyright holders, and apologise if any acknowledgement has been omitted.